Proceedings
of the Second
National Conference
on
Business Ethics

A collection of addresses and discussions at a conference sponsored by The Center for Business Ethics, Bentley College. Qualified and respected corporate, government, and academic leaders discussed such issues as accounting ethics, membership and role of corporate boards, corporate responsibility, ethical problems raised because of the managerial hierarchy, employee freedom and rights within organizations, advocacy advertising, and bribery. Since business ethics is a relatively new and developing field of inquiry, the bibliographical material throughout the volume would be a tremendous help to anyone interested in gaining some familiarity with the general area of business ethics or with any one issue included in the volume as mentioned above. Three extensive case studies of real world happenings are included, presented by qualified individuals of varying backgrounds, giving the reader insight into how differently trained individuals handle case analysis. Recommended for purchase by upper-division undergraduate libraries with serious collections in philosophy, management, and/or applied ethics and by all graduate libraries.

University Press
of America™

University Press of America, Inc.™

4710 Auth Place, S.E., Washington D.C. 20023

Copyright © by Bentley College, Waltham, Massachusetts, 1979.

ISBN: 0-8191-0762-X

Library of Congress Catalog Card Number: 79-64514

PROCEEDINGS OF THE SECOND

NATIONAL CONFERENCE ON BUSINESS ETHICS

Power and Responsibility in
the American Business System

April 7 & 8, 1978

Edited by
W. Michael Hoffman
Director, The Center for Business Ethics
Chairman, Philosophy Department, Bentley College

Sponsored by
The Center for Business Ethics, Bentley College, Waltham, Massachusetts

PREFACE

This volume consists of the addresses and discussions of the Second National Conference on Business Ethics (April 7 and 8, 1978) sponsored by the Center for Business Ethics at Bentley College, Waltham, Massachusetts. Bentley established this national Center in 1976 for the primary purpose of providing a non-partisan forum for the exchange of ideas on business ethics in an industrial society, particularly as these ideas relate to the activities of corporations, labor, government, and the professions.

The Proceedings of the Center's First National Conference on Business Ethics (March 11 and 12, 1977) has been purchased by hundreds of organizations and individuals and is being used as a text in many business ethics courses throughout the country. Having as its theme "Business Values and Social Justice: Compatibility or Contradiction?" this First National Conference heard addresses from twelve corporate, government, and academic leaders, including: George Kneeland, Chairman of the Board of St. Regis Paper Company; Daniel Bell, Professor of Sociology, Harvard University; David Cohen, President, Common Cause; Edward Gibbons, President, F. W. Woolworth Company; George Cabot Lodge, Professor of Business Administration, Harvard University; Thomas P. O'Neill, Speaker of the U.S. House of Representatives; Alasdair MacIntyre, Professor of Philosophy, Boston University; and Elliot L. Richardson, Ambassador at Large. The ideas that were discussed at this Conference, including the public opinion poll on business ethics conducted by The Gallup Organization especially for the Conference, attracted major national attention and concern to the practical and ideological problems in this newly developing field of study.

This First National Conference established an important conceptual framework and receptivity for the more particular discussions in this Proceedings of the Second National Conference on Business Ethics with its theme "Power and Responsibility in the American Business System." Over fifty of our nation's leaders and thinkers participated in this Conference speaking on a wide range of issues such as: accounting ethics; corporate boards; managerial hierarchy; employee freedom and rights; the philosophical foundations and the nature of the corporation; multinationals; advocacy advertising; apartheid; environmental protection; private property; and bribery. These issues were delivered at the Conference through major addresses, workshop paper presentations, panel discussions, and case studies. We

v

are confident that the readers of this volume will gain insight into timely and important ideas relative to many ethical dimensions of business activities.

This Conference was made possible partially from grants from the following organizations: Arvin Industries; General Mills Foundation; Rexnord, Inc.; Semline, Inc.; Stop and Shop Manufacturing Companies; and Woolworth Company. On behalf of Bentley College's Center for Business Ethics, I wish to thank all these contributing organizations and all the participants for sharing with us their ideas.

A special thanks must go to the members of the Business Ethics Conference Planning Committee who spent many long hours in structuring and overseeing this Second National Conference. I want to also thank Theresa Armstrong for her able assistance in the preparation of this manuscript. Finally, my deepest gratitude goes to Jeanne Sprague, who not only was primarily responsible for the preparation and organization of this volume but who also has devoted generously and unselfishly her time and energies to the success of the Center for Business Ethics since its inception.

W. Michael Hoffman

CONTENTS

GREGORY H. ADAMIAN

Introduction

Many of us are perhaps still not fully accustomed to the
juxtaposition of the words "business" and "ethics." Not that we
conceive of business as an unethical pursuit, but rather that we
tend to think of ethics in the more traditional sense of a moral
code for the individual or as a particular branch of philosophy.
I suspect that ethics, to many, somehow does not seem practical
enough, nor communal enough, to deserve institutional attention
in the rigorous, competitive world of business.

This perception is both misguided and ironic. Over the
last few years, we have seen virtually every form of institution
in America come under strenuous attack for alleged violations
of law and unethical conduct. In many instances, these charges
were found substantially true. Though the gravest symbols of
our ethical failures -- the Vietnam War and Watergate -- are now
largely behind us, even a casual familiarity with "headlines"
informs us that the American public still deeply questions --
and often rightly so -- the integrity and truthfulness of our
foremost institutions. The misuse of our environment; the dishonesty of politicians; the abuse of authority in government,
at all levels; and what seems the corrupting influence of many
business practices, all suggest that we have yet to penetrate
the heart of our ethical problems, let alone resolve them. And,
according to a Gallup survey announced at last year's Conference
at Bentley, three-fourths of America's public believe that big
business, despite government regulation, can still do whatever
it wants, ethical or not.

If any doubt the critical pertinence of the study and application of ethics to American business, I would remind them that
the study of ethics was born in the marketplace, the child of
commercial and industrial democracy. In the Greece of Socrates,
with whom the study of ethics may be said to begin, a centuries
old agrarian monarchy was rapidly giving way to the development
of democracy and the rise of a powerful commercial class. Men
not of noble birth came to power and influence precisely through
their commercial success.

These men were not inheritors of the ancient sense of honor
and espirit de corps of the landed aristocracy; rather, in a new
business world where money counted more than title and all men
stood as equals as buyers and sellers, these men needed a more

1

practical, explicit, and reliable code of conduct than their
journey to success could itself provide. In their rapidly
changing world of democracy and business, the study of ethics
began as a realistic, utilitarian, practical, workday critique
of conduct for men of the world. Ethics was born not in the
serenity of an ivory tower, but in the dealings of Greek traders
and merchants. Twenty-five hundred years later, in an immeasur-
ably more complex industrial democracy, the United States, we
are slowly learning, as did ancient Greece, that the need for
business and ethics to be joined in a practical way becomes more
critical as a society's commerce advances and its democracy dis-
perses authority and power.

Although last year's Conference was widely praised and
accomplished much, I believe this year's program, with greater
attention to the real nuts and bolts of power and responsibility
in business, represents progress and improvement. Yet we would
all concur that few of our nation's ethical crises or dilemmas
are truly solved. More accurately, all of us are still working
toward a proper appreciation of the scope and magnitude of the
problems before us. The scandals of the past year alone, are
firm proof that a thinking machine as complex as American business cannot be set right by one timely repair, but that a constant program of preventative supervision, self-examination,
mending, and fixing is timelessly needed.

I offer one bit of guidance concerning these problems: there
must be a far greater and more creative partnership between business and the academic world than ever before. It is insufficient that colleges and universities educate students to meet
specific business needs for accountants, lawyers, managers and
comptrollers. We must talk with one another more frequently,
and with greater attentiveness, and with a greater appreciation
of each other's vital concerns. And business should demand <u>and</u>
<u>support</u> -- both morally and financially -- centers like Bentley's
for Business Ethics and conferences like this. We are each
other's <u>greatest</u> <u>resource</u>, and one another's <u>partner</u> in any future success.

I thank you all for coming to our Second National Conference
on Business Ethics. I hope you will find this experience worthwhile and rewarding, and the beginning of closer and more productive relationships among us all.

SESSION I

"Business Ethics Is <u>Not</u> a Set of Rules"

Kenneth Olsen
President
Digital Equipment Corporation

KENNETH OLSEN

Business Ethics is <u>Not</u> a Set of Rules

   With the Conference that we have here today, it should
become very clear to you that my position is not to be academic
or elegant. For that there are people much more qualified than
I am. Instead, I will try to tell you some of the experiences
and attitudes that I have encountered in the 20 years during
which Digital grew from a small group of men to a company employing 37,000 to 38,000 people. I don't know if what I'm going
to say will sound like bragging or sound like confessions, but
I will try to tell you exactly what our thoughts, our experiences,
our worries, and our concerns were.

   When some people in business look at the title of this Conference, they will say that the pressure groups on the outside
have all the power and business has all the responsibility. I'll
try to put it in a little bit better perspective than that. I'll
probably cover a lot of detailed items, some of which may seem
tedious, trivial and dumb, but then that's part of the message I
want to get across. Ethics is not always found in the stories
that make the newspapers. It's in the day-by-day decisions which
create very little interest on the outside.

   Now, our company is particularly interesting from an ethical
point of view. It's new. Our products are technical. People
buy these products for technical reasons and we have very little
opportunity to take part in the ethical wrongdoings which bother
society the most. We have a product which does almost universal
good, and has little opportunity to harm. Our manufacturing
facilities have little opportunity to pollute. There are no
unusual safety problems for our employees and as far as I know
we've never been tempted to make bribes outside the country.

   One point I'd like to make is that the major decisions --
ethical, ecological, community -- are made by many people through
an organization. Important decisions are made by other people
on the management scale and the president only sees those that
he makes and is directly involved in.

   The interesting part of the experiences we had, starting
with just an idea at MIT, raising money, and then continuously
raising money for 20 years, is that we had a very simple and clear
view of the position of profit in American business. When we
started we were young; we had only worked at Massachusetts In-

5

stitute of Technology but we had an idea. We thought we knew
how to make high speed, transistorized computers. The world
smiled at us and said, "You're just academics." Interestingly,
that's what we say to people at MIT today.

We made a proposal that we go into business and show the
world how to build these computers. We went to a risk capital
company in Boston called American Research and Development Corporation (ARD) and gave them our proposal. It was a bad time
in 1957. A recession was starting. The Korean War was over.
Businesses starting then weren't doing very well and no one was
interested in starting a business. But ARD was fascinated by
the idea.

The staff at ARD gave us three bits of advice. First,
they told us not to use the word "computers" because _Fortune_
magazine said that no one has ever made any money in computers
and no one is about to. So, we took that out of our proposal.
We had written our proposal by going to the Lexington Library
and looking through all the books, including Moody's, where we
looked at the financial statements of all the good companies.
They seemed to make about five percent profit so we put five
percent into our financial statements.

Their second bit of advice was that we had to promise more
profit because if someone was going to risk their money, there
had to be more promised returns than what they would get in a
savings bank. The last bit of advice they gave us was to promise
quick results because most of the ARD board was over 80 years of
age. So we redid our statements, our plan, and promised to make
a profit in a year.

After one year we really did make a profit. It was infinitesimal, but, it was very clear. ARD's stockholders were in
turn savings banks, insurance companies, trust funds, probably
union pension funds, company pension funds and mutual funds. In
general, they were basically a large cross-section of the people
in the United States. They had a social contract to use that
money effectively, for all the people involved. When we started
the business it was very clear to us what our responsibility was:
We had to make a profit for the people who had invested in us.
It made for a very simple relationship within the company. When
we hired people we said we had received $70,000 from our investors,
had promised to make a profit, and that's why we're here. We
could tell people that was our goal and it worked very well. We
reach our employees consistently with this message. Most of the
people understand exactly what the meaning of profit is.

Every year of two, we go out and look for more money.

6

Digital has been growing 30, 40, and sometimes 50 percent a year
and that growth needs large amounts of money. So, when we go
looking for money, people look at our history and our consistent
level of managing profits. They have been very willing to invest.
Our employees work hard because they know how important it is
if we're going to raise money for the next time.

There is a question that is perpetually asked from an academic point of view: What is more important, the profit or the
social obligation of the company? Now, from my point of view,
I think that's nonsense, and I can't take part in that discussion.
It's like saying to a football team, is it more important to make
a goal or to be ethical? It's obvious when you're playing a game
that the goal is to win. You assume you're going to obey the
rules and you assume a level of ethics and sensitivity. There's
no conflict. Everything we do has a goal and you assume a level
of ethics.

One question which I have never been able to settle completely in my mind is the role of corporations in making contributions to charities. We are logically stewards of somebody
else's money. We are professional managers of these funds. Are
we then in a position to make contributions with somebody else's
money to our favorite charity? It seems to me that's all confused. Digital makes contributions. We probably do it more than
most, but I never want to take any credit for it because I'm
giving away somebody else's money. I think it's clear that corporations really deserve no credit.

Because of this situation I've always had a list of reasons
why we gave somebody else's money away if society ever turns
around and challenges us. There's a whole list of reasons. Some
we give away for business reasons. We used to give a lot of
equipment away for business reasons when the tax laws made it
very favorable. Then with great brilliance, Congress discouraged
that, just when colleges were in financial trouble. How they
could be so brilliant I don't know, but it's not as profitable
for corporations to give away equipment as it used to be. But
whenever possible, because of the unique product that we have, we
make contributions to hospitals, colleges, and the like. We
justify part of them because they are part of the cost of our
employees, for example, the local hospitals, things like this.
The rest of the contributions we justify because society expects
it. Even though it's not logical, society expects it, and there's
never been a complaint.

But my main point is that when society asks for and expects
contributions, we should always be sensitive to the fact that
we're giving away somebody else's assets. Now, I think the way

7

my company happens to do it is very wise. I'm not involved in
it at all. The last thing I want is to be responsible for giving
contributions to my favorite charities. So we have a committee.
The committee makes the decisions. They don't do it the way I
would do it. Like a committee, they tend to give fewer dollars
to more organizations, but it's a lot safer than me being personally involved.

Another question that comes up is, what is the position of
the board of directors in a company? Well, it's quite clear to
me. We have a goal, we have standards of ethics -- often not
written down because ethics are principles more than written
rules -- and the board is very important for maintaining these
principles. The board is part of the team.

Our goal is clear -- make profit and survive as an organization. We have many constituencies. We have all our employees
who are very dependent on us. We hold their pension funds and
this is a tremendous responsibility to the town, to the state,
and to the country. We're in business to stay successful and to
survive.

The board of directors is an important part of the corporate
team, and they all have to work in the same direction. I've been
on a number of non-profit organization boards where board members
sometimes serve in order to represent a specific interest group.
They don't care about the total organization. They are there to
make sure that their group has its rights. They're not part of
the team to make sure the entire organization is successful. The
last thing I think I would want on a board is for someone there
to worry about their specific interests. There have been some
classic examples of this where organizations have just disappeared
because people on a board had special interests. The social obligation of a board is quite clear and that is to make the organization survive and be successful.

There are a number of other ethical questions regarding the
board. The board of directors, as individuals, should respect
the confidences that have been given them. They should not reveal board secrets nor tell anything that they've learned, as
board members, about the company. It's a gross corruption in our
society where we encourage people to break confidences.

Our experiences in ecology have not been as exciting as
some firms, but I can tell you a little bit about our attitudes
and problems we've encountered. We wanted to buy a building in
the northern part of Massachusetts which was going to be empty.
It fit our needs perfectly and it had land for expansion. We
had a consultant look it over and the consultant said, "No way.

To expand there, you're going to need five governmental agencies in Massachusetts to approve it and you will never get five agencies to agree at one time." There is the feeling, largely in this area, that you do good for ecology by hassling the companies who want to do things. Now, logic says that is not a contradiction. You just discourage people.

About this same time we went to Phoenix and said we wanted to build a building. We picked the site very quickly. Arizona agencies clearly established guidelines for what we had to do. We were a little shocked at how expensive it was. We had to build a pond, a fountain. We had to build a hill between us and housing. We had to do extensive landscaping, and several other things necessary to the ecology. But unlike Massachusetts, they gave us this list of guidelines immediately. Their attitude was take it or leave it. We took it and our site is beautiful. Our firm, we feel, has made a real contribution to the ecology. If they had had dozens of people hassle us for years, no good would have come out of the project. But the agencies knew exactly what they wanted, and we followed their rules.

Another question we're often faced with is airport noise. We're very dependent on communication. We fly a lot of cargo out of Boston at night and fly a lot of people around New England. It's quite clear, I think, how you take care of airport noise. The government has to decide what it will allow and corporations will have to decide whether they can do business under those guidelines or not. I think it's that simple. There's no way a corporation can go out and make everybody happy. In one of the areas we're in, people were complaining about airport noise. At that time, it wasn't our airplane. They tried to do some research but they couldn't make any measurements there because the highway noise overwhelmed the airplane noise. There's another area where we can't fly our helicopter after 7 p.m. but there's no way you could measure our helicopter noise because we're right on a road filled with trucks. The government just has to decide the rules and then we have to decide whether we can go along with them or not. Nobody can ever afford to be continually in the middle of hassles on things this subjective.

On another ecological matter, several years ago our firm built a plant in western Massachusetts. We were going to do some chemistry there, some plating, etching, and out of that facility came water which had certain metals in it. We could purify the water to the point where supposedly you could swim in it or drink it. We had accepted the plan. The state had accepted the plan that we could put the water in the ground. The ground surrounding the plant was all sand and all water would go into it.

9

Then the state changed its mind. We had built much of the facility and it suddenly became impractical to reverse our decision. The state wouldn't allow us to put water which was drinkable into the ground but, at the same time, they would allow us to put human sewage into the ground. It turns out that they were right. If you put human sewage into the ground, it deteriorates and becomes part of the soil with no danger. On the other hand, if you put water containing infinitesimal amounts of metals into the ground, over many years the metals will collect and in time become poisonous. So, in this case, they were right. The state was wise. It cost us something. We wish they had been wise a little earlier, but this was good ecology.

Another time, we were accused in the press of not living up to the limits set on us for copper in the drinking water. When this came out in the newspapers I was angry; I was going to go to the President and tell him the whole story. Wiser heads, however, prevailed and they said these people in the ecology department are good. They're sensitive. They're very cooperative and they made a mistake. Don't jump on them. So we didn't and the ecology department apologized quickly and the whole thing worked out very well.

Some time ago I was on the President's Science Advisory Committee. We learned that there was a chemical which hadn't created public attention, but it was worse than DDT. It seemed so passive that we all used it. It was in a lot of products such as latex paint, and we never worried about it. They used this chemical in laboratories all the time because it was so passive. But when they were measuring for DDT, much of the time they were measuring this chemical. It turns out that this chemical has the same problems as DDT and maybe caused many of the disasters that DDT was blamed for. When I heard about this I immediately went home and told our people to find out where we were using it and to be sure and dispose of it carefully. We didn't use it in manufacturing, but it turned out we did use it in latex paint to paint equipment such as transformers and the like.

Well, I think employees dealt with this matter like they do with a lot of other things. The workers said, "Ah, the boss is on a kick. Let's go along with it but let's not take it seriously." A few years later the government came in wanting to know the same things I did; where were we using the chemical and how were we disposing of it? Now, they got a lot better reaction than I did. I think this example points out the good the government can do as well as the responsibility government has. But above all, government has to operate in a very positive way and not polarize people.

10

Now as you well know, the government has not always done things wisely. A few years ago, Congress voted to have zero pollution in the water. But, as long as we human beings are here, waste has to go somewhere so you just can't win with a position like that. They also voted to cut out 90 percent of all major pollutants in the automobile. They didn't know what the words meant. They didn't know how to measure them, and they weren't sure if they were harmful. But they voted to get rid of 90 percent of them. We're still paying the price, largely through poor gas mileage and higher car prices.

Another subject that comes up is how you treat employees. When we first left the academic world, we just fell into the idea of participatory management and consensus management. We got people involved in most of our decisions. We did a lot in giving people the opportunity to take responsibility for the projects they proposed. Because of our 20 years of experiences with this practice, I can make some comments on it. With many organizations, it would seem they never could have enough parti- cipation or communication with their employees. But there are limitations on this. First of all, people after a while don't want to participate in every decision. There are just too many things going on. Second, it turns out that participating in decisions in which one is not an expert is just foolish. You should only really listen to those who will be responsible.

Now, we forget once in a while. Some of our managers get the idea that they have to get everybody involved. If there's a question coming up, they'll get two, four dozen people in a room and think they'll all participate and come to a decision. Needless to say, the solutions become more and more divergent. So they meet a week later and the people who spoke up the week before have changed their minds and the longer you carry it on the more divergent the question becomes. So, participation and en- couraging people to participate in the community, and definitely in business, is great. It does tremendous things for commitment and for communications. But we should learn it has to be done with responsibility.

Digital has also been exceedingly successful in letting people propose what they want to do and then giving them the responsibility to do it. But, this also has its limitations. People can get themselves too deeply involved and end up working too hard. We have to protect our employees from getting in over their heads and still let them have the freedom to propose and do what they think they should.

Above all, we must hold people responsible for doing the job that they were hired for. In our modern society, people

11

come to work and they want to do what they see everybody else doing which is solve somebody else's problem. Now, there was a story a few years ago of two pilots who flew an airplane into a hill and killed everybody aboard. When they took apart the flight recorder and listened to it, they found out that before the crash the pilots had been arguing over the ethics of Richard Nixon. Now, as citizens, they indeed had a right and an obligation to consider the ethics of their leaders. But at the same time, they had their job to do which was to keep that airplane out of the hills. If we could make sure that everybody, including Nixon, did their jobs, we would be better off.

Work is one of the most important things in a person's life. We have a consultant from MIT who claimed that work is the most important thing in a person's life. Now, I would argue with him that a person's family was the most important, but it doesn't make any difference. Work was either number one or number two.

By assuming that work is the most important thing and treating this concept as one of the most important values that we can pass on to our employees, we've had tremendous results. We've had enormous results in the ghetto where people were considered unemployable. We treated them with dignity. We treated them like we'd like to be treated, and not any differently. We said we'd hire them if they were good and fire them if they were bad, and if they were good, we'd promote them. The results have been just amazing.

Another topic concerns the fact that Accounting in business has received a great deal of attention lately. Having come from the academic world, I'm always amazed at the brilliance of accounting as we have it in this country. It is intelligent, sophisticated, and clever. I say this from a scientific, mathematical background. Having been involved in higher education, religion, and government, I think business is the most honest of all the communities I have had contact with. One of the main reasons for this is that bankers will only want to do business with you if you're honest and if your accounting system is good. I chaired a committee which looked at every agency in the State of Massachusetts, and it's clear to me that if government followed normal business accounting practices where every year all expenditures were reviewed, all long-term commitments were taken into account, and as in business, published a report once a year which criticized and made suggestions, many of the problems we see in government would disappear. The two agencies in Massachusetts that follow normal business accounting practices are the best run ones in the state.

I have great admiration for accounting. Now, accountants have done unwise things in the past. A few years ago, if you re-

member, they used to call the item on the bottom line "undistri-
buted surplus." Well, they got some of the names confused. That
really upset people because they wanted that surplus, and of
course it really wasn't there. The other word they used wrong is
"profit." To many people, profit is something you get for free.
For instance, if I bought a car for $100 and sold it for $200,
and didn't make any improvements to the car, I made $100 profit.
But if I loaned $100 and got $105 back, you wouldn't call that
real profit.

The problem I see is that people keep wanting to change
accounting procedures. One thing we need in order to run a business, understand a business, and for people outside to understand
a business, is some stability in the recording. Making changes
all the time, I think, causes confusion. Look at annual reports.
One idea that somebody very cleverly came up with was to put
everything in big type in the same size type so nothing would be
hidden in fine print. Well, I no longer read annual reports.
They are so dull, so useless, and contain so much insignificant
information. It used to be you could just pick out what was important. Then if you were suspicious, you'd look at the smallest
type. You understood what was going on. Now it's all the same
size type and there's just no message at all. We keep wanting
to make changes like this, which on the surface look helpful but
really cause no end to confusion.

Let me briefly mention a few other items that relate to
ethics. We often look at the big company. We really ought to
look at the little company because that's where the people are
going to come from who will eventually run the big companies.
We think a little company can do no harm. But, small businesses
frequently follow shady practices trying to get started. For
instance, a small company will buy something from a big company
and then not pay for it. When you ask for the money, they
answer, "You were small once. You know how hard it is to get
cash. We just won't pay you for six months." I never said it
but I was thinking I gave 70 to 80 percent of the company away
in order to pay my bills on time. These small businesses are
trying to get risk capital from others for free and that's
basically immoral.

A small company will steal a design from IBM and when IBM
changes the design, they'll sue IBM for anti-trust. Or they'll
buy equipment from IBM and depreciate it over 10 years when IBM
depreciates it over five. They'll rent it for less, and when
IBM changes, they'll yell 'anti-trust.' We are sympathetic for
the little company, but basic morality isn't there. When we
allow this, how do we expect people to be moral when they get
hired by big companies? Now, some people will say, "We'll make

13

a whole list of rules and they'll become ethical." No way. People have to become ethical in every part of their life, at all steps of their life, and then you can trust them when they work for a big company. You're not going to make them ethical by hassling them from the outside. We must find people who are ethical all the way and we as a society should influence it.

Another item: Many companies, including the U.S. government and Massachusetts, will set up a business that lives off the unemployment compensation laws. They'll only work for a few months at a time, put the people on unemployment and give them a reasonable compensation. I think this is basically unethical.

The stock market is an interesting phenomena. We sometimes worry so much about ethics but we should stop and consider the stock market. What an amazing phenomena. All of that business, all that transfer of funds, is done by word of mouth, often over a telephone. That is the height of integrity, honesty, and trust. With all the problems we have, there are so many things that run by simple integrity and simple trust and the stock market is one of our greatest examples.

Another issue which we're often questioned on is lobbying. The State of Massachusetts passed a law a year ago saying companies cannot lobby against the graduated income tax. The implication of the law is, I think, that the rich vice presidents would use company funds to protect their income tax situation. But on many issues like this, there is no one to argue the other side if we outlaw it or say it's immoral. In the case of the graduated income tax in Massachusetts, it's not the rich vice presidents who are effected. It's the middle class, the people who are well paid, with the husband and wife working, who feel they must leave Massachusetts or won't come to work here. If we scare all the technical, management-type people away, or say it's unethical for companies or someone to present the other side, we lose an important voice.

Another quick item. We always worry that a company is unethical because it doesn't pay enough. The major temptation on my company's part is that we pay too much. If we pay an individual too much, an engineer, a manager, and he can't get a job somewhere else because of that high salary, we can destroy a man's life.

Most people don't ever think of that. They always think the problem is not getting paid enough. But if you have to leave for one reason or another and you can't get another job, many people are destroyed. Similarly, Digital is one of the largest corporations on the western side of Puerto Rico. If we pay too

14

much there we could wipe out the economy of Puerto Rico because no one else could afford to go in and pay the rates we pay. It's very important what we pay. Now, it's not easy because it's always a compromise and sometimes expediency, but it's a moral obligation in areas and with individuals not to pay too much.

A final point. Several years ago there were 600 colleges without a president. The academic world of professors in the college community would make more points by hassling their presidents. There was no incentive to be president or to take the responsibility. There is a danger that we do that in business. If everyone is hassling business, no one will want to take responsibility, and this is something we should be very careful of. We give the oil companies and the power companies a hard time, often very unfairly. We should remember that we have a very clear social contract with the oil companies to keep us warm in the winter and with the power companies never to run out of power. The day they want to become ecologists because it's easier and there's nobody to take the social contract to make sure we have lights, heat, and power, we as a society are going to be in trouble. We assume that these power companies and oil companies can take hassles forever. But, all we have got to do is destroy that social contract they have along with other businesses and we'll pay dearly for it.

To sum up, we shouldn't polarize companies and outsiders. We must work together. We should never think that a code of ethics solves the problem. Codes of ethics help. There are certain things today that we don't do that we used to think were okay. It's just so much easier if you say these things are illegal. It just makes life easier, but no way can we say that then we are ethical.

In closing, I would like to say once again that we have to remember that the major decisions are not made at the top. It's important that we train people, educate them, teach ethics, teach traditional values, and expect it at all levels of society. Then, we'll see it also at the top. Thank you.

DISCUSSION

COMMENT: I would like to have you explain more clearly your doctrine of the morality of ceiling labor wages. Where is it immoral to pay too much?

OLSEN: Most areas are dependent on many businesses, and if one goes in and raises the labor rate so that other businesses leave or can't enter, the whole area can be economically destroyed.

COMMENT: You raised a very interesting point when talking about the morality of paying wages which do not destroy the community. Would you like to apply the same logic in terms of not making too much money so that the other firms could also have adequate capital?

OLSEN: It doesn't work that way. If the large company prices to make a large profit it allows the small company to price to make a profit.

It is illegal for a large company to price so low that it makes little or no profit in order to force the small company to do the same. A big company can tolerate the loss; the little company would disappear.

COMMENT: Perhaps you covered this point, but I wonder if DEC has attempted to write a code of ethics and publish such a document?

OLSEN: We have statements for our people of what our policies and attitudes are, and we are very clear on things we will not tolerate. I hate to use the word code of ethics because the implication is: If you do this you are ethical. We do things today which tomorrow might be unethical. For example, when we go to New York City and have to make a slide presentation, we'll pay a union member to sit in the back of the room while our lecturer uses a slide projector himself. In a few years that might be very unethical. Today, we say it's a tradition in this country to do these things.

COMMENT: You are the President of a very successful small company in the computer field. How would you feel as presiding officer of that company if IBM wanted to take you over. Would you welcome that act or would you resist it and why?

OLSEN: Fortunately, anti-trust laws protect us from large com-

16

panies like IBM, and besides, IBM has not shown an inclination to increase market share by acquisitions. IBM is a strong competitor but also a most ethical organization.

To specifically answer your question, no, we would not like to be taken over at this time. There are times when companies should be merged, and many times smaller companies do well with the discipline and help they get being part of a large organization. But we do not feel that we are in that situation.

Sometimes companies get bought because the management gets tired of the hassle with local communities. It is sometimes easier to avoid the hassle if you are part of a large, distant company. If communities want to keep local ownership they should show some respect for the people who are managing it. If someone is running a local company and is part of the community but everyone seems to hate you and you are pressured from everyone and every housewife in town seems to have more power than you do, and if the government is changing rules all the time, and if your children would love you more if you became an ecologist rather than a manager, selling your company seems to answer many problems.

Ethical questions are often harder for a small company. Everybody watches the big company. The small company has to work harder to be sure it is ethical, particularly when in contest with a larger company. It seems obviously ethical, moral and neighborly to go directly to your neighbor when he does something wrong rather than sue him even if he is a fierce competitor and even if he is a giant corporation. At least a couple of times in history we have gone to IBM and suggested that they were doing something wrong. One time they backed down and another time they convinced us we were wrong and we backed down.

SESSION II

"Accounting Ethics"

Richard S. Kraut
Assistant Director, Enforcement Division
Securities and Exchange Commission

Abraham J. Briloff
Emanuel Saxe Distinguished Professor of Accountancy
Baruch College, CUNY

Daniel Sweeney
Director of the Professional Ethics Division
American Institute of Certified Public Accountants

Kenneth P. Johnson
Vice Chairman and Technical Counsel
Coopers & Lybrand

RICHARD S. KRAUT

[The Securities and Exchange Commission, as a matter of policy, disclaims responsibility for any private publication or speech by any of its members or employees. The views expressed are my own and do not necessarily represent those of the Commission or its staff. Ed.]

*   *   *   *   *   *   *   *

Our capital raising system, of which we should be genuinely proud, is unique and salutary in the extent to which it provides for broad public participation in the capital raising process, and in the extent to which it provides opportunities for members of the public to obtain income and capital appreciation. Public companies, in turn, from the largest to the smallest, look to private individuals for sources of capital. It is a rare public company, indeed, which disdains the public entirely in favor of solely institutional financing.

The public, however, has become leary about participating in the capital-raising process. With news about illegal political contributions, foreign and domestic political and commercial bribes, hidden corporate "perks" and misappropriations and sudden, unanticipated bankruptcies, among other things, it is not difficult to comprehend why. Avoidance of the capital markets by private individuals, however, is an unhealthy trend in my opinion since it may portend a return to the days of concentration of a large proportion of our nation's wealth in a relatively small group of persons or financial institutions. This result might effectively shut out young or new companies from the capital markets. Few would dispute that this would be an undesirable result.

To stop this unhealthy trend should be the objective of anyone who wishes to preserve our capital-raising system. In the forefront of such efforts should and must be the independent auditing firms which report on the financial statements of our public companies. The importance of the integrity of such financial statements cannot be over-estimated since they are relied upon by those who invest in newly offered securities and by those who provide liquidity for such securities through investing in the trading markets. However, revelations through public and private litigation and disciplinary proceedings involving public accountants in cases such as Penn Central and Equity Funding have

21

shaken the public's confidence in what it reads in financial statements.

Expressions of concern have taken several forms. If humor is one reflection of and way of dealing with the concerns of society, consider the well-worn anecdote about the company president who interviewed prospective independent auditors and asked each: "How much is 3 plus 2?" He rejected all who gave him the answer "5" until he got to one who responded: "How much do you want it to be?" He got the job. A cartoon in the New Yorker a few years ago showed a member of senior management introducing a bright young man to other senior management: "In examining our books," he said, "Mr. Matthews promises to use generally accepted accounting principles -- if you know what I mean." A recent cartoon depicted a chairman addressing his board of directors: "Another successful year, gentlemen. We broke even on operations and pulled a net profit on accounting procedures." And only a few weeks ago, also in the New Yorker, appeared a cartoon where a senior management member was introducing a recent business school graduate to another member of management: "Young Mr. Moncure here is that Harvard M.B.A. I was telling you about who has the keen sense of depreciation." It seems even our business schools are not exempt from suspicions of fostering financial chicane and deception.

If the anecdote and cartoons reflect society's perceptions of the role of the public accountant, it is easy to see why many would-be investors are loathe to rely on issuers' financial statements. The public's perceptions as well as certain aspects of the realities must be corrected if the present form of our capital system is to survive.

The accounting profession presently has an excellent opportunity to correct what hopefully are misimpressions. As you may know, committees of the Senate and the House of Representatives have been holding hearings to determine whether additional regulation of the accounting profession by the Federal government is warranted. The Commission has expressed its views to Congress on the question of regulation of accountants; it prefers self-regulation to direct Commission oversight, but has indicated it is prepared to assume a more active, direct role if the profession, through the AICPA, does not achieve a meaningful structure for professional self-regulation. The Commission has also committed itself to report to Congress on July 1, 1978 concerning the profession's overall efforts in this regard. SEC Chairman Williams testified before Congress in February that the Commission was not wholly satisfied with the profession's efforts. While time prohibits a detailing of the criticisms, a generic criticism may be stated as the view that the proposed self-regulation structure may be dominated by the major firms with the result that the public may perceive a lack of objectivity, regard-

22

less of the reality. The profession's success at enhancing objectivity -- or stated otherwise -- enhancing "independence," may be the most important criterion against which the Commission will be measuring the AICPA's program of self-regulation.

"Independence," as between the independent auditors and the client, may also be the criterion upon which public investors will or will not decide to have confidence in audited financial statements and come into or stay out of the capital markets. If there is one ethical standard to focus upon, I believe it involves this issue of "independence." Quoting Chairman Williams' testimony before Congress:

> "Independence -- in fact, in appearance and in mental attitude -- is fundamental to the work of the outside auditor. In many ways, the public has expectations of the profession and of what the auditor's report means that exceed reality. To the extent, however, that the public views the auditing process as a wholly unbiased review of management's presentation of the corporate financial picture, I believe that the expectations are fully justified and must be fully met. Independence is the auditor's single most valuable attribute -- indeed, it is perhaps the single attribute which justifies the existence of accounting as a separate profession. If the profession cannot satisfy its obligation to maintain both the appearance and the fact of independence, I suspect that legislation is inevitable."

The presence or lack of "independence" is clearly the substantive issue which underlies the 'hiring the auditor' anecdote and the described cartoons. Can the independent auditor ask his client what results the client would like to show, in the manner of the applicant who answered the 3 + 2 question? Is adherence to generally accepted accounting principles -- period -- all that is required for the auditor to do his duty, as evidently did the new accountant in the first cartoon? Do financial statements accurately present results of operations and financial condition where operations are break-even but where profits are shown through accounting gimmickry? And is it right or wrong for an auditor to apply a "keen sense of depreciation" and other keen accounting senses, as did the "recent Harvard M.B.A."? When does application of a generally accepted accounting principle become "creative accounting" or misleading "gimmickry"? These admittedly rhetorical and pejoratively-phrased questions are clearly related to the issue of independence in that they suggest circumstances under which the independent auditor acts at the behest of management and leaves behind the interests of shareholders and the investing public who,

23

I believe, are his real clients.

Practitioners of accounting and auditing might want a road-map to help answer the foregoing questions since, just as nature abhors a vacuum, so do those who must act ethically abhor uncertainty in standards. Experience has shown, though, that tightly defined, as opposed to flexible, standards usually provide a road-map for avoidance of standards by enabling those so-minded to avoid negotiating the too sharply drawn corners and curves. Accordingly, I believe that ethical standards relating to accounting should not be overly exact.

While perhaps not providing a road-map, judicial decisions, allegations in the SEC's Complaints filed in its civil actions where it has been a plaintiff, Commission opinions issued in its own administrative disciplinary proceedings, and the AICPA's Code of Ethics have contributed to the evolution of ethical standards. I expect what may be viewed as newly evolving standards may be the subject of debate by the panel.

Since I have the podium alone for these few minutes, I would like to mention a discrete problem I have seen emerging which I believe also raises ethical issues. So long as it is the Commission's statutory responsibility to investigate possible violations of the Federal securities laws arising out of possibly misleading financial statements, the Commission will continue to seek the cooperation of accounting firms which reported on such statements. However, I perceive an unhealthy trend in the profession toward a lessening, rather than an increasing, amount of cooperation in the Commission's investigative enforcement function. More frequently, we find that we have to go to court or go to the brink of going to court to obtain compliance with subpoenas issued to accounting firms in investigations of their clients. With the body of law so clearly weighing in favor of enforcement of subpoenas and the non-recognition, for example, of an accountant-client privilege, I have to wonder whether segments of the profession are not, in essence, seeking to frustrate the Commission's investigative efforts. We are also seeing the formation abroad of foreign or international partnerships in which what are essentially domestic and foreign branches of the same accounting firm become partners. On paper, the U.S. and foreign branches appear to be related only as partners of the foreign international partnership. The structure is then used as a basis for refusing to comply with Commission requests for records of the foreign branch which audits the foreign sub of the U.S. parent on the ground that the U.S. accounting firm, while it has a relationship with the foreign firm, does not own it and therefore cannot compel it to cooperate. If the foreign sub's financials are consolidated in or a part of the U.S. parent's financial statements, the SEC cannot be precluded from investigating

24

the financial statements. I suspect, unfortunately, that this
foreign dodge, which also frustrates the Commission's investigative efforts, will have to be tested in the courts since such an
evasion cannot be tolerated.

Accountants' responsibilities in the foreign area will also
be heightened as a result of the recent passage of the Foreign
Corrupt Practices Act of 1977, whose passage was mightily urged by
the Commission. The Act, as its name suggests, generally makes it
a crime for U.S. companies, both publicly and privately owned, and
their officers, directors and employees, to pay bribes to foreign
officials and foreign political parties and candidates. As you
may be aware, the Act in large part obtained its impetus from the
Commission's Report to Congress on Questionable and Illegal Corporate Payments and Practices which discussed the Commission's civil
injunctive actions and voluntary disclosure program. I do not intend to fully discuss the Act since I see there is a panel tomorrow on "Business, Government and Bribery" which I assume will do
more than touch on it.

In my opinion, the Act enhances the preexisting role of the
independent auditor in uncovering and preventing improper or illegal transactions. Almost a year before passage of the Act, John
Biegler of Price Waterhouse wrote that "the independent auditor
should increase his sensitivity to such transactions and plan his
examinations with a heightened awareness that material improprieties
may exist. He should ensure that appropriate disclosure is made
when he detects material improper acts." Certainly he should not
assist or participate in such improper acts. However, we have seen
in our investigations instances where foreign employees of branches
of U.S. accounting firms have aided in improper practices abroad,
through acting as conduits for improper payments or counselling a
foreign subsidiary of a U.S. parent how to evade, and I don't mean
avoid, foreign taxes. Such conduct by a company's auditor now may
be not only unethical but illegal since Congress made clear that
the legal concepts of "aiding and abetting" and "joint participation" would apply under the new Act.

The accountant can perform a real service to his clients, the
company's public stockholders, by assisting in the prevention of
such misuses of corporate assets. A "sleeper" provision in the
Act certainly provides the impetus: it is the section dealing with
and entitled "Accounting Standards," which requires companies that
file reports with the SEC or that have had a public offering of
securities to make and keep books and records which, in reasonable
detail, accurately and fairly reflect the transactions and disposi-
tions of the assets of such companies and which requires them to
construct and maintain a system of internal accounting controls
sufficient to provide reasonable assurances that transactions are

25

executed in accordance with managements' authorization.

The new subsection is especially significant in that it imposes affirmative obligations and is not restricted by its terms to payments to foreign officials. This provision includes within its coverage, for example, domestic commercial bribes, undisclosed corporate "perks," or, as in the first invocation by the SEC of this new section in a suit filed on March 9, simple misappropriation of assets and concealment by means of false and improper accounting in the company's books and records; in other words, anything under the sun.

To comply with the affirmative provisions of this new provision, then, is to go a long way toward preventing violations of other Federal securities laws since accurate public disclosure will be better assured. The independent auditor will clearly have a significant role to play in assuring compliance by assisting his clients in devising the required system of controls and by insisting on detailed documentation of every significant financial transaction and tighter procedures for disbursements. In this connection, it has been urged that independent auditors include in the scope of their work a report on management's internal accounting and policy controls, which report, to my knowledge, they are not currently required to prepare. It has also been suggested that the report go to the company's stockholders as well as to senior management or the audit committee of the board.

What underlies these suggestions, the new legislation and the judicial and Commission decisions is that accounting firms may not be passive and do the unquestioned bidding of their client companies. They have a higher duty to their real clients -- the investing public. They must take initiatives to do their job not only properly in the professional sense, but in the ethical sense.

By July 1, the accounting profession must convey to the Commission and then to Congress and the public that it recognizes a duty of openness, fairness and candor to the public and that it proposes to deal meaningfully, and not merely cosmetically, with the plethora of problems facing the profession. Whether the profession is motivated by self-interest or ideals and principles, or both, the capital raising capacity of our system will be the ultimate beneficiary of improvements within the profession.

26

ABRAHAM J. BRILOFF

Accounting Ethics and the Accounting Establishment

Last fall a Federal District Court Judge referred to me as
the "Cassandra of Accountants." I must admit that at times I feel
that I share that lady's fate--no one appears to be listening. I
then feel also like another character out of the Greek myths--
Sisyphus, destined for an eternity to push that rock up the moun-
tain--only to have it come rolling down once again (and like that
character, picking myself up again, with despair but yet not de-
spondency). More often I might appear to be like Pandora playing
with a certain box.

But today I am moved to be like Martin Luther nailing his
accusations on the very door of the Establishment. Thus, I am addressing the theme of "Accounting Ethics and the Accounting Establishment" in the presence of stalwart exponents of that Establishment: Kenneth Johnson, a Vice Chairman of one of the eight
giant firms comprising that Establishment; then there is Dr. Daniel
Sweeney, who sits at the head of the Establishment's disciplinary
apparatus, as Director of the Professional Ethics Division of the
American Institute of Certified Public Accountants. In addition,
there is Mr. Richard Kraut of the Enforcement Division of the
Securities and Exchange Commission. The SEC is, of course, a
governmental agency; nevertheless, as I will seek to demonstrate,
in the matter of enforcing ethical standards for accountants (at
least) it has formed a symbiotic relationship with the Accounting
Establishment.

By way of a tangential prologue, I had originally intended
to include in my remarks reference to the activities of another
firm comprising the Accounting Establishment, namely, Touche Ross &
Co. That was because the original program listed that firm's
managing partner in the slot now occupied by Mr. Johnson. After
he realized that I was to be on this panel (possibly even because
of it) Mr. Palmer found it necessary to go abroad. Had he been
here, my roster of matters to which I would have asked my colleagues today to address their consideration would have extended
from Ampex to U.S. Financial (i.e., the roll of Touche Ross'
fiascoes which appear to have escaped the reach of the AICPA's
Ethics Division.

So it is that I am constrained, instead, to confront the
panel with a most aggravated matter involving Mr. Johnson's firm--
also a matter which seems to have escaped the censure of the

27

Accounting Establishment. I am alluding to the activities of one, Robert L. Vesco, who sat at the head of one of Coopers & Lybrand's clients, International Controls Corporation ("ICC").

This is not entirely a new matter for me; in fact, I devoted some pages thereto in my More Debits Than Credits, published two years ago. But yet the Vesco manipulations take on new and added interest from the voluminous report promulgated last winter by the Special Counsel designated by the SEC to study the ICC matter in order to recommend what action, if any, might be taken against various persons (including ICC's auditors) who might have been involved in transactions whereby assets of ICC and Investors Overseas Services ("IOS") were dissipated.

According to that report, central to the accounting aspects of this ICC-IOS tangled web of deception was a transaction whereby, as an incident to a loan arranged by ICC to IOS the former received 3 million warrants to acquire IOS shares. Through a subsequent (1971) amendment these warrants carried a penalty clause, whereby IOS would be constrained to pay $3.6 million ($1.20 per warrant) on the occurrence of certain contingencies. ICC, in its 1970 and 1971 income accounts, picked up $3.6 million as additional income, pretending that the IOS default had occurred concurrently with the 1971 amendment so that ICC, the accounts said, earned that sum as additional loan interest.

In my More Debits Than Credits I questioned the highly suspicious circumstances whereby Coopers & Lybrand was dropped by the SEC from the roster of defendants at the last minute -- just as the SEC vs. Vesco complaint was about to be filed in the courthouse.

But as I said, I am not here to again recite that saga. Instead, I turn to the Special Counsel's Report (Chapter VII, "The Warrant Income"). Sprinkled through that chapter are choice nuggets like the following:

Alternative methods of reporting and valuations which might also have been used would have reduced or eliminated reportable income from the warrants. That they were not is consistent with Vesco's attitude and demands on his financial advisers that accounting principles be applied in a manner which assured that the most favorable possible presentation be made of ICC's financial position. For purposes of financial reporting, the warrants might have been treated as additional interest income on the loan or as an investment in securities in which case income, if any, could not be realized unless and until the warrants were exercised or sold. ICC with the concurrence of Lybrand, opted for the reporting of warrants as interest income.

Another area in which judgments had to be made for
financial reporting purposes was the valuation of the
warrants. The possible range was between $.10 and
$1.20 per warrant, and the $1.20 figure was chosen.
It was also necessary to determine whether any portion of the income should be reported in 1970 or
await reporting until later years.

   To justify this booking of $3.6 million as a putative asset
the auditors felt called upon to ascertain whether there was an
ability on the part of IOS to pay such a sum. Here the Special
Counsel quotes from the auditors' workpapers, to wit:

"A consideration in the valuation of the IOS warrants
was IOS' ability to pay the $3.6 million (the penalty
if the reorganization did not occur) either from its
own resources or from the money on deposit with Butlers. LRB & M (Lybrand) did not confirm the (amounts)
on deposit. However, LRB & M (Lybrand) was aware
(per J. D. McMenamin) (a Lybrand partner-ed.) of the
amounts on deposit through a) review of AA's (Arthur
Andersen & Co. -ed) confirmations with Butlers in connection with the IOS (warrants) and b) from contact
with C & L (Coopers & Lybrand) which audits Butlers.
Through these means, LRB & M (Lybrand) was aware that
such deposits did exist in the (amounts) indicated
(and) for the contractual purposes they were intended.

"AA (Arthur Andersen) did not release their report
until after LRB & M's (Lybrand's) release of ICC
financials. Accordingly, at LRB & M's report date
IOS audited financials were not available. However,
through C & L's (Coopers & Lybrand's) review of AA's
(Arthur Andersen's) papers and contact with IOS, LRB &
M (Lybrand) was aware of IOS's financial position and
IOS's ability to pay the penalty (amounts). Based
on audited report (which denied an overall opinion
but which did not take exception to the relevant current position) IOS does have the ability to pay for
the reasons indicated in JDM's (McMenamin's) memo to
Graham Garner of C & L (Coopers & Lybrand)."

   I have no idea as to when that Lybrand workpaper was prepared. Notice the implicit reliance of Lybrand partner McMenamin.
As my More Debits Than Credits demonstrated, he was made overtly
aware of the diversion of a quarter of a billion dollars of IOS-
controlled Dollar Funds, and yet stood silent.

Significantly, there is a curious omission in the Lybrand
rationalization for permitting the $3.6 million to be booked as an
ICC asset and income.

Thus, logical reasoning should dictate that an ICC asset
would correspond with an IOS liability. Nowhere does the Special
Counsel's Report refer to this symmetry.

I infer that IOS did not during the years in question reflect
the presumptive complementary liability to ICC. Be it remembered
that Vesco was Chairman of the Finance Committee of both companies
and Lybrand audited the IOS complex after Vesco asserted his hege-
mony.

While I might understand such a schizoid, manic-depressive
mode of accounting from Vesco's mentality, I cannot thus reconcile
it with the presumptive sane and cool objectivity of a prestigious
member of The Accounting Establishment.

What does the Special Counsel's Report conclude on this warrant issue?

Fairness of Reporting and Disclosure

Special Counsel's accountant, Hertz Herson has reviewed
the reporting of the warrant income, including the valuation applied. Hertz Herson has expressed the view the
warrants would more appropriately have been accounted
for as an investment rather than interest income. As
such, this would result in the IOS note and warrants
being carried at an aggregate cost of $5,000,000. In-
come would be reflected only from the interest earned
currently, including amortization, of the discounted
note to its par value until the sale or disposition of
the assets.

Assuming, however, that the warrants were appropriately
reported as interest income, Hertz Herson has expressed
the view it was incorrect to ascribe to them a unit value
of $1.20. It believes there were significant uncertain-
ties which precluded such a valuation.

Hertz Herson nevertheless recognizes that professional
judgment may differ. Its criticism of the reporting is
based on its view that when faced with a choice of accounting methods ICC regularly opted for the method
which maximized currently reportable income. As noted,
this practice obscured the fact that during the years
1967 through 1971, the net earnings from operations re-

ported by ICC resulted almost entirely from acquisition accounting.

Alas, how sad to see Hertz Herson go up the mountain and then collapse. Surely the exercise of professional judgment demands the exercise of an independent judgment. Surely the firm recognized that C & L was going along with the Vesco proclivities for creating income through the bookkeeping office. Surely this in and of it-self should have impeached C & L's performance for having abdicated its presumptive independence.

I am deeply troubled by my sense that Hertz Herson were not as sanguine in their evaluation as the Special Counsel reported. Regrettably, my efforts to obtain a copy of the Hertz Herson report have been unavailing. Could Mr. Johnson or Mr. Kraut help me in this endeavor?

Clearly, I do not share the Special Counsel's absolution of C & L in this important respect, just as I fail to comprehend the SEC's 1972 apparent absolution of the auditors in the enormous Dollar Fund diversion and the warrant accounting.

And what of the Ethics Division of the AICPA? Have they taken cognizance of this situation? I expect that Dr. Sweeney might say that "a file has been opened on the matter." Query: Is the opening of a file an appropriate disciplinary response in the face of such action by the high priests in the temples of our pro-fession?

Be it remembered that at the very times these Vesco shenani-gans were being tolerated by C & L, its managing partner sat at the head of the Accounting Principles Board. Are accounting prin-ciples intended to serve as the Catch-22s for our profession, whereby they would be interpreted and applied in a fashion designed to accommodate the particular proclivities of the particular client? Is a body of principles to be thus bent, folded and mutilated?

I raise this cause celebre at this time and in these circum-stances not to embarrass Ken Johnson, who served so valiantly as the technical advisor to Phil Defliese when he was on the APB; in-stead, I do so to get an open response to the pervasive underlying issues from those heregathered round -- each of whom represents a sector of the Accounting Establishment.

Lest I nevertheless be accused of imposing on Ken Johnson by zeroing in on his firm, let me flesh out for you another, possibly even more aggravated, chain of circumstances.

In July, 1975, the Securities and Exchange Commission promulgated its monumental Accounting Series Release Number 173 exposing the actions of Peat Marwick Mitchell in no fewer than five major fiascoes: Penn Central, National Student Marketing, Republic National Life, Tally Industries and Stirling Homex.

For these transgressions PMM was prohibited, for a brief period, from taking on some new public corporations as clients, and was constrained to expose some aspects of its mode of conduct to a special review committee (one acceptable to the firm and the SEC). In addition, the firm had to consent to decrees of the court enjoining it from violating the Securities Laws again in the future

So it was that in mid-1975 the firm was subjected to an elaborate tongue-lashing, made to do some brief penance and to foreswea future violations. Significantly, the firm obtained a clean bill of health from one of its peers, Arthur Young & Company, in late 1975, and a limited clean bill from the special review panel required by ASR 173.

So enthralled was the SEC with the report of the Special Committee required by ASR 173 that, by a special ASR 173 supplement (ASR 173A), the Commission permitted PMM to move to self-regulation rather than being subjected to the continuing oversight by an external SEC-approved committee.

But lo!! Just last fall the SEC filed a complaint against Sharon Steel Corporation, its holding company (NVF) and several individuals, especially Victor Posner, alleging a catalogue of corporate and individual misconduct (e.g., using assets of public corporations as though they were those of a strictly private fiefdom). Aside from these enormous perquisites which apparently escaped the auditor's attention, the SEC complaint spelled out the following distortions in the audited financial statements of Sharon Steel:

In 1975, Sharon reported $25,520,000 pre-tax earnings, $13,878,000 of which earnings were overstated because of a number of improper accounting devices used by Sharon...

Among these improper accounting devices, we are told, were

In 1975 approximately $7,050,000 of Sharon's pre-tax earnings were properly attributable to Sharon's 1974 earnings...

In 1975 Sharon improperly revalued virtually its entire iron ore inventory, by creating a certain type of iron ore pellet (called ITPV)... This device created $4,929,000 in 1975 pre-tax earnings of under $12,000,000...

There were further allegations of "Misrecording of Iron Scrap Inventories," "Recording 1976 sales as 1975 sales," and several other categories of the fouling of GAAP and GAAS in Sharon's audited financial statements for 1975.

That reference in the SEC complaint to the Inventory hoax is especially intriguing--it may be worth our consideration for a few minutes.

Sharon, like most steel companies, has been maintaining its iron ore inventories on a LIFO basis. Consequently, these stocks are carried on their balance sheets at debased, historical costs.

Assume now that Sharon had three piles of such ores labeled, respectively, "L", "S", and "D" -- each with a LIFO carrying value of $1 million.

Alchemist Posner takes the three piles (all having a consistent metallurgy) and combines them, and Abracadabra! He says he has a new product; he puts an $8 million price tag on it, and into the 1975 closing inventory it goes with that number, producing a $5 million hypo for that year's income.

Why, it's so deceptively and cleverly simple--one wonders why it isn't done each day-- who knows, maybe it is.

And now, it should be noted, that among those who saw and were bedazzled by the Posner Alchemy (according to an opinion by Federal District Judge C. F. Poole of California) were "members of (Sharon's) outside accountant staff." The court branded the 1975 financial statements as "at best the cultivated product of questionable fluctuations and self serving maneuvering of accounting procedures." This, he said, was perpetrated "with some concurrence of respected outside accountants."

And here it must be told, Sharon's "respected outside accountants" for 1975 happened to be, you guessed it, Peat Marwick Mitchell & Co. Now, mind you, that 1975 audit was performed after PMM had been inculpated in ASR 173, pleaded mea culpa and promised to mend its ways (and, it might be added, after AY earned its more than a half million for its PMM peer review and its "A-OK" published seal of approval).

If it had been PMM which "blew the whistle" on its client after it discovered the ways in which it "had been had" I might manifest some compassion. Instead, it would appear from a Business Week article that this mare's nest was uncovered by Haskins & Sells, another member of the Accounting Establishment -- and not because the firm was engaged in a pro bono expedition. Instead, H & S's client, Foremost-McKesson & Robbins, was being threatened by a take-over by Sharon. Since Foremost chose not to fall into the Posner empire, it had its auditors do a review of the Sharon accountings--and lo!! while much of the detailed evidence is still under a court order of confidentiality, enough has surfaced to demonstrate the ineptness and/or scienter on the part of PMM. (It was in a proceeding brought by Foremost to enjoin Sharon from proceeding with the take-over that Judge Pool made the foregoing pronouncements.)

For present purposes, I challenge the SEC: Is not the firm in violation of its 173 undertakings and in contempt of the judgments of the Court in the several consent decrees? What are you doing about it? Are the auditors to be absolved of the Sharon shenanigans? Will PMM be permitted to "brazen it out"?

But also of important interest, what of the profession's disciplinary machinery -- that which is presently headed by Dr. Sweeney? Has it heard of Penn Central? National Student Marketing (other than of the members of the firm convicted of a felony)? Stirling Homex? Republic National Life? Tally Industries? And now Sharon Steel?

Mind you, the Ethics Division is alive and well, as can be demonstrated by the box score of its reported actions over the eight year period, 1970 through 1977. My analysis of these actions discloses 130 reported cases, thus:

For conviction of bribery	23
For failure to file (or for false filing) of personal returns	22
Because of revocation or suspension of member's certificate by this state-licensing body (where specific reasons not indicated)	21
For conviction of grand larceny, embezzlement, extortion, theft, perjury and corresponding high crimes	14
For conviction of mail fraud	8
For failing to disclose (or for false disclosure) to the SEC or IRS	6
For substandard auditing and reporting	5
For conviction of involvement in the Equity Funding fraud	5
For lack of independence	5
For moral terpitude and other undisclosed crimes	4
For solicitation and advertising	4
For violation of securities laws	3

34

```
For fraud on CPA exams or applications thereof     2
For refusal to cooperate in grand jury or
    state investigations                           2
For failure to pay for securities                  1
For obstructing justice                            1
For failure to acquire sufficient information      1
For threatening to inform on a client              1
For filing false reports with HUD                  1
For inadequate disclosure in footnotes             1
                             A TOTAL OF:  130
```

Study these constabulary actions with all your might and you will not find the perpetrators of the causes celebres, those who have induced the crisis in confidence or the credibility gap in our profession--excepting for the inexorable disciplining of those who were convicted of the felonies in Equity Funding and National Student Marketing.

I indict the ethics machinery of the Establishment for its inability to cope with the major aberrations on the part of my colleagues. Whether it be by design or the consequence of circumstances, the Ethics Division is rendered impotent in the face of a cause celebre. I will leave it for Dr. Sweeney to explain why and how come the Division is thus rendered ineffectual.

I have on several occasions accused the Establishment's disciplinary apparatus as being like the blind guides of Scriptures, those "who strain at a gnat while swallowing camels." This is dramatically epitomized by juxtaposing items which appeared in the initial 1976 and 1978 issues of the CPA letter, the AICPA biweekly newsletter which carries the message from the Establishment. Thus, from the 1976 publication:

AICPA member Maurice H. Stans, former Secretary of Commerce, has been found by a sub-board of the Trial Board of the AICPA to be not guilty of charges brought by the AICPA's division of professional ethics.

The ethics division's charges arose from Mr. Stans' plea of guilty in Federal Court in Washington in March of last year to five misdemeanors relating to his conduct as Chairman of the Finance Committee to Re-elect the President. It was alleged that the subsequent conviction tended to bring discredit to the profession. Mr. Stans contended that the offenses were minor and technical, that they had been found by the court to be unwillful and that the transactions upon which the convictions were based had been handled by him in good faith.

Following a full-day hearing, the sub-board, on
October 28, 1975, found that the charges of the
ethics division had not been proved. Mr. Stans requested publication of this finding and the sub-
board has authorized this notice.

And now from the first of this year's crop:
On September 9, 1977, a hearing panel of the Joint
Trial Board Division's Tenth Regional Trial Board
voted to expel a member of the AICPA and the New
Jersey Society of CPAs for acts discreditable to
the profession.

One of the discreditable act charges was failure
to take CPA courses as he had promised a trial board
hearing panel in 1973. That panel had found the
member guilty of performing substandard work in connection with a client's financial statements in violation of the AICPA Code of Professional Ethics. In
view of his statement of intention at the hearing to
take CPA courses on reporting standards, the panel
limited his penalty to an admonishment.

The other discreditable act charge was refusing to
deliver a W-2 form, which the ethics charging authority characterized as a "client record," until his
fee for accounting services was paid.

In addition, the member was charged with failure to
respond to requests by the AICPA ethics division to
produce audit work papers in connection with a subsequent examination of financial statements of the
same client that had been involved in the 1973 hearing.

The member did not appear at the September 9th hearing.
After hearing the charges, the panel found the member
guilty of the discreditable acts charges but not guilty
of the charge of refusal to deliver the client record
because of insufficient evidence that the document was
in fact a client record. Based upon its guilty findings,
the panel voted to expel the member from membership in
the New Jersey Society of CPAs and the AICPA and to
withhold publication of name from the notice of disciplinary action.

The member was advised of the hearing panel's decision
and did not request a review. The decision therefore
became effective on October 10, 1977.

36

Editor's Note: A Council resolution was recently amended to require disclosure of the member's name following a finding of guilty in a disciplinary action. The above decision was made prior to this amendment.

I will leave it for Dr. Sweeney to answer whether in his "heart of hearts" he believes the profession's credibility was made more contingent by the 1978 scoundrel than by Mr. Stans. I have made clear my considered view in other contexts. Again, I accuse Dr. Sweeney's apparatus of being very effective in straining out a gnat--while swallowing camels.

I further maintain that in his administration of the Division he has determined to be oblivious of the "Sunshine Standards" which should govern the activities of all agencies charged with a public interest. By so doing he is helping to protect those in the power structure of the Accounting Establishment who have contributed importantly to the prevailing malaise--and by this protection he is contributing to the perpetuation of this power structure.

In sum, I recognize the significance of the book of rules called the Code of Professional Ethics of my beloved profession, that of certified public accountancy. I maintain that the evil is not in the Code but in the ways in which it is administered in practice. In this circumstance, I find that the Securities and Exchange Commission has failed to fulfill its oversight responsibility.

To help strengthen the regulatory process for my profession I especially welcome this opportunity for a dialogue with representatives from what is subsumed in the epithet The Accounting Establishment.

DANIEL L. SWEENEY

Professional Ethics Enforcement

Much as I would like to respond to the humor of the previous
speaker, I have so much to convey to you in this brief period, I'll
just get to work. I would like to begin with an introduction for
those of you who may not know the precise background of the American
Institute of Certified Public Accountants. It is a national, voluntary membership, professional association, whose objectives are to
enhance the quality of practice of its members and at the same time
to improve the stature of the profession in the eyes of the public.
Our Code of Ethics is an important means of achieving these two
objectives and our disciplining mechanism is designed to give both
educational support and enforcement teeth to our Code of Ethics.

The AICPA Professional Ethics Division interprets and ad-
ministers the Code of Ethics, and that Code defines members' responsibilities for a number of the things that Mr. Kraut was talking
about; for independence, integrity and objectivity. It also defines
members' responsibilities for technical professional competence and
for adherence to professional accounting and auditing standards, and
there are certain other responsibilities to clients and the public
as well as to the other members. The Division investigates complaints against members and if justified, the Division disciplines
them either with administrative censure or it summons them before
the Joint Trial Board Division. The latter is an independent unit
that we say is within the Institute because it's physically housed
there and yet the Joint Trial Board Division likes to think of itself as a totally independent unit composed of the Trial Board Division of the Institute and representatives of each of the independent State Societies of CPAs. The State Societies of CPAs are
not units of the American Institute. They are independent bodies
and they pride themselves on that independence.

The Ethics Division does not wait for complaints to be filed
before it opens an investigation. The publication of a newspaper
story alleging misconduct or a notice in the SEC docket can trigger
an investigation. One of the features of our enforcement effort
is a program between the American Institute and a good many of the
federal agencies which receive accountants' reports on the disbursement of funds by local organizations which receive funds from
the sponsoring agency. When a federal agency encounters what it
believes to be substandard auditing by a CPA, it can submit the
allegedly substandard work to the AICPA Professional Ethics Division
for appropriate action and it is investigated as every other com-

38

plaint is. We also receive complaints from concerned members, bankers, or others who receive financial statements in the course of their business.

It would be useful for you to have some background on the environment in which our ethics enforcement activity takes place because this will supply some of the reasons why we do some of the things that we do. I would like to note first that every complaint is investigated as expeditiously as possible. The procedures that we follow in an investigation are thorough. They are consistent. And they are fair and firm for each member, in each investigation. It is as costly and time consuming for us to complete an investigation that is closed with a finding of no violation as it is to complete an investigation with a prima facie case of a violation of the Code which goes to the Trial Board. Because we are dealing with a professional person's reputation, our files and the decisions on closing actions taken on them are confidential. This is true up to the point where, if a Trial Board finds a respondent guilty, there is publication of the respondent's name. Our files are confidential for the very simple reason that a professional reputation is the most valuable asset that any professional person can have. If a member's technical competence is considered suspect in even the slightest manner, it can prove to be totally damaging to that individual. We have seen cases where word has been leaked in a small community that an ethics investigation was underway against an individual, and where there was no violation or a minor violation so that the decision would not have been published, but the gossip alone was extremely damaging to that person's ability to earn a living. This kind of gossip has damaged the member's professional reputation, his ego and that is the place where a professional person lives, with public disclosure of the simple fact that an investigation was underway. It does not require a finding by the Trial Board that this person was not professionally competent to cause this to happen.

The Ethics Division observes legal due process rights for all members when matters are in litigation. We do not have subpoena powers in the Institute so that anything in our files has been obtained voluntarily from our members. All such material is discoverable in a legal action by persons bringing suit against the member. We feel that in these circumstances, we cannot compel a member to voluntarily give us information which later could be used against him by a lay court or jury, and I stress the word "lay" there because it is extremely difficult to impart professional judgment to a jury which will enable it to evaluate technical standards, on a hindsight basis, in a complex business situation.

As you may have gathered from my remarks, our investigations are conducted only with respect to individuals. We may investigate a total situation in which more than one individual is involved, but because the action that we take can be taken only against an individual, we think in terms of dealing with files on individuals. The closing actions that the Division can impose, such as comment letters or the administrative censure, have to be given to an individual. If a person is going to be expelled or suspended from membership in the organized profession (a State Society or the Institute), this action has to be taken by the Trial Board against an individual. I will say a little more later about the fact that the profession is trying to gain a different type of enforcement capability with respect to firms, but that will be in the future.

One other feature I'd like to mention is that in an effort to avoid duplication of investigative effort, the American Institute operates with 43 State Societies of CPAs what is known as the Joint Ethics Enforcement Program. Briefly, this means the State Society investigates complaints which have local impact, and the Institute investigates those which have multi-state impact or broad national interest. There must be concurrence on the issue of administrative censures and on taking a case to the Trial Board. With most of these states, their bylaws are structured to be comparable to ours in disciplinary matters, and there may or may not be a formal contractual arrangement. With other states there may be neither of these arrangements but the Division continues to cooperate very closely with the Ethics Committee in enforcement cases. The purpose of these arrangements is to avoid a duplication of effort. The idea is that if the State Society investigates a case, the AICPA accepts their closing action as ours. If the AICPA investigates a case, the State Society accepts our closing action, and in that way we avoid a repetition of investigative effort. As you will see in my next remarks, there is enough investigating going on of certified public accountants to make them the most righteous people on earth at the present time. It is the Division's belief that there is no need to do any more overlapping of investigative activity, at least within the organized profession. We also feel that this process, by avoiding duplication, enables us to accomplish more enforcement activity. It promotes consistency in the processing of complaints and in the granting of closing actions. And it provides a basis for a more complete reporting of disciplinary actions taken by the profession now that we have decided to take that significant step.

To emphasize the reason for our interest in not duplicating ethics enforcement actions, let me detail for you the potential discipline that can face a person who is accused of violating technical standards within the public accounting profession. First of all, there are lawsuits brought in state or federal courts. Depending on the court, it can assess money damages in civil liability suits, or it can levy fines and/or imprisonment if there is a finding

40

that criminal acts were involved. In addition to the courts, there are actions by the State Boards of Accountancy, which are administrative arms of the state and which thus have subpoena powers. They can suspend or revoke a certified public accountant's certificate and his right to practice. They can take away the major asset which he has for earning a livelihood. If the practitioner is involved with clients who are required to file reports with the Securities and Exchange Commission, the SEC can take two very effective disciplinary actions. They can issue injunctions against continuing alleged violations of the Federal Securities laws and they can also take other remedial actions which include such things as required participation in a supervised peer review or a quality control type of review and either a temporary or permanent injunction against practicing with SEC listed clients. Next comes the American Institute and the State Societies working together to reach a closing action that can involve either a private or a public censure and suspension or expulsion from membership. If you happen to be practicing in one of the few states that is not a participant in the Joint Ethics Enforcement Plan, you could be faced with the AICPA functioning in one investigation with one closing action and also have the State Society conducting another investigation and concluding with still another closing action. The ultimate outcome of this duplication of discipline would be that a member could be expelled from both bodies of the organized profession or suspended from either or both for a specified period of time.

At this point, I would like to digress slightly and respond to some of Mr. Kraut's concerns about what the organized profession is doing to respond to some of the charges made by members of the Congress, by the recent report of the Cohen Audit Commission and by others who have expressed concern about the quality of financial statements and the manner in which they are presented. Probably the major emphasis that the profession has perceived in the area of things that need to be done, is for the profession to have the ability to discipline firms. We have been promised this is going to be the subject of legislation if it is introduced at the federal level, and in order to set up a structure within the organized profession that can deal with firms, there has been organized within the AICPA a newly structured Division for Firms. This is made up of two parts, the public firms, those that deal with clients who have to submit reports to an organized securities exchange and to the SEC, and the private sector firms, which is an organization for those firms which do not wish to operate in this very public arena. A number of technical quality control procedures are required for membership in this Division which should reduce the ethics actions needed in the future. The objectives of both sections are very similar. They want to control and to improve the quality of professional performance of the people who are going to be members within this group. Among the required steps in this process are: that a member of either section must submit to a peer review, that is, a quality control type of internal review, every three years; that sanctions can be provided against firms which are found to have inadequate control procedures over technical professional engagements or for those whose method of operation and conduct of their practice does not come up to the level that is considered appropriate for public practice; and it is required that there be continuing professional education for the entire professional staffs of the member firms. And the Public Oversight Board for the Public Section can do something that none of the other organizations can do, and that is, provide monetary fines against firms if they do not meet the standards of practice demanded for membership. There are other requirements for membership that I'm going to have to move quickly beyond, but one of the points I would stress is that the Division for Firms is going to be overseen by a public oversight board of five distinguished members of the public who have no connection with the public accounting profession. With this technical performance control at the Firm level, combined with the other enforcement activities that I have mentioned which provide potential disciplinary action against members, it should be possible to keep the members of the organized profession aware of and alert to their responsibilities to the public. If this combination of forces cannot do the job of policing the profession, I doubt that anything else can.

There are other things we are trying to do to improve the effectiveness of ethics enforcement. I mentioned earlier this matter of the avoidance of publicity, and since the start of this year, when there is a finding of guilty by a Trial Board panel, that fact will be published. A practitioner's greatest concern in the publication of his name for a proven lack of technical competence is for the great harm that this does to one's professional reputation. Seeing this done in those cases where a person is found guilty should cause many practitioners to consider most carefully the work that is before them at all times. The Ethics Division is now disclosing statistics on the number of files that are being processed by the Institute and how they are closed. We are trying to shed as much light as we can on our operations to show that the profession is working in this area.

As has been pointed out by our other speakers, these are unprecedented times in the history of the profession. We are concerned about openness for public view and understanding of all the activities of the senior committees of the Institute. There have been allegations that these activities are dominated by major firms. Let me assure you that when any of you take time to visit one of the open meetings of the senior committees of the Institute, you will find that everyone on the committee participates and has an opportunity to influence the outcome of the actions taken. Representatives of the large firms are as diverse in their views as are those of the smaller practice units, and representation is balanced. I would also just like to mention one other activity that is getting publicity at this time. The AICPA engaged in a major effort to modify the profession's advertising and solicitation rules and others including the general standards provisions of our Code. This was initiated within the profession in response to an observed trend in consumer groups' pleas for information and the trend of court decisions related to regulation of the professions. This change was approved by the Institute's membership. The vote just ended last Friday night and in response to requests from the publics we are trying to serve, including many governmental agencies, practitioners are going to advertise and solicit for new clients almost at will. It was in response to a request from another governmental agency about 50 years ago that the Institute made its members stop advertising. Now again, at least in part at the government's request, we're going to permit them to start it. It will be interesting to see how long it takes before they want us to stop it again.

The public accounting profession is trying to be responsive to its publics; in rapidly changing times that is as hard for us as it is for you. We ask that you withhold judgment, until we can show what we are doing and what we can do, before wasting more governmental effort on an already heavily repetitious effort at disciplining this group of professional practitioners.

KENNETH P. JOHNSON

I hope everyone noticed that the three other panelists
are doctors and were so introduced. You probably noticed that
there was no special title fixed to my name, which allows you to
conclude that I am the patient. Now, you could ask yourself,
and if you don't you should, what I'm doing here today. You've
heard me, in my professional capacity, abused by the well-intentioned
regulator. You've also heard me, and my firm, dealt with in a
reasonably inaccurate way by a distinguished professor. What's
my role? Well, my role, I think, is to bring balance to this
position, particularly to the students, for I feel those that are
farther along in matriculation can easily understand the generalities
with which the regulator dealt with the topic, the half-statements
and suggestions that my colleague, Dr. Briloff, so skillfully employs.
So I'll talk to the students and say, don't let these guys scare
you. It's true that public accounting today is a profession of
takers of risks. But dealing with the topic of our presentation,
ethics, there is no group in the U.S. today whose ethics are as
high as those of public accountants.

Dr. Kraut ticked off three cases where there were management failures, and please note that that's important, for the
first line of defense against these matters is the management
and directors of the companies, who are elected by thousands of
shareholders and are given duties to perform and fill. In those
three companies, as illustrations of expansion of ethics, a
closer analysis will show that two of those cases are violations
of good sensible business judgment and there is one where clearly,
and the court has said, the auditor who was involved apparently
was violating his own professional responsibility and, in fact,
was in league with an apparently dishonest client. Just to bring
a sense of balance, let me tell you that Coopers & Lybrand has
600 publicly held clients. You've heard the term "Big Eight" —
there are seven other firms that have about equal sized clients,
give or take a little. Against that spectrum, an example of five
would be few indeed. Let me bring a sense of balance in this way:
There are approximately 135,000 members of the AICPA, and the people
that have been involved in these actions number roughly 100.
Included in that hundred, for the list is not quite accurate, are
some who were guilty of violations while attempting to achieve
the CPA examination.

Our rules are tight. The penalties for failure in our
business are severe. Dan's mentioned some of them, for example,
imprisonment. There was a partner out in Tulsa, Oklahoma, in the

44

firm of Arthur Young and Co., who went to jail because he was trying to protect his client's rights by refusing to surrender certain
documents that belonged to the client but were under subpoena by
a court. The partner went to jail. I talked to him. He didn't
like it. We get sued. And we have difficulty buying insurance
because of some boxcar settlements that read well in the newspapers
but are awfully hard to cover out of a firm's income. We lose
our reputations. I think Dan is totally correct; there is nothing
that's more valuable to me as a professional man than my reputation
for being someone who is honest and fair in his dealings. And
so we've developed a defensive sort of code: a set of rules that
don't allow me to accept gifts from a client, that don't allow
me to make investments in client companies, that don't allow me
to enter into business with people that are even officers of corporations. And, by and large, we live by those rules. Is it hard?
Of course it is. The rules, by the way, apply even to the spouse
and children of partners in public accounting firms. The fact that
they still apply shows how far behind our ethical requirements are -
as you know, about the worst thing in the world that one can do
today is attempt to give clear direction to one's wife.

Nevertheless, I think all these burdens are worth bearing
because the rewards of participating in this profession are greater
than the costs. The rewards are numbered in a couple of different
ways. Recently, I spoke to a group of attorneys in San Francisco.
I was trying to describe some of the many events, some of the many
investigations and changes, that were going through the public
accounting profession. Someone in the audience came up and he
said, "I envy you." He said, "You happen to be in the profession
at the time it is going through a very dramatic change and you have
an opportunity to contribute to that to make your profession
better." And he said, "I envy you for it." Up until that time,
I don't think I'd really thought too much about it because there's
a sense, when you're beat on the head and shoulders, to be a little
reluctant to stick your head up much over the top of the fence.
But after he told me that I thought that this is the challenge
and this should be the attraction for young people that seek to
come into our profession today. We are undergoing change; Dan
has mentioned quite a lot. The most significant change that he
has mentioned is the fact that, for the first time, we're going
to divide into a group of public company auditors, those that
have responsibilities to thousands and thousands of small shareholders and some larger ones, all around the United States - the
very backbone that keeps our system of allocating capital resources
alive. Some of the new disciplines will impact the managements
of the firms. So that now, or in the future at least, should I
happen to go to jail for an alleged improper activity in connection
with a client audit, I will have company. My managing partner
will probably be with me.

We are accepting those changes, I think, with remarkable speed. I don't think we've quite gone far enough. Coopers & Lybrand, my firm, testified before the recent Moss Committee hearings in which we offered some statements for additional reforms. A very interesting one was this, that we felt that disciplining of auditors should be outside the framework of the new division of public company auditors. The reason for this is that we think it's impossible for anyone, even a professional group, to serve as both judge and jury. We offered an alternative plan, a better mechanism, that is more easily accepted by the lay public, to provide the right kind of discipline. We're willing to accept those costs.

Now, I can't respond to all of the things that Dr. Briloff said. Unfortunately, I didn't have an opportunity to share with him exactly the case that he intended to bring up, so I couldn't quite prepare myself. But I will tell you that the record of the public accounting profession is really pretty good. I'll tell you that the public accounting profession is going to get a whole lot better. And I'm going to offer an opportunity for those of you who wish to participate in part of the exercise to come and join us. Let me tell you some of the things you will find very interesting. We are working out new relationships with the SEC. The first panelist mentioned the fact that the SEC, in July, is going to report to Congress. He also mentioned the fact that, at the present time, Chairman Williams' view is that the establishing of standards and ethics in the private sector can be done with some additional changes to the mechanism, which Dan Sweeney has already described to you. We are undergoing an immense attack on our auditors' independence; this is an area where we still have some additional work to do. For I think our independence, our credibility, is really the thing that makes our service worthwhile.

There are areas under attack as to the scope of the auditor's service. Should we be restricted from providing services that go beyond the attest function? The Cohen Commission has dealt with that. Their conclusion is that there is no evidence in the area of management consulting services, save only one case, where management consulting services impacted the auditor's ability to serve as the attestor to financial statements. This area needs new development; the topic will be under study, and possibly under change, as time goes along. We are paying more attention to the appearance of independence, reminding you, of course, that the facts of independence have always been dealt with very carefully by the profession. Listen to this new rule promulgated by the SEC: it would cause the auditor to be non-independent if he is sued by a bonding company because of a defalcation that has occurred in the client company environment. This obviously is an extreme. It illustrates that

46

the SEC doesn't totally understand the way that activities go on
in the commercial world. But it's another aspect of the interaction between the conflicts of interests which don't have much
to do with independence, conflicts of interests between an auditor
and his client. These topics, again, are under study and possibly
will be under change in the future.

Let me sum up in this way. You've heard some serious criticisms and some misstatements about accounting ethics. Most of
the people in our profession, in fact, keep very high standards
of ethics in practice and they will probably get better in the
future. There's room for the students. There's opportunity for
you to come and contribute to our continued improvement.

DISCUSSION

KRAUT: Dan Sweeney stated before that the AICPA is now going
to publish its so-called guilty verdicts, and I understand that
this action resulted from considerable pressure. I would like
to ask him: Why was the public for so long denied the right
to know that the persons or firms that performed the audits and
prepared the reports on the financial statements were either
incompetent or dishonest or unethical?

SWEENEY: The only thing I can tell you is that the requirements
for publicity in a guilty verdict came about because of the concern expressed by the Cohen Audit Commission that this be done.
I can't give you a specific reason why it wasn't done previously
in all cases. The Trial Board panel probably did not think the
public would be better served by that publicity at that time.
But for now, the profession is saying that any time a person is
found guilty of a charge brought before the Trial Board, the
name and the charge must be published. Previously, there were
cases where this information was published, as Dr. Briloff pointe
out. He has very carefully monitored everything that's been published on this. And in the past, we have published names where
the Trial Board felt that the charge was of such a magnitude
that the public ought to be protected from the individual involved.

KRAUT: Why was the AICPA so reluctant, though, to publish the
results of its disciplinary proceedings? Or doesn't the AICPA
believe that the public investor is entitled to know that he may
have a cause of action where he has relied on the report of the
individual, which report is probably prepared by an individual
as opposed to the whole firm, even though the firm's name goes
on it?

JOHNSON: Well, let me answer your question in a practical way.
(Excuse me, Dan, let me just step in here for a minute.) Because you see, this illustrates your misunderstanding of how the
system works. The fact is that the management and the board of
directors of an enterprise are so significantly sensitive to any
suggestion of a failing on the part of their auditing firm that
publicizing a name as an attempt to protect the investors really
would have no practical, meaningful effect. What would happen
to anybody that happened to be before the AICPA Trial Board on
a charge of lack of confidence is that they would begin to find
their clientele silently eroding away. Because remember, the
auditor's stock in trade is credibility and there is no manage-

ment that I know of, and of course we have 600 public companies, that would be willing to stay with an auditing firm whose reputation for competence has been brought into question in a serious way. Management has an interest in the improvement and the adding of credibility to their financial statements. So that while publication seems, on the surface, to be a useful thing, as a practical matter it adds very little at all to the process.

KRAUT: How can you say it has no practical effect? The SEC filed a civil injunction action under the federal securities laws in 1974 against U.S. Financial and various individuals. The SEC also instituted a disciplinary proceeding under its rules against Touche Ross, the first such proceeding that resulted in peer review of a major accounting firm. The disclosure that the SEC made pursuant to its findings gave stockholders of the company and bond holders ammunition to seek redress in private civil actions. Actions were brought in federal court and in state court, and several months ago a $35 million judgment was obtained in a state court in California against Touche Ross, which is appealing the judgment. Now, isn't it the fear of civil liability that has really kept the AICPA from releasing information with respect to misconduct by its members?

JOHNSON: I don't know. I'd have to speculate. My guess is that there may be an element of that. In fact, I would also suspect that in this private enterprise system, which doesn't have the protections that are graciously offered to a regulatory agency like the SEC, that frequently serves as both judge and jury, we are hesitant to deal in a public and reckless manner with the reputation of some man who has taken four years of college and many years of apprenticeship and is trying to make a living serving the public.

KRAUT: I've got a question for Dr. Sweeney. How can your people effectively investigate the facts when they don't have power to compel the firms or the individuals to produce information? Now, I have been involved in enforcement work at the SEC for approximately 10 years, and I can tell you that when the SEC operates informally we almost universally don't obtain the amount and quality of information as when we do utilize the subpoena power. I've also been involved in civil litigation where civil rules of procedure provide for issuance of subpoenas or notices to produce with the compulsion, or potential compulsion, of a court order standing behind it. I have found that this measure of compulsion, unfortunately, provides the only truly effective way to get to the truth. Now, how can you say that the AICPA's procedures afford a means of getting to the truth, which I think should be your objective, if you have absolutely no power to compel any of your member firms or member individuals to cooperate?

49

SWEENEY: Admittedly the only compulsion that we have is the threat of removal from membership for the person if he doesn't cooperate, and I agree that we are at a disadvantage. I'd love to have the SEC's powers in the conduct of my investigations. If I'm going to have people throwing darts at me from all directions, as if I ought to be able to accomplish great things in this spot, it would help to be able to move directly into an investigation and immediately get at the critical evidence. I will concede that we've got some beautiful "foot draggers" in the profession. Where the respondent is being advised by an attorney, who is serving him as an advocate, whether the respondent is right or wrong, to the very last ditch, the attorney will allow him to concede nothing. The attorney seems to feel it is his duty to make any investigation as difficult as possible. Whether they believe there is evidence to support or to oppose their position they make it as difficult as possible to get to the essential data needed whether or not it will show an actual prima facie violation. That process is all part of the game we play. In a sense it's sort of a chess game. With our requests for information, we keep zeroing in, we keep closing them off, and closing them off, and closing them off, until, finally they have to come up with what we want. I'll concede, it's a long process, but the operation of the law itself, or justice itself, is a slow and careful process, unless you want to do the kinds of things you read about in the newspapers everyday. Look at the Los Angeles police; how many people have they arrested for being the "midnight strangler," or whatever on earth they're calling him out there. It is easy to make an arrest; it is easy to publish names; it is easy to destroy someone's reputation in the press, but you sure don't read about it when they find out he is the wrong party and they have to let the guy go. We are concerned about making false moves, Dick; it's just that simple. I'm as eager as you and I'm as eager as Professor Briloff to expel the "rascals" in our profession. We surely have some; I wouldn't deny that. But it's something you have to do carefully, step by step, and you want to be sure when those building blocks are laid down that when you're finished you've got a solid structure that's going to really prove a violation and remove the offender from the ranks of professional respectability.

KRAUT: How many people have you expelled from your membership for failure to cooperate?

SWEENEY: I couldn't tell you that just off the top of my head but there have been people expelled for this.

MODERATOR: Dr. Briloff, would you care to get into this match?

BRILOFF: I believe that the audience really has sensed what it

50

is that brothers Johnson and Sweeney have been suggesting, namely, that the AICPA process is, as far as discipline is concerned, very frequently debased into a CYA process - meaning a "cover your anatomy" process. As Dr. Sweeney knows, it costs a hell of a lot of money for the "foot draggers" to bring in these important advocates; and so the process ends up as a two-tier system of justice -- one for the rich and the powerful, and the other for the poor and powerless. And it's just this kind of a circumstance that I'm inveighing against. I applaud so very much and so very sincerely and intensely an important message that Ken Johnson gave to you, the students. And it's the message I want to applaud and concur in. And that is when you, literally you, move into these positions of power and responsibility that some of you will be moving into, whether in academe or in practice or in corporations, remember these commitments that we have all been addressing ourselves to today. Dr. Sweeney has referred importantly to the two-divisional system that has now recently been implemented by the AICPA. I'll close by reciting a story, undoubtedly apocrypahl, about the lady who wanted to buy an exotic bird as a present for her family for some anniversary. She went to the pet shop, saw a parakeet she wanted to buy, but the owner said, "Now wait a minute, tell me who is in your family before I permit you to buy it." She said, "Well, I have two daughters and my husband." The owner replied, "No, you're not going to buy it." "Well, why not?" "Because this parakeet happens to have lived for a number of years in one of the most famous bordellos in New Orleans, and has picked up some choice language; and I wouldn't permit it in a house with young ladies." The lady persisted, and so, she took the bird home. At the appropriate moment, with the family gathered about, she lifted the cover off the birdcage and the bird shook its head, whistled and said, "Hmmm, a new house," looked at the lady, whistled again and said "a new madam," looked at the girls... "new girls," and then looked at the husband and said "same customers."

Just one point, who is it that has been put at the head of the executive committee of the AICPA-SEC Division? -- the managing partner of Peat Marwick. Now, I don't deny his qualifications, but I say let him answer a few questions. "Where were you when your firm's monstrous aberrations took place? What did you do when you found out? How are you cooperating with the AICPA, your litigation notwithstanding, to bring about the judgment by your peers?" He should respond just as Bert Lance and William Miller were made to respond to demands from the public, without their reputations being necessarily destroyed - excepting to the extent that they should be. Let him answer publicly because the accounting profession is public. And just by way of a footnote to history, when, just seven years ago, in March or April of '71, Peat Marwick brought an ethics complaint against one Abraham

51

Briloff, they published their action in their firm's newspaper.
Why did they bring this ethics complaint? -- because Briloff
dared to criticize the Peat Marwick accountings in the Penn-
Central case. By way of reciprocal courtesy, as Dr. Sweeney
notes, I brought an ethics complaint against Peat Marwick, based
on Penn-Central. When I write to Dr. Sweeney, to inquire as
to where it stands, his response is, "It's in an open file."

SESSION III

"Membership and Role of Corporate Boards"

Joel Seligman
Professor of Law
Northeastern University

Franklin Gill
Chief Corporate and Finance Attorney
Administrative Services Group
Sun Company

Martin Krasney
Executive Director
Aspen Institute of Humanistic Studies

Brother Leo V. Ryan
Dean
College of Business Administration
University of Notre Dame

JOEL SELIGMAN

For close to eleven months, the Securities and Exchange
Commission has been involved in a comprehensive reexamination
of the rules bearing upon corporate governance, at least for those
firms subject to its jurisdiction. During September of last
year, the SEC began a series of hearings and one of the striking
aspects of these hearings, which may ultimately result in proposals to amend the SEC's proxy rules or perhaps proposals for
new legislation, was the consensus that existed among a number
of individuals, ranging from say Ralph Nader types like myself
all the way to American Bar Association and corporate executives
on certain aspects of the selection and role of the board and
how it might best be improved. There was obviously great concern on the part of virtually everyone who spoke that, at least
in the past decade, the board hasn't done well enough. Whether
you look at the close to 400 bribery disclosures that have
been made to the SEC, or periodic financial disasters such as
the Penn-Central case, or cases of extraordinarily aggressive
fraud, such as Equity Funding, you see a record that speaks
very poorly of the board. By September 29 of last year, there
were probably relatively few people who would have disagreed
with the statement of Ohio Senator, Howard Metzenbaum, when
he testified before the SEC, "The controversy is not over
whether something should be done. Everyone agrees that reform
is necessary. The controversy is over how much should be done,
and, more importantly, how should the reforms be implemented."

Now I certainly agree with Senator Metzenbaum and, as one
who has taken a polar position in the corporate governance debate,
advocating generally the need for new federal corporation laws
and specifically the need for a board of directors wholly independent
of operating executives, perhaps I can best serve the panel and
this audience by distinguishing those questions concerning the
board where there seems to be a broad concensus from those of
enduring controversy.

As of this date, I should suppose nearly everyone would
agree that directors should work harder, meet more often, be better
informed and better remunerated than they were say a decade ago.
There is nearly as broad a concensus that a majority, or most
members of the board should be outsiders; that is, nonfull-time
employees of the corporation they direct so that the board will
possess independence from senior operating executives. For similar
reasons, many urge that attorneys, accountants, and investment
bankers employed by a corporation should not serve on a board.

55

There is also broad agreement that the board should possess
audit, compensation, or nominating committees composed entirely
or nearly entirely of outside directors.

Now, I would not argue with the adoption of any of these
reforms. I would certainly urge that the adoption of these reforms
by all U.S. firms would be salutary. But I doubt these reforms
taken alone would make that much difference. So let me highlight
some of the areas where there is enduring question.

First and perhaps most decisively is the question: Who
shall nominate directors? Unless and until mechanisms are established to remove senior operating executives directly or indirectly
from the nominating process, I am doubtful that boards really
will possess sufficient independence to effectively review the
actions of senior executives. Presently, most boards remain passive
because senior executives control the proxy machinery by which
directors are nominated and elected. Only if senior executives are
barred from serving on the board or nominating directors can we
expect democracy to function in any meaningful sense. For the board,
like the separate branches of the federal government, best functions
when it can freely check executive violations of laws, executive
self-interest, or gross errors of judgment.

A second enduring controversy revolves around the question
of the staffing of the board. An effective board in a billion
dollar corporation requires a small but effective full-time staff
to adequately monitor the performance of senior executives. For
the same reasons that Congressional hearings are aided by full-
time staff attorneys, boards of directors require the aid of a
loyal and competent staff to research and frame pertinent issues.

The third major controversy concerns whether new rules for
the selection and performance of boards should be mandatory or
merely suggested by guidelines. Now, this type of question tends
to draw a kind of paradoxical response from the corporate community.
Typically, you'll find the most responsible executives coming forth
and saying, "We don't need mandatory rules because honest and
well-managed corporations will voluntarily comply with well-intended
guidelines." But this misses the point entirely. We generally
don't need new rules for the majority of American corporations that
are honest and well-managed. We need them specifically for the
corporations that are dishonest, poorly managed, or subject to
executive conflicts of interest, and these are the firms least
likely to follow guidelines and where the public would be most
served by new laws. If new legislation is seen not as an attempt
to punish anyone but as a wise expedient to prevent incompetent
or negligent actions, self-serving actions, or fraudulent actions
from ever occurring, perhaps the case for new legislation is best

56

put. To put it simply, if corporate executives were angels, there would be no need for boards of directors in the first place. It's only because they're not angels that we need boards and the basic question is: How can we make the boards effective?

Now the final open question, and a seriously debated one by some is: Who should adopt and enforce new laws, the federal government or the states? In light of the fact that states have used lax corporation laws as a mechanism for generating tax revenues for close to 100 years, there are very few who see the need for reform on the board who believe that reform should be adopted by the states. This is a little bit like asking Las Vegas to come up with anti-gambling rules. I thought we were going to be fortunate today to have Mr. Samuel White, the General Counsel and Vice President of Sun Oil Corporation, here as one of the last of the true romantics to defend the state's prerogatives and the ability of the state to reform laws, a task almost as improbable as gaining Vanessa Redgrave membership in the Jewish Defense League. Unfortunately, Mr. White is not here and I do not know whether his pinch hitter from Sun Oil Corporation wants to take up that particular gauntlet.

It's a hard one to take up. To this date, corporations can choose their state of incorporation. Because of the perceived advantages in choosing the state with the laxest laws – and we have states like Delaware which derive 15-20 percent of their income from marketing, in a sense, lax laws – it's very unlikely that serious reform will come at the state level. It's for this reason that those who most strenuously advocate reform tend to say it either must come from SEC rules or from new legislation enacted by Congress and presumably enforced by the SEC.

In sum, the four major issues, I think, that would divide this panel and divide any reasoned discussion of the selection and role of the board and that are open to serious debate at this point are: First, who shall nominate the board? Second, will the board have sufficient staff so it can do its full job? Third, will reforms be presented merely in a package of voluntary guidelines, say similar to a recent Business Lawyer article suggesting corporate directors' guidelines, or will they be mandatory in the form of, say a new Congressional enactment? And finally, will reform come at the state level or will it come at the federal level?

57

FRANKLIN GILL

As a pinch hitter for Mr. White, the General Counsel of Sun Company, I shall follow his proposed remarks. But, in the interest of assuring some controversy, I shall do so by seeking to respond to some of the arguments so ably made by Professor Seligman and shall add my personal views.

It is notable that there is little or no controversy on so many questions of corporate governance. We share the view that all corporations registered under the Exchange Act should be managed under the supervision of a Board of Directors with a majority of the Board composed of persons who are not employees of the corporation, and who are not partners of law firms, accounting firms, or investment banking houses which give regular counsel to management. We share the view that such corporations should establish three committees: an Audit Committee and an Executive Compensation Committee, each with a majority of outside directors, and a nominating committee composed entirely of outside directors. Just how "outside directors" or "independent directors" are to be defined is the subject of some differences of view. The attorney, accountant, or banker of an outside firm employed by a corporation may be highly interested in supporting the policies of management which another disinterested party would look at differently. However, this may not always be true. It is noteworthy that the New York Stock Exchange, in requiring that the Audit Committee be composed of directors independent of management, left the decision of what kind of relationship would interfere with independence up to the Board itself. A rigid formula would not meet the needs of the diversity of American corporations. We believe that the SEC could contribute importantly to an improvement in corporate governance by adopting guidelines covering these matters.

Professor Seligman identifies the first open question as: Who shall nominate directors? He is searching for a mechanism to remove senior corporate operating executives from the nominating process. I doubt that this would be desirable even if it could be achieved, because senior executives certainly should be able to contribute significantly to the identification of the needs of the Company and the people who can fill them. But this does not mean that they need to control the selection process. We suggest that a nominating committee of directors be composed of outside directors and that it seek recommendations from shareholders and senior executives, as well as other sources of information inside and outside of the corporation.

58

The second question posed concerns the staffing of the Board. Professor Seligman advocates a full-time staff. I heartily disagree with this proposal. I believe that all administrative experience suggests that a full-time staff would eventually be put in the position of a rival, rather than an aid, of the corporate staff to the detriment of both. Of course, any director should have access at the Company's cost to outside consultants for legal, financial, engineering or other advice on specific problems. In over 20 years of work in corporate law, I am familiar with many cases where directors have employed lawyers, accountants, and investment advisors to review specific problems on their behalf and have requested the corporation to pay their fees. Although I have read cases where disputes have arisen, it has been my experience that the corporation has always agreed to such requests. This is entirely proper and suggests that it may be desirable to have a policy approved in advance for employment of such advisors and reimbursement of reasonable expenses. But, it is unlikely that a permanent staff would be well equipped to deal with unforeseen problems, and it surely could become an administrative nightmare.

The third area of controversy is whether or not guidelines should be mandatory. We have suggested that guidelines be adopted by the SEC for guidance as the name suggests. No rules can adequately deal, in my opinion, with the infinite variety of situations in which American corporations do business. Flexibility is important. Mandatory rules immediately bring into play elaborate procedures for review, staff interpretations, no-action letters. I believe that guidelines would influence the behavior of all regulated companies without being imposed by the force of law.

Finally, Professor Seligman raises the question whether new laws should be adopted by the federal government or the states. He says that states have no interest in revising their corporate laws and he doubts that nonchartering states have the constitutional power to adopt laws bearing on the selection and role of the board.

Suppose a large commercial state, say California, adopted a statute providing for the "minimum" standards supported by Professor Cary and required each corporation maintaining its principal office in the state to be subject either to the entire corporate law of that state or at least to specified minimum standards. And suppose that, thereafter, other large commercial states such as Illinois, New York, Ohio, Michigan, Pennsylvania, and Texas followed suit. It would seem that few major corporations would, under such circumstances, continue to be available as prospects for the so-called "race for the bottom." How many companies would, for example, want to establish their corporate headquarters in Nevada where the corporation laws have been cited as unreasonably promanagement? Corporations generally are not going to move their corporate headquarters for corporate governance purposes. The economic considerations of proper headquarters location would be far more important.

Is such a proposal possible? I suggest that examination of the New York and California statutes shows a trend in this direction with their sections on "pseudo-foreign corporations." In the case of California, the statute is applicable to foreign corporations, including a foreign parent corporation that does not transact business in the state, if the average property factor, payroll factor, and sales factor for taxes is more than 50 percent and if more than one-half of its outstanding voting securities are held on record by persons having addresses in the state. An exemption is provided for companies listed on a national securities exchange. In New York, certain sections of the corporation law are applicable to foreign corporations with an exemption for companies listed on a national securities exchange or where less than one-half of its income was allocable to the state for tax purposes. These statutes cover some of the matters with which Professor Cary is concerned.

About ten years ago, Professor Stanley A. Kaplan of the University of Chicago Law School, in an article entitled "Foreign Corporations and Local Corporate Policy," 21 <u>Vanderbuilt Law Review</u> 433 (1968), concluded that there were no jurisdictional or constitutional obstacles to host states, as compared to the states of incorporation, adopting statutory requirements concerning the internal affairs of the corporation. In regard to the policy of the states in pursuing such an objective, he indicates that there has been a lack of interest. One of the possibilities he cites as a reason for this is the dramatic growth of federal "intervention and inventiveness in this area." He then goes on at page 479 to make the following observation:

If, however, several important states chose to use this statutory directive device for protective purposes and asserted it with vigor, it might have some effect in reversing the accelerating tendency of all corporation statutes to become mere enabling acts.

We have already seen the U.S. Supreme Court set limitations on an expansion of Rule 10b-5. It is somewhat evident that the reason for this has been the ever increasing caseload burden on the federal courts. The adoption of minimum standards does not eliminate this problem, since it suggests litigation as a method of administering the law.

The Commission can ignore this signal from the Supreme Court

and urge Congress to pass federal legislation. There is no doubt
about this. I, personally, would prefer to see such an alternative
held in reserve. Let us see if the responsible people who manage
our corporations, their counsel, both inside and outside, and
legal scholars, cannot exert sufficient pressure in the key states
I have suggested to get this matter properly handled there. If
the job does not get done within a reasonable time, then the
federal alternative is obviously still available. Thank you.

MARTIN KRASNEY

A Plea for Extensive Boards

The question of the appropriate composition of corporate
boards has been a source recently of considerable controversy.
I shall try to demonstrate that the controversy is largely the
result of misperceptions by the corporate sector with regard to
the kind of board membership most likely to serve their best
interests. A corporation should not perceive a highly-independent
and diversified, outsider-dominated board as a threat inflicted
by hostile adversaries, but rather seize upon such a structure
as a highly useful instrument in the advancement of corporate
goals.

Survival and independence are the two most basic and essential
corporate goals. All other corporate accomplishments are piled
up on these foundations. The primacy of survival is rarely stated,
but universally acknowledged.

The act of incorporation is relatively swift, uncomplicated
and inexpensive. It takes place scores of times daily. Its opposite
is similarly a frequent occurrence. We sometimes forget this second
phenomenon, since even in today's climate of mergers and takeovers,
most of the more visible corporations survive. The wreck of the
Penn Central or the bailout of Lockheed reminds us that even the
most seemingly solid corporations are vulnerable to extinction.
Less apparent is the fact that many smaller companies are acquired
or suffer bankruptcy daily. Survival is not automatic. It has to
be worked at and much of the responsibility for it ultimately resides
in the board.

Survival is obviously a prerequisite for the attainment of
any of the criteria by which corporate vitality and viability are
commonly measured: sales, earnings, assets, growth, diversification,
innovation, and even social responsibility. But if survival is
the clutch, independence is the accelerator. Independence and
the discretion it allows are at the core of our free enterprise
system. Decisions about what to value and what to pursue are highly
discretionary and again it is the board which has the ultimate
responsibility within social and legal constraints to guide and
govern the independent behavior of the corporation.

The concepts of survival and independence are evolving and
board composition must evolve with them. The kind of structure
best suited to the corporation of a half-century ago or more is

62

unable to provide the kind of direction necessary today. Defenders and adversaries of the traditional board are in agreement about its homogeneity. They merely differ in describing and connoting it. Ingrown, incestual, inward looking, and tending toward intolerance would be among the terms some critics would use. Such boards usually got started with the owners and a few close advisors - former officers, lawyers, bankers, and others whose interests coincided closely with those of the owners. Their histories and responsibilities with regard to the corporation make such board members professional loyalists and large stock holdings or options make them personal loyalists as well. I would like to label such boards "intensive."

Intensive boards were the rule in the 19th century and early 20th century companies and are still appropriate today to those corporations new enough and small enough to be regarded as private property. The stockholders of such companies are frequently individuals - rather than institutions - and are likely to have a somewhat long-term interest in the company. They are owners, not merely investors, and have the right to expect management, including a board, to move responsively, quickly and effectively on behalf of their economic interest. And the economic interest is primary. Such private property corporations have slight social or political importance.

With the exception of anomalies like Cargill or Mars, however, the designation of private property is no longer applicable to large American companies. And, in fact, by and large it has not been applicable for half a century. In their incisive and groundbreaking 1932 book Private Property and the Modern Corporation, Adolf A. Berle and Gardiner Means pointed out the schism between ownership and management that was apparent even then:

"The typical business unit of the 19th century was owned by individuals or small groups; was managed by them or their appointees; and was, in the main, limited in size by the personal wealth of the individuals in control. These units have been supplanted in ever greater measure by great aggregations in which tens and even hundreds of thousands of workers and property worth hundreds of millions of dollars belonging to tens or even hundreds of thousands of individuals are combined through the corporate mechanism into a single producing organization under unified control and management... The property owner who invests in a modern corporation so far surrenders his wealth to those in control of the corporation that he has exchanged the position of independent owner for one in which he may become merely recipient of the wages of capital."

63

Such publicly owned corporations now predominate in America's "private business sector" and it might be observed in passing that public ownership has become the established fashion among non-profit organizations as well. The universities and hospitals and orchestras which in simpler times were beholden for continued existence to the handful of wealthy entrepreneurs who owned America's corporate sector are now dependent on an increasingly democratic base of support and ultimately in many instances on the government itself for the margin of survival. It can be argued that after a certain point, private sector success, whether by an M.I.T. or a Ford Motor Company, creates an entity which can not ultimately be contained in the private sector.

But that is the subject for a different panel. To return to boards, I would concur with the analysis that an intensive composition of directors -- close-knit and united in a rather narrow purposefulness -- provided the necessary governance (and probably the sufficient governance as well) for corporations in the private property state of development. But I believe with equal conviction that such a board is not the best leadership - either from the standpoint of the corporation or of the society - for today's large, publicly owned, economically regulated, politically involved and socially impacting companies. Instead I would strongly endorse a fairly rapid and voluntary transition from traditional boards to boards of independent directors like those described by Harold M. Williams, Chairman of the Securities and Exchange Commission, in a much-discussed address on corporate accountability last January in San Diego.

The Williams Design advocates that the chief executive officer of a corporation should be the only internal representative on the board, that the chief executive ought not to be chairman of the board with consequent control of the agenda, and that persons who sell services to the corporation (outside counsel, bankers, and the like) ought to be excluded from board membership. Chairman Williams did not label the structure he described, but I would like to propose the designation "extensive." It contrasts with and complements the term "intensive" which I selected to describe traditional boards and it calls attention both to the broad-based membership desirable for the comtemporary board and to the wide range of issues essential to its concern. Roderick Hills, Williams' predecessor as SEC Chairman, substantially concurred with the position of the incumbant chairman regarding extensive boards. Hills told the Senate Commerce Committee in June of 1976 that in his judgment "the larger companies ought to have substantially all of their directors outside." Many progressive executives are moving closer to this position. Their views are reflected by A. W. Clausen, President and CEO of BankAmerica, who wrote in a recent issue of Chief Executive Magazine that "strong outside directors should constitute a clear majority of the board of public corporations." And practice seems to be following theory with the average current board membership (as reported in the March 31

64

New York Times) being nine outsiders out of 13 seats.

In the face of such statements and tendencies, however, there is considerable unuse with regard to the emergence of extensive boards. Arguments raised against them include the following:

A) Lack of information by outside directors

B) Lack of requisite skills

C) Usurpation of management prerogatives

D) Divided loyalties causing erosion of corporate interests.

The first two objections are questions of expertise, the last two of orientation. I believe that all four can be satisfactorily laid to rest and that persuasive arguments can be raised on behalf of the opposite position: the desirability of extensive boards.

With regard to information, the answer is a simple one. Directors ought to have access to any information they desire and should automatically be provided with such information as they require to operate effectively. The chief executive must charge employees to provide board members with any information and must develop staff and systems to assure they can assimilate any they need. Total access to information is not a privilege but a necessity. With information, intelligent and dedicated men and women can acquire expertise, particularly if they are given sufficient incentives to do so. The March 31 Times report indicated that the average director of a company with 1977 sales of $5 billion or more was compensated $18,000 for 115 hours of work that year, or about three short work weeks. Companies that size can and should compensate directors sufficiently to encourage more devotion to corporate concerns, to give them an income commensurate with their responsibilities and risk-exposure, and to preclude their having to knit together a fragmented patchwork of income sources.

The situation with regard to usurpation and orientation is much more complex and of critical importance. As I noted above, the function of the intensive board was to direct the management of the company. Usurpation could not have been invoked in this context. The intensive board had the luxury of ignoring most extra-corporate concerns and concentrating on the owner-management interface. That interface is now an anachronism. As George Lodge and others have noted, we've moved from an ownership ideology to a participatory ideology. The modern board must interface between management and

65

other participants in the corporate orbit; government is primary, but labor, consumers and ultimately the society at large have legitimate claims. To respond suitably and effectively, a company needs a board with an exceedingly broad range of interests, experience and expertise. Usurpation of management prerogative is not the issue today that consideration if it ever genuinely existed is now also anachronistic. Protection of remaining management independence within a newly constrained operating environment is today's and tomorrow's challenge and I believe that an extensive board with full access to internal corporate skills and information can best serve that end.

A final point must be made concerning orientation. The stance of the traditional corporation was self-protective and self-promoting. The contemporary and future corporations must be sector-protective and sector-promoting. The issues today transcend single corporations - capital adequacy, labor relations and job fulfill-ment, corporate legitimacy, government regulation, social and poli-tical status - and the solutions must be comparably transcendent. Survival and independence cannot be attained by one or several firms if the private sector itself is not secured and perpetuated.

And right now the private sector -- and I use the term in-clusively -- has its back to the wall. The demands of individuals are increasing while their trust and support is wanning. More im-portantly, government pre-emption, intervention and reaction is constraining the private sector on all sides and pushing it below the threshold of vitality. Once there, it is quite possible it will never re-emerge. Pluralism of initiative and response would die with the subordination of the private sector. With it would go the catalyst for both our individual freedom and our economic accomplishment, replaced perhaps permanently by the monolithic totalitarianism De Tocqueville identified as the dark side of democracy.

Intensive boards by their very nature are disinclined to meet such challenges. Self-protectiveness and sector-protectiveness seem antithetical. The incentive of the intensive board is un-bridled corporate growth toward pre-eminence within a market, a competitive attitude which moved us toward today's summits of cor-porate achievement, but seems unlikely to brake the descent down the opposite face of that summit. Only an extensive board free from inside pressure is likely to have the objectivity necessary to guide the CEO, the internal manager of the firm, away from nar-row corporate self-interest toward free-enterprise sectoral self-interest and consequent societal self-interest. And only by making the society work, can the private sector endure and the individual corporation survive as an independent entity.

66

LEO V. RYAN

My reflections for this panel are drawn from two perspectives. My initial observations reflect an academic concern about the evolving nature of corporate governance -- the composition and mix of corporate board membership and the changing nature of their role in the management of corporate life. My further reflections are drawn from my own participation as a director of several cor- porations -- family held in one instance; closely held in the case of another parent corporation with three wholly owned subsidiaries; my further concern arises from the need to respond soon to invita- tions from two publicly held corporations to become a member of their boards of directors. In each case, my role is that of the "outside director" as distinct from the "inside director" or "specialist director." It is a case of serving as a "single capa- city director" to use Robert K. Mueller's distinction rather than serving as a "dual capacity director" or "triple capacity direc- tor."[1] My preliminary remarks will focus on the role of the cor- porate board rather than the question of board membership.

All corporations operate under the general dictum, described by different phrases in different state statutes, that the corpo- ration "shall be managed by a Board of Directors." Just what it means to "manage" and how the Board "manages" is not very clearly defined. Robert M. Estes, General Counsel and Secretary of General Electric Company, reminds us that the law on director responsibi- lity is still ambigious, and the general environment in which it is applied today is both fluid and frequently hostile.[2]

Certain duties are clearly the responsibility of the Board of Directors. Courtney C. Brown would say that, "Policy, person- nel, procedures, and performance have been called the 'four P's' for the proper attention of board members. Together, they con- stitute the hard core of the governing board's responsibility to the stockholders."[3]

The 1978 Statement of the Business Roundtable defines four key board functions more fully:

"We can describe the four key board functions - provision for management and board succession, con- sideration of decisions and actions with a potential for major economic impact, consideration of major social impacts, and the establishment of policies and procedures to assure law compliance - as the care of the board obligation to 'manage' or 'direct the management of' the corporation."[4]

Thus, from an academic perspective it would seem rather clear what is expected of a member of the Board of Directors. While none of the functions aforementioned specify a concern for the ethical, it is clearly implied in the concept "to manage" if that phrase is taken in the fullness of the professional concept "to manage." Moreover, to accept the "good and prudent man" rule in corporate governance is to propose a sensitivity to many issues beyond basic economic and financial concerns.

In fact, as a participant in the current American Assembly meetings on "The Ethics of Corporate Conduct,"[5] I was involved in the adoption of this resolution during the National Capital Assembly:

"The Board of Directors has a continuing responsibility to monitor not only the financial, but also the ethical health of the organization. This obligation entails an extensive use of checks and balances. To fulfill its responsibility, the Board must be competent to review ethical audits at every level, and be prepared to consult outside professionals when deemed necessary."[6]

An earlier Report from the American Assembly adopted nine recommendations concerning corporate governance including the prescription that:

"The board of directors must recognize its ultimate responsibility for the ethical conduct of the corporation."[7]

The American Assembly Sessions have all placed considerable emphasis on the importance of Codes of Ethics. I indeed also favor Codes of Ethics, as much for the process as for the outcome; but, I defer discussions of Codes of Ethics to another time and place.

During recent years Boards of Directors have been undergoing major challenges and substantial changes.[8] Much of that change involves broader representation, increased accountability, director liability, concern for social change -- corporate response to public issues, social responsibility and greater concern for and sensitivity to ethical corporate behavior. Boards are hopefully becoming less advisory and more action orientated, less spectator and more participator, more diligent in monitoring corporate behavior, and more insistent on the observance of the legal, social and ethical obligations arising from corporate economic activity. The perpetual problem for the outside director is the problem of keeping informed, the need for a system of information flow that is both appropriate and accurate.

As a corporate director from academe, my board service is hopefully characterized by a critical and inquiring mind for my talent as teacher should be that of asking questions, being critical and examining whether the data provided me supports corporate conclusions.

As a corporate director who is also a cleric, my very presence on the board prompts questions that might not otherwise be asked, or, more accurately, my participation permits the sharing of perspectives on agenda items that might not otherwise be present. Yet, I would never presume to describe my service as that of "an angel's advocate" or even corporate ethics specialist.[9]

Yet my experience tells me that meeting after meeting the agenda of corporations are filled with topics that are not only economic and social in their significance but also moral. In a definition of moral significance that interprets moral to be matters of rights and obligations, it would be my contention that almost every issue before the Board of Directors is a moral issue.

All business activity has economic, social and moral significance. It is a natural corollary that business ethics, moral questions and issues of rights and obligations are, and necessarily must be, the constant concern and preoccupation of the Board of Directors.

NOTES

1. Cf. Robert K. Mueller, <u>Board Life: Realistics of Being a Corporate Director</u>. New York: AMACOM, American Management Association, 1974, p. 32. "The heavy liability of corporate directors leads to a growing legal distinction among three classes of directors, with liabilities defined accordingly:

1. The single-capacity director, whose sole significant relationship to the board is in his board membership. This is a typical outside nonexecutive director.

2. The dual-capacity director, who either represents a major shareholder bloc and is not a part of management, or is on the board because he is a company executive.

3. The triple-capacity director, who is a substantial shareholder or is closely allied with the major shareholder group. In addition to a place on the board, he has a place in the management. This is the case particularly in closely held corporations.

There is a trend in both federal and state legal decisions to impose the highest standards on the triple-capacity director, relax it progressively in favor of a dual-capacity director, and accept from a single-capacity director a performance considerably less arduous, provided there is good faith evident." Ibid.

2. Cf. Robert M. Estes, "Outside Directors: More Vulnerable Than Ever," Harvard Business Review, January-February, 1973. Also Cf. Board of Directors, A Harvard Business Review Reprint Series, No. 21024, 1976.

3. Courtney C. Brown, Putting the Corporate Board to Work. New York: Macmillan Publishing Co., Inc., 1976, p. 25.

4. "The Role and Composition of the Board of Directors of the Large Publicly Owned Corporation," Statement of the Business Roundtable. New York: The Business Roundtable, 1978, p. 15. An elaboration of duties of the board of directors appears in J. Keith Louden, The Effective Director in Action, New York: AMACOM American Management Association, 1975.

"There are many matters that are exclusively reserved for the board. These include selection and removal of executive officers; declaring dividends; appointment of auditors, legal counsel, and other outside experts; approval of the financial structure of the organization, including budgets; mergers and acquisitions; disposition of capital assets; long term and substantial leases; the payment of salaries to the officers group; and, last but not least, the election of the chief executive officers."

J. Keith Louden, The Effective Director in Action. New York: AMACOM, American Management Association, 1975, p. 34. Also see J. M. Juran, and J. Keith Louden, The Corporate Director, New York: AMACOM, American Management Association, 1966.

5. Cf. Clarence Walton (editor) The Ethics of Corporate Conduct. Englewood Cliffs, N.J.: Prentice-Hall, 1977. This speaker participated in the National Capital Assembly at Catholic University of America (Washington, DC), November 10-12, 1977 and the 20th Air Force Assembly, U.S. Air Force Academy (Colorado Springs, CO), March 15-18, 1978; both assemblies addressed themselves to the Ethics of Corporate Conduct and several additional regional assemblies are planned on this same theme. Corporate Governance will be the next American Assembly topic. "New Trends in Directorships and Corporate Governance" is also the object of an extensive Public Policy Study of Business International Corporation, a public interest organization concerned with multinational corporations and headed by Orville L. Freeman.

6. Ethics of Corporate Conduct, Final Report, The National Capital Assembly, November 10-12, 1977, Washington, D.C.: The Catholic University of America, 1978, Resolution 3, p. 5.

7.   The Ethics of Corporate Conduct. Report of the Fifty-
Second American Assembly, April 14-15, 1977. New York: The
American Assembly, Columbia University, 1977, Corporate Governance,
Resolutions 1-9, p. 5-6. The quotation is from Resolution 3 which
reads in full: "The board of directors must recognize its ultimate responsibility for the ethical conduct of the corporation.
The corporation should develop and promulgate statements of
operating principles or codes of conduct. Management's commitment
to such principles must be impressed on every employee, compliance
therewith required and adequately monitored." (p. 5).

8.   Cf. "Even the Future is Not What It Used to Be: The
Ranks and Roles of Corporate Boards Are Changing Rapidly Now."
A series of six statements by Carnegie-Mellon faculty directors.
Novus, Winter 1977-78, p. 12-18. Also Cf. The Changing Board:
Profile of the Board of Directors. Chicago: Heidrick and Strug-
gles, Inc. 1977 and Director Data, Heidrick and Struggles, July
1977 4 pp. Two rather typical examples from the business press
would be: "Corporate Governance: New Heat on Outside Directors,"
Forbes, October 1, 1977 and "Citizens and Southern Shake-Up
Underscores Evolution of Boards." Wall Street Journal, Vol. LVIII,
No. 109, March 21, 1978, p. 1.

9.   Theodore V. Purcell, "Electing An 'Angel's Advocate' To
The Board," Management Review, May 1976, p. 4-11. Purcell advocates a three fold ethical process: Examinations of general
ethical principles; examination of middle-level ethical principles;
and, in-depth study of specific cases and classes of similar cases
(p. 7-9). He proposes that "we should institutionalize ethical
expertise at the board of directors and top-management levels,
focusing on one director, but with responsibilities shared by a
committee of the board." (p. 9).

DISCUSSION

COMMENT: I'd like to ask Mr. Gill a question. You mentioned that a staff for the board of directors was unnecessary, since the independent directors on the board had access to the staff. I was on a panel very recently and when I started talking about how directors ought to fulfill their responsibilities by obtaining information as much as they could and to go to the staff if they weren't getting it from senior management, particularly senior management which held more seats, I was interrupted and the others on the panel were horrified at the prospect that outside directors would make an end-run around senior management and go directly, for example, to middle management on the staff. They indicated that this kind of approach would be terribly disruptive, that there would be a feeling that they were snooping around, that it would be demoralizing to management. I'd like to have you comment on that and maybe clarify what you mean by access to the staff in the absence of the board having its own staff. Do you mean that directors would be able to freely go to members of the staff for information or with particular questions?

GILL: It is my legal opinion that directors, at least under the laws of Pennsylvania, do have the right of access to all personnel and information that is in the possession of the corporation of which they are directors. I recognize that as a matter of personal relations and effective functioning (the relationship of the board with the management of the corporation), to suddenly appear in the accountant's domain and commence asking some probing questions without having advised the chief executive officer could create some serious problems. But I think they have the legal right to do that. In our corporation, where directors, particularly in the audit committee, have from time to time requested interviews with various people in the corporation, they have advised the chief executive in advance. In fact, they regularly do have direct access to the chief auditor and the controller. They freely review on a quarterly basis with those officers of our corporation any questions they have, because there's no one else present. Furthermore, they have an interview with our outside independent accountants, Coopers & Lybrand, without the presence of other corporate officers. I think this is not unusual in large, well-managed, publicly held corporations. I think there's an even greater problem with the suggestion of a separate staff for the board of directors. I think it would inevitably become a rival to their comparable persons, say, in the Legal Department, the Accounting Department, the Financial Department, Personnel Departments, and could create serious per-

72

sonnel problems that would be way out of proportion to their value.

COMMENT: If the permanent staff were composed of representatives of those departments, then you wouldn't have that problem of rivalry, I should think.

GILL: Sounds to me quite unnecessary and cumbersome, but perfectly possible. Since the directors, at least in my experience, do have access to these officers, the controller, the chief auditor, and any other members of the staff they want to talk with, I'm doubtful that any useful function would be accomplished by creating a separate committee of these people. We do have what is called a Financial Information Committee of the Board of Directors at Sun, and this is composed of directors, the chief financial officer of the Company, the controller and the general counsel. Perhaps that's something like what you're suggesting.

SELIGMAN: Might I cut in for a minute with a question. The base line from which this debate probably emanates is a book written by Myles Mace that appeared in 1970, I believe. It basically stated that the leading problem of boards of directors was that they tended to be the passive nominees of the corporate chief executive officer of some clique of leading corporate chief executive officers and the biggest problem was that they didn't ask questions at all. Now, in the last six or seven years, we have had, through the SEC bribery scandals, the revelation of more data concerning the board of directors than we have historically ever had. The disclosures and reports in those scandals show that there was one consistent theme: the directors were asleep. If nothing else, by creating a board not nominated by management and then giving it an independent staff, the staff would play the function of keeping it awake and keeping it active.

Quite contrary to the assertion that Mr. Gill has made in his remarks, that he knew of no instance where a director had sought independent advice and a corporation had not agreed to it, it was exactly because an airplane corporation on whose board Arthur Goldberg sat refused to provide him information that he resigned and began writing his series of articles. His own research confirmed that of Myles Mace that the surest way to get yourself "de-selected" from a board of directors was to ask tough questions. In other words, although boards have made progress in the last seven years, they still are chosen by senior corporate executives. They don't ask tough questions. They don't do thorough examinations, particularly in large billion dollar corporations as distinguished from closely held

73

ones. They don't keep their ears as open as they might to
problems and prevent them from developing into full-fledged
legal or ethical questions. This is why an independent staff
is so absolutely essential.

COMMENT: It is a typical American pattern to try and solve one
problem by making it larger. When we couldn't revitalize the
cities, we made them into regions and tried to revitalize the
regions. It seems to me that if you've got a board of directors
that doesn't ask questions, and you give them a staff, which
presumably they pick, which would have investigative functions
within the corporation, if that staff sought to ask questions
of some mythical corporation, that staff could be just as easily
hoodwinked as the board members could. The internal problems
in a corporation of having an internal police force reporting
to some outside members of the board seem to be horrendous, and
the consequence of solving that problem would be to make the
staff even larger, until you've got a parallel management.
Then, running the corporation in two separate but equal managements would be interesting. Perhaps Conrail would serve as one
example of how that worked. I don't think there's any question
that anyone would disagree that the board of directors needs to
be more active. It needs to be more independent, and so on.
But the assumption of management culpability which seems to
exist here, from my experience, and I come to the business
world from an academic and an activist world, just doesn't exist.

SELIGMAN: Well, it's hardly an assumption of corporate or
business person's culpability, but the reality is that business
people aren't perfect. We have had abundant evidence in the
past decade, whether it's the bribery scandals or fraudulent
actions as in the Stirling Homex and Equity Funding cases. I
can go on with a parade of horribles of illegal actions. We've
had a far greater number of negligent or poor business planning
type actions. The question is really, do we want business ultimately to be reviewed by federal agencies in a court system
or do we want to create internal deterrent devices so we can
have a form of effective self-regulation. Now, for the same
reason that the army has an inspector general, that the bar
associations of this country have disciplinary committees (I
was told, to my surprise, in this morning's Accounting Ethics
panel, that the AICPA apparently feels it has one too.), it is
possible to create in a sense, a watchdog, a small trim staff
to help frame questions and frame issues to enable the board to
do its job, which is not to manage the corporation but to prevent management from making grossly negligent, grossly illegal,
or grossly self-dealing decisions.

COMMENT: Wait a minute, you're trying to divide the functions of this separate staff into two separate areas, one of which is illegality so that they have a legal parapolice function, and the second is economic misdecision. It seems to me that the most effective way of taking care of the economic misdecisions is to leave it to the marketplace.

SELIGMAN: Excuse me, do you want to show me one example where the marketplace alone has replaced, say through a proxy decision of some sort, an incompetent management over the past decade.

COMMENT: Many bankruptcies.

SELIGMAN: That's a kind of a high price for shareholders to pay.

COMMENT: You talk about passive directors and that's a generality that I have not seen. The subtlety of the difference between a board member and a board member's staff investigating the management is also a distinction that I have a very difficult time making. There was a comment about compensating a director for the risk that he takes as a director. I'm not sure you can compensate a director for that risk as it is presently evolving. I think that one of the most important decisions that has to be made by the management of the company is how you run the company. Now, how is a director to determine the technological currency of a company such as Digital, such as IBM, or such as Xerox? As a director, I'd like to know the answer to that question. How is a director to do that? Is he charged with that?

SELIGMAN: In a sense, when we look at laws which, as Brother Ryan said, begin with the assumption that a corporation "shall be managed by a Board of Directors," obviously the board cannot do that. The only real role a board can play, one which I would argue is extremely necessary, is to review management decisions, particularly important business initiatives for compliance with existing laws and for determination that there has been a rational thinking process, a rational business process involved when you're about to invest great sums of shareholders' money in a particular new venture.

COMMENT: Why is there the assumption that that's not done?

SELIGMAN: Because when you go through the pathology of corporations that fail, whether it's a W. T. Grant or a Penn-Central, or on and on and on, you find time and time again that business decisions were made on the basis of assumptions that could not have been proved or confirmed and that were inaccurate. A classic example was the vote of the Pennsylvania Railroad's Board of Directors to merge with the Central Railroad because

75

of "cost efficiency savings" of (I believe) 70 million dollars. There was no study to determine this. There was no outside counsel sought in trying to estimate it. In other words, a board of directors' function should be at least to say, show me the study. Have you made it? Can you prove it? It's not to run the corporation. It's not to make the business initiatives, but to insure to the shareholders whom they represent that business decisions are rationally based.

GILL: Studies had been made for almost 10 years, that were presented to the Interstate Commerce Commission and argued over with the Interstate Commerce Commission, that the Penn-Central and New York Central merge. I'm rather surprised by your comment that the subject had not been adequately studied.

SELIGMAN: There was none apparently by the Board of Directors at the time of the Pennsylvania Railroad's decision to merge with the Central Railroad. It made the decision on the basis of inadequate information. It did not ask the right questions.

GILL: Extensive studies were presented to the Board of Directors according to the record of Penn-Central, and furthermore had been presented to the Interstate Commerce Commission over, I don't know how long, but a large number of years. The problem was that the railroad was over-regulated and the merger was studied to death, so that by the time the decision was made, nobody could put up with reading the documents once again.

COMMENT: I'm surprised that we've been here listening to the panel for several hours and I haven't heard a single mention of any corporation misconduct involving blood at the same time that we're talking about ethics. In recent times, we have had disclosures of the following:

  -Drug companies that have falsified animal testing on
   potent drugs which can cause cancer and other diseases.
  -A coal company, a consolidation to be exact, which is
   under a 172-count indictment charging it with falsifying
   safety data for coal miners. Miners carry dust cassettes
   into the mines to record dust levels. The company was
   substituting, according to the indictment, fake cassettes
   for those that came up from the mines dirty.
  -We recently had a jury out in California award (I think
   knowing that the judgment would be overturned, but they
   wanted to send a message) $126.8 million, I think it was,
   against the Ford Motor Company, for the manufacture of a
   Pinto, knowing it was equipped so that it burst into flame
   when rammed from the rear. A poor man there lost his nose
   and suffered other injuries from the horrible fire.

And what is the result? You don't hear a damned thing about
any board of directors of any of these companies doing anything
about this. Henry Ford popped up last week in _Newsweek_ with a
full page to whine and moan about government regulations. That's
his answer.

I'd like to go back to a book written in 1907. It has an interesting title: _Sin and Society_. Edward A. Ross was the
author. I put this before you because I don't think things are
working well - not when Henry Ford can do what he did; when G.
D. Searle can do what it did in false and/or fradulent drug
testing, a matter before a grand jury; when a company called
Industrial Biotest Laboratories, which is the single biggest
tester of pesticides, drugs and other chemicals for the government, is found to be falsifying data, and nothing happens. You
don't hear directors raising their voices.

Let me read this from Ross, if I may.

"The directors of a company ought to be individually accountable for every case of misconduct in which the
company receives the benefit, for every preventable deficiency or abuse that regularly goes on in the course
of the business. Hold them blameless if they prove the
inefficiency or disobedience of underlings, but not if
they plead ignorance. Consider the salutary side-effects
of such severity. When an avalanche of wrath hangs over
the head of the director of a sinning corporation, no
one will accept a directorship who is not prepared to
give a good deal of time and serious attention to its
business. Strict accountability will send flying the
figurehead directors who, when the misdeeds of their
protégés come to light, protest they 'didn't know.'"
[But Olin Industries protested it "didn't know" that its
subordinates were dumping mercury into the Niagara River.]

I put this before you. What about this kind of individual accountability, this kind of monstrous conduct that I have just
sampled here? What is the point of having boards if Henry Ford
and his people can do this kind of thing and not even be repri-
manded? Where should the accountability be if the executives
buy insurance to prevent them from being individually liable?
I find that intollerable.

COMMENT: Do we hang a police chief each time a murder is done
in his city?

COMMENT: Oh no. No, that's ridiculous.

COMMENT: I think it's analogous.

COMMENT: Every time a murder's committed in a city, the police chief ought to be hung? That's analogous? That's ridiculous.

COMMENT: It's his role to protect. . .

COMMENT: Well, I think it's different.

COMMENT: Are you implying that the crooks report to the police chief?

COMMENT: No, I'm not, but I don't see how, in a company as large as, say, Digital, you can hold an able man trying to do a conscientious job in a director's slot as liable for every subordinate's actions.

COMMENT: Well, this is not what Ross said. He said hold them blameless if they prove the inefficiency or disobedience of underlings, but not if they plead ignorant. Maybe that's too strong. My only point really is not to advocate this, but if we could try and get this into the question of individual accountability, where is the accountability? If you're not going to put it in executives, because they buy insurance, or if you're not going to put it in directors, who you say can't be held accountable, where is it? Where is the responsibility for this kind of misconduct that I talked about?

RYAN: There is a well accepted principle that you must exercise the prudent man rule in the management of the affairs. That does not mean that you will of necessity know everything that goes on in the name of the corporation nor be aware of the actions of all people in the firm. But it is incumbent upon one as a director, especially an outside director, to see that the system of successor management, the system of advancement of employees to positions of responsibility, is, in fact, a system and is, in fact, a process that can be identified and is reviewed periodically and is tested. That would take you back all the way to examination of corporate policies of recruiting, screening, hiring, placing, training, and evaluating. That may seem a long way back, but that's exactly how one builds the organization. You have to decide among other things what qualities of persons you're looking for. One has to be very careful, it seems to me, whether you are hiring someone in the financial area or in the sales area. It's a fact that in both of those areas the principles that the people have are the principles that are going to govern their actions, and their actions are going to become representative of the firm. The firm has a way of making some guarantees about how people will act. The firm must have a plan for taking action, equally taking action, when people sin. Those things have to be thought out. There has to be a system. And I think that one of the things that an outside director can constantly do is raise questions -- What is our system? What is our policy? What is our procedure? How is it in principle and in fact? Is it being monitored? Is it being evaluated?

That is not a very glamorous kind of role. It is a very tedious one. It is sometimes offensive. I mean, it may be hard to raise questions in a publicly held corporation. It is a lot less difficult, I think, to raise them when 9 out of 13 directors are outsiders. It's a lot more delicate, I might say, to have to raise them when you're the only outside director, but you have to look at the fact that you probably wouldn't have been invited to that directorship unless the corporate leadership wanted you. However delicate it might be on a given occassion, if it is done from the spirit that the whole aim is to assist the system to improve itself, then I think progress is made.

COMMENT: Brother Ryan, do you think the action of the Board of Directors of G. D. Searle was appropriate? As I recall, they discharged the chief executive officer and replaced him with Mr. Runsfield. He took the office from the Chicago Airport out to N. Chicago, where their plant is located, I believe. He discharged the senior vice president in charge of research, and I think that used to be a fairly closely held corporation.

RYAN: It is a family corporation. He is the first outside senior executive in the firm. I don't know all the details. I know he took very strict action against the director of research. In fact, they had him intercepted at the London Airport, flown back to Chicago, brought in and dismissed, on the basis that he should not be ignorant of what was going on in his division. His division having failed in its professional responsibilities, he having failed in his management responsibilities, there was no way to cover that up but to act.

SELIGMAN: The colloquy suggests maybe a final open area which any modern debate on the role of the board should come to grips with regarding the duties of the board -- what it actually should do; what it actually should be accountable for. You look at virtually every modern corporate law, every securities law, whether it's in the trust indenture field, the public utility holding company field, and so forth and so on, and you have responsibilities for particular individuals laid out. A trustee, say, for a bond, shall do the following, shall give reports on the following. There's a conscious effort by the legislatures to distinguish between those functions which are

79

very, very important and which someone should take responsibility for and those which are less important. By contrast, in the corporate law field, we have seen the erosion of two concepts -- one, the prudent man test you referred to has not been effective at the state corporate law level. There was a study done by Professor Bishop of Yale in the post World War II period. He could only point to four cases over something like a 30-year period where a negligence claim had been stated and gotten beyond summary judgment. In the state of Delaware, you have a so-called business judgment rule, which is a virtually impregnable shield to alleging incompetence or negligence on the part of a director. At the same time, we have retained at the state level a very vague description of directors' duties. I would submit that we would be in a far preferable position if the responsibilities of the board were spelled out, if they were primarily in the form of reports. It shall report that it investigated, say, the safety of new products, compliance with law, and so forth. You would have a mandate that could be met. You would have a responsibility that was clear as a matter of law and within the corporation. The functions of the board could be clearly distinguished from those of operating management. You have seen that in the modern securities' laws. You don't have it in the state corporations' laws and they are crying out for it.

SESSION IV

"Corporate Responsibility: A Critique of
    John Ladd on Formal Organizations"

Thomas Donaldson
Professor of Philosophy
Loyola University of Chicago

K. E. Goodpaster
Professor of Philosophy
University of Notre Dame

John Ladd (Commentator)
Professor of Philosophy
Brown University

TOM DONALDSON

Moral Change in the Corporation

Despite the fact that it has been called the representative
institution of modern Western society, the corporation has been
repeatedly criticized for failing to harmonize its interests with
those of society. A common complaint made about the modern corporation is that its structure cannot accommodate certain moral
and social goals. For example, it has been said that the corporation's explicit goal, to generate profit, gives rise to inevitable conflicts between that goal and certain moral principles,
e.g., the principle of honesty, and with social goals, e.g., a
pollution-free environment. Many critics suggest that, short of
doing away with the corporation and short of thoroughly regulating
it from the outside, the answer lies with making certain alterations in the structure of the corporation. Some rather specific
recommendations of this sort have been made. W. Goedeke and
others have suggested that corporations be forced to obtain renewable federal charters. John K. Galbraith has proposed requiring
corporate stockholders to exchange their stock for government
bonds, thus allowing the corporation's board of directors to consist entirely of public representatives. And, as a less radical
alternative to the Galbraith idea, it has been suggested that at
least one-fourth of the membership of corporate boards of directors should consist of public representatives who are not stockholders of the corporation.

I shall not attempt to criticize or defend any certain one
of these proposals, but I shall defend the general moral desirability of making structural changes in the corporation, especially
ones affecting internal corporate structure. My principal thesis
shall be that alterations in the structure of the corporation,
namely, ones which will institutionalize ethical and moral goals
within the corporate structure, are desirable so long as certain
assumptions are made, and so long as such changes are viewed
within the context of the historical evolution of the corporation
and society. In defending this thesis, I shall isolate some
specific moral criticisms of the corporation, and then explore
possible means of resolving those criticisms.

Two fundamental moral criticisms of the corporation deserve
our attention: the first attacks the overall goals of the corporation, while the second criticizes its organizational form. The
essense of the first criticism lies in the simple claim, made by
Karl Marx and others, that the most obvious goal of the corporation,

83

namely profit, conflicts directly with moral and social needs of the culture.[1] Although the nature of the conflict may vary depending upon the instance, its general form may be presumed to remain the same: the conflict is between profit and human well-being. Although those offering this criticism often do not refer specifically to the conflict between profit and moral norms, the fundamental role typically assigned to economic forces by such critics is easily extended in order to account for moral conflicts. So, to take an obvious example, the corporation's pursuit of profit through the use of misleading television advertising can be argued to be at odds with the moral requirement to communicate honestly or to provide reliable information to consumers. Or, taking another example, the corporation's pursuit of profit by attempting to increase productivity from its workers can be argued to be at odds with the moral requirement to provide reasonable and safe working conditions. For convenience we shall label this type of criticism as one of "profit versus moral norms."

The second of the two criticisms suggests that the corporation fails to adhere to moral norms because, in contrast to human individuals, the corporation exists as a _formal_ organization. Put simply, this means that because corporations, just as all formal organizations, are organized in accordance with the idea of some agreed upon purpose (the corporation represents a voluntary association of stockholders who typically invest their money for the purpose of economic security), it follows that moral issues can only be relevant to a corporation insofar as they affect this fundamental purpose. John Ladd is the best known proponent of this view; he argues that the general characteristic of all formal organizations is that they are "planned units, deliberately structured for the purpose of attaining specific goals." For such organizations the sole standard of evaluation must be the "rational" one, namely, maximizing the achievement of the organization's goals.[2] The implications of this argument for corporations are clear: the corporation is an organization established for the purpose of achieving certain goals, so moral considerations _per se_ cannot, as a matter of necessity, be significant to the corporation.

Yet this criticism, which we may label the "institutional" criticism, stands in need of additional clarification concerning the presumed inability of formal organizations to use moral norms. Why would it not be possible for a corporation or any other formal organization to regard moral principles as limiting conditions which would act as self-imposed guidelines restricting the pursuit of fundamental goals? Those defending the institutional criticism, however, deny that moral norms can serve as such limiting conditions. Ladd admits that certain factual conditions, which he calls "limiting operating conditions," are used in organizational decision making, e.g., scarcity of resources, legal restrictions and employee morale, and yet he insists that moral considerations cannot qualify as limiting operating conditions. Limiting operating conditions on this view could only include factual matters which relate directly to the achievement of the organization's goal; yet, morality is not even a matter of empirical knowledge -- or so Ladd argues. The only way in which morality might enter into organizational decisions is when considered as purely a factual matter; for example, the moral attitudes of the customer might be considered as a factor influencing the achievement of the organization's goal.[3] Thus, the institutional criticism seems to throw into question the very possibility of a moral reform of the corporation.

It should be noticed that the organizational criticism overlaps with the profit versus moral norms criticism in important ways. The latter criticism identifies a conflict between one specific goal of the corporate organization, namely profit, and the need to adhere to moral norms. But although the former identifies a conflict between corporate goals and morality, it is the mere existence of organizational goals -- whatever they may be -- which gives rise to the conflict, and not the specific goal of profit. Interestingly, both criticisms share the feature of locating difficulties at the general level of the goals of the corporation.

Even if both criticisms were correct, it is at least possible that no single or unique solution exists for the difficulties they raise. The problem of a unique solution occurs because even if there are ways in which the profit orientation of corporations can be weakened or eliminated by restructuring the corporation (thus resolving the profit versus moral norms criticism), the second criticism remains in force since it applies to all formal organizations, including not-for-profit organizations; and thus no restructuring of the corporation which weakened the profit motive could have the desired effect. Despite such a restructuring, the corporation would maintain its status as a formal organization. Hopefully, a closer look at the overall problem will reveal some means of resolving these difficulties. With this hope in mind, let us next examine both criticisms in more detail and offer some appraisal of each, in order to shed light on a plausible overall solution.

The objections to claiming that a conflict exists between the pursuit of profit and social well-being are widely known: the arguments of Adam Smith and others for the social benefits of self-interested, profit oriented behavior in the marketplace constitute the classical objection to this criticism.[4] Indeed, the doctrine of the "invisible hand," or some modern version of it, seems to be the dominant position in the business schools and departments of economics in Western culture. There seem to be a great many who subscribe to Smith's famous remark that "It is not from the benevolence of the shopkeeper that we expect our dinner, but from his regard to his own self-interest."

But although we may agree with Smith that self-interest instead of benevolence motivates the shopkeeper to provide our dinner, this should not lead us to disparage benevolence -- or the need to cultivate moral behavior in general. The shopkeeper who fails to act morally fails to achieve an almost universally recognized human good, that is, virtue; and he fails in this regard despite whether he achieves, or fails to achieve, his self-interest. Smith himself was not unaware of the fact that virtue is a desirable human end, and in his The Theory of Moral Sentiments he writes at length about the unfortunate fact that "...wealth and greatness are often regarded with the respect and admiration which are only due to wisdom and virtue..."[5] He calls this tendency to admire wealth "the great and most universal cause of the corruption of our moral sentiments," and insists throughout his writings that, although men may pursue wealth to the best of their ability -- thus giving rein to their own self-interest -- they must, all the same, observe the fundamental moral norms which facilitate the security and well-being of human society. Thus we may borrow an argument from Smith for our own purposes: the need to allow self-interest its proper due in the marketplace does not obviate the requirement for both individuals and organizations to act morally.

In his recent article in Ethics, Warren Samuels has brought this aspect of Smith's philosophy to light by showing how Smith neither proposes nor defends the a priori optimality of market solutions.[6] Smith believes that the effectiveness of the market system depends, in part, upon the role of moral institutions and other forces of social control, and views the market system as functioning best when it is able to rely upon a strong moral foundation which itself is grounded in the quality of society's laws and the structure of its institutions.[7] It strikes me that Smith is generally correct in his analysis of the market system's need for a solid moral foundation. In order to maximize its benefits to society, an economic system should produce high quality products at reasonable prices, and it is in the service of this end that Smith and others believe a free market system has optimal results. But also in order to maximize its benefits to society, the market system must achieve another goal, recognized as having fundamental human value, namely, the adherence to moral norms. The market system can benefit society the most when it both satisfies society's economic needs, and lives up to society's moral expectations. This conclusion holds good for corporations participating in the market system every bit as much as it does for individuals. We may agree with Adam Smith that there need be no necessary conflict between the idea of the optimal market system and the idea of a market system which observes moral norms.

Society's demand that corporations behave morally, then, cannot be negated even in the context of a free market economy. The pursuit of profit in a free market economy may require the imposition of certain moral restraints, or the recognition by the participants themselves, including corporations, of the existence of certain moral requirements. Keeping this in mind, let us turn briefly to the other criticism of the corporation under consideration, i.e., the charge that the corporation, because it is a formal organization, possesses a structural incapacity to perform morally motivated actions. This argument is in a way the more troublesome of the two since there appears to be no remedy for its problem; it applies to all formal organizations regardless of their economic orientation.

The difficulties raised by the institutional criticism may be partly illusory. I would like to suggest that one of the fundamental claims associated with this criticism, namely, that moral norms cannot function as limiting conditions, begins to lose plausibility when one looks at what is meant by the expression "limiting conditions." To begin with, the claim stands or falls with one's acceptance of two premises: (1) that only matters of fact can count as limiting conditions, and (2) genuine moral considerations cannot be matters of fact. Yet there may be good reasons for denying one or both of these premises. Although it may be true that the corporation and consequently its individual members are necessarily constrained and evaluated in terms of the special goals which constitute the organization's formal objectives, it is nonetheless possible that genuine moral and social goals might come to constitute an important part of the institution's formally established goals. Thus, moral considerations could constitute a special kind of limiting condition by serving as a particular kind of goal; for example, it could happen that a corporation would formally incorporate the goal of performing its activities within the scope of certain moral norms. This leaves the door open for a kind of institutionalization of moral and ethical goals within the corporation, and it also means that, even if correct, this criticism allows a moral remedy for formal organizations. We do not need to look far in order to discover examples of formal organizations which have obviously integrated moral goals into their formal constitutions: religious organizations, state agencies, and overseas aid organizations are obvious examples. Whether or not it is proper to label a specific organizational goal as a "limiting condition" need not concern us. I see no reason why an organization could not establish as one of its formal goals the goal of adhering to certain moral norms while in the pursuit of its other fundamental goals. But if it is objected that this characterization misuses the concept of limiting

87

condition, on the grounds that limiting conditions must be empirical matters of fact and not moral norms, then this objection may be granted. The more important truth for our purposes is that even formal organizations -- and this includes corporations -- can improve their capacity to adhere to moral norms by incorporating moral goals into their formal structure. The institutional criticism does not succeed in showing that formal organizations cannot take morality seriously as an internal matter.

We are now in a position to relate the organizational criticism to the earlier criticism (of profit versus moral norms) and to suggest a common resolution for both. Two conclusions that we have reached so far possess a special significance: (1) that the need to allow self-interest its proper due in the marketplace does not obviate the requirement for individuals and organizations to act morally; and (2) the organizational criticism leaves the door open for an institutionalizing of moral goals within the corporation. Both conclusions suggest that one special kind of structural change within the corporation, namely, that which involves the institutionalization of certain ethical and moral goals within the formal structure of the corporation, could have the effect of reducing or eliminating the problems posed by both criticisms. Because both criticisms derive their force from the identification of a conflict between the goals of the corporation and the requirements of morality, it follows that an institutionalizing of moral goals within the formal structure of the corporation should eliminate or reduce the conflict.

The way in which such goals might best be institutionalized remains undetermined. The task of determining practical solutions lies far beyond the scope of this paper. Even so, we may anticipate some of the general criteria which any potential practical solution must satisfy. First, a change in the formal structure of the corporation would very likely imply a change in the concept of the corporation as recognized by the government, since the corporation exists in virtue of an abstract system of concepts which, in turn, requires formal recognition by the government. It is worthwhile adding that in the case of democratic governments the particular formulation of the concept of the corporation which actually is endorsed by the government should accord generally with the will of the citizenry.[8] Secondly, whatever changes are made in the formal concept of the corporation must be ones which will introduce moral goals into future corporate pursuits; in other words, goals must be introduced which are different from ones of mere profit, growth, technological advance, etc. Otherwise, the problems raised by the two criticisms we have examined would not be resolved or abated.

Given these parameters for possible solutions, it is note-

worthy that the three practical suggestions mentioned in the beginning of our discussion all attempt, each in its own way, to
achieve some institutionalization of moral and social ends. To
repeat, those three are: (1) require corporations to exist under
renewable federal charters; (2) require corporate boards of directors to consist entirely of public representatives; and (3) require that one-fourth of the membership of the boards of directors
of corporations consist of public representatives who are not
stockholders. The implementation of any one of these changes
would almost certainly require substantial revisions in the formal recognition of the corporation by the government and legal
system. Although I believe that proposal #2 represents an overly
radical, and ultimately unacceptable, solution to present corporate
problems, its modified counterpart, i.e. #3, might, by placing
public representatives on boards of directors, introduce relevant
moral and social goals into the formal structure of the corporation.
Public representatives on the boards of directors of major corporations would presumably represent the interests of consumers and
employees, and one may assume that adherence to moral norms, all
other things being equal, is in the interest of those groups. Or,
if corporations were required to exist under renewable federal
charters (in contrast to the unlimited state charters which are
now required), it would be possible to make adherence to moral
norms one of the criteria for the granting of charter renewal.
Interestingly, both of these changes have an additional benefit of
not requiring continuous, external regulation of the corporation
by the government. Our conclusions, then, strongly suggest that
proposals #1 and #3 be given some attention.

As a final note, it should be mentioned that the suggestion
of altering corporate structure to accommodate social and moral
needs is thoroughly consistent with the historical pattern of
evolution for the corporation. Indeed, the very concept of the
corporation has undergone a constant evolution -- often in response to social and moral demands -- ever since its beginnings in
the Middle Ages.[9] The evolution of the corporation seems to correspond closely to the tendency on the part of society to demand
more and more social responsibility from its institutions. One
need not look far to discover the justification commonly used by
society in its demand for change in the corporation; as F. H.
Lawson has remarked, "the corporation is granted qualities not
possessed by ordinary citizens, e.g., limited economic liability
and unlimited longevity."[10] As a consequence, the corporation has
always been required to assume special social obligations which
reflect its special privileges.[11] Thus, insofar as this paper
has argued for the desirability of instituting moral goals within
the formal structure of the corporation, its conclusion appears to
be consistent with the direction of corporate evolution.

NOTES

1. It is worth noticing that even if one accepts John Kenneth Galbraith's claim that the modern corporation is not controlled by its stockholders and that motivations other than profit, e.g., growth and technological advance, are crucial goals of the technostructure, it remains possible to view the mere existence of a strong need for profit as being at odds with certain moral and social goals.

2. John Ladd, "Morality and the Ideal of Rationality in Formal Organizations," The Monist, 54 (1970), 489-499.

3. Ladd, "Morality and Rationality in Organizations," 498.

4. Recently Antony Flew has taken a position similar to Smith in his article, "The Profit Motive," in Ethics, 86 (1976). He contrasts selfishness, which he admits is always wrong, to what he calls "interestedness." Interestedness, in contrast to selfishness, need not be bad: for example, we are displaying interestedness when we eat our dinners, yet wanting our dinners does not constitute selfishness. In turn, the interestedness of the corporation towards the creation of profit is not necessarily bad -- especially in a free market.

5. Adam Smith, The Theory of Moral Sentiments (London: Henry G. Bohn, 1853), p. 84.

6. Warren J. Samuels, "The Political Economy of Adam Smith," Ethics, 87 (1977), 189-207.

7. Samuels, "Political Economy of Smith," 197.

8. For an account of the impact which democratic political theory can have on the concept of the corporation, see Joyotpaul Chaudhuri's "Toward a Democratic Theory of Property and the Modern Corporation," Ethics, 81 (1971), 271-286.

9. Walter R. Goedecke, "Corporations and the Philosophy of Law," The Journal of Value Inquiry, 10, No. 2 (1976), 83-88.

10. F. H. Lawson, Introduction to the Law of Property (Oxford: Clarendon Press, 1958), p. 4.

11. As long ago as 1279, the Statute of Mortmain in England prohibited giving land to corporations without a license from the Crown. Lawson explains this by referring to the fear that corporations, since they never die and consequently never divest themselves of property, might have the undesirable effect of taking property out of commerce. (Lawson, Introduction to the Law of Property, p. 143).

K. E. GOODPASTER

Morality and Organizations

In what follows, I propose to examine the applicability (and desirability of <u>rendering</u> applicable) such notions as 'virtue' and 'moral responsibility' to formal organizational agents (paradigmatically, business corporations and government agencies) in the face of certain conceptual barriers which have been thought to attend such a move. Motivation for such an inquiry stems from several sources. The last decade of American life has witnessed a deep intensification of concern about the quantity and quality of large-scale technological growth, in terms of both social and environmental impact. Clearly the vehicles of this growth have been corporate and bureaucratic agents whose presence in modern society is as ethically mysterious as it is pervasive. Ethics, as traditionally conceived, is a discipline which concentrates on the values and proprieties of individual conduct. That corporate conduct has in fact come to dominate the lives of individuals is only slowly beginning to occur to the moral philosophical community, together with an attendant imperative to accommodate this fact to ethical theory. One important stage in this accommodation process includes a shift in levels of agency (and consequently, moral responsibility or virtue) from the individual to the corporate or organizational decision-maker. On the face of it, what is demanded is a rather straightforward inversion of Plato's avowed methodology in the <u>Republic</u>. Instead of taking our cues from the macrocosmic or organizational level in the quest for a deeper understanding of virtue on the microcosmic or individual level, we seem to be faced with the task of searching for clarity about corporate moral responsibility through a close scrutiny of its necessary and sufficient conditions in the lives of ordinary human agents. This is, at least, the strategy that has suggested itself to more than one laborer in the vineyard of "technology and values" including the present writer.[1] Christopher D. Stone, in a recent and important book on law and the corporation has summarized the strategy nicely:

> If people are going to adopt the terminology of 'responsibility' (with its allied concepts of corporate conscience) to suggest new, improved ways of dealing with corporations, then they ought to go back and examine in detail what 'being responsible' entails -- in the ordinary case of the responsible human being. Only after we have considered what being responsible calls for in general does it make sense to develop the notion of a corporation being

91

responsible.[2]

Thus the picture which emerges sets a clear, if not widely appreciated and accepted, project: if certain current social and environmental problems are related to the conduct of large-scale technological agents, we need to provide both a descriptive-explanatory account of the ethical style of such agents as well as a normative account of what moral responsibility for such agents might amount to. I have elsewhere labeled this double-purpose enterprise "ethical diagnostics" -- invoking both the descriptive-explanatory and the therapeutic suggestions of the medical metaphor.[3]

This project (with its strategy) has been challenged, however. Usually the challenge is implicit and subtle, as in the context I shall focus on presently. But sometimes it is overt. Quotations from corporate executives such as the following carry the message:

The social responsibility of business is to make profits.

The owners of each business enterprise should define the social responsibility of their enterprise as they see fit. This is the only way compatible with the rights of their owners.

I can't believe that social responsibility was ever invented by a businessman; it must have been made up by a sociologist.[4]

The idea that corporate agents should be thought of in the categories of ethical theory at all is what seems to be at stake in these remarks. And the challenge which this provides to the project sketched above is apparent. What should be noted, however, is that though the challenge is significant, it is at least manageable in the sense that it represents a difference in viewpoint of a quasi-ethical sort (sometimes ethical disagreements are actually to be preferred to other sorts!). That is, the disagreement seems to turn on whether we should think of or treat organizational agents as morally responsible beings. And we can entertain arguments and counterarguments in an effort to resolve such a disagreement.

But there is a more subtle and deeply rooted challenge to the project to which I propose to devote most of my attention in this essay. It does not come from the business world, but from ethical theory and allied disciplines. And the issue appears not to be the advisability of construing organizational agents in

92

ethical terms, but rather the very _intelligibility_ of doing so.
The sort of view I have in mind here is paradigmatically articulated by John Ladd in a penetrating article entitled "Morality and
the Ideal of Rationality in Formal Organizations."[5] Ladd's thesis,
if I read him correctly, is that there is a logical or conceptual
barrier to the project of ethical diagnostics and its moral intent.
According to Ladd, if one expects corporate or organizational a-
gents

> . . . to conform to the principles of morality, he
> is simply committing a logical mistake, perhaps even
> what Ryle calls a category mistake. In a sense,
> . . . organizations are like machines, and it would
> be a category mistake to expect a machine to comply
> with the principles of morality. By the same token,
> an official or agent of a formal organization is
> simply violating the basic rules of organizational
> activity if he allows his moral scruples rather than
> the objectives of the organization to determine his
> decision.[6]

Ladd bases his contention in part on a rather uncompromising account of the ideal of rationality in formal organizations gleaned
from organization theorists like Herbert Simon,[7] Chester Barnard,[8]
and, more indirectly, Max Weber. Essentially, the picture is that
of organizational decision-making involving

(A) Imputation of joint decisions to the organization;
(B) A set of constitutive goals in terms of which the
     organization is defined and its rationality is as-
     sessed; and
(C) The exclusiveness of a means-ends conception of
     rational decisions in the "language game" of the
     organization.

And one of the most significant results of the pervasiveness of
this organizational standard, in Ladd's view, is a kind of moral
schizophrenia which sets in upon participants (and recipients).
For standards of moral responsibility are binding on individuals
as individuals, whereas the corporate agents in which and toward
which individuals operate are (logically) marching to the beat of
a nonmoral drummer.

     This last point needs expansion, for it contains by implica-
tion the other main part of Ladd's basis for his general contention.
Besides the account of rationality in formal organizations, there
is also an account of the nature of moral responsibility at work
in Ladd's discussion which is broadly Kantian in character. Though
it is not set out explicitly in the essay under discussion, the

reader can piece it together in outline, at least as containing the following elements:

(A') Moral decisions are imputed to the individual agents who are their authors, not to (or from) something else;

(B') Moral responsibility is not (simply?) a matter of pursuing efficiently a goal or set of goals, i.e., it is not essentially instrumental in character; and

(C') Morality involves a conception of rationality in which respect for the integrity and freedom of persons is central.

Thus Ladd embraces the interesting, if controversial, view that standard utilitarian-style approaches to decision-making are, as a matter of logic, incompatible with morally responsible decision-making, at least as it is ordinarily understood. Expediency and moral responsibility are like oil and water.

The upshot, then, in light of the fact that organizations are such an integral part of modern civilized life, is that we find ourselves in a practical, ongoing dilemma which is rooted in a conceptual impasse between individual and institutional forms of rational agency.

II

Now, though much more could and should be said to do justice to Ladd's provocative discussion, perhaps enough has been set out for my present purposes. For if one is reluctant, as I am, to permit the project described at the outset to run aground in the face of what appears to be a challenge to its intelligibility, the alternatives become relatively clear: It would appear that we must either

(1) Abandon Ladd's account of the ideal of rationality in formal organizations, or

(2) Abandon Ladd's implicit views as to the nature of moral responsibility, or

(3) Abandon both (in whole or in part).

The problem is that none of these courses is, in my opinion, easy.

Alternative (1) might seem at first glance to be the most appropriate on several counts. For one thing, it is phrased in terms of an "ideal" of rationality, and the natural response is: Whose ideal? After all, if we are simply dealing with certain

94

idiosyncratic conceptions of what it is reasonable for an organization to do, then this should give us no pause in trying to articulate a ("therapeutic") model of what organizations ought to do
morally. The problem with this response is that Ladd's account of
the ideal of rationality in formal organizations is not idiosyncratic, either in terms of popular opinion or in terms of social
scientific theories. It undoubtedly represents the dominant model
of organizational behavior, both in terms of descriptive-explanatory
studies of that behavior and in terms of people's expectations (if
not ultimate appraisals) of that behavior.

There is, however, an important respect in which this account
is incomplete, and I propose to argue that it is this fact which
provides some flexibility in what is otherwise a tense dichotomy
between corporate rationality and moral responsibility. In outlining the "ideal" of rationality for formal organizations, Ladd,
drawing largely upon H. A. Simon, emphasizes the analogy with game
rules (e.g., chess). The constitutive conditions which define what
is a 'move' and what is not are compared to the decision-making
premises ("organizational goals") which define what is and what is
not a genuine organizational decision (as against, say, a personal
decision by a member of an organization). But there is a crucial
disanalogy here which is not emphasized. It is that, for the most
part, game rules are static while organizational premises tend to
be more dynamic. In other words, though we are dealing perhaps with
differences of degree, the irrelevance of morality to chess is of
a different order of magnitude from the irrelevance of morality to
organizational rationality. For organizational mandates and goals
(the decision-making premises) are subject to constant stress,
even evolution, in the presence of complex pressures both from
within and from outside the corporate coalition. The limits of
willing identification and cooperation among managers, stockholders,
workers, customers and the general public (in the case of private
organizations) and legislators, administrators, staff, voters,
etc. (in the case of public organizations) result in considerable,
though possibly incremental, changes in organizational premises.
By contrast, it would be surprising to find such changes in the
rules or objectives of chess over time.[9] And the explanation is
not hard to discern. Chess, unlike organizational decision-making,
is pretty clearly insulated from morally significant impact. My
guess is that one could think of limiting cases of game rules
which do exhibit developmental characteristics due to their impact
on human life (e.g., rules of war, or rules of language or rules
of etiquette). But for the most part, the moral irrelevance of
constitutive rules varies in direct proportion to the 'artificiality'
or 'abstractness' of the games which they constitute. Thus we
should expect that the stark separation between organizational rationality and moral responsibility is overstated. Organizational
rationality, to be sure, includes a purely 'means-to-ends' compo-

95

nent, but the 'ends' which are often taken as 'givens' are rarely taken as unalterable. This being the case, efficiency can only exhaust the concept of rationality in formal organizations if it is also rational for such organizations to abdicate control over the development or change of those ends. If it is not rational to do this, and I hazard the opinion that it is not, then the ideal of rationality in formal organizations must include more than the efficient pursuit of given or static decision-premisses (by analogy with games like chess[10]). It must include criteria for the scrutiny and modification of those premisses ('ends') themselves. And it seems less likely that a case can be made for the irrelevance of morality to these criteria than for the irrelevance of morality to any (given) premisses or ends.

Simon himself seems to me to acknowledge this perception implicitly when he writes:

> . . . although it is correct to say that organization behavior is oriented toward the organization objective, this is not the whole story; for the organization objective itself changes in response to the influence of those for whom the accomplishment of that objective secures personal values.[11]

Thus, though Ladd seems right in interpreting organizational theorists as less sensitive than they might be to the ramifications of controlled adaptation of organizational goals or premisses, he goes too far in inferring from remarks about the givenness of organizational goals[12] such conclusions as that:

-- organizational decisions "cannot take their ethical premisses from the principles of morality" and
-- "for logical reasons it is improper to expect organizational conduct to conform to the ordinary principles of morality."[13]

What is crucial is that it is an empirical question whether the principles of morality find their way into organizational premisses, and that the "givenness" of those premisses is only a part of what is involved in the ideal of rationality for formal organizations.

I conclude, then, that we must enrich the account of rationality for formal organizations to accommodate the phenomenon of controlled adaptation of organizational goals or decision-premisses. This modification permits us to conceive of moral principles as candidates for organizational premisses, or at least as criteria for the control of those premisses, in a way which Ladd's account precludes due to its emphasis on the static "givenness" of those premisses. With respect to alternative (1) above, then, it seems

96

unreasonable to abandon Ladd's account altogether, though it seems reasonable to do so in part.

III

Let us now turn to alternative (2). Here we find difficulties of a procedural sort, since Ladd does not develop explicitly an account of morally responsible decision-making. Determining whether to abandon it in whole or in part, then, is problematic. My strategy will be simply to isolate one feature of the account and suggest that it is overstated as it stands, and then trace the implications of this fact for Ladd's general argument.

As I pointed out earlier (B'), a key element in Ladd's contrast between organizational rationality and morality is the issue of instrumentality. As Ladd puts it, instrumental rationality

> . . . reduces the relationship between human beings
> to the category of means to an end, a category in
> which they do not belong. It makes the only point
> of a rational action the function that it plays in
> 'means-ends' chains. The only point of keeping a
> promise, for instance, is the effect that doing so
> will have on my ends or the ends of others. This
> way of looking at rationality reflects what seems to
> me to be essentially an amoral position, for it re-
> duces morality, which is a matter of the relations
> between human beings, to what is useful or expedient
> for some purpose or other.[14]

Now, I have no desire to maintain that a non-instrumentalist conception of moral responsibility is untenable, quite the contrary. But I do wish to point out that there are two importantly different interpretations or versions of what has come to be called "deontological" morality. On the first, consideration of consequences for persons' ends is held to be relevant but insufficient for morally responsible decision-making, while on the second, such consideration of consequences is held to be irrelevant and unnecessary.[15] To the extent that Ladd is embracing the latter, more radical, view of morally responsible decision-making, his thesis of incompatibility between morality and organizational rationality is enhanced. To the extent that he is embracing the former, more moderate, view the incompatibility thesis becomes less plausible. For on the moderate view, there is a definite, even essential, place for consequential "means-ends" reasoning in moral decision-making -- even if this sort of reasoning does not exhaust morality. This observation, joined to my earlier point about the place for controlled adaptation in organizational rationality, begins to complete the

97

picture of a reconciliation where Ladd seems to have seen only conceptual impasse.

The question in the present context, then, becomes: Which of the two general forms of deontological morality is more plausible, if we assume with Ladd that a purely teleological account of morality will not do?[16] It seems to me that we have to answer in favor of the moderate form. The implications of relegating consequences to _irrelevance_ are simply intolerable. In terms of Ladd's example of promise-keeping, it is salutary to be reminded that there is more, morally, to our responsibilities in this matter than expediency, but this is no reason for thinking that the effects on persons' ends of keeping or breaking a promise make no moral difference _at all_.[17] The moral ambiguity at work in such slogans as "whatever the consequences" has been too amply demonstrated (to most philosophers) to bear the weight that the radical deontologist wishes to place on it.

I conclude, then, that Ladd's account of the general nature of moral responsibility needs a moderation which is not clearly present, and that with this moderation we again perceive a lessening of the tension between the ideals of organizational rationality and the demands of morality. Thus alternative (2), though too strong, leads us to alternative (3).

The pattern which emerges is as follows. The project of "ethical diagnostics" and its point, the molding of corporate "conscience," appeared to be threatened at the outset by what was claimed to be a logical or conceptual barrier. The ideal of rationality in formal organizations was simply _inconsistent_ with the ideal of morally responsible decision-making. On examining Ladd's accounts of the respective ideals, however, I argued that each required modification. Organizational rationality cannot be conceived as _purely_ instrumental with no criteria for guiding the development of the goals or premises from which efficiency departs. Nor can moral responsibility be conceived as _purely_ noninstrumental with no attention to the consequences of conduct on the ends or interests of those affected by it (including, I might add, the agent himself). Thus what I claim to have provided so far is rather negative: a kind of _space_ for the working out of a solution to our problem. The logical or conceptual barriers to describing and developing formal organizations through moral categories were seen to depend upon unduly strong construals of ideal rationality and ideal morality, respectively. The moderation of these ideals (or better, the clarification of them) relaxes the barriers a bit and allows for the possibility that rationality might be moralized and morality rationalized.

But it is important not to overstate the case. Though per-

98

haps exaggerated, Ladd's approach is a healthy caution to a naive conception of corporate (or organizational) description and reform. There is, in other words, a clear tension between the joint demands of efficiency and adaptation in decision-making, not to mention complications involved in the proper understanding of each demand taken separately. My own view is that this tension (not inconsistency) represents an essential structural feature of rational as well as responsible agency. Both for purposes of empirical analysis and for purposes of reform, our conception of corporate agency (like our conception of individual agency) must reflect the fact that action is not simply the mindless pursuit of antecedently given ends. The static model must be replaced by the dynamic one in which action is seen as a mutual accommodation between organism (organization) and environment in which the organism monitors both means and ends. And the monitoring process involves feedback between the agent and the results of his pursuit. Sometimes this feedback will dictate alteration of means, sometimes it will dictate alteration of ends. Rationality in action will depend upon an agent's capacity, among others, to make appropriate adjustments in both areas in an effort to maintain stability and long-term integrity. Whether and in what way an agent engages in this tuning operation is a more important indicator of its conscience or lack of conscience than any given set of goals which it may pursue at any given time. Thus an ethical profile of an organization's decision-making will need to attend not simply to organizational premises, to use Simon's term, but (more importantly) to the adaptation patterns which control those premises. In the case of a private organization like a corporation, such goals as profit, growth, market shares, etc., represent a typical corporation's ongoing behavioral premises -- but they do not, in themselves, provide us with a picture of the corporation's action-guiding principles in the fuller sense under discussion. To get at these, we need to attend to such features of the organizational structure as:

-- information-gathering and processing priorities;
-- criteria of management selection; and
-- authority relationships between participants.

As with an individual agent, an organizational agent exhibits his ethical commitments as much (perhaps more) in the procedural controls he places on his goal selection as in the goals selected. One of the most difficult (and interesting) tasks of the diagnostician is to isolate the key control variables in a given organization, relating them to patterns of organizational behavior and the results of that behavior.

A natural way in which an organization's goals (premisses) might be controlled would be in terms of some more general or basic goal such as corporate expansion or community esteem, etc. This might manifest itself in selectivity regarding information-gathering, choice of managers, and degree of centralization of authority. Such a "teleological" organizational ethic might be more or less morally defensible. And there could be combinations of "metagoals" as well. A power company might control its goal selection in terms of both local community satisfaction and company growth.[19]

But the control need not be provided in this way. Indeed, in the end the selection of the metagoals themselves would seem to require criteria of some sort. If an infinite regress is not to be the result, there may well be standards of goal selection of a more formal sort, e.g., law abidingness, justice, acceptability to a certain class or type of persons, etc.

Conclusion

The general implication is that organizational agents (and corporate agents in particular) do exhibit structural features which permit the working out of both a diagnostic and a therapeutic ethical inquiry, once we understand the categorical compatibility (however fragile) between rationality and morality. This is not to say that all formal organizations can be analyzed and modified toward more responsible decision-making without serious disturbance, or even that such modification can be accomplished at all in every case. We should not expect more in our interactions with human organizations than we expect in our interactions with human individuals.

However, if we are convinced that modern life with its large-scale technology presents serious problems due to a lack of reflectiveness and responsibility on the part of our more powerful institutions (private and public), and if we are also convinced that our main model for purposes of analysis and reform is the very human person in whose image and likeness those institutions are fabricated, then perhaps enough has been said to vindicate the intelligibility (and desirability) of a new task for ethics.

NOTES

1. Goodpaster, K. and Sayre, K., "An Ethical Analysis of Power Company Decision-Making," in Values in the Electric Power Industry, K. M. Sayre, ed., University of Notre Dame Press; (1977), pp. 238-287.
2. Stone, Christopher, Where The Law Ends, Harper & Row (1975), p. 111.

3. Goodpaster and Sayre, op. cit. p. 280.

4. Silk, L., and Vogel, D., Ethics and Profits, Simon and Schuster (1976), quoted on p. 138.

5. The Monist, Vol. 54 (October 1970), pp. 488-516.

6. Ladd, op. cit. p. 500.

7. Simon, H., Administrative Behavior (New York: Free Press, 1965). Third edition now available, 1976.

8. Barnard, C., The Functions of the Executive (Cambridge: Harvard University Press, 1938). Also see Barnard's Forward to Simon, op. cit.

9. I do not mean to suggest that the constitutive rules of chess do not, or have not, undergone evolution. They clearly have. What is important is that this evolution (a) has been very slow since initial formulations of the game and (b) has not been due to the impact of the game or the players on others' lives or well-being (since there is next to no impact here to speak of -- which is why chess is "only a game").

10. The other analogy employed by Ladd, the machine, seems to me to clarify the point even more: the picture is of rigid givens, inflexible and unalterable (or at least uncontrollably so) a picture which human organizations exhibit only in superficial ways over short periods of time.

11. Simon, op. cit. p. 114.

12. Remarks like Simon's: "Decisions in private management, like decisions in public management, must take as their ethical premisses the objectives that have been set out for the organization." (p. 52) My point is that the "setting" is not outside the realm of organizational control.

13. Or even more strongly, Ladd writes: "We cannot and must not expect formal organizations, or even their representatives acting in their official capacities, to be honest, courageous, considerate, sympathetic, or to have any kind of moral integrity. Such concepts are not in the vocabulary, so to speak, of the organizational language-game." (Ladd, p. 499).

14. Ladd, p. 515.

15. Cf. Frankena, W. K., Ethics (Prentice-Hall, 1973, second edition), Ch. 3.

16. As for the assumption that a purely teleological theory is implausible, too much needs to be said. My opinion, in view of the long history of controversy here, is that the operationalizability of the key maximandum for such theories appears inevitably to vary inversely with its plausibility. I suspect that this was Kant's point when he observed in the Foundations that the notion of 'happiness' could not sustain an ethic.

17. Cf. Frankena, op. cit. and W. D. Ross, The Right and the Good (Oxford, 1930).

18. Goodpaster and Sayre, op. cit.

JOHN LADD

Is "Corporate Responsibility" a Coherent Notion?

Mr. Goodpaster and Mr. Donaldson have offered us some interesting and instructive comments on the article entitled
"Morality and the Ideal of Rationality in Formal Organizations,"
which I wrote almost ten years ago.[1] I want to thank them for
singling it out for so much attention and for the care and
thoughtfulness with which they have prepared their comments on
it.

A few remarks concerning the article under discussion may
help to put its main contentions in perspective. When I originally wrote the article, I did not really have business corporations in mind; my main focus was on governmental bureaucracies
such as the IRS, the FBI, the CIA, the Pentagon, and other
governmental decision-making organizations. The paper that
formed the basis of the article was written for a conference
concerned with moral issues connected with the Viet Nam War and
covered topics like political obligation and civil disobedience.
In thinking about these issues, it had seemed to me that a better
understanding of the concept of rationality in decision-making
might throw light on how and why we became involved in Viet Nam,
why it was so difficult to extricate ourselves from the war, and
how it was possible for so many "bright" and idealistic people
to become submerged in a process of decision-making that seemed
to "outsiders" quite obviously to be immoral and stupid and to
portend grave consequences for the nation. I contended that it
was impossible to discuss political obligation and civil disobedience in the Viet Nam context without first examining some
more basic moral issues concerning compliance and disobedience
within formal organizations, e.g. the military bureaucracy.[2]

In the meantime, although the Viet Nam War is behind us,
we are still confronted with the same perplexing moral problems
associated with formal organizations that I discussed in my
article. Now, however, they are connected with a different type
of formal organization, namely, large private corporations.[3]

On rereading the article, it is clear to me that what I say
in it about public formal organizations applies equally to large
private organizations, including, of course, multinational corporations. If we find many of the same moral problems in private
as well as in public organizations, then it would seem clear
that there are some important moral problems connected with cor-

102

porations that do not turn on the specific nature of their goals, but, to put it crudely, involve the morality of the kinds of means that, by its very nature, any formal organization has to use to realize its goals, whatever they might be. Finally, I should make it clear that I do not pretend to have any ready solutions; my only purpose is to lay open a complicated moral problem that has not received as much attention from philosophers as it deserves.

I should like to pursue the point about goals a little further. It is natural to try to base moral evaluations of the operations of corporations on the consequences for good or evil that they have for society. A good corporation is one that brings more benefits than harms to society; for example, it may provide for peoples' needs at a minimum economic cost and with the least social disruption. (Public utilities such as electric or telephone companies are often held to be good in this sense.) A bad, i.e. morally evil, corporation would be one that brings more evil than good; it might be an organization that unduly exploits its employees, clients, or consumers for private purposes of its own (e.g. profit). Thus, for example, multinational corporations, according to some reports, are said to use their power to exploit indigenous populations in underdeveloped nations for their own economic advantage.[4] Consequentialistic evaluations of this kind, pro or con, have an understandable appeal, although it should be pointed out that they are more cogent and persuasive when the benefit or harm in question is clearly discernible and specific. If we attempt a more general consequentialist analysis of the costs and benefits of the private corporation as an institution, we run into difficulties simply because it is not clear what we should compare it with.[5]

Likewise, we will not get very far if we try to evaluate corporations morally in terms of the personal character or motivation of the persons who participate in corporate activity, e.g. as managers or employees. I do not subscribe to a conspiracy theory of moral evil and I am quite ready to admit that corporate officers are moral people or at least that they are as likely (or unlikely) to be honest, hardworking, kind, unselfish and patriotic as the rest of us. But whether they are or not is beside the point. My thesis is that the special moral issues connected with formal organizations, including corporations, are institutional (or ideological) rather than personal.

Mr. Goodpaster has summarized my position very well, so I need not review it here. The main point that I make is that organizations, viz. corporations, are governed by special standards of conduct that serve to guide, justify and explain the particular actions of the corporation's officials. For reasons

103

given in my article, I also suggest that organizational standards must by their very nature deviate in significant ways from moral standards that govern the conduct of individual persons. As a consequence, many people in our society find themselves operating under a double standard of morality: one at work and the other at home with friends and neighbors. The resulting tension produces what could be called a kind of "moral schizophrenia" -- or as the Marxists would say: a condition of "alienation."

Accordingly, I maintain that both a consequentialist evaluation, on the one hand, and a moralistic evaluation, on the other hand, miss the point; for they take for granted that the same standard will be employed in the evaluation of corporate activity as is used for the evaluation of other types of conduct.

As Mr. Goodpaster points out, I take the problem of corporate responsibility to be a conceptual problem and not merely a problem for what he calls "ethical diagnostics," that is, a problem calling for a 'descriptive explanatory analysis' and 'ethical therapy.'[6] Indeed, I am prepared to defend the more general thesis that most of the perplexing and disturbing moral problems of morality that face our society today are conceptual problems of some sort or other. As such they cannot be resolved by 'patching up' or corrected by ethical therapy. The conceptual aspects of many basic ethical problems are not always clearly recognized because so many of the concepts that we use in ethics consist of both factual and ethical elements intertwined with each other, usually inseparable and sometimes almost indistinguishable. At the bottom of many of our problems is the fact that "is" and "ought" often cannot be separated simply because the concepts in which they are imbedded are so complex from the analytical point of view. Consequently, many ostensibly factual issues in ethical controversies actually involve concepts that, upon closer examination, turn out to be ethically loaded and, on the other hand, many ethical concepts that they employ are founded on factual presuppositions that may actually be entirely false.

All of this has a bearing on the notorious doctrine of a value-free social science, a doctrine that has been shown in numerous instances to be untenable in dealing with institutions and institutional behavior. Without going into details, a descriptive analysis of corporate decision-making is bound to be normative in a certain sense, since it can be carried out only in terms of a theoretical framework of rational decision-making. ("Rationality" is, of course, a normative concept.) Similarly, the particular concepts employed in describing and explaining institutional behavior, e.g. the concepts of rules, policies, positions, information, and authority, are in the final analysis themselves normative or, broadly speaking, ethical concepts.

104

Consequently, any less than superficial ethical analysis of corporate goals, corporate structure and corporate decision-making must be based on an extensive conceptual analysis of the sort that could be called a "logico-ethical analysis."

From an ethical point of view, many of the problems presented by the existence of a double moral standard in corporate life can be attributed to a basic conceptual confusion about what a corporation is. This confusion leads to treating a corporation as a person and endowing it with various personal moral attributes such as responsibility, rights, obligations, and so on. Mr. Goodpaster puts the point I make about corporations very well when he suggests that we are dealing here with a straightforward inversion of Plato's analogy in the Republic; instead of moving, as Plato does, from the larger unit (the State, the organization) to the individual, the conception that I am concerned with moves from the individual to the larger unit, e.g. the organization or corporation. Plato tried to analyze the morality of individuals by assimilating it to the morality of the state; the organizational ideology, if I may call it that, assimilates the morality of organizations to the morality of individuals. I contend that the analogical arguments that both procedures employ represent what Ryle calls a category mistake.[7] The kind of category mistake involved here can be illustrated by the difference between a baseball game and a baseball team; it would be a category mistake to suppose that the game itself was a tenth member of the team! In this case, it is easy to see that the game is simply a pattern of behavior adopted by the two teams, viz. eighteen persons, in a certain kind of situation; and, like corporate activity, it is a collective activity defined by rules, strategies and goals.

A few more words about the ontological status of organizations (or corporations) may help. It is tempting just to say that an organization is a 'fiction,' but to call it a fiction does not help us very much; one might just as well say that a baseball game is a fiction. Calling them both fictions is misleading simply because organizations and baseball games are real in the sense that they can be used to explain behavior and they have a certain kind of causal efficacy (i.e. agency). Bearing this in mind, it might be more accurate to say that organizations, and especially corporations, are mythical entities, for, like many powerful myths that are about fictitious beings, corporate myths exercise immense influence over the lives of individuals and of society.[8] Leaving aside its mythological aspects, however, an organization might be defined, in Simon's words, as a "pattern of group behavior."[9] The pattern describes a way in which people make group decisions, systematize and coordinate their activities, deliberate and frame projects, and so on. In

105

other words, it is a "decision-making structure." In all these respects, an organization is more like a baseball game than it is like one of the members of a baseball team, that is, it is a way of structuring the behavior of a group of individuals rather than being itself another individual.

The distinctive thing about corporations, as contrasted with other patterns of group behavior, is the accompanying "mythology," namely, the attribution of the group behavior described as corporate activity to the organization itself. By that account, the organization is considered to make decisions and to act on its own so to speak. The real people involved are viewed as the instruments (agents) or recipients of organizational actions, that is, they are the organization's representatives and perform the actions for and on its behalf ("in its name") or, as its subjects, they benefit or suffer from the consequences of the organization's actions.

In this connection, it should be observed that ambiguities in the word "agent" tend to conceal some ethically significant differences between organizations and persons. Philosophers customarily use the term "moral agent" to designate persons acting freely and 'responsibly.' But we should remember that in everyday English the term "agent" is used much more broadly to designate things that act as well as persons; thus, the dictionary defines an "agent" as "one who or that which acts" or simply as "an efficient cause."[10] Accordingly, insofar as they act and bring about changes, many different categories of things besides persons can be properly characterized as "agents," e.g. chemical substances and social systems such as organizations.[11] It would be clearly fallacious, however, to conclude that, because corporations are agents in the causal sense, they are also agents in the moral sense. In order to avoid this trap, it would be better to follow the lead of sociologists and call acting persons actors.[12]

Again, the fact that corporations possess a legal personality should not deceive us into concluding that they are therefore also moral persons. As artificial or fictitious persons, corporations do indeed have legal rights and duties, powers and responsibilities (=liabilities?), and as corporate persons, they can, of course, perform various kinds of legal acts such as buying and selling, making contracts, and perhaps even committing crimes - although the latter presents some conceptual problems even for the law. In any case, it should be obvious that we cannot infer anything about the moral status of corporations from their legal status.

Another frequent source of confusion about the ethical

106

status of corporations is the supposition that every aggregate of persons that possesses a unity of some kind and has some way of differentiating its members from outsiders must on that account be an organization. I do not deny that there are many different ways of dividing and classifying social aggregates and social systems in general and that for certain sociological purposes it might be useful to put organizations and other social systems, e.g. communities, in the same category. For ethical purposes, however, it is absolutely necessary that we differentiate between organizations, as patterns of group behavior, and associations, as aggregates of individuals. Thus, moral principles relating to associations such as friendship groups, gangs, families, communities, nations, and perhaps even universities, are quite different from those relating to formal organizations such as corporations.

We can see some of the important ethical differences between them if we contrast what constitutes the unity and identity of an association with what constitutes the unity and identity of an organization. The bond that brings and holds the members of an organization together is provided by the goals of the organization and the rules adopted to realize those goals. The unity of an organization might be said to be teleological! The unity of associations, on the other hand, is not teleological; individuals are identified as members of an association by reference to a particular fact about them as individuals, such as that they have something in common, say, a certain non-teleological and perhaps quite incidental trait that may be entirely situational; for example, they may be bound together by the fact that they live near each other as neighbors, that they have blood ties, a common religious or cultural heritage, or perhaps just that they have mutual concerns or mutual affections. To put it very crudely, associations achieve their unity, identity and continuity from contingent historical factors rather than teleologically, i.e. through deliberate planning with a goal in mind.[13] According to this conception of associations, it is absurd to ask for the goal of an association as such, that is, a goal over and above the goals of the particular individual in it. It is absurd, for example, to ask for the goal of the family, or of friendship, or of a village or of a university. Thus, Aristotle and Aquinas were conceptually (and ethically) mistaken in trying to reduce all human groups (including friendship, families, communities) to groups organized teleologically around a goal of some kind; in effect they make all groups into what I have called "organizations."[14]

From the ethical point of view, it is important to note that, in contrast to organizations, the goals, actions, projects and decisions of an association are not any different from the goals, actions, projects and decisions of individuals within it.

107

Hence, although the individuals in an association may share the same goal and jointly undertake an action in pursuit of it, the goals and the actions themselves are nonetheless attributes of the individuals participating in them, severally and jointly. More generally, the fact that two individuals join in the same action makes the joint action an action of both and it is not any less the action of one of them because it is performed by someone else as well. The same sort of consideration applies, of course, to common goals, projects, and plans. Accordingly, we must be careful not to confuse shared goals and joint actions with the goals of a collectivity or the actions of a collectivity, say, of an organization. It also follows that the rights, duties, and responsibilities of an association are indistinguishable and inseparable from the rights, duties, and responsibilities of persons who make up the association. If I do something for an association, I do it for most or all individuals within it and if an association has a duty or responsibility that means that a certain number of individuals within the association have the duty or responsibility. An association has no "life of its own" so to speak; it does not exist apart from its members - and, indeed, cannot be defined apart from its members.[15]

The arguments that I have given here concerning the moral status of corporations differ slightly from those that I gave in my earlier article on formal organizations, because I have tried to meet some of the objections that the commentators have brought against my position as it relates, specifically, to corporations. In that article, I stressed the ethical aspects of the logic of organizational decision-making; in particular, I argued that the kinds of premises that organizations must (logically) use in their decision-making are incompatible with morality. It is quite understandable that Mr. Goodpaster and Mr. Donaldson should ask about the ethical assumptions underlying my critique. I shall therefore try to sketch briefly the ethical point of view that makes me reluctant to accept organizational decision-making as a moral (or conditionally moral) activity. At the outset, however, I feel that I should point out that in order to be valid an ethical critique need not be based on premises derived from an hypothesized alternative theory. A critique, as I have argued elsewhere, may be purely negative, that is, skeptical or destructive; it does not, as such, depend for its validity as a critique on the prior acceptance of another ethical theory. Hence, I hope that the critique that I originally presented can stand on its own feet so to speak.[16]

Is the ethics I presuppose teleological or deontological? Mr. Goodpaster asks. In reply, I can only say that I find this commonly accepted distinction to be almost useless. I am not sure, for example, what is meant by the terms "teleological" and "deontological," and whether or not the division is supposed to be exhaustive and exclusive, and so on. (Even Mr. Goodpaster has to qualify the distinction before he can apply it.) On my view, the basic subject-matter of ethics is not acts (or kinds of acts) but relationships between people. Sometimes these relationships are defined by rules (deontologically?), sometimes by goals (teleologically), and sometimes by other things such as attitudes and mutual concerns. One gains a better insight into what is involved in social relationships, morally speaking, if one connects them to virtues and vices. Virtues like honesty, trustworthiness, integrity, kindness, care, concern, love, loyalty, generosity, responsibility and respect indicate the parameters for more specific moral requirements relating to acts, such as duties, rights and responsibilities. Similarly, vices like deceit, cruelty, insensibility, neglect and irresponsibility set the parameters for wrongful conduct. It can be seen at once that virtues and vices of the kind mentioned cannot be attributed to organizations, except metaphorically.[17] They can, on the other hand, be attributed to associations, for in that case all that we mean is that they are attributable distributively to many or most of its individual members. By the same token, virtues and vices can be attributed to managers, employees, and clients of corporations, providing they are taken as individuals. In such cases, we can, of course, make general statements of the form: "In general, the members of association X or the managers of corporation Y are honest, etc." But when we make such statements about virtues and vices, they always refer to persons and not to fictitious or mythological entities such as corporations.

When it comes to specific kinds of actions, the ethical position I have in mind concerns itself with what one person (or group of persons) can do to or for another person (or group of persons). Acts to be avoided would include lying, deceiving, killing, hurting, and abandoning another person. Such act-types can be defined non-consequentially. In addition to acts of that kind, one person can do something to or for another person by doing something that has good or harmful consequences for him. This general category of moral requirements can be called "responsibilities." A person's responsibilities comprise those possible states of affairs for which he is responsible in the virtue sense.

The term "responsibility" has, of course, many meanings. Some of them are applicable to corporations and some are not. To begin with, "responsibility" is frequently used in a causal sense, so that physical objects as well as persons and organizations can be said to be 'responsible' for a disaster, e.g. the death of a large number of people. (To be responsible in this sense is tied up with causal agency, which has already been discussed.)

109

Second, "responsibility" is often used to describe a task or a role: the janitor is responsible for emptying the wastebaskets. I have elsewhere called this kind of responsibility <u>official</u> responsibility. An interesting logical feature of both causal and official responsibility is that they are exclusionary, that is, if A is responsible then others, say, B and C, are not responsible. It is obvious that every social structure, such as a corporation, uses the concept of official responsibility as a principle for organizing its activities.

Moral responsibility, which is our concern here, is different from both kinds of responsibility just mentioned in that it implies a moral ought of some kind. Here we must begin by distinguishing between <u>retrospective</u> moral responsibility, i.e. responsibility for something that has already happened but ought not to have happened, and <u>prospective</u> moral responsibility, i.e. responsibility for what might happen in the future and ought or ought not happen. Both kinds of responsibility call for anticipating and planning for outcomes that one could have done or now can do something about. Philosophers have almost entirely devoted their attention to retrospective moral responsibility. Inasmuch as moral responsibility in this sense is exclusively ascribed to persons and implies a free will of some kind, it is doubtful that it can be applied to corporations as entities, although it can, of course, be applied to individual persons who happen to be the managers, employees, or subjects of a particular corporation.

Too little thought, in my opinion, has been given to the other kind of moral responsibility, namely, to what I call prospective moral responsibility. This is responsibility for future outcomes that are foreseeable as consequences of one's present acts or omissions. It has also been called <u>responsibility in the virtue sense</u>.[18] Responsibility in the virtue sense is what distinguishes a responsible from an irresponsible person. Essentially it calls for a concern for what might or might not happen to another person or group of persons over whose welfare or fortunes one has some sort of control. In the sense that it involves this kind of indirect control over what happens to others, responsibility defines a moral relationship between the actor and other persons.

It should be observed that moral responsibility of the virtue kind, unlike the other kinds of responsibility mentioned, is non-exclusionary. If one person is responsible, say, for the health and safety of another person (or group of persons), it cannot be assumed that no one else is responsible. Responsibility in the virtue sense cannot be abdicated or transferred! So one cannot "escape" moral responsibility for what happens to others by foisting it onto someone else or onto an organization. It also follows that there can be such a thing as joint responsibility or collective responsibility, that is, there may be circumstances in which a number of individuals are jointly and separately responsible for X's health or welfare, etc.[19]

Without arguing the matter in detail, I hope that it will be evident that prospective moral responsibility, as I have just outlined it, cannot be attributed to organizations, although, of course, it can still be attributed to individuals within an organization, say, to managers and employees, and it can be attributed to others who deal with an organization, say, its clients and the public at large. And, as I have pointed out, the responsibility of any one individual or of any single one of these groups does not exclude others from being responsible as well.

One other facet of moral responsibility in this last sense needs to be mentioned. This kind of responsibility is intimately related to power; for where there is power to affect the future of others, there is also responsibility. We might even say that power creates responsibility.[20] It is obvious that managers of large corporations wield an enormous amount of power, power to influence the behavior of others and to affect the happiness, welfare, health and lives of large numbers of people. This power is exercised through the medium of the organization which they manage. But the moral responsibilities that this power creates are personal, that is, they are attached to persons and aggregates of persons, rather than to organizations as such.

In conclusion, I want to make it quite clear that by denying that corporate responsibility is a coherent moral concept I am not claiming that moral responsibility is an unimportant ethical notion or that no one is responsible for what corporations do. Rather, I am simply saying that responsibility should be placed where it belongs, namely, on people rather than on fictitious, mythological entities. That is, it rests with the people who run and work for the corporation as well as with those who deal with it - perhaps, indeed, it rests with our whole society. To attribute moral responsibility to a corporation, on the other hand, simply provides all of us with a good excuse for not taking the responsibility on ourselves and for not demanding it of those in power.

NOTES

1. _Monist_, vol. 54, no. 4 (October, 1970). Hereafter referred to as _MIR_. An abridged version of this article is reprinted in Thomas Donaldson and Patricia H. Werhane, editors.

Ethical Issues in Business. Englewood Cliffs, N.J.: Prentice-Hall, 1979, pp. 102-13.

2. See, for example, Richard J. Barnet, *Roots of War: The Men and the Institutions*. Penguin, 1973.

3. Henceforth, I shall use the term "corporation" to stand for large, private corporations that are also formal organizations. Most of what I have to say does not apply to small corporations, e.g. businesses, where everyone knows everyone else.

4. For details, see Richard J. Barnet and Ronald E. Müller, *Global Reach*. New York: Simon Schuster, 1974.

5. The point of my analysis will be missed if anyone concludes that the same sort of problem that I discuss here does not exist for socialism or communism as well.

6. "Therapy," Goodpaster writes, "is a procedure for the correction of disorders." Kenneth Sayre, ed. *Values in the Electric Power Industry*. Notre Dame: University of Notre Dame Press, 1977, p. 280. Conceptual problems, on my view, are not disorders that can be corrected!

7. See Gilbert Ryle, *The Concept of Mind*. London: Hutchinson's University Library, 1949, p. 16. In passing, it should be pointed out that the category mistake committed here has grave moral consequences, whichever way the inference is made. See Renford Bambrough, "Plato's Political Analogies." Reprinted in Gregory Vlastos, *Plato II*. Garden City, NY: Doubleday, 1971.

8. Myths, as they are used in ethics, are not always objectionable. They may serve important functions of one sort or another, e.g. to encapsulate an ethical doctrine or to bring out other facets of morality. The main point to note about myths, as I conceive them, is that they are literally false or at least they make ostensible factual claims about reality that are empirically unverifiable. For a discussion of the kind of claims that I have in mind, see John Wisdom, "Gods." *Proceedings of the Aristotelian Society*, 1944.

9. H. A. Simon, *Administrative Behavior*, 3rd edition. New York: Free Press, 1976, p. 100.

10. See the *Shorter Oxford English Dictionary*, p. 34. Italics are mine.

11. In addition to the causal sense of "agent," we should note the legal sense: "a person authorized by another to act for him, one intrusted with another's business." *Black's Law Dictionary*.

12. Using the term "actors" will also help us to avoid confusing "moral agents" with "legal agents." It should also be noted that the use of the term "agent," as in the concept "moral agent," easily permits one to slip into an "agency" theory of action or some other kind of causal theory of action. For a description of the agency theory of action, see Alan Donagan, *The Theory of Morality*. Chicago: Chicago University Press, 1977, pp. 37-52. I attribute many common errors con-

cerning organizations to the unquestioned assumption of a causal theory of action. See MIR.

13. I have set forth this conception of associations and, in particular, of communities, in "The Idea of Community," New England Journal, American Institute of Planners, New England Chapter. Vol. 1, August 1972. An earlier version, entitled "The Concept of Community: A Logical Analysis," may be found in Community: NOMOS II, ed. Carl J. Friedrich. New York: Liberal Arts Press, 1959.

14. Thus, Aquinas defines matrimony in organizational terms; it is an organization for producing, supporting and educating children! See Summa Theologica, supplement, question 44.

15. Defining an association in terms of particular members is often, however, a complicated matter. For details, see references in note 13.

16. Positive and negative arguments against an ethical position may conveniently be referred to as confutation and refutation, respectively. For further discussion, see my "Are Science and Ethics Compatible?" in Science, Ethics and Medicine, ed. Daniel Callahan and Tristram Engelhardt, Jr. Hastings: Institute of Society, Ethics and the Life Sciences, 1976.

17. It is interesting to speculate on various possible interpretations of such statements as: "The Corporation has been kind to me."

18. See Graham Haydon, "On being responsible," in The Philosophical Quarterly, vol. 28, no. 110 (January, 1978).

19. I have argued these points in more detail in "The Ethics of Participation," in J. Roland Pennock and John W. Chapman, editors. NOMOS XVI: Participation in Politics. New York: Atherton-Lieber, 1975.

20. See Steven Lukes, Power. London: MacMillan, 1974.

DISCUSSION

COMMENT: Professor Goodpaster, you say you did a study of the utilities. Let's introduce a little factual discussion here. Couldn't a corporation decide that out of concern for senior citizens it should offer the so-called life line discount rate if you're sufficiently poor or sufficiently old. I'd like to hear if you'd thought about that in your investigations. And I'd like to hear Professor Ladd say why it's a mistake to ask some companies, e.g., utility companies, to do that.

GOODPASTER: Okay. Good. In our study of the utilities we concentrated on a different subject matter. We were worried about the decisions to expand capacity, especially in the nuclear direction. We did, however, informally talk about other issues with these decision makers and among them the one you mention did come up. And there was some division among them, as you might expect, about the advisability of life line rates. But to answer your question quite simply, it seems clear to me that a corporation, say Edison in Chicago which was one of the ones which we dealt with, could decide to institute life line rates for moral reasons, and not only could but should.

LADD: What I think I'd want to say is that sometimes people who are managers of corporations and directors are human beings as well as managers, and that in a sense they're cheating on the profit.

GOODPASTER: Can I add something to that because it fits in with something that Professor Ladd said at the outset of his commentary. He said that corporations are not human beings, and, for that reason, moral categories are not appropriate in their decision making or we shouldn't expect that of them. That is exactly where we differ, I think. It seems to me that there is no a priori reason why something that is not a human being can't be morally responsible and held morally responsible. It might even be morally idealistic for that matter. It may be the case that a corporation is making all sorts of altruistic contributions and that it is thereby cheating its stockholders. But it doesn't seem to me that it's cheating its stockholders by using corporate revenues to be morally responsible, because a promise to a person to maximize his return on investment, whatever methods one might use, is an invalid promise. It doesn't seem to me that stockholders have any right to expect a manager to maximize their return unless it is subject to the conditions of moral responsibility. That promissory argument, as some people call

114

it, seems to me to be invalid. There are some promises we ought
not to keep.

COMMENT: I wonder how the three of you would respond to the following kind of thing. Suppose workers and people who live near
some plant that generates a lot of noise put pressure on the company to reduce the noise and eventually it's effective. What
happens is that whatever mechanisms the company uses for dealing
with the noise become business costs and can't really be described as a moral response to public or employee concern. I
think typically what happens is that when there's a response it
just becomes a new business cost.

LADD: I agree with you. And that's the point that I was making.
I would say responses to people's moral opinions, to popular
opinion, sometimes have an effect on corporations or business in
the same way as changes in the weather or availability of oil.
My principle that I came up with was that the only way to get a
response is from some kind of pressure from the outside and that
this is the rationale for having utility commissions and so on.
The only trouble is that then you usually, as came out in the
discussion this morning about accountants and the SEC, have to
set up another bureaucracy to handle the first bureaucracy and
you're back where you began; namely, you have two bureaucracies
both of which are non-moral enterprises.

DONALDSON: It strikes me that there might be another problem
here which has to do with the so-called rational model of formal
organization. I take it that Professor Ladd is raising a fundamental issue having to do with the conceptual side of responsibility. Are corporations the sort of things that you can
pattern after rational individuals? Now if they're not and if
ought implies can, then it sounds very strange for one to hold
the corporations morally responsible in the same way that we
would have individuals held responsible. My view would be that
in the same way that one could pursue self-interested ends and
have moral constraints, one might also pursue virtue and have
certain self-interested constraints.

SESSION V

"Ethical Problems of Managerial Hierarchy"

Archie B. Carroll
Professor of Management
University of Georgia

Arthur H. Walker
Professor of Management
Bentley College

Joseph A. Litterer
Visiting Professor of Management
Tuck School
Dartmouth College

ARCHIE B. CARROLL

Managerial Ethics and the Organizational Hierarchy

When discussions of business ethics transpire, it is inevitable that the topic of discussion will turn to the source of
a manager's value system and, hence, ethics. Many have taken
the position that the manager's ethics emenate out of the broad
sociocultural surroundings in which the manager resides. For
example, it has been suggested by Keith Davis and Robert Blomstrom that a very important aspect of the conduct of business
is the value system of its people. Such values as technical,
economic, social, aesthetic and spiritual, among others, represent
the types of values that must be balanced in decision-making
situations. George Steiner reinforces this view by positing that
religious, philosophical, cultural, legal and professional values
influence business decision-making.

Obviously, these broad environmental factors weigh heavily
in shaping the manager's value system, and they are not to be
taken lightly in any appraisal of what determines a manager's
ethics. However, I would like to take the position today that it
is the specific organizational context or environment -- especiall
the superior-subordinate dyadic relationship -- that most significantly influences organizational ethics. To put this differentl
I am suggesting that managers and employees ethics are shaped by
the transactions taking place between superior and subordinate,
and especially by the expectations placed on the latter by the
former.

Proving the causality link between superior and subordinates
may be quite hard with available research evidence; however, there
is research that is suggestive of such a linkage. I am referring
specifically to a survey I conducted several years ago in the
immediate post-Watergate period. There were three findings, in
particular, that were quite interesting. Let me describe the
survey briefly to you and point out the three findings.

The study was conducted soon after the Watergate incident,
and involved a survey of managers across the nation in an effort
to determine the validity of several propositions that were being
suggested concerning the relationship between business ethics and
political ethics. Questionnaires went out to approximately 400
managers chosen from various management levels and were constructed to elicit responses indicating the extent of the respondent's agreement or disagreement with selected propositions.

119

Out of the 400 questionnaires mailed, 238 were completed and returned, representing a response rate of approximately 59 percent. Three of the 10 propositions tested are pertinent to our theme today and the results of each item suggest a hierarchical pattern of response.

The first proposition and response follow:

Proposition 1: Managers today feel under pressure to compromise personal standards to achieve company goals.

Response	No.	Percent
Disagree	58	24.6
Somewhat disagree	26	11.0
Somewhat agree	102	43.2
Agree	50	21.2
Total	236	100.0

It is particularly insightful to examine the 64% who agreed with the proposition categorized by management level. The results are as follows:

Level	Agreement
Top Management	50% agreed
Middle Management	65% agreed
Lower Management	85% agreed

Notice the pattern -- the lower the respondents were in the organization hierarchy the more they tended to feel that "managers today feel under pressure to compromise personal standards to achieve company goals."

The second proposition and responses in my study were as follows:

Proposition 2: The junior members of Nixon's reelection committee who confessed that they went along with their bosses to show their loyalty is just what young managers would have done in business.

Response	No.	Percent
Disagree	58	24.6
Somewhat disagree	38	16.1
Somewhat agree	84	35.6
Agree	56	23.7
Total	236	100.0

When we examine the 59% of respondents who agreed with this proposition by management level, we see a response pattern similar to the first:

Level	Agreement
Top Management	37% agreed
Middle Management	61% agreed
Lower Management	85% agreed

We can see that in each case the lower one was in the organizational hierarchy, the more one perceived ethical problems. There was one other proposition that suggested a similar pattern of response. The proposition was: "I can conceive of a situation where you have sound ethics running from top to bottom but, because of pressures from the top to achieve results, the person down the line compromises." The pattern of findings on this proposition was similar to the other two.

The pattern of response is particularly troublesome in these findings. The lower one is in the organizational hierarchy the more one perceives pressures toward unethical conduct. Though there are a number of reasonable explanations for this phenomenon, one seems particularly attractive because of its agreement with conversations I have had with a number of different managers over the past several years. This interpretation is that top level managers simply do not comprehend how seriously subordinate managers perceive pressures to go along with the boss -- and, hence, do go along -- to please them. These differing perceptions down the organizational hierarchy suggest that higher level managers are not "in tune" with how pressures to behave are perceived at lower levels. There seems to be a gap in the understanding of higher managers and lower managers regarding the pressures toward unethical behavior that exist, especially in the lower parts of the hierarchy. This breakdown in understanding, or lack of sensitivity by top management as to how far subordinates will go to please them, can be conducive to lower level subordinates behaving unethically out of a fear of reprisal, misguided sense of loyalty, or distorted concept of the job.

Top level management may quite innocently and inadvertently create a condition conducive to unethical behavior on a subordinate's part. For example, take the case of a manager setting a sales goal of 25% for next year, when in actuality, a 15% increase is all that could be realistically expected even with outstanding performance. In the absence of clearly established and articulated ethical norms to the contrary, it is easy to see how a subordinate might feel that he is to go "to any lengths" to achieve the 25% goal. The manager failed to see, thus, that there is an ethical dimension to even the most routine of managerial decisions. As John Biegler, senior partner of Price, Waterhouse & Co., asserted in a recent talk: "Many corporate employees have behaved improperly in the misguided belief that the front office wanted them to. If standards are not formulated systematically at the top, they will be formulated haphazardly and impulsively in the field." (Wall Street Journal, February 24, 1977.)

Lending support to this view that the superior-subordinate relationship is at the core of much unethical behavior are the findings by Steven Brenner and Earl Molander in their 1977 survey of 1,227 Harvard Business Review readers. They conclude:

. . . relations with superiors are the primary category of ethical conflict. Respondents frequently complained of superiors' pressure to support incorrect views, sign false documents, overlook superiors' wrongdoing, and do business with superiors' friends. (Brenner and Molander, p. 60.)

The above citations do not exhaust the literature; however, they do point toward the organizational hierarchy as a significant source of ethical problems today. If managers are at the core of the problem as I believe the data presented above suggest, this constitutes a useful point of departure for discussing actions managers can employ to effectively address this problem that has serious current and future implications for organizations and society. It is only by beginning this serious discussion that impetus can be found for improving the ethical behavior of managers and employees alike.

SOURCES

Brenner, Steven N. and Earl A. Molander, "Is the ethics of business changing?" Harvard Business Review, January-February, 1977, 57-71.

Carroll, Archie B., "Managerial Ethics: A Post-Watergate View," Business Horizons, April, 1975, 75-80.

Carroll, Archie B. (ed.) Managing Corporate Social Responsibility (Boston: Little, Brown and Company, 1977).

Davis, Keith and Robert Blomstrom. Business and Society: Environment and Responsibility (New York: McGraw-Hill, 1975).

Hill, Ivan (ed.) The Ethical Basis of Economic Freedom (Chapel Hill, North Carolina: American Viewpoint, Inc., 1976).

Steiner, George. Business and Society (New York: Random House, 1975)

ARTHUR H. WALKER

I am particularly excited not only about being here with
Dr. Litterer, but because I also see some real connections between what I have to talk about today and Dr. Carroll's comments.
I agree that one of the areas to look at is the area of the
superior/subordinate relationship. What I want to do is to
develop a concept which may in part explain some of what Dr. Carroll found which in turn will lead into what I consider to be some
very serious ethical issues in superior/subordinate relationships.

Perhaps a way to start is to comment on an event that occurred
a while ago. I had a call from a large corporation and the person
calling said to me, "Do you know of someone really good who will
come in and help us turn this corporation around?" I said, "Well,
I do happen to know of a very competent person and I will call and
see if she's available." I called back and sure enough she was.
She went out, was interviewed, and was hired. Three years later,
almost to the day, she left the corporation. The Vice President
of Personnel called me up and he said, "You know, you really referred a very fine person to us and we're really sorry to have her
leave. She was really excellent." I asked, "In what way was she
excellent?" He said, "She never questioned our policies or our
practices." I replied, "Isn't that a pity."

That event introduces for me the issue of power. The way
I'm thinking of power is the ability to influence what people do.
I will look at the sources of power and how they are used or mis-
used and how they get placed in the hands of people in superior/
subordinate relationships.

We are all familiar with what I would call the rational
sources of power. You have a position, you have authority to
hire, to fire, and so forth. You also have knowledge about what
needs to be done. This gives the person in the superior position
at least two sorts of power to influence the behavior of a person
in the subordinate position. Of course we are also familiar with
the notion that power that comes from position or of knowledge
is not effective if it's not accepted. In essence, therefore,
you have these formal kinds of power or of influence which not
only reside with the person in the superior position but are
accepted based on the formal aspects of the relationship between
the superior and the subordinate. I'm not going to elaborate on
the formal aspects of power.

123

What I want to do is look into a more subtle kind of power
which relates to the formal sorts of power and which emerges out
of the formal aspects of power. By this I refer to the power
by which people unwittingly and almost unconsciously exercise
powers far beyond the intentions of the rational system and
influence the behavior of subordinates in ways that we may
consider to be unethical. I'm talking specifically here about
the emotional content of the relationship (for those of you
that are academicians, I would mention that I'm working here
with a translation of some of the work of Wilfred Bion). How
do these subtle forms of power emerge and what are they like?
There are four parts to the construct that explains what these
powers are like. First of all, there is the assumption that
any event that occurs between a superior and a subordinate
contains both rational and emotional content. There is some
sort of feeling there. We are not machines. We are human
beings. The fact that we are human leads to the question:
"What difference does it make that what we do is done by people
instead of machines?" You know, you plug in the machine, you
set the feed and the speed and off it goes. You put people
in a circle and present them with work, and it's a very different
matter. This is what keeps behavioral scientists scratching
our heads saying, "What's going on?" In any event, what we are
saying is, because the work is done by people there is an
emotional content that affects what is done. That's the
first principle involved in the idea that I am developing.
The second principle is that one of the emotional ingredients
that is present is the wish or the assumption that somebody
out there knows better, that someone is going to take care of
our needs, that someone has ideas on which we must depend for
our work, over and above the rational content. It's almost
like we're waiting for the duck to come through the ceiling
with the magic word on it. The third principle is that if
someone out there can take care of our needs, there is a wish
and an expectation on the part of the subordinate to be taken
care of. That's a very comfortable place to be. It is easy
to think that President Adamian is going to solve the problems
of Bentley College. Or the President of the country is going
to solve the problems of the nation if not the world. In this
respect, then, the person in the position of formal authority
may be seen as virtually omnipotent, all knowing, and the provider
of security and protection for the members of the organization.
This is over and above the rational content of the formal relationship.

The interesting thing about these principles that I have
observed in work that I've done is that there seems to be a
collusion that emerges between the superior and the subordinate,
in that the subordinate colludes to become deskilled and become
impotent while the superior on the other hand gets a feeling that

124

there's a lot of power in the role and accepts it. It's a collusive type of process which leads to a further movement of power up the ladder. This results in a much greater ability of superiors to influence the behavior of other human beings who work for them than the formal system intends.

When you look at behavior of people in these relationships, we can also use some of the concepts of Eric Berne. In his terms, we say we're teaching that we're behaving in adult rational ways; that when we conduct business, when we run a government, when we run a hospital, all of the decisions are rational. All the data, all the decisions are based on current information which is processed and from which the decisions are reached. By contrast what you often see happening is that the superior in superior/subordinate relationships does not behave always in a rational and factual way, but very often in a way that reflects a sort of Parent type of attitude towards one who might be viewed more in the Child state of mind. "Do this because I want you to. It's for the good of the organization. It's for the good of the country." I've heard that one! Here again the subordinate in this sense may respond "from the Child," more or less, in the sense of responding as if she or he has no choice but to carry out that instruction. So again, in terms of behavior, when you look you see two things happening. One, behavior on the part of the supervisor which may well go well beyond the formal definition of power of that role. At the same time, you often see a reciprocal response by the subordinates who accept without question what they're asked to do. Again, the two components: one, the presence of the power; and two, the acceptance of the power.

There are three ethical considerations here. One consideration is that the result of this kind of transfer of power is that people in the subordinate ranks are living lives which are far below their capability and contributing far less than possible. I think this is, in terms of the nation's needs and the people's needs, a very serious problem. I think further that just the existence of the movement of power unnecessarily up the ladder through this collusive process is not, in my mind, an ethical thing. I think that that's a serious problem. I further think again that if there are norms and values here, as Dr. Carroll's paper tends to suggest, then the multiplying power of not just the rational execution of the order but the emotional collusion to execute expands the ability to conduct unethical practices on an institutional basis. I'm convinced in my own mind that many people who conduct what in retrospect seem to be unethical or undesirable practices are people who are well-meaning, well-intentioned and who are trying to do what they think is right. But their assumptions about what they think is right are coming from people to whom they are giving up immense amounts of power, again, far beyond that which the architects have intended.

125

JOSEPH A. LITTERER

Ethics in the Management Hierarchy

Ethics in managerial hierarchies are often pursued like
zoological specimens. We pursue them as individual entities
noting their absence or presence, the variety among them, the
clarity with which they are stated, and how widely they are
dispersed throughout an organization. Thus, we isolate the individual standard of behavior: "always be honest" or "meeting
the shipping schedule is more important than meeting the safety
standard." We note who has heard the standard and who holds to
it. Such knowledge about the contents, demography and commitment
to ethics in a business organization is obviously important. But
this mode of advance ignores the consequences of ethics or behavioral standards on organization life. What can be missed is that
standards of behavior, each "good" in its own right, when acting
in concert with others can lead to consequences both unanticipated
and lamented by those who first promulgated them. It is the thesis
of this introductory comment that: (1) we have to be concerned not
only with the content of an ethical position but the function that
those ethics or standards of behavior will actually have in an
organized setting, and (2) we cannot look at ethics or standards
of proper conduct individually but must look at the synergistic effect
of them in combination.

My comments grow from a paradox encountered on a consulting
project. The firm is very successful and one which espouses and
attempts to practice many ethical beliefs that I, at least, find
very attractive. Many in the organization say these beliefs make
the firm one of the most exciting places to work they have ever
encountered. The president, a charismatic figure of powerful influence,
has articulated the belief that work should be fun and fulfilling.
Further, that individuals, if given challenge and freedom, will reach
out to accomplish amazing things. Individuals should not be held back
by education, birth, or many of the other social hindrances, but be
allowed to rise as far as their natural abilities will take them. These
general propositions have been translated into a series of norms or
codes of behavior that, while not written down, are frequently articulated throughout the organization, used to guide decisions, and to
explain why action was or was not taken. Among these are:

The Less Structure the Better. Repeatedly as proposals are made to
    create new systems of work, controls -- or further divisions of
    work -- the explanation given for not adopting the suggestion is
    that structure of any type is bad in that it limits people, hinders

126

the flow of communication, creates unnecessary hurdles and divisions among individuals, and serves the minimum of detailed reporting systems. Written reports are frowned upon in favor of oral and face-to-face communication. Creating specialized positions proceeds very slowly and only when absolutely unavoidable.

The Fewer Status Differences the Better. A close derivative of the former is the anathema of status differentiation. Going from one office to another, it is extraordinarily difficult to deduce the occupant's actual position in the organization. A key vice president has an office which looks very much like that of a plant manager, which in turn looks very much like that of a middle level plant supervisor. They are all extremely simple, sparse and, for the most part, unattractive. Desks are of metal, tables are almost all identical. Rarely do the walls go to the ceiling, instead an office consists of a partitioned off area of a larger office or production floor. Among the tales company raconteurs regale the visitor with are the blistering notes the president has sent out to managers who mistakenly thought their offices should have a little class.

The Right Person Can Make it Happen. Supporting the idea that individuals freed of constraint and given challenges will be highly motivated and able to accomplish great things is the slogan, the right person can make it happen. This is used and reflected in two ways. It is a call of encouragement to the individual given a demanding assignment. It is also a reminder of how important it is to carefully select people to be hired into this firm to fill a managerial or professional position. A job candidate will commonly interview 20 different people and 30 is not uncommon. From these extensive interviews, gradually a consensus is formed that someone will or will not fit.

Go Do the Right Thing. Consistent with the belief in the individual's capabilities of accomplishing things and the other belief that structure and restraints should be kept to a minimum, instructions to individuals when given a new challenge are usually minimal, often little more than a target, and then to be told, "Go do the right thing."

This system of beliefs has been in effect for some years and there is ample evidence of their success. Key executives are often very young and some with minimal technical education in a firm dealing with a very sophisticated technology. Walking through the plants, people do seem excited by their work, taking pride in the company and that they are members of it. Repeatedly one hears in different ways that the BLANK company is a great place to work.

Yet in all of this, I gradually detected that a sizable number

127

of people were very unhappy and often almost being ground up in the
process. Exactly how wide this condition is, I do not know. However,
it is far more widespread than I originally would have suspected.
For one thing, I come across these people one at a time who, only
after they've known me for a little while, begin to open up about
how wretched they feel. At first, I concluded that they were a
collection of people any organization of this size is likely to
have who have their own individual personality problems connected
with work. Only when gathering information about their condition
and hearing the same structure of conditions again and again did I
begin to realize that the way they felt and what they were experiencing
was the result of them being in the organization and, in particular,
the result of them being exposed to the ethics of this particular
organization.

In reviewing many of the incidents that came to my attention,
I found a common series of steps:

1) <u>Failure in a new managerial assignment</u>. Many of the
individuals had previous track records of success, either within
the firm or in other firms. They had recently failed in a new
assignment that was looked upon as a real challenge and opportunity.
Looked at more closely, the new assignment could frequently be seen
as one in which it was impossible to succeed.

The company was growing rapidly. Middle level managerial
personnel were continually changing jobs. It was rare that an
individual would be more than two years in one position and often
a year was all the experience a person would have in one place.
Consequently, while in a position, a manager would find him/herself
working with a constantly changing coterie of colleagues. Information
about almost anything was slow in coming to a large extent because
of the underdeveloped systems of reports, controls and accounting
procedures, concomitant with the philosophy of the less structure
the better. In addition, the new position was usually only vaguely
defined, again in line with the philosophy of the less structure
the better, and the person often told to go "do the right thing,"
with inadequate information in a rapidly changing context, working
on a poorly defined task which often required far more resources
and time than anyone, including the incumbent initially appreciated.
The fact that there were not more failures is perhaps the most
remarkable thing about the situation.

2) <u>Personalizing failure</u>. When failure occurred the common
pattern was for the individual to blame him/herself. They remembered
too vividly the phrase, "the right person can make it happen." The
feeling often was, "I was not the right person"; "I was not adequate";
"I was not able to make this great challenge into a success."

3) <u>Reinforcement of a sense of personal failure and isolation</u>
<u>from corrective feedback</u>. A not uncommon thing when a person meets
failure and is hurt is to call out for help or to try to explain or
justify or even excuse oneself from what happened. Attempts to do
this were met with several social mechanisms which frustrated any
opportunity to interact with others and alleviate the feeling of
personal failure. First, if the individual was aware that there was
more than a personal failure, that there was a failure in the
assignment and an inadequacy in the organization, he or she would
have to start pointing a finger at the organization and saying, "it
contributed or set me up for failure." This sort of statement
would immediately run counter to the prevailing value that one only
says positive things about this organization. "The BLANK corporation
is a fine place to work." "There is a real opportunity there for
anyone who wants to work and make it." This was the common, prevailing attitude. Many people seemed to respond as if it were
disloyal to hear bad statements about the organization.

The second factor which occurred grew from the sense of
heady excitement of challenge and advancement which permeated the
organization. People were continually moving, often upward.
It was a place of winners. Being recognized as a winner was very
important. Consequently, there was a quick, almost instantaneous,
reaction to identify and turn away from those who were seen as losers.
An individual's reputation could change almost overnight from being
a winner to a loser as soon as there was any indication of an
impending defeat or failure. One personnel manager, observing this
phenomenon, referred to it as the "jackal syndrome." Hence the
rest of the organization personalized failure and socially separated
themselves from the loser.

Looking at the way the values and norms of this organization
operated, there is no denying that they fostered a particular
climate, one of heady success and excitement. And yet, interesting
enough, in combination in more cases than were ever recognized, they
worked in combination to be a cruel system. Failure is seen in
intensely personal terms. One effect of this was that the organization
and higher management are absolved of any responsibility. When a
person did not succeed, he or she had only their own inadequacies
as an explanation -- an attitude and interpretation which is
curiously reinforced by the way the system operates.

This is but one illustration. There are many. And this is
but one company. I feel sure the same processes exist in other
companies which would bring out the two points introduced at the
beginning. The first of these is that we are all too inclined to
look at a value or ethic in an organization and examine it for its
intrinsic worth. In short, we ask, is that a good or positive
statement? Is that a desirable thing to want? We rarely ask the

question, what will happen if we behaved in accordance with that
ethic or standard of behavior? Would we in truth get the good intent
that the statement conveys?

Secondly, we, to my knowledge, never have examined how different
values or ethical propositions work in concert. What happens when
standards of: as little structure as possible; enhancing individual
growth and potential and a norm like, this is a fine place to work,
are combined? The results are sometimes, as we have seen, quite
different than the attractive picture the intent contained in the
individual statements would convey.

There is a third point. The need to face the basic paradox
managers always encounter, namely, that every action they take, every
value or ethic they espouse will have both positive and negative
aspects. This leads to a painfully personal decision for which there
is never any easy or obviously right answer. It is, I would hold,
unethical to allow oneself to be unaware of the negative consequences
that accrue to positively sounding value and ethical statements. But
that only opens up the more serious, more difficult problem that a
choice still has to be made as to whether or not the desirable things
which accrue outweigh or are more important than the undesirable.
Because of these complexities, I personally conclude that the ethical
issues faced by members of managerial hierarchies are among, if not
the, most perplexing and challenging of all.

DISCUSSION

COMMENT: I'd like to ask Dr. Carroll a question, if I may. I followed your chain of thought that many of the ethical pressures that emanate from the organizational hierarchy come from the top level of management. I'm wondering if you've given any thought or looked into the fact that many of these pressures are not the responsibility of management but originate above them from the Board of Directors and from the demands of the stockholders.

CARROLL: Though I haven't given much thought to it, I think what I said about top management and middle management would similarly hold between Boards of Directors and top management. First off, no, I don't think that pressure of this kind would come from the stockholders except as isolated cases of corporate gadflies raising points in an annual meeting or something of this sort. But I don't think there are great pressures, other than the always implicit pressure of the bottom line, to make profits.

CARROLL: Concerning the difficulty of getting lower level subordinates to make socially responsible decisions and to be imbued with the same concern for social responsibility that perhaps top management has verbalized, my only comment would be that, in most cases, that's all that's happened on top management's part. In other words, they have verbalized these concerns but have not followed through on their own with reinforcing reward systems for their lower level subordinates. I am addressing particularly the pressures to do wrong as I describe in this analysis here. In other words, the perceived pressure that a subordinate receives or the implicit pressure that a subordinate has to perform and hence to perhaps do something that is not right in order to achieve these performance objectives.

COMMENT: Which reinforces your point that the directions from the top have to be very specific. If you build it into the reward system, they will respond, but if it's a general policy, let's do a better job of promoting women within the organization, you're not likely to get that kind of a response.

COMMENT: May I make a comment on that. You talked about the unrealistic reading of the request from top management. Wouldn't some of that be eliminated by a better system of control, going out and checking to see if the desire of management is being taught clearly?

CARROLL: I don't think there's any question that control would aid that process. Yes. I think this relates to Dr. Litterer's comment. Just go and do right. In other words, give a kind of a general directive for the subordinate to take, leaving it to them to shoulder the burden of having the utmost of insight as to what is right and what is to be done by them.

COMMENT: I'm very much interested in addressing the panel from the standpoint of human nature. I would like to toss out a proposition and invite them to comment. Most people, executives and managers included, are nearly 100% conditioned. They come to their jobs preprogrammed. Debugging personal "programs" is necessary if they are going to be aware. Awareness is necessary if we are to be ethical. Unfortunately, this is a lifelong process and if our undebugged personalities produce victims and victims produce more victims, we get the vicious cycle that you have described. It strikes me that you're suggesting that good management is necessary. More particularly, we need a management which can provide those structures, those processes, and that climate which gets results and prevents the victimization of people. Would you care to react?

LITTERER: Yes. We have to take into account that organizations are going to shape what people are going to do and, therefore, the people who set up organizations have to take that into account. We cannot set up organizations just to be efficient in delivering a product. Instead, when creating an organization it needs to be understood that the way we set it up is going to shape the decision processes, the content, the form of information available for decision making, and the cues as to what values are to be used. If that was your point, I couldn't agree more. I think that is one issue all three of us are addressing.

WALKER: I agree. I think that could be the thesis for our next conference. That is, how to do what you have suggested. To add to what Dr. Litterer said, he has talked about the organizational systems and I have talked about human systems within organiza- ·tions. I think you can also intervene at the individual level. So, in summary, you can intervene in terms of organizational systems, but then you can also intervene at the level of people as individuals and in groups so that they avoid the collusion that I was talking about, depending on which side of the coin they're on. You've got to come at it from several different levels, not just one or two.

SESSION VI

"Some Operational Models of Corporate Responsibility"

Norman D. Axelrad
Vice President, Public Affairs
McDonald's Corporation

J. W. Kiermaier
Vice President for Corporate
Contributions and Civic Affairs
CBS, Inc.

Paul Turley
Regional Director
Federal Trade Commission

NORMAN D. AXELRAD

Can Corporate Social Responsibility Work? -
-The McDonald's Model

While the general concept of Corporate Social Responsibility
has been around since the turn of the century, it certainly has
become more than an idle philosophical debate during the last several years. From World War II to the late 1960's, what people
wanted and what business produced seemed to be in excellent harmony. If business operated efficiently, provided the goods and
services, created jobs and paid its taxes, society seemed satisfied, management was considered successful and its "corporate social
responsibility" was more or less acknowledged.

Since that time, however, public opinion polls have reflected
the emergence of widespread public distrust and dissatisfaction
with many of our institutions. The social, political, economic,
and environmental traumas of the last decade as well as a societal
shift in values have, in large part, accounted for this phenomenon.
Those polls reveal a public expectation that American business
should be directly responsible for solving those social and environmental problems that have become the by-product social cost of our
advanced industrial society. And since our other institutions seem
to have failed to adequately cope with other national and local
social problems, there is the further expectation that American
Business should tackle many of these problems as well. Indeed, a
recent Harris survey confirmed a current public attitude that business should be less concerned with profits and more concerned with
its "corporate social responsibility" -- whatever that means.

The central issue now facing business is the growing conflict
between a corporate sector presumed to be solely concerned with the
pursuit of its narrow economic objectives and a popularly elected
government attempting to respond to the demands, aspirations, and
new values of its electorate. The question is whether or not the
private sector can long afford to ignore the implications of an
emerging social policy embodied in the government's new social regulation. In my judgment business cannot be indifferent to today's
social and political realities without inviting growing government
intervention. The consequent impact of such regulation may strangle
its ability to function, and, ultimately, its loss of freedom.

But what can and should business do? First it must be willing
to re-examine its goals, purpose, and vision. It must establish
new management tools for being as socially and politically adapt-

135

able as it has been industrially. It must identify a pragmatic role for its self-interest and profit motive to bring its performance into better congruence with public interest expectations, concerns, and the needs of society. In the following remarks I will propose a model in which corporate self-interest, the profit motive, and serving social objectives can be compatible.

But first, let's consider whether the concept of corporate social responsibility is the way to the Promised Land? Its popularly stated premise is that business should adopt a mode of performance which more fully takes into account the human, environmental, and social affects of its activities. In the broadest sense, it has been defined as the voluntary restraint of profit maximization by directing corporate activity towards objectives that are less economically attractive and more socially desirable. It is rationalized as the ethical and moral obligation of "power," viz., that power must be exercised responsibly and be used beyond narrow self-interest. Although it has a lofty moral appeal, let's examine its utility.

First, the moral-ethical perceptions of corporate social responsibility have distinctive connotations and meanings to different people and companies. This adds to a definitional and semantic sponginess which tends to zig zag its purposes, image, boundaries and potential. Under its rubric, the private sector has been inveighed to hire the hard core unemployed, cease advertising on TV shows containing excessive sex and violence, eliminate pollution, undertake affirmative action programs, donate to charity, refrain from doing business in South Africa, keep open unprofitable operations, and so on.

Next, a fundamental deficiency of the concept is its failure to recognize the importance of self-interest as the premise for such activity. The ill-fated Corporate Responsibility Index recently proposed by the U. S. Department of Commerce illustrates the problem inherent in attempting to define the concept as an activity or quality of performance that operates outside the direct self-interest of the corporation. One of the principal criticisms of the proposed Index is that business self-interest motivation differs markedly as it relates to any of the activities proposed to be indexed. Those advocates of corporate responsibility who argue that business does good only when it departs from its profit objectives, are engaging in self-deception. "Doing good," not based on logical self-interest, is and should be suspect. It suggests a saintliness of human individuals and institutions which would be Utopian. Democratic capitalism rests on a more realistic assumption of enlightened self-interest. Self-interest, properly identified and utilized, would be a more effective way of serving the needs of society than the concept of "corporate social respon-

136

sibility."

Reviewing a couple of its applied perceptions and the moral, ethical, and practical issues they raise will demonstrate why the popular, altruistic concept of corporate social responsibility is ineffective to meet the needs of the large, modern corporation or society. Then I will offer an alternative approach and application of the concept that may serve both.

Let's begin by asking if there is a level at which the corporation should be "doing good" for its own sake? I would say "yes," but only if it is in the form of financial support to institutions that are presumably capable of directly or indirectly serving the long-term self-interest of the corporation. Charitable gifts to education, the arts, and for social welfare contribute to a healthy and viable social order, and promote a desirable and necessary business environment.

But should the corporation undertake a variety of initiatives in the social problem-solving arena on the basis of moral, ethical grounds, or "good conscience" only? The experience of the late 1960's, where a lot of money was squandered on social programs for which corporate management had neither the understanding, time, resources or commitment to sustain them makes me say, "no"! Those corporate forays into many "pie in the sky" social programs were a disappointing and costly lesson. It was philanthropy, pure and simple, with no real self-interest and consequent stake in its success. The predictable and disappointing result was a negative experience with "corporate social responsibility" - and an image which lingers on.

Altruistic programs undertaken by business may make some corporate folks "feel good." And it might make for some good public relations. But, by and large, it makes for better rhetoric than results. In my opinion, it is only when such activity is related to the economic function and objectives of the business institution, and its self-interest is thereby promoted, that such ventures are likely to succeed. And it is a good deal easier to translate and merchandise such projects to management, secure the resources, and sustain the program - in good times and bad - when this criterion is applied. That's the way most of our "corporate citizenship" programs are measured at McDonald's.

It is ironic that government leadership has been calling upon business for corporate responsibility and to become more involved in the social problem-solving arena. Concurrently, politicians win elections by promising their constituents that they will see to it that the economic resources of the country will be directed by government into the social problem-solving arena and

137

into various entitlement programs. Government is increasingly defining social problems (and, more recently, even the conditions
under which goods and services are produced) as being outside the
role of the private sector, while taxing business for government
imposed social programs and regulation. While being admonished
for lack of social initiatives, the business sector is being rele-
gated to nothing more than a financial and technological support
system for the political decision makers, the government bureaucracy, and the quasi monopolistic social service institutions. To
date, there have been no economic incentives and limited opportunities for business to enter this arena.

However, the dramatic and costly growth of our social service institutions, the vested interest of its bureaucracy in a
dependent clientele, and the failure to efficiently or effectively
deliver on its social programs is becoming increasingly clear to
the public - which is becoming increasingly out of patience.

In addition, the enormous costs imposed on society in the
form of government social regulation during the last several years
as compared to the presumed benefits to society is becoming more
evident. I speak particularly of those regulations such as OSHA
and EPA where the final incremental improvement to achieve a typically unrealistic objective yields small benefits relative to
costs or even great costs relative to benefits. The public is becoming more aware that the ultimate costs it ends up paying are
far more than necessary to achieve the legitimate goals of government social regulation. A 1978 Harris poll reflected a high level
of public approval for tax incentives to reward those companies
that meet standards which are "socially desirable." This self-
interest concept is reportedly gaining favor among economists and
members of the House Ways & Means Committee.

Perhaps when the government has no further resources to invest in the social service field it will find a more collaborative
and less adversarial relationship with business. Government
might then create a "market" for the private sector through tax
incentives or similar devices in order to invite it to compete
with government operated delivery systems on some of these social
needs. Given a level of self-interest, and working within a profit discipline, I am convinced that many of the social problems
and services could be handled more effectively and economically
by the private sector. Competition and the profit discipline
could be a much more effective gauge of identifying and satisfying
social needs and delivering services efficiently - and for calling
it "quits" when a market demand no longer exists or the service is
inefficiently delivered. Under a new set of conditions, corporate
social action and involvement would be invited not on an illusive
"corporate social responsibility" basis, but rather on pragmatic

138

economic grounds.

This leads to the next inquiry as to the role of the business corporation and whether it can operate as a social as well as an economic entity. I believe that it is difficult to establish a moral/ethical system or frame of reference at the corporate level beyond a commitment to deal honestly, openly, fairly, without fraud or deceit, and within the law. Beyond this level of self-interest, is there a higher moral level required to be socially responsible? Apart from an executive's personal convictions, competitive and business pressures make it very difficult for a profit conscious manager to make moral/ethical judgments which will result in voluntary restraint of profit maximization. The free enterprise system is an economic and not a moral system. The larger society and its social institutions should establish those moral values and have them reflected in acceptable and legally codified standards of conduct. If the business executive is expected to make a purely moral judgment, where does it stop? I find some examples of "selective morality" being demanded of the corporate sector by certain elements of its stockholders as well as some other publics. For instance, why is it morally wrong to do business in one politically repressive country but not another? Unfortunately situational ethics as affected by competitive, special interest group pressure, or national politics is the standard by which corporate social responsibility is currently defined and measured.

Another perception of corporate social responsibility is that the corporation should voluntarily restrain or eliminate corporate activity which results in incidental social injury, such as pollution. I part with the conservative view that free market forces alone will eventually make such activity uneconomical to sustain in the long run. It is an intellectually neat argument, but it flys in the face of all the evidence.

Indeed, the early 1970's ushered in a series of government interventions that placed a new corporate focus on social issues. It was then that the private sector became aware of how quickly social injury issues become codified into costly and burdensome government regulation. Business had only to reflect on the costs and burdens of compliance with the regulations such as promulgated by EPA, OSHA, EEOC, etc. to recognize the cost of indifference. Through this new perceived self-interest, business soon became much more sensitive to the potential adverse impact or social injury of its actions on the range of its constituencies. This period signalled the beginnings of a new corporate awareness and response to _social_ and _political_ as well as to market forces. They _all_ affect sales, costs, and profits. For the first time some business corporations identified their self-interest with these new social and political realities. They began evolving

139

organizational structures and strategies to systematize inputs
which affected their present and proposed activity. These inputs
became an added dimension to corporate decision making and affected internal change and performance. In this model, the popular, altruistic notion of corporate social responsibility was inappropriate and too limited a management tool to deal with the new
social and political environment. As we have identified its role
at McDonald's, corporate social policy became the core component
of a larger external relations management system.

This management model can go beyond the traditional concepts
of corporate social performance and government or public relations. Its responsiveness mode is shifting from reactive, to pro-
active, and even anticipatory. With it important and negotiated
accommodations with the public and government as well as needed
self-regulation are becoming viable self-interest alternatives.
This emerging and dynamic model is more likely to achieve a congruence of business interests and the public interest than the
doctrine of corporate social responsibility. Intrinsic to this
entire process, of course, is a quality of substantive and responsible corporate performance that becomes the basis of credibility, negotiation, and communication. Flashy, external "do good"
projects, expressions of "concern," or slick advertising messages
fool no one. Corporate policies and practices and how they serve
the company's employees, the consumer, and the public are coming
under increasing public scrutiny. The day of building libraries
while polluting the rivers is past.

These broader perceptions of self-interest and profitability
are being reflected in a more responsive corporate performance.
It has also resulted in the development of a new type of executive
- the corporate external relations practitioner. These executives
are designing organizational structures and strategies to monitor,
analyze, prioritize, and respond to emerging demands and expectations of important publics of the corporation. This type of
management system may develop a very pragmatic self-interest criterion with which the corporation may examine a variety of responses to either avoid social and political confrontation, to seize
initiatives, or to identify market opportunities. By identifying
and serving socially relevant needs that can satisfy its important
publics and benefit the corporate enterprise, corporate communication can deal with substantive issues and programs of interest to
the public - rather than imagery. At McDonald's, programs are
identified which benefit an important constituency, the broader
public, as well as the company and its local restaurants. Our
programs and performance are also measured by their value in establishing credibility, goodwill, and earning the company a role
in shaping socially desirable change.

This external relations management model can go much beyond designing self-interest motivated social initiatives or avoiding social injury. It can be utilized as a very useful discipline in self-appraisal for internal management efficiency. Or it may be employed as a new marketing tool. In a growing service oriented economy, external relations management can serve as a vital R & D resource, sensitive to a changing social, technical, economic, and political environment. It can provide key inputs to corporate planning, and also identify market opportunities.

Even corporate philanthropy has an important role to play in this management model. The criteria for gift giving should also include as its purpose the improvement of the social, political, and economic environment as it relates to the business of the company. And philanthropy can be a valuable corporate resource. The matrix of contacts and relationships established within the not-for-profit sector through a thoughtfully managed program can be an important source of input, data, an early warning system or even an ally on emerging issues for problems.

In summary, the broader gauged external relations management model, grounded on self-interest rather than the "good conscience" rationale of corporate social responsibility, works better for society and the corporation. It merely requires a broader vision of self-interest and profitability. The practitioner, irrespective of his or her personal moral and ethical motivation, finds resources and commitment easier to obtain by merchandising the proposal in concepts that management can relate to. And the program is easier to sustain in good times and bad when the activity affects the economic functions and goals of the company or the local problems of the environment in which the corporation operates.

At McDonald's we organized this external relations function under the name "Public Affairs." Components within this structure include Government Relations, Corporate Social Policy, Affirmative Action, Corporate Philanthropy, Consumer and Environmental Affairs, Stockholder Relations, Media Relations, and Corporate Communications. The Public Affairs Department is designed to perform several functions. They are: 1) developing contacts and relationships with external organizations and institutions that may provide needed "inputs"; 2) identifying emerging issues among the company's important publics that may have a significant future impact on the company; 3) providing inputs to senior management for consideration in major corporate decision making and performance; 4) acting as a catalyst and resource to various management departments to deal with identified issues as it affects its activities; 5) communicating responsible and socially relevant corporate performance in the frame of reference and in the "public interest" of the company's key constituencies. All of these component disciplines,

141

centralized within Public Affairs, work as a team – identifying
the problems, the opportunities, and contributing to the solution.

Admittedly, the state of the art has a way to go yet before
the impact of some external relations programs lend themselves to
concrete measurements and impact on corporate profits. The so-
called "social audit," and similar techniques do not yet adequately measure progress with some of the illusive and general, but very
important corporate goals, particularly for a consumer retailing
company. I refer to achieving a distinctive corporate "personality,"
"character," and reputation for integrity. This in as important
to a company's employees as it is to its customers. A positive
reputation in the community; the credibility of its advertising
and products; attracting and retaining high quality employees; establishing positive relationships with opinion leaders on issues
of importance to the company; reflecting a sensitivity to the
public's interests and needs; and so on, are the "soft" but increasingly important goals of our programs. Many other activities
can be related to much more specific and measurable corporate objectives.

By way of illustration, I will review just a few McDonald's
programs, the reason they were undertaken, and the self-interest
benefits we perceived to the public and the company.

Through relationships established with external organizations
in health care and nutrition with our contributions program, we
became aware that 10 million diabetics, and possibly their families were, for all practical purposes, foreclosed or inhibited from
eating meals away from home. As a result of this input, we designed a Diabetic Exchange Unit Card which we delivered along with
the assistance from the National Diabetic Association. Since that
time more than 2 million cards have been requested and distributed
throughout the United States by local diabetic associations, doctors, hospitals, etc. Diabetics now have additional options in
eating meals away from home. In addition to the favorable public
reaction flowing from a perceived sensitivity and awareness to the
needs of diabetics, we have considerably enlarged our customer
base.

In examining the need for adopting an Affirmative Action
program, we did not sell it on the issue of morality or "doing
good." Nor did we concentrate too heavily on the legal liability
consequences of potential violations. Nor were we obliged to institute an Affirmative Action program on the basis of federal
government contracts. Instead we communicated the potential for
improving our capacity to successfully do business with 25 million
Americans by hiring more minority employees. We would thereby be
better able to relate to the special needs of our increasing num-

ber of minority licensees and the special challenges of doing business in the Black and Hispanic communities. We have made excellent progress in meeting those objectives. And they were based on self-interest business principles rather than compulsion. I'm also pleased to report that our minority licensees contributed $135,000,000 in sales during 1977. Inevitably, when we are obliged to re-examine our corporate performance in terms of new and evolving demands, we learn from the experience. In the course of our Affirmative Action program, we re-examined our entire employment practices and policies. We discovered areas where our existing employee relations program could be improved to better serve all our employees.

McDonald's is the largest single employer of young adults in the United States. We are acutely aware of problems they face in the years ahead as they enter the job market. By examining the problems of lack of access to information, such as career counseling, and educational financial aid, we designed a program for young people working at McDonald's restaurants. We are currently testing it in a major city. First it will translate the initial on-the-job experience to life skills which can be utilized in a variety of ways to contribute to the future success of the individual. Secondly, we are assisting these young people in identifying a variety of vocational career paths. Data will also be furnished regarding schools, scholarships, and financial assistance. By making these programs available to the 300,000 part-time young people working at McDonald's stores, we demonstrate our sincere interest in them. And we hope that in turn we will attract a high calibre, well-motivated individual to work at McDonald's, and hopefully, one who will stay on and make a career with us after completing school. This program can translate to higher productivity and lower training and turnover costs at our restaurants. In a service business, the attitude of that employee when he or she meets the customer is where it's at. McDonald's huge financial investment in facilities, advertising, management philosophy, and training mean little to the customer who may be treated poorly or have a bad experience. We hope that this extra investment in the future of these youngsters will be repaid in the understanding, pride, commitment, and dignity they can bring to their job - and to the quality of service given to our customers.

Of course, the illustrations could go on. It could be an immunization project, sponsoring a conference on arts in education, social study programs for school systems, or underwriting quality children's programming on PBS. Each program would, however, deal with an important issue affecting the company, establish positive relationships, or help attract or retain customers. I say this unabashedly and without shame. As a corporate executive and a reasonably sensible human being, I am immensely turned on by the opportunity to both help people and my Company at the same time. Profit and conscious are not antithetical. They can pull together!

143

J. W. KIERMAIER

When I first got involved in this panel the subject was
Theories of Corporate Responsibility. I was prepared to talk forever and a day on the theories. Now that it has been transformed
into Operational Models of Corporate Responsibility, I am here
under false pretenses. We do not have an operational model as
such but to the extent that I have some rather strong notions
about corporate responsibility, perhaps I am not.

I will give a reasonably large reward to anyone in this room
who can define corporate responsibility in one crisp, brief definition without sounding pretentious or without being out of touch
with reality. That elusive phrase differs in meaning from corporation to corporation and also has a multitude of other names: social
responsibility, public service, public accountability, social
performance. It is a concept which should not be and really can't
be measured (although a great many people are trying to do so); a
concept which does not lend itself to graphs or charts or numbers.

Rather, I have concluded that it is an attitude, an awareness,
a belief on the part of management that each corporation has a continuing opportunity to improve the lives of those who work within
the corporation and those whom it touches outside its limited
boundaries. These opportunities vary in their scope and nature.

Corporate responsibility really represents the cumulative
impact of a wide range of activities -- everything from scholarships for children of employees to a creative, generous, activist
program of philanthropy to special seminars which help Blacks and
women within the corporation adjust to the realities of corporate
life to active concern for the communities in which we do business.

The important thing is that management constantly seeks and
is open to opportunities to do more than the minimum by way of
service to employees and to the outside world. This, of course,
is the ideal. That particular management instinct finally emerges
over a very long time and most importantly (and probably only) from
the example of the executive core of the corporation.

We did try to institutionalize corporate responsibility at
CBS through a small department. We also established a management
corporate responsibility issues committee. In the end, we departed
from that formal approach. We realized since we were so heavily
involved in the creative process, it was extremely difficult to
devise and administer standards from a central source which had a

144

realistically consistent and evenhanded impact on broadcasting, publishing, records and a fourth group which involves everything from the manufacture of harps to retail record stores. The spread was too wide. The creative subtleties too complex.

That we gave up a formal approach is probably a reflection of the type of corporation we are and has little to do with its useful application in other corporations which are more integrated and carry out a traditional and more or less common business function.

One of the major conclusions I have reached is that a corporation's long-term relationship to its thousands of employees, if properly and constructively handled, might be one of its greatest points of beneficial impact on society. Indeed, it may well be the only area of corporate responsibility which is relatively within the predictable control of the corporation. We can become so enthralled with external corporate responsibility that we forget the internal potentials.

I also concluded that it was more of an ongoing management spirit of corporate responsibility that we have to foster within the organization. We are attempting to do that on a daily operational basis by constant re-emphasis, sometimes not as well as we might like -- our winner-take-all tennis episode is one example of failure -- but certainly, given the high visibility of CBS, we are more than usually conscious of the need to be in the vanguard of the public interest and trust.

In recent years, the church, schools and other like institutions which have for so long been groping for answers to life's problems seem to be under stress and strain and in confusion as never before. It is not impossible that the corporation may be potentially among the strongest and most flexible of the institutions in this democracy. Preservation of that strength and flexibility is inevitably tied to how well we serve the society in which we function. This is a perception that must be fostered at the very top. It does not roll from the bottom up. Corporations which cut corners in their corporate conduct will in the end damage themselves and, of greater importance, will damage one element of the private sector which is still strong and cohesive enough to help bring leadership and stability to the society.

Someone has described the voice of conscience as that small voice in the night which tells you what's going to happen if you get caught. Needless to say, the type of corporate responsibility we ought to be practicing responds to louder and clearer and more sensitive voices.

Not one of you in the corporate world needs this conference to tell you what's right and what ought to be done. In our business life each of us really does know. If enough of us at the upper levels of corporations actually do it, we won't have to worry about defining or analyzing corporate responsibility a decade from now.

PAUL TURLEY

When I was asked to come here and speak - particularly
given the contrast between these corporate pillars and our own
generally perceived biases - I assumed that I was to be the
resident rabble-rouser. But after this morning's session, I
guess that is not my role. Now I'm not sure why I was asked
to be here. My position probably needs to be explained because
my perception of corporate accountability and the ethical considerations that are laid before corporations and the way that
they respond to ethical problems is pretty much a policeman's
view of society. We at the FTC don't have a great deal of exposure to the socially conscious efforts referred to by Mr.
Axelrad. The confrontations that we have with corporations
almost invariably represent a breakdown in their effort to have
some form of ethical considerations applied to their decision
making.

Believe it or not, I am sympathetic with Mr. Kiermaier's
difficulties at CBS in attempting to decide how they can apply
ethical principles to their operation. My experience with corporations has been with executives and lawyers who appear to be
fairminded and ethical. On the other hand, I'm confronted with
a consumer problem, a group of people who have had a great deal
of difficulty, who in my mind appear to have been mistreated,
who appear to have been treated unfairly, defrauded, ripped-
off, however you want to say it. I suspect that there is a
dilemma of sorts that is involved. The problem is that it is
tremendously difficult to have a division of ethics in a corporation because the ethical decisions are made throughout the organization.

One of the criticisms that I have of corporations is that
sometimes they attempt to compartmentalize ethics. They make
some "Vice President in Charge of Doing Good" and perpetuate the
kind of problem that Mr. Axelrad referred to that corporations
build libraries while polluting the rivers. I hope that it is
true, as Mr. Axelrad said, that such times have passed, but it
seems that one of the difficulties that still occurs is that
the guy who is in charge of polluting the rivers doesn't seem
to have the same degree of accountability for his ethical choices
as the guy who's in charge of building the libraries.

Some of the problems that we encounter with corporations
in their ethical decisions deal with the fact that they haven't
been able to integrate ethics into their basic day-to-day business-

147

making decisions. I am not able to propose a model for integration of ethics but I have had some bad experiences in decision making and I think they represent the failure of corporations to accomplish this integration.

When I was a law student, I worked on a case involving a major nationwide retailer. The retailer sold books of script or coupons that would allow a consumer to charge individual items up to $200. The script or coupons were printed in $10 increments and could be used, with that retailer, like cash. The problem was that if you got $200 worth of script and bought a shirt that cost $10, you started paying interest on a $200 installment loan from the time you spent the first $10. Repayment of the $200 installment loan also began when the first coupon was spent. In Wisconsin, that appeared to be usury and a lawsuit was filed by the attorney general. Subsequent to filing the lawsuit, we began a long series of delays. Filing motions, requests for continuances and other almost traditional methods lawyers use to buy time. The delays are very expensive to the court system and the attorney general's office, both of which are paid for by tax money. The respondent utilized virtually every available means of delaying the trial and in each instance there was little or no substantive basis for the delay and there was always a high cost being imposed on the taxpayer. That company eventually went bankrupt and perhaps the example of social responsibility is born out.

There are tremendous costs that go into the judicial process and the people who are being injured by such costs are not just the people who got ripped-off by the purchase of the script. It's the taxpayers. In our agency and throughout the government, we continually hear tremendous cries of pain and anguish from the law firms and particularly from the corporations about the tremendous burden of government regulations. The corporations do a great deal of complaining but they are more than willing to impose immense costs on the public when they think it is in the best interest of their corporation. That is socially irresponsible!

The FTC had a little problem with CBS. It's tiny, miniscule, given the size of CBS. CBS has a Publications Division, the Publications Division apparently subcontracted with a company that does magazine solicitations. They sent out mailings and they asked people to return the card and participate in a sweepstakes. You also check a box to indicate whether you want a subscription to Field & Stream magazine. Everyone who didn't check NO received the magazine and was also billed. If you checked neither YES nor NO, you received the magazine and, of course, you got billed. If you didn't pay the bill, you got

148

dunned. Unfortunately for CBS, a judge in Boston returned the card and he didn't like getting dunned very well so he complained to the Federal Trade Commission.

When we first reviewed the problem, it appeared that a small firm in Marion, Ohio, was doing unlawful magazine solicitations. After some investigation we discovered that and there was CBS standing at the top of the problem. To their credit, when it was brought to their attention, they resolved it very quickly. They made restitution to the people who had received the dunning letters and ultimately paid their bill. The fact is that I'm sure that this gentleman here would not sit down and make an objective decision: "Hey look, everybody that doesn't check NO, we will dunn them until they pay." I don't think he would do that. The problem is that there are breakdowns in the system and the pressure is applied at the wrong points.

This morning Mr. Olsen talked a little bit about business being like a football team and I suspect that that's somewhat true, that they have a goal and the goal is quite clear. They are there to make money and that's, I'm sure, what they better be doing as far as their stockholders are concerned. I'm not quite as optimistic as he is that they recognize that the only way that they are going to obtain that goal is to not break any of the rules. Even some of the best football teams occasionally shade the rules a bit if they think they can get away with it. I think that the corporations are involved in the same kind of process. They are people that are part of the system. If you've ever played football, for example, and you're an offensive lineman, and some guy's running around you and he's going to get the quarterback, at some point you say, "I've got a tremendous amount of pressure on me to stop that person. Maybe I can get away with holding." And at some point in the corporation's structure, there is some guy who's got a lot of pressure on him to make that goal; to get those profits, and as that pressure builds up, he says, "Maybe I can shade a little bit. Maybe I can cut an edge here." It's not as if the Chairman of the Board or the Board Directors of CBS says, "We can rip off an extra $40,000 this way." Forty thousand dollars to CBS probably wouldn't be worth it. But the system breaks down and unethical decisions are made.

The FTC obtained a consent order against K-Mart a year or so ago. K-Mart had an in-house credit plan. Some people in the State of Ohio defaulted. K-Mart subcontracted to a debt collection agency the responsibility of collecting the debts. K-Mart didn't tell the debt collectors how to collect the debts and they didn't know what the debt collectors did but the debt

149

collectors simply filed lawsuits in Cincinnati against defaulting
creditors in Cleveland, which is almost 300 miles away. Most of
the debts were relatively small and the collector got default
judgments, took them to Cuyahoga County and got them executed
and saved a lot of time and made his money.

This poses a slightly different ethical problem. K-Mart
said, "My God, we didn't tell him to do that." And the FTC response was, "Did you tell him not to do that?" You can't subcontract your ethical responsibilities away and say, "We didn't
do it. It wasn't our fault. We didn't order him to do it that
way. We didn't order him to handle it that way and if we had
known about it, we would have told him not to do it." The result
was that some people were denied due process of law and they
were given a bad deal because some place in the K-Mart system,
they failed to take into account the fact that bad ethical results can come as clearly from someone who makes the conscious
decision, "I'm going to cut a corner," as it can come from the
person who says, "Just go out and do it and don't tell me what
you're doing."

Not long ago there was an article that was published in
the London Times. I won't vouch for the veracity of the article.
The only thing I know about the facts of the situation is what
I read in the newspaper. I'm not telling you that the Federal
Trade Commission is going to sue anybody. The story was about
a lawsuit brought in California by a person who had been in an
accident in a car made by an American manufacturer. It was a
small car. The car had been hit from the rear and burst into
flames. The person who was riding in the car was killed and
the driver had been severly burned. The person who had been
burned filed the lawsuit.

In the course of discovery, the attorney for the young man
who was bringing the lawsuit obtained documents from the automobile manufacturer that indicated that the manufacturer knew
that the gas tank was dangerous and if the car was hit from the
rear at relatively low speeds, the chances were very good that
a stream of gasoline under pressure was going to spurt into the
passenger compartment of the car and when that happens, instant
explosion is likely. But the cost to the manufacturer was $9
a car. If the gas tank was left unchanged the manufacturer
calculated that a certain number of people would die, a certain
number would be badly burned. A certain number would sue. The
damages were calculated to be about $49 million. On the other
hand, the cost of moving the gas tank would cut into profits.
The manufacturer did some cost/benefit studies and determined
that they were going to be about $70 million ahead if they left
the gasoline tank where it was. I thought to myself, "Son of a

150

gun, they really do it, don't they!" I seriously doubt that
there is an individual in that entire corporation who would cost/
benefit away human lives.

I went to theological school. I won't try to pass myself
off as being a biblical scholar nor an ethics scholar, but one
of the things that I was impressed with while I was going to
theological school was that in the Old Testament they talk about
corporate ethics and they don't mean corporations. They mean
groups of people as opposed to individuals. I think that there's
a lot of validity in the Old Testament principles that basically
say, "If groups of people do good things, good things happen to
their society. If people live with a sense of trust, love, for-
giveness, humility, things that we might be able to agree are
positive values, that good things will happen to their society,
that they will prosper, they will grow, they will be strong."
I guess I believe that. On the other hand, if groups of people
live in a society where they lie, cheat, steal, and rob, their
society becomes suspicious and it degenerates.

From my viewpoint it is very essential that we give a great
deal of attention to ethical considerations that are made by corporations because corporations really are the essence of our
society. If we do not do that, our society will degenerate. On
the other hand, if the corporations can go beyond where they are
now and can learn not to have a vice president in charge of doing
good, but can learn to integrate ethical considerations into
their basic business considerations, their basic marketing, distribution, purchasing, and selling decisions, it will be good
for us all. Our country will be strong. We will be strong and
we will be part of a strong society.

DISCUSSION

COMMENT: It would seem to me from what you have said that, as
far as management goes, there was the hint that there are two
kinds of models that are somewhat exclusive of one another; an
integrated or dispersed kind of function on the one hand and a
centralized one on the other, which you put in terms of a vice
president for doing good. I wonder if those things really are
exclusive of one another or if it might not be that a centralized
function can promote an integration or disbursement of management
responsibility.

KIERMAIER: Well, I think if I had responsibility for McDonald's,
I would do precisely what they're doing. It makes sense because
it is a one product kind of thing, it's a one-service kind of
thing. Their problems are pretty much constant no matter where
you go. You know if you're serving a bad hamburger. It's very
different to know when you're serving a bad program or you're
serving up a bad book or a bad record. The whole atmosphere in
which we operate at CBS is so subjective, so much a matter of
taste that, in truth, unless you have somehow permeated from the
top the notion of the ethic of which Mr. Turley spoke, there's
really no way at the problem. You can't send out guidelines and
directives that will apply equally to a book by Erica Jong, and
a half-hour television series that goes into the home. It's
just impossible to do it. And when you get into other things,
such as the alleged damage to children through violence on television and what time they watch television or the damage to kids
from advertising, there are very subjective studies on which
people of great scholarly eminence disagree, and disagree very
violently.

COMMENT: Are you saying there shouldn't be an internal attempt
to assess those things?

KIERMAIER: No. What I'm trying to say is that we do have internal mechanisms, but we do it at the level at which they occur
and not from the corporate level, which I think is the distinction between McDonald's and what we're trying to do now.

COMMENT: A number of you have made comments about saving face,
public relations and having a good image of the corporation in
the community as being a motivating factor towards corporate
social behavior, and I was wondering whether that really makes
a difference. The fact that the automobile companies have·lost
face doesn't mean that people will stop buying automobiles. So,

152

does losing face or losing respect in the public's eye really make a difference to the corporation ultimately? How does that relate to the self-interests of the corporation? The public interest groups, let's say with regard to CBS, that condemn CBS and networks in general for the violence on television and the low quality of evening prime time TV don't seem to have a major impact, and even if they did have an impact, they don't seem to ,change the situation.

KIERMAIER: I think you're implying that criticism is loss of face. Criticism becomes loss of face if, indeed, the criticism is proved to be accurate. They are two different things. I think any interest group in this country that wants to criticize CBS should do so and should do so by its own rights as vigorously as it wishes to. I think we have a right to respond if we so wish or to be silent and take the consequences of whatever that silence might represent in the public eye. But, in many cases, we are criticized for absolutely the wrong reasons. And, therefore, it doesn't affect the public because the public is rather smart too, and they sometimes perceive the criticisms directed against the corporation are not necessarily true. Because after all, all these millions of people are watching television every night and all these millions of people have children who are watching it, and they're not without their capacities to make some subjective decisions of their own about what's happening and where the criticism should lie. In the face of their own experience, the criticism isn't going to mean very much.

COMMENT: Mr. Turley, you obviously fully understand some of the pressures that bear upon people employed in industries, particularly those with sales and marketing responsibilities. I am curious about one thing that you did say in reference to the K-Mart case study, and I'd like to go over part of it with you if you will. You said that ethical responsibilities cannot be contracted away, and I think of a particular grand jury that investigated certain improprieties in my industry in packaging, at least so I'm told. There was a significant effort to implicate senior management of the many packaging corporations involved with a price fixing violation, a supposed willful violation of a section of the Sherman Act. Do you feel that senior management does not have the responsibility to subcontract away their ethical responsibilities? Is it the responsibility of the Chief Operating or Chief Executive Officer? Do they carry the responsibility for their employees?

TURLEY: When I lived in a different city, I had a friend who was a vice president of a major corporation, and he stated very candidly, "We know that our people attempt to engage in price fixing and we tell them, don't tell us about it, we don't want

153

to hear that." If there's a serious decision at the top of a corporation where they say to their people in a candid manner, "Do not engage in this kind of activity, and if you do and you get caught or if we find out about it, you're going to at least be fired, and if you get caught, you're going to go to jail and we're not going to assist you," then I think that a corporation has behaved in an appropriate manner. But the fact that there is an intraoffice memo of some sort that says, "All employees are hereby informed that they should not engage in price fixing (chuckle, chuckle). Keep the bucks rolling in fellas," indicates that there should be a serious effort by any agency that's engaged in prosecution to affix culpability at the level where it resides. If we are talking about prosecuting people who are involved in drug trafficing, we recognize the futility of catching a bunch of pushers. And I think that if we're concerned about doing something about price fixing, if doesn't help to get a bunch of salesmen and send them off to jail.

COMMENT: I think there has been a decision within the past couple of years, where the chief executive officer of a corporation was held liable for the willful, wanton neglect of one of its subsidiaries in keeping its premises clean and wholesome; I think it was a meat packing company. And there has been some precedent for holding the chief executive officer accountable for the acts of subordinates, even though the chief executive officer was probably not privy to that information. That might be a trap.

TURLEY: The Justice Department enforces criminal statutes and has criminal remedies. From our viewpoint, we're not as anxious as the Justice Department might be to name a chief executive officer. My impression is that there is a certain degree of punitive treatment that results from being sued by the government and that, particularly for publicly held corporations, there is some form of conventional wisdom among stockholders, that they don't like their companies to be sued. And it's not just economics. It would be possible to persuade me that stockholders only consider lawsuits from an economic standpoint. They say, "Boy, our guys ripped off five million and they're only going to lose two and we obtained extra profits in the process. We don't care if we get sued." I don't think that it works quite that way. Even if the corporation engages in conduct that's unlawful and makes money and gets caught and gets sued, and still comes out ahead on a cost/benefit analysis, the stockholders don't like that. They don't like to own stock in companies that break the law. I believe there is a degree of deterrence without having to name the chief executive officer.

COMMENT: I'm perplexed by Mr. Turley's comments about Ford Motor

Company for this reason: I think any company that's doing its job is going to constantly be making trade-offs between costs and risks, in chemicals, in auto safety, and whatever else. So, the very presence of a memo seems to me to perhaps reflect a strength of management, rather than a weakness of management. Perhaps the application of how much a human life is worth was wrong, but the point that existed seemed to me to be a good sign. And very deliberately, hopefully, corporations are coming to make decisions about the trade-off between X amount of extra steel in the door of an automobile versus the cost of a human life, because you could theoretically save all lives in all automobile accidents if you wanted to.

TURLEY: Right.

COMMENT: So, I guess I'm troubled by that because I think there will always be an implied cost to the human life in decision making, be it corporate or government or whatever else.

TURLEY: It doesn't bother me that they've fixed a price for lives. It bothers me that . . .

COMMENT: It was so low?

TURLEY: No. That when the gap was so narrow that they made the choice they did.

COMMENT: Well, that's that the price was set so low. How high can you set the price?

TURLEY: Perhaps they set the price correctly. You must teach ethics instead of law. This kind of question is for people who teach ethics. It's not that they set the price too low on a life, but that the annual sales of the corporation involved are $8 billion, $10 billion, maybe $25 billion, and that talking about $60 or $70 million they would make that kind of trade.

AXELRAD: I'd like to throw my two cents into this too, since we're off the operational models of corporate responsibility and into ethical issues. There are trade-offs. There are a number of ethical judgments which are extremely difficult to make in a corporation. A profit conscious manager may be asked, "Shall we do business in South Africa or not?" "Our competition is there." "It's an important market." Now, obviously, there are some very serious moral questions. But is it really appropriate for "situational ethics" resulting from public or special interest group pressure, or whatever, to make those kinds of decisions? If it is not morally right in South Africa, why is it okay in Iran or Uganda, or some place else, where perhaps equally

155

or worse repressions may exist? Or how about the computer manufacturer who may be asked not to sell hardware to X country because it might be used for politically repressive purposes? Why
is it okay to do business with the Soviet Union? These are
difficult moral judgments which should not be made in essentially
an amoral system like business. It is more appropriate for the
larger society to have the responsibility for establishing those
types of norms and ethical behavior, and to reflect those standards politically by laws.

KIERMAIER: Well, I certainly understand the subtlety of the
point you're making, but it seems to me that there is a difference
between a corporation trying to make social policy and making an
ethical decision about it. They are a little different. Sometimes they overlap but more often than not they are fairly discrete and you can recognize the difference. For example, although people think CBS has immense powers in terms of persuasion
of the American people, the truth is that we don't do that and
we are less apt to do that and less able to do that than the
average corporation in the United States, simply because we have
a news operation. And it will be very seldom you'll even see
CBS take a position on a major national issue at the corporate
level, because it would simply be a revelation to anybody who
wanted to think so that we were sending a signal to the news
department. So, we don't do it. But we are accused of doing
it, and so we don't get into the social policy issues, simply
for that reason. Other corporations do and I think probably
with good effect if they wish to. A corporation has a potential
for being socially responsible which, in the end, will mean more
business, better business, a better society, a better country.
One flows from the other.

SESSION VII

"Employee Freedom within the Organization"

Phillip I. Blumberg
Dean
School of Law
University of Connecticut

David W. Ewing
Executive Editor-Planning
Harvard Business Review

Morton Mintz
Reporter and Author
Washington Post

PHILLIP I. BLUMBERG

I am glad to be here today and to have the opportunity to
review with my distinguished colleagues, David Ewing and
Morton Mintz, this important topic which is of increasing concern in American society.

The freedom of employees to challenge publicly the acts
of their employers in response to their own personal judgments
on a moral level or a political level or in terms of their own
concepts of social responsibility involves some of the basic
questions of our times. It vitally involves three constituencies.

Firstly, we tend to think primarily in terms of employees,
who constitute the most important constituency:

How do we preserve individual freedom in a society increasingly
conducted by immensely large and powerful corporations?

There are two other important constituencies to be considered
as well. The second constituency is the corporation itself:

How do we achieve greater accountability on the part of these
large organizations that play such an important role in our
society and thereby strengthen them and, incidentally, strengthen,
or if not preserve, free institutions in a democratic society?

The third constituency is the public:

How do we assure that the public has sufficient information
to make full and informed discussion and decision on matters
of major public concern?

I find the problems presented to be complex and their answers
obscure because we have a clash between these important objectives
that I have mentioned and the traditional values of confidentiality,
obedience and loyalty which are clearly essential for the functioning
of any large organization. As with any tough problem, when fundamental interests clash, it is not easy to resolve them. Unless one
wants to argue for an essentially anarchistic society where any
employee is free to disclose anything about an employer for any
reason that he/she may deem valid, we are committed to the principle
that there must be some limitations on employee disclosure and that
disclosure or dissent or whistle blowing or disobedience, however
it may be expressed, is only justified under certain circumstances.
The very hard problem is to define the circumstances that justify
such conduct.

159

What I would like to attempt today is to try to do what I would regard as the law professor's job of dissecting the problem and exposing its components rather than struggling to come up with sweeping answers. I do not believe that answers are going to be readily available in this area.

I would like to start by distinguishing problems of this nature that are related to the job and problems that have no relationship to the job at all.

The employer's effort to restrain an employee's off-the-job conduct that has no relationship to the job obviously involves fundamental concerns of human freedom for the individual on the one hand and a very attenuated nexus, if indeed there is any nexus at all, to the employer's legitimate interests on the other. This obviously presents a very different clash of interests than the conduct of the employee that is related to the job.

We should, of course, recognize that we do not escape the problem of job relation and the employer's legitimate interests simply because the conduct occurs off-the-job. Even in his/her "private life," the employee may be identified with the employer. If you work for a bank, people in your community know you are a banker. If you also happen to be known as a gambler, this may well be a matter of legitimate concern to the bank, however theoretically right and proper it may be for you to seek your individual fulfillment in whatever manner you choose, including gambling.

The problems are not easy and they do not go away. Nevertheless, where we are talking about off-the-job conduct, we have an area of discussion that is visibly different from something that is on the job.

On-the-job conduct involves a number of problems. It can involve disobedience. It can involve dissent. It can involve unauthorized disclosure. Each of these activities presents an entirely different sort of conduct. Let me try to describe various ways in which the exercise of individual freedom in this area can clash with the fundamental values of employee confidentiality, loyalty, and obedience in which the employer has a legitimate interest.

First of all, we have conduct that represents an act of abstention, that is essentially private. An example would be the decision of an employee not to participate personally in some conduct that he/she finds highly offensive. Whether this is a matter of conscience or a matter of professional ethics, or a matter of political concern, it is a private matter between the employer and the employee. It does not become public unless the employer chooses to make it public in taking some sanction against the employee to which the employee is forced to respond. This presents conflicting interests that are quite different from the situations that involve public conduct or public acts.

On the public side, there are at least three different types of conduct that deserve examination.

The first is disobedience. Statutes may call for certain employee rights as citizens. An employee may be responding to a right that is guaranteed by statute. Let us say, applying for a workman's compensation when the employer says: "Don't you apply." Or serving on a jury when the employer says, "We're too busy around here to have our people serve on juries." Or testifying truthfully before a state investigating committee when the employer says, "We want to tell the following story." In these examples taken from actual cases, we have the disobedience of the employee in acting in response to a statutory right or a statutory duty. Disobedience, of course, may occur for many other reasons as well.

A second type of conduct is one that I would call participation. The employee wants to make employer conduct public because the employer has not yet made its decision and the employee wishes to influence the decision-making process by getting it into the newspapers, having the public aware of the situation and influencing the board or the management. This is the sort of leak which occurs every day in our government in Washington. In Washington, governmental secrets so-called often get disclosed because the side of the government that is afraid it is losing in the bureaucratic process involving the decision of an issue is hoping that through broadening the scope of the discussion and getting the public involved, it may yet be able to prevail. This is disclosure by way of participation in an effort to influence the decision-making process. It is quite different from disobedience. It is quite different from abstention.

The third classification is dissent. The decision has already been made. The employee strongly disagrees with the decision and goes public in order to get the employer to stop the conduct or to penalize it. Typical examples would include the employer that is making products that are believed to be unsafe by an employee, or the employer that is contributing to environmental pollution.

In addition to the different ways the clash of values may arise between employer and employee, we have important differences in the nature of the employee's motivation. It is not enough to examine the conduct in question. One must also inquire into the motivation of the employee.

161

First of all, we have what I would like to call the area of civic rights particularly where articulated in statutes. These are the cases hastily described above where the law gives citizens generally certain rights, which the employee in question wishes to exercise. Examples were jury service, workmen's compensation, and testimony.

Secondly, we have another type of civic motivation, where the employee wishes to inform the public about a crime or fraud or otherwise iniquitous conduct. This is a very important citizen's duty, recognized by federal statute in this country since 1790 and recognized from very early times under the English common law.

Thirdly, there is the impact of ethics on the employee. The employee may be responding to ethical considerations in a philosophical sense as a matter of conscience. Alternatively, the employee may be responding to ethics in a professional sense. This may have very little to do with conscience as such, but will represent the organized view of the employee's profession as to the manner in which the professional should conduct him/herself to comply with the professional code which the profession seeks to have followed by (or to impose upon) its members. A code of professional conduct is a powerful influence on a professional person, although it may not involve conscience in the sense that ordinary ethics do.

Fourthly, we have the area of concern with social responsibility which, in its very intense form I would suppose, may become almost indistinguishable from political attitudes.

Fifthly, we have concerns that relate to freedom of self-expression. As a citizen, an employee may be interested in a particular question and may want to participate in the public debate whether or not the employer approves of the participation or the point of view expressed.

Finally, to move along the spectrum, you may come to less attractive motivational factors. What about the employee who is primarily interested in making some money out of the disclosure by selling something to the press which he/she thinks the press will buy. To carry it to the extreme, what of the employee who acts out of malicious motives; the employee who wants to injure someone in the corporation or the corporation itself for whatever reasons.

Clearly, as we range over different possible motives we evoke different responses from each of us in evaluating the worth of the employee's conduct and the desirability of protecting the employee.

Let us now inquire into the process by which these problems
arise. They come to the fore with the employer who wishes to
impose some sanction on an employee for conduct that breaches
the employer's view of the employee's duties of loyalty, obedience,
and confidentiality. The sanction may involve the capital
punishment of discharge. It may involve demotion. It may simply
be a failure to promote.

This is the way the law gets into the act. We are discussing employee rights. We must recognize that all that we mean
when we inquire whether employees have rights in this area, is
that we are seeking to ascertain whether the law will provide a
remedy to an employee in order to set aside, or compensate him/
her for that sanction? If discharge is the sanction in issue,
the question becomes: Can the employee be protected, either by
reinstatement or by way of damages? Employee rights in this area,
thus involves a determination of the available legal remedies.
Does the employee have legally cognizable rights by which he/she
may obtain relief against the employer's sanction?

At the outset, we have to distinguish between employees of
government, state and federal, and employees of all the other
enterprises, however large or small.

Government employees are protected against governmental
reprisal by the Constitution of the United States through the
Bill of Rights and the Fourteenth Amendment. On the other hand,
employees of corporations or other non-governmental organizations
or persons have no constitutional protection against employer
action.

Protection for private employees must rest on an entirely
different basis. Let us assume that the employer's response
to the employee's conduct is the extreme sanction of discharge.
The legal analysis must begin with certain fundamental notions
about the employment relationship. In the United States, the
traditional view has been that unless an employee is covered by
an employment contract, the employee is employed at will. In
the traditional view, in the absence of contract or statutory
prohibition the employer may discharge the employee for any
reason at all or for no reason whatsoever. The question before
us is to what extent the developing common law will cut back
the harsh implications of employment at will to protect an
employee against discharge when the employee's conduct is regarded
as socially desirable.

Let me briefly review the state of the law. Since the last
century, the common law has provided protection for an employee's
disobedience or dissent that was related to concern about an
employer's conduct that was criminal or fraudulent or involved

163

what an English court called "iniquitous" behavior. You will
note that these all involve areas of conduct where everyone would
agree that the employer's conduct was very wrong indeed. The
common law has subsequently indicated protection for the professional employee who refuses to violate accepted professional
ethics. Where the employer imposes a sanction for employee disobedience or dissent related to employer criminal, fraudulent,
or iniquitous acts or demands that the employee violate professional
ethical standards, the traditional law already provides a remedy
and, therefore, the employee may be said to have legal rights.

There have been emerging further developments in recent
years. Where there is a public policy that is expressed in
statute, such as the duty of the citizens to serve on juries
or a program of workmen's compensation, we have had an increasing
number of cases that have provided relief for an employee discharged for exercising his/her statutory rights. There are
not many such cases thus far, but there are certainly enough to
conclude that this is accepted law today. In the Frampton and
Sventlow cases, employees discharged for filing workmen's
compensation claims received relief. In the Nees case, an
employee who was discharged for serving on a jury received relief.
In the Petermann case, a teamster's union employee who refused
to commit perjury and was fired for his disobedience received
relief.

Where however the public policy is not embodied in a statute
we see only limited signs of change. The only case that actually
upholds employee's rights in the absence of a statutory policy
is a recent decision in New Hampshire dealing with sex harrass-
ment. A female employee discharged because she rejected the over-
tures of her supervisor was able to recover damages. To reach
this result, the Supreme Court of New Hampshire overruled centuries
of law with respect to employment at will and the right of an
employer to discharge an at will employee. Other decisions look
the other way. Where a steel mill employee was allegedly discharged for protesting the sale of an allegedly unsafe product,
the Supreme Court of Pennsylvania by a 4 to 3 vote refused
recovery. Where a General Motors' employee was allegedly discharged
because he protested that the company was lying in its public
statements about a matter of public concern, the court found no
liability.

It is clear that the growth of the common law is slow.
Where we are dealing with problems of general social concern in
which public policy has not yet been embodied in statute, the
development of the law has begun but the conclusion still appears
decades away. This is very slow for impatient people. What, then,
are other alternatives?

An obvious first alternative is legislation. We already
have, as you know, federal statutes and an elaborate administrative apparatus that seek to protect employees against discrimination for age, for sex, for religion, for national origin.
One could simply add another category to that sort of statute.
However, alleged discrimination for age, or sex, or religion, or
national origin presents a relatively narrow issue, and where
groups of employees are involved can be analyzed on a statistical
basis. Alleged discrimination for conduct or points of view
reflecting conscience or social values presents a more difficult
problem. The feasibility of establishing and operating an administrative apparatus in this area is open to some question.
Senator Kennedy has presented a much heralded "Employee's Disclosure Act." This was the most minimal sort of statute. It
was intended to protect federal employees against reprisal for
making public those things that an agency was required by law
to make public anyhow or to protect federal employees against
reprisal from testifying before the Congress. It never got off
the ground. The failure of this modest proposal dealing only
with two very narrow circumscribed areas clearly indicates the
difficulties in looking forward to any prompt legislative solutions. Legislative action on the state level is even more
doubtful because as the development of corporate law clearly
indicates, states are unwilling to take any reform action that
may be perceived as "anti-business" and thereby threaten employment or employment growth.

A distinguished author has suggested a constitutional
amendment to provide employees, particularly of very large corporations, with the same type of constitutional protection that
the employees of the federal and the state government already
have. Aside from the question of the desirability of such an
amendment, I would think we would agree that the political
feasibility of such a solution is very, very doubtful.

Aside from governmental action, there are at least three
areas that promise some measure of progress in this area.

First of all, the corporation itself can do a great deal
to deal constructively and affirmatively with this problem by
providing an internal forum for dissent and an internal chan-
nel for communications to enable employees who feel strongly
about aspects of corporate conduct to express their concern
within the organization. Professor Austin of the Harvard Business School suggested such a program years ago. The corporation
is not monolithic. Like any other institution, the corporation
is comprised of human beings. With most questions within the
corporation, there will be differences of opinion. The development of internal channels of communication to enable employees

to voice opinion and particularly dissent in matters of public concern would reduce the scope of the problem, although it obviously would not eliminate it. A system of corporate appointed inspectors general or ombudsmen would serve very much the same function. Such systems could be reinforced by corporate codes of conduct or policy guidelines in areas of social concerns. These would provide the platform for employees to say, "Our corporation is supposed to be doing this; in this particular instance which I am bringing to management attention, we do not seem to be doing it." Although these suggestions are not complete solutions to the problem of employee dissent, they should be helpful.

Secondly, union contracts are another alternative of interest. Almost all union contracts provide that the employer may not discharge an employee except for "just cause." In the United States today, this clause is the most effective instrument in the land for protecting employee rights. When an employee speaks up and challenges a corporation, if he/she is protected at all, he/she is protected by the union, operating under that clause. We have an increasing body of law being developed by arbitrators under collective bargaining agreements on the definition of "just cause" within the meaning of the union agreement. The arbitral process is providing significant protection for employees. On the other hand, unions, as you know, represent only 20 million employees in a work force of over 90 million. They cover only a small part of the work force. However, they are concentrated in manufacturing industries and therefore are more significant than might appear from numbers alone.

A third area that promises progress is the sharply increased concern on the part of professional societies, particularly in the area of science and engineering. We are becoming increasingly a technological society and the attitudes of technologically trained people will be increasingly important. To the extent that professional societies without divisiveness or politicization can agree on professional responsibilities for their members we will have the enactment of standards of conduct that will represent private law-making, which courts will be more likely to enforce. The common law has recognized that professional employees cannot be expected to violate the ethical standards formally accepted by their profession.

It is clear that the climate in this area is changing. Remarkable progress has been made in the last ten years. Conferences of this sort obviously help, but I must emphasize that we are dealing with a very murky and a very complex problem. We still do not have any adequate bench marks to distinguish

166

appropriate employee conduct on the margin or to determine where the law should draw the line in doubtful cases. We can only hope that continued discussion will in time provide some better answers.

I read a little item in a magazine the other day I'd like
to read to you. It's called "Only in America." Only in America
do they lock up the jury and let the prisoner go home; do we play
baseball under a roof and go to the movies outdoors; do we make
instant coffee and spend an hour dawdling away drinking it; does
a mother drive her kids three blocks to a physical fitness class;
and only in America does it take more brains to make out the income
tax return than it does to make the income (which many of us feel
strongly right now.) And I would like to add to this list that
only in America do we make a big production of guaranteeing such
civil liberties as free speech, privacy, conscience and due process
to all the people except from the hours of 9-5, Monday through
Friday. This prompted one cynical friend of mine to add that only
in America do they classify your book, <u>Freedom Inside the Organization</u>,
as a nonfiction book.

Mark Twain once said that this country has three unspeakably
precious things: freedom of speech, freedom of conscience, and
the wisdom to practice neither. But unfortunately, George Geary,
who is the subject of one of the cases that Phil Blumberg just
mentioned, didn't know this. George Geary worked for a large steel
corporation in Pennsylvania. He'd worked for it for 14 years,
doing a pretty good job, getting raises, and then he learned that
his company was going to market a new tubular steel casing that
apparently hadn't been tested properly and that could be exceedingly
dangerous to customers if it malfunctioned.

After learning this, George Geary went to the boss and said
he didn't think this product was ready to be sold yet. And the boss
said, "Stop worrying, George. You just go out, sell and do your
usual good job." So then George Geary went to other sales managers
and got the same reaction: "Forget it George. Don't rock the boat."

So then George went to the vice president in charge of sales,
and this was to be a tragic mistake, like passing on third down
against the Dallas Cowboys or pitching high and inside to Jim Rice.
The vice president reminded him that he'd gone to the senior managers
and they had told him to shut up and then blew his own stack and
said, "Haven't they told you not to worry about this? George Geary,
you're fired. You're out!" Or in the chilly language of personnel
administration: "You're terminated."

Now, so far, this isn't a very newsy story and you're probably
thinking to yourself, well so what else is new? Well, actually,
there are two new things about the George Geary story. First, he

took his case to court, and when his case got to the Supreme Court of Pennsylvania, the decision went against him only by a judicial whisker. As Phil Blumberg said, it was a 4 to 3 vote of the Supreme Court. Now legally that vote is astounding. It's the equivalent of, say, Bentley College's hockey team playing the Boston Bruins and losing 4 to 3. And then particularly in the traditional law of the master/servant relationship, it's absurd that George Geary should have lost by a 4 to 3 decision. He should have been voted down by every judge on the bench. That's the way it would have been 25 years ago or any other time in the past. So, the significance of the case is that first, it represents a crack in the legal wall.

The second way that it's significant is in businessmen's reaction to it. Last year I gave this case -- in disguised form of course; I didn't tell them that it had been decided in a law court -- to about 2,000 of the business subscribers who read the Harvard Business Review. And do you know how they responded? Only 14 percent backed up the vice president who fired Geary! All of the rest, about six executives of every seven, said that they would not back up the vice president. They did not condone what he did. Now you can deflate that reaction a little. You can say, well, that was just a questionnaire. Or you can say, Harvard Business Review subscribers, who are they? But even if you discount those figures I gave you, you're still left with a strong vote in favor of giving George Geary a break -- a pretty impressive sign that the times are changing because if we'd given that question 10 years ago or 20 years ago, we wouldn't have come out anywhere near that result.

So the wind in employee relations seems to me to be shifting, and all of us in management, up in the corporate crow's nest so to speak, should be taking notice. I see five types of rights making their way into the organization -- not just the corporation but also the goverment agency and the university. These rights don't mean that corporations and other organizations will become democratic, but they do mean that corporations will become Americanized, so to speak, a great deal more than they are today.

First is the right to privacy. As an employee, you should be able to leave your office or your locker or your place of work knowing that your papers and possessions won't be rummaged through. Your boss should have no right to search through your files or locker on some flimsy excuse. The right of privacy also means that your telephone conversations will not be monitored without your knowledge. The right of privacy means that your home will not be spied on by a managment agent, and the right of privacy means that you can check your personnel files to be sure that they are accurate and do not contain false accusations, heresay, or irrelevant information. And the right of privacy means that your private personnel

169

data will not be given to outsiders -- to landlords, banks, creditors, credit bureaus -- without your consent.

Do you want an example of a corporation that protects the right of privacy for the employees? -- IBM. IBM has enacted a privacy code that goes even farther than the rights I have just mentioned. (This is discussed more fully in an interview I had with Frank T. Cary, chief executive of IBM, in the Harvard Business Review, September-October, 1976.) And from what I can tell, IBM has found that it can enforce this privacy code without great expense and without any major inconvenience. Other companies with advanced privacy codes include Bank of America and Cummins Engine. A scientist might have been burned by this once. He wrote a little ditty which is found on the company bulletin board: "I do not like thee Dr. Fell, but why this is I cannot tell. Meanwhile to erase those smiles, we plan to rummage through your files."

The second right is outside activities. As an employee, you should be free to engage after hours in political, social, and cultural and economic activities of your choice without being penalized in any way by your company. If you want to spend your weekends with some unpopular group or cause, that's your own business and your company has nothing to do with it. Now, of course, this is not an absolute right -- what rights are? One limitation, for example, is that you can't go out evenings and weekends and compete with your company. If you work for Burlington Ford during the week, you can't spend weekends selling Chevrolets.

Right number three is conscientious objection, one of the most precious rights on the list. As an employee, you should have the right to refuse to carry out a directive or order that violates your religious or moral principles. Phil Blumberg talked about this briefly. For example, you shouldn't have to fudge the figures in a profit statement so that your company can get a loan from a bank if you feel this is wrong. You shouldn't have to make secret illegal recordings of telephone conversations with outsiders if that's against your principles. That was the subject of the famous Shirley Zinnman case in Philadelphia several years ago. You shouldn't have to carry out a directive to pollute the water or air in violation of antipollution laws if that's against your principles. You shouldn't have to sleep with the boss in order to keep your job. You shouldn't have to engage in illegal price fixing in order to get your pay increase next year.

Now does this give you the right to object to the boss finding someone else to do the work? No. Does it give you the right to keep on objecting if after some sort of a hearing procedure

170

it's decided that you're unrealistic and naive? Well, no. There's
a sign on a church door down in Boston, a little brass plate,
and it says, "If you're tired of sin, come within." And somebody had written under that sign, "If you're not, call Kirkland
7-5432." That also reminds me of a sign that I understand is on
an executive's desk in a company out on 128. The sign says,
"Age and treachery will always conquer youth and skill." In
other words, this right of conscientious objection is purely to
enable you to be faithful to your conscience. You are not being
asked to be your company's brother's keeper or some sort of
corporate chaperone. It's your conscience, your moral values.
What happens to simple human dignity when there's no right of
conscientious objection? What happens to your pride in the
private enterprise system? What happens to your confidence in
yourself? What happens to the attitudes of your children towards
the business system when they see you come home with guilt and
shame on your face because you had to do something that was in
violation of your personal principles?

The fourth right is qualified free speech. I am continually
amazed at the emotional resistance to this right, which is
certainly one of the most beautiful ones that we have in this
country. Obviously, it has to be a limited right, as almost
all rights are. You can't yell fire in a movie theater and,
similarly, this doesn't mean that you should have the right to
criticize the boss' judgment on normal operating matters. You don't
have the right to slur your company or any executive in it and
you shouldn't have that right. But you should have the right,
more and more employees are feeling, to blow the whistle on
wrongdoing. You should have the right to commit the truth, as
Pentagon whistle blower Ernest Fitzgerald calls it. You should
be able to go to the corporate house organ editor and say, "This
company is violating the law, and I think people should know."
You should have a right to tell a legislative committee or the
Attorney General that "figures we're putting out on safety are
wrong in my opinion."

Commit the truth as you see it. Is there any right more
precious and human than that? Now I've been told and warned by
some corporate managers, such a right is impractical and that it's
terribly naive and very, very wrong to urge such a right in the
business system. But if this right is so naive and unrealistic
and dangerous, then how come it works so well in a few leading
companies where it's been tried? New England Telephone has a
system called 'private lines' wherein you can call in any fact
or criticism, personal or impersonal, anonymous or not anonymous,
without suffering any retaliation. Dow Chemical Company,
American Airlines, New Jersey Bell, and a number of other companies
publish house organs where, as an employee, you are free to
criticize wrongdoing in the corporation and many do without fear

of retaliation. It works. These companies aren't going out of business.

The fifth right is due process -- the right to a prompt, impartial and fair hearing when you feel that you have been treated harshly, immorally, or illegally by your boss. This could be the most important right of all. Why? Well, for one reason, it's important to human dignity and for another, it's excellent for the sake of morale. But that's not all. This right is also necessary if we are to enforce the other rights. For example, suppose you blow the whistle on wrongdoing and then you get fired on some trumped-up charge. Or suppose you refuse to engage in illegal price fixing and then for some mysterious reason you get transferred to a miserable job in the boondocks. If there's a fair hearing procedure in your company, you can go to it right away and you can save yourself, at least if you have a good case. And this isn't theory. This happens every day in a few legal organizations in this country. It happens at Polaroid, where there is an employee-elected committee which hears complaints and grievances, accusations of abuse. It happens at Donnelley Mirrors in Michigan where the employees elect delegates, sort of like groups of the population elect delegates to the State Legislature, and where every week they hear problems that come up. It happens at organizations that have ombudspeople. For me, a reasonably good system of due process is where civil liberties and constitutionalism in business should start.

Skeptics complain, "How do you know that the employee judges or the ombudspeople will always be fair?" You don't, but the courts aren't always right either. The Supreme Court can be wrong. But it's a fair system that we know of, and it's a lot fairer than any other system, or having no system at all. "What's in all this for business?", people ask. "Will civil liberties and constitutionalism make a business more effective? Will they improve labor/management cooperation? Will they reduce costs?" In all probability they will, although we don't really know yet.

However, in my view these questions are the wrong questions. They're irrelevant. They're spinach. The case for employee constitutionalism has nothing to do with efficiency or cost effectiveness or productivity. The case for employee constitutionalism is built on human dignity. Good pay and working conditions are not enough to meet the needs of dignity. Equal employment opportunity, wonderful as it is, is not enough to meet the needs of human dignity.

Max Frisch once wrote a play in which a businessman comments on the refusal of employees in the factory to act like robots. And in one sentence, the businessman says it all. He says, "We hired workers and human beings came instead."

172

MORTON MINTZ

I have found, in long years as a reporter, that there is
very little discussion outside of our business about the very
kinds of matters my fellow panelists talked about as they apply
to the press. I come before you independently but I also am an
employee of the Washington Post, one of the many who tries to act
as if professional but nonetheless is an employee, meaning a person who legally could be fired, just like that, were it not for
some union protection.

The question that concerns us is more complicated than that
in non-press corporations, because of the First Amendment.
A. J. Liebling, the late, great press critic of the New Yorker
said that freedom of the press belongs to the man who owns one.
The difficulty is that it doesn't belong to press employees.
I don't have a solution to offer you, but I'm happy on this
occasion to put before you the question of what rights we employees
do have, and what rights we ought to have, other than those insured
by union contract. As one more preliminary, may I note that
the Minneapolis Tribune and Star have a contract with the Newspaper
Guild which provides for a Voice Committee. The function of the
Voice Committee is to meet once a month with top managers and
to talk about problems that are not grievances but professional
problems. Suppose I say something here today, and I will, that's
critical of the Post, and I were to be disciplined for it, which
I will not be; but suppose I were. What rights would I have? The
Voice Committee is a mechanism to deal with that. It's assured by
the union contract. But when we, the Newspaper Guild of the Post,
proposed such a committee to our company, the Post sat on it for
a year without discussing it and then said: We don't have to discuss this in collective bargaining and we're not going to. The
essence of the company message was: We have no real rights except
those granted to us.

I want to get down to what I think are some fundamentals that
bear on the question of employee rights in news organizations, and
it's going to be a kind of awkward path to follow. I just haven't
found any way of greatly simplifying it.

In the American constitutional system, the people are (at
least theoretically) sovereign. To rule intelligently, a sovereign
must have information about matters that concern, we'll say, him.
What the sovereign does with the information is of course the
sovereign's business.

173

The sovereign public has no system of its own to gather and distribute information. Instead, the press relies on the owners of the press whose mission, Liebling said, is to inform the public but whose role is to make money. To a degree, the mission and the role tend to coincide. Without money the mission cannot be performed and, indeed, without a lot of money much indispensable reporting, long-term investigations, and foreign correspondence, can not be provided. And, surely, profits ought to be used to maintain and improve quality. But individual greed in a few cases, and the imperatives of the publicly owned corporation in many more, lead to the trimming or sacrifice of the moral and ethical obligation imposed by the constitutional protection of the First Amendment. Editors throw away much of the news that flows into newsrooms because time and space are money and they can get away with it. That's what A. M. Rosenthal, Managing Editor of the New York Times, said in a speech in 1975. The consumer who would raise hell if he were short-changed at the supermarket or who found himself buying watered milk, says nothing and does nothing to try to persuade the local editor or publisher or broadcaster that he does want to know what is going on in the world, Rosenthal said. But if the consumer does not know of the news of which he is being deprived, how on earth can he complain? Omissions often are more important than commissions in this business, I assure you. The press is often criticized for what it does when the real criticism ought to be what it does not do. What, if any, are the rights of the reporter who feels that something important is being omitted?

If you want to take a glamorous case that you'll all recognize, think of Watergate. Let's suppose that Carl Bernstein and Bob Woodward had acquired devastating information about people in the Nixon White House or about the President himself and had taken it to the management and the management had said, "My God, if we do this we might lose our television licenses. We are about to go public. Our stock will be depressed in value." Katherine Graham said no such thing. I'm very grateful, but suppose she had? What rights would Carl Bernstein and Bob Woodward have had if they had taken such information outside in the belief that it was their duty to do so? I don't know. I am trying to struggle through some of these questions and have not had to be in a sharp confrontation as yet where I have to draw some kind of final conclusion.

"It is startling, or would be except we are used to it," says Charles Rembar, a lawyer who's an authority on the First Amendment, "that the means by which the citizens of the democracy get their news, information that they must have in order to run their country, is a form of private property." Henry Fairlie wrote in The New Republic, "The root of almost every weakness of the American press just now will be found to be not with individual journalists but the management whose concern with profit has become no different

than that of any other corporation." A digression which is
striking to me: We had a discussion in this room before this
session began about directors of corporations. To my knowledge,
there is not a public director (public in the sense of representing
a broad interest, rather than merely being from another corporation)
on any of the large media corporations in this country – not CBS,
or NBC, or ABC, or Washington Post, or New York Times, or any of
these. The message is plain enough. Press owners subordinate
First Amendment responsibilities to profits often, and in doing so,
impede the flow of necessary information to the sovereign. This
is an exercise of power over the sovereign.

I now want to go on to a couple of related matters, quoting
mainly from an article of mine in Politics Today. A couple of
things have been proposed. Stephen Barnett, who was until recently
a professor of law at the University of California at Berkeley,
said that in the case of the broadcast media, the FCC could forbid
licensees to fire news employees without due process. Perhaps
that is conceptually possible in the case of broadcasting media,
but not in the case of print press, I don't believe.

There was a book written in 1907 by Edward Ross called Sin and
Society which contains much that I find relevant to this question.
Basically, what I want to tell you, through what he perceived so
acutely 71 years ago, is that the press has a primary role, I think,
in trying to assure that corporate behavior is what it should be;
that is, in the service of the broad public. A few weeks ago, Olin
Industries was indicted in New York for concealing the discharge
of 38 tons of mercury into the Niagara River. The mercury poisoned
the fish. People in Niagara Falls and other communities along the
river and along the shores of Lake Ontario, into which the river
empties, ate the fish. New York Health authorities said there was
a serious hazard. The New York Times, to its credit, played the
story on page one.

The Washington Post reacted differently. On that same day,
there was a Congressman indicted, Charles Diggs of Michigan, who
was Chairman of the House District of Columbia Committee; it was
kind of a local story, I suppose. We devoted 89 column inches to
the Diggs indictment, starting with two stories on page one; a
third was inside. We devoted 1 3/16 inches to the indictment of
Olin Industries and it was the third item in the "Around the Nation"
wrapup on page A6. The attention, just in space terms, was 1/75th
as much. What had Diggs done? He had diverted $101,000 from
federal payroll into his own pocket or for his own purposes. That's
according to the indictment. I have difficulty, and I so told an
editor, in divining the rationale for assuming that a congressman
stealing – which is not an especially startling occurrence – should
be given all of this attention (I mean, to the point where you couldn't

stand it), and I can't get any rationale. What am I supposed to
do about it, exactly? It doesn't make any sense to me. I can't
get a rational explanation. I'm told (and I believe it absolutely)
that there's no policy that required that we do this. But there's
no policy that required that we didn't.

What's troubling to me is that when we did not pay attention
to that Olin indictment we made it easier, inadvertently, for
corporations to stray from the straight and narrow. What lash did
Olin Industries feel in Washington from public opinion? Ross, in
1907, deplored the grading of sinners on the basis of their character.
He wrote: "The patent ruffian is confined to the social basement
and enjoys few opportunities. He can assault or molest, to be
sure, but he cannot betray. Nobody depends on him, so he cannot
commit breach of trust, that arch sin of our time. He does not
hold in his hand the safety, or welfare, or money of the public.
He is the clinker, not the live coal; vermin, not the beast of
prey." He's talking about street crime in our times, I would say.
Ross went on: "Today the villain most in need of curbing is the
respectable, exemplary, trusted personage who is strategically
placed at the focus of a spider web of fiduciary relations. He
is able from his office chair to pick a thousand pockets, poison
a thousand sick, pollute a thousand minds, or imperil a thousand
lives. It is the great scale, high-voltage sinner that needs the
shackle. [Olin was that according to the indictment.] To strike
harder at the petty pickpocket than at the prominent and unabashed
person who, in a large and impressive way, sells out his constituents,
his followers, his depositors, his stockholders, his subscribers,
or his customers is to strain at a gnat and swallow a camel." Thus
Ross provided reasons why the press has a crucial role to play
in auditing corporations. We run into trouble when the press doesn't
do it, and when its employees have no rights.

Ross again is eloquent on the corporation: "It feels not
the restraints that conscience and public sentiment weigh on the
businessman. It fears the law no more and public indignation
far less than does the individual. You can hiss the bad man,
egg him, lampoon him, caricature him, ostracize him and his. Not
so with the bad corporation. The corporation moreover, is not in
dread of hellfire. You cannot Christianize it. You may convert
its stockholders, animate them with patriotism or public spirit
or love of social service, but this will have little or no effect
on the tenor of the corporation. In short, it is an entity that
transmits the greed of investors but not their conscience, that
returns them profits but not unpopularity." When the press fails,
again, corporations lie unrestrained. They can't be imprisoned.
They can't be sent off into battle. The more some of them are
punished with indictments (and there are many recidivist criminal
corporations), their profits go up. The press has a role to play,

176

to be redundant about it. Ross dealt way back then with that
role. He said that citizens can restrain the corporation by
public opinion, as well as by statute. And at another point
he said, "We dream that we live under a government of laws.
We are actually under a government of men and of newspapers."
[There wasn't television in his day.] He also wrote, "Public
opinion is impotent so long as it allows itself to be kept
guessing which shell the pea is under, whether the accountability
is with the foreman, or the local manager, or the general
director, or the president, or the directors." It puts a
burden on us, which we seldom fulfill, to try to find out why
some corporate atrocities happen. Who was responsible? Or,
at the very least, we have a burden to seriously report court
proceedings and trials, whether they result in acquittal, which
may be deserved, or in conviction, which may also be deserved.
Finally, Ross offered a solution which is at least interesting,
and that is that "the directors of a company ought to be individually
accountable for the misconduct of which the company benefits."
In this context, he suggested that "the newspapers ought to print
along with the news of the exposure of corporation misconduct
the names of the directors, in order that the public indignation
may not explode without results but find rather a proper target,
for just indignation is altogether too precious a thing to be
wasted."

　　Well, if the corporation is to be disciplined, disciplined
not in a punitive or vengeful way, in which I genuinely have no
interest, but disciplined to make it perform its true function,
which is to serve society as a whole, again, the press has a major
role to play. Today it plays that role erratically, unreliably,
and unsatisfactorily while it increasingly becomes big business
itself. I cannot imagine anything more morally repugnant than
the repeated deceptions by pharmaceutical companies of physicians
with false advertising and false promotion of drugs - overclaiming
safety, overclaiming effectiveness, in order to broaden markets,
particularly when it's the patient, not the physician, who pays
the bill. The Food and Drug Administration, starting in the mid
1960's, undertook a campaign to require drug companies to write
physicians saying, "Dear Doctor, we misled you in such and such
an ad," or to write a corrective ad saying, "We misled you in an
ad, or the FDA says we misled you." By any standard I have learned
to accept or embrace in 30 some years as a newspaper man, I don't
know how to defend the nonperformance of the New York Times, a
pacesetter for the press, in never printing a story about one of
these. I made it my business to write dozens of them. I thought
it was news, and my editors agreed with me. But suppose I'd
been at the Times, felt as I did, and said, "Aren't we going to
print this?" And they said, "No, we don't think it's news." Well,
then what? Again, I don't know the answer. I think it's important.

The former chairman of the Federal Trade Commission,
Lewis Engman, once announced what he called the "Washington
Post Rule" for corporations: How would you like it on page one
of the Washington Post tomorrow morning? If the press is to do
better, there must be protections for people within its own ranks
who want to be professional but who are employees subject only
to the protections of union contracts. There are many press estab-
lishments where there are no union contracts.

Again, I don't know what the answers are. I just feel there's
a problem.

DISCUSSION

COMMENT: I have a question for anyone on the panel who might care to answer it concerning an area that Dean Blumberg referred to. I was wondering if you could address yourselves to a specific example that was reported in the New York Times where perhaps employee rights might collide with reasonable regulations on conflict of interest. A suit has been brought against the EEOC by Sears Roebuck Company, charging that a staff member of the EEOC was in a conflict of interest situation when he acted on a complaint of NOW against Sears Roebuck because he was also a Board member of the NOW Legal Defense Fund. I was wondering about your reaction, just on a gut level, to that set of facts.

BLUMBERG: I would say this question pushes us to the ultimate. We've been talking about the employee who has been hostile to an employer attitude. Here we have an employee who is in fact shaping the employer's attitude in terms of his own view of the universe as reflected by his affiliation with the complainant. The question is whether such an affiliation invalidates the employer's decision which has been made by the employee. This is beyond the area with which we have been traditionally concerned. It is clear, however, that if we conclude that employee conscience is so important that in certain circumstances it justifies disobedience, or dissent, or disloyalty, or unauthorized disclosure, the next question we must face is whether it may properly provide the basis for influencing employer decisions.

COMMENT: This is a question that perhaps is peripheral to what you're talking about, but I think the business community generally feels that the press is hostile to us, that the media is hostile to us, which would suggest that the corporations, the big organizations, would feel that a dissident employee, someone who comes up and whines, is going to get a disproportionate attention; that is, there will be a tendency to say, this is the good guy and he's right, and the corporation is wrong. Do you think then there's a balance? I think that is probably the reaction in the business world and I think there's some validity to it myself.

MINTZ: I don't think there's any validity whatsoever. First of all, you have to understand that the press finds it relatively easy to go after government. We have a Freedom of Information Act. If we have the slightest whisper of something wrong in the CIA, the FBI, the FDA, the CAB, you name it, we have the right, and the public has the right, and corporations have the right, to seek out information which is often terribly embarrassing to the

179

organization involved. Just as we heard from the other panelists
that employees have no constitutional rights in the private work
place, we have no rights, we have no Freedom of Information Act
to get information about corporations or anybody in the private
sector. Moreover, I can tell you that in 16 years of reporting
on the drug industry and the American Medical Association, I
never had anybody come to me from a drug corporation and say:
"Here is some horror." And there were plenty of them, believe
me. I got the information only because government got it, not
because somebody came out of the woodwork.

But as for the basic attitude, I operate from the assumption that
any large organizations, including press organizations, exercise
power, power that ought to be audited and checked and balanced.
When we find out that a corporation has exercised power, as Ford
Motor Company did in the Pinto case, building cars that would
burst into flame if hit in the rear; when we find falsified drug
tests; falsified tests for pesticides; pollution of the Niagara
River; whatever, this is as much government, in the sense that
it affects life, property, liberty, as something done by the so-
called legitimate government. It ought to be reported. I do
not believe that I, or other reporters I know, are hostile to
business. What business construes as hostility is a desire to
report misconduct. It has nothing to do with being hostile to
business. I don't know what alternative there is to business,
but much of what passes for business and is defended, comes down
to something such as Henry Ford whining about government regulations when he's building those damned Pintos. He thinks the
press is hostile, I suppose. I don't believe it. How is the
corporation, when it engages in misconduct, to be kept on the
straight and narrow? Well, only by a whole series of things, the
conscience of certain individuals in the organization, the press,
directors who care, whatever. But, there has to be a whole array
of things. The press is one of them, and if the press lets down
its guard, then we're in more trouble than we know about. It
wasn't the press that found out about all this corporate bribery.
It was government that found it out for us. And I just don't
know what the basis for saying we're hostile is. I don't believe
it's true.

COMMENT: Mr. Ewing, your second point of your five employee rights
was the right to participate in outside activities of their own
choosing. Suppose an employee decided to protest, for example,
the construction of a nuclear power plant and a governor decided
to lock them all up in an armory. It could happen, right! What
do you do then when that employee doesn't come to work on Monday
morning? Suppose the employee was not able to perform his assigned tasks for a certain period of time?

180

EWING: Well, I should think that, personally, you'd put that in the category of sickness and other acts of God that you can't really hold an employee responsible for doing. It does verge on an outside activity that interferes with performance but if they get sick or if there's a terrible tragedy in the family, we don't penalize them for being out a couple of days for that.

COMMENT: Can I follow up from that? Suppose, in that case, in the Seabrook case, someone went and sat down in violation of a court order and was taken to jail and then was offered the opportunity to make bail and refused. It seems like there's two chances there for that employee to get back to work and still have made his point in terms of freedom of speech and freedom of assembly.

EWING: Yes, if he had the opportunity to get out, then I'd find it harder to be sympathetic with him. But, if he didn't have that opportunity, I really don't think it should be held against him. I think that's one of those things that happens where most companies would be reasonably lenient. This goes in the category of some of those situations that happen to take an employee away, but which in good conscience he or she wasn't able to control.

COMMENT: But he broke the law.

EWING: Lots of employees in management break the law, too, in payoffs and in lots of other ways, but, of course, that doesn't usually come right to the attention of others. If I go out and I'm guilty of reckless driving or I get convicted of homicide or larceny, I don't think my employer would hold that against me.

COMMENT: I don't think he reimburses you for it.

BLUMBERG: I would say that the question this gentleman has asked is a typical question that comes before arbitrators: Has a discharge been made with "just cause" within the meaning of a union contractual provision? Do we have any arbitrators here? I think I could guess how arbitrators would respond to the situation described. It seems to me they would probably just deprive you of the pay for the period.

COMMENT: This is a question for Dean Blumberg. If a corporation has adopted a code of ethics, would that give rise to an implied contract between the employee and the corporation which would be enforceable by the employee against the corporation? For instance, a code might touch on some of the moral issues of doing business and so on and a corporate official ought to follow that code of ethics. Would a complaining employee who was discharged for pushing the matter have a cause of action against the corpora-

181

tion?

BLUMBERG: I can't imagine that a code of ethics would be drafted
in such a fashion as to give rise to any contractual rights on
the part of the employee. However, if you have a case that might
otherwise be appealing, a judge might see this as a further occasion for erosion of the strict view of employment at will. The
existence of a code of ethics that set the standard for the situation to which the corporation has not responded might have
some influence on a judge.

GILL: At Sun Company, we have a condition of employment for a
number of employees to sign, an agreement that they will assure
compliance with corporate policies relating to not making improper payments or paying bribes to various people and that sort
of a thing. I would think that it might be possible to imply
such a contract.

COMMENT: If, as Dean Blumberg said, any solution via common law
is a long way off, what are the prospects for a legislative
solution to the problem of employee rights? Should we look forward to an employee's bill of rights or a bill which stipulates
certain kinds of due process coming out of Congress in the next
couple of years?

MINTZ: God knows what's going to come out of Congress. I share
some of the concern that the business community feels about
erratic actions by Congress. But it is conceptually possible to
have a federal chartering bill which would require in one of its
titles, an employee rights section, due process in the work
place. It could be done. There have been hearings about the
idea of federal chartering but, in my perception of what's going
on, it's light years away, if it's ever coming.

SESSION VIII

"Ethics and Values Research in American Business"

Agnes Missirian
Professor of Management
Babson College

Max Wortman
Professor of Management
Virginia Polytechnic Institute

Martha A. Brown
Professor of Management
Angelo State University (Texas)

Robert L. Bjorklund
Professor of Management
State University College at Utica/Rome

Harvey Kahalas
Professor of Business
SUNY at Albany

MAX S. WORTMAN, JR.
and
AGNES MISSIRIAN

What Ever Happened to Ethics?

To suggest that managers are any more or less ethical than
other members of society appears absurd on its face. Yet, if you
ask a group of college students, "Do managers have a code of ethics?"
or put another way, "What do they think of the ethics of managers?",
the answers will vary imperceptibly from "Are you kidding?" to
"It's how they can put it over on the other guy," and "They're a
bunch of chislers," or "Rip the other guy off before he rips you
off." This is a strange commentary in a free society enjoying the
highest standard of living and the greatest economic equality the
world has ever known.

What is astonishing and alarming about these replies is that
they come from business majors--young men and women in their junior
and senior years of college, all of whom presumably have chosen
business as their profession. What prompts a student to pursue a
profession for which he or she has no respect and for whose members
he or she shows such contempt?

It is just this paradox which demands a closer look at the
bases of ethics in American business and the values from which they
are derived.

Ethics, Morals, and Social Responsibility

An investigation of business ethics is complicated by the
confusion that exists in the literature between the terms "ethics,"
"morals," and "social responsibility." These terms are used in-
terchangeably and may render spurious and tangential conclusions.

Philosopher Sahakian in his book, Ethics, defines ethics as
the branch of philosophy which explains and analyses moral judgments, choices, and standards. While philosophers disagree about
the scope of ethics, the central motif generally is accepted to be
the study of moral value judgments and the bases for these judgments.

The term ethics refers to the study of morals and moral
issues, i.e., a theoretical or rational interpretation of moral

phenomenon. Whereas, the term _morals_ refers not to a study of discipline but to the standards which individuals are directed to observe in their conduct; i.e., ethical behavior.

Traditional professions--law, medicine, and theology--have prescribed codes of ethical conduct. While there is still some debate as to whether businessmen and businesswomen are professionals, we submit that they are indeed professionals. In the absence of a generally accepted business code, Peter Drucker suggests, "Primum non nocere"...not knowingly to do harm..., prescribed by Hippocrates 2500 years ago, should serve as a guide to ethical business conduct.

Definition of the concept of social responsibility is much more difficult. Because of differing views as to the moral obligation of the business community, there is no consensus.

Milton Friedman's often quoted position, "The business of business is business" is interpreted to mean that business should concern itself only with its performance in providing goods and services and interaction with its direct constituencies. A manager has no mandate to commit corporate resources to activities beyond the scope of its mission.

Following a fundamental Kantian precept enunciated by the Committee for Economic Development, the "doctrine of enlightened self-interest" reflects the changing public expectations. It recognizes that business functions by public consent, and that the corporation is dependent upon the goodwill of society. Therefore, it is in its best long-term interest to promote the public welfare in a positive way. In the extreme, John Kenneth Galbraith, recognizing the concentration of power and influence which exists in the megacorporation, suggests that the social responsibility of a manager extends to the international community. That is to say, a manager has a moral obligation to be concerned about such things as pollution of the ionisphere, the concentration of economic power in a few corporations, the increased sovereignty of multinationals and the complex relationship between business interests and the threat of war.

Clearly, problems of business ethics at an organizational level and problems which are societal and political in nature need to be differentiated. The problems just enumerated are societal and/or political and are beyond the effective responsibility of most individual managers.

In the wake of Watergate, the Equity Funding scandal, and the Lockheed disclosures, public demands for a more responsible and ethical leadership are understandable. However, much of the business response has been defensive and rhetorical. Many well-

186

meaning chief executive officers write and lecture about their
concept of morality and corporate responsibility; but this approach
to the problem is in reality dysfunctional and presents a spurious
image to the public. Managers have an obligation, as do all citizens, to be actively concerned about the needs of society, but they
are not empowered to act for society--nor is it desirable that they
should do so. This is a political function, not an economic one.

It is far simpler for managers to discuss the ethics of doing
business in South Africa, for example, than it is for them to confront the effects of their own behavior on the ethical conduct of
the young men and women of organizations they lead.

The former is remote, enmeshed in a political, societal, and
economic web which would defy a Solomon. So, after the rhetoric,
they throw up their hands and say, "How can any one man or woman
be expected to assume responsibility for the ultimate consequences
of their behavior?" And, indeed, how can they? The latter problem
--that of ethics in organization is discrete--and completely within the realm of a chief executive officer's sphere of power and influence.

Research in Business Values

The personal value systems of managers are significant because they set the limits for the determination of what is and
what is not ethical behavior. Moreover, as Chester Barnard points
out, they determine the extent to which a manager will accept or
resist organizational pressures and/or goals which conflict with
his or her value set. In other words, a manager's values influence
his or her perception of situations, people, decision-making, and
the inevitable trade-off between individual and organizational
success and achievement.

George England's theoretical model of personal value systems
postulates two major classes of personal values: "operative"
values, or those values that have the greatest influence on behavior; and "intended or adopted" values, those that may be pro-
fessed but do not directly influence behavior to any great degree.
The model also indicates two primary ways in which values can influence behavior: "behavior channeling" and "perceptual screening."
Behavior channeling would be illustrated by the behavior of a
manager who places a high value on honesty and integrity when approached with a proposition which involves deception and questionable ethics. His or her behavior would be channeled away from
the questionable behavior proposition as a direct result of his
or her "operative" values. Common expressions such as, "He sees
what he wants to see," and "She only hears what she wants to hear,"

describe the phenomenon of perceptual screening. The power of personal values to select, filter, and influence interpretation of what one "sees" and "hears" is well known in common experience and in the scientific study of behavior.

The results of England's extensive survey show that while "intended" values such as loyalty, trust, and honor may have been considered by managers as important throughout most of their lives, they are not viewed as leading to success in the organizational context. Therefore, these intended values are suppressed by managers in favor of "operative" values such as ambition, ability, and skill whenever they are in conflict with organizational norms and/ or goals.

In 1972, researchers Lusk and Oliver repeated England's study on a comparable national sample of U.S. managers. Their prediction that the widespread examination of environmental, societal, and political issues during the 1966-1972 period would be reflected in a change in the value systems of managers was not confirmed. Personal value systems of managers appear to be relatively stable over time and change slowly. This conclusion was confirmed by Milton Rokeach in his extensive research of human values.

The following year, Henry Singer explored the relationship between human values and leadership. He reported that the successful executive places a high priority on moral standards and personal integrity. The manager is less interested in defeating communism or advancing capitalism than in being happy. However, they place power and economics at the top of their scale of values, even though they are significantly higher in their concern for people than less successful executives. In England's terms, these results represent managers' cognitions or "intended" values, not necessarily their "operative" values.

Scott and Susan Myers discovered sources of potential conflict in organizations when they compared the value profiles of individuals at various hierarchical levels and functions. They concluded that supervisory style or systems characteristics at any level are most suited to the levels just below, except at the highest level. This suggests that the immediate supervisor still has position power and maintains his or her influence over operative values. Since conflict and dysfunction result when values differ widely, there is a strain toward consistency.

Rama Krishnan conducted a survey of business leaders across the country which focused on their value systems or philosophy of business and their attitudes toward certain managerial practices. He arrived at two revealing conclusions: Younger managers are not convinced that business organizations will behave ethically when confronted with situations conflicting with the goals of the organization as seen by upper management. Most managers surveyed still believe in the profit maximization philosophy and the absoluteness of the prerogatives of management in operating the business organization as they perceive it. It would appear that not much has changed in the values and philosophy of business executives. The most recent survey of HARVARD BUSINESS REVIEW readers underscores this conclusion.

Research on Business Ethics

While there is a dearth of empirical data on questions of business ethics, the following field studies provide some revealing insights into the sources of conflict between values espoused by managers and their actual behavior.

Raymond Baumhart, in his classic study of business ethics, attempted to examine and interpret motives behind business decisions. The following conclusions were drawn from the integrated findings of three research projects. Managers believe that:

1. They are more ethical than the average manager and more ethical than their corporate peers.

2. They have the same ethical standards at home and at work, but that it is more difficult to live by these standards at work because of the competitive pressures.

3. Competition is the greatest influence upon ethical behavior in business. Unethical practices result from both too little and too much competition in an industry.

4. A written code of ethical practice would be useful for improving business practices in their industry.

5. The values of the chief executive are ultimately accepted by most subordinates.

Baumhart's data revealed a tendency in every age group, company milieu and management level for a person to accept the values of his or her supervisors. His findings are significant not only because they have been supported by subsequent research, but because of their broad behavioral implications. For example, the Stanley Milgram studies involving the behavioral responses to authority elicited by the experimentors under stress-provoking conditions are directly related to his findings.

189

Newstrom and Ruch compared managers' beliefs to perceived peer and top management beliefs. They found that action-oriented overt behaviors such as blaming others, falsifying reports and large padding of expense accounts are repugnant; whereas, the more covert behaviors involving the use of time and company services are more acceptable. Moreover, managers perceived their peers to have a significantly weaker set of values than they do. In general, managers thought that their ethical beliefs were highly congruent with those of their superiors. We may postulate that top executives actually serve as a key reference group to provide an important source of the managers' ethical standards.

Given that the peer group typically provides a strong reference model for individual behavior, here it appears to be a consistently "negative" model, if only in the mind of the manager.

Surveying managers over a cross-section of industries, age, education, and management level, Archie Carroll concluded that managers experience pressure, real or perceived, to compromise their personal moral standards to satisfy organizational expectations. Moreover, middle and lower level managers perceive this pressure more than top managers. The following hypothetical statement used in the survey illustrates this point with alarming clarity: "The junior members of Nixon's reelection committee who confessed that they went along with their bosses to show their loyalty is just what young managers would have done in business."

Almost 60 percent of the respondents agreed with the above statement. This suggests the real possibility that top management may be consciously or inadvertently insulating themselves from organizational reality with respect to ethical issues.

Conclusion

The research clearly defines a gap between perception and reality where ethical conduct is concerned. Subtler, yet apparent, is the distinction drawn between those who would manage and those who would lead.

We live in a pluralistic society and thus our institutions, public and private, are peopled with men and women from every segment of the social milieu. In this sense, our institutions are representative of society as a whole. So while business may well be afflicted with ethical degeneracy, the malaise cannot be ascribed to the business community alone, but must be shared by the society as a whole.

Why is it, then, that managers are so often the target of

societal frustration and wrath? Perhaps it is because they epito-
mize our society's notion of success; and therefore, they are particularly vulnerable to the opportunity to use the discretionary
power which success brings. Moreover, they are protected by the
anonymity which corporate life affords them--as distinct from their
private lives.

What ever happened to ethics? Ethics has simply disappeared
behind the corporate veil, which until recently was sufficient
protection personally and legally.

We can better understand the organizational environment and
the power of the organizational norms which shape the behavior of
corporate participants if we view the corporation as a microcosm
of society.

Psychologist Harry Levinson in The Exceptional Executive
points out that even under ideal conditions, leadership climate
is not a simple imitation of one hierarchical level by the level
below it; rather it is a process of interaction in which the values
and role models offered by higher levels of management are transformed in keeping with the needs of the followers and the requirements of the organization.

Since the power structure of most organizations is still
hierarchical, the impact of the chief executive officer's behavior,
both explicit and implicit, permeates every level of the organi-
zation--perhaps softened or intensified by each manager's internal
set of values--but nevertheless paramount in the organizational
context.

Therefore, whenever leaders fail to define the parameters
of ethical behavior--whenever they say simply, "Don't tell me how;
just do it!"--whenever they look the other way instead of providing direction or sanction, they create the atmosphere and
generate the pressure which forces men and women to abandon
principle for expediency.

Business managers must begin to recognize that as professionals they are also teachers of their profession; that they have
a responsibility to, and a profound influence upon, the ethical
conduct of the next generation of business leaders.

Thoughtful examination of one's own personal value system
may well be helpful in the effort that all must make in the strain
toward consistency between what one believes and what one is.
Ethical codes of conduct exist in a civilized society to fill the
gap between behavior constrained by codified law and behavior
constrained only by mutual respect and mutual restraint.

Alfred North Whitehead expressed this notion of responsibility simply and succinctly when he advised that, "Businessmen should think greatly of their function."

BIBLIOGRAPHY

Reference Books: Business Ethics and Values

Barnard, Chester I. The Functions of the Executive (Cambridge, Mass.: Harvard University Press, 1948).

Barnard, Chester I. "The Elementary Conditions of Business Morals," The Barbara Weinstock Lectures on the Morals of Trade (University of California, Berkley, 1958).

Baumhart, Raymond. An Honest Profit (New York: Holt, Rinehart and Winston, 1968).

Drucker, Peter F. Management: Tasks, Responsibilities, Practices, "The Limits of Social Responsibility," Harper and Row, New York, 1974.

Drucker, Peter F. Management: Tasks, Responsibilities, Practices, "The Ethics of Responsibility," Harper and Row, New York, 1974.

Festinger, Schacter, and Back. Social Pressures in Informal Groups (New York: Harper and Row, 1950).

Garrett, Thomas M. Business Ethics, ACC Business Series, Meredith Publishing Company, New York, 1966.

Hill, Ivan (editor). The Ethical Basis of Economic Freedom, American Viewpoint, Inc., North Carolina, 1976.

Levinson, Harry. The Exceptional Executive: A Psychological Conception, Mentor Books, New York, 1968.

Milgram, Stanley. Obedience to Authority: An Experimental View (New York: Harper and Row, 1974).

Rokeach, Milton. The Nature of Human Values (New York: The Free Press, 1973).

Sahakian, William S. Ethics: An Introduction to Theories and Problems, Barnes and Noble Books, New York, 1974.

Articles: Business Ethics in American Society

Benson, George C. S. "Business Ethics in American Society," Journal of Contemporary Business, 4, No. 3 (Summer, 1975).

Birdzell, L. E. Jr. "The Moral Basis of the Business System," Journal of Contemporary Business, 4, No. 3 (Summer, 1975).

Carr, Albert Z. "Can An Executive Afford a Conscience?" Harvard Business Review, 48, No. 4 (July-August, 1970), 58-64.

International Christian Union of Business Executives, "A Case of Business Creed," International Studies of Management and Organization, 1, No. 2 (Summer, 1971), 150-154.

Long, John D. "The Protestant Ethic Reexamined: What kind of

Value System is Implied?" Business Horizons, 15, No. 1
(February, 1972), 75-82.

O'Brien, John C. "A Plea for Ethics," Business and Society, 14,
No. 1 (Fall, 1974), 28-36.

Purcell, Theodore V. "A Practical Guide to Ethics in Business,"
Business and Society Review, No. 13 (Spring, 1975), 43-50.

Steiner, John F. "The Prospect of Ethical Advisors for Business
Corporations," Business and Society, 16, No. 2 (Spring, 1976),
5-10.

Strother, George. "The Moral Codes of Executives: A Watergate-
inspired Look at Barnard's Theory of Executive Responsibility,"
Academy of Management Review, 1, No. 2 (April, 1976), 13-22.

Wilkens, Paul L. "The Case for Ethical Absolutes in Business,"
Business and Society Review, No. 13 (Spring, 1975), 61-63.

Wilson, James A. "Morality and the Contemporary Business System,"
Journal of Contemporary Business, 4, No. 3 (Summer, 1975).

Research on Values

Connor, Patrick E. and Boris W. Becker. "Values and the Organization: Suggestions for Research," Academy of Management
Journal, 18, No. 3 (September, 1975), 550-559.

England, George W. "Managerial Value Systems--A Research Approach,"
in Ethics and Employment: A Symposium (Minneapolis, Minnesota: Graduate School of Business Administration, University
of Minnesota, 1967), 11-34.

Hay, Robert and Ed Gray. "Social Responsibilities of Business
Managers," Academy of Management Journal, 17, No. 1 (March,
1974), 134-143.

Krishnan, Rama. "Business Philosophy and Executive Responsibility,"
Academy of Management Journal, 16, No. 4 (December, 1973),
658-669.

Myers, M. Scott and Susan S. Myers. "Toward Understanding the
Changing Work Ethic," California Management Review, 16, No. 3
(Spring, 1974), 7-19.

Powell, Reed M. and K. Tim Hostiuck. "The Business Executive's
Role in Politics," Business Horizons, 15, No. 4 (August, 1972),
49-56.

Singer, Henry A. "Human Values and Leadership," Business Horizons,
18, No. 4 (August, 1975), 85-88.

White, J. Kenneth and Robert A. Ruh, "Effects of Personal Values
on the Relationship Between Participation and Job Attitudes,"
Administrative Science Quarterly, 18, No. 4 (December, 1973),
506-514.

Research on Managerial Ethics

Carroll, Archie B. "Business Executives and Moral Dilemmas,"
Business and Society Review, No. 13 (Spring, 1975), 51-57.

Carroll, Archie B. "Managerial Ethics: A Post Watergate View," Business Horizons, 18, No. 2 (April, 1975), 75-80.

Newstrom, John W. and William A. Ruch. "The Ethics of Management and the Management of Ethics," MSU Business Topics, 23, No. 1 (Winter, 1975), 29-37.

Newstrom, John W. and William A. Ruch. "The Ethics of Business Students: Preparation for a Career," AACSB Bulletin, 12, No. 3 (April, 1976), 21-29.

Sturdivant, Frederick D. and A. Benton Cocanougher, "What are Ethical Marketing Practices?" Harvard Business Review, 51, No. 6 (November-December, 1973), 10-12; 176.

MARTHA A. BROWN

The Measurement of Values

Donald Crieghton has remarked that "History is the record of successive encounters between values and circumstances." This points up, I think, the importance of values. The <u>difficulty</u> with the study of values, and particularly research in this area, is that they are imprecise, have an integrated nature, are largely invisible, and show great variability........this list of problems with values could be very long. In order to pursue value research I have assumed that human beings vary in how much they care about freedom, dignity, and other values; that they can indeed be said to possess values; that values determine behavior; and that value change leads to attitudinal and behavioral change.

Values are personal, so the critical interface is between individuals. In the work scene, a particularly critical relationship is between the superior and the subordinate. If values are as basic to behavior as they appear to be, then they are communicated both verbally and nonverbally to subordinates and/or superiors. When the manager (or employee) realizes, consciously or unconsciously, that his or her basic values are different from those of the other member of the dyad, respect and confidence are reduced or disappear: honest, open communication suffers, and grounds for conflict (or more often apathy) are present. The relationship proceeds downward until the employee quits, the manager terminates or transfers the employee, or the manager leaves or transfers.

The basic hypothesis with which I have worked is that job satisfaction is at least partially dependent on the "value match" between subordinate and superior. In the Rokeach Value Survey I found an instrument that simply asks respondents to rank eighteen instrumental and eighteen terminal values in the order of their importance to the respondent. In a small pilot study I asked work groups (one superior and multiple subordinates) to so rank their values. Additionally I asked respondents to complete the Smith Job Description Index, which gives a numerical measure of job satisfaction. The assumption implicit in the research was that a relatively close match between the values of the subordinate and the superior would produce relatively higher job satisfaction on the part of the subordinate.

Although this assumption tends to make good common sense, the pilot study did not support it. Apparently too many other variables contribute to job satisfaction. While one may doubt the validity and/or reliability of ranking values....or of the Rokeach instrument particularly, I tend to support the instrument. The Value Survey is simple in design, economical to administer, provides reasonably reliable and valid measures, is easily grasped by literate users, and produces responses directly expressed in quantitative terms. While it is clearly a projective test (eliciting responses that come from internal demands), it does not have to be disguised, does not allow free responses, and does not require trained personnel to administer it.

The problem, as I perceive it, may be the use of job satisfaction as the dependent variable. Job satisfaction is the result of such ingredients as type of work, pay, opportunities for promotion, and co-worker relationships, as well as superior-subordinate relationships. The preferable dependent variable may be motivation, although, of course, it has other ingredients also. In addition (to my knowledge) there are no available adequate instruments to measure motivation. There are, of course, multiple job satisfaction instruments available. However, I have no reason to doubt the Job Description Index, for reasons stated above. I simply think job satisfaction measures are such composites, that they are not useful as a dependent variable.

So the dilemma....I am hopeful this conference may offer some insight into this quandry. It is reassuring to be reminded by Will Rogers that "Everybody is ignorant, only on different subjects."

ROBERT L. BJORKLUND
and
HARVEY KAHALAS

Ethics Among Engineers and Managers:
Constructs Linking Values to Actions

The contemporary importance placed on the subject of this
conference can be measured in part by the sheer volume of the ink
spilled in its behalf. In the eighteen months preceding September
1977, five times as many articles on business ethics appeared in
the popular and professional press as in the prior eighteen months.
Besides being the bicentennial year, 1976 was a year of increased
examination of the conduct of American Business. That examination
continues with articles that criticize specific business organizations, condemn or defend the business community in general, or
discuss macro-societal philosophical issues. They are often
written by journalists, academicians and social reformers, but also
occasionally by business executives seeking to explain or improve
the ethical performance of their own industries and firms.

Furthermore, a number of major studies of business ethics
have been conducted and reported. Most recently, Silk and Vogel
reported on a series of conferences and interviews with chief executives of major corporations who were painfully aware of negative
public scrutiny.

In 1977, Brenner and Mollander described their replication of
Baumhart's 1961 ethics research and Bjorklund and Hebert replica-
ted Gautschi's 1973 work. In both cases cited, the authors looked
at and reported the changes in ethical judgments made between the
original study and the replication. Further, both studies focused
on the impact of ethical decision-making on the society at large.
A summary study recently conducted by Wortman and Missirian (panel
members in this session) examined the research of others in this
area. Citing work by England, Rokeach, Singer, Meyers and Meyers,
and Krishnan, they proposed a series of important research hypotheses for further study. However, it appears that the thrust
of the contemporary research has been on the impact of corporate
decision-making on the society. With few exceptions, the research
has not looked at the adverse effect of purposeful and specifically
definable unethical practices on the firm in which they are condoned
or allowed. We suggest that both the firm and the individual suffer
as a result, and that the model of outcomes involved should be expanded to become parallel as shown in Table 1. That is, the effect
on the firm should be considered as a separate and co-equal effect

197

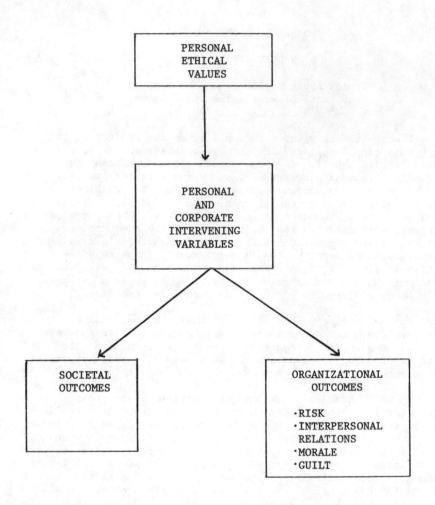

TABLE 1.

198

in the business ethics problem. When research examines the internal effects, it is quite likely that additional serious attention will be paid by the firm to the problem.

The research reported here originated with the Bjorklund-Hebert replication of the Gautschi study of 1973. Gautschi enumerated eight situations and required respondents to select from a list of actions, the one that they would choose if they were the actor and the one that they expected a generalized "other" would choose. Inasmuch as this research was conducted in a "pre-Watergate" setting, the replication was proposed to gauge the level of changed opinion over the four year period.

The method was to ask respondents of the first research to answer the same questionnaire and compare the results. Because of a limited sample, the results were somewhat inconclusive. There was an indication that respondents reported more ethical decisions, but also felt that the "other" would adopt a less ethical choice. When cross-tabulating on demographic variables such as religion, age and number of children, there were certain interesting observations. However, it was determined that two problems with the research method invalidated the results. First, the sample was too small. Second, it became evident that the researchers were making value judgments concerning ambiguous distinctions in terms of what was ethical.

Therefore, the researchers set out to conduct a two-phase study. The first phase was to allow the respondents to specify from a pilot-tested list, which of twenty-seven activities would justify the violation of five unethical behaviors (dishonesty, illegality, manipulation, unfairness, and wastefulness). The second phase asked the respondents to define their own ethic by rating an expanded list of the five behaviors on a four-point Likert scale that ranged from "totally unethical" to "not particularly unethical." Approximately 350 responses were received from a national sample of engineers and technical managers. Figures 1 and 2 show the question and the distribution of responses to both phases of the questionnaire. This data was analyzed and many demographic variables, situational variables and definitional variables were cross-tabulated against one another.

Value Dissonance

The concept of cognitive dissonance is well-known in the field of psychology. Defined originally by Festinger and Lewin, cognitive dissonance is a state of non-fitting between two cognitive elements. Pressures are known to well up in individuals to reduce these tensions and various manifestations occur as a

199

PERCENT OF RESPONDENTS WHO INDICATE THAT THEY BELIEVE
THE ACTION BELOW IS JUSTIFIED BY THE SITUATION DESCRIBED.

For each reason listed below, please indicate (with a check) those behaviors that may be justified.	DIS-HONEST	ILLE-GAL	MANIPU-LATIVE	UN-FAIR	WASTE-FUL
1. There are no situations that justify this behavior.	63	65	23	26	25
2. This behavior is almost always justifiable.	2	2	31	8	10
3. To improve your job security.	5	2	49	17	16
4. To avoid losing your job.	9	5	57	29	26
5. To maintain an advantageous personal status in the corporation; i.e. promotions, budgetary advantages, etc.	4	2	46	15	15
6. To improve a poor personal status in the corporation.	4	2	48	17	16
7. To obtain an extremely advantageous personal status in the corporation.	4	2	43	18	12
8. To obtain an advantageous interdepartmental status in the corporation.	3	2	43	15	12
9. To improve an extremely poor interdepartmental position in the corporation.	4	2	50	21	18
10. Under the direct orders of your superior.	8	5	48	42	55
11. At the implicit direction of your superior.	6	3	43	30	42
12. To make a critical sale.	5	4	48	26	34
13. To make a routine sale.	3	3	34	11	16
14. To avoid the loss of a critical customer.	6	4	50	28	39
15. To avoid the loss of an average customer.	2	3	38	13	18
16. To reduce the effectiveness of a key competitor.	5	2	44	23	25
17. To make a breakeven profit.	5	3	40	19	25
18. To avoid a serious financial loss.	9	6	53	34	36
19. To increase profits to meet a goal that has been established by your company.	3	2	42	16	21
20. To increase the price per share of your company's stock.	3	3	34	13	13

	DIS-HONEST	ILLE-GAL	MANIPU-LATIVE	UN-FAIR	WASTE-FUL
21. To increase the price per share of your company's stock because it is dangerously low.	5	3	38	20	19
22. To obtain an extremely high price per share of your company's stock.	3	2	32	12	11
23. To maintain a high credit rating.	4	2	35	14	14
24. To increase a dangerously low credit rating.	7	2	40	20	23
25. To gain an advantage with public officials.	6	5	39	15	15
26. To pirate a particularly valuable employee from another company.	7	2	38	21	19
27. To screen out potentially disadvantageous employees.	6	4	51	29	23

DEGREE OF UNETHICALNESS AS DEFINED BY RESPONDENTS

	AVERAGE RESPONSE	TOTALLY UNETHICAL 1	VERY UNETHICAL 2	MILDLY UNETHICAL 3	NOT PARTICULARLY ETHICAL 4
A (1) DISHONESTY	1.3				
(2) DECEIT	1.6				
(3) FALSIFICATION	1.3				
B (4) UNFAIR TREATMENT	2.3				
(5) INEQUITABLE TREATMENT	2.4				
(6) NEPOTISM	2.6				
(7) PREJUDICE	2.2				
C (8) MANIPULATION	2.8				
(9) COERCION	2.2				
(10) EXPLOITATION	2.2				
D (11) ILLEGAL ACTIVITY	1.2				
(12) CONSPIRACY	1.4				
(13) CORRUPTION	1.2				
(14) EXTORTION	1.1				
(15) PERJURY	1.2				
(16) THEFT	1.2				
E (17) WASTEFUL ACTIVITY	2.7				
(18) WASTEFUL ECONOMICALLY	2.6				
(19) WASTEFUL ENVIRONMENTALLY	2.5				

FIGURE 2.

202

result.

In this research, value dissonance occurs as a result of
ethical dilemmas. In the more critical situations, fairly large
groups of respondents said that they could justify conduct that
they later rated as totally unethical. This was true in all five
groups, but most pronounced in the highly unethical activities.
One can surmise that ethical dilemmas lead to critical feelings
of value-based dissonance.

Table 2 highlights the contrast between dissonance and con-
sonance in ethical activity. When there exists an action of different ethical standards than an ethical value, then one can define
that situation as value-based cognitive dissonance. The stress
that occurs as a result is deleterious to the person and the firm.

Situational Ethic

There was a clear situational pattern to the responses.
First, the various behaviors, as revealed in Phases I and II, are
viewed in two separate lights according to their severity. Illegal and dishonest activities are viewed in the same category.
Well over half of the respondents said that no situations justified these two activities. Also, these two activities were rated
as much more unethical than the other groupings.

Second, as an additional measure of the situational nature
of the result, the respondents indicated that the rules, which
were inviolable in relatively routine settings, were not so in
critical and particularly personal situations. For instance, improving one's job security is less critical than saving one's job.
Implicit orders of one's superior is less critical that explicit
orders and so forth. The respondents fully supported the contemporary notion of the situational ethic. Third, the situational
nature was revealed in that the respondents agreed to conduct
themselves unethically, even in less severe activities, most frequently in cases which would obviously be instrumental in improving
the situation. For instance, 55% of the respondents would be
wasteful at the explicit order of their boss, but only 18% to improve an extremely poor interdepartmental situation. However, 50%
would be manipulative to improve an extremely poor interdepartmental situation. Clearly the engineers and managers discriminated
on the basis of instrumentality.

Career Equilibrium

The research has lead to a further observation. When ethical

203

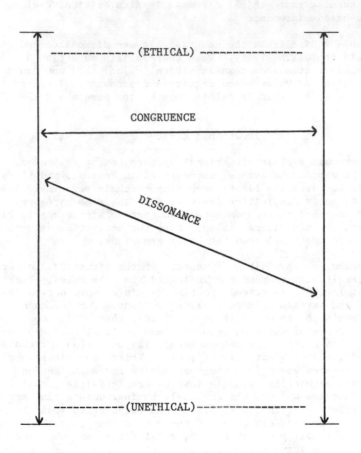

STATED
VALUE

BEHAVIOR

-------------- (ETHICAL) --------------------

CONGRUENCE

DISSONANCE

------------- (UNETHICAL) --------------------

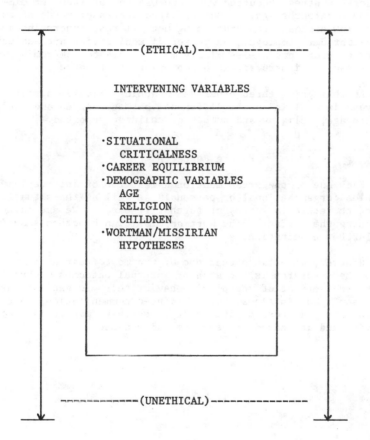

STATED
VALUE

BEHAVIOR

------------(ETHICAL)------------------

INTERVENING VARIABLES

·SITUATIONAL
   CRITICALNESS
·CAREER EQUILIBRIUM
·DEMOGRAPHIC VARIABLES
   AGE
   RELIGION
   CHILDREN
·WORTMAN/MISSIRIAN
   HYPOTHESES

------------(UNETHICAL)------------------

dilemmas arise, certain persons more frequently admitted a willingness to compromise personal values. Specifically respondents who expressed dissatisfaction with their career progress compromised their expressed ethical values significantly more often. The concept of "career equilibrium" was developed to explain. Sheehey and others have talked about mid-life crisis and male menopause. Thompson, Dalton and Price discussed career stages and implied considerable stress occurred when one was out of step, at mid-life, with one's career stage. Barber cited increased cases of expressed low ethical standards among medical researchers in career disequilibrium. Employees in career disequilibrium are subject to greater pressure and are seemingly more liable to compromise when it is viewed as instrumental to improving their career.

At this point three other demographic variables appear to intervene in explaining the difference between values and actions. They are age, religion and number of children reported.

Future Research

Each one of the areas mentioned in terms of intervening variables (organizational or personal) as well as the situationalness of the ethic is worthy of further research. We are just scratching the surface. The Wortman/Missirian hypotheses merit much further examination.

However, we believe that one of the most fruitful areas for further research is the area of internal outcomes. What is the internal effect of unethical behavior to the organization and the person? Not in fines, but in reduced communication, increased decision risk, decreased rationality, decreased managerial productivity and increased stress from value dissonance.

DISCUSSION

BJORKLUND: I'd like to suggest that in any organization -- no matter what level of the corporation you're at -- while we tend to think of corporations as being a fictitious individual, the fact of the matter is that corporate decisions are made by people and the limitations of their decisions, whether the behavior is ethical or not, are consequences of the values of the particular individual and how he or she finds himself or herself in that situation. Now, in that context, I'm not sure I see a great deal of difference between individuals and corporations. I don't think corporations can absolve themselves from ethical responsibility by saying that they're corporations and not individuals.

COMMENT: Let's just look at it on the individual level. You don't expect the same level of responsibility from a juvenile that you expect of an adult because of their capabilities and capacities, and so on. And, in the same context, I would suggest to you that the responsibility of corporations behaving in an ethical way, particularly in social affairs, is greater than that of the individual because their power to exercise their will is greater, and so they really ought to be looking at the effects their decision making has in areas where they have some direct contact. Dealing with issues within their corporate structure or within direct constituencies, I really think that they do have a responsibility and it's one that they can identify.

COMMENT: The thing is that individuals in corporations do make decisions within their given parameters of action, but their problems are compounded by the fact that we have so many international regulations. What is acceptable in the United States may not necessarily be acceptable in Saudi Arabia. There are just too many international regulations.

WORTMAN: Agnes has a copy of our paper here from an Academy of Management meeting. There are a couple of hypotheses that we'd like to test on values with respect to the top corporate executives, and I think maybe Agnes ought to read one or two of those that deal specifically with how the values of the top executive, the chief executive officer, really impact upon everyone below them. That's what we're really after. Let's face it.

MISSIRIAN: Some of the hypotheses that we wanted to test: Top management value profiles will be consistent with subordinate value profiles. That's one. Top management value profiles will

207

be inconsistent with the immediate subordinate's perception of actual behavior. That's saying two different things. The third one is that the farther away from top management you get, the less consequence will be observed between the top manager value profiles and the attributed values perceived by subordinates. I haven't tested these, by the way, they're suggestions.

BJORKLUND: I would like to add a little force to what Agnes has said. There was an article recently in Personnel in which someone did that comparison. It suggested that there's a strong likelihood that people lower in the organization have a very different value structure than those higher up in the organization. I suggest that you might want to glance at that if you're interested.

COMMENT: This is one of the things that bothers me in these kinds of explanations; in the corporate decision making process, the decisions are not made by individuals but by groups. We have a group-think, for instance, and we know that information is systematically kept from reaching the higher levels if it is disturbing in some ways. These kinds of things mitigate against the ethics of the chief executive permeating the organization.

COMMENT: On the contrary, I would suggest to you that that is an underscore of their understanding of what the real ethics, or the operative ethics, of that chief executive are, if they know that he doesn't want to hear something. It isn't that they want to keep it from him because they think that it isn't good, but because they know that if he hears it he's going to do something about it and he doesn't want to do anything about it. So they keep it away from him. That would be my explanation of that particular phenomenon.

BJORKLUND: My research indicates that managers and engineers are far more willing to violate their own personal codes of ethics at the explicit order of their boss, rather than the implicit order of their boss. That's one point. Another point is that in the previous session both Joe Litterer's comments and Archie Carroll's comments confirmed this. I talked recently with Rosabeth Canter, who wrote a book, Men and Women in Organizations, in which it appears that the people on the fast-track filter up through the organization. It appears that they have a little stronger value structure, that they are more immune to some of the pressures around them because they're on the way. I think that merits further understanding. I agree with you that there is a group pressure to conform to something that seems to be implied but I'm not sure how you measure the ethic of a corporation.

COMMENT: We've sort of glossed over the situation. I was a mem-

208

ber in a small oligopoly where the ethical thing was entirely situational. We had to behave as other firms in the oligopoly did. If we did not, we couldn't protect the interests of our employees and our stockholders and our community. So there's a dicotomy there.

BJORKLUND: I have researched individuals, not corporations. I would drop back to some economics background, the economics of oligopoly which suggest that there are leaders and there are followers, and in an oligopoly situation, perhaps the leader firm sets the tone for the whole industry. I was interested, for instance, in Ken Olsen's (Digital) comments this morning about his corporation juxtaposed against IBM. One of the vice presidents of IBM commented regarding an ethical issue, "People come to us and say: 'Well, that's easy for you because you have $14 billion to fool around with.'" And he said, "Well, we've had this particular ethic (he was referring to what they call their full employment policy and some other things) ever since we started, so we're wondering if perhaps we have $14 billion because we had that ethic." I'm stuck in terms of answering how you compare corporations and even the relevance of it.

WORTMAN: I'd like to get back to a prior question. In the same sense (I attended this Conference's "Membership and Role of Corporate Boards" session and have done some work in this recently), if you have a chief executive officer who indeed, as we are proposing, basically sets the ethical standards of the corporation and then has basically an internal board of directors, that really does set the tone for the ethics of that particular corporation. There's no question. It would set the question of the ethics all the way through that corporation unless you happen to be one of those radicals who is far removed, way down at the bottom of the organization. So, I would argue, as some people did in that session, that the sooner that we have external boards, the better off we would probably be from an ethical standard standpoint, depending on what the ethics of the people are who you're putting on.

BJORKLUND: I just observed something in the last couple of weeks that's been conducted by Montgomery Ward's retail company. They have a lot of managers all over the world, particularly in the United States, and they have just instituted a program where each manager is required to go through an inventory of ethical propositions. There were about five or six pages on a number of issues: ownership; whether they do business with the friends of their superiors; what kind of stockholdings they have; and this and that and the other thing. It was very complicated. And the manager was required to sign each and every page and make a statement about their understanding of what the corporate ethic was intended to be.   So that's a company that is trying to take a very thorough manager-by-manager approach to dealing with corporate ethics.

COMMENT: What do you see as the basis for either IBM having taken such a stance from the start or for Montgomery Ward doing this now?

BJORKLUND: In the case of IBM, I think it was the ethic of the entrepreneur. Watson started with the notion that, in this particular area that I was talking about before, they wanted to employ people and that they never wanted to lay anyone off. They wanted to be responsible for the people that they employed. And they have never laid anybody off, ever, according to them. They have a number of ways of dealing with that. They've canned a few people, but . . .

COMMENT: I think it's important to realize it's no "layoffs." They fire but they don't lay off people in slack time.

BJORKLUND: That's right. And they do that in part because they're very highly centralized in the human resources area. That's one example. Ken Olsen is another example of a company that hasn't had them because of the entrepreneur's personal commitment. In the case of Montgomery Ward, I think that is a result of litigation and just the popular position. As I said in my paper, in the 18 months before September of '76, I counted over 100 articles just in the popular press and in the 18 months prior to that there were only 1/5 as many. So there's a growing feeling that corporations and managers have to be concerned about their personal conduct.

COMMENT: How important would you say a formal code of ethics is in closing this communication gap between the higher echelon of the management and the perceptions that the lower echelon have? Does a code of ethics do any good?

BJORKLUND: I think, as Max mentioned, there are codes and there are codes. For instance, take some of the professional codes: the engineering codes, the American Medical Association codes, the Bar Association codes. I think the people are subject to some action. They are subject to being disbarred. In the case of the Montgomery Ward code, false statements lead to being fired. People are very concerned about something that they know has action, but I think a code, in general, is just a first step. I think they require some communication channels, some role modeling. That's what a number of corporate presidents are striking out to do -- to become visible and professional role models for their organization.

210

WORTMAN: I agree with Bob, particularly in suggesting that if you're going to have a code of ethics for your particular company, the issues that are dealt with ought not to be generalized for the whole world. They ought to deal with realities that exist in your company or your particular industry, and there should be a stipulation on what happens when you don't subscribe to that particular code of ethics, and it needs to happen quickly. If it doesn't, then you might just as well take the thing and throw it out because it isn't worth the paper that it's written on. Secondly, is the fact that the enforcement of something that is so specific as that is really a function of the ethic of the chief executive officer.

COMMENT: I know a couple of companies that are doing periodic performance evaluations using as one of the elements public affairs activities or public relations activities. That is being done in a few companies, but is that kind of thing done with adherrance to a company code of ethics per se? (For example, saying I lost $2 million because I refused to pay that bribe. Is anyone doing that?)

WORTMAN: I thought for a minute we were into social indicators here. What we're really trying to do is to say to our corporations: Are you really being socially responsible? And that is beyond the law, beyond all the things that we are requiring by law.

BJORKLUND: Norton Abrasives Corporation is doing this sort of thing in the Worcester, Mass. area, but there's some question, once again (which Ken Olsen brought up), about going beyond the law. What are the requirements of the corporation to do something with somebody else's money?

MISSIRIAN: However, I would like to underscore one thing Olsen said that impressed me. He said that ethical behavior ought to be ethical in every aspect of one's life. I think that's a thing not to lose sight of, that while there is a question of situational ethics, the fact of the matter is that each individual does have a set of values, does have some ethical behavior. Unfortunately, the thing that forces people into unethical conduct often times is their sense of powerlessness in a given situation. It is the question of economic expediency. Are you prepared to pay the price to maintain your own particular ethical standards or values? That's very hard if you happen to be a young man in a corporation or a middle manager in a corporation and you have two children that you just put into private school, you just moved into a house that's next door to the country club, and you see yourself as the next vice president of the company, and somebody is asking you to do something that you know damn well is unethical. That's a dilemma. Those are the real issues for

211

most managers. Not the question of whether or not you're going to pay a bribe in South Africa or Saudi Arabia when that's the culture of the area.

COMMENT: I'd argue that it doesn't even have to be as dramatic as that.

COMMENT: Well, I was trying to make it as dramatic as possible just to emphasize the point.

BJORKLUND: One of the things that I've observed and I heard Joe Litterer and a lot of other people talk about today is the relationship between superior and subordinates. There are packets of people in organizations that think, "Oh my God! Here I am; I'm stuck in my career, and if I don't make some moves in the next year or so, I'm going to be stuck." (These are people, incidentally, that Rosabeth Cantor called "the stuck.") If the stuck people perceive that they have to make their moves now and that their career is in jeopardy, they'll do a lot of things that are personally repugnant to them, and against their ethical standards. So, one thing to add to your laundry list of how to deal with this in the corporation might be to go to the human resource planner and try to understand people's attitudes about their careers. I think this is vital. I think a lot of people's decision-making hinges on their view of themselves -- where they are, where they're going, if they're about to be destroyed, walked over.

SESSION IX

"Corporate Responsibility: Some Philosophical Foundations"

Max Oelschlaeger
Professor of Philosophy
North Texas State University

Howard Sohn
Professor of Religion
Mount Holyoke College

James B. Wilbur, III
Professor of Philosophy
SUNY at Geneseo

MAX OELSCHLAEGER

Corporate Power and Social Responsibility: Reflections on
The Prospects of Business Civilization

This paper explores one aspect of the vague but significant
concept of social responsibility. Perhaps no issue is more important to the future of what Robert L. Heilbroner characterizes
as "business civilization" than the question of how corporate
power is to be held accountable to government, environmentalists,
and other groups who serve to influence or regulate the social
good. Serious talk about the concept of social responsibility is
engaging more and more members of both "the business" and "nonbusiness" communities. Both groups seem to agree that corporate
power needs to be exercised in a more socially responsible fashion,
since such action is thought to be necessary to solving or ame-
liorating social problems, such as poverty, unsafe working conditions, and the environmental crisis.

Typically, in discussing social responsibility, the focus
tends to be on ethical dimensions of the concept. A. M. Sullivan's
viewpoint is representative; he writes that in "the 20th century,
a more sensitive breed of management has recognized that human
values come first and the profit system must include a responsibility to society as well as stockholders."[1] Furthermore, Sullivan
continues, "responsibility begins at the top and filters down
through middle management and supervisors. It includes the complex and relative ethics of wages, workrules, seniority, fringes,
profit participation, and pensions."

Careful inquiry into the ethical framework of managerial
responsibility has been a very important part of business ethics.
But, if the dialogue about social responsibility is confined to
this one area, the potentially revolutionary implications of the
concept are ignored. As Thomas Petit observes, "it is not self-
evident whether the trend toward secondary noneconomic corporate
functions is a forerunner of the development of a new type of noncapitalistic economic system or whether it is a prudent step
necessary to preserve the best features of capitalism."[2] Thus it
appears that much more is involved in the concept of social responsibility than strictly ethical considerations.

The very idea of social responsibility raises, in other
words, questions about the future of our socioeconomic system. It
is manifest that our society is facing problems, such as the environmental crisis, which threaten its long stability and possibly

215

survival.[3] It is also apparent that the traditional socioeconomic
processes by which business civilization has ordered and controlled
its behavior appear inadequate to deal with some of these problems.
Government appears to many to have been laggardly in its responses,
and, furthermore, governmental solutions seem almost antithetical
to a free enterprise system; yet business appears to many to have
been oblivious to a need to respond. Thus has a cry arisen for
"socially responsible behavior" by businessmen.

Some understanding of the idea that business must assume
secondary noneconomic functions, outside the historically evolved
scope of business concern, can be gained by factoring the concept
of social responsibility into its component parts. The "social"
part of the concept refers primarily to nonmarket phenomena, such
as pollution or consumer's interests, which have not customarily
been a part of managerial concern. The "responsibility" component
of the concept implies that managers of firms are to be held accountable, in some way, for working toward solutions of nonmarket
problems.

However, it is not self-evident, given the above discussion,
what the idea of social responsibility implies about the future of
business civilization. Granted that there is a wideshared public
opinion that business must be socially responsible, and granted
that nonmarket considerations are to be introduced into the framework of managerial decision-making, it is obvious that the social
role of business is changing. But it is not clear what that future
role of business is to be.

Neil Jacoby suggests that, "Want of an adequate theory of
the ideal behavior of the large business corporation lies at the
heart of current confusion over the social role of business. The
basic difficulty is not so much ignorance of corporate social involvement, but rather the lack of an adequate criterion by which
it should be judged."[4] How is the businessman to know when he has
made a socially responsible decision or even when he is required
to admit nonmarket variables into the decision-making process?
How are representatives of the public interest to distinguish between socially responsible corporate behavior and self-interested
behavior which harms the public's interest? How is government to
safeguard the public interest without destroying the liberty and
freedoms which are the cornerstone of the American way of life?
A theory of social responsibility which has any pretense to being
adequate must somehow come to grips with such questions. The
answers that theory provides will have much to do with determining
the future configuration of our socioeconomic system.

Classical economic theory, which has long dominated the
American mind, did provide an explanation of how the businessman,

in serving his own self-interests, also served the public interest. In what might be termed the Classical Model of social responsibility, the businessman had a clearly defined role; namely, his goal was to maximize his own profit. The so-called "invisible hand" would see to it that the greatest amount of social good was produced. The role of government, according to Adam Smith's laissez faire ideology, was simply to serve as an impediment to impediments so that each man could freely pursue his own self-interest. Thus, in the Classical Model, socially responsible behavior and decision-making could be defined and determined by a profitability criterion: given the assumption of perfect competition, the more profitable a businessman was, the more he contributed to the public interest; or, in other words, by striving to maximize his own profits, the businessman contributed to the maximization of the social welfare function.

History, however, has served to reveal certain shortcomings in the Classical Model of social responsibility. Air pollution, for example, is one facet of the environmental crisis which seems to contradict Smith's theory. In seeking to maximize profits, an individual corporation cannot afford to bear the costs of protecting the commons; the so-called "invisible foot" can sometimes lead self-interested individuals to kick the common good to pieces. Thus the Classical Model has given way to what is sometimes called the Managerial Model of social responsibility. In this model there is an expectation that the businessman will act in socially responsible ways because, when operating in markets that are not perfectly competitive, he no longer seeks profits exclusively, but rather tries to maximize his own satisfactions by seeking other goals.

This model offers an advantage over the Classical Model of the social role of business, since it is evident that completely self-interested behavior can damage the common good. But criticism has also exposed certain weaknesses in the Managerial Model of the social role of business. In the ideal case the managerial preference function will coincide with the community's preference function (e.g., interest in clean air); but simply recognizing the autonomy of corporate decision-makers to choose goals other than profit does not guarantee either that managers will choose goals which coincide with the community's preferences or that they will optimize their preference at the same level the community would choose.

Furthermore, and more crucially, the Managerial Model of social responsibility does not account for the influence of political and other nonmarket forces on the behavior of corporate decision-makers. In the first place, this model offers no way in which disputes as to the nature of the public interest can be

217

resolved. As the recent report of the Advisory Committee on National Growth Policy Processes notes, "In a free society, commons problems are notoriously intractable. Almost by definition their resolution requires outside intervention, because individuals must be induced to ignore their perceived self-interests."[5] By not accounting for actual interrelations between the power of the non-business community and the business community, the Managerial Model assumes, in effect, that a pre-established harmony of interest exists. But the very existence of social problems makes that assumption false, and the political process a necessary component of any adequate account of the social role of business.

In the second place, by failing to account for the influence of political forces on the business community, the Managerial Model places the burden of making socially responsible decisions on the manager's conscience (or humanitarian propensities). The model, in other words, expresses a hopeful idealism that the businessman will intuitively know society's preferences. But no self-consistent account can be given of how it is that a business manager internalizes standards of behavior (or preferences) of the nonbusiness community. By definition, the businessman is part of the business community of interest; although the corporate decision-maker may share some preference functions with the nonbusiness community of interest, there can be no prediction that he will do so in all cases.[6] Thus, the community at large, and various representatives of the public interest, can be none too certain or confident that corporate decision-makers will act in socially responsible ways.

These difficulties in the Managerial and Classical Models have led to the appearance of the Social Environment Model of social responsibility. This model attempts to visualize the social role of business in the context of American society as a dynamic system in which all the parts mutually affect each other. The Social Environment Model especially attempts to explain how, through the political process, the nonbusiness community and the business community interact so that the firm or corporation can perform its functions in accordance with the needs of society itself. The theoretical emphasis of this model is, then, on the empirical relations between the corporation and its sociocultural environment.

By recognizing the direct influence of nonmarket forces on business, the Social Environment Model seems to overcome the flaws inherent in the two previous models of social responsibility. The Classical Model merely assumed an a priori connection or identity of interest between business and the public; the a priori criterion it offered for defining and determining socially responsible behavior is not in fact workable, since there is no necessary connection between maximization of profit and maximization of the community's preference function. The Managerial Model overcame this difficulty by recognizing that if the community's preference function is to be optimized, then managers will in fact be required to make decisions based on other than market criteria. But this model provides no criterion by which either the public or the business community can know (i) when business is obligated to act, since there is no theoretical account of the empirical relation between the business and nonbusiness communities, and (ii) how socially responsible behaviors are in fact to be determined, since introspective or subjective criteria (i.e., the conscience or humanitarian propensities of the manager) only are presumed to be sufficient.

The great advance in thinking made by the Social Environment Model is that it provides a system level perspective on business civilization. Corporate behavior is understood or explained in relation to the complex process of interaction between the many parts of the cultural system. The firm itself is no longer seen in misleading anthropomorphic terms as the locus of social control, but rather as part of a cultural whole where the parts mutually interdetermine their own behavior. From a system level viewpoint, business civilization is seen as a set of interacting subsystems or vectors, political, economic, social (e.g., environmentalists, consumers), and so on. Each cultural vector has its own objectives (or interests) and characteristic institutions, and each has a magnitude or power to influence other vectors.[7] Vectors can cooperatively interact as well as mutually obstruct each others interest and, collectively, they determine the behavior of the system as a whole. Corporate business itself is a "powerful subsystem, which is generally supportive of the other subsystems, but which comes into conflict with some of them at various points of intersection."[8]

Thus, the Social Environment Model makes it apparent that "In order to function effectively and, in the last analysis, to survive, a system must realize a synthesis among its several parts-- a working harmony among them--and it must subordinate part to whole."[9] Some kind of social planning for the well being of the system itself is necessary. In other words, as Neil Jacoby puts it, "The art of social policy is to find ways of reconciling the conflicts and of mutualizing support of the different social subsystems and their institutions."[10] Such system level planning, or establishing of macrolevel goals, could serve to direct corporate behavior into socially responsible channels. Thus, system level goals or objectives could stand as normative criteria by which both the business and nonbusiness communities could know in fact when socially responsible behavior is obligatory.

What is not clear is whether system level goals can be established in a manner compatible with primary structural features of business civilization, such as the separation of private and

219

public sectors, and private profits. This vagueness thus hides or
disguises the revolutionary potential implicit in the concept of
social responsibility. In the present socioeconomic system, tremendous discretionary economic and political power has been given
to corporations; despite widespread governmental regulation of day-
to-day business operations (and the performance of certain other
financial functions by the federal government), the system remains
one based on free enterprise. Government, or the public sector,
serves primarily as an impediment to impediments, providing an organizational superstructure for the short-term functioning of a
private enterprise system. Yet, as we have already see, a variety
of social problems is forcing reconsideration of the relation between the private and public subsystems or sectors of our national
life. The environmental crisis, poverty, and other system level
problems have made social planning virtually mandatory.

Some individuals have argued that our social problems can be
solved while simultaneously maintaining the key structural features
of business civilization. Neil Jacoby, for example, thinks that
corporations can act in socially responsible ways without the profit
system being jeopardized and without the growth of a noxious and
costly bureaucracy. He persuasively argues that, in fact, "the
contemporary corporation must become socially involved in order to
maximize profits."[11] Thus, as Jacoby sees the future, the idea of
social responsibility becomes perhaps the salvation of business
civilization.

But others, such as Robert L. Heilbroner, believe that the
solution of social problems necessarily involves the evolution of
a noncapitalistic economic system. Heilbroner argues that over
the next 25 to 30 years, "the drift of business society will be
toward a business-government state" where the historically placed
lines between the private and public sectors of our national life
will become increasingly blurred.[12] "As the business world becomes
merged with or submerged beneath a national economic state, the
social responsibility of corporations or ministries becomes less
and less distinguishable from that of government itself."

Willis W. Harman provides a perceptive summary of the two
apparent futures of business civilization. Recognizing the existence of system level nonmarket problems which presently go unresolved, Harman argues that there are two paths of advance open
to our society. "The first approach is to continue the collectivist trend which has characterized the last four decades, perhaps
by moving toward 'new socialism.'"[13] This is the future as Heilbroner sees it. "The second approach," according to Harman, is
". . . to reverse the collectivist trend and revitalize the role
of the private sector. Such a reversal might be possible, but
would not consist of moving back to some previous state [of the

220

system]: Instead, we would need to go on to something we have never known." This is close, though perhaps not identical, to the future as Jacoby sees it.

Future historians will be in a position to tell whether some kind of "new socialism" triumphed over business civilization, or whether some workable model of social responsibility emerged in time to revitalize decision-making in the private sector. It seems clear, on one side of the coin, that a failure on the part of the business community to engage in socially responsible behavior will lead to the demise of business civilization. But what of the other side of the coin? Is there any evidence to suggest that the Social Environment Model of social responsibility is workable? Is there any reason to think that the Social Environment Model is compatible with the primary structural features of our present system, yet flexible enough to allow business to respond to present-day social problems?

The answer to these questions is a qualified "yes." In the first place, the Social Environment Model of social responsibility is workable in principle because it is a system level model and the social problems confronting business civilization are system level problems. The behavior of a system as a whole represents a synthesis of its component subsystems or vectors. As the systems theoretical paradigm makes clear, to function effectively, an over-all harmony (i.e., initiation and maintenance of mutually beneficial and amelioration or elimination of mutually detrimental patterns of interaction) must be created.[14] "For maximum effectiveness--in an ideal system--syntheses should be effected in all areas and at all levels leading to the top of the system [emphasis added]."[15] Once macrogoals are identified and established, then microlevel decision-makers can act in a manner compatible both with their own self-interests as well as those of the culture itself.

Given the present structural configuration of business civilization, top-down or totalitarian kinds of decision-making to establish macrogoals is not, in fact, workable. However, as the Social Environment Model reveals, planning for system level goals does not require top-down decision-making. What it does require is cooperative interaction among public and private decision-making sectors of our society. "If the political and economic sub-systems of American society are to interact in the public interest, it is desirable that the business community facilitate rather than obstruct the political and market changes called for by shifts in public views."[16] What is called for, once the systemic nature of the concept of social responsibility is recognized, is planning. As the Social Environment Model shows, planning can be done in a way compatible with the primary structural features of business civilization. This means that cooperation among various subsystems

221

is essential.

The question is, however, can such cooperation be achieved in fact (granting that it is in principle a possibility)? There is some evidence to suggest that it can. For example, there are some cases where corporate decision-makers have effectively worked with representatives of the public interest in defining mutually acceptable goals.[17] One particularly noteworthy example was launched early this year; leaders from both environmental groups and industry have been trying to reach a consensus on some of the difficult and unresolved issues involved in the mining and burning of coal.[18] Using the "rule of reason," the two groups attempted to resolve the many points of difference between them; interestingly, mutual accommodations were made on most points, environmentalists being won over in many cases by industry arguments, and industrialists being won over in others by the environmentalists.

A second reason to think that system level goals can actually be established is that public discussion of the concept of social responsibility is increasing in frequency. Furthermore, talk about social responsibility is no longer confined to an inner circle of academics and a few far-sighted business leaders. For example, the Advisory Committee on National Growth Policy Processes was able to agree on the necessity of planning for system level goals and building social accountability into the American socioeconomic system. Especially significant is the fact that this committee included representatives from most major subsystems of American life, including finance, industry, labor, state and federal government, education, and public interest groups. Further manifestations of increasing public concern over social responsibility are also apparent; for example, a proliferation of courses in business ethics, conferences of both a regional and national nature on business ethics, the development of scholarly specialities in business ethics, and the funding of a retraining institute for humanists concerned with business ethics are all positive signs.

What conclusions can be drawn from this brief study of social responsibility as to the future of business civilization? With the caveat that no one can predict the future, two provisional forecasts can be made. First, self-adaptation of the system we have characterized as business civilization is not only possible, but a strong possibility. The increasing public attention to the concept of social responsibility highlights growing awareness (among the many subsystems) of the necessity of cooperation in defining macrogoals. The recognition that mutually acceptable system level goals must be established does not mean that opposition among various interest groups is a priori eradicated. Rather than obviating the political process, the Social Environment Model of social responsibility underlines the fact that diverse interest groups must begin working together through political channels (e.g., the NEPA) in order to resolve the question of what is in the public interest. Political power and authority is a necessity of civilized human existence. The question is whether the future will bring a kind of top-down or socialistic form of politics, or whether the future will bring a revitalized kind of bottom-up politics. In any case, system level goals will be established; but collectivistic solutions are not compatible with the present configuration of our system. The Social Environment Model at least shows the way toward a cooperative system of establishing system level goals.

Second, the Social Environment Model of social responsibility manifests an increased sophistication in our understanding of our own social behavior. Because the Social Environment Model is a systems paradigm, it counters an unscientific tendency to think of social responsibility in moralistic terms. Of course, the established "free will" ideology is well entrenched, and the idea that the businessman's conscience is the seat of socially responsible behavior will not be easily displaced by the Social Environment Model. There are some very difficult and fundamental philosophical issues involved in this matter which cannot be discussed here. But, suffice it to say that the Managerial Model of social responsibility is moralistic in that it exhorts business managers to conform to some communal standard of the social good which, in fact, can not be clearly defined; the Managerial Model merely assumes that some kind of consensus on goals exists, and that the manager then intuitively knows these. The Social Environment Model, by recognizing that when we talk about the social good we are in fact talking about system level goals, places the emphasis on establishing rational macrogoals rather than conforming to pre-established (and largely imaginary) definitions of the common good.

The Social Environment Model redirects, in effect, our attention from an anthropomorphic concept of social responsibility to a scientific one. An increased scientific understanding of business culture increases the likelihood that rather than haplessly drifting into collectivism, actively anticipatory responses to social problems will be made by the system of private enterprise. The behavior of business civilization as a system has been justifiably characterized as "unintelligent, reflexive, and tropismatic," which is the lowest stage of systems behavior.[19] What the Social Environment Model does is underscore the fact that, at the present juncture of history, the continued operation of the system as per usual is tantamount to resignation to blind fate or destiny.

Given 200 years of American history, we can look back and see that the controlling mechanisms of our culture were adequate to propel us to the highest levels of socioeconomic achievement in the world's history. As the cultural anthropologist Leslie White remarks, "It is no wonder that American institutions have been extravagantly extolled for a century or more."[20] But the fact remains, as we have already seen, that these mechanisms of control are no longer adequate. "The behavior of a nation is an expression of the coordination, the integration, and the synthesis of . . . [its] multitude of parts, . . . myriad of vectors, economic and political."[21] The Social Environment Model thus points the way toward a revitalization of our institutions. While the Social Environment Model is no panacea, it perhaps symbolizes the hope that corporate power can be held accountable to diverse public interests which serve to influence or regulate the social good.

NOTES

1. A. M. Sullivan, Human Values in Management (New York: Thomas Y. Crowell Co., 1968), p. 67.
2. Thomas A. Petit, The Moral Crisis in Management (New York: McGraw-Hill Book Co., 1967), p. 138.
3. See, for example, Robert L. Heilbroner, Business Civilization in Decline (New York: W. W. Norton & Co., Inc., 1976).
4. Neil H. Jacoby, Corporate Power and Social Responsibility (New York: Macmillan Publishing Co., Inc., 1973), p. 190.
5. "Forging America's Future: Strategies for National Growth and Development," Challenge: The Magazine of Economic Affairs, 19, No. 6 (January/February, 1977), p. 18.
6. See, for example, Peter L. Berger and Thomas Luckman, The Social Construction of Reality: A Treatise in the Sociology of Knowledge (Garden City, New York: Doubleday and Company, Inc., 1966); George Gurvitch, The Social Frameworks of Knowledge, trans. by M. A. Thompson and K. A. Thompson (New York: Harper and Row Publishers, 1971); C. Wright Mills, The Power Elite (New York: Oxford University Press, 1956); and G. William Domhoff, The Higher Circles: The Governing Class in America (New York: Vintage Books, 1971). Recent work in the sociology of knowledge and social stratification indicates that predictions of identity of either perceptions or interests between the business and nonbusiness communities cannot generally be made.
7. The systems paradigm, in the opinion of many scientists and humanists, promises to revolutionize our understanding of man and society, and thus our understanding of the concept of social responsibility. See Ludwig von Bertalanffy, General System Theory: Foundations, Development, Applications (New York: George Braziller, 1968) and Ervin Laszlo, Introduction to Systems Philosophy: Toward a New Paradigm of Contemporary Thought (New York: Harper and Row Publishers, 1972) for a general introduction to systems theory.
8. Jacoby, Social Responsibility, p. 17.

9. Leslie A. White, *The Concept of Cultural Systems*: *A Key to Understanding Tribes and Nations* (New York: Columbia University Press, 1975), p. 166. (Both White's book, and Jacoby's book, *Social Responsibility*, employ the systems paradigm.)

10. Jacoby, *Social Responsibility*, p. 17.

11. *Ibid.*, p. 197.

12. Heilbroner, *Business Civilization*, p. 34.

13. Willis W. Harman, "The Coming Transformation," *The Futurist*, XI, No. 1 (February, 1977), p. 9.

14. Cf. Laszlo, *Systems Philosophy*, pp. 106-112.

15. White, *Cultural Systems*, p. 167.

16. Jacoby, *Social Responsibility*, p. 190.

17. Of course, it must also be noted that there are numerous examples of private interest groups working in opposition to public interest groups.

18. Luther J. Carter, "Coal: Invoking 'the Rule of Reason' in an Energy-Environment Conflict," *Science*, 198, No. 4314 (21 October 1977), pp. 276-280.

19. Cf. White, *Cultural Systems*, pp. 93-97.

20. *Ibid.*, p. 99.

21. *Ibid.*, p. 97.

HOWARD F. SOHN

Prevailing Rationales in the
Corporate Social Responsibility Debate

In the discussions of "corporate social responsibility" over the last few years, there have emerged numerous rationales for and against business involvement in social issues. The views expressed range between two extremes: from those who see business responsibility as that of returning a profit to investors within a set of constraints, to those who would have business direct its resources toward the solution of social problems unrelated to its operation.

What I propose to do is enumerate several major types of rationale regarding corporate social responsibility and demonstrate that underlying each rationale is a certain perception of the relationship between business and society. My contention is that one's perception of the business-society relationship, or the emphases that dominate that perception, determine one's position in the corporate social responsibility debate. Although this connection in itself is rather obvious, the enumeration of various perceptions and the rationales that emerge from them is very helpful in organizing, analyzing, and clarifying the major views. The purpose of this essentially descriptive enterprise is to bring into focus the distinguishing features of the various rationales and to make explicit their underlying assumptions about the business-society relationship. Unlike some participants in the debate who believe that corporate responsibility is a management issue not significantly served by discussions of ethics,[1] perceptions, and values, I believe that clarity as to rationale and awareness of perceptual emphases is of real importance and practical effect.

My procedure will be to summarize four major ways of perceiving the relationship between business and society, and in each case spell out the resulting views on corporate social responsibility. In the first major view the relationship is perceived in classical functional terms, in the second a constituency model dominates, in the third the legal framework is the primary medium of perception, and in the fourth a sharp distinction between private and public spheres is the salient feature.

In a prevailing traditional view, the business-society relationship is perceived in functional terms. In response to the question--What is business _for_?--business is defined as a functional unit in society having clearly defined and limited tasks to perform. A society is seen as dividing up the various things that need to be done. Some tasks are assigned to business, some to government, some to non-profit and voluntary organizations, some to individual citizens and their communities. The word "assign" suggests more order and intentionality than is really there, but the functional perception of the business-society relationship often sees this division of labor as a matter of design.

What functions receive emphasis in the traditional functional view? The primary function of business, and certainly the primary motive in establishing a business, is to make money. Business is, in a sense, a medium of exchange. Persons who put time, skill, effort, materials, money, etc. into a saleable product receive access to other goods and services in return.

From the standpoint of society at large, the function of business is to provide needed goods and services. This is not why most people start or participate in a business, but it certainly is a way of perceiving a primary social function. Most functional definitions of business would combine the two functions mentioned: business exists to provide goods and services to consumers and a reasonable profit to investors.

In the functional perception of the business-society relationship, then, certain tasks in the society fall to business to perform. The social responsibility of business, in this view, is to perform those limited tasks well. If business does, and if other units in this division-of-labor scheme perform their functions well, the society as a whole will thrive. It is not appropriate--in fact it is irresponsible--for business to take on social tasks that belong to other units in the society. Lee Preston and James Post refer to this view as fundamentalism:

> [A]ccording to fundamentalists, what management cannot and should not do is expand the scope of its activities beyond those functions necessary to the successful accomplishment of the task itself, including execution of the resulting transactions. If each individual and organization seeks to accomplish in the most efficient manner the highest-valued specific tasks of which he (it) is capable, the value of the total product of society will be as great as possible.[2]

Among the fundamentalists are Theodore Levitt and Milton Friedman who argue that the functions of business are economic. To perform its economic tasks efficiently--that is the social responsibility of business.[3]

227

There are fundamentalists, however, who, while sharing the traditional functional view of business' role in society, put forth a rationale for corporate social involvement that extends responsibility beyond narrowly defined economic tasks. The rationale takes various forms and is essentially defensive in posture, intended to guard the traditional functions and place of business in society. The idea is to expand social functions enough to substantially protect traditional functions. In their report for the Committee for Economic Development on the social audit, John Corson and George Steiner report that the rationale most frequently articulated by businessmen for involvement in social issues focuses on the need to maintain a social climate in which private property and private profits are respected. "It is reasoned that the majority of the people are content to continue with laws and regulations that are hospitable to corporate operations when business leaders assume non-profit responsibilities voluntarily."[4]

In other words, corporations must promote a public image in which they are seen as significant contributors to social well-being, not as perpetrators of social harm, in order that a political and legal system conducive to private enterprise can be maintained.

In another perception of the business-society relationship articulated increasingly in recent years, business is seen as related to society through its various constituencies. A constituency is a group of persons linked to a company on the basis of some common interest. The most prominent constituencies are those at either end of the business cycle: stockholders or other investors whose capital initiates or makes possible the production process, and the consumers who receive and pay for the goods or services. These two constituencies are part of society, essentially external to the company, and constitute a two-fold link of the company to society.

If limited to these two groups, the constituency approach looks very much like the classic functional approach (described above) in which business exists for a two-fold function: to satisfy a consumer need and to provide a profit to investors. Although in the functional view the focus is on function rather than composition of a constituency, the two views are very similar.

In the context of the corporate social responsibility discussion, however, these two views diverge considerably. When corporate social responsibility is articulated in light of a constituency-type perception of the business-society relationship, the number of constituencies expands significantly. Not only are consumers and investors constituencies, but so are employees, suppliers, the community, and perhaps even the larger society,

228

governments, and future generations. All constitute links between business and society.

According to this multiple constituency perception of the business-society relationship, what constitutes corporate social responsibility? To act responsibly is to take the well-being of all constituencies into account when making policy. The assumption is that all constituencies whose interests are affected by company policy have a legitimate claim to consideration in policy matters. William P. Drake, Chairman of Penwalt Corporation, has summarized the constituency obligation this way: "Penwalt's purpose is to provide profitably, socially useful products and services through efficient use of the resources available to us for the benefit of our five major publics: our employees, our customers, our shareholders, our suppliers, and the general public. This last public includes, of course, federal, state and local governments and the communities in which we operate."[5]

This statement does not acknowledge the fact that numerous dilemmas of social responsibility arise because of conflicting claims from different constituencies or "publics." Human Resources Network, a research and consulting firm, sees corporate responsibility as "the obligation of the corporation to balance its impact on and contribution to its various constituencies: customers, employees, suppliers, shareholders and the larger society."[6]

"Balance" is of course the loaded word here. How a company evaluates and compares the interests and claims of the different constituencies, what constitutes a balance, where priorities lie given limited resources and capacities—these are the hard questions raised by the constituency approach to corporate social responsibility.

The rationale for corporate social responsibility that arises from a constituency view of the business-society relationship may take either a positive or negative form. The difference between the two is not absolute, but a matter of emphasis. In both forms a company is seen as responsible for the effects of its operations on its constituencies. In the simplest terms, it is responsible for what it does. But those who share the negative or minimalist form of the argument will focus on—and perhaps limit their concern to—ill effects directly caused by company operations, while a subscriber to what we have called the positive view is more likely to be sensitive to indirect and longer-term effects. The latter is also more likely to include the concerns of more remote constituencies such as future generations. More important, however, is the fact that those of the positive constituency rationale will emphasize positive contributions to constituency well-being. They will establish a bias in company

229

policy in favor of constituency well-being, making enhancement of well-being the goal. They will seek out opportunities and take initiatives for such enhancement. Those of the negative constituency rationale are not really negative--they are essentially neutral: constituencies should not be harmed by company operations.[7] Executives of this persuasion will be responsive to the claims of constituencies regarding ill effects and may go a step further and monitor operations in order to better discern harm or potentially harmful effects. The difference, as we said at the outset, between positive and negative forms of the multiple constituency rationale is a matter of emphasis. But differences in emphasis ought not to be minimized. Like forks of a road, they can end up in very different places.

Another rationale based on this multiple constituency perception begins with assertions regarding the public character of corporations. A large corporation's effects are so far-reaching, in social and political as well as economic terms, that no one can pretend that their proper concerns are narrowly economic. Neil Chamberlain argues that "the corporation has become, by virtue of its size and scope, more of a public institution than a private one."[8] Kuhn & Berg argue that business decisions are no longer merely intramural, limited in their effects to the industry or private sector as a whole. "Corporate influence spreads far afield; a decision that a board of directors imagines to be of concern only to those in the company may have repercussions in the highest councils of government as well as in the homes of ordinary citizens."[9]

The consequent argument for corporate social responsibility is rather obvious. Extensive power and influences carry commensurate responsibility. "When men command large, prestigious organizations whose influence reaches far, they become, by virtue of their position, consequential members of the national polity."[10]

So much for the rationales based on multiple constituency perceptions. They have received a good deal of attention here because of their prominence in social responsibility discussions of the last ten years.

In another perception of the business-society relationship, the salient feature is the legal framework. The foundation of a corporation, in this view, is its charter which gives it legal standing in the society and legal rights. When the state, as representative of the society, grants a charter and "creates" the corporation as a legal entity, a legal relationship is established which becomes the model or pattern for future relationships between the corporation and society.

230

The legal relationship begins but does not end with chartering. As a chartered corporation, the business becomes subject to
the various laws--federal, state, and local--that apply to such
entities. It becomes subject to whatever legislation the law-
making representatives of society wish to enact in its regard, particularly to that body of legislation referred to as government
regulation of industry. So in this perception of the business-
society relationship, the law stands out as the primary link. The
charter, the general laws of the society, and regulative legislation dominate the character of the relationship between business
and society.

On the basis of this perception of the relationship, what is
the social responsibility of business? Essentially, it is to obey
the law. The laws that apply to business collectively constitute
the society's statement of what it expects of business with respect to societal well-being. If society expects more of business,
it can pass more laws. "Unless and until it does so," says Christopher Stone, "we are all better off if corporations steer themselves by profit, rather than by the manager's various and vague
personal notions of what is best for the society."[11]

Closely related to the legal approach to the business-society
relationship is the corporate citizenship view. By virtue of its
charter, the corporation becomes a legal entity with a standing in
society similar in many respects to that of the individual citizen.
As an "institutional citizen," the corporation has duties as well
as rights and privileges. Donald MacNaughton, president of
Prudential Life, put it this way: "[We] believe that, as a corporate citizen, we have the same responsibility to contribute to
the welfare of the community as does any leading citizen."[12] Or
to put it in more explicit social contract terms: if there is a
more or less identifiable "common good" (perhaps "quality of life"
in contemporary terms) toward which society as a whole strives,
then the various units of the society, individual as well as institutional, have a responsibility to contribute toward it.

This rationale for corporate social responsibility is sometimes formulated as the "capacity argument." Corporations should
contribute to the solving of social problems and the promotion of
social well-being because they have the capacity to do so. That
is, in certain social-issue areas, corporations have expertise,
competence, talent, as well as power and influence, that can be
directed toward a social issue. But capacity implies responsibility only if one accepts the notion of a "common good" to which
all social units have an obligation to contribute. (It should be
noted here that there is also an incapacity or incompetence argument used in support of limits on corporate social responsibility.
It says that corporations should steer clear of involvement in

social issues precisely because they do <u>not</u> have the competence and expertise in these areas.)

In part, the citizen rationale for corporate social responsibility is based on the notion that the chartering process lifts legal responsibility from individuals (managers, owners) and places it in the new legal entity, the corporation. Hence the corporation ought to assume those responsibilities that accompany that transfer in legal standing.

To those for whom the legal framework is central to the business-society relationship, then, social responsibility entails obeying the law or being a good corporate citizen. The former is a restrictive notion that limits corporate social responsibility, while the latter embraces the former and implies a positive, an initiating role in the social sphere.

Finally, we turn to another version of the traditional view of the business-society relationship, one which emphasizes the distinction between the private and public spheres. It sets the one over against the other, perceiving the spheres as distinguished from each other, not only in terms of function, but in terms of value emphases as well. The private sphere is the realm of entrepreneurial opportunity, of individual freedom, freedom to "make it," to get ahead. On the other side is the public sphere, consisting primarily of government. The less there is of government, the better, for although it should, in this view, be supporting the same values, it in fact restricts freedom and threatens fundamental entrepreneurial values because of its expansion of influence, power, and control. This extension of influence emphasizes collectivist values and by implication, at least, puts equality and justice on a level with freedom—sometimes even ahead of it. In this perception, then, the private and public spheres are essentially distinct, but the name for the whole emphasizes the proper dominance of the private sector. It is a "free enterprise" system.

Where the business-society relationship is perceived with this emphasis, at least two types of corporate social responsibility rationale emerge. One line of reasoning argues that the greatest threats to the autonomy of the private sector, and the free-enterprise values it embodies, are the increase in government regulation of industry and the expansion of government-sponsored social programs such as welfare, employment programs, and health care. The way to thwart this expansion is for business to assume responsibilities in areas where government will otherwise step in.[13] Industry can minimize regulation by taking initiatives on its own and by establishing effective self-regulatory mechanisms. Where there is no need for regulatory legislation, there won't be any.

Some representatives of this viewpoint argue for corporate social involvement not only on the grounds of avoiding regulation, but extend the argument further with the assertion that private social programs can keep government social programs small. If companies provide good employee benefits such as pensions and health care, good training and re-training programs for both the able and the handicapped, and so on, then government will be inclined to do less, and its so-called socialist tendencies and general expansion of influence and control will be minimized.

There is another type of rationale, too, that stems from the perception of business and society as two separate and rather distinct spheres. It might be called the reciprocation argument. Corporations benefit in numerous ways from the society in which they exist, and not only because people buy what they produce. Companies also have access to, make use of, and benefit from many public goods which are usually taken for granted. There are public roads and other publicly funded or subsidized transportation facilities that make the movement of goods and personnel easy and inexpensive. There are schools which provide capable employees. There is a whole range of public goods and social institutions from which business benefits to a degree that exceeds its contribution to them.[14] They represent, in a sense, assets whose costs are not borne by the business sector. The reciprocation argument asserts that as a result companies owe society, owe the public, some favors returned. Reciprocation should take the form of a greater corporate role in promoting social well-being.

I hope this summary has clarified some of the dominant rationales regarding corporate social responsibility and has shown how each is rooted in a certain perception of the relationship between business and society. Obviously, not all such rationales are of equal validity, nor are they always expressed in the form articulated here. Most persons and institutions, in expressing themselves on this matter, would combine more than one of the rationales enumerated here into a kind of composite. Few would articulate a rationale that doesn't touch some of these bases. An awareness of which types of rationale are called upon and what emphases dominate perceptions of the business-society relationship may assist the maturation of a movement that is still in its infancy.

NOTES

1. For example, Robert W. Ackerman, The Social Challenge to Business, Harvard University Press, 1975, p. 1.
    2. Private Management and Public Policy, Prentice-Hall, 1975,

p. 31.

3.   Theodore Levitt, "The Dangers of Social Responsibility," Harvard Business Review, Sept.-Oct., 1958. Milton Friedman, "The Social Responsibility of Business is to Increase Profits," New York Times Magazine, Sept. 13, 1970.

4.   John J. Corson and George A. Steiner, Measuring Social Performance: The Corporate Social Audit, C.E.D., 1974, p. 16.

5.   Penwalt Corporation, "Corporate Citizenship" brochure. The concept of constituencies as real "stakeholders" with legitimate claims on the corporation is dominant in two important books: John Hargreaves and Jan Dauman, Business Survival and Social Change, London: 1975, Pehr G. Gyllenhammer, People at Work, Addison-Wesley, 1977.

6.   "Evolving toward a Social Policy Professional," Human Resources Network, Corporate Responsibility Planning Service, 1-28-77, #353.

7.   A significant expression of this view is found in John G. Simon, Charles W. Powers, and Jon P. Gunneman, The Ethical Investor, New Haven, Yale University Press, 1972.

8.   Neil W. Chamberlain, The Limits of Corporate Responsibility, Basic Books, 1973, p. 203. Such assertions are common and come from sources other than obvious ones like John Kenneth Galbraith in Economics and the Public Purpose. Harold Williams, Chairman of the Securities and Exchange Commission has argued similarly. See Corporate Public Issues, Vol. III, No. 4, March 1, 1978.

9.   James Kuhn and Ivar Berg, Values in a Business Society, Harcourt, Brace, and World, 1968, p. 60.

10.   Ibid. p. 62.

11.   Christopher D. Stone, Where the Law Ends, The Social Control of Corporate Behavior, Harper and Row, 1975, p. 75.

12.   As quoted in: Human Resources Network, Corporate Responsibility Planning Service, S.P.M., 7-2-76.

13.   Corson and Steiner, op. cit. pp. 15-16.

14.   This view is expressed, for example, by E. F. Schumacher: "Large amounts of public funds have been and are being spent on what is generally called the 'infrastructure,' and the benefits go largely to private enterprise free of charge." Small is Beautiful, Harper and Row, Torchbooks edition, p. 257.

JAMES B. WILBUR

The Foundations of Corporate Responsibility

Without any doubt at all, corporate structure is the most
pervasive form of organization in our society. It has been the
engine of our growth and development over the last one hundred
and fifty years. It has been given special considerations by
government in recognition that its activity is central to our progress as a people and as an inducement to more of the same. And
it has been filling up the social space between the individual and
the nation state (and beyond) by leaps and bounds. Even government structure itself at all levels is perhaps best understood in
the same terms, as a variant on general corporate structure. But
setting aside the sense in which government on the federal, state
and local levels is corporate, my concern lies with the huge number of public corporations which are, again past doubting, by far
the most powerful elements in our society.

Much is being said now about the responsibilities of the corporate community starting at the traditional center with duties to
stockholders, radiating outward through those to consumers and the
general community and coming to rest on corporate responsibility
to the total environment including the support systems for the
biosphere. But all the while, very little helpful is being said
about the foundations of all this responsibility. Why should corporations be responsible? What is usually given in reply is a
litany of the duties of business and the attitudes of managers
which rests either on some assumed sort of "self-interest" which
becomes more "enlightened" as it reaches beyond narrow selfish
concerns or on the fact of community pressure. The former might
work very well if in fact my interests fall somewhere along this
range of increasing enlightenment, but it says precious little
about why I "ought" to be interested at all. The latter is straight
power talk of the "might makes right" variety and provides no basis
for the determination of which pressures should be bowed to and to
what extend and which pressures should be resisted. Both of these
attempts to ground responsibility deprive such talk of any sense
of obligation, in fact of any moral nub at all.

Another way of writing about these matters, much in use now,
is the ideological approach. Corporate activity is found to be an
expression or function of a certain set of beliefs or values at a
certain time. Now, under changing conditions, this set of beliefs
and values is being modified to handle the new circumstances. The
old ideology is no longer adequate and the wave of the future is

235

the new set shaping up. The implication here is that anyone who is not an antiquarian, anyone who wants to be where the action is, will point his nose in the direction of this future and get with it. There is much to be learned from this kind of developmental analysis and comparison provided that somewhere along the way questions of truth and obligation are treated. But in the total absence of these considerations this approach reads· like a fashion report.

There are even some pious references to the moral, accompanied by the use of moral language (the use of "responsibility" is a case in point), but until and unless some attempt is made to ground obligation, to step the moral mast, so to speak, the whole concern with corporate responsibility is at the mercy of the winds. Philosophical ethics might have been expected to remedy this, but hasn't done much but confirm the vagaries of wind and current during the last generation. Having shown to its satisfaction that the "ought" cannot be grounded on the "is", it appears that the moral enterprise is adrift.

The question "What are the foundations of corporate responsibility?" presupposes yet another question: What would a responsible corporation be like? How should I think about corporate structure and activity? Professor James Coleman in his little book Power and the Structure of Society tells us "if you want to know what is new in the modern world, it is the modern corporation." (W. W. Norton, 1974, p. 14) How are we to understand this new phenomenon?

My answer to these questions is that corporate activity can best be understood on analogy with the activity of persons. Let me start by giving what I take to be three good reasons for taking this thesis seriously and then I want to sketch an answer to the problem of obligation and consider some of its implications.

The first of these reasons is historical and based upon the fact that the legal conception of the corporation was fashioned after the legal conception of the natural person. It has come down to us as the corporate person and is known as a legal fiction. Such corporate persons are understood functionally as having rights and obligations at law analogous to those of natural persons. The fact that the legal idea of the corporation developed historically along these lines argues at least for the initial plausibility of the suggested analogy.

The second reason is that while the corporation may have rights and powers as well as duties, these cannot be exercised except by persons acting as corporate agents. This instrumental function of persons within the corporation framework includes not

236

only management but employees as well. In fact, by extension, two
other types of persons can be included as effecting corporate activity, the investor and the consumer. In speaking of the "active
wealth" of corporate management, Berle and Means say[1] "The group
in control of a large modern corporation is astride an organism
which has little real value except as it continues to function
[and]... is dependent for [its life] on its security holders, ...
workers and consumers, but most of all on [its] mainspring, --
'control'." (p. 348) Corporate activity is surrounded by, shot
through with and totally dependent upon the activities of persons
and this leads to the third and best reason for thinking of corporate activity on analogy with persons.

Originally corporations were the instruments of the people
who formed them but in their modern development it is the people
who have become instruments of corporate purposes. The result has
been a widespread loss of freedom by persons. But perhaps more
important is the loss of power -- the sense of being reduced to
something less than a person should be, or even, used to be. The
classic example is the consumer with a just complaint looking for
satisfaction. Locating someone with responsibility is no easy
job. There are exceptions, but very often you get nowhere unless
you are willing to make an occupation of your complaint and a long-
term investment of time. The only real defense against being completely reduced is to consider corporations to be like persons, to
hold them responsible to ourselves and society in the same way that
persons are held responsible to each other and to society in general. Nothing will dehumanize our society more completely than to
have the most powerful elements in that society treated and thought
about in non-human ways. When I first began to study philosophy
I remember reading that anthropomorphism, the attributing of human
characteristics to non-human things, was unscientific and wrong.
This complaint is at least as old as Zenophanes who, about 510 B.C.,
vilified Homer for writing about the gods in that way. And it must
be admitted there is some "right reason" in the complaint. None
the less, there are limits and where human creations such as society
and its institutions are concerned, a certain bedrock anthropomorphism is positive virtue, in the absence of which, for man, to borrow a phrase, "nothing beside remains."

There is yet a further reason for taking the proposed analogy
seriously in the way we talk about corporations and their activities
(the aforementioned phrase "corporate responsibility" is a case in
point). So far as I know no one tries to show that any kind of
finite being other than humans can be responsible and even that is
roundly debated every so often. To attribute responsibility to
corporations suggests that proposed analogy, whether correctly or
incorrectly.

237

Lastly, consider as example the wording of the Sherman Anti-Trust Act of 1890:

> Every person who shall monopolize, or attempt to
> monopolize, or combine or conspire with any other
> person or persons to monopolize any part of the trade
> or commerce among the several states, or with foreign
> nations, shall be guilty of a misdemeanor...."

Only persons can "combine", "conspire" or even "be guilty".

A "caveat" is appropriate before proceeding: I am not saying that a corporation _is_ a person, but only that in certain ways a corporation is _like_ a person, and, since the corporation is a human creation and only persons can be responsible, if we want the corporation to be responsible, we ought to take these ways of being alike very seriously.

Prior to the historic study of Berle and Means in 1934, entitled The Modern Corporation and Private Property, it was assumed that the corporation was an instrument of its owners and that it would operate within the purposes for which the owners formed it. As long as this instrumental relationship obtained the locus of responsibility for corporate action was simply assignable to the owners. But as the separation of ownership from control developes, this traditional locus of responsibility evaporates. The result has been likened to a corporate Frankenstein monster, having all the power of pooled resources, the ability to perpetuate its own power and no responsibility for its actions beyond what the law covers. The prospects for the misuse of such power are at least as frightening for ordinary mortals as was the older and less so-phisticated era of the "robber barons". There are those who in the fact of this situation see nothing but a tight-fisted set of laws for the protection of society. And of course much of the regulation that has come about through the years has been in response to just such a peril. I shall turn to the topic of regulation later on, but want to return at present to the separation of ownership and control for a longer look.

Berle and Means point out that when this split comes about the purposes of the managers need no longer be those of the owners (p. 121ff). There is general agreement that corporate objectives in the post-World War II era have been "survival, growth, profit, economic contributions and social obligations" (Luthans and Hodgetts, p. 38).[2] Obviously, the order listed is from the most to the least basic. The interesting thing about this list of objectives is how it differs from the objectives of corporations prior to the coming about of the split. As instruments, corporate goals were obviously those of the owners, presumably profits. But with

238

the split between ownership and control something striking comes
about which is implicit in the objectives of survival and growth
and indicative of an important stage in the development of the corporate idea; with the coming of the split, the corporation clearly
becomes an end-in-itself with its own objectives. Management ac-
quires a vested interest in the survival of the corporation it
controls and the giving of an adequate return on investment to the
owners becomes just one of the conditions of survival. And, since
nothing stands still, growth is also a condition of survival as
well as of increased power for management.

Previously, in mentioning the results of the split, it was
noted that its occurrance removed the traditional grounds of responsibility, the owners, from the picture leaving a monster on the
loose. That is partly true, but there is more to the story. For
when the split made the corporation an end-in-itself, apart from
the ends of the owners, it created the basic condition without
which there can be no responsibility whatsoever. The corporation
becomes something in its own right. Prior to that point, the
courts' consideration of corporations as persons was an acknowledged fiction. Since then, the basic building block of responsible
activity, self-standing individuality, has been present. Or put
in another way, the courts have developed the idea of the corporation on analogy with the person for several hundred years and in
large part this development has occurred in our country over the
last one hundred and seventy-five years. As long ago as 1819 in
Dartmouth College vs. Woodward, Chief Justice Marshall, referring
to the "artificial being" of the corporation, wrote of the properties of such being,

> Among the most important are immortality, and if the
> expression may be allowed, individuality; properties
> by which a perpetual succession of many persons are
> considered as the same, and may act as a single in-
> dividual. They enable a corporation to manage its
> own affairs....[3]

But it wasn't until the split between ownership and control came
about that the independent status which is a precondition of personhood came into existence. (The parallel between the corporation
and the nation state in this light is compelling and the corporation
has been characterized, especially in its multinational form, as
being like a nation state in its independence. But this goes beyond present concern.)

There is a further point to be made concerning the split
however. The classical tradition in economics holds firmly to the
view that the primary objective of the corporation should be the

239

maximization of profits. For an instrument of the owner's purpose, maximization of profit must mean one thing, the fulfillment of the owner's purpose, presumably profits. But for an end-in-itself, maximization of profits takes on a wholly different meaning; at best profit becomes a means to the goals of survival and growth. To put it in language which I will use a little later on, as instrument, corporate activity is purely acquisitive. As end-in-itself, however, corporate activity aims first at satisfying those demands which must be met to maintain itself. The concern for profit is very different before and after. The former is analogous to pure egoism in human behavior while the latter involves not only self-regarding but other-regarding motives as well. As has been suggested, the latter "makes 'profit' more than an economic concept."

It is one thing to point out that with the split the corporation becomes an end-in-itself, an individual, but the problem of responsibility remains. John Maurice Clark in <u>The Ethical Basis Of Economic Freedom</u> (Westport, Ct., The Kazanjian Economics Foundation, Inc. 1955) poses the problem as follows:

> To talk of the business corporation as facing a 'crisis of legitimacy' does not imply that there exists any significant controversy as to whether it should exist; there is none. Rather it is to suggest that corporate leaders are being confronted with two basic questions: By what right do you who manage these huge corporations exercise your power? And what means do we have to insure that corporate power will be exercised in accord with some generally accepted notion of the public interest? (pp. 128-9)

Clark expresses the matter in terms of the distinction between "public" and "private" and looks for some assurance that corporations will be concerned with the former and not merely the latter interest. In traditional moral terms this is the problem of egoism and altruism in the field of human motivation and behavior and it is the nub of the notion of obligation.

The ground for the analogy between corporations and persons lies in the conception of activity which is common to both. Responsibility has to do with the activity of persons and it is the activity of corporations which needs to be made responsible.

The best analysis of activity that I am aware of appears in a little book by Alburey Castell entitled <u>The Self in Philosophy</u>[4] and occurs in the context of distinguishing activity from process. In the exposition that follows, the ideas are Castell's and my summary explication of them aims at a faithful rendering though I may miss the mark. But the uses to which they are put are upon my own head.

Castell begins by considering astronomy, the science which studies the nature and movements of the solar system. Such solar movement is a process. Astronomizing, on the other hand, is the discipline which studies the nature and movements of the solar system. Such a discipline is an activity and the following characteristics belong to activity but not to process. Activity is fallible, purposive, experimental, critical (performed by reference to criteria), reasoned (asks for justification), a locus for choice, a locus for responsibility, corrigible, meaningful, judgmental, presuppositioned, requires the distinction between real and ideal, educable, and involves response to challenge.[5] Clearly some of these presuppose or involve others but before entering into such comparisons to flesh out the nature of activity, we must follow Castell's argument one step further.

For Castell, it seems true beyond question that there are activities, and I tend to agree, because the denial of activity is itself an activity.[6] Notice, this is not a proof of activity, it merely cuts the ground from under the opposition in the same way the skeptic is silenced (what C. I. Lewis called a "pragmatic contradiction").[7]

While all of those characteristics listed above are important in that they reveal the differing aspects of activity some of them mark out the outlines more clearly than others. Such, for example, is "purposiveness" - all activity is directed towards some end. (We will speak of "purposive activity" throughout this paper just to keep this characteristic of activity in front of us.) Further, purposive activity is "critical" in that certain criteria are used to assess progress towards the goal. Perhaps the most important characteristic of activity is that it has "presuppositions" - that is, there are certain conditions which must be the case or the activity in question is not possible. As an example, consider the so-called three laws of thought; -Identity, Non-contradiction and the Excluded Middle. If you reflect upon the activity of thinking you will see that there can be no thinking -- dreaming or fantasy perhaps -- but no thinking unless these three laws are adhered to. Thinking presupposes them. It is perhaps not as informative to say that these laws are true for all thought as to say that these laws are normative for all thinking. C. I. Lewis observed that they constitute "the morality of thought".[8]

Being a "locus of choice" is another characteristic of purposive activity - if I cannot choose which measures will further my purpose and ignore those that do not, there can be no purposive activity. Freedom of choice, then, is a presupposition of pur-

241

posive activity. Notice, this is not a proof of freedom, there can be none. But for me to be able to do what I'm doing in writing this paper it is necessary that I be free to choose.

There are other presuppositions of purposive activity - conditions necessary for it to come about. Since purposive activity involves someone doing something in some context, there are two groups of necessary conditions, those pertaining to the agent and those pertaining to the context or world of the agent. We have already seen that "freedom" pertains to the agent, but since freedom would amount to nothing unless there were real alternatives, the world of the agent must contain real "multiplicity". In summary fashion, the other two conditions pertaining to the world are "continuity", -- in a world of atomistic states the perdurance of directed effort would not be possible, and "structure", -- unless there were stable connections between the things of the world no goal could ever be attained and you couldn't go about getting somewhere from anywhere else. The other two conditions pertaining to the agent are "concern", -- an agent must be able to exhibit continuous concern to carry out purposive activity, and "consistency", -- an agent must act in a stable and connected manner, that is, not in a willy-nilly sort of way and not in such a way as to cut the ground from under his previous actions. By far the most important of these presuppositions of purposive activity are "freedom" and "multiplicity" for with them come the possibility of choosing wrongly as well as rightly. But notice, there are two senses of choosing rightly or wrongly here. In one sense, with reference to fulfilling ones purpose, choice may be right or wrong. But in another sense, choice may be right or wrong as it either maintains or cuts the ground from under the very possibility of purposive activity itself.

It will have become clear at this point that I am on the edge of an interpretation of the Kantian ethic. I wish to acknowledge this and to say something about why it is important to our topic.

The problem of the legitimacy of corporate power raised by the separation of ownership and control is not a new problem. Rather, it is a species of a very familiar problem in the modern world. In the so-called Modern Period in Western European Civilization it is almost a truism to say that the basic interest has been with the individuality of man. This, of course, translates directly into the importance of freedom and is expressed in the Protestant Reformation as well as the political theory of the state. The difficulty has been to square authority and obligation with the fact of freedom so as not to undercut the integrity and independence of the individual. This is not easy to do as a moment's reflection will show.

242

Of all the theories of political and social organization put
forward in the last four hundred years to answer this difficulty
only that of Kant sets out to locate the source of authority and
obligation within the individual himself. This means that for
Kant the individual is ultimate in ways which I will make clear and
which bear, I believe, very heavily upon our problem of corporate
responsibility and the worth of the analogy between corporations
and persons suggested in this paper.

As I was saying, freedom to choose makes attaining your goal
possible, but it also means you can undercut the possibility of
your own activity - i.e., you can vote away your right to vote.

It is one thing when external conditions remove the possibility of purposive activity, but it is quite another when you by
your action undercut those possibilities for yourself. Just as
the laws of thought are normative for that special kind of purposive activity called thinking, so there are similar conditions
which are normative, obligatory for purposive activity in general.
It is the maintenance of these conditions of purposive activity
which is constitutive of responsible personhood. Each of us discovers these by reflection upon those conditions without which
purposive activity would be impossible. It is this capacity in
each of us to carry out purposive activity, and, by reflecting
upon such activity while engaged in it, to recognize the enabling
conditions of it as obligatory, that constitutes the moral dimension of human nature. Kant calls this capacity "practical reason"
and characterizes its enabling conditions as "categorical" and un-
conditionally imperative. This doesn't mean that you _must_ do
something, you have the power of choice, but it does mean that
you _ought_ to do something on pain of undercutting your own nature
as responsible person, if you don't. One of Kant's examples: it
is wrong to lie because if everyone could lie there would be no
truth and lying would lose its meaning. This is generalized as
"act so that the principle of your action can be universalized
without self-contradiction", and called the Categorical Imperative.
In contemporary ethical theory this is the criterion of universalizability, nothing is right for me unless it would be right
for everyone, and captures very well the usual moral meaning of
the term "right". But the connection between lying and purposive
activity can best be seen if we take universalization to apply
only to my own behavior. It would be right for me to lie in this
instance only if it would be right for me to lie in every instance,
to be a consistent and concerned liar.[9] If you had to lie all the
time, you couldn't do anything, nothing would have any meaning and
purposive activity would be impossible.

I do not believe that the criterion of universalizability
relies so much upon an act being right for me only if right for

all others - which would place the criterion of obligation outside of the individual - as much as it relies upon the traditional notion that the essential attributes of a thing are those which are always present whenever the thing in question is present - that is, lying can only be moral, an essential, rather than an accidental, part of the moral, if it can be present in or consistent with all instances of the moral, in this case, with the dimension of purposive activity. Of course, lying makes utter nonsense of this dimension, and each individual upon reflection can see this for himself.

The considerations just mentioned lead to one of the most important and I think striking aspects of this view of individual responsibility. The conditions which maintain the possibility for me to be responsible are the conditions which maintain that possibility for all persons. The best example I can give of this idea comes from an understanding of the slogan "Support Your Better Business Bureau" and the realization of how best this can be done. It is widely recognized that the best way to give such support is to conduct your business affairs in an honest manner because by so doing you establish a climate in which other businesses and your own can do likewise. In short, the conditions which best support you in your purposive corporate activity are the ones which best support all purposive corporate activity. We are all involved in maintaining the conditions of personal responsibility for ourselves as well as for others. It would seem that this is the primary and supportive relationship of society to its members and of the members to each other and to themselves. Off hand, I can think of no duties founded on other grounds than these.

There are those who would found corporate responsibility upon a contractual agreement between the corporation and the community, but reflection upon what such a contract presupposes on the part of the parties to it, will, I believe, lead us back to the foundations we have just been considering.

There are a number of very fine books on the corporate problem whose authors at the outset deny the adequacy of treating the corporation as a person in the manner of the law. They often hold that such a way of looking at corporate enterprise may have been useful and meaningful in earlier conditions of our history, but that such is no longer the case. And then they proceed very carefully to suggest ways and means of making corporate activity more critical, more reflective, more broadly concerned and purposive, in a word, more responsible in exactly the functional and organic ways that have been suggested here. Such proposals as upgrading and standardizing the corporate charter, giving the responsibility of the board of directors an active and critical dimension and many others, all of which suggest nothing so much

244

as the characteristics of the purposive activity of responsible persons sketched previously. To say that the corporation is like a person is not the anatomical comparison so dear to the middle ages and the early modern era with the monarch as the head of the body politic nor even of the military with the cavalry as the eyes and ears of the army. Rather, it is a thoroughly functional analogy, a self-conscious, reflective and purposive way of acting, and to my mind it is like nothing so much as the purposive activity of responsible persons. It is often pointed out that there has been an organizational, and managerial revolution in the last forty years and much of it is organic in nature and functional in aim in just this way.

Professor James Coleman in comparing the purposes established in the corporate charter under which the corporation must act with the motives of persons makes the excellent point that the purposes of a corporation are so much more simple and monolithic than the complex of motives and sensibilities of the average person that they tend to dominate and cancel out the interests of natural persons in our community.[10] It would seem that in our present era of concern with ecological, consumer and equal rights we are watching the upgrading of corporate sensibility and motivation to a level more nearly commensurate with the complex sensibilities needed by responsible persons.

So far I have presented a conception of activity which is purposive, reflective, and presuppositioned. I have been concerned primarily with the latter characteristics, the presuppositions of activity, as the locus of obligation and the source of responsibility and have called this aspect the maintenance dimension of activity. Freedom of choice brings about concern with moral matters of maintenance. And in the light of this, purposive activity is seen to be double-ended. No matter to what external end activity may be directed, there are inner conditions of activity itself which must be maintained. This requirement is best expressed in Kant's Third formulation of the categorical imperative: "act so as to treat humanity, both in your own person and in that of another as an end and never as a means only." With respect to our treatment of others and ourselves this statement very nearly says it all.

While this inner purposiveness or maintenance function is neither derived from nor dependent upon the external ends of activity, the obligation to be concerned with the acquisitive or external dimension stems from the maintenance function and is categorical.[11] Man is not independent, he has needs and these ought to be taken into account and purposive activity is goal oriented. Then too, there are forces outside as well as inside us which can effect our activity for good or evil and constitute opportunity or peril. It is here that the whole utilitarian, cost-

benefit form of analysis in terms of consequences comes in but
within the framework of the moral concern with maintenance. The
concern is categorical but assessments of individual ends and
their consequences within that concern, are complex, chancy, and
very often endlessly arguable. While each individual matter of
prudence is not categorically obligatory, the general concern with
prudence as such is one of the presuppositions of purposive activity and the maintenance dimension. It is on these grounds for
example, that a corporation moving into a new community should take
seriously the concerns of that community even though their own
line of business may be unrelated. And it is in these terms that
the myriad possible ends that present themselves for choice are
assessed both in their expected consequences and in the light of
the presuppositions of purposive activity "both in your own person and in that of another," and accepted or rejected. It is a-
gainst the moral backdrop of the maintenance dimension of purposive activity that contracts involving the interests of the
parties to them can be entered into in good faith. And it is
against this dimension that the general rights and duties of persons whether stockholders, employees, consumers or the corporate
entities themselves can be legitimately marked out.

     In the rest of this paper I want to be concerned with the
topic of regulation as it relates to the analogy suggested and the
ideas set forth. As might be expected from the historical comments
made earlier, it is the topic of regulation which poses the
severest challenge to the analogy we are considering. To repeat
the question in the quote above from John Maurice Clark, "...what
means do we have to insure that corporate power will be exercised
in accord with some generally accepted notion of the public interest?" It is clear that there are only three avenues of approach to this problem of regulation: the corporate charter, the
persons who carry on the corporation's business and the community
itself.

     The corporate charter could go a long way towards insuring
responsible behavior and could very well specify certain general
conditions of activity as well as the external goals of the activity. But the present chartering by state on a competitive basis
gives little hope for the upgrading and standardizing of charters.
However, closely akin to charter provisions are the by-laws and
operating policies which corporations establish for themselves.
This is a very important source of improvement because it is almost a rule of thumb that if a corporation doesn't take steps to
control its own operations, it is inviting outside regulation.
The commonest complaint of the corporate community against regulation is that it robs them of the freedom of decision needed to
carry on business properly. There is an extremely significant
truth here; regulation deprives them of their ability to act re-

sponsibly. It can, but need it do so?

The very heart of responsible activity is the phenomenon of
self-regulation; such activity is "critical", that is, it is performed with reference to standards for guiding choice. In the
bringing up our children we cannot produce responsible behavior
without extending them the freedom to exercise such critical choice.
Ham-handed regulation of our children's behavior can preclude the
possibility of their ever being really responsible. This is no
apology for a standard-less permissiveness, just the recognition
that in matters of regulation the community can throw the baby
out with the bath water. The power to regulate is the power to
destroy and we must regulate so as to allow the freedom and
autonomy needed for responsible activity. And this is where the
shoe pinches, for the very possibility of responsible action by
any person includes the possibility of irresponsible action, the
moral includes the immoral within it as possibility. Considering
the power and influence which corporations exert upon society this
is not a prospect to be viewed lightly. And yet I see no complete
remedy from the outside for this risk without slowly but surely
reducing the areas in which purposive activity as spoken of here
will even be possible. Again, this is not an apology for corporate
freedom. Much regulation, enabling as well as restricting and
prohibiting, is both possible and desirable, but the capacity to
be an end-in-itself must not be removed or else the conditions of
purposive activity by responsible persons will be severely crippled
in our society. It is for this reason that many business firms
are trying to be self-governing and set standards of their own.
There are different levels or kinds of regulation and we should
look at them briefly in the light of our analogy.

The surest way of regulating the flow of traffic across the
front yard is to fence it in. If the threat is from small children, unruly mobs or any and all free-wandering animals, you may
have to do just that. However, if the threat is from the comings
and goings of individual people in daily commerce, signs saying
"Keep off the Grass" located strategically may well do the job.
But notice, this form of regulation presupposes something about
the regulated other than the capacity to move around. It requires
the ability to read and understand the sign as well as the capacity
to see the meaning as applying to the person reading the sign,
"this means me", and the ability to direct my movements in con-
formity with the message. This type of regulation, simple as it
is, requires purposive activity on the part of the regulated to
carry it out. The very same assumptions are in force with laws
and regulations, except that the problem is more difficult. Because the conditions stipulated in laws and regulations are
general in nature and because those being regulated are always
in some particular situation a judgment must be made that this

247

situation comes under this regulation and not some other and this requires choice and critical activity. As mentioned before, you can regulate by requiring that certain things be taken into account (pollution) or not be taken into account (race, color or creed) in the decision process and the ensuing activities. This narrows the available options, puts uninteresting consequences behind non-compliance and sharpens the sensibilities of those involved. And as long as such regulation doesn't get on the other side of what are "reasonable" operating conditions in a given industry, regulation and responsibility can go hand in hand. The relationship of government regulatory agencies and the industries they regulate is much in the public eye at the moment and rightly so.

You can put the question another way: Is the public interest so narrow and confining that there is no room within it for private interest? And we have that peculiar combination of business and government, the private-public corporation, which draws its initiative and techniques from the private sector and its accountability procedures from the public. Or perhaps one of the most important public interests is exactly the preservation of the enabling conditions of private interest? It is perhaps worth noting in passing that that is the main function of a bill of rights, a public document grounding the rights and duties of each.

The degree to which this latter question is answered in the affirmative is the degree to which the problem of regulation has a large dimension of education within it. We often think we lay down the conditions for responsible activity by just leaving the room needed for such activity and we are often tragically disappointed by our children, by our cities, where the pressures against civilized behavior increase daily, and even by our government. We are learning however, that we have to get inside the decision activity with our corporations not to dictate restrictions so much as to instill sensitivity to the awareness of the basic values and conditions that permit responsibility and the freedom that goes with it for everyone.

By way of summary, the common ground for the analogy between corporations and persons lies in the nature of activity and activity is the only basis for responsibility. Activity is distinguished from process in that it is, among other things, purposive, critical, involves choice and has presuppositions. Reflection upon activity reveals its double-endedness - it aims to acquire some thing or condition extrinsic to it while maintaining itself in so doing. Hence, there are external conditions of purposive activity as well as internal conditions. The external conditions are multiplicity, continuity and structure. The internal conditions are freedom, concern and consistency, and these

248

latter three are normative for purposive activity in that they embody the conditions without which there would be no purposive activity and no responsibility. And because these are the general conditions of all purposive and responsible activity and not just my own, they constitute the moral dimension for man.

I have been laying out the conditions of the class of purposive activities, have pointed out the presuppositions which are normative for this class and have taken membership in this class as the locus of responsibility. But the question remains: What makes the conditions of the class of purposive activities obligatory and necessary for the individual? Such obligation would impinge only upon members of the class and could be considered as only hypothetical and not categorical for each or any individual. But in so far as human beings carry on purposive activity, and a good case can be made that such activity is descriptive of the peculiarly human, these norms apply to what humans do, and the obligation can be seen to apply to anyone so engaged by reflection upon the conditions of his own engagement. I doubt that I can fail to be purposive in my behavior and still remain responsibly human, and I recognize this responsibility as applying to all members of the class, including myself. But each individual must recognize this for himself.[12]

In conclusion it could be argued that the development of the corporate idea and structure has increasingly taken on the character of persons. Since they are conceived by, activated by and reflect the purposes of persons, it would be unlikely that they should do otherwise. And this tendency has increased in the face of the mounting need and pressure to make corporate activity responsible. The continued upgrading of their reflective and critical awareness of the conditions of their own purposive activity as being the conditions for any such purposive activity will strengthen the comparison. Only in this way can the difficult combination of individual initiative and choice and the awareness and sensitivity to the enabling conditions of the human and the corporate community and the values they reflect be brought about. Who knows, under the continuing pressure of the general community and with an increased awareness of the norms to be taken seriously backed by sanctions where needed, corporate purposive activity might wind up among the most responsible activities in the community of persons. Considering the power it possesses for good and evil, it needs to be. Only in this way can corporations be good to work for and to live with.

NOTES

1. The Modern Corporation and Private Property, Berle,

Adolf A. Jr. and Means, Gardner C., New York: The Macmillan
Company, 1934.

2. Compare: "As a permanent institution, the large corporation is developing long-term goals such as survival, growth, and
increasing respect and acceptance by the public." Social Responsibility of Business Corporations, Research and Policy Committee,
Committee for Economic Development, #42, June 1971, p. 22.

3. 17 U.S. (4 Wheat.) 518 (1819).

4. The Self in Philosophy, Castell, Alburey, New York: The
Macmillan Company, 1965, Chapter 2 & 3.

5. Ibid., pp. 21-25.

6. Ibid., p. 26f.

7. Values and Imperatives, Lewis, Clarence I., John Lange
(ed.) Stanford, Ca.: Stanford University Press, 1969, p. 124.

8. Classroom remark, Harvard, 1948.

9. Cf. Foundations of the Metaphysics of Morals, Kant, I.,
L. W. Beck (trans.), New York: The Library of the Liberal Arts,
Bobbs-Merrill Co., 1959, p. 58. "The action which can be compatible
with the autonomy of the will is permitted; that which does not
agree with it is prohibited." and my application of it only to
my own behavior as illustration fulfills the universalizability
conditions.

10. Power and the Structure of Society, pp. 49, 49fn, 50.

11. Cf. The Ground and Nature of the Right, Lewis, Clarence
I., New York: Columbia University Press, 1955, p. 82; "The Hypo-
thetical Imperative," The Philosophical Review, Vol. LXXII, No. 4,
Oct. 1973, pp. 429-450.

12. This recognition of something as necessarily valid for
and impinging upon myself is an example of the classical criteria
of knowledge, knowing that you know, and it occurs in the reflective
framework brought to the fore by Descartes' Cogito.

DISCUSSION

COMMENT: I'd like to address myself to Professor Wilbur. First of all, I'd like to say that I'm sympathetic with the point of view that you take. My only question has to do with the reasons for your view. I'd like to make two challenges to your suggestion that there's an analogy which can be drawn between the individual and the corporation. As I understand it, you argue that because corporations, just as individuals, are purposive, rational, experimental, etc., that an analogy can be made between them. Isn't it true though that corporations don't bear some characteristics which individuals do have and which we often, as a matter of fact, associate with morality. For example, corporations can't love, show compassion, sympathize, and so on. So, I guess one question would be why the former set of characteristics and not the latter is the basis for the analogy. The second challenge is this: Insofar as we assume the corporation is rational, how are we to regard the American Tobacco Corporation, or a corporation of that sort, which seems to just lumber ahead in the face of all sorts of evidence testifying to the damages of cigarette smoking by defending cigarette smoking, pursuing profits, and so on?

WILBUR: Well, let me answer the second one first. Probably you know that if you are Hindu, you couldn't be a butcher. And I think the same thing applies here. You can engage in many different forms of making a livelihood, but in some of them you might be doing your soul no good. And I guess that I feel the same way about the tobacco company. Those may be hard words, but every time I hear their arguments against the evidence that smoking does cause cancer, I begin to wonder. And there's no argument that I can give there. That whole thing is just beyond the pale of what I would take to be moral. That's the answer to that, from my point of view. Notice they've diversified themselves tremendously over the last ten years. Secondly, however, my concern is with responsibility, with what I take to be the moral. It's nice if you don't beat your mother because you love her, but I don't know as any moral quality is reflected by those grounds. Maybe my Kantianism in this sense comes out here. It's very nice if one loves one's mother or feels compassion for people, and we try to bring people up who feel that way. But, at the same time, what I was trying to do is give some kind of rational basis for obligation so that one could say, "Why should I be responsible?" or "What is my obligation?" and have a reasoned answer. It's no answer to say: "Well, if you feel compassion, you'll know what I'm talking about. If you don't feel compassion, I'm sorry for you." From the point of view of justification, love, compassion and sympathy are important, but

251

secondary, virtues.

COMMENT: I've got a question for Professor Wilbur that comes out of the third point of the Kantian theory. And that is, if we preserve this analogy completely between corporations and persons, one of our obligations to persons is that we treat them as ends, rather than as means. Should we also treat corporations as ends rather than as means and not seek their dissolution, for instance?

WILBUR: Well, after all, the courts do disband corporations, and for good reasons. They just don't say go away. They're tried or they're found wanting in some way and they are dissolved. Their ability to initiate activity is taken away. They are no longer ends in themselves in the business community.

COMMENT: But I, as a major stockholder in the American Tobacco Company, for example, couldn't do that.

WILBUR: No, I grant you that. Is there an analogy here between it and corporal punishment?

COMMENT: It's beginning to come that way, isn't it?

WILBUR: Well, it's in the same family if we're going to apply the analogy. But I'm not quite sure about corporal punishment. That one gives me some trouble, the problem being that I have to treat everybody, including myself, as an end even if everyone doesn't treat everyone else as an end. The condition of being treated as as end makes us individuals or persons. It begins to appear that reason is a social affair. In other words, one cannot be a reasonable creature in a community of unreasonable people. Try it, try being liberal in a group of conservatives and see what happens. It won't work. There must be reciprocity between the individual and the social in this matter. I have to be in a community where other people respect these same requirements. This is one reason why the universality of the conditions of the moral is to be emphasized.

COMMENT: But, I still bring up the major question that I see, and that is, we treat the people as ends rather than as means because, I suspect from Kant, God made them. But if we're going to treat corporations as ends, assuming they're nice law-abiding corporations, rather than as means, surely we can dissolve them if we wish. But, if they're something more than that, maybe God made them too.

WILBUR: Well, at that point, the analogy begins to run into trouble. But, I'm not bothered by the question for this reason: If we can increase the sensibilities of corporations, for instance, make them write operating procedures which take into account the fact that there are reflective human creatures that are ends in themselves that work for them and are operating in the market- place in conjunction with other reflective human beings, then it seems to me people can operate in those corporations much more ef- fectively than they can in a more monolithic type of organization with respect to motivation. Now, maybe that's not clear. What I'm trying to say is, the trouble with most corporations is that they have very narrow and monolithic motivations which are built into their stated purposes and they go on fulfilling those purposes come hell or high water. No human being can operate that way. You and I come into contact with each other and we are mutually ad- justing our expectations and hopes all the time as we operate. It is very much more complex. And it is very nice to say, "Well, I'm an executive and must work here in terms of these corporate pur- poses." But many times they undercut the responsible human acti- vity they require. The problem of an executive, who has to do things for a company that he might not approve of from his own moral point of view, is a very basic one in our society. Any activity which fails to take into account the conditions of its own possibility is immoral. If, in this manner, you upgrade the sensibilities and ways in which the purposes and rules are set up within the corporation itself, I take it that problem would be alleviated somewhat, maybe not ever completely, but it would be alleviated.

COMMENT: Professor Oelschlaeger, after you presented your two models of classical economics, you moved on to another model. I was wondering how that really works. You did talk about vectors and taking into account the various vectors, but isn't that seeing some sort of automatic measures that are taking place there or working there to counterbalance various other factors?

OELSCHLAEGER: That was the third model, the Social Environment Model. The critique essentially of the first two models was that they assume some sort of mechanism exists to balance off the kinds of interest that businessmen have with other sorts of interest in the community at large. Yet neither the classical nor managerial models of social responsibility can identify or describe any em- pirical process by which a balance of interests might be struck. The advantage of the Social Environment Model is that it does not make a covert appeal either to a preestablished harmony of in- terests or to the humanitarian propensities of businessmen. Rather, this model emphasizes that solving public interest problems, such as pollution, necessitates various interest groups, including business, working toward a consensus as to what is in the general interest. When the general interest can be identified, then, and only then, does there exist a standard which will define corporate social responsibility. Once defined, then the businessman is obligated to live up to that standard.

COMMENT: Just a quick comment about Mr. Wilbur's response to the two questions that he got. To quote an old teacher of mine, Bill Frankman, "I'm more on your side than you are." It seems to me that there's a much stronger way that those two questions could be responded to. The analogy is not a partial one. It's a full analogy, and we're not to accept the implications of it right down the line. It doesn't seem to me that there's any asymmetry between certain features of human psychology and corporate capacity to love or show compassion, or whatever. It seems to me that there are structural analogs for all of those human psychological capacities and it also seems to me that we're going to have to bite the bullet on the question of whether corporations ought to be respected as persons as well. I'm prepared to bite that bullet. I don't see any nasty implications just yet why we shouldn't. I think organizations deserve respect just as persons deserve respect. The ultimate, the bottom line of this kind of view, I think, is the recognition that persons, in a very real sense, are themselves organizations.

WILBUR: Yes, that's turning the analogy around. But, it has to work both ways.

SESSION X

"Private Property and the Corporation"

Lawrence Becker
Professor of Philosophy and Religion
Hollins College (Virginia)

James V. Fisher
Professor of Philosophy
Bentley College

Barry A. Stein
Managing Partner
Goodmeasure, Inc.

LAWRENCE C. BECKER

Property Theory and the Corporation

My recent work on property has had two foci -- one on the
concept of a property right itself, the other on the general justification which can be offered for systems of private property
rights.[1] The former focus -- on the concept of a property right --
has a direct bearing on the issues of this conference because it
can shed light on two perplexing questions: first, on the question
of who owns the corporation; and second, on the question of the
moral obligations of corporate managers. What I want to do here
is to rehearse briefly an analysis of the concept of a property
right, and then to show the relevance of that analysis to the
questions just mentioned.

I

I begin with the banality -- known to every first year law
student -- that a property right is always a bundle of rights;
rights to possess, rights to use, rights to exclude others from
a thing. But this banality is not very helpful -- even when
coupled with the realization that there must be many varieties of
property rights; some restricted to temporary possession and
limited use, for example, and others not. The most helpful place
to start, in getting an appreciation of the complexity of the concept of property, is with an analysis of the concept of ownership -- specifically, with a systematic exploration of the
varieties of ownership; the varieties of property rights.

A. M. Honoré (an Oxford legal philosopher) has produced an
illuminating analysis of the concept of full ownership.[2] I shall
use his analysis -- modified in some important ways -- as the basis
for explicating two theses about the concept of property: first,
that an idea of full, unlimited, private ownership of anything is
now and always has been largely a fiction; and second, that a
proper understanding of ownership arrangements in the real world
requires a systematic survey of the wide variety of "less than
full" ownership rights. (Throughout what follows, I will be
speaking just of legal rights, not moral ones.)

Property rights, as I think of them, then, are the rights
of ownership; and the rights of ownership may be conveniently
divided into the following elements:[3]

257

1) the right to possess a thing;
2) the right to use it for one's own benefit and enjoyment;
3) the right to manage it;
4) the right to the income from it;
5) the right to modify it (short of destroying it);
6) the right to consume or destroy it;
7) the right to transfer or abandon ownership;
8) the right to transmit ownership by a will.

When these eight rights are secured -- that is, when the state grants the possessor of such rights a legal immunity from expropriation of them -- then I shall say that full ownership exists. Full ownership, in other words, is having legally secured rights to possession, use, management, income, modification, consumption, alienation and transmission.[4] We must therefore add a ninth element to full ownership:

9) the right to security (immunity from expropriation).

Now it is clear that each of these elements of full ownership is typically subject to a wide variety of limitations. The right to security, for example -- that is, to immunity from expropriation -- is typically restricted by the state's power to tax, and by its right of eminent domain. Further, Honoré claims (I think correctly) that ownership, in all developed legal systems, includes some version or other of the following:

10) the specification of term -- that is, the specification of a time limit on the ownership rights (or, in the case of unlimited ownership, the absence of a time limit);
11) the prohibition of harmful use of the thing owned;
12) the liability (of the thing owned) to execution for debt; and
13) residuary rules, defining the disposition of abandoned property, for example.

Here again, it is clear that the elements can be defined in a wide variety of ways. For example, the prohibition of harmful use can sometimes be defined so as to require productive use -- anything less being considered harmful to society.

We therefore have two versions of full ownership:[5] one without limitations of any sort; the other with a wide variety of possible limitations. Either version of full ownership -- i.e., the unlimited or the limited version -- can be either private or public; and if private, it can be either individual, or joint, or common ownership. Think of the following tree:

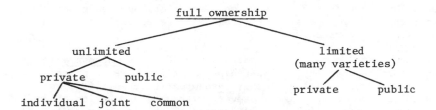

Except for rather trivial cases, it is clear that full unlimited ownership is a fiction. <u>Private</u> ownership is virtually
always limited by the state's power to tax and to take, by liability to execution for debt, by the prohibition of harmful use,
by limitations on transfer and transmission, and so on. <u>Public</u>
ownership is virtually always limited by the power of officials
(to the exclusion of others) to manage, possess, and use, for
example. So full, unlimited ownership is a rather empty notion
-- except as a zero point against which to describe the variety of
instances of full, <u>but limited</u>, ownership.

For present purposes, however, it is more important to describe the varieties of ownership which are limited in another
way -- the varieties of ownership which are less than full: the
varieties which include only a subset of the rights of ownership
I have listed. The new tree looks like this:

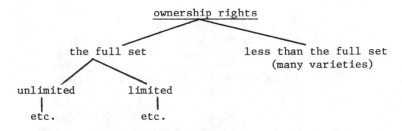

For example: when a trust fund is established for me, and I have
no management rights over the principal, I have a variety of ownership in that trust which is significantly less than full ownership.
The question is, then, what subsets of the rights of ownership
constitute varieties of (less than full) ownership?

I suggest that <u>any one</u> of the first eight rights -- <u>when</u>
<u>secured by an immunity against expropriation</u> -- constitutes a pro-
perty right. That is, I want to say that any <u>secured</u> right to
possess, or to use, or to manage, or to income, or to modify, or
to consume, or to transfer, or to transmit is <u>by itself</u> a property

right. My authority for this is merely our ordinary usage of the term property. I hope a brief remark will be sufficient to convince you I am correct.

Consider: surely the right to security is a _necessary_ ingredient in any variety of ownership. If a right -- to possess, use, or whatever -- is completely _unsecured_ (that is, if it can be withdrawn on any pretext whatever, without any question of due process or compensation), then it stretches things too much to speak of it as a property right. It is better regarded simply as a liberty, revocable at the pleasure of the state. But when any one of the rights of ownership _is_ secured (that is, when its revocation involves a question of due process or compensation or both) then it _is_ a property right in a sense recognized by our law -- that is, in a sense which brings it under the purview of the takings clause of the Fifth Amendment and/or the due process clauses of the Fifth and Fourteenth Amendments.

Now a moment's reflection will show that, if the foregoing analysis is correct, there are _very_ _many_ varieties of ownership -- over 4,000, in fact -- ranging from full, unlimited ownership through the varieties of full but limited ownership to the many types of less than full ownership.[6] The question now is: how does such an abstract analysis relate to the issues I mentioned at the outset: the ownership of the corporation and the moral obligations of managers?

II

First, take the question of who owns the corporation. This has been something of a puzzle to theorists, for the obvious reason that stockholders have such attenuated ownership rights. They are the natural candidates for owners (I think of a Texaco commercial which Bob Hope opens by saying something like: "Let me show you where some of Texaco's owners live" -- and then proceeds to show the houses of some minor stockholders.) Yet what rights of ownership do stockholders have? They have virtually no rights to possess or use corporate property; and virtually no rights to manage it. They do have limited rights to _income_. And they can transfer and transmit those rights. But the corporation's creditors have similar rights. So the claim that stockholders are "the" owners of the corporation is hollow. On the other hand, holding that the board of directors owns the corporation is just as unsatisfactory.

Now why does this matter? If a convenient set of legal fictions about corporate ownership is sufficient to keep things going, why quibble? The answer is that the identification of

260

owners has a direct bearing on the responsibilities of the corporation's managers -- at least as those responsibilities are defined in a social order such as ours. A manager's primary responsibility (as conceived by free market political theorists) is to act -- within the constraints imposed by morality and the law -- on behalf of, and for the benefit of, the owners. Milton Friedman, for example, in an oft-quoted passage, has oversimplified this into an obligation to make money for the stockholders.[7] That is inaccurate -- both because there may be things more important to the owners than making money, and because (as we have seen) the stockholders are not "the" owners of the corporation. But the general point is the same: the ideals of classical liberalism -- from Adam Smith through John Stuart Mill to Hayek and Friedman -- is that persons free to act out their own self-interests will maximize not only their own welfare but social welfare as well. Corporations are to be treated as persons in this scheme, and they too must be free to act out their self-interests -- meaning, of course, the interests of their owners.

Now I don't want to enter here into a discussion of the merits of classical liberalism. I merely want to point out the relevance -- to a discussion of corporate responsibility -- of an accurate answer to the question, "Who owns the corporation?" If it is not just the stockholders, then who is it? Some have said that the managers are the de facto owners; others have suggested that corporations are instances of collective ownership.[8]

In fact, I think it is evident from the analysis of the concept of property rights just given that the corporation is an intricate and interesting example of divided ownership,[9] and that the managers' responsibility -- at least as given by liberal political theory -- is to act for the benefit of all those owners. That means not just stockholders, but anyone with a secured (i.e., legally guaranteed) right to possession, use, management and so on in corporate property. And that includes any employee of the firm who has legally recognized job security (for example, by way of a collective bargaining agreement); it includes directors of the corporation, to the extent that their positions as directors are secured; it includes creditors; it includes employees without job security (to the extent that they are creditors); and it even includes customers who -- under the rules of negligence, product liability or contract law -- have been awarded judgments against the corporation. All of these people have property interests -- rights of ownership -- in the corporation.[10]

What emerges from this is a dramatically different picture of corporate managerial responsibility than that painted by the naive assumption that "the" owners of the corporation are its stockholders. Here it is evident that a decision, for example, to

forego profit maximization in order to keep a factory open should
not be seen as a magnanimous sacrifice of the owners' interests on
behalf of the corporation's social responsibility to its workers.
It should rather be seen as the resolution of a conflict between
the interests of one set of owners (stockholders) and another set
of owners (workers with job security arrangements). It is conflict
resolution analagous to that which goes on when one group of stockholders is interested in short-term income gains and another group
is interested in long-term development. Legally, it may be that
neither group has a claim on the managers' favor. Legally, the
managers may be able to make whatever choices they want. But we
would certainly say -- even from the narrow standpoint of classical
liberal theory -- that managers who simply failed to consider the
interests of a significant group of owners had failed to carry out
their managerial responsibilities.

    Now I suppose it might be objected to this whole line of
argument that it simply stretches the concept of ownership too
far. Why not just admit that there is a difference between having
a property interest (or right) in a thing and owning it -- and
that the modern corporation just doesn't have "owners" as we ordinarily use the term? Why not say instead that there are a lot
of people with different (and severely limited) bundles of property
rights in each corporation, and that the legal fictions of corporate personality and corporate ownership are simply convenient
ways of assigning rights, powers, duties and liabilities to this
essentially "ownerless" entity? Or, on the other hand, why not
take the view that since ownership of a corporation (as we ordinarily understand the term) cannot be assigned to any identifiable
subset of individuals in a society, corporations must be in fact
collectively owned by the society at large?

    My answer to these objections is, briefly, that they lack
the conceptual precision which is made possible by the notion of
divided ownership I have explicated, and that as a consequence,
the alternative accounts of corporate responsibility which they
suggest are not as satisfactory as they might be. In the first
place, it is seriously misleading to insist that owning something
-- as opposed to having a property right in it -- must mean that
one has full ownership of it. We just do not consistently speak
this way about ownership. My trust fund is mine -- whether I have
control of the principal or not, or can alienate it or not, or
transmit it or not. But it also belongs, in a very significant
sense, to the trustees. (If you think it doesn't, just try removing the trustees.) To fail to specify the division of ownership rights here is to ignore a powerful analytical tool for understanding the division of rights and responsibilities with regard
to the trust. Similarly for the corporation. Legally recognized
property rights in the corporation are divided, but that does not

262

mean we must think of it as ownerless any more than we must (or ought to) think of a trust as ownerless. The ownership rights in a large corporation are widely scattered across the population, but they do not rest equally on everyone -- and they do not rest at all on some people. To think of the corporation as collectively owned obscures this.

In short, it is not wise to distinguish ownership from having legally secured property rights (however limited these rights may be). It is not wise to do this because it encourages a misconception about the nature of most kinds of ownership recognized by our law (most kinds are instances of significantly less-than-full ownership). And it is not wise because it tends to obscure the division of rights and responsibilities which appear clearly only when we recognize the wide variety of types of less-than-full ownership.

III

Now I expect that it will also be objected to what I have said so far that the "theory" of corporate responsibility it suggests -- if, indeed, it can even be called a theory -- is pitifully thin. What of people who do not have property in the corporation? Is nothing owed to them? What of the impact of corporate activities on non-owners generally? Is there no place in the "theory" for concern about these things? If not, we have not gone very far beyond Milton Friedman's position.

My answer has two parts. First, we must recognize, after all, that property theory is only a small part of moral theory. Property rights are only a subset of moral rights: the duties of ownership are only a subset of moral duties; and so on. We must not expect to be able to develop a full-fledged moral theory of corporate responsibility from such a small subset of moral considerations.

For example, individuals have duties of citizenship which sometimes complement, sometimes conflict with, and sometimes supercede their property rights.[11] Individuals have obligations of reciprocity which similarly complement, conflict with and supercede their property rights.[12] And we ordinarily think that _moral_ individuals strive to exemplify various ideals -- of concern for others' welfare, and of generosity, and of commitment to social goals, for example.[13] Now it doesn't take a shift from individualist to communitarian political theory to see that the corporation as a fictional "person," in law, can have fictional duties of citizenship in law, and that it ought to live up to various ideals analogous to personal virtues. Those duties of citizenship,

263

and those virtues, may occasionally conflict with the property rights of owners, just as personal duties and personal virtues occasionally conflict with them.

In short, this panel is about the relation of property theory to corporate responsibility and power -- and I think that there is an important relation between the two. I just do not think that it is an all-important relation. I therefore oppose any attempt to exhaust the topic of corporate responsibility by discussing questions of ownership. There is more to the moral life than the rights and duties of property; and there is more to the question of corporate responsibility than the ownership obligations of corporate managers. That is the first part of my answer to the objection.

The second part is that, even with respect to ownership obligations, we have so far spoken only of rights and duties with respect to "insiders" -- rights and duties with respect to the people who have property rights in the corporation. There are, however, a few things -- not many, perhaps, but a few -- that property theory can contribute to a discussion of "outsiders" -- to a discussion of corporate responsibility to people who do not have property in the corporation.

First, there is, of course, the question of who ought to have legally secured ownership rights in the corporation -- that is, which people who are by current law defined as "outsiders" should be redefined as "insiders." The most vexing problems of this sort that we currently face are those concerning job and educational opportunities.[14] Is one's "place" in a medical school class a property interest? Is discrimination in hiring or admissions the denial of a property interest? These are questions which cannot be answered by property theory alone -- at least not by the purely analytical branch of property theory. We need a comprehensive view of what justifies a person in holding something as property, and how that justification fits into moral theory per se. (I have done work on the former issue, but as yet I have very little to offer on the latter.[15])

The second contribution property theory can make to the question of managerial responsibility to "outsiders" comes from the notion of harmful use. Recall that Honoré argues (and I think correctly) that all developed legal systems prohibit some harmful uses of private property.[16] It is this prohibition which provides part of the foundation for nuisance law, for example, and for tort liability generally. Just what things count as harmful uses, however, and which of those things should be prohibited, are matters of continuing controversy.

264

In particular, there are four crucial questions here for a theory of corporate responsibility: (1) How is 'harmful use' to be defined? (2) What harmful uses are to be permitted by law only upon the condition that the corporation is liable for the cost? (3) What harmful uses are to be permitted by law without making the corporation liable for the cost? And (4), what harmful uses of its property, permitted by law, ought the corporation nonetheless refuse to make? These are large questions and I have no carefully considered general answers to them. But let me conclude this presentation with a few very sketchy suggestions for further reflection on them.

In the first place, the leading problem in defining harmful uses is to decide whether the prohibition of harmful use ever, or always, includes the requirement of some "productive" use. Is a patent owner's refusal to market a needed product a harmful use? Is a strike -- by workers with job security -- a harmful use of property rights? Communitarians and individualists have fundamental differences on such issues, and these differences need to be worked on. Whether they can ever be resolved is difficult to foresee -- but it is not difficult to foresee that very little progress toward a resolution will be possible in the absence of sophisticated analysis of the concepts of harmful and productive use. If such analyses exist -- analyses, that is, which are not just self-serving set-ups for either libertarian or communitarian theories -- then I am not aware of them.

Secondly, on the questions of what harmful uses should be permitted with or without corporate liability for the cost, the best recent work comes from lawyers and economists working on the problems of social costs and their relation to liability rules.[17] Much of that work is at present very narrowly conceived -- e.g., within the assumptions of welfare economics or public choice theory -- but it is useful nonetheless.

And finally, on the question of what harmful uses a corporation ought morally to refrain from -- even though they are permitted by law -- I think property theory itself has very little to offer. Here I can only repeat what I said earlier: there is more to the good life than the joys of ownership; and more to the moral life than the rights and duties of property.

NOTES

1. See my Property Rights: Philosophic Foundations (London and Boston, Routledge & Kegan Paul, 1977).
2. A. M. Honoré, "Ownership" in A. G. Guest (ed.) Oxford Essays in Jurisprudence (Oxford, Clarendon Press, 1961), pp. 107-147.

3.   It should be noted that Honoré combines elements 5, 6, and 7 below into one, which he calls "the right to the capital." See Honoré, op. cit., pp. 118-119.   I think these three rights should be kept separate, for they are often assigned to different people.

4.   Here again I depart from Honoré's presentation.   He treats all the elements in his analysis as "incidents of full ownership."   I prefer to divide them into rights of ownership and (standard) limitations on ownership.

5.   I here leave Honoré's analysis, though it obviously forms the basis for my remarks.

6.   There are $2^8 - 1$ (i.e., 255) combinations of the eight rights of ownership.   Each of these may either stand alone (with the right to security -- element (9), or be combined with any subset of the remaining 4 elements (elements (10) through (13)). There are thus 2^4 (i.e., 16) variations possible on each of the 255 combinations: 16 x 255 = 4080.   This number has a specious exactness, of course.   There is some arbitrariness in dividing ownership into 13 (or 11, or 15) elements.

7.   Milton Friedman, Capitalism and Freedom (Chicago, U. of Chicago Press, 1962), p. 133.

8.   See, for example, Barry A. Stein, "Collective Ownership, Property Rights, and Control of the Corporation," Journal of Economic Issues, vol. X, no. 2 (June, 1976), pp. 298-313.

9.   Honoré suggests as much in a very brief discussion of "split ownership," op. cit., p. 142.   It may be of interest to note that anthropologically, divided ownership of this sort is not uncommon.   See the descriptions of varieties of ownership in preliterate societies in the writings of economic anthropologists such as George Dalton, Raymond Firth, and Melville Herskovits.

10.   See Perry v. Sinderman 408 U.S. 503 (1972) and Board of Regents v. Roth 408 U.S. 564 (1972) -- both concerning tenure for college teachers.   But Bishop v. Wood 426 U.S. 341 (1976) -- concerning job security for policemen -- modifies matters somewhat. See also Goldberg v. Kelly 397 U.S. 254 (1970) (property interests in welfare benefits), and an analogous argument with regard to a driver's license in Bell v. Burson 402 U.S. 535 (1971).   The constitutional law defining what counts as a property interest for the purposes of the due process clauses of the Fifth and Fourteenth Amendments is rapidly changing.   A good place to start one's inquiry into these matters is in Chapter 10, §7-12 of Laurence H. Trive, American Constitutional Law (Minneola, N.Y., Foundation Press, 1978).

11.   I think here of public health and safety cases, for example: Surocco v. Geary, 3 California 69 (1853) -- destruction of private property by city fire marshall to stop the spread of a fire; Harrison v. Wisdom et al. 7 Heis 627 (1872) -- uncompensated taking of liquor to prevent public disorder upon the arrival of Federal troops during the Civil War; North American Cold Storage

<u>Co</u>. v. <u>Chicago</u> 211 U.S. 306 (1908) -- seizure and destruction of
poultry without prior hearing on the grounds that an emergency
existed; and <u>Miller</u> v. <u>Schoene</u> 276 U.S. 272 (1928) -- requiring
cedar tree owners to cut down infected trees without compensation.

    12. Here I think not of legal duties but socially recognized
moral obligations. See the social science literature on social
exchange theory: e.g., Peter M. Blau, <u>Exchange and Power in Social</u>
<u>Life</u> (N.Y., John Wiley and Sons, 1967), and Peter Ekeh, <u>Social</u>
<u>Exchange Theory: The Two Traditions</u> (Cambridge, Harvard U. Press,
1974). See also Alvin W. Gouldner, "The Norm of Reciprocity: A
Preliminary Statement," <u>American Sociological Review</u> 25:161-178
(1960).

    13. I have elsewhere argued that "ideal morality" -- or the
"virtues-vices" approach to moral questions -- is equal in importance to maximization-of-value theories and rights-duties
theories. See my <u>On Justifying Moral Judgments</u> (London and New
York, Routledge and Kegan Paul and Humanities Press, 1973) and my
"The Neglect of Virtue," <u>Ethics</u> 85:110-122 (1975).

    14. See, for example, the recent case of expulsion from
medical school: <u>Board of Curators of the University of Missouri</u>
<u>et al</u>. v. <u>Horowitz</u> (Slip Opinion) No. 76-695, Decided March 1, 1978.
See also the case of <u>Ross</u> v. <u>Pennsylvania State University</u> (decided by a U.S. District Court in Pennsylvania and reported in
the February 21st issue of <u>The Chronicle of Higher Education</u>, page
4). There the judge ruled that a graduate student -- who had been
summarily expelled -- had a property interest in the continuation
of his studies.

    15. See, on the former issue, my <u>Property Rights</u> (1977).

    16. Honoré, <u>op</u>. <u>cit</u>., p. 123.

    17. A good source for recent work on this topic is Bruce
Ackerman (ed.), <u>Economic Foundations of Property Law</u> (Boston,
Little, Brown, 1975).

JAMES V. FISHER

Property and Liability*

The notion of private property is in trouble today. Consider these comments of George Lodge of the Harvard Business School and a participant in last year's conference:

> A curious thing has happened to private property --
> it has stopped being very important. After all,
> what difference does it really make today whether a
> person owns or just enjoys property?... The value
> of property as a legitimizing idea and basis of
> authority has eroded as well. It is obvious that our
> large public corporations are not private property at
> all.... It was to (the) notion of community need,
> for example, that ITT appealed in 1971 when it sought
> to prevent the Justice Department from divesting it
> of Hartford Fire Insurance.... Note that here, as
> so often happens, it was the company that argued the
> ideologically radical case.[1] (emphasis added)

This readiness to give up the notion of private property reflects what in the last four decades has become 'conventional wisdom', i.e., the observation that in the modern corporation ownership has little to do with control. It is a view that goes back not only to Berle and Means' pioneering study on The Modern Corporation and Private Property (1932) but even before to Walter Rathenau, the German industrialist cum philosopher, in his essay on Things to Come (1917) -- and it is an important link in the theory of what is often called the 'managerial revolution'.[2]

Both Professor Becker and Mr. Stein have challenged that readiness to give up the notion of property, focussing on factors internal to the corporation. I want to challenge it, however, by going back for a moment to a brief analysis of one aspect of the concept of property itself. The focus will be on the external relationship of the corporation to others in society. I think I would disagree with Professor Becker that the concept of property gives us little guidance here. In fact I want to argue that the theory of the 'managerial revolution' rests on an unacceptable gerrymandering of the definition of private property rather than an innocent discarding of the idea.

In what follows I will be concerned in particular with two of the rights traditionally seen to be part of the bundle of rights

268

which define the notion of private property, i.e., (1) the right to exclude all others from the benefit of something, and (2) the right to transfer or discard something (what was traditionally meant by alienation).

I will begin with two preliminary definitions drawing on the Canadian political philosopher C. B. Macpherson:[3]

(1a) Something (x) is the private property of someone (S) only if S has the right to exclude all others from the benefit of x.

Common property, on the other hand, must be defined in such a way as to include the individual rights of those who share ownership as well as the collective right of the owners to exclude all others.

(2a) Something (x) is the common property of two or more people (S_1, S_2, etc.) only if S_1, S_2, etc., together have the right to exclude all others from the benefit of x, and S_1, S_2, etc., each has the right not to be excluded from the benefit of x.

These definitions which emphasize the right to exclude or the right not to be excluded are, it will be argued, incomplete. There is, in fact, a double-edged exclusion which will become obvious when we consider the right to alienate or dispose of something.

To elaborate further the concept of common property let us consider what it means for something to be common property. Suppose an apple tree is the common property of S_1, S_2, etc., and suppose further that it is autumn and the apple tree in question is now full of ripe apples. If S_1 were to pick one of those ripe apples and eat it, and assuming no prior agreement to refrain from eating any apples (say, for example, to save them all for pressing cider), then it would make little sense for S_2 to say to S_1: 'You had no right to eat that apple since it was common property and you have now excluded the rest of us from the use or benefit of it'. Here being common property would appear to mean (again in the absence of some specific agreement) that while S_1 had indeed excluded S_2 from the use or benefit of that apple, nevertheless S_2 had not been excluded from the use or benefit of the apple tree -- at least as long as there is another ripe apple for S_2. The problem becomes somewhat more complicated if that autumn the apple tree in question were to have borne only one edible apple (each gets one bite?), but clearly any individual commoner's right not to be excluded cannot be taken to mean an absolute preclusion of any other individual commoner's actual use of the common property.

269

What this suggests is that any notion of common property is incomplete without some (implicit or explicit) procedure for 'fair-taking/using'.

There are two preliminary points that should be emphasized. The first concerns the value of owning. It was Hegel who pointed out, though no one seems to have followed up on the point, that owning something is an action. To put the same point somewhat differently, a necessary condition for S's owning x is S's intention to own x. As Hegel put it, "...a person puts his (or her) will into a thing -- this is just the concept of property..."[4] Clearly I may possess, use, or benefit from something without intending or claiming to own it. I cannot own something accidentally (though possible modifications of this will be noted in a moment). Without S's intention to own x, S's possession of x is no more ownership than S's arm moving would be S's action without S's intending that S's arm move. It follows, then, that S's property is S's in precisely the same way and for the same reasons that S's action is S's. Since this is true for any theory of property, the (perhaps surprising) consequences apply for any and all theories of property.

The second point concerns the nature of common property or shared ownership. In modern Western society it has sometimes been assumed that the term 'property' automatically (or even necessarily) meant private property. It should be clear, however, that if we can talk about common or joint action, we can also talk about common property. We need no such notion as that of some (fictitious) corporate intention (the intention of the whole as if there were such a thing as a group mind). In other words, there is a clear parallel between 'S$_1$ and S$_2$ together do something (joint action)' and 'S$_1$ and S$_2$ together own something (common property)'. What should be said is not that property necessarily takes the form of private property, but that property is a right which necessarily takes the form of an individual right. And this is true whether it is a right to exclude, on the one hand, or on the other, a right not to be excluded, i.e., whether it is a private property or a common property right.

We can talk about at least three modes in which an individual makes a claim (at least a de facto claim) to own something: (1) taking possession; (2) use; and (3) alienating or disowning it. I will elaborate (1) briefly and then move to (3), since it is of greatest interest for the argument being developed in this paper.[5]

Under the first category, taking possession, at least three elements can be distinguished: directly grasping something physically -- what is referred to in legal contracts as 'taking possession'; shaping, forming or developing something; and taking possession by simply marking something as one's own. Note the

270

function of the concept of <u>intention</u> in all three of these activities. Not only is it a necessary element in ownership, its scope
extends beyond the immediate relation to the thing itself. Thus
the claim to ownership extends to not only such things as unknown
parts (mineral deposits, etc.) and organic results (eggs, the off-
spring, etc.), but also connections made by chance subsequent to
the original acquisition (alluvial deposits, jetsam, etc.). This
is even more explicit when I take possession by shaping or forming
something. By shaping or forming it, I take more than just the
immediate constituents into my possession. This applies to the
organic (breeding of cattle, etc.) as well as to the reshaping of
raw materials and the 'forces of nature'. The point that needs to
be emphasized is that marking something as my own is an action that
extends my intention to ownership beyond the immediate thing itself,
a principle long accepted in legal theory and in social practice
(and in fact is at the basis of our patent laws, etc.).

It is with the third category, however, that we come to the
most interesting move. In a sense when I <u>disown</u> something (e.g.,
by selling it) I intend the thing in its entirety (I intend, so to
speak, to be rid of it) and so presuppose the claim that it is/was
most completely my own.

It is at this point that we can see clearly the missing half
of our definitions of property. Note that it is generally held
that there are two ways of <u>disowning</u> something:

(1)   I may yield it to the intention (will) of another,
      i.e., to another's claim to ownership (usually in
      exchange for something I deem valuable, though it
      may be an outright gift as long as the recipient
      accepts it as his or her own);
or (2)   I may abandon it as <u>res nullius</u>, the property of
      no one? (or as now the common property of all?).

The first option is clear enough and if we pursued that discussion
the questions would center around the issue of what constitutes a
fair exchange. But what about the second option? Where does the
logic of disowning lead us? Consider the following case:

Suppose S, being perceptive and industrious, notes that
there is a good market for tiger skins (well tanned,
handsome to the eye and luxurious to the touch). Furthermore, there are wild tigers in S's vicinity and the
tigers may rightfully be appropriated by anyone and thus
become the private property of the one who appropriates
them (there being plenty of tigers in the vicinity relative to the number of people, etc.). By virtue of
S's physical strength, cunning and dexterity (as well as

271

industriousness), S is able to capture several of
these tigers intending to breed them in captivity for
their very fine skins. Suppose further that S is successful initially in breeding the tigers, but it soon
develops that they do not live long enough in captivity to grow to a size to produce sufficiently luxurious skins. But S is undaunted and eventually by
ingenuity and much hard labor is successful in breeding
stock that is long-lived, very handsome and adequately
large.

Let's suppose further that as a result of this in-
genious breeding process S produces a tiger, we can call
it T_n, which not only has the above characteristics, but
marvel of marvels, T_n has two very special and advantageous characteristics: (a) T_n regularly sheds its
skin, leaving each time a very fine tiger skin ready
to be tanned and sold; and (b) T_n appears to be immune
to the aging process and even impervious to anything
which might harm or even kill it. T_n appears to be indestructible, a source, it seems, of an infinite number
of fine tiger skins.

Can it be doubted that T_n is the private property of S,
that S has the right to exclude all others from the use
or benefit of T_n? If anything could ever satisfy the
traditional property accounts like those of Kant, Locke
and Hegel, surely S's ownership of T_n could.

Now let's imagine that one day T_n begins to show signs
of a developing nasty temperament, and finally it becomes painfully clear to S that T_n is a serious danger
to S (far outweighing the amazing advantages which T_n
manifests), and as well a danger to those in S's immediate living unit, S's neighbors, and even S's whole
community. But T_n is indestructible (or at least no one
has yet found a way to do away with T_n). What is S to
do? The danger is critical.

Aha! S, using what precautions are possible, takes T_n
one day to the village green and in the presence of the
(not too happy) villagers makes the following announcement: "I, S, who have rightfully acquired this tiger,
T_n, as my private property, do here and now publicly
renounce, relinquish and abandon my property in T_n." We
are assuming, of course, that S has attempted to transfer
property in T_n to someone else, to yield S's property in
T_n to the will of another and so into that person's possession, but understandably has found no takers.

Imagine then that the next day S's neighbor appears at S's door, cut and scratched and bearing the remains of a flock of sheep which had been destroyed during the night. "Look what your tiger has done," says the neighbor to S. "My tiger," responds S, "I renounced and abandoned my property in that tiger yesterday. That's not _my_ tiger." No doubt we would be more than a little sympathetic with the neighbor's reply: "The hell it's not _your_ tiger!"

It is interesting to observe that philosophers from Aristotle to the present all treat property _only_ as if it were a good, i.e., as if the right to exclude all others was something always desirable (note our use of the term 'goods'). Why is it that these pillars of modern Western social and political philosophy have apparently ignored what we might call the 'garbage factor'? (Which is not to say that those involved with the practice of law and politics have likewise ignored this factor.) Is it because we no longer live in an age when people commonly throw their garbage out the window? Or because there are now so many of us? Or because of such things as radioactive nuclear wastes and breeder reactors? No matter. It is in any case clear that the initial definition of private property must now be revised along the following lines:

(1a) x is S's private property only if S has the right to exclude all others from the benefit of x _AND_

(1b) each of these others has the right to be excluded from liability for the maleficence of x.

The term 'liability' ('responsibility' does equally as well) is chosen for etymological reasons -- the root of 'liability' being _ligare_, to bind. It is not intended in any technical legal sense. This is what we may call the _double-edged_ exclusionary definition of private property.

What will become obvious on reflection is that IF S's PROPERTY IS S's IN PRECISELY THE SAME SENSE AND FOR THE SAME REASON THAT S's ACTION IS S's, THEN THE DISCUSSION OF MORALITY IS ALSO A DISCUSSION OF PROPERTY.

Consider for a moment the question of the relation of intention to responsibility. In one sense I cannot be held responsible for an act that was not, in some significant sense, intentional. But I doubt that we want to take this in the strictest sense, i.e., that I have a right to recognize as my action -- and to accept responsibility for -- only those aspects of the deed of which I was conscious in my aim and which were contained in my original purpose. Surely, even though one may intend only to bring about

273

a single, immediate state of affairs, there are consequences which are implicit within that state of affairs or connected with it empirically of which I ought to be aware and for which I am therefore morally responsible.

There is a clear parallel between how we deal with the question of someone's liability and how we deal with the beneficial additions to someone's property (by nature, chance, etc.) which, though subsequent to the time and intention of the acquisition of that property, are judged to be part of that property. It is directly analogous to the distinction between having an action imputed to me and being responsible for the consequences of an action. I may be responsible for a criminal act, though it does not follow that the thing done may be directly imputed to me. To apply this to our case of T_n, we might say that on the one hand we do not want to confuse S with T_n, though on the other hand, we may want to hold S responsible for the consequences that follow.

Hegel observes: "To act is to expose oneself to bad luck. Thus bad luck has a right over me and is an embodiment of my own will (intention)."[6]

It is fair, I think, to paraphrase Hegel: 'To acquire property is to expose oneself to bad luck.'

The case of T_n, I submit, demonstrates that we are inclined to hold T_n's owner liable for the consequences, an inclination that finds expression in positive legislation in contemporary society. If we hold S liable for T_n, it is clear that what we are saying is that not only does S have rights in reference to T_n, but all others do as well. All the story of T_n does is to make explicit that the double-edged exclusionary definition represents what has always been, and indeed must be, implicit in the notion of private property.

The abandonment mode of disowning makes sense, then, only if property is only considered a good. Or rather we might say, it is morally justified only if what is abandoned is good. If it is acknowledged that property also entails liability for maleficence, then it follows (especially where the negative consequences of something are serious) that such a mode of disowning is really tantamount to ascribing to the thing in question the de facto status of common property of all -- and that without the express (or implied) consent of those to whom the liability is transferred. Or perhaps we should say that the thing in question ought to be the common property of all, since in fact the negative consequences may fall more heavily on some than on others. Note that the definition of common property must also be revised to pick up the double-edged aspect.

(2a) x is the common property of S_1, S_2, etc., only if
      S_1, S_2, etc., together have the right to exclude
      all others from the benefit of x and S_1, S_2, etc.,
      each has the right not to be excluded from the
      benefit of x
(2b) BUT not the right to be excluded from liability
      for the maleficence of x.

Given this interpretation of the logic of the notion of property, now reconsider a view which is current these days among
some social theorists and popularized in Lodge's eclectic The New
American Ideology, the view that the notion of (private) property
is passé in our 'post-industrial' era. Recall that Lodge argued
that "...(t)he value of property as a legitimizing idea and basis
of authority has eroded ....(and that it) is obvious that our
large public corporations are not private property at all."

This 'ideological' change, reflecting the operational changes
in management practice in large 'public' corporations, has been
characterized as a managerial revolution. If we are to use a metaphor like 'revolution' here, then it might be said that the managerial revolution is a revolution, to be sure, a revolution in the
concept of property. That is, what seems to be implicit in the
theory of the managerial revolution is not merely a move away from
the notion of private property to some new basis of legitimation
for the modern corporation. It is rather a radical change in the
concept of property itself. The implicit change (or revolution) is,
I suggest, a gerrymandering of the concept of property out of parts
of the concepts of private and common property. It would then appear to be something like the following:

(1a) S has the right to exclude all others from the
      benefit of x BUT
(2b) these others do not have the right to be ex-
      cluded from liability for the maleficence of x.

This is, of course, a bit oversimplified, but recent cases
like that of the Lockheed Corporation suggest that it is not far
off the mark in characterizing our contemporary situation. We
should entertain such (implicit) proposals for a gerrymandered definition of private property, I suggest, with considerable hesita-
tion and even skepticism. Too easily giving up the notion of private property runs the danger of giving up the right to hold
accountable for x those people who have the sole right to the
benefit of x. What would be more rational (and not merely conceptually conservative, I am arguing) is to say that WHEN ALL OTHERS
ARE TO BE HELD LIABLE FOR S's X, THEN EACH OF THOSE OTHERS SHOULD
ALSO HAVE THE RIGHT NOT TO BE EXCLUDED FROM THE BENEFIT OF X. In
other words, that x become common property. Or, one might say,

logically some kind of social revolution is what is called for, not a conceptual revolution.

One of the many questions which now arise concerns the problem of symmetry (or fairness). Why should it be considered right to put a limit on liability (or to recognize a de facto limit, e.g., bankruptcy laws, etc.), but not to have some sort of similar limit on the benefits? (But would that not turn private property rights into common property rights, i.e., some procedure for fair taking/ using?) The question becomes especially critical in situations where the negative consequences of something are actual while the benefits only potential. Thus, for example, S may declare the intention to assume liability for x commensurate with the potential benefits from x (or even commensurate with the total assets of S), but how does this help when the negative consequences are actual and the benefits only potential (or when the potential negative effects far outweigh the potential benefits)?

Lest one think that this is a purely hypothetical situation, consider the case of the 1957 Price-Anderson Act cited by Morton Mintz and Jerry Cohen.[7]

In 1954, when the government decided to encourage electric utilities to venture into nuclear power, the companies at first were enthusiastic; but after studying the consequences of a possible major nuclear accident, they and such equipment manufacturers as General Electric and Westinghouse backed off. They feared damage claims that could bankrupt them. Insurers refused then and refuse now to provide full coverage. And so the utilities told Congress they would build nuclear plants only if they first were to be immunized from full liability. Congress responded with the Price-Anderson Act of 1957. Because of this law -- a law that legalized financial unaccountability -- nuclear power technology exists and is growing today.... In 1965, when it recommended that the Price-Anderson Act be renewed, the Congressional Joint Committee on Atomic Energy "reported that one of the Act's objectives had been achieved -- the deterrent to industrial participation in the atomic energy program has been removed by eliminating the threat of large liability claims"... In December 1975... Congress voted to extend the law for ten more years....

In the face of such policies I have attempted to show that the logic of property leads one from the notion of private property (the right to exclude) with a kind of inevitability to the notion of common property (the right not to be excluded) -- unless one proposes gerrymandering the concept of private property. At least this is true with respect to certain kinds of things which have traditionally been seen to fall within the range of what can rightfully become (and remain) private property. A more elaborate specification of what kinds of things these might be is a topic that goes much beyond the scope of this paper.

NOTES

1. George C. Lodge, The New American Idealogy (New York: Alfred A. Knopf, Inc., 1975), pp. 17-19. Also see his article "Business Ethics and Ideology" delivered at Bentley College's "First National Conference on Business Ethics," published in the Conference Proceedings, edited by W. Michael Hoffman, Center for Business Ethics, 1977).

2. The classic analysis which generated much of the contemporary discussion is A. A. Berle, Jr., and G. G. Means, The Modern Corporation and Private Property (New York, 1932). See also A. A. Berle, Jr., Power Without Property (London: Sidgwick and Jackson, 1959).

3. These definitions are adapted from C. B. Macpherson, "A Political Theory of Property," in Democratic Theory: Essays in Retrieval (Oxford University Press, 1973), p. 128.

4. Hegel, Philosophy of Right, translated by T. M. Knox (Oxford University Press, 1952), §51A.

5. A more detailed discussion of this issue is contained in J. V. Fisher, "Hegel and Private Property (or, The Case of T_n the Tiger)" (unpublished mss.), from which portions of this paper were adapted. See also Lawrence Becker, Property Rights: Philosophic Foundations (London: Routledge and Kegan Paul, 1978).

6. Hegel, §119A.

7. Morton Mintz and Jerry S. Cohen, Power, Inc. (New York: The Viking Press, 1976), p. 513f. Other such liability exclusionary examples could be cited.

Note to title

*This paper is an adapted version of part of a paper presented jointly with W. Michael Hoffman at the Conference on "Ethics and Economics" at the Center for the Study of Values, The University of Delaware (1977) which is to be published in Ethical Theory and Business, edited by Norman E. Bowie and Tom L. Beauchamp (Prentice-Hall, forthcoming).

BARRY A. STEIN

Who Owns Corporations:
Implications for Social Responsibility

I'm going to try to be relatively brief, although it's not going to be easy, because the subject is complex.

I'd like to say, by way of preamble, that I propose to bring the horse into the classroom. Medieval scholastics, as you probably know, believed that the way to find out such things as the number of teeth in a horse's mouth was to conceptualize a horse, discuss the essence of a horse and draw a conclusion, based on such authorities as Aristotle, about how many teeth an ideal horse had. It was not considered fair game to bring the horse into the classroom and count the teeth. So I'd like to do something that is slightly unfair; bring the horse in.

I believe in private property. I think it's an extremely important institution both in principle and in practice. It also turns out that private property, in one form or another, is an absolutely universal feature of all societies; modern, traditional or ancient. In every case about which we have information, there is always a sense in which individuals are allowed to own property, and to have private property rights in certain things. What differs, of course, is what those things are, how those rights can be exercised in different conditions, what sanctions exist, how property can be acquired, and so on. But the institution of private property is of extremely ancient roots, and exists everywhere.

The problem with a corporation is not that it might not or ought not be considered property, but that we apply an inappropriate model of property to it. The way ownership tends to be defined in present American society is inappropriate for the nature of the beast, and for the kind of society we live in. I argue that what is essential about private property, or the institution of property in general, is the important social and individual functions it serves, functions that are not duplicated by other institutions. Its reason for existence lies not in natural rights, as some philosophers have held, but rather in the fact that its functions importantly link individuals to their society. It's because of that, that it is universal. The questions then are: 1. what are those key functions, and 2. how does the idea of property in corporations square with those functions?

278

In short, let us inspect the horse before drawing conclusions.

I'd like to start by describing the social construct that is property, and the functions it serves. Very briefly, it offers individuals an essential means by which they can exercise their competence and shape their own environment to some degree. This follows from the right, given me with respect to my property, to control certain things, physical and nonphysical. It is that ability, the exercise of certain rights, very largely at my discretion, that is fundamental to the idea of the private property of individuals. People need to own things -- that is, to control things unilaterally -- even if that only includes the clothes on their back and some tools. Even the most collectivist or communist societies have permitted this sort of private property.

The only limits on these rights derive either from interference with other's rights (my right to use my lawnmower can not allow me to mow your lawn), or more to the point here, from the fact that property rights also serve important social functions. The critical one is that they decentralize decision making. Societies are extremely complex. Property is one of the main mechanisms that makes individual decisions legitimate within a social context. Clearly, well-established rules are needed for that purpose. It would be impossible to require everyone to test in advance the validity of their decision-making rights every time they use them.

The institution of ownership provides one particularly elegant way of solving that problem. Ownership enables people, within specified limits (themselves socially defined) to make unilateral decisions about the appropriate use of the property owned. The presumption is in favor of the owner as determining what those appropriate things are. As a practical matter, property thus serves as an important link between individuals and society, setting boundaries between individual actions and collective social actions. That also makes clear the relationship of property to markets. Markets don't necessarily require "private property", but they do require decentralized decisions and property is the most straightforward basis for that.

But it's not the only possible basis, no more than it's the only basis for rights in general or for distributing and decentralizing decision-making. All property rights of action can be conveyed by another means; that is, by contract. The difference between rights of contract and property is critical. In particular, contracts are between persons, with the state serving as referee and arbiter.

Property is an arrangement between individuals and the state, acting as the agent for society. In fact, property is the only mechanism that really makes a direct deal between the state and individuals. Through property, a circle is drawn that bounds the rights of the owner from all others. Within it, the owner is empowered to act and others are not. Responsibilities of the owner also follow from this. The fact that they do is a good demonstration that property serves a social function, which is itself defined by the state. The Price-Anderson Act is an elegant recent example of one way that can be done.

This and other distinctions between rights of property and of contract make it clear that it is important to distinguish between the two mechanisms. What is central to the institution of property is, in fact, its non-contractual nature and the presumption in favor of owners. Contracts are narrow and specific; property rights are broad and general. Contracts involve a quid pro quo, some exchange; property rights do not. Contracts permit only what is stated; property rights permit everything except what is excluded.

Thus, even though any given right that can derive from property ownership can also be conveyed by contract, the context in which that right needs to be viewed is different. Therefore, the existence of a right that _can_ flow from property does not demonstrate, as Professor Becker asserts, that there _is_ a property right. Both socially and individually, the availability of two very different sources of rights of action, with very different sorts of responsibilities, provides flexibility that would otherwise be lacking. Moreover, the distinctive qualities of property rights need to be sustained, especially in a world where encroachment on individuals is steadily increasing.

To return to the corporation, we now need to ask: in what sense is the corporation property, and who owns it? I have never heard anyone suggest that it is _not_ property at all (though one could), merely that it's not the same kind of property as such items as chairs or automobiles or even ideas. I agree with this. The corporation (meaning conventionally a business firm) is property; it is even private property. But it is not simple, nor individual property, and its owners are not merely stockholders.

Let us return to the horse again. Organizations change. Societies change. Private property and other legal institutions change. Corporations in their present form developed in the mid-nineteenth century; property institutions then in existence had a certain historical form. Thus, corporations tend to be rooted in much earlier principles. Listen to Blackstone, the great British legal theorist: "So great is the regard of the law for private property that it will not authorize the least violation of it; no, not even for the general good of the whole community." Now, here is an authoritative mid-nineteenth century view of private property. That view tends to treat private property as a natural right, rather than a reflection of the fact that property is a creation of the state, serving social functions.

Present discussions of ethics, corporate responsibilities and the like are clear illustrations of the fact that present social norms suggest that that earlier definition of property rights is no longer appropriate, though what should replace them is less clear. In any case, the law has yet to catch up. There is, after all, no reason to assume that what is felt to be right at any given time and place precisely corresponds to existing law. As a matter of fact, in general, those two things cannot change together. Social norms change smoothly, slowly, in infinitesimal steps, and with variations and inconsistencies. Laws necessarily change discretely, sharply, and consistently. So there is always some out-of-jointness between the actual laws and the norms that they reflect and that in turn underlie them.

I might add also that one present visible effect is a loss of respect for private property. I interpret that to mean a weakening of the consensus on which it rests. George Lodge's comments about its loss of importance is one aspect. More important is the very clear reluctance to believe in its appropriateness. The increase in crimes against property are one manifestation of this. I believe that underlying this is a general feeling, that property rights, as presently exercised and as embodied in the law, are increasingly inconsistent with the realities of our present society, and that the times are out of joint with respect to this particular social institution.

Corporations were intended to be quasi-permanent devices permitting a group of people to act as an entity. In the process, they became cloaked with the mantle of simple private property, which I think is entirely untenable. There is nothing sacred about "private property" in connection with corporations and there is nothing new about society modifying what is meant by property rights. It has always done so, because property rights are a creation of society. The mid-nineteenth century ideology of the sanctity of private property was itself a cultural creation of the time. As all these things change, and that is what we see going on today, elements that once were congruent are no longer so: inevitably, conflicts arise. This incongruity serves as a notice that the existing institutions may no longer be serving their purpose. Conflicts arise among various claimants against the corporation, some of whom we call owners. That was, I think, one of Professor Becker's points.

281

However, there is no logical need to assert that <u>all</u> of those
claimants and all of those kinds of rights derive from property;
rather, we can see that property is only one origin of rights
that intersect in the corporation.

It is interesting to note that almost everywhere in the
western world, the idea of the corporation as simple private
property is under attack. In France, the Sudreau report of
several years ago specifically suggested several potential alternatives. Here in France, a bastion of classical property
rights, a blue ribbon commission was suggesting that they were
no longer adequate. Several Parliamentary commissions in Britain
have explored similar options. All across the European continent, worker representatives sit, by legal mandate, on corporate boards of directors. Everywhere what is being questioned
is the assumption that only stockholders have ownership rights.
I myself would argue that one set of owners (presently unre-
cognized) is the set of all employees (including managers, of
course, but not limited to them). Those who labor in an organization are themselves creating value. By doing so, they
develop ownership rights that we do not recognize legally.

I'd like to quote a British <u>conservative</u> statesman: "The
known association which in fact produces and distributes wealth:
the association of workmen, managers, technicians, and directors,
is not an association recognized by law. The association which
the law does recognize: the association of shareholders and
directors, is incapable of production or distribution." We
still recognize one important root of ownership as the creation
of the property, that aspect which traditionally (notably in
John Locke) was the <u>most</u> basic source of ownership. Yet the
creation of value in a corporate organization cannot be attributed permanently and alone to the initial activities of an
entrepreneur, to say nothing of investors, whose role is merely
an enabling one. Therefore, the permanence of rights of ownership in their classical form, and their vesting in entrepreneur
and investors makes no sense. There's no reason, for example,
why we shouldn't have term equity in corporations; that, in
effect, is what a patent is.

So then, who do managers serve? How does the issue of
property arise in connection with corporate ethics and responsibility? The answer is unfortunately complicated. Reality
doesn't always conform to elegant definitions. I disagree
strongly with Professor Becker that mere conceptual precision
constitutes an important argument in favor of one set of definitions over another. Life happens also to be complicated and if,
as Occam's razor has it, things ought not be complicated beyond
necessity, they ought not also to be simplified beyond utility.

282

(That is a rather free interpretation of some important recent work in philosophy.)

In fact, a manager serves several masters, as indeed we all do. The notion that "no man can serve two masters" is clearly untrue. We all do, and it is a necessary part of our lives, and of social arrangements, to find ways to balance them. Who then do managers serve? They serve themselves, in their own self-interest. They serve their family, which clearly has legitimate claims. They serve their community, their country, their state, or any other political unit to which they are attached, and its laws. They serve values, and religious and ethical standards of one kind or another. They serve owners of several sorts and they serve their managers, who are probably not the same. There's no reason to assume that these ought to coincide. On the contrary, it is one of managers' key tasks to have to balance those and other claims.

Why should the corporation, a largely fictional creature, be a vehicle exempt from the demands of citizenship? Why should people, acting in their corporate roles, be exempt from the more general claims of society or its ethical standards? The answer is: they should not. Managers' responsibilities should take account of all legitimate claimants (or stake-holders). Ideally, society's interests should be exercised through control over the "rules of the game"; for example, by creating appropriate ownership rights, setting up desired claims, responsibilities and rights related to property, and establishing the types of property that can exist and how they can legitimately be acquired. If such "rules of the game" were sufficiently precise, then one could more comfortably say that managers serve owners. Of course, that would not eliminate conflicts of interest, but it would make the conflicts legitimate and that is what is really at issue. Then we could stop arguing about side issues such as who owns the corporation, and instead start addressing the resolution of genuine and important differences, and the modification of such central institutions as property to accord with present realities.

COMMENT: Mr. Stein, I'm not clear where you disagree with
Becker's definition of a property right. Do you reject some of
the elements in his list?

STEIN: We disagree only in whether all of those elements necessarily constitute property, and overall, whether that is a
serviceable way of talking about property. I don't think that
differentiates property from other sorts of claims. The point
that I was trying to bring in, very much too briefly, concerned
looking at the ways in which property rights and ownership have
been defined in different places at different times. I noted
the fact that these things do change routinely over time, and
can be looked at in terms of the functions they serve. I certainly admit that I didn't make the point as nicely as I'd like
to, but that's the nature of the disagreement.

BECKER: Yes. I don't think there's that much disagreement, except that I want to say that I think the anthropology of property
reinforces the analysis. Economic anthropologists, as a matter
of fact, were a good deal in advance of legal and philosophical
theorists in developing something like the notion of divided
ownership that I was proposing. They too began by operating with
the notion of full ownership. That was ownership; that was private property. And the arguments (at the turn of the century)
over the existence of primitive communism really depended on
going into a society, seeing that in some societies there wasn't
anything like full ownership for any significant range of objects,
and concluding, then, that things weren't privately owned in that
society. The revision of that line of argument, beginning at
least with Raymond Firth, was to point out that in many preliterate societies there were intricate cases of divided ownership.
Property in a canoe, for example, might be divided so that one
person would have the right to manage the canoe and to transmit
it, but not the right to modify it, and certainly not the right
to destroy it. And the right to manage it might be limited by
the fact that, if he did not want to go out himself, he had to
let others go out. So, I think the anthropology supports this
analysis.

COMMENT: Professor Becker, would you like to comment on the
State's police power to take property without compensation --
something like the eminent domain power and its use -- and how
it fits within your theory of some of the limitations of private
property?

BECKER: Well, I regard takings law as essentially a stab at defining the limitations on the right of security. And I haven't yet been able to generate anything interesting about takings out of the analysis that I presented to you -- anything that reaches substantive issues about takings law and just compensation law. One can locate the problem in terms of the right of security, but what beyond that one can do, I just don't see at this point. I don't see any way of making a normative argument (or even a significant conceptual one) about takings simply from the analysis that I've given.

COMMENT: I'd like some clarification on the nature of our right to security. It seems to me that, insofar as rights are claim rights, they necessarily provide security. The right to security, then, may be a redundant element whenever we are dealing with a claim right to possession, or use, or whatever.

BECKER: Good point. If we were discussing only moral rights I might have to revise the list to take account of that objection. But security seems a significant thing to isolate in the case of legal rights, simply because the interesting variety of limitations that are imposed on security make it important to look at security separately. (Consider takings law again.) It is a little hard to think what the difference would be between a moral right to possess and a morally secured right to possess, that's true. But in the legal context, Honoré convinces me, at any rate, that you have to sort the two out.

COMMENT: To explain that answer a little further, parts of rights to security may be rights not to have certain risks imposed upon you. These rights may not be captured in the other eight.

BECKER: Or in the prohibition of harmful use. That's where I would locate most of the liabilities Professor Fisher was talking about.

FISHER: We have laid out a number of different rights calling them property rights. There seem to be some things that are not secured by contract and, therefore, you're going to have to call them something other than property rights.

BECKER: There is a growing list of recent cases involving the definition of what counts as a property interest, particularly for purposes of the due process cause. For example, the right that a tenured professor has in his job at a state institution. In one recent case the Colorado Supreme Court decided 4 to 3 against the claim that a divorced woman had a property interest in her husband's Masters Degree (which she had financed). And apparently some of the argument turned on how many elements in (something like) my list had to be present before you could say that a property right existed. In any case, a whole lot of things like that are going on which I find illuminating to understand in terms of this scheme.

STEIN: I'd like to make a point about practically all of the foregoing. This, to me, plainly illustrates that property is redefined all the time, that property rights are redefined all the time, and that the things called property are redefined all the time. They are, in fact, virtually created out of whole cloth by societies for their own needs. The problem is that we often assert, partly because of American traditional roots, that there is something special and peculiar about property that makes it immune to such monkeying around. The consequence is that although we have very plainly transformed property rights drastically over the years -- for example, there are property rights increasingly in jobs -- we don't like to admit it. Often the underlying reasoning is incredibly torturous because of this presumption that there is something special, like natural rights, about property. And so, it is very difficult for courts to find ways to modify these, but, in fact, they plainly do.

The trade-offs you were all talking about a few minutes ago, and such issues as eminent domain are redefinitions that are eventually forced because of the increasingly untenable gap between what we feel is and ought to be a legally sanctioned property right and the traditional definitions that are hanging on. The law is excessively conservative in this respect. My whole argument was that if you look at the matter broadly, including the perspective of the economic anthropologist, and focus on the functions those divided rights serve, you see how many ways property has been used to modify the ways in which various social and individual functions can be carried out. In that sense, property rights are really instruments. That's the way I think that property needs to be seen, not an abstract ideal, but a flexible set of socially sanctioned claims that are redefined from time to time. I think the only basis for defining property rights otherwise is the extent to which people literally create it. Unless you believe in natural rights, Locke's argument is still the only fundamental one, although it's much too simple-minded to use in any obvious way.

SESSION XI

"Power and Responsibilities of Multinational Corporations"

William A. Mackie
Executive Vice President
Ingersol-Rand Company

WILLIAM A. MACKIE

The Multinational Corporation:
A Ton of Responsibility, a Pound of Power

They say our society can solve just about any problem it wants to once it's motivated. But I read recently that a question which has perplexed us for generations had to be resolved by an ancient, but sage, African culture. The question dealt with how to pry long-winded dinner speakers away from the podium without breaking their fingers. The African answer was simple but entirely effective. Speakers can talk for as long as they like, but they must stand on one foot while doing it. When the other foot falls, so does the curtain.

Although I plan to keep both feet planted firmly on the ground this evening, it's the though that matters and I promise to keep brevity uppermost in my mind.

I was asked to talk tonight about the extent of a multinational corporation's ethical responsibilities and power. Both our critics and supporters agree that we garner an exorbitant amount of one while sharing little of the other. Their difference of opinion revolves about which is the exorbitant measure, the power or the ethical obligation.

I have been associated with a multinational company for a quarter of a century and believe that if we could weigh the two, multinationals would end up with a pound of power and 2,200 pounds or a metric ton of responsibility. And I hope before the other foot falls this evening, I can convince you that multinationals are not the irresponsible, power-hungry ogres they are sometimes made out to be, but more often a beneficial economic force in the nations where they do business.

But I'm no Pollyanna, and I won't stretch my credibility by denying the problem--God knows, we business people have to enhance what credibility we have left these days.

Imperialistic policy--often a reflection of their nation's government--was the policy favored by the early generations of multinationals. Doubtful payments have been made; they may well continue in the future, more than likely by foreign multinationals trying to undercut the U. S. firms bidding for contracts.

In recent years, we have all been made terribly aware of the transgressions of a few by the well-publicized cases involving attempts to rig an election in Chile, a $20 million Dutch connection --euphemistically called commissions--and a $50 million political contribution in Italy.

Some of these examples represent violations of just about every nation's ethical codes--and my own. Most, however, are not so much a malignant grasp for economic power as they are a benign offshoot of unilateral moralizing on the part of individual governments. Such cases are illustrative of a very delicate question, and one I shall return to.

Suffice it to say that I believe the majority of cases are more a question of confused ethical standards than outright felonious intent. And I believe as well, that the extent of the power a multinational does have today is derived from the quality and the competitiveness of its products and services in the world market. I call it power of performance with the customer.

If a multinational's products and services are better and less expensive than its domestic counterparts, the multinational will be successful. In a very real sense then, it is the multinational's world-wide customers--those who choose to buy its products--who are the primary source of the company's power. Ask yourself why many of your neighbors drive Japanese and German cars-- or why many American women wear Italian shoes. In fact, I defy any multinational to produce a less then superior product and maintain its customers.

This is the way it's been since trading between countries began. Although today's multinationals are basically a product of the industrial, transportation and communication revolutions, their ancestry--and the trading principles upon which they were formed--originated long before.

I don't know who was the first multinational. Perhaps the Phoenician pot merchant who opened a successful branch in Carthage because the Carthiginians found his pots better in some respects than their own. The Venetian-based multinational trading firm of Polo and Polo grew because it brought to medieval Europe entirely new products, such as a string-like flour, later called spaghetti. Centuries after, the Hudson's Bay Company built pelt-power--selling Canadian beaver hats to London dandies.

While the products were as diverse as the companies that sold them, the principle itself never varied. The multinational grew in power because it provided better or newer products or introduced unavailable natural resources to the countries it served.

290

The principle holds true today. Some 3,500 U. S. multinationals
have $100's of billions of direct investments abroad. Conversely,
foreign multinationals have invested billions internationally,
much of it in the United States.

These investments supply developing nations with technolog-
ically-advanced products and services which are as unavailable to
them as spaghetti was to pre-Polo Venice. They also add to the
diversity of available products in the most well-developed nations.

It is in this way, through the desire for their products,
that the multinationals gain their real pound of power. Government
intrigues, bribery and other corrupt acts, while attempted by a
few, are shunned by the many as ultimate strategies of failure.
They suggest that a few companies--possibly for reasons of lagging
technology or poor productivity--are incapable of competing fairly
in the world marketplace.

If a multinational's products define the parameters of its
power, then how it sells them would seem to encompass its ethical
uprightness.

Of course, all businesses, domestic or multinational, large
or small, have ethical obligations to shareholders, to employees,
to their communities and to their customers. But the ton of a
multinational's responsibilities are necessarily more complex
because of the innumerable moral and ethical shadings which color
the world's cultures. Those subtleties can distort the meaning
of right and wrong. They cast misleading shadows over the gray
areas of doubtful payments and human rights and many other issues.

It is my opinion, and one that reflects the formal policy
of my company, that our basic ethical responsibility is to be a
good citizen of the nations in which we operate. We've been trying
to do this in many countries since before the turn of the century.

In fact, if we did not obey the laws and practices of these
individual nations, we could not remain in business very long. Why?
Because, in the event of a confrontation between a company and the
state, it is the host government which holds all the aces, not the
multinational.

That multinationals are beyond government control may have
applied to the imperialistic 19th Century but it is a fallacious
argument whose rhetoric does not apply today. Frankly, I think
such thoughts may be fostered by governments which are unable to
use the multinational as a tool to achieve their own political
aspirations.

While I say that we are good citizens and obey the law of the land, that does not preclude that we offer constructive ideas for change. This is an important point to remember when dealing with the human rights equation.

To remain good citizens, Ingersoll-Rand and many other multinationals hire locally. In this way, we ensure that plants and working arrangements are harmonious with a nation's standards. Of I-R's 16,000 employees working abroad, all but a handful -- over 99%+ -- are based in their homeland. And I'm not simply speaking of non-management. Most of our overseas managers also are nationals who are cognizant of local customs and behavior.

But being a good citizen of one country doesn't automatically make a multinational a good citizen the world over. And herein lies the problem, whether it deals with doubtful payments and human rights -- topics which I shall address momentarily -- or codes of conduct.

When governments or world organizations involve themselves with global ethical standards, inherent ambiguities arise. Today, ethical codes are under examination in the United Nations, Congress and the Organization for Economic Cooperation and Development, the OECD. I will not dwell on the individual points raised in each since most of you, as avid followers of international trade, are already aware of them.

While I grant that such efforts are noble in scope, the end results are often less so. Their final form rarely is equitable. And once written, their interpretation and application are usually open to wrangling debate.

The draft code of conduct submitted by the OECD, for example, apparently stresses American values against bribery, demonstrating our single-minded attention to the noisy event of the moment, rather than a deeper understanding of the importance of encouraging multinationally-oriented economic activity.

The bottom line of any formalized standard of world-wide ethics is to attach a structured code of oscillating principles. It's as if we were to apply football rules to the games of tennis, soccer and baseball and hope there wouldn't be any confusion.

The paradoxes generated by such formalized efforts also cloud other issues, often placing the multinational's ethical obligations squarely in an ambiguous circumstance.

You've heard much about doubtful payments, boycotts and human rights today, and you'll hear more tomorrow, but let me comment

292

briefly about each as they relate to a multinational's responsibilities.

Doubtful payments. Two points. Are they all ready doubtful and are they made as frequently as reported?

Idealistically, every business transaction should be completed on the basis of competitive and evaluative analysis. Pragmatically, this just isn't the way it happens all the time. Payments were and <u>can</u> be involved. But who is to say what is ethical and what isn't when dealing with different cultures? Are we to export our ethical standards as well as our services?

In some of the Mid-east oil states, for instance, there is no real distinction between the private wealth of the ruling sheiks and the national government's resources. In other cases, payments by business concerns are integral parts of a nation's culture. The reduction of such payments would demand wholesale changes in the country's culture.

As to the size of this purported ethical crisis, to my mind it is greatly exaggerated. We've all heard about companies with Latin American business developing their so-called "black box" accounts for customs official payoffs. Or firms which provide Middle East purchasers with as much as 10 percent off the top. Or others who supply Eastern Bloc state purchasing agents favors. Sure it happens, but the waters have been so muddied so deeply that we <u>and</u> governments have been all but blinded by what are basically isolated acts by a few. If doctors over-reacted in a similar fashion, anyone who ever suffered a stomach cramp would have had his appendix removed long ago.

The American economists, authors of <u>Bribery and Extortion in World Business,</u> uncovered what I believe to be a more realistic perspective after having interviewed dozens of multinational corporate executives. They conclude, and I quote:

"Prevailing ideas about payments contained serious errors... (They) have in fact been a relatively small and immaterial factor in the foreign business of the vast majority of United States companies. Most of these payments have been responses to extortionate demands by officials of foreign governments, who demanded them as a condition for the performance of their regular duties or for deterring them from harming American corporate interests by punitive taxation, regulation or expropriation..."

Despite this, and despite the fact that we and most multi-nationals now have corporate codes which strictly forbid improper payments, direct or indirect, to any public servant or public office

293

holder, the United States has become the only industrial country
that legally forbids its business people from making such payments to secure orders.

Although I think the law may be unnecessary, I nevertheless
support it wholeheartedly. It may cost American-based multinationals
some business -- probably less than 10 percent of their' sales,
according to some estimates -- but it will have a salutatory effect
in stifling the urge to pay when the demands do arise.

Now let me turn briefly to boycotts. Today, we have legislation which explicitly describes a multinational's correct reaction
to an unsanctioned foreign boycott. This particular law, of course,
is aimed primarily at the Arab boycott of Israeli products -- but
it does apply to other countries.

Here's the paradox: Can a multinational balance the controls
on foreign boycotts with that of the need to continue business
relationships with the countries using them?

Many multinationals do business with both Israel and the
Arab states. Whether they will be able to do so in the future
is a tenuous question and one that is only complicated by Congressional pressure.

Finally, the human rights question which right now is centered
over South Africa. Activities of some 350 American multinationals
in the land of apartheid are being scrutinized by everyone from
universities to labor unions. Stockholders at more than 20 American
corporations have raised resolutions which demand total withdrawal or an elimination of further financial activity. Others
suggest that multinationals should be doing more to instigate
social reform.

Again the paradox: At one extreme, we're being asked to
withdraw our entire investment. At the other, we're being
asked to intervene in the internal affairs of a sovereign nation.

We're in the midst of the dilemma. Like many other
American corporations, we have a subsidiary in South Africa.
It's been there for nearly 80 years. My own personal feeling
is that we should stay and work from within -- using all the
legal resources available to us -- to change the system as best
we can. Already, 56 American companies have supported a program
designed to promote fair employment practices. In addition,
if we leave, our influence leaves with us, robbing hundreds of
South Africans of both races of employment and the benefits of
our products.

Taking a harder line might be idealistically satisfying --
but it hardly would be any more effective. As we have seen with
President Carter's recent and laudable human rights initiative,
little has been accomplished in changing Soviet society. In fact,
that policy may be more severe than ever, if we accept recent
news accounts. What <u>has</u> changed, though, is the number of trade
opportunities between the U. S. and the Soviet Union. Having
been to Russia on several occasions, I believe we'll accomplish
more through commerce than through political pressure. And
what we need in these days of increased protectionism and
worsening world political events and economies, are policies which
do not inhibit relations and international trade, but stimulate
them.

Sometimes I wonder just how many people are aware of the
importance of the multinational to our economy. In our country,
the world economy absorbs the products of one out of every three
acres of U. S. farmland; it is the source for nearly one of every
three dollars of U. S. corporate profit, and it keeps one out of
six Americans employed in manufacturing. I might add that, despite
the claims of organized labor, multinationals effectively <u>increase</u>
employment at home by building overseas businesses and plants which
become markets for many ancillary and domestic products.

In addition, our international markets serve as a balance
against the effects of variations in domestic supply and demand.
Each of these contributions add to the betterment of our living
standards -- and <u>that</u> is the number one ethical obligation of
any business.

If I failed to state it clearly at the outset, by now you
know I'm an unabashed advocate of multinationals -- American or
not. Like many of you, I've owned a car and TV set made in Japan,
enjoy French and German wines as well as those from California
and still appreciate British woolens. In essence, these multinationals have enhanced my own lifestyle as I believe most are
basically doing worldwide. And as I was taught at the HBS in near-
by Cambridge, Mass. that's the bottom line.

And now, my watch - the product of a Japanese multinational -
tells me it's time to close. I believe the foot is about to fall.
Thank you and good night.

SESSION XII

"Ethics and Advocacy Advertising"

S. Prakash Sethi
Professor of International Business
and Business and Social Policy
University of Texas at Dallas

William A. Latshaw
Manager, Advertising Division
Bethlehem Steel Corporation

Paul Weaver
Associate Editor
Fortune

Carll Tucker
President
Saturday Review

William H. Weed
Executive Vice President
Ogilvy and Mather, Inc.
(Delivered a multimedia presentation
on advocacy advertising)

S. PRAKASH SETHI

I will start out by saying I have no objection to advocacy advertising. Some of the best companies do it, but that doesn't mean they do it right. Before starting, I'll make three propositions: 1) I believe corporations do have a right to communicate their views to the public through paid communication advertising, or any other means possible. 2) I would also like to state that most of the current advocacy campaigns, with some exceptions, not necessarily of Bethlehem Steel, but some exceptions, are not effective on either economic, social, or political grounds. 3) I believe that this type of advertising is expanding at a rapid rate, and therefore it raises some serious issues of public policy, notably that of providing media access to non-business viewpoints. In dealing with these issues, Bill Weed[1] has raised the question of "legitimacy"; this provides a good starting place.

At any given point, one could say that there is a gap between societal expectations and business performance. One could call this a "legitimacy" gap. While other social institutions, including government, religious bodies, and academia, have also suffered a lot in public trust and credibility, the decline in the case of business has been more precipitous and widespread. Nor is the loss of credibility in business institutions, and especially large corporations, confined to the United States. It can be found, to a greater or lesser degree, in most of the non-Communist countries, both the industrially advanced nations of Western Europe and the less-developed countries of the Third World.

One of the ways by which business in the United States has attempted to counteract public skepticism of its social role and criticism of its activities is through the use of publicity campaigns called advocacy advertising. These campaigns are adversary in character: Business institutions take a public position on controversial issues of social importance, aggressively state and defend their own viewpoints, and criticize those of their opponents.

Advocacy advertising has had a long history of sporadic use by businesses in the United States, the United Kingdom, and other Western European countries.[2] Public interest groups by their very nature have resorted to advocacy oriented themes in their external communications aimed at specific groups of the general public. However, as a systematic corporate strategy, advocacy advertising has significantly expanded in the United States since 1973, following the Arab oil boycott and the resultant energy crisis. There is every indication that this trend will continue in the foreseeable

future. Their sponsors include some of the largest and most presti-
geous U.S. corporations, ranging from Allied Chemical to U.S.
Steel. Although exact dollar expenditure figures are not easily
available, there are currently more than 30 such campaigns in
various stages of execution.[3]

This upsurge in the use of advocacy advertising by business
institutions has generated considerable controversy and debate in
the United States. It has also raised questions of public policy
that are likely to have long-term consequences for the public's
perception of the role of business in society and how that role is
being performed.

Advocacy Advertising Defined

Advocacy advertising is part of that genre of advertising
known as corporate image or institutional advertising. Some other
terms used to define one or more dimensions of advocacy advertising
are "issue-oriented advertising," "counter advertising to counter
the news," "public interest advertising," "information advertising,"
and "adversary advertising." It is advertising concerned with the
propagation of ideas and elucidation of controversial social
issues of public importance in a manner that supports the position
and interests of the sponsor while expressly denying the accuracy
of facts and downgrading the sponsor's opponents. Corporate-image
advertising is aimed at creating an image of a specific corporate
personality in the minds of the general public and at seeking maximum favorable images among selected audiences, e.g., stockholders,
employees, consumers, suppliers, and potential investors.

It would improve our understanding of the situation if we
were to analyze the logic of business actions in terms of the role
of business in society. Business is a social institution and
therefore must depend on society's acceptance of its role and activities if it is to survive and grow. If, at any given time, a gap
develops between business performance and societal expectations,
it will cause business to lose its legitimacy and threaten its
survival. Business must therefore strive to narrow this "legitimacy" gap in order to claim its share of society's physical and
human resources, and to maintain maximum discretionary control
over its internal decision making and external dealings.[4] The
legitimacy gap can be narrowed in one of four ways, as shown in
exhibit 1.

Traditional corporate institutional advertising is aimed at
changing public perception of business performance, as in strategy
one of exhibit one. Strategy two encompasses the whole spectrum
of corporate social responsibility movement wherein businessmen
concede that corporations should contribute to the alleviation of

EXHIBIT 1

BUSINESS STRATEGIES FOR NARROWING THE LEGITIMACY GAP

Business Performance	Legitimacy Gap	Societal Expectations

1. Do not change performance, but change public perception of business performance through education and information.

2. If changes in public perception are not possible, change the symbols used to describe business performance, thereby making it congruent with public perception. Note that no change in actual performance is called for.

3. Attempt to change societal expectations of business performance through education and information.

4. In case strategies 1 through 3 are unsuccessful in completely bridging the legitimacy gap, bring about changes in business performance, thereby closely matching it with society's expectations.

society's problems but insist that such effort must be voluntary, must not interfere with a corporation's business activities or impinge upon the management's prerogatives, and management must have the final say as to how much and in what form the corporation expression takes place. The logical outcome of this emphasis has been to render the social responsibility totally meaningless since it could mean anything. Even where corporations have made good-faith efforts, generally they have been lost in the morass of cosmetic changes by a large number of business entities.[5]

Advocacy advertising is used to achieve the objectives of both strategies 2 and 3. Advocacy advertising covers a broad spectrum of attempts to change or sustain public opinion and social policy on specific short-term issues, as well as on long-term fundamental values that underlie social and political institutions. Nevertheless, all advocacy advertising campaigns share certain common characteristics in terms of the corporate posture, depiction of the adversary, and claim to social legitimacy via identification with widely held social beliefs or representation of public interest. Strategy 4 calls for a substantive change in corporate behavior, is long-term in character, and carries substantial uncertainties and risks in execution.

The managerial context of advocacy advertising is that of defending the corporation's activities and modus operandi. The behavioral and social context of advocacy advertising is that of changing public attitudes toward a corporation's actions and performance from skepticism and hostility to belief and trust. The strength of advocacy advertising for the corporate sponsor lies in two elements: (1) the content of the message is controlled and defined in a manner most favorable to the sponsor; and (2) the sponsor's message is presented within the controlled and sponsor-determined advertising copy, thus making otherwise one-sided viewpoints appear objective and balanced.

THE RATIONALE FOR ADVOCACY ADVERTISING

The rationale for advocacy advertising - and Bill Weed mentioned some of these points - could be classified into four categories: 1) Business claims that it used advocacy advertising to counteract public hostility because of ignorance or misinformation; 2) it uses advocacy advertising to counteract what's euphemistically called the spread of misleading information by the critics, or to fill the need for greater explanation of complex issues -- business being a complex issue in itself; 3) it uses advocacy advertising to foster the values of the free enterprise system; and 4) it uses, or at least claims to use, advocacy advertising to counteract inadequate access to and bias in the news media.

1. To Counteract Public Hostility Because of Ignorance or Misinformation

This is one of the more prevalent and persistent explanations given not only for advocacy advertising but for all institutional advertising. Surveys conducted by Opinion Research Corporation in the United States in 1972 show that the public's image of business and approval of its actions is now at its lowest since the early 1960s. For example, 60 percent of the people have a "low" opinion of business, one-third of the public thinks that government should limit profits, and two-thirds think that government should control prices. More than half the people think that industry is doing "very little" about air and water pollution, and more than three-fourths think that "consumer" laws are necessary. Furthermore, the public thinks that after-tax profits of corporations average 28 cents on a sales dollar, compared with an actual level of slightly over 4 cents.[6] Business sees this public antipathy as a harbinger of greater public pressure for further intrusion into and increased regulation of its activities by government agencies and private groups.

Historically, business has favored the strategy of education to counteract public antagonism, since it is the least painful and easiest to undertake. But there is overwhelming evidence that media campaigns to educate the public have been singularly unsuccessful. As early as 1952, William H. Whyte, Jr., noted that the billion-dollar attempt of the two earlier decades to "sell business to America" had failed utterly.[7] More recently, authors like Irving Kristol have criticized this approach, contending it is absurd to think that institutional advertising can serve any educational purpose.[8] Paul Weaver, in his article a while ago in Fortune magazine, mentioned a survey that was done, a cross-section of national population where seven questions were asked of the people on complex economic issues, and a majority of them responded to them correctly. Marshall Loeb, a senior editor of Time magazine, states that "Americans understand the free enterprise system. Everyone knows what it is. Campaigns to 'educate' the people about free enterprise have tended to be loaded with cliches, which nobody listens to."

There is little attention in these campaigns to the possibility that the disagreement between the corporations and the public may not be owing to lack of recognition of business's contribution to society, but instead may have resulted from the corporations' failure to appreciate and understand their role in a society whose expectations have changed. Such an education program seldom considers the need for a change in business performance, because to do so would be to attack the status quo and thereby frustrate the purpose of the campaign. Any obvious lapses in performance are

attributed to individual businesses and explained away in terms of
the rotten apple theory.[9]

Even some of business's strongest supporters have been struck
by the ineptness and poor timing of some of the public relations
campaigns.[10] Furthermore, the media blitz has been often so heavy
that it has had the effect of overkill, leading, Preston Tisch,
president of Lowes Corporation, to comment that business leaders
"have fallen into the habit of thinking of public opinion as something to be molded and manipulated for their own purposes. What's
really needed are new higher standards of openness and accuracy."[11]

2. To Counteract the Spread of Misleading Information by Critics and to Fill the need for Greater Explication of Complex Issues

Businessmen attribute a large part of the public hostility
to the rise of groups opposed to business on intellectual grounds,
opposed to economic growth, and proposing a socialist society and
public control of the nation's productive resources. According to
a National Association of Manufacturers' discussion paper, "One
of the causes of the antibusiness bias arises from a power struggle
being played deliberately by intellectual thought leaders."[12]
Furthermore, complex issues are often oversimplified, left un-
explained, or given one-sided treatment by hostile critics, thereby
creating false impressions in the minds of readers.[13] In justifying
its advocacy ads, Mobil has contended that the oil industry's critics do not have an in-depth understanding of an extremely complex
industry. Therefore, unless the public can get a better grasp of
the real problems, the future of the nation is likely to be ad-
versely affected because a poorly informed public could press for
the adoption of counterproductive measures. However, an analysis
of various recent advocacy ad campaigns indicates that their prime
emphasis is on getting the attention of the public. Ads are just
not the place for long-drawn-out complicated arguments. Thus,
issues are presented with catchy headlines and simple messages,
with the primary emphasis on reinforcing the sponsor's position
rather than explaining both sides of a controversy.

The idea of balanced presentation of facts does not imply
that a given advocacy campaign will present all significant arguments, pro and con, on an issue. Businessmen maintain that,
through advocacy campaigns, they present their side of the issue
to counterbalance the information given the public by their opponents. Thus, the information balance is achieved in the marketplace, where everyone has an opportunity to express his or her
viewpoint. On an admittedly controversial issue, the sponsor is
not likely to present the opposition view in a sympathetic light,
because to do so would be to reduce the credibility of his own
message. The same logic applies to presenting one's own side with

all the qualifying or cautionary remarks necessary to be objective about it.

The above-given explanation, however, presumes away the question of the ad content and the kinds of details being provided by the corporation. In most of the antipollution ads, not only is there little balanced information about both sides of the issue, but the corporations by and large make no effort to present an accurate picture of their own role in both the creation and the abatement of pollution, or of the relationship of their activities to the overall magnitude of the problem. At least in some cases, the corporations that engaged most heavily in antipollution advertising were found to be the biggest polluters.[14] Although this argument is not being presented to suggest regulation or control of such advertising, it certainly raises doubts about corporate claims that this advertising was being employed to restore sanity and bring more rationality into the public debate on the issues.

In a sense, the above argument is another version of the "public education" strategy applied to specific issues and against specific critics. But in the example of the environment, advocacy ad campaigns dealing with pollution and other environmental problems have taken one or more of the following three forms: (1) Industry efforts at controlling pollution are often exaggerated and projected as voluntary while in fact they may have been undertaken under threat of government prosecution. (2) The adverse consequences of pollution are downplayed and the adverse economic consequences on jobs and incomes overemphasized. (3) There is an implication that voluntary individual action will largely solve the problem, thereby absolving the firm or industry of substantial responsibility for controlling pollution.

3. To Foster the Values of the Free Enterprise System

Business argues that advocacy advertising is needed to foster the values of the free enterprise system, which have been eroded by the ever-expanding shadow of the welfare state, the sapping of individual initiative, freedom, and the work ethic. Thus, reinforcing traditional values and beliefs will support the foundation on which free enterprise is built.[15]

The claim of American businessmen of upholding the American values, e.g., free enterprise and individualism, runs through all of American history. This belief logically leads to the notion that no change in the system is needed and that public education is called for. Thus, Richard S. Gerstenberg, then chairman of General Motors, was being historically quite consistent when he complained in 1972: "The average American has only a hazy idea of what free enterprise means, and much less how it works." He at-

305

tributed the lowering of business ratings in public opinion polls to the public's ignorance.[16]

In the long run, this argument is perhaps more dangerous and likely to be more counterproductive for the large corporations than all the other arguments combined. The modern corporation in size, scope, and operations bears no resemblance to the classical model of free and competitive markets, private enterprise, and individualism. Thus to seek legitimacy through traditional ideological values is to make corporations highly vulnerable to attack on their own grounds. Furthermore, as Professor George C. Lodge argues in his book, The New American Ideology, American businessmen have seldom behaved as if they believed in these traditional values.[17]

The same corporations who decry the erosion of the great American traditions and values and the decline of the capitalistic system are quick to espouse a different framework for the measurement of corporate legitimacy and performance when circumstances call for it. For example, during the Senate hearings examining the circumstances of ITT's acquisition of Hartford Fire Insurance Co., an ITT attorney stated: "Don't visit that old idea of competition on us. The public interest requires ITT to be big and strong at home so that it can withstand the blows of Allende in Chile, Castro in Cuba, and the Japanese in general. Before you apply the antitrust laws to us, the Secretary of the Treasury, the Secretary of Commerce, and the Council of Economic Advisors should meet to decide what, in the light of our balance-of-payments-problems and domestic economic difficulties, the national interest is."[18] At the same time, internal company memos showed that ITT was actively conspiring to undermine and overthrow the Allende government under the guise of protecting "liberty" and "individual freedom," which were "under attack everywhere."[19]

The image business and business institutions would like to have of themselves and would like the general public to have is not exactly congruent with reality both as business sees it and as the public experiences it. Some elements of reality do correspond with both the image and the underlying ideology. But business behavior and rhetoric abound with internal contradictions in such critical areas as government regulation, open competition, the working of the market mechanism, and the role of the individual in society and in enterprise. Yet, such inconsistent behavior and rhetoric is justified as being within the basic framework of the American private enterprise system.

The point is not that private enterprise is irrelevant or outmoded -- far from it. But business cannot legitimize its behavior or freedom of action on ideological grounds that bear little resemblance to reality. The justification therefore must rest on

306

criteria that are relevant, and more important, credible to large
segments of society. Otherwise, in a free society, it is not in-
conceivable that people will reject these rationalizations and the
institutions supporting them.

4. To Counteract Inadequate Access to and Bias in the News Media

There is a widespread belief in the business world that an
antibusiness bias in the news media and among journalists prevents
it from getting fair and objective exposure. Furthermore, businessmen contend that their access to the various media is grossly inadequate when compared with the importance of the issues being
covered and the space and air time devoted to discussing the viewpoints of the opposition. Thus, business has lumped the news media
with its adversaries. In a recent speech, Professor Louis Banks
of the Harvard Business School, a former editor of Fortune, suggested that in the case of everyday news coverage,

> We are fed a daily diet of authoritative ignorance, most
> of which conveys a cheap-shot hostility to business and
> businessmen. Here is where the nation sees a persis-
> tently distorted image of its most productive and per-
> vasive activity, business. . . . The reporters and
> the editors in the general media are woefully ignorant
> of the complexities and ambiguities of corporate opera-
> tions, and being so, are easy targets for politicians
> or pressure group partisans with special axes to grind
> at the expense of business.[20]

In a similar vein, Rawleigh Warner, Jr., chairman of Mobil
Oil, says that the purpose of Mobil's ad campaign is to defend
the company against slander. "We've been willing to react because
we feel we've been treated unfairly."[21] Herbert Schmertz, a
Mobil vice-president and the architect of its advocacy campaign,
believes there is too much accusatory journalism.[22] Similar comments have been made by spokespeople for large corporations and
industry associations such as the American Association of Advertising Agencies (AAAA), American Petroleum Institute, Exxon Corporation, and Shell oil.[23] John O'Toole, president of Foote, Cone
& Belding advertising agency, also does not find it surprising
"that the voice of the adversary culture is more dominant in the
media than that of the system. One role of the press is to
question established institutions, directions and processes. They
deal in crisis and confrontation, the stuff of which news is made."[24]

Despite the vigorous denial of the majority of media people
of the charge of antibusiness bias, the question of inadequate or
poor coverage of business news has received some grudging acceptance.
According to John Oakes, editorial page editor of the New York Times,

It is normal that business would accuse the press of
bias and inadequate coverage. This is true not only
in the case of business, but of political parties, and
every other kind of special interest group -- profit
or non-profit.

Editorially, The New York Times has been very critical of many business practices, not only this year,
but also in earlier years. Over the years, we have been
editorially critical of every special interest group
that exists. Newspapers wouldn't be doing their duty
if they did not express their opinion. We reserve the
right to express our views in our columns. If oil companies or any other group wish to call this bias, that
is their privilege.

The editors of Time, Business Week, and Fortune, however,
stated that in the general press, daily newspapers, and television
news, the coverage of business-related stories is of poor quality.
They assign the cause of poor coverage more to the lack of training
in economic matters on the part of news reporters than to the
existence of an antibusiness bias in the press. The media people
also deny the charge that businessmen do not have adequate access
to express their viewpoint. They contend that:

1. Before a news story is reported in the press, its contents are checked for accuracy with all the interested parties and
their views evaluated and reported.
2. Where businessmen disagree with a news story or are critical of an editorial, the "letters to the editor" columns are open
to them. Many newspapers have special editorial space, e.g., the
Op-Ed page in the New York Times, which is made available to outside spokespeople including top corporate executives.
3. A large part of the inadequate coverage is due to the
general unwillingness on the part of top corporate executives to
talk with reporters.

Although there may be an element of truth in the business complaints, it does not justify a blanket charge against all news
media. First a distinction should be made between special-purpose
print media (business and trade magazines) and general (mass)
print media (newspapers and magazines). Second, a distinction
should also be made between a large majority of small-town newspapers, newspapers of conservative orientation, and a few large
newspapers considered liberal, e.g., the New York Times and the
Washington Post.

Obviously, business news media will provide fair coverage
for the business viewpoint. Nor should there be too much concern

for the vast majority of newspapers with primarily local orientation. Constrained by funds from hiring a sufficient number of
reporters and heavily dependent on advertising, they are only too
happy to accept press releases from the public relations departments of various companies and print them as news stories. Moreover, the hostility of small-town newspapers to "radical" and
"left wing" groups is not a secret. It is therefore unlikely that
the business viewpoint will not get fair exposure.

Similarly, a distinction should be made between the network
news in television broadcasting and the news programs of local independent stations. The station programs generally concentrate on
local news and seldom venture into national controversies on
economic issues. Furthermore, these stations have been known to
yield to pressure by business. It has been reported that TV
stations in some localities had either fired their consumer affairs
reporters or changed their assignments when advertisers threatened
to withdraw their advertising from those stations.[25]

It would thus appear that the complaints of business are
primarily confined to the network news programs, major newspapers,
and nationally distributed news magazines. It can be argued that
business does not fully realize the necessity for these news media
to cater to a diverse and heterogeneous audience. A large part of
what business might consider unfair presentation might simply be
a fair presentation of news seen from another viewpoint.

Nevertheless, business is in a dilemma. In its attempt to
reach opinion leaders, it must use the media of their choice. Yet
the environment in these media is hostile because the media are
being inundated with revelations of activities that business would
like to describe as necessary evils but that other groups consider
illegal, unprofessional, and unethical. Thus we find that while
Phillips Petroleum is extolling the virtues of free enterprise in
paid advertising, the news stories tell us of a court case in which
the company admitted to making illegal political campaign payments
in the United States.[26] Or as the Council on Economic Priorities
reported in 1970 in a study of the pulp and paper industry in the
United States, the companies with the best track records on pollution control kept the lowest profile, while the worst polluters
did the most advertising. The strength of a company's statements
is considerably weakened when its integrity and social performance
are being questioned.

CONCLUSIONS

The preceding analysis leads us to conclude that advocacy
advertising by large corporations, as it is being currently practiced, is of questionable value on ideological, economic, and

sociopolitical grounds. It is not likely to yield significant benefits in terms of good will. Nevertheless, restraining or regulating of the use of institutional advertising is not warranted. Corporations have every right to express their position in paid advertising space and through other channels of communication open to them. However, both corporate objectives and public purposes would be better served if business would undertake to improve the quality of its communications through advocacy advertising and to respond positively in other ways to public criticism.

Advocacy advertising, however, is a sensitive tool and, unless used with care, could have serious negative consequences for the corporations. A high level of intellectual integrity in the discussion of controversial issues must be maintained if business expects the opinion leaders—who are the major target of such advertising—to give serious consideration to an admittedly partisan communication.

Advocacy advertising should be an integral part of a corporation's total communication program, which in turn must bear a close relationship to the activities of the corporation, the role it projects for itself in the society, and the expectations of the society for corporate performance. Too often advocacy advertising is confined to what the corporation wants the world to hear rather than what the world wants the corporation to talk about.

No amount of advocacy advertising will help unless there is a recognition that some of the criticism directed against business institutions is indeed valid. There must be a demonstrated willingness to change where current methods of operation and standards of performance fall short of societal expectations. Business must take steps to put its own house in order. Generalized statements of self-righteousness are ineffective in presenting one's case. Nor does it help to explain away wrongdoing, e.g., illegal political payoffs and bribes at home and abroad, in terms of the "rotten apple theory" when such behavior is persistent and widespread, and equally well reported in the news media.

Advocacy advertising can either be a cutting edge in the process of further opening corporations to the public or one more step in continuing efforts by businessmen to defend today's reality and status quo with yesterday's ideology and raison d'être. In the event that there is a mass move by corporations to pursue the partisan propaganda made in their public communications, the consequences will affect every aspect of American society. Such a course will not reduce the scope of conflict, but enlarge it. Nor will it contribute to the quality and diversity of public information. By escalating the level of noise, it will increase public antagonism, which will show itself through greater government re-

310

strictions on the conduct of business than are necessary or desirable.
If this happens, business will have no one to blame but itself and
no recourse but to buy more ad space to bemoan public ignorance,
media hostility, and political opportunism.

NOTES

1. William H. Weed, Executive Vice President, Ogilvy and
Mather, Inc. Member of the Panel: "Ethics and Advocacy Advertising,"
The Second National Conference on Business Ethics, April 7 and 8,
1978, Bentley College, Waltham, Mass.

2.

3.

4.

5.

6. "America's Growing Antibusiness Mood," Business Week,
June 17, 1972, pp. 100-103.

7. William H. Whyte, Jr., Is Anybody Listening? (New York:
Simon and Schuster, 1952), p. 8.

8. Irving Kristol, "On Economic Education," Wall Street
Journal, February 18, 1976, p. 20. Kristol's analysis is similar
to the findings of a 1950 study by the Brookings Institute on the
effectiveness of attempts at economic education by business. The
study concluded that real improvements in economic education can
be best achieved through improved teaching efforts in established
educational institutions. "How Good is 'Economic Education'?"
Fortune, July 1951, pp. 84-86ff. The study was conducted by Dr.
Harold Moulton and Dr. C. W. McKee.

9. For some case histories of corporate corruption and payoffs, see S. Prakash Sethi, Up Against the Corporate Wall, 3rd ed.
(Englewood Cliffs, N.J.: Prentice-Hall, 1976).

10. "Oil Meets the Press: The Image Has Been Smeared and
the Companies Are Largely To Be Blamed," Dun's, April 1974, p. 62.

11. "The Embattled Businessman," Newsweek, February 16, 1976,
p. 56. Paradoxically, emphasis on the positive often provokes a
negative reaction. If the audience is critical of corporate failures,
avoidance of the issue by repeating a list of contributions tends
to create further alienation. William Whyte points out: "Even
with those facts for which business rightfully claims credit, the
message represents business as essentially static and defensive.
It concerns what was done. That we have achieved more telephones,
more bathtubs and so on per capita is fine fact, but it is not a
fact that answers the aspirations and gripes of the people business
is seeking to win as friends." (Is Anybody Listening? p. 14).

12. National Association of Manufacturers, The Public Image
of Business in a Time of Changing Values (New York: The Association,
June 1973). Emphasis in original. See also, Lewis F. Powell, Jr.,
"Attack on American Free Enterprise System, Confidential Memoran-

dum, August 23, 1971," reported in Washington Report Supplement (Washington, D.C.).

13. Testimony of Herbert Schmertz, of Mobil Oil Corporation, in U.S. Senate, Energy and Environmental Objectives, Hearings before the Subcommittee on Environment of the Committee on Commerce, Part 2, Washington, D.C., 93rd Congress, May 6 and July 18, 1974, pp. 99-100.

14. According to a study by the Council on Economic Priorities, the number of companies treating the environment as a gimmick in an attempt to boost the sales of their products include American Tobacco, Bulova, Cott Beverage, Hask, Liggett & Meyers, Publix Shirt, Pittsburgh Plate Glass, and Texaco. "Corporate Advertising and the Environment," p. 19.

15. Whyte, Is Anybody Listening?

16. For an early history of the defense of business by businessmen as the guardians of American ideological values, see George C. Lodge, The New American Ideology (New York: Knopf, 1975), chapter 4. Gerstenberg's statement appeared on the Op-Ed page of the New York Times, December 29, 1972, and is cited in Lodge.

17. Lodge, The New American Ideology.

18. Cited in Lodge, The New American Ideology, p. 91.

19. Cited in Sethi, Up Against the Corporate Wall, 2nd ed., pp. 102-211.

20. Louis Banks, "Media Responsibility for Economic Literacy," speech given at the Annual John Hancock Awards for Excellence in Business and Financial Journalism. "A Bicentennial Examination of the Free Market System," John Hancock Mutual Life Insurance Co., Boston, October 28, 1975. See also "People in Business: Executives vs. the Newsmen," New York Times, October 22, 1975, p. 59.

21. Connor, "Mobil's Advocacy Ads."

22. "The New Concerns About the Press," Fortune, April 1975, p. 130.

23. Letter by John Crichton, president, American Association of Advertising Agencies, to Senator Philip A. Hart (D.-Michigan), dated July 16, 1974. For comments by other industry spokesmen, see U.S. Senate, Energy and Environmental Objectives, Hearings before the Subcommittee on Environment of the Committee on Commerce, Part 2, Washington, D.C., 93rd Congress, May 6 and July 18, 1974: "Donald Cook Takes on the Environmentalists," Business Week, October 26, 1975, p. 70; Connor, "Mobil's ads"; Donald S. MacNaughton, "The Businessman Versus the Journalist," New York Times, March 7, 1976, section 3, p. 14; "The Embattled Businessman," Newsweek, February 16, 1976, p. 58; Kristol, "On 'Economic Education,'" p. 29; Deridre Carmody, "Reporters Chided on Business News," New York Times, May 5, 1976, p. 38.

24. John E. O'Toole, "Advocacy Advertising Shows The Flag," Public Relations Journal, November 1975, p. 15.

25. Liz Roman Gallese, "Boston's Sharon King Becomes Local TV Star by Knocking Products," Wall Street Journal, October 20,

1975, p. 1.

    26. William E. Blundell, "Phillips Petroleum to Turn Over Control to Outside Directors in Settlement Suit," <u>Wall Street Journal</u>, February 19, 1976, p. 7.

WILLIAM A. LATSHAW

Good evening ladies and gentlemen, those of you who have survived this long day.

Many observers, both within and outside of the advertising business, have expressed great concern about the ethics, propriety, legality, goals, tone, and financial accountability of corporate advocacy advertising.

Bethlehem Steel has been carrying out an advocacy advertising campaign since 1976. I am an advocate of advocacy advertising. With that background, some of you might anticipate that I resent and disagree with much of the criticism expressed about what is wrong with advocacy advertising. Not so. Especially in the area of practical criticism as opposed to philosophical.

I applaud the critics' interest, share much of their concern, and agree with many of their observations. And I will defend, through an entire three-martini lunch, the critics' right to express their views.

By the same token I will defend unto the death, or until such time as my vice president changes my mind, the corporation's right, no, it's duty to communicate on public issues through advocacy advertising as well as other appropriate outlets.

Just what is wrong with advocacy advertising? Dr. Sethi's recent book has outlined the philosophical arguments. I could quote chapter and verse from many sources within the industry, but perhaps Robert S. Marker, Chairman of the Executive Committee of Needham, Harper, and Steers, summarized the professional communicators' viewpoints most cogently.

Said he, "In perhaps no other area of American advertising is there as much waste and ineffectiveness as there is in public issue advertising. Abuses are prevalent. Why?

"I contend," said Marker, "that some of the managements of companies and associations running public issue advertising don't understand it. I contend," he continued, with greater conviction, "that many of their advertising agencies don't know what they're doing.

"Corporate managements often use this kind of advertising to vent their angers, not to inform their publics...their objectives

314

are murky. Their knowledge of their audience is in error. Their
budgets are either too small for large problems, or too large for
small problems. The copy is indistinct...the media plan incestuous.
And the measurements of results too emotional. Some of these
campaigns are totally useless."

But Mr. Marker concludes, "business should be less reluctant
to cry 'foul' when a foul has indeed been committed." Or, I might
add, when a foul is about to be committed.

And Alex Kroll, President, Young and Rubicam, U.S.A., observes,
"this whole area of corporate advertising is...very subjective, and
the constructive criticism is just as subjective."

I share Mr. Marker's critical views, and I agree with Mr. Kroll's
observations.

But I believe that Bethlehem Steel's advocacy advertising has
avoided most of the sins and pitfalls attributed to such advertising.

Our corporate advertising does not vent corporate anger. Nor
does it attack or demean those who hold opposing viewpoints. Our
objectives are clear. Our knowledge of our audience's viewpoints
is profound. Our budget is modest. Our media plan is unique. Our
copy is lucid, informative, and direct, and offers positive alternatives. And our measurements of results are soundly based, tinged
perhaps with the sole emotion that we believe our advocacy advertising
to be intelligent, responsible, and as balanced as subjective advocacy
can be.

This conference is sponsored by the Center for Business Ethics.
And I'm sure that many of you would hope to hear more philosophy
and less bolts and nuts about advertising per se. I'm not much of a
philosopher and what little I have to say in that area I'll save
for last.

But some bolts and nuts are appropriate, if only to provide
you with a frame of reference for Bethlehem Steel's advocacy ad
program.

What are we doing, why are we doing it, and how are we going
about it? If you don't know where you're going, any road will take
you there.

In 1975, Bethlehem Steel's public affairs department isolated
six issues of national concern, vital to the health of our corporation -- tax reform and capital formation, environmental clean-up,
the energy crisis, steel imports and foreign trade, over-regulation
of business, and business concentration.

Before embarking on a print advertising campaign on some of these issues we defined our target audience -- the opinion-leader readership of national magazines. Their demographics include: a 100 per cent professional/managerial background, some college education, 25 to 64 years old, $20,000 annual income or above, and active politically in their communities. That's our primary audience.

Secondary audiences include employees, shareholders, customers, suppliers, and members of our plant communities.

Those, in brief, to whom members of Congress, agency heads at the state and federal levels, turn when taking the pulse of their constituencies. Our primary goal is to inform these audiences, to shift their views where we can, in the hope that their educated views will impact on those in the legislative and executive arena. Beyond shifting opinion, we hope to create a better awareness, and we wish to position Bethlehem Steel in a leadership role in dialog on national issues.

We're talking about our corporate concerns, our problems, and presenting our views, our suggested solutions on them. These problems of ours are the readers' problems too, although they are not always perceived that way. They are national problems.

At the start, we surveyed 13 national business, cultural, and newsweekly magazines and studied the attitudes of our target audience on the 6 issues of concern to us. It was a unique study that enabled us to improve the targeting of our corporate messages, to reach readers who are willing to listen and then draw their own conclusions, to improve the effectiveness of our media buying, and to set up a monitoring system that would accurately measure the results of our advertising efforts.

We carried out advocacy advertising on four issues during 1976 and 77. We measured results, using a control group as a check. We have informed and we have shifted attitudes.

We have attempted to contribute in our own way to the public dialog Dr. Sethi wishes to take place. And it is perhaps appropriate here to note that while I have some reservations about Dr. Sethi's proposed solutions, and I do not share all of his fears, anyone who has read his recent book, Advocacy Advertising and Large Corporations will find that he has explored this subject thoroughly and fairly.

As I read his book, I noted that sprinkled throughout were such normal qualifiers as "few, most, some, as a rule." These modifiers served to point out exceptions to his critical appraisals. Dr. Sethi may not have had Bethlehem Steel in mind when he allowed for exceptions, but in that context, and in any other context, I'm convinced that we have carried out an "exceptional" advocacy advertising campaign.

The final point I'd like to touch on is the basic premise of the appropriateness, the validity, the ethics of corporate advocacy advertising.

On this point, Antonio Novarro, Vice President, Corporate Administration Group, W. R. Grace & Company, has commented, "Many corporations face a dilemma today. To speak, or not to speak. It is inescapable that we live in an age of information. It is an age of questioning and challenge, of accountability and disclosure. In such an age we really have no choice but to speak, and in the process, justify our behavior to both ourselves and our publics. Because what is really at stake is the survival of the public corporation as a legitimate form of business enterprise.

"Legitimate self interest is not radical or shameful. In these rapidly changing times, the ability to anticipate issues and challenges will be the ultimate test of a corporation's capacity for survival.

"Silence buys its own penalty."

To quote Harold Burson, Chairman, Burson-Marstellar International, "Businessmen must learn to stand for something as well as to be opposed. They must gain the courage to make their views known, not only as responders -- on the defensive -- but by taking the initiative in an aggressive manner. Very frequently, paid advertising is the only vehicle available to do that."

Corporations have the same legal rights as others, under the first amendment, to communicate their views on political and legislative matters, to debate on public issues, or to criticize the government. Indeed, it is more than a right, it is an obligation.

Increasingly, corporations are being run less by their boardrooms and more by the decisions, sometimes ill-informed, of federal and state legislatures, governmental agencies, and their executive branches.

Advocacy advertising is only one facet of Bethlehem Steel's corporate communications effort. But it is an important facet, and one which we intend to continue to use -- honestly, intelligently, measurably, and responsibly.

Thank you.

PAUL WEAVER

It is a pleasure to be here this evening. I don't want
anyone to misunderstand; everyone couldn't have been nicer to
me this evening, but I want to confess to you that I am irri-
tated and depressed by the fact that we are meeting here tonight
to discuss and debate the topic of "Ethics and Advocacy Advertising." I wouldn't be troubled too much if this were only a
discussion of an abstract, ethical and intellectual question.
But, of course, the discussion comes in the context and at a
time when there is a movement in certain parts of the American
political system to inhibit and discourage, in any case, to regulate the conduct of advocacy advertising. And I find this
depressing because I was under the impression that this was
supposed to be a free, liberal society and that in such a society
the right of free expression of institutions, even institutions
that conduct business, was not to be questioned. Apparently
that is not altogether so these days.

It is also depressing because when people start putting
aside in one case or another case basic principles of freedom
and of liberal values, all of a sudden it turns out that the
least attractive human characteristics and the most famous human
vices and sins quickly become evident. All of a sudden the sin
of envy is everywhere apparent. Seeing envy is never an attractive thing. You also see the emergence of the sin of pride;
the sense on the part of any person, actor, or critic that he
is inherently superior, that his own views are sufficiently
superior to those of other people, that he is legitimate, that
he is justified in trying to impose his views and his tastes
and standards on others' conduct, whether through government or
any other means. Finally, I suppose it is irritating and worrisome to me that we are discussing this topic at this time in
this context because it is always worrisome in a free and liberal
society to see manifestations of what can only be called a fear
of freedom. Still, I am happy to be here tonight despite these
reservations because I am, in fact, an ardent advocate of advocacy advertising, at least as an idea, and I would like to
explain just a bit if I could why I am such an ardent advocate
of advocacy advertising, why I think companies, corporations of
all kinds, should be free to engage in it, and also why I wish
more of them would engage in it and do it better, and in a way,
do it harder.

My basic reason for being such an enthusiast has to do
with my belief, which I think is now being backed up by an in-

318

creasing amount of evidence, that the American political system, and in particular the system of representation in the American political system, has undergone a large, rapid, and by now an absolutely devastating change over the last 10-20 years. And as a result of that evolution, almost revolution, in our political system, I believe that we need advocacy advertising on the part of business in the way that we never did before. Now to understand the change that is taking place in American politics, I hope you won't mind if I raise with you a distinction made almost a century ago by one of the most interesting tory critics and observers of modern democracy, Sir Henry S. Maine. Maine said that in any democracy, ultimately one of two kinds of people would dominate. And he named these, in his inimitable way, the wire pullers and the hasty generalizers. Wire pullers are exactly what they sound like. That's to say they are machine politicians. They are people whose business is the organization of interests of all kinds, the leadership of interests, the management of interests, the bringing together of interests into coalitions, and the management and operation of a political system and of a government, and the effort to interpret the public interests through the mode of interest group politics. I suppose I don't need to mention the fact that in this country we have had no paucity of wire pullers running American institutions at various times. The hasty generalizers, of course, are very different. They are people who excel not in the management and mobilization of interests but in talk, not in the arrangement of groups and forces but in the manipulation of symbols and in the moving of people by touching their sentiments and affecting, if possible, their minds.

The basic change that has been happening in this country for some time now and that has accelerated rapidly lately is that the United States' political system, from having had a system of representation based heavily on wire pullers and the organizations that those people are involved in, increasingly is based on the art of hasty generalization. That is to say we are entering rapidly into an era in which talkers, writers, intellectuals, the press, universities, research institutes, and professionals in government bureaucracies are dominant. Now this has its merits, not the least being the fact that it gives people like me work.

On the other hand, there are real disadvantages in such a system. The biggest of these disadvantages is that, for a variety of reasons, the institutions, the groups and the professions that tend to dominate the system of hasty generalizing politics in this country at this time tend to share, alas, a basic, profound, really worrisome misunderstanding about the nature of American politics. To wit, they are victims of what

319

I think is fairly described as the populist myth; the notion
basically that behind and underneath any important political
undertaking or issue you will find, if you look hard enough and
are willing to push aside the surface of events, a conflict between self-interested special interests on one hand and the
good but exploited and pushed around people on the other. That
is a profound mistake. It is never the case, never purely the
case, that there is an opposition between the people on the one
hand and special interests on the other. The public interest
has to be composed of an amalgam of self-interests, and every
self-interest contains within it, however faintly, an image of
a genuine public interest.

In the system of hasty generalization that we live in and
live with today, an important kind of understanding and an important set of interests are increasingly being shut out. There
is a liberal press in this country and it doesn't like business.
Liberals in general aren't especially fond of business and
never have been. But that isn't the problem. The problem is
that people in this country whose business is hasty generalization don't understand and don't appreciate basic perspectives
that certain kinds of practical institutions, notably business,
are concerned with. And it is to correct the emerging and
growing institutionalized deficiency in American public discussion that I would like to see more advocacy advertising being
practiced in this country.

On the other hand, I have looked at corporate advocacy
advertising campaigns and I have come away feeling very dis-
satisfied and in certain cases contemptuous. Let me explain
what I mean. I do not object to the fact that corporate advocacy advertising is touched by the corporation's self-interest.
We all have self-interests. It is no bad thing and, even if it
were, we couldn't avoid it. It doesn't bother me that self-
interest affects the content, the balance, and the spirit of
what an advocacy advertiser says. That's inevitable too. And
it doesn't bother me that there might be factual distortions
in advocacy advertising campaigns. Of all the advocacy advertising campaigns I have looked at, none has as many distortions
and as many willful distortions in my judgment as a typical
book issued by Ralph Nader. If we're not going to regulate
Ralph Nader's speech, let's not regulate his corporate opponent's
speech. The problem is not the sort of things that are usually
adduced as being the weaknesses and shortcomings of advocacy
advertising. The underlying problem is a kind of intellectual
cowardice that reflects in turn a kind of personal moral
cowardice on the part of corporate executives. That is to
say, when they engage in advocacy advertising, they too often
engage not in honest advocacy reflecting their own knowledge,
understanding, and feeling, but they engage in what we all

320

recognize as phony corporate public relations junk.

For an example, one of the most famous advocacy advertising campaigns that we've seen in the last several years is the one that was run starting in 1974 by American Electric Power Corporation, which objected to an emerging requirement on the part of the EPA that coal fire utilities attach very expensive machines called scrubbers to their power plants. There were all kinds of good reasons for AEP to oppose EPA scrubber requirements. They're enormously expensive. They deliver very modest benefits. The benefits themselves are very problematic. Indeed, it's not clear that sulfur dioxide, which is what scrubbers take out of smoke, is a problem anywhere in the country of any importance. In approaching this, therefore, AEP was advocating its own self-interests but on an issue where its self-interest had at least a very close relationship with the broad public interest. And yet, given the magnitude of this problem and the many good reasons for AEP to argue against scrubbers, AEP decided to pull its best intellectual punches in this campaign. Instead of arguing, as was the case, that the most recent scientific evidence had called into serious question the legitimacy and validity of EPA sulphur dioxide standards, instead of pointing out that an EPA study had discovered that while scrubbers take sulphur dioxide out of the air, they create enormous amounts of another pollutant that EPA's scientists think is even more dangerous to public health, instead of focusing on those things, which were controversial and which might have made AEP look like it didn't care too much about public health, like it was calling into question the authority of' doctors of public health, AEP decided to focus on the mountains of sludge that scrubbers could produce as a waste product. It decided to focus on this relatively minor shortcoming of scrubbers in a humorous rather than a serious or angry spirit. I think that almost every advocacy ad campaign that I have seen shares a comparable weakness.

Therefore, although I am an advocate of advocacy advertising, I don't mean to suggest that the practice of advocacy advertising has been all that terrific, nor do I mean to suggest that it would be all that easy for corporations to do it right. For corporations to start acting as honest and unfearful advocates would entail rather large and difficult changes in the self-conception that prevails among American corporate executives today.

321

CARLL TUCKER

There have been a number of attitudes towards the relationship between the unalligned press (or, in some people's eyes, the
liberal press) and business expressed both at this table and during
the day. I gather that Mr. Morton Mintz earlier today said that the
excesses or abuses in reportage that business attribute to the press
are, on the contrary, responsible reportage of the abuses of business.
At dinner Mr. Mackie asked the question: "Are doubtful payments as
frequent as the media would like you to believe?", the assertion
being that the media would like you to believe that companies were
making lots of doubtful payments -- a doubtful assertion at best.
I want to suggest a reason why I think advocacy advertising is
tremendously important: It's important for the same reason that
having good reporting and a wide variety of opinions in our national
press is important. Because dialogue leads to understanding between
the special interests -- the people who know an awful lot about
what's going on in their particular expertise -- and the general
interest population, the people who are trying to make sense out of
what's going on in the world, and trying to arrive at some opinions
about how to deal with what's going on in the world.

Before I get there though, I would like to comment on what
some other people have said on this panel. I strongly agree with
Paul Weaver that it's the right of business to advertise. I think
there's no question about that and there are not many people who
would advocate disallowing advocacy, at least in print. That ignores
the whole complicated question of advocacy in the electronic media,
which is something that I don't want to get into, electronic media
being more coercive perhaps than intellectual. The argument that
Prakash made that there's no quality in this advocacy advertising
is probably true, but not much to the point. There's very little
quality in the media at all, but the fact that there is little
quality does not discredit the attempt to communicate. The reason
that I want to put forward for advocacy advertising is that it
broadens our awareness. Advocacy advertisers may not always speak
the truth. They may not always speak accurately. They may not
always speak, as Paul's example showed, to the point. But they
enlarge our dialogue and, more importantly, improve the relations
between business and the public.

During the past decade, the antagonism between the press and
big business has escalated into something of a cold war. Sensible
chief executives swear that the news media are bent on wrecking
their profits and their reputations, while newsmen who are otherwise objective assume that they have failed to get a business story

unless they have uncovered unconscionable greed, callousness or corruption. An armed camp mentality is growing. Instead of pondering how business and the press can cooperate with each other to improve the quality of business reportage, newsmen and executives scheme to circumvent or sabotage each other by sensationalizing on the one hand, or lying and stonewalling on the other. And if anybody looks into the public relations department of a major corporation, they will see that an awful lot of time is spent on worrying about how either to lie and get away with it or to tell only as much truth as won't hurt.

I find that a terrible shame because I don't think it's necessary. I think the differences between the press and big business are not ideological as they are in some European countries. In other words, we do not have a communist press squaring off against capitalist businessmen, although Spiro Agnew once intimated that that was the case. Excepting a few extremists on the right and the left, newsmen and businessmen recognize each other as legitimate partners in our national enterprise and they agree that the free press and profits are essential to the workings of our system of government.

Then the question arises, why do they fight with each other? In an article (I hate to mention a competitor, but...) in the _Atlantic Monthly_ this month, called "Memo to the Press: They Hate You Out There," Louis Banks, a former managing editor of _Fortune_ and now an adjunct professor of management at MIT, talks about the problems between the press and business. He says businessmen fault newsmen for careless reporting of facts, oversimplification, chronic negativism, treating good news as no news, and abusing the power of the press. Newsmen on the other hand fault businessmen for obfuscating facts, squandering journalists' time with bromidic press releases (some of these bromidic press releases they put into advocacy ads), not making themselves available to answer questions, and in some memorable cases, lying. Yet neither business nor the press object to the fundmental goals of the other. In business' case, the fundamental goals are to produce goods and services, jobs and profits. And in the case of the press, the fundamental objective is to report the news. What business and the press _do_ object to is the way in which the other pursues its goals.

Now, as with many wars, the root of the problem is misunderstanding and the way to alleviate the problem is to talk to each other. And this takes time, energy, money, and a certain courage. Now it goes without saying that the time, energy, and money could be otherwise allocated and the courage is very often lacking, but unless such a commitment is made to talking to each other, this argument over methods could escalate into an idealogical war in which the newsmen will clamor that capitalism, dishonest and uncontrollable, should be replaced and the capitalists will insist the press, uneducatable and incendiary, should be muzzled. That may sound like scaremongering and I don't mean to say that we're on the verge of that kind of situation now, but it certainly has happened in other countries. Our situation is dynamic: It can get better or it can get worse. But it's not going to stay the way it is.

Madame de Staël wrote, "To understand all is to pardon all." If businessmen and journalists knew better about what was going on in each other's operations, they would treat each other better, I suspect, and might even try to help each other out. Businessmen, for instance, should understand why people become journalists. They become journalists because journalism is intellectually various and stimulating. It's in the public eye. But most importantly, journalists consider what they do in the public interest. And to do their jobs well, journalists need honest information. Journalists respect a good source. But there are very few good sources in the business community. When a journalist seeks information, he is either evaded or referred to thrice-removed assistants in the corporate relations department who say they'll get back to them in three months and then never do. And so the journalist writes, "I wasn't able to get an answer," and then the corporate relations department angrily insists that it was going to deliver an answer if the journalists had given them time to prepare.

The problem is mutual misunderstanding and the solution to the problem, or at least part of the solution, is education. Now I'm not saying that journalists oughtn't to do better, in any case. But I think they also need to be made aware, as the public needs to be made aware of the businessmen's point of view. And I think advocacy advertising is one way of doing that. It alerts journalists and the people for whom journalists work (that is, the general public) that there are other points of view. Herb Schmertz's campaign for Mobil has been tremendously contro- versial (and I know Prakash disagrees with me on this), but one of the things that his campaign has done is that it has forced journalists to ask before they report negatively on the oil com- panies, might not there be another defensible point of view? Now that isn't to say they buy Schmertz's point of view, but it does mean that they are much more careful in their reportage with the result that the quality of our national dialogue is improved.

Another Frenchman said, "There are always reasons." I think business should make it its business to alert journalists and the general public to its reasons for doing what they do. That doesn't mean we have to support everything that the businessmen do, but I think it enhances our knowledge and our sensitivity towards

324

what business is going on. I, like Paul, believe very strongly
in advocacy advertising because finally, the more voices you have
in the national dialogue (and this is a Jeffersonian notion
which I adhere to), the greater the chance that the national
dialogue will be a dialogue of quality and that the mean which
will be derived is one that is closer to the just mean.

Most advocacy advertising is bad. It's bad because there's
timidity in the board rooms and there are multiple approval processes. But the fact is those are people with opinions who are
trying to say something, trying to change people's minds; they
encourage and enhance dialogue, which leads to better understanding, which leads to more reasoned and circumspect action.

DISCUSSION

LATSHAW: There are two thoughts I have in regard to Dr. Sethi's
remarks. The Association of National Advertisers in a study
conducted last winter surveyed some 250 corporate advertisers,
and two things became apparent as a result of that study. First,
there were only three corporations which were carrying out corporate advertising with advocacy as the prime goal; and secondly,
it concluded, based on previous benchmark studies that advocacy
advertising by corporations is waning, not expanding. And to
the point about corporate press releases: When corporations
send out press releases to newspapers, especially to small town
newspapers, of course, they'd like them to be reprinted as they
were written. And, of course, the pride of most newspapers calls
for a rewrite. And it's in the rewriting, by reporters who are
not trained in business, economics and finance, where the news
release becomes misinterpreted, or misleading. And that's what
draws the ire of the corporate press relations people. I can
understand the local newspaper attitude, but I think we wish
they'd either educate themselves in the field of business better,
or run the release as it was issued -- which is probably asking
too much.

SETHI: I have also two comments to make: Paul Weaver, Carll
Tucker, Bill Weed and Bill Latshaw, they all seem to agree that
advocacy advertising is difficult and that advocacy advertising,
by and large, has not been very successful. But then we hear
the comments from Carll and Paul saying, but it creates good
dialogue and we should support it. Well, where the heck is the
dialogue? All you have is one hysterical noise of the Ralph
Nader type and the other nonfactual glossy type of message from
the corporate advertisers. If dialogue is what we are looking
for, this is not the way to do it. All it would do is to increase
the level of noise. It would not contribute to the quality of
discussion or diversity of public information. On the contrary,
it would create greater public antagonism which would assert
itself through overreaction by the government in imposing greater
restrictions on the conduct of business than are necessary or
desirable. What you would then see is businessmen taking more
advocacy advertising to say that they were being unnecessarily
restricted and regulated.

TUCKER: Well, Prakash always gets me going. The fact is that
advocacy advertising does increase dialogue because advocacy
advertising very often attacks or broaches issues which are not
discussed, or are not of particular interest to the press. In

the general interest press you will very rarely see a piece about
the importance of profits. That doesn't happen to be a subject
which is of much interest to the general interest press. However, it is quite obviously a subject which is of great interest
to corporations, and I think that they raise the issue and in-
culcate their argument in the minds of the readers. Similarly,
the whole question of protectionism. Protectionism, as it relates to the steel industry for instance, is a very complicated
issue. As an editor, I have run one article about it, which was
a rather complicated article. It's a tough nut for an editor
to approach, and it tends to seem a little dry for the general
interest reading public. Bethlehem Steel, for instance, has a
great concern with this question, as well they should, and the
fact that they talked about it and gave their point of view on
the subject put the awareness of that as being a public issue
into the public's mind. So, from an editorial point of view, I
think it increases the dialogue. Of course, it will also increase the level of noise, but I think there is productive noise
and unproductive noise. And I would argue that advocacy advertising stimulates the former.

SETHI: Carll, you have been had. Because, what you're saying
is not good dialogue; it is a damage to good dialogue. I think
it's almost diabolic. What business is doing through advocacy
advertising is really forcing the journalist and the editors to
look at the issues that business wants them to look at, and to
avoid looking at and investigating the issues that business
doesn't want them to. Well, that may be good advocacy, but it
certainly isn't public interest.

TUCKER: I would say that, insofar as it discourages journalists
from looking into questions of corporate malfeasance or various
other things, it is bad, but I don't know of any case in my publication, or the New York Times, or various other places where
corporate advertising does appear, where the fact that corporate advertising appears discourages reporters from going and
investigating those companies. I really don't, and I don't think
the fact that advocacy advertising is run in our magazine increases our coverage of business or of the issues that are of
concern to business. I think it enlarges their side of the
dialogue, but I don't think it discourages us from trying to get
an objective appraisal of what's going on.

WEED: I do have an observation, and I guess it's an observation
of hope. Historically, it's absolutely true that business,
business executives, and business individuals have hidden from
the press, and the dialogue that was repeated here earlier has
happened hundreds and hundreds of times -- the press can't get
to the head office. They get meaningless vacuous statements

from some public relations man -- and it has gone a long way,
I think, to giving business the black eye that it has with the
editorial community and with the academic community. But I
really have seen very specific and positive evidence that this
is changing, and that presidents and chairmen of some important
corporations have finally -- and I hope it's not too late --
realized that they can't conduct their affairs this way any
longer. They are taking speech courses and they're doing all
kinds of things so that they are equipped to talk to the public
and to appear on television talk shows, and I really have a
very firm hope and belief that this situation is going to improve and that the dialogue that I think all of us here are
longing for will occur. It won't be a dramatic change, but it
will be a gradual and a real change.

MODERATOR: Let me ask the audience: Do you have questions?

COMMENT: I just want to say that I sat here listening to this
tonight, appalled. I came to hear a serious discussion on
advocacy advertising and what I saw was an example of advocacy
advertising that exemplifies every fault that was pointed out by
the speakers. To have to sit and listen to someone from Fortune
magazine, the magazine itself being advocacy advertising and
part of an empire of advocacy advertising, say that there is a
need for dialogue is just shocking. That this College would
seriously have presented this as a study in business ethics is
a criticism of the very possibility of a serious conference of
this type. There probably are laws on the books to deal with
advocacy advertising. They are the laws on obscenity.

COMMENT: Mr. Weed, I was very disturbed by the Armco Steel ad
you showed in your visual presentation. I spent a year in
Houston. As I recollect, there were two fellows accompanying
the executive. The fellow on the left in the helicopter and the
fellow who introduced him were two local anchormen at Houston
television stations. Wasn't there any concern on Armco's part
and your own that you'd be appearing to buy out the media, as it
were, or that it was improper for a journalist to be a participant in an advocacy ad?

WEED: They were reporting the facts as they understood them.

COMMENT: Was that a news report or an ad? It looked like an ad.

WEED: It was an ad.

COMMENT: Boy! It's one thing for Barbara Walters to sell dog
food, but it seems to me that a journalist is not supposed to
get that close to a corporation.

MODERATOR: Maybe we could ask one of the people here who work for a magazine to make a comment on that.

WEAVER: I agree with you; a journalist shouldn't have done that.

TUCKER: So do I. I think it was rather clever of Ogilvy and Mather to persuade them to do it. I certainly think those journalists, if you can call them that, were had, or let themselves be used.

COMMENT: But don't you think that depends upon their view of their role in their community?

COMMENT: I agree with the observation of my colleagues in the audience that we certainly have been put upon, but I'd nevertheless like to try to put the best face on the evening's proceedings I believe that Mr. Weed (related to the ethical implications) set the tone for his commitment. Remember, he said that one of the standards that his firm uses is to treat the audience and the objects of the advertising as though they were human beings. I say they are human beings, Mr. Weed, not as though they are. And using those anchormen as ploys is to abuse us. Secondly, journalists who think of their writing with the anticipation of brainwashing have certain audience objectives: How do you slant it? What headlines do you use? If any respectable journal or journalist were to proceed in that fashion, he should be drummed out of the profession forthwith. This is not journalism -- it's brainwashing and propaganda. Mr. Weaver's remarks bothered me too. When he described our history, our nation's history, as moving from wire pullers to hasty generalizers, I can think of no more beautiful hasty generalizations than we hold these truths to be self-evident. These were not wire pullers, these were generalizers in behalf of the most beautiful of our ideas and our ideals. And they did not have to use paid advertising to get the message across. I'd like to put a question to Mr. Latshaw of Bethlehem Steel. If I want to influence legislation, I try to write a letter to the Times, and it might or might not get published. If I were to advertise that, I would have to pay for it without a tax deduction. Is Bethlehem Steel using my money, that I'll be contributing and have contributed through the tax process, in order to get Bethlehem Steel's message across?

LATSHAW: Well, the answer to your question is that the dollars spent for advocacy advertising are not taken as a tax deduction. No, in effect, the (our) corporation is paying for that twice.

COMMENT: What about the personnel that are being used in the development of the advertising? Are they being deducted as part of the corporate payroll?

329

LATSHAW: You mean their wages and salaries?

COMMENT: Yes, yours for example.

LATSHAW: Yes.

COMMENT: My question is related to the previous one asked, and I think it also relates to an issue that really wasn't developed very well by the panel. And that is, aside from the mixed evidence on whether or not advocacy advertising is effective and whether or not it is legitimate, there's the question that Dr. Sethi, I think, brought up, of whether it enhances the dialogue. It seems, instead, to be a monologue. It doesn't relate just to taking tax deductions or not, or to the whole question of public subvention of advocacy or lobbying, but it also relates -- even aside from the tax deduction -- to the tremendous resource advantage that corporations would enjoy with advocacy advertising versus the limited resources that other people have with which to respond or to initiate their own voice. Now, I suppose that one could say, "Well, you already have the leader of the environmental defense fund and many other groups quoted in the major press, and a lot of people believe that the press is biased in favor of those groups in the first place." But I think those are really disparate kinds of quotations. You never really get a coherent view of what any interest group is saying unless they are able to afford to buy a full-page ad. I think that not too many years ago, when a major newspaper refused to run a full-page ad from Mobil, Herb Schmertz actually said, "In order to get away from the mainstream mishmash that this newspaper puts out, I'm willing to pay for an ad by the opposing public interest group if you're willing to run my ad too." But I think there are very few corporate executives who would take that beneficient position.

INTERRUPTION: I don't think Mr. Schmertz thought he was going to be taken up on it though.

Okay, granted. But I would still go back to my position that very few other corporate executives would even utter it, would take the risk. But my large question to the whole panel is: What measures do you propose to enhance the dialogue, that is to eliminate the disparity, the resource advantage that any particular company or industry would enjoy vis-a-vis its opponents?

LATSHAW: Well, Dr. Sethi, I think, has suggested certain courses of action in his book -- one of which, for example, would be for corporations who are doing advocacy advertising to take, let's say, 25 to 50 percent of the funds they're expending for advocacy advertising and make those dollars available to those who are

330

less affluent, if you care to use that term; that is, they have
less resources to advance their proposals. And I think he has
indicated that when he talked with business executives about
this point, he found a certain reluctance on their part. I don't
find that surprising. I don't think Sethi does either. I think
it is a fascinating proposal. But I don't think that it's about
to come about. It's difficult enough to get dollars for any
kind of advertising, whether it be advocacy or commercial, or
what have you. You're not about to supply those who hold contrary viewpoints with the dollars to come forward and present
those viewpoints -- not at your expense. If that seems awfully
damned self-serving, I'm sorry but it's very realistic, I believe.

COMMENT: What about alternative mechanisms, then?

LATSHAW: Well, I think one of the problems this evening is that
when we have concentrated on advocacy advertising, we have shut
out many of the other opportunities that corporations take advantage of through other media or through other events, to explain their points of view. I think we have built advocacy
advertising into a far more gigantic being than it really is.
Insofar as to how to make other forums available for opposite
points of view, well, Dr. Sethi, would you like to touch on that?

SETHI: You did make the point, and this is true, that there is
almost a total reluctance on the part of business to undertake
or entertain any kinds of proposals that would provide a better
opportunity, not to say an equal opportunity, for public exposure
to alternative viewpoints. And I choose the term alternative
very carefully, because business has a tendency to use, or to
flaunt, Ralph Nader as a "red herring." Every time one talked
to them, they'd say, "But Ralph Nader gets free access to the
press. He's already heard so often. All I can do is just keep
up with him." But it's not Ralph Nader we are talking about.
We are talking about alternative viewpoints. If business is
willing to accept intelligent and informed public decision making,
then business people should be willing to risk giving the public
better information on nonbusiness viewpoints as well. I don't
see it coming, and this is where you find that advocacy advertising is really adversary advertising. And it's not intended
to enhance the public's understanding of the issues. Instead it
might confuse them about the issues and give them a distorted
version of what is the right answer, namely, the answer business
prefers to use at a particular point in time.

COMMENT: I would enjoy Mr. Weaver's outlook on that as well.
But I thank you for answering it.

WEAVER: Your first question was: What can be done to equalize

the resources of companies as against other participants in public discussion, insofar as their ability to buy ads is concerned?
Whatever <u>might</u> be done, I don't think anything <u>should</u> be done,
for a number of reasons. For one thing, it would involve government and public policy and the shaping of conditions of access
to one important form of public discussion, advertising in media.
And for another, I think it's a mistake to focus only on the
dimension of financial resources. It's true on that dimension
that business is overwhelmingly potent compared to Nader type
groups and compared to many other participants in public discussion. But there are other dimensions that are also very important in shaping public discussion and moving public opinion
where there are imbalances the other way. For example, there's
some evidence to suggest -- and certainly my observation suggests
to me -- that in comparison to activist groups, whether on the
left or on the right, business organizations and business executives have very low feelings of legitimacy and political efficacy.
For example, if you poll corporate executives and ask them about
the credibility of corporate communications, more than two-thirds
routinely say corporate communications have little or no legitimacy, and you wouldn't get comparable answers from a poll of
leaders of citizen activist groups. Now, there's a very big imbalance that has a powerful effect on the relative ability of
the two categories of participants to affect public opinion.
Should we have some public policy to rectify that imbalance?
The fact is, there are lots of different kinds of resources that
are relevant, and they are distributed very unevenly. I don't
see that the maldistribution is cumulative; it seems to me that
it cancels itself out.

TUCKER: I'd like to speak to this point. I think it is very
easy to mistake the dialogue. It you're talking about the dialogue between one individual, as this gentleman did, and a corporation, obviously it's unequal. No individual can afford to
buy ads, probably even in his local newspaper, much less in
national media. But I think the public is represented in our
national dialogue in a number of ways. First of all, I think
our public dialogue is formed by power groups, not by individuals,
versus the government. And the general public is a member of
a number of power groups. One is as a voting power group. The
general public can become members of consumer groups. The general public can become members of unions. We haven't touched on
this here, but unions have engaged in advocacy advertising recently, so it's not just big business that uses the print media
to express its point of view. And, also, it's the business of a
representative press to watch out for the public's interests and
to make it its job to adequately, honestly, and fairly report
the news to its publics. Take a magazine like <u>Saturday Review</u>.
Our readers are a tremendous pressure group because if I don't

332

report fairly; if I don't deliver the truth, they can, and occasionally they do when they're angry, defect. So, I think that
yes, Paul's absolutely right that there is inequality in terms
of power, but I don't think it's fair to say it's the individual
versus the corporation. The individual has access to power
in terms of membership in power groups. And I think that's the
way our national dialogue is formed.

LATSHAW: May I speak to a point that was raised earlier. I
don't think there's anything insidious about a corporation, an
advertising agency, a publisher, scientifically surveying his
audience. Anyone who is trying to communicate with anyone else
tries to find the best route to communicate to that person. So,
of course, you wind up tailoring things to that particular
audience. But that doesn't mean that that's brainwashing. I
think the readers to whom we address our advertising have enough
intelligence to either, if they read our ad, believe it may have
some validity or not, to accept it or not. But brainwashing,
it seems to me, implies dishonesty or lying. And I simply would
point out that that's not the case in my view.

SETHI: I'd like to make just one point. Paul Weaver mentioned
that giving the opposition access to paid communication media
would involve government. I don't see why this should be the
case. There's no reason why voluntary arrangements cannot be
set up to provide or to distribute funds collected along the
lines that I had earlier suggested. Nor am I too bothered about
the inequality point. Sure enough, business has very low credibility, but they don't need balancing of power for that. All
they need is more accuracy in their communications. One more
point, Carll: I still disagree with you. If the press is so
competent to take care of the public interest, why is it incompetent to take care of the business interest? If business
feels that the press is incompetent and can buy paid communication media, what about the consumers who feel that the press is
incompetent to represent their interests. What about the environmentalists who feel that the press is incompetent to represent their interests? Don't they have a right to have paid
access to communication media? Just because they don't have
money, that doesn't mean that they shouldn't have access to
public communication space. And, that being the case, either
the press is competent in all the areas or is competent in none.

SESSION XIII

"The Bay Area Rapid Transit (BART) Incident"

Robert M. Anderson, Jr.
Ball Brothers Professor of Engineering
Purdue University

James Otten
Professor of Philosophy
Purdue University

Dan E. Schendel
Professor in Industrial Management
Purdue University

ROBERT M. ANDERSON, JR.,
JAMES OTTEN
and
DAN E. SCHENDEL

The Bay Area Rapid Transit (BART) Incident*

On the morning of March 2, 1972, Holger Hjortsvang was busily
at work in his office. Hjortsvang, at the age of 61, was employed
as an engineer for the Bay Area Rapid Transit system (commonly
known as BART), a modern rail transit system in the San Francisco
area. Suddenly the phone rang. It was the secretary of Hjortsvang's
superior, Mr. Ray, calling. The message was that Mr. Ray wanted
Hjortsvang to come to his office for a meeting of some kind.

When he arrived, Hjortsvang found himself in a meeting not
only with Mr. Ray, but also with Mr. Kramer, another of Hjortsvang's
superiors. These two men informed Hjortsvang that the General
Manager of BART had made the decision that Hjortsvang must either
resign or be dismissed. According to Hjortsvang, however, neither
man would give any specific reasons for the decision. At first
Hjortsvang refused to resign, but he changed his mind after considering the benefits that he would receive. A security officer
accompanied Hjortsvang back to his office so that he could collect
his belongings and then leave the premises.

Later that morning, around 11:00 a.m., Hjortsvang received
a phone call from Max Blankenzee. Blankenzee, at the age of 30,
was also employed as an engineer at BART, and worked in the same
department with Hjortsvang. Blankenzee was calling to say when he
would be returning to the office after a meeting with a BART contractor. Hjortsvang relayed the bad news that he had just been
dismissed, and told Blankenzee that Blankenzee's superiors wanted
to see him when he returned.

Soon after Blankenzee returned to his office, he was summoned
to a meeting with Mr. Ray and Mr. Kramer, his superiors. He too
was told that he must either resign or be dismissed. According to
Blankenzee, when he asked why he had to resign or be fired, Mr. Ray
said that it had to do with "your affiliation with Burfine, I

---

*Although Professors Anderson, Otten, and Schendel presented the
BART case study at the Conference, Sandy Dukes, Robert Perruci
Lea Stewart, and Leon E. Trachtman of Purdue University also
aided in coauthoring this document.

337

guess." Edmund Burfine was a private consultant who had written a report on alleged safety problems in BART's Automatic Train Control System, and had presented the report to BART's Board of Directors. Management was upset by this because it had not commissioned the report, and Burfine would not say exactly who had commissioned it. At any rate, Blankenzee refused to resign, and was fired. Blankenzee was then accompanied back to his office by the head of security, and was instructed to gather his belongings and vacate the premises.

The next morning Robert Bruder, 49 years of age, who was also an engineer with BART, but who was not in the same department with Hjortsvang and Blankenzee, was called in for a meeting with his superiors. When Bruder was asked if he had any involvement with Burfine, he answered that he had not. His superiors responded by saying that they had good reason to believe that he had in fact been involved with Burfine, and they proceeded to ask for his resignation. When Bruder declined to offer his resignation, he was fired.

BART's dismissal of these three engineers--Hjortsvang, Blankenzee, and Bruder--marked the culmination of one chain of events within BART, and marked the beginning of another chain of events which ultimately involved hundreds of interested people and organizations. The first chain of events centers around the three engineers' acts of "organizational disobedience." (An act of organizational disobedience, as we define it, is the deliberate violation of organizational policies, procedures, or accepted organizational standards of behavior; it is an action that an employee takes with the intention of overturning some organizational policy which the employee thinks is harmful to the public welfare or to the organization's welfare.) The second chain of events is comprised of reactions to and consequences of the dismissal of the three engineers for their acts of organizational disobedience. In the following pages we shall be tracing out the various links of these two chains of events.

The Early History of BART

The most appropriate place to begin is with the early history of BART. The formative idea for the BART system goes back to 1947. In that year a joint Army-Navy Review Board recommended construction of a tunnel under San Francisco Bay for the use of a high-speed electric train system. Actually the idea for such a system is a very natural one when you consider the geography of the Bay Area. San Francisco, shaped like a blunt-ended thumb and surrounded on three sides by water, is the center of tourism and commerce in the nine-county area surrounding the Bay.

In the years following World War II, intense political pressures were mounting for the creation of a transportation system that could reach out from San Francisco to serve the spreading cities and suburban communities in the Bay Area. Responding to these political pressures, the California State Legislature created the San Francisco Bay Area Rapid Transit Commission to undertake a detailed study of the transportation needs of the Bay Area. After six years of deliberation, this 26-member Commission recommended the formation of a nine-county rapid transit district which would coordinate its plans with the Bay Area's total plan for economic and social development. In accordance with the Commission's recommendation, the California State Legislature created BART in 1957. However, the plan for a nine-county BART system was not to survive. By 1962 only three counties remained in the BART plan--San Francisco, Alameda, and Contra Costa.

In late 1962 the voters of these three counties approved a design for BART and a proposal for bonding support for the system's construction. The difficult task of recruiting then began. BART's management decided not to hire its own technical and support staff to design and build the system. Instead, it formed a consortium of three outstanding engineering firms to design and build the system. The consortium was called Parsons, Brinckerhoff, Tudor and Bechtel (PBTB), and was comprised of Parsons, Brinckerhoff, Hall and MacDonald of New York; Tudor Engineering of San Francisco; and the Bechtel Corporation also of San Francisco. B. R. Stokes, who was General Manager of BART from 1963 to 1974, said of BART's recruiting plan: "We did not want to build a huge staff for the construction effort, that would later have to be disbanded... The decision was made to rely very heavily on...consultants in the various disciplines and to only build a staff based on largely permanent needs as we transitioned into an operating status." As a result of this recruiting decision, the BART staff was rather small, and perceived itself as a permanent group with a long-term commitment to both the construction and operation of the BART system.

The Role of the Three Engineers in BART

Construction of the BART system finally began in 1966. It was in September of that same year that Holger Hjortsvang came to work for BART. He was hired as a Train Control and Communications Engineer. In the beginning Hjortsvang received drafts of the specifications for the Automatic Train Control System from PBTB, which he would read and comment on regarding clarity, additions, and corrections. Later, after Westinghouse Electric Corporation had been awarded the contract for the Automatic Train Control System, Hjortsvang began to oversee Westinghouse's activities.

In 1969 Hjortsvang's superiors approved his request to accept an invitation from Westinghouse for BART engineers to go to Pittsburgh and work with the Westinghouse software design group in developing the Automatic Train Control System. Hjortsvang worked for ten months with the Westinghouse designers in Pittsburgh before resuming his regular job activities at BART.

According to Hjortsvang, it was during his stay at the Westinghouse facility that he first became concerned about the Automatic Train Control System and about general organizational problems at BART in trying to monitor the activities of PBTB and Westinghouse. At this time Hjortsvang prepared five or six reports detailing his concerns, and sent these to his superiors. These reports were acknowledged, but Hjortsvang indicated that there was "no response in reality. Nothing changed because of my reports." He added that Mr. Wargin, one of his superiors, "seemed to agree with what I had to say, but said, 'That's nothing. There's nothing I can do about it. BART's policy is that this is PBTB's business and not our business. Let's not rock the boat.'"

In November, 1969, a few months after Hjortsvang left for Pittsburgh, Robert Bruder joined the BART organization. His job involved coordinating train control and communication contracts. Whereas Hjortsvang worked in the Operations Division at BART, Bruder worked in the Construction and Engineering Division. In his position, Bruder had to maintain contact with the Operations Division at BART and with outside contractors, especially PBTB and Westinghouse. Bruder felt that he did not have a very good working relationship with his supervisor at BART, Mr. Fendel. On many occasions Bruder urged Mr. Fendel to do something about the lack of test scheduling by Westinghouse and PBTB, but, according to Bruder, Mr. Fendel did not respond because he felt that such matters were not the responsibility of his department. Bruder said that Mr. Fendel's reaction to his concerns could be summed up in this statement: "Hey, thank God it's not in our group, its downstairs or in operations."

In May, 1971, Max Blankenzee came to work for the BART organization. His position was that of a senior programmer, and he worked in the Operations Division with Hjortsvang. Concerning his job responsibilities, Blankenzee recalled that he was told that he would have "to do the hardware and the software, more or less work along with Westinghouse, stay abreast of them, get involved with the development in such a way by trying to find out what Westinghouse is doing so that later on we could maintain the central computer complex." His analyses of some of BART's technical problems were shared by his colleague Hjortsvang, with whom he worked on a daily basis.

340

All three engineers--Hjortsvang, Bruder and Blankenzee--
claimed that within BART there was a freedom to determine one's
own work activities and an absence of specific job descriptions
and assignments. Looking back, Blankenzee speculated: "I think
if BART would have had a little bit better controlled environment,
they probably not only would have seen these things we've talked
about, but they would have stopped us, would have stopped us long
before we ever got started on it (the organizational disobedience)."

Rising Concerns

Through 1970 and 1971 the character and complexion of the
BART effort slowly changed. The massive construction phase of
BART development was slowly coming to an end, and connections were
being made between the various structural components of the system.
Now BART was beginning the great effort to use the subway, surface
and aerial rails which had been laid in order to test the proto-
type car, and to install and check out the Automatic Train Control
System. As summer turned to fall in 1971, BART experienced a full
quota of technical and managerial problems. Of course, the BART
system was very innovative in its technical design as well as in
its managerial and contract-monitoring methods. Consequently,
management was not really surprised when problems arose with the
Automatic Train Control System.

Through 1970, the concerns of Hjortsvang and Bruder persisted about the Automatic Train Control System, the lack of adequate schedules for testing, and the failure of BART management to
monitor the work of PBTB and Westinghouse. Sometime early in 1971,
after Hjortsvang had not received an adequate response from his
superiors to the concerns he had been expressing, he decided to go
"outside normal channels" to present his concerns to a Director of
BART. A third party arranged for Hjortsvang to meet with Mr.
Blake, one of BART's Directors. However, the meeting never took
place because Hjortsvang changed his mind. Later Hjortsvang said
that the reason he had changed his mind was that "I did not want
to...start anything, anything that could be dangerous for me personally."

Several months later Hjortsvang tried another approach. He
set up a luncheon meeting with Robert Bruder and Jay Burns, two
other BART engineers. Bruder later recalled the meeting in this
way: "I think at the time even he (Hjortsvang) wanted to go to
some member of the Board. He wanted us to support him and go with
him. To ring the bell or whatever you want to call it." But
Bruder and Burns both refused to support Hjortsvang. When
Hjortsvang was rebuffed by these two men, he again lost interest
in pursuing his concerns. "I sort of gave up," he said. "I had

to do what I'm supposed to do here and not concern myself with BART's management."

Meanwhile Blankenzee's concerns about the Automatic Train Control System began to intensify. In the fall of 1971 he sent numerous memoranda to management expressing his concerns. He was afraid that he and others at BART would inherit a system from PBTB and Westinghouse which they could not understand and could not maintain. Blankenzee's assessment of the BART situation re-awakened the concerns of Hjortsvang and Bruder.

In November, 1971, Hjortsvang distributed an unsigned memo-randum to as many levels of the BART organization as he could reach. In this memorandum he proposed the creation of a Systems Engineering Department. In the memorandum he stated: "Most of the personnel can be extracted from existing departments, but a number of new specialists should be hired." Later management was to interpret this remark as indicating that Hjortsvang was seeking power for himself in the form of a department which he would head.

The Burfine Report

In November, 1971, the three engineers began trying to ar-range a meeting with a BART Director to express their concerns. Contact was made with Mr. Blake, one of BART's Directors. There was talk of a possible meeting between the three engineers, Mr. Blake, and Mr. Bianco, another BART Director. According to the three engineers, Mr. Blake thought that an outside consultant should be obtained before any such meeting took place. Presumably an outside consultant would be able to strengthen the case the three engineers wanted to make.

Blankenzee contacted an independent consultant, Edmund Bur-fine, to confirm the engineers' views. After spending one day discussing the BART situation with the three engineers, Burfine produced a seven page report entitled "Review of BART Operations." It was dated January 12, 1972. Finally, after all the effort to get an independent consultant to back up the engineers during their proposed meeting with Mr. Blake and Mr. Bianco, that meeting never materialized.

What happened instead was that another BART Director, Daniel Helix, became interested in meeting with the three engineers. In early January, 1972, Hjortsvang and Blankenzee met with Mr. Helix in a local union headquarters in Oakland. Hjortsvang said of this meeting: "My first comment was that this meeting was con-fidential and I pointed out to Mr. Helix that we had some con-cerns about BART's management, and we would like him to know about

342

it and...perhaps use his influence as a Director to get these problems solved in the interests of BART and the taxpayers...But I
pointed out very strongly that I had a family and I was sixty years
old and I was not going to expose myself to any open fight against
BART. And he assured me that he would respect that and that
nothing would happen to me or Blankenzee." During the meeting
Hjortsvang gave Mr. Helix some copies of memoranda he had written
about the need for a Systems Engineering Division at BART. Two
days after the meeting, the Contra Costa Times published a story
about BART's internal problems in which Hjortsvang memoranda were
reproduced in their entirety.

BART management immediately started trying to discover who
had been releasing information to Mr. Helix and the Contra Costa
Times. Hjortsvang, Blankenzee, and Bruder were each asked whether
they had any responsibility for this release of information, and
each firmly denied responsibility.

On February 22, 1972, Burfine, at the behest of Mr. Helix,
presented his report to the Engineering Committee, a subcommittee
of the BART Board of Directors. Blankenzee summarized what happened at this meeting by saying: "Burfine was slaughtered."
Three days later, on February 25, 1972, Burfine made his presentation to the BART Board of Directors. The Board voted 10 to 2 to
reject the Burfine report. B. R. Stokes, General Manager of BART,
said of the Burfine report: "My first reaction to the report was
that it was a ridiculously unprofessional, incomplete...almost
silly effort in terms of anything smacking of professional engineering." Interestingly enough, Burfine asked the BART Board
to pay for his effort in preparing the report. The Board declined
to do so.

The Firing of the Three Engineers

Soon after the Board meeting at which the Burfine report was
presented and rejected, management learned that Hjortsvang,
Blankenzee, and Bruder were involved with Burfine. As described
earlier, the three engineers were dismissed on March 2 and 3, 1972.

General Manager Stokes said of the dismissal: "I specifically authorized it, and directed it after satisfying myself that
we had no other recourse, after repeated exhortations for people
to come in and talk, after the material continued to flow into
the press, and after continued frustration at getting...the havoc
that was being caused among the staff."

Apparently there were at least four major considerations in
management's decision to dismiss the three engineers. First, the

three engineers' acts of organizational disobedience were, in Mr. Ray's words, "causing a lot of dissension...Work wasn't getting done. It was causing a lot of disruption." Second, management was upset by the fact that the three engineers had lied about their involvement with Burfine and Mr. Helix. Mr. Tillman, one of Bruder's superiors, remarked: "I'm not used to having people tell me one thing while they're doing something else." Third, management found that the three engineers were guilty of repeated insubordination in their activities. And, fourth, management believed that the three engineers were not acting out of concern for the public interest or for BART's best interests when they engaged in organizational disobedience against BART, but rather management thought that the three engineers were acting out of self-interest. General Manager Stokes recalled the last few days before the dismissal in this way: "At this point, some of the true motives (of the three engineers) were beginning to come out... it was not so much that anything was wrong with what was going on at the moment, but (that) it could be done better with a... Systems Engineering Group, (and the) three of them would be very very highly...involved at a very high level (in this group).

Involvement by Societies

One society which became involved with the three engineers was the California Society of Professional Engineers (CSPE). Bill Jones, president of CSPE, tried to arrange a meeting with BART management to discuss the dismissal of the three engineers. But BART management would not agree to such a meeting. Mr. Hammond, Assistant General Manager of BART, commented: "I don't believe professional organizations ought to act like unions; they ought to act like professional organizations...They saw three engineers who were fired and they felt, like a union, 'they can't fire our members.'"

The three engineers filed suit against BART, and Bill Jones instructed the CSPE attorney to give legal assistance to the engineers. Although the engineers asked for a total of $875,000 in damages, they eventually made an out-of-court settlement with BART under which each engineer was awarded $25,000.

Especially active in its support of the three engineers was the Diablo Chapter of the CSPE. The Diablo Chapter was spurred on in its support by two of its members, Roy Anderson and Gil Verdugo. These two men were instrumental in bringing about an investigation of BART by the California State Legislature. This investigation eventually led to great changes in BART, including the ouster of Stokes as General Manager.

Another society which became involved with the three engineers was the Institute of Electrical and Electronic Engineers (IEEE). After much internal struggle, the IEEE filed a friend of the court brief in the lawsuit brought by the three engineers against BART. Rather than support the particular position of the three engineers, the brief proposed a definition of a proper standard of ethical behavior for an employed engineer, thus indirectly supporting the three engineers.

The Aftermath

The reaction of the engineers to being dismissed was first surprise and then anger. They felt that they had been led to believe by Mr. Helix that there would be no reprisal for the actions they had taken. Furthermore, they viewed their actions as morally right, and in light of this their dismissal seemed to them unjust. As time moved on, the sudden loss of income and the inability to find new positions became the central experiences of their lives.

For a period of about fourteen months after the dismissal, Hjortsvang had a total income of $5,000, and when he finally did get employment his starting salary was $2,000 below what he had earned at BART. It took Blankenzee fifteen months after the dismissal to find a job with which he was fully satisfied. In this period, he experienced several months of unemployment or partial employment, and a cross-country move to Rochester, New York, which threatened the stability of his family. The impact of being fired by BART had its greatest effect on Bruder. He worked for a circus for a week, receiving about $20 that week for "putting up the middle of the ring." He held a sales job in which he lost more money than he made. After holding a low-paying consulting job for three months, he found a satisfactory job in November, 1972, with Singer Business Machines. All three engineers felt that the BART experience had a negative influence on their chances for finding employment.

Bruder later recalled with some bitterness the promises that Mr. Helix, the BART Director, had made to the three engineers when they were undertaking their acts of organizational disobedience: "(Helix) said, 'Gentlemen, don't worry...It's still up to you. You will not be in trouble...You won't starve.'" Obviously Mr. Helix was only partly right.

DISCUSSION

ANDERSON: The engineers' viewpoint might be summarized this way. There were serious problems with the Automatic Train Control System in the view of these three engineers. They did everything they could think of to get their management to listen to them, to understand and to appreciate the problems that existed. They wrote memos to their boss, to their boss' boss, to their boss' boss' boss. They had meetings with their boss, with their boss' boss, with their boss' boss' boss. In fact, they went up four levels of management trying to attract the attention of the management structure. They couldn't get what they felt was an adequate hearing of their point of view.

COMMENT: Would it be worthwhile to say they sound like they were really in three different technical areas? Did they work together or were they in different departments? How did they get together?

ANDERSON: That's a very complicated kind of situation. They worked together at times. They were arguing about separate issues at separate times. They did have different bosses to go through and they merged in and out over the course of two or three years, until finally they were together when the axe fell. Finally, they felt they had no choice, that they weren't getting anywhere with the line management structure. We know that they had an opportunity to go public and they turned it down. They made a conscious decision not to go public. They instead said, "We have to stay inside the organization," and they went to a member of the Board of Directors.

COMMENT: Could you tell us when they got together, the three of them?

ANDERSON: Well, they knew each other. The BART organization in the late 60's was not a large organization; they knew each other and they interacted with each other. Holger Hjortsvang and Max Blankenzee worked together, they were in the same group. Holger Hjortsvang car pooled on occasion with Bob Bruder, who was in a separate part of the organization. That's the kind of relationship that they had.

COMMENT: You said they had a chance to go public.

ANDERSON: A reporter heard that there was trouble and came to them and said, "Tell me what's wrong," and they said, "No."

That's the opportunity to go public that we feel they turned down.

COMMENT: He came to them as a group, or to an individual?

ANDERSON: He came to at least one of the three engineers. Then the consultant came in and after the contact with the Board, the whole thing finally became public. The management identified them and fired them. They had so much difficulty in getting work that the engineers feel that they were, in a sense, blackballed. And, finally, they sued the organization.

COMMENT: In your presentation, you said that they had contact with at least three members of the Board: Bianco, Blake and Helix. Did this issue ever come before the Board? Did one of those three Board members bring it before a formal meeting?

ANDERSON: Yes.

COMMENT: And the minutes are there?

ANDERSON: Yes, very cryptic. Two sentences convey very little information on what really went on. Newspaper articles at the time had far more detail.

COMMENT: Was it an open meeting of the Board?

ANDERSON: Yes. All meetings were open.

COMMENT: Was the firing done without prior approval of management?

ANDERSON: As we understand it, a phone conversation took place between one of the engineers, Blankenzee, and one of the members of the Board, Blake, and in the course of that conversation, they were discussing the credibility of the argument that the engineers were trying to make about the safety and reliability of the train control system. In the context of that kind of a conversation, apparently it sort of happened -- it's not clear who suggested it or how it came out of that conversation -- but the idea came out of that conversation that they needed a third opinion, an impartial opinion. Well, Max Blankenzee knew a guy by the name of Ed Burfine who was doing some consulting on the side, who knew something about train control systems and computer systems, and Max said, "Well, we'll ask Ed to come in and look at it." So Ed Burfine, the consultant, came in and talked to Max Blankenzee, Holger Hjortsvang, and Bob Bruder, collected information and wrote a report. The report in essence said, "There are serious problems in this area."

COMMENT: He was not under contract to BART in any way?

ANDERSON: No. He was an outsider.

COMMENT: Did you say the consultant only spent about a day doing this?

ANDERSON: Yes.

COMMENT: That sounds incredible on such an involved and complicated project.

ANDERSON: That's exactly what management said.

COMMENT: If they had spent so long on this and so many years, how could a consultant come in and in one day make a decision, short of just adopting whatever people he talked to told him?

ANDERSON: That's exactly what the Board said and that's exactly why the Board said it was a ridiculous piece of paper and not worth their time to consider it.

COMMENT: Did anyone of the three engineers appear at the open Board meeting in which the two lines were written? Were they present or were they entitled to be there?

ANDERSON: No sir, they were not present, but they were indeed entitled to be. Helix asked whether or not they would want to appear and they said, "No way." They were not at all interested in being identified. Helix promised them that he would do everything he could to preserve their anonimity and he tried.

COMMENT: They had already written memos, right?

ANDERSON: They had been identified as dissidents, but they had not been identified as the engineers who had gone to the Board.

Discussion After Study-Groups Come Back Together

SCHENDEL: I'm a policy teacher by heart, and I suggest that the strategy any particular organization wants to follow is going to have some very important influences on the organizational structure -- the reporting kinds of relationships, the hierarchical distributions of authority, and so on, that we associate with structure. But strategy will also have something to say about the managerial processes that are used: planning processes, decision-making processes, resource allocation, and so on. And there are certain kinds of behavior that you want to evoke and certain kinds of people that are going to be part of this structure, and these three items -- structure, processes, and behavior

--create a climate in which things occur.

Well, it's clear that if you were to look at the BART climate,
there were some things that were vitally wrong with it. Well,
here are the study-groups' conclusions, filtered by our perceptions, as to what went wrong, what the reasons were behind what
happened at BART, and what might have been done differently.
The first point that seemed to get your attention was: there
should have been more facts collected by management and much more
control over these engineers and what they did. If I can interpret that to mean more interest in what they did, more investigations of their own opinions, one might take that even further
and say: there should have been much more built into the organization's structure that controlled what their contractors did.
It's not clear at all that the goals of the contractors were co-
incident with the goals of BART or with the public. The Board
didn't get involved with that. Management didn't get involved
with that.

There was a question of the priority of objectives that management had. I probably caused some of these perceptions by saying
what the great pressures were on management. How do you trade
safety, cost, timing, the need for publicity and notoriety?
After all, management claimed they were building a very innovative
system and people from all over the world were coming to see
them. How do you trade off those kinds of issues in a not-for-
profit organization like BART (although one could argue every
organization had better make a profit if it's going to survive).
But how do you trade those objectives off? Management was trading
them off one way. Engineers wanted to trade them off another.
Who was right? And who was to decide? Should the Board do it?
If so, why didn't they?

What mechanisms, or processes, if you will, existed in this organization for hearing dissent and with what kind of objectivity?
Did BART management really have an open-door policy? And if they
really acted with an open-door policy, what would have had to
take place to insure it? One group pointed out that Stokes' expertise, which was considerable, was directed upward and not
downward in the organization. I would concur on that. He was
very much more interested in what went on above him, as general
manager, than he was in what went on below him. But all of his
early efforts had to be directed, first of all, to the bond issue.
He was instrumental, incidentally, in helping to get the 66-2/3's
reduced to 60%. He spent a lot of time in Sacramento. He had
to be a publicity man to get his job done at all. But when his
attention needed to shift internally, he was unable to do it, and
the Board was unable to see the necessity for such a shift.
Somebody said, use an ombudsman, an inspector general. Should

we have one in an organization like this? I don't know. There are pros and cons to that.

The engineers were organizationally naive. I think that's true. I've written the word coalition, something that's occurred to me and is to my mind similar to Capote's thesis, In Cold Blood. Would this incident have happened if the three engineers hadn't gotten together? If just two had met? Would the incident have occurred then? I don't know. But how do you discern the potential for such coalitions in organizational design and how do you assess people's capability for joining such coalitions? Better organizational structure. Sure. Better design. Less hierarchical responsibility for a very technical system. There's enough evidence around to suggest that organizational structure for a technological organization should not be as hierarchical as this one. It should be flatter. More information had to flow. Better information systems. That's probably true. A control system for the expenditure of money and for the accomplishment of goals. I think they were very naive about that. The technical expertise itself wasn't really what it should have been. What technical expertise they had, for the most part, had to do with the rails and the concrete, and not with the cars or with the electronics, which was really important and very significant to BART's attempts at innovation.

What was the role of the Board of Directors in this incident? I've been concerned with the Board's viewpoint but I'm fairly critical of the Board. I think for many directors it was a political plum to be on the BART Board and the role models that these people needed to guide behavior just weren't there. There weren't people on the Board who were associated with big organizations or experienced with what it took to run them, or with policy-making in them, or what the Board might have done vis-á-vis General Manager Stokes, who, in fact, really ran this organization lock, stock, and barrel, and who was very good at controlling what the Board saw and heard. One other thing that I'll just add as a little fillip before I sit down is that each Board member was paid $50 for every meeting attended, and that included any committee member at committee meetings, but only up to five per month. And they met more frequently than five times per month, so after five meetings people wouldn't come. Stokes knew that and he used it tactically, I am told, or so it's alleged by people like Director Helix. That sort of thing went on, all of which suggests the organization structure should have been much more carefully designed.

And the one question I'd leave you with, that goes beyond the incident of the engineers and has more interest to me is: How do you design third sector organizations -- and we're going to

350

see more of these collections of not really public, not really private organizations? And who do they answer to? There are, after all, expenditures of great sums of money in such third sector organizations and to what good end? Could BART, for example, have had a transit system for less money if it had done its work in a different way? I don't know. Jim, I'm going to turn it over to you to deal with some of the individual questions.

OTTEN: Well, I see that you've had a lot of the same reactions that we had to the BART case. Only one study-group came out and really took a stand on the issue of whether the three engineers were morally justified in their actions, and that group said that the engineers were justified and that the proof of that was their willingness to endanger their careers. Well, let's take a look at some of the other reactions. One group claimed that BART ruled out acting on principle because of the way the organization was run. Okay, well, it seems like there would be disagreement about that. I think the BART management wouldn't want to agree with that. Like we said before, the engineers thought that BART was run like a military organization, whereas management thought that they had an open-door policy. Another reaction was that management should discourage circulation of unsigned memos, and maybe this is really saying that the engineers weren't justified in all of the actions they took. Another opinion: Was it really a matter of principle for the three engineers? And that's something that we're all still puzzling over. Some groups pointed out that there are always mixed motives and maybe the engineers had a whole bunch of different motives. Another reaction: How serious was the issue? One group said that at least the three engineers felt it was a serious enough issue to engage in the organizational disobedience. I'm not sure what the upshot of that is. If they felt it serious enough, were they therefore justified in it? Well, as I said, it seems like you had a lot of the same reactions we did. It's not a black and white issue. It seems like there's a lot of gray areas here. There aren't any heroes or villains. Maybe we can have a few minutes of general discussion now about these issues.

COMMENT: It seems that insofar as it's an organizational issue, or there's an organizational issue in it, you could get the most flexible organization setup you wanted to, but if you were under public pressure, with $2\frac{1}{2}$ billion over cost, under those conditions it might freeze the whole backbone of command right down through. You'd say, "No objections boys. Wait until we get into process and then we will refer you. We'll do what we can on this business and then we'll bring it up. But right now, we are under the gun." And that's not an unreasonable attitude, because their primary obligation almost is to the people who wrote the bond.

The other thing I wanted to get at was -- and this is an informational question -- how did the three engineers present their
case? Did they come up and say: "Yeah, we know we're in a hur-
ry. We're behind. But, somewhere down the line we've got to
start thinking about these kinds of things because we've got
operational problems when we get in here." Or did they come back
and say: "Gee, it's no good. Turn it back to Westinghouse.
Stop the whole thing." Which way did it go? Because, after all,
management came up with the idea that they were dissidents.
And that's, in a way, a strange kind of notion because they've
got qualifications. Now, unsigned memos don't help as far as
dissidence is concerned, but where did they get that view that
they were undesirable people?

COMMENT: Holger Hjortsvang was there first, and because he was
there first, he was most well-known in the organization, and his
personality has been described variously as abrasive, hard-
headed, etc. He wasn't a smooth politic man and that clearly
colors the way people react to his concerns.

COMMENT: I'd like to ask a question of Dr. Otten. I'd like to
know exactly what he thinks is the ethical content in all this
material, because one could interpret this as dealing merely
with good management procedures or operational questions about
how management should have proceeded. It's alleged by some that
BART ruled out acting on principle when, in point of fact, their
principle may have been: Secure our objective with the least
possible cost overrun in an acceptable time and with acceptable
risk. And looking through all of the comments that have been
made here, exactly what is the ethical content that we might be
dealing with and what are some of the ethical principles in the
NSPE code that would apply, if any?

OTTEN: What do you mean by the ethical content? Are you asking
me what I think the ethical issues are, or what my ethical judgments are?

COMMENT: What are the ethical issues without your own personal
judgments?

OTTEN: Well, I think we have to evaluate all of the actions
that were taken by management, by the societies, by the Board,
by Helix, by all the individual members of the Board, by Burfine,
by the engineers. So I think there are ethical questions all
around on this. What else were you asking?

COMMENT: Well, I'm asking, how can we make a determination if

352

we're concerned with ethics on what was the right thing to do in terms of right or wrong, as against what was the right thing to do in order to pursue certain better management procedures, and so forth?

OTTEN: Okay, well, I think there are no simple principles you can follow. Like I said, there are a number of considerations you have to take into account where you can't state them neatly in any principle and say that organizational disobedience is justified when such and such occurs.

COMMENT: Did anybody violate a code of ethics as established by any of the professions involved here?

OTTEN: Yes, you could say that the three engineers violated the NSPE's code of ethics, because they have some provision in there which says that you shouldn't make derogatory comments, I think, about other engineers.

COMMENT: Don't you want to add to the response to that question the concern that our group raised. Appeals to minimizing cost, getting the job done, and then the factors that you mentioned are important appeals. But what about the appeal to the safety of the end product? If there is a clash between those first appeals and that appeal, I think you have a good example of an ethical question.

COMMENT: All right, well that's what I would say, that the ethical question turns on the safety of the product. But who is right about that? The engineers had certain kinds of expectations; management had still others. And who would you believe without a serious testing program or without operation?

COMMENT: Am I right that a model was built in the desert somewhere -- a mile-long model -- and the features of that were not actually transferred to the final product?

SCHENDEL: No, the test track was really a part of the system, as I understand it, and it was used for car testing and other things. But you see the big problem they ran into was the TransBay Tube. You've got to funnel three lines into that tube and they were going to go through with two-minute headways. Well, you think about merging three systems like that, that's where all the problems come. Incidentally, when they opened, they only ran up and down the East Bay from Richmond to Hayward. And if you recall those three lines coming in right at Oakland, going right across that tube, that's where the big problem was. And to run two-minute headways with no operator takes a very sophisticated system. How do you control -- they talk about blocks in train

control -- how do you move from one block to another, making sure
it's unoccupied? Well, they ran into such things as: overnight,
the rails would oxidize (because the system wasn't running all
the time) and in sections they couldn't detect trains. That's
what the engineers were concerned about. The equipment was not
sensing that a train was there. And, so, when they finally did
operate, they had human controls. One operator would say, "This
train has left this block" to another controller, "Yes, okay."
This could not be a very advanced system, but that's the way
they started running and were forced to operate like that.

COMMENT: What's the ethics in that?

COMMENT: Safety should be very important.

COMMENT: I think the priorities listed here touch upon that. I
imagine everybody here would have named safety as the number one
priority in the whole program.

OTTEN: Of course, you can never have perfect safety. If you're
going to make a train as safe as possible, it would never run.
So, you have to consider: How seriously unsafe was it?

COMMENT: But the way that was presented, if that was presented
to the Board, they've got to consider safety more than the timing.
That's a basic technological unsafe thing that you could make an
ethical decision on. Was it presented to the Board that way?

SCHENDEL: I could tell you a little story about that. George
Silliman was the President of the Board. I interviewed him and
asked him, "What did you think of all of this?" And he said,
"Well, of course safety was first," but he said, "Hell, if it
was unsafe, it wasn't going to run. I was concerned with making
it run." And he said, "When it was all done, I got my people
together and we went to Westinghouse," and he talked about being
at Westinghouse and talking with Don Burnham, who was the Chairman of the Board at that time, and they said, "Well, you know,
this is something we can determine; either it's safe or it isn't
safe." You know, just as cavalier as that. Now, George Silliman
is a fine gentleman for all I can tell, but his background was
as a newspaperman and a banker. He didn't know much about technical matters. But he felt it was as simple as that. It's either
safe or it wasn't safe.

COMMENT: But what did they determine later?

SCHENDEL: Well, it's all relative. What's safe? You know, I'm
going to go on an airplane this afternoon and I guarantee you
it isn't 100% probability that I will get to Chicago. But I

354

think it's safe enough, so I'm going.

COMMENT: It seems to me there's another ethical question involved here, and that would be from the standpoint of Westinghouse being the contractor. If Westinghouse is the contractor, as a major corporation, they certainly cannot sell to the Bay Area Rapid Transit System because their ulterior motive is going to be additional sales. They cannot stop there and say that they're not going to sell an unsafe system.

COMMENT: So.

COMMENT: That's the argument that BART management had; "Of course, Westinghouse isn't going to give us a bad system."

SCHENDEL: But that doesn't guarantee it.

COMMENT: That would be my position. Which source are you going to go to?

SCHENDEL: Well, let me try to shatter your faith in Westinghouse. One of the things that the California state legislature did when they got into it was appoint what they call a "blue-ribbon" investigating committee, and one of the members of that three-man committee was Barney Oliver, who is the Vice President of Hewlett-Packard and knows something about electronics. And he wrote a personal letter to a vice president of Westinghouse Corporation who he knew very well. And one of the sentences in that letter says, "It's clear that the ATC (the Automatic Train Control System) did not occupy the attention of your better people." That's a verbatim quote out of that letter. It's a three-page letter, by the way, single spaced and very detailed. But in that one sentence, it seems to me that Barney Oliver, who looked at the electronics of the train control system, concluded that it was a poorly designed system from a technological point of view. There were better ways to do what Westinghouse was trying to do. And Westinghouse, in fact, had made some poor technical decisions, in Barney Oliver's opinion, and that's the issue, you see. Who do you believe in things like this, in high technology situations especially, where there is no extensive experience to draw upon, where you are trying to advance the state of the art, and where you have competing and alternative ways to accomplish ends?

COMMENT: The problem with the "blue-ribbon" committee is that Westinghouse could assign its own "blue-ribbon" committee that said that it's an outstanding system.

SCHENDEL: Along that same path, there were several other ways to go, from a management point of view. And it seems to me one can make a strong case here, that managerial expertise was missing. Oliver said, "There are other ways to go if you're going to follow a high technology strategy." Isn't there some kind of an ethical obligation on the part of an organization if they are to bring people in, manage them, set up expectations, expect a certain kind of behavior, that that kind of expertise be in the organization. Isn't there some kind of ethical responsibility to make sure that it is there?

COMMENT: I would believe that there would be. You talk about high technology; they never began to employ the technology that management knew about. Think about a billion dollars being expended. They went at it like it was mom and pop's grocery store. Really. It sort of grew like Topsy.

COMMENT: Mostly Uncle's money.

SCHENDEL: No. Twenty percent of it was Uncle's money. This was very much local money. It's a very unusual project in that regard.

SESSION XIV

"Polaroid and South Africa"

Dharmendra T. Verma
Professor of Marketing
Bentley College

DHARMENDRA T. VERMA

Polaroid in South Africa (c)

On Monday, November 21, 1977, Polaroid Corporation announced
its decision to terminate its distributorship in South Africa thereby ending the "Experiment in South Africa" which it had begun six
years earlier. In making this announcement, an official of Polaroid stated:

> We were presented on Wednesday, November 16, with in-
> formation which suggested that Frank & Hirsch Pty. Ltd.,
> the independent distributor of Polaroid products in
> South Africa, has been selling film to the government of
> South Africa in violation of a 1971 understanding. That
> understanding stipulated that the distributor refrain
> from selling any Polaroid products to the South African
> government.

> As a consequence of this new information, we initiated
> that same day an investigation from which we have now
> learned that Frank & Hirsch has not fully conformed to
> the understanding with regard to sales to the government.

> Accordingly, Polaroid is advising Frank & Hirsch that it
> is terminating its business relationship with that com-
> pany.

> In 1971, when the question arose as to whether it was
> appropriate for Polaroid to continue to sell to a dis-
> tributor in South Africa, we examined the issue care-
> fully. We abhor the policy of apartheid and seriously
> considered breaking off all business with South Africa.
> We felt, however, that we should consider the recom-
> mendations of black Africans before making a decision.
> They urged us to maintain our business relationship
> and try to accomplish improvements in the economic and
> educational opportunities for black workers. We did
> succeed in persuading our distributor to give to black
> employees responsibilities much greater than they had had
> in the past and substantially to improve black salary
> rates. We also made contributions, which aggregate
> about one-half million dollars, to black African scholar-
> ship funds and other programs. In much of this activity
> our distributor cooperated effectively. We were there-
> fore shocked to learn that the understanding not to sell

to the government was not followed.

With the termination of this distributorship in South
Africa, we do not plan to establish another one.

The South African Distributor: Reaction

Polaroid Corporation's 1977 sales were over one billion dol-
lars.   The South African business was worth between three and four
million dollars.   This amounted to about half of the revenues of
Frank & Hirsch (Pty.) Ltd., the South African distributorship.
Helmut Hirsch, the owner of the distributorship is a "66-year-old
German-Jewish emigree who escaped to South Africa from Nazi Germany.
In the South African political scene he is considered a liberal.
He is a member of the Progressive Party and a friend of Helen
Suzman, a well-known critic of the Vorster regime.   He has been
the chairman of Dorkay House." (The Boston Globe, November 23, 1977.)
The company has distributed Polaroid products for the past 18 years
and it also handled Japanese cameras, watches, and other imported
equipment.

Following Polaroid's announcement, Helmut Hirsch issued a
statement in Johannesburg on Tuesday, November 22, 1977, that said:

On hearing allegations that Frank & Hirsch have supplied
Polaroid products directly to departments of the South
African government, we made an immediate investigation
that revealed over the past several years a very small
number of isolated cases where unbeknownst to us there
were deliveries to the South African government.
Frank Hirsch regrets these isolated instances because
they are not in keeping with the agreement between
Frank & Hirsch and Polaroid.   Immediate steps have been
taken to avoid any recurrences.

The Boston Globe reported that in a telephone interview Hirsch
confirmed that some sales of Polaroid products to the South African
government violated the agreement with Polaroid.   According to
Hirsch, his investigation of the records showed three sales in
1975, two deliveries in 1976, and 12 transactions so far in 1977.
The records do not go back further.   However, he insisted that
other sales to South African government agencies had not been restricted by the ban agreed upon in 1971.   Hirsch claimed that "only
some agencies were restricted--the Security Department, the Bantu
(black) Reference Bureaus, and the military.   Muller's Pharmacy
(a large Johannesburg drugstore) was officially permitted to supply anyone.   They were tendering government contracts.   Polaroid
was well aware of it.   They knew the government was putting orders

360

through pharmacies." (<u>The</u> <u>Boston</u> <u>Globe</u>, November 23, 1977.)

In the same interview, Hirsch explained to the <u>Globe</u> that his firm supplied many government agencies, including hospitals, water supply agencies, and airports. These transactions apparently were prearranged with the government agencies through Muller's Pharmacy. Other deliveries were done as a favor. "It's possible the customers phoned, and I was not aware of it." ... he "begged" Polaroid management not to sever the relationship... Hirsch said he is planning a trip to the United States this weekend to try and repair his relationship. "If they give us an opportunity to talk to them, we have a good case for not abandoning Polaroid from South Africa. It's become a way of life here." Hirsch was planning to bring Sidney Kentridge, a prominent South African attorney, to represent him in discussions with Polaroid over the weekend. (Kentridge represented the Biko family at the inquest into the death of Steve Biko, a well-known black political activist.)

Circumstances Leading to the Polaroid Decision

Polaroid products were sold through the distributor to drugstores and photographic supply houses in South Africa. Polaroid management had known the South African government was using its film, but believed the purchases were made in the open market and not from its distributor. A 1971 agreement between Polaroid and its distributor had specified that no sales were to be made to the South African government.

Allegations of secret sales of Polaroid cameras and film to the South African military and Bantu (black) Reference Bureau that issue identification documents "passbooks" to blacks (an instrument of apartheid) were made by Indrus Naidoo, a former employee of Frank & Hirsch. Naidoo made a photostat of a delivery note covering one shipment of Polaroid film going to the Bantu Reference Bureau on September 22, 1975. This photostat copy was passed on to Paul Irish, an official of the American Committee on Africa (ACOA) in New York City. Irish released the copy to the press in mid-November 1977, only after Naidoo had left South Africa as an exile.

The <u>Boston</u> <u>Globe</u> (November 21, 1977) reported that Naidoo was interviewed by telephone while in Bonn, Germany, where he was on a speaking tour for the African Liberation Movement and he detailed the transactions between Frank & Hirsch and the South African government:

Frank & Hirsch billed all the shipments to the South

African government through Muller's Pharmacy, a drugstore in downtown Johannesburg. The films and cameras
were placed in unmarked cartons and then transferred to
unmarked transport vans for the drive to their desti-
nation... There were regular deliveries to the
Voortrekker Hoogte military headquarters outside Pre-
toria, periodic deliveries to several local reference
bureaus, and at least one large shipment of sunglasses
to the Air Force... Since all billing was done through
Muller's Pharmacy, there would be no record of funds
being received from the South African government.

Polaroid management was informed of the charges on Wednesday, November 16, and they dispatched Hans Jensen, the Export Sales Manager
and a British auditor, to South Africa to investigate. Polaroid
officials stated:

Helmut Hirsch told us many times he was not selling to
the South African government, As far as we were able
to determine he had stuck to the agreement. However,
we never took for granted they would follow our stipulation. That's why we have sent people there every
year.

Mr. Jensen found several deliveries to the South African
government in his examination of Frank & Hirsch records. In his
telephone conversation with Polaroid officials, Jensen reported
that Hirsch, the owner of Frank & Hirsch, was shocked: "He claimed
he had no idea this was going on."

On Monday, November 21, 1977, in announcing Polaroid's decision to discontinue the distributorship, Robert Palmer, Director
of Community Relations at Polaroid, described Polaroid officials
as distressed.

People are upset and disappointed... Over the past 6
years Polaroid influenced Frank & Hirsch to substantially raise its black employees' wages and we have
contributed almost half a million dollars to several
black groups in South Africa. Hirsch followed the
program we outlined--equal pay for equal work, and
black employees were moved into jobs the whites
held. The distributor had only 200 black employees
but I think our influence had a ripple effect on
other U.S. Corporations... Now this "Experiment in
South Africa" has come to an end.

Polaroid's Experiment in South Africa and Consequences: A Perspective

In late 1970, internal (corporate) and external (community) questions were raised regarding Polaroid Corporation's involvement in South Africa.[1] Specifically, questions focused on the use of Polaroid's ID system by the government of South Africa in its passbook program. These passbooks had to be carried by all non-white South Africans and were seen as a means whereby the government enforced its apartheid system. In response, a Polaroid team was sent to South Africa to study the problem first hand. Based on its report, Polaroid management stated that they had reviewed their operations in South Africa and in January, 1971, announced an "Experiment in South Africa." The announcement included the following statements:

- We abhor Apartheid.

- We want to examine the question of whether or not we should continue to sell our products in South Africa.

- We do not want to impose a course of action on black people of another country merely because we might think it was correct.

A group of Polaroid employees, both black and white, then toured South Africa and returned with a unanimous recommendation to undertake an experimental program for one year with these goals:

- To continue our business relationship there except for any direct sales to the South African government.

- To improve dramatically the salaries and other benefits of the non-white employees of our distributor there.

- To initiate through our distributor well defined programs to train non-white employees for important jobs within that company.

- We would commit a portion of our profits earned there to encourage black education.

At the end of the year, in December, 1971, Polaroid management issued their report outlining the benefits of their year-long experiment (see Exhibit 1). The report concluded:

In a year's time the visible effects of the Polaroid experiment on other American companies had been limited, but the practical achievements in increased

363

salaries, benefits, and education had shown what could
be done. Therefore, the company decided to continue
the program for the present.

In November, 1977, following a series of reviews and audits,
Polaroid issued a report specifying some of the consequences of
the six-years following the initial decision to undertake the "Experiment" (see Exhibit 2). In conclusion, the report pointed out:

We believe that it is still too soon to make a final
judgement on our relationship to South Africa. We have
found that the lack of knowledge concerning American
business in South Africa has been as difficult to deal
with as has the complexity of issues surrounding business practices in that country.

We will continue to press, as constructively as possible, for change in South Africa. We will not, however,
decide for black Africans what they need. The final
determination will have to come from South Africans
themselves. We intend to stay as long as black South
Africans and moderate whites feel that progress is
being made and that our presence there is helpful.
We should acknowledge that our decision to continue is
made easier by the fact that our South African distributor has been a willing participant in the changes
affecting his work force.

We agree with our thoughtful critics that the specific
accomplishments of the Polaroid experiment affect relatively few black people. A growing number of people,
however, are beginning to share our hope that the
possibility of change in South Africa is real.

U.S. Corporations & South Africa: A Different Perspective

The non-profit Investor Responsibility Research Center (IRRC),
Washington, D.C., released a study indicating that about 320
American companies have operations in South Africa. Some of the
largest (with 1976 sales in South Africa) are Mobil Corporation
(over $500 million); Caltex, a joint-venture of Standard Oil of
California and Texaco ($500 million); Ford ($208 million); General
Motors ($250 million); Chrysler (through a 24.9% interest in Sigma
Motors, $190 million); IBM ($163 million or less). The U.S. Com-
merce Department estimates book value of U.S. Investments in South
Africa at $1.7 billion in 1976. For most American companies,
South Africa represents 1% or less of their total sales. However,
in the South African economy, some are significant. IRRC reported

364

that American companies control 43% of the country's petroleum market, 23% of its auto sales and 70% of its computer business. (The Wall Street Journal, December 5, 1977)

The article further stated that some companies, such as General Motors, Ford and Control Data, have indicated they will limit further expansion there. Chrysler, International Telephone and Phelps Dodge have merged their subsidiaries into South African companies. Burlington Industries, Weyerhaeuser, Halliburton and Interpace have completely closed down their South African operations.

The call by a number of groups for complete withdrawal of U.S. investments in South Africa has been voiced on numerous occasions. Following the Polaroid announcement, a church group introduced a shareholder's resolution calling on the Eastman Kodak Company to ban all direct and indirect sales to the South African government. This was seen as a first step in a phased withdrawal of Kodak from South Africa. The resolution called on the corporation not to "make or renew any contracts or agreements to sell photographic equipment, including cameras, film, photographic paper and processing chemicals to the South African government."

Eastman Kodak Corporation has been in South Africa since 1913. It employs 470 people, half of them black and has sales of about $27 million in South Africa out of total sales of $5.4 billion. The Boston Globe (December 14, 1977) reported that a Kodak spokesman, Ian Guthrie, had confirmed sales to the South African government. However, it was pointed out that Kodak had no equipment that could be used to make passbooks or ID cards. Moreover, Kodak's policy was to stay in business in South Africa because of "strong" commitment to the 470 employees in its subsidiary, Kodak (South Africa) (Pty.) Ltd.

Kodak and 53 other U.S. companies to date have signed a "Statement of Principles" regarding their operations in South Africa (see Exhibit 3). These companies point to steps they have taken to improve the lot of their black employees and express confidence that in time the existing racial barriers can be pulled down. This "Statement of Principles" was drawn up by Reverend Leon Sullivan, a black minister from Philadelphia and a director of General Motors Corporation. The Los Angeles Times (December 29, 1977) reported:

South Africa's Minister of Information, Connie Mulder, officially approved it (Statement of Principles). "In expressing a desire to contribute to the well-being of the black workers in South Africa, these American companies are to be commended," he said.

In a press release issued September 15, 1977, Dr. Leon Sullivan commented on the 54 corporate endorsements and the situation in South Africa:

> We are pleased with the response to date, but we will continue to invite other companies to participate... Some encouraging progress has been made during the last six months. I have been informed that racial signs are coming down; in some instances walls are being broken out to end segregation and new integrated facilities are being constructed; blacks are being selected and promoted to supervisory positions; and all companies are developing plans for aggressive future implementation of the six points. Within the next year we shall see if the effort is only a "ripple" or becomes a "tide for change."

At a business recognition dinner on October 5, 1977, attended by many senior corporate officials, Dr. Sullivan informed the executives that the Statement of Principles was being endorsed by non-U.S. groups such as the Federation of Swedish Industries and expressed the hope that "a world-wide effort against segregation and discriminating practices will be developed by businesses on a global scale." He pointed out that the European Economic Community recently announced its South African code of ethics which are very similar to the American Statement of Principles. (The EEC Code goes further in pushing companies to recognize black trade unions and to practice collective bargaining as pointed out in Business Week, October 24, 1977.)

At the same dinner, U.S. Secretary of State Cyrus R. Vance said:

> ...I think that all of you recognize by your presence here tonight the international business community operating in South Africa has an extremely important role to play. By adopting progressive employment practices for your South African Subsidiaries, you not only enhance the lives of those who work for you, you also demonstrate the promise of a society based on racial justice... We believe that your efforts will set an example which will hasten the day when all the people of South Africa will realize their full human and spiritual potential...

Exhibit 1

POLAROID IN SOUTH AFRICA (C)

Polaroid's "Experiment in South Africa," 1971

October, 1970 - Frank & Hirsch (Pty.) Ltd., South African Distributor, pay and benefits, black employees

- Range R303 to R56, average salary R75 per month (South African
  Rand = $1.15).

- Pension plan applied to both blacks and whites

- No medical plan for black Africans

- Interest free loans for all employees

- Christmas Bonus of one month's salary after three years

- A black employees committee in existence

May, 1971 - Report to Congressional Sub-Committee on South Africa

- We decided whatever our course should be it should oppose the
  course of Apartheid.

- Polaroid is a small economic force in South Africa, but we are
  well-known and, because of our committee's visit there, highly
  visible. We hope other American companies will join us in
  this program.

- South Africa articulates a policy exactly contrary to everything we feel our company stands for. We cannot participate
  passively in such a political system. Nor can we ignore it.

- Both our distributor and one of his suppliers have granted
  wage increases to all their non-white employees ranging from
  13 to 33%.

- An additional increase of 28% for a group of 20 non-white
  Frank & Hirsch employees was announced last week (April 25, 1971).

- Frank & Hirsch and one of their suppliers have agreed to guarantee the educational expenses for the children of their non-
  white employees through the high school level including the
  cost of school tuition, transportation and books.

- The first installment of a financial grant to ASSECA (The

Association for the Educational and Cultural Advancement of the African People of South Africa) has been completed.

- A grant has been made to USSALEP (United States South African Leader Exchange Program).

- We have been working to set up an educational foundation in South Africa. The foundation will be charged with selecting 500 black students and providing financial assistance to them. Administration of this program will be handled by the Institute of Race Relations.

- We are not sure what the longer term decision will be regarding Polaroid's relationship with South Africa, but we are convinced that the basic approach of working for change from within deserves this kind of trial.

December, 1971 - End-of-the-year Report

- The average salary including bonus for black employees (at Frank and Hirsch) had now been increased by 22%.

- Individual increases had ranged from 6% to 33% - the average pay was now R91 up from R75 of a few months earlier.

- Eight black supervisors were appointed during the course of the year in the Computer, Administration, Services and Distribution departments. Some of these positions had been formerly held by whites and they were being paid on the same pay scale as their predecessors.

- The pension plan with death benefits and the employee education plan were in full operation.

- A grant of $15,000 was completed to the Association for the Educational and Cultural Advancement of the African People of South Africa (ASECA).

- A second grant of $10,000 was made to the U.S.- South African Leader Exchange Program (USSALEP).

- A third grant of $50,000 was used to establish a foundation to underwrite educational expenses of black students and teachers in South Africa - The American - South African Study and Educational Trust (ASSET).

- A fourth grant of $1,000 was made to the American--S.A. Institute.

368

Exhibit 2

POLAROID IN SOUTH AFRICA (C)

Polaroid's "Experiment" Update, November, 1977

- Our contributions are continuing to ASSECA, though some concern has been expressed as to the slow pace of programs of
  this organization based mostly on the problem of a lack of
  full-time leadership. ASSECA has requested a full-time
  person from the United States. (See graph)

- Our financial contributions have also continued to ASSET.
  In addition we made up for the loss suffered by the recent
  devaluation of the dollar. Several other companies have also
  made substantial contributions to ASSET.

- We have also made additional contributions to the United States
  South African Leader Exchange Program, the African-American
  Institute, and a contribution to AIESEC in South Africa – an
  organization of students in economics and business administration.

- With our encouragement and assistance, the Addison-Wesley Publishing Company of North Reading, Mass., donated over 22
  thousand new text books for use in black South African schools.

- Training programs, medical benefits, legal aid, bursaries
  (scholarships) and loans have also been expanded at Frank and
  Hirsch.

There are some who sincerely believe that complete cessation of
business with South Africa is the only solution to the existing
problems. We respect that view though we continue to disagree with
it. We believe that constructive engagement is the responsible
course of action for an American company already there. Though
Polaroid does not have plants, investments, subsidiaries or employees in South Africa, we have for a number of years sold our
products through a local distributor, Frank and Hirsch (Pty.) Ltd.
We feel for that reason alone we have a responsibility not to walk
away from the problem.

We are pleased that some major U.S. (and other) employers in South
Africa have initiated affirmative action programs. The Company's
general feeling continues to be hopeful. We are aware of a number of companies with large investments there who have started
serious new programs in the country. We will continue to review
our efforts with our distributor and the programs to which we are
making financial contributions on an annual basis. Visitors from
South Africa and many other people with whom we have corresponded
have encouraged us to continue. Press reports of the effects of
our experiment have reinforced our decision to proceed.

Exhibit 2 (continued)

POLAROID IN SOUTH AFRICA (C)

POLAROID'S CONTRIBUTIONS IN SOUTH AFRICA (1971-1977)

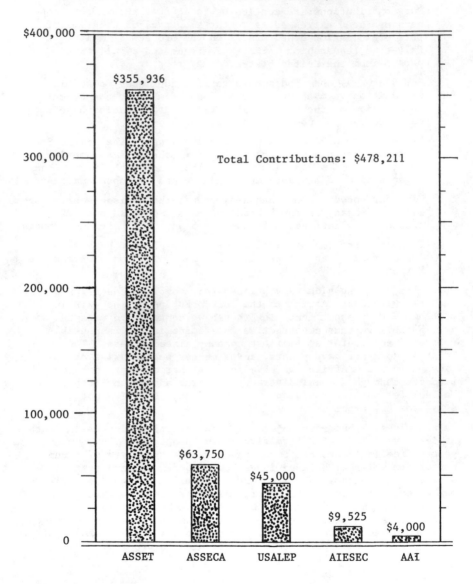

Exhibit 2 (continued)
POLAROID IN SOUTH AFRICA (C)

FRANK & HIRSCH PAY SCALE FOR BLACK EMPLOYEES   (1970-1977)

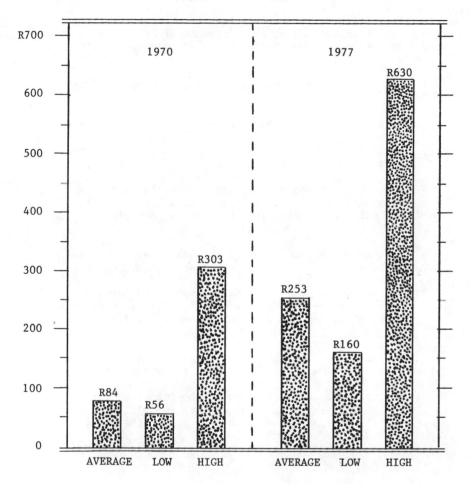

NOTES: · In addition to pay raises, benefits have been expanded.

· Costs in this report do not include other costs of the
Experiment such as time, travel, audit, etc.

· Total number of black employees: 1970 - 180
1977 - 190

371

Exhibit 3

POLAROID IN SOUTH AFRICA (C)

Statement of Principles

Each of the firms endorsing the Statement of Principles have affiliates in the Republic of South Africa and support the following
operating principles:

1. Non-segregation of the races in all eating, comfort,
   and work facilities.

2. Equal and fair employment practices for all employees.

3. Equal pay for all employees doing equal or comparable
   work for the same period of time.

4. Initiation of and development of training programs
   that will prepare, in substantial numbers, blacks
   and other non-whites for supervisory, administrative,
   clerical and technical jobs.

5. Increasing the number of blacks and other non-whites
   in management and supervisory positions.

6. Improving the quality of employees' lives outside the
   work environment in such areas as housing, transportation, schooling, recreation and health facilities.

We agree to further implement these principles. Where implementation requires a modification of existing South African working conditions, we will seek such modification through appropriate channels.

We believe that the implementation of the foregoing principles is
consistent with respect for human dignity and will contribute
greatly to the general economic welfare of all the people of the
Republic of South Africa.

Exhibit 3 (continued)

POLAROID IN SOUTH AFRICA (C)

Companies Endorsing "Statement of Principles" *

Abbott Laboratories
American Cyanamide
American Hospital Supply Corp.
Avis, Inc.
The Bendix Corporation
Burroughs Corporation
Caltex Petroleum Corporation
The Carborundum Company
Carnation Company
Caterpillar Tractor Company
Citicorp
Colgate-Palmolive Company
Control Data Corporation
CPC International
Deere & Company
Del Monte Corporation
Donaldson Company, Incorporated
Eastman-Kodak Company
Envirotech Corporation
Exxon Corporation
Ford Motor Company
Franklin Electric
Gardner-Denver Company
General Motors Corporation
The Gillette Company
Goodyear Tire and Rubber Company
Hewlett Packard Company

Hoover Company
Hublein, Incorporated
Inmont Corporation
IBM Corporation
International Harvester Company
Kellogg Company
Eli Lilly & Company
Masonite Corporation
Merck & Company, Inc.
Minnesota Mining and Manufacturing Co.
Mobil Corporation
Nabisco, Incorporated
Nalco Chemical Company
NCR Corporation
Otis Elevator
Pfizer, Inc.
Phelps Dodge Corporation
Phillips Petroleum
Rohm & Haas Company
Schering-Plough Corporation
The Singer Company
SmithKline Corporation
Sperry Rand Corporation
Squibb Corporation
Sterling Drug, Inc.
Union Carbide Corporation
Uniroyal, Inc.

******

*As of September 26, 1977

NOTES

1. For details describing the initial protest demonstrations and Polaroid's response, see the author's case, "Polaroid in South Africa (A)," ICH 9-372-624. The Polaroid "Experiment" along with local and worldwide reaction, are described in the sequel case "Polaroid in South Africa (B)," ICH 9-372-625. Both are distributed through the Intercollegiate Case Clearing House, Harvard University.

DISCUSSION

VERMA: Mr. Robert Palmer, Director of Community Relations,
Polaroid Corporation, Cambridge, Mass., could not be here for
our discussion of the "Polaroid in South Africa (c)" case. However, he agreed to a videotaped interview. The first segment
includes a review of past activities leading to the decision to
withdraw from South Africa. This is followed by Mr. Palmer's
responses to a series of questions I asked him regarding the
case.

VIDEOTAPED DISCUSSION

VERMA: On November 21, 1977, Polaroid Corporation announced
its decision to terminate its distributorship in South Africa.
Polaroid has been involved in South Africa now for a number of
years and has been the focus of a lot of attention since the
early 70's. Mr. Palmer, could you give us some background of
the events leading up to the decision to terminate your distributorship in South Africa.

PALMER: I'd be glad to. I think the best thing that I could
do would be to, in about ten minutes, walk you through a very
brief but overall view of what happened to the company from the
day that two black employees protested outside corporate headquarters about our involvement in South Africa, through the internal strife that we went through of how to respond to it and
deal with it, to the decision which was, at that time, to stay,
and finally to the decision, which was very recent, to withdraw.
First of all, I ought to add for the benefit of the audience that
Polaroid has never had any plants, any subsidiaries, any investments, or any employees in South Africa. We have worked through
an independent distributor -- not owned by us but entirely independent -- Frank and Hirsch Ltd. in Johannesburg. As you know,
that relationship lasted almost 20 years before it was terminated.
There was also an earlier independent distributor for sunglasses
and filters for about 10 years that Mr. Hirsch was associated
with.

In October of 1970, two black employees of Polaroid announced
they were going to have a demonstration outside of corporate
headquarters in Cambridge about South Africa. There was a lot
of confusion within the company -- no real interest -- wondering
particularly what one of them was up to because he'd been in
some other problems in the past. So, a lot of us went out there
that day around noon while these attacks were made. The attacks

375

were essentially that Polaroid should get out of South Africa.
Most of us really didn't know that we were there, and if we were,
in what way. They made three demands, as I recall it: One was
to withdraw immediately; the second was to announce our view or
policy regarding apartheid; and the third was to turn over all
profit to black liberation or revolutionary groups in South
Africa. There was very little media attention at the time. A
few newspapers were there and about 100 people, all of whom were
employees. And then questions were asked -- What's the issue
about? What are you doing? Why are you so mad? -- that kind
of thing.

The lights burned late that night within the company while we
ran around trying to figure out what all this was about. We were
giving, in my judgment, all the wrong responses. Initially,
management was saying: "That's unfair. You can't say that
about Polaroid. We're a good company. Look at our hiring practices," and all that kind of thing. Almost no one was asking
what the issue was, at least on the first day. The thing that
also troubled several of us at this time was that we really didn't
know what we were doing there and couldn't find anyone who did.
I think that bothered me, perhaps more than anything else.
Usually in a subsidiary or even a distributorship (which this
was) you could instantly look up what you sell, what the sales
are, and what the profit is on the product. We couldn't find
that out at the time. We sent, almost immediately, one of our
people over to South Africa to get a first-hand report and come
right back to report to us what we were selling, what it included,
and so on. I issued a statement to the press that day (which was
the beginning of my learning how to deal with an issue like this)
that we would not negotiate in the street, that we condemned
apartheid in South Africa or anywhere else in the world, and
that we were going to examine the issue.

The next day the papers -- the Boston papers -- were saying Polaroid refuses to negotiate. The issue started heating up at that
time. More demonstrations were called. We made the mistake of
answering each one when I think, at that time, it would have
been very wise for us to have simply been quiet and start examining the issue. Dr. Land, who, as you know, is a very unusual
person as the head of the company, at this point said that we
have a social issue. It's going to involve the company. It will
not be simply a management decision. We want to involve interested parts of the population of Polaroid (which has a large
black population) to examine the issue. And we sent out a call
for those interested saying, "Come on and meet and we will start
examining it." Fifteen people did -- about half were black and
half white, which was by accident. We sat down and started
looking at the issue and got bogged down almost instantly. The

pressure was building up now with people saying, "Polaroid isn't doing anything; they're just meeting about it," when we were actually looking at it very intensely. I started talking with anyone who called the company and said they had an expert opinion. I found every expert opinion was different. We found black and white South Africans who said: "Get out." "You have got to stay." "You are the best." "You ought to buy your own distributorship." "You ought to cancel this one and set up another one." Every possible view was represented by several hundred people, with no pattern. The committee bogged down until one black member (who has a very strong approach to the problems of race, corporate problems and others) stood up one day and said, "I realize what you have done. For a hundred years, you have told me what I needed, and not asked me, and all of a sudden you've now put me in the same boat regarding South Africa. You are asking me to decide for them what's best for them without any knowledge of them, without talking to them." And that was it. The committee disbanded and immediately there was a vote taken to send four people -- two blacks, two whites -- to South Africa right away to review the situation. It became an international incident at that time. Once the decision was made to tour, the issue became not only national but international.

We have not released the results of the tour detail, and that is really for the protection of the people we talked to. But four went over. Within a very short period of time, a pattern was established. First, they found that they could talk to no one where other people were around, like in an office. Even a brother with his brother would not talk, the oppression was so real. A lot of talking happened just walking along the street. They talked to about a hundred black individuals, employees and others, and there were a lot of other late night odd gatherings and meetings. The pattern turned out to be exactly the same. "We believe you're serious." "There is pressure coming from the United States through corporations' employees -- that's good." "We will decide our future. You will not." "If we choose revolution, that's our choice; it's not yours." "Here are a number of things you can do if you really want to help." And they named them: tripling salaries, granting monies to black education training, medical benefits, and a number of other efforts.

Of the four who went over to South Africa, three went over pretty well convinced to withdraw and one went over with an open mind. They came back unanimously to stay. When they arrived back in the United States, pressure again was working in reverse saying that we were brainwashing the four, when exactly the opposite was happening. The committee was ready to withdraw and the four came back to persuade us to stay. A vote was taken to stay

377

and an announcement was made in January of 1971, which was dubbed
the 'Polaroid Experiment,' in full-page ads across the country
outlining the problem, what we were doing, what we thought our
responsibility was, and that we were going to stay. We didn't
know for how long, but we would audit it annually to find out
how the experiment was doing. In thousands of letters on that
ad, I don't remember one complimentary one. Everybody wrote in:
How much did the ad cost? Why an ad? We felt that it was the
only way we could get our full story across, that it was not
getting across any other way. Many from the far right condemned
it as a liberal, crazy sellout. Others said it was a sellout
also and that we ought to stand up and get out. Everybody wrote
in that what we did was wrong. At that point, I think the entire incident changed.

The then Executive Vice President of Polaroid, Tom Wyman, and
I went down to testify before Congress and we were told by Congressman Biggs that we had a half hour to read our statement.
Mr. Wyman said he resented that, that the Committee on South
Africa did not have subpoena power, that he expected to give a
statement, and he expected to be heard and wished to have their
attention. We testified till almost six o'clock that night and
again the same reversal occurred. We found that the Committee
on South Africa was uninformed, other than from an American
perspective, and was saying: "What do we do?" We ended up
telling them what we did and said they should go and do the same
thing. Go over. They did, as you know, and came back with their
minds changed and Congressman Biggs saying that maybe there can
be constructive engagement in South Africa.

I'd like to skip the intervening years. At that point, we did
all the things we promised to do in the experiment. We found
they were very easy. We heard from very few companies about it
since we were not an investor there. I had no idea really what
their views were. I'm always asked about our contracts in the
South African government; there's never been one of any kind,
at any time, including recently. We audited the effort each
year, although I cannot say in a substantive way. We sent a
knowledgeable person over every year who would go over the sales,
go over agreements, how we were doing, wouldn't find much problem, would report that, would report where we'd given money, how
operations were going, how foundations were going that we'd given
grants to, etc.

Beginning about a year ago, I began to get some odd mail saying:
"Do you know that your agreement with Frank & Hirsch is being
violated?" Our agreement, from way back when the experiment was
announced (not before), was that they would not sell directly
to the South African government and that there would be no in-

direct sales to the South African government. Now, there are
two kinds of indirect sales. One is where the South African
government purchases from a dealer. We can't do anything about
it. We didn't and they occurred. The other is where the distributor would say: "If you need that much, wait and pick it
up at such and such a place." I would call that an indirect direct
sale and one which would violate our agreement. A Globe reporter came into the office one day and said, out of the blue,
"I have evidence that your agreement's been violated with indirect sales to the South African government." He showed us
the evidence and it was convincing. We said that we wanted a
few days, if we could have it, to send someone over with an
auditor immediately, unannounced, to examine the records. They
arrived. They found the evidence that there had been those
sales. They called Polaroid and the decision was made that
afternoon to withdraw. The statement was written, agreed to,
and announced. It stated simply that we would terminate our
agreement with our distributor in South Africa, that our agreement had been violated, we regretted it and, perhaps more importantly, that a new distributor would not be named. And that
was, in effect, withdrawal. Our goods are available there.
Anyone can buy them anywhere on the world market, but in terms
of a formal relationship it's ended. I think we ought to stop
here and perhaps get into some questions and discussions.

WORKSHOP DISCUSSION

VERMA: Well, there you have their version of what went on.
Would any of you have any comments based on what they went
through?

COMMENT: Could you elaborate on his very last remark that
their goods are still available there? I mean, will this decision in any way affect the amount of Polaroid film and other
equipment going into South Africa? Is the decision really a
public relations decision? If the South African government
wants to, they can still buy Polaroid products.

VERMA: All shipments to South Africa have been stopped. However, nothing can stop the South African government from going
to any other country to buy Polaroid products. As Mr. Palmer
indicated, there's no way to stop that unless Polaroid goes
out of business.

COMMENT: Polaroid is in South Africa to make sales and to provide a service to the people. By what right does Polaroid
decide whether or not it's going to be selective in its customers? Where does it get the ethic, the right to determine
whether or not to sell to somebody? It is in business to serve

379

the general public. I think this is the heart of the question.
Maybe I'm playing the advocate but their decision appears dis-
criminatory.

VERMA: Would anybody like to respond to that?

COMMENT: I'd like to ask the gentleman a question. Suppose
somebody were making gas ovens which the natives were buying to
exterminate people at Auschwitz. Would there be any burden on
the manufacturer of those ovens not to sell them?

COMMENT: I don't know.

COMMENT: Well, that's in the same ball park. I thought maybe
you could answer that. I think you have a point. It can get
way out of hand. On the other hand, it can get to a point that's
so morally offensive that a company would have to say no. I
think that's the issue here: Was selling to South Africa so
morally offensive?

COMMENT: But your product is a little different. You're selling
a weapon of war, which is inhumane and Polaroid is selling film.

COMMENT: It's not so different because the film was being used
for making passports that the whole black population had to
carry within certain regions, and to further apartheid in particular. It would be different if we were only talking about the
product itself but we're talking about a very particular use of
the film.

VERMA: Anybody else have any thoughts?

COMMENT: If I could, I think there's another question which
might be: Why should the burden be on Polaroid, rather than on
national policy? If Congress said, "We will not permit business
in South Africa," the problem would be solved as a legislative
one.

VERMA: Are you suggesting that as long as the United States
government sanctions sales that the company should not be involved in evaluating the ethics of their decision?

COMMENT: No, I'm not really in any position like that except to
say that as the government doesn't ban it or condemn it, certainly a company can say, "The government doesn't ban it or condemn it; what are we doing that's wrong in violation of management policy? We're kind of stuck."

COMMENT: One of the interesting points about this thing is that an easy way for Polaroid to avoid any problems would have been to simply do what almost every other American corporation that's in South and North Africa has done, which is to ignore or fend off the question. Polaroid, because of Dr. Land, chose to respond and got into the soup, so to speak, right from the beginning, and became symbolic. And in terms of ethics, it's interesting to see how many corporations have avoided the problem by simply ducking and fending off any serious investigation of their role in South Africa.

VERMA: Are there any other questions you would have liked to have asked him if he were here -- I'm trying to see if you can anticipate some of my questions.

COMMENT: Well, it seemed to start when they discovered, almost by accident, that materials were falling into the government's hands. I find it rather appalling that this incident should happen and I get a picture of everybody scurrying around at Polaroid trying to find out what their international division is doing. I would think that if they had monitored their international sales more closely and had at least known what was going on, it would have alleviated a lot of this problem. There's an element of negligence in monitoring their international sales which I don't understand.

COMMENT: If Dr. Land were here, I would be interested in asking him on what basis he feels that a company has an obligation to become involved in the social and political issues of the country in which it deals, which I think is probably the underlying question.

VERMA: Anybody else?

COMMENT: At any time during the period in which their experiment in South Africa was operational, did the government find it was unable to continue its Polaroid passbook identification program? In other words, did their relationship with this distributor in any way inhibit that or were they able to take pictures of people they wanted to take pictures of throughout that '71 to '77 period?

VERMA: Let me raise that as a question because that is one of the questions I did ask him as to what extent Polaroid products were actually being used in the passbooks.

COMMENT: . . . For security purposes.

VERMA: Right. The assumption is that Polaroid film was being used for the passbook system. Rather than anticipate his response, I'll raise that as a question that you might like to have

381

answered.

COMMENT: How did the decision to withdraw from Africa happen to come about? Who made it? And what was the process by which it was made?

VERMA: Something that is related to this, that struck me as being rather unusual, was the immediacy with which the decision was made. They found out on November 15 that sales were being made to the South African government. Two days later they sent an auditor to South Africa to check it out. I think he arrived there on Saturday and the decision to withdraw was announced public-ly on Monday. And the question arises here: What was the rush? When you've been in business in a country and you've established a relationship with a distributor over the last 30 years, if an issue like this comes up, how quickly do you make a decision? I think that most of you familiar with corporate decision making realize that decisions are not usually made that quickly, es-pecially when there is a sensitive issue such as this involved.

COMMENT: You're overlooking Polaroid's unusual relationship with Dr. Land, who is Polaroid.

VERMA: That's right. That's part of it, and the other part of it is that it's something that had been bothering them for the last six years.

COMMENT: Sure. They knew what the issues were.

COMMENT: The question I would have liked to have asked them is: Why only in the last six years? Where were they 15 years ago? What was their feeling 15 years ago? Why didn't they start this at that time? It seems as if it's nothing more than a reaction to the stimulus imposed upon them by society. What was the feeling of Land 15 years ago? What was the feeling of Polaroid 15 years ago?

COMMENT: Of course, a corollary to that is to develop an active sense of corporate responsibility as opposed to simply reacting to this. Do they examine their operations elsewhere, or is it solely confined to incidents such as the demonstrations which then pointed out to them where a problem may exist?

COMMENT: Following up on that, unless I've missed something, this is being dealt with in a kind of international vacuum. Last night, we heard a man from another company extolling the selling of his products in the Soviet Union, which engages in repression, unless we've been misinformed all these years. Are we saying we will not sell to South Africa but we will sell to the Soviet Union?

COMMENT: I think the main response to that question is that
you really do not have an absolutely unique, but a relatively
unique situation in South Africa -- one in which there is a very
extreme form of repression. There may be some of that in the
Soviet Union too, but this is a kind of repression that is coun-
trywide and, as a matter of government policy, open and explicit,
and probably unlike anything that we've seen since the Hitler
period in Germany. And, therefore, it really stands out as
unique.

COMMENT: I think we're missing where the substance is in terms
of the Polaroid decision and where the symbols are. The speed
of the decision, it seems to me, is based not on suddenly dis-
covering that the passbooks that everybody in South Africa carries were made with equipment made by the only company that made
that equipment any place in the world, but on the fact that the
press was about to get hold of the story. Sales in South Africa
are running about 3-4 percent of worldwide sales of Polaroid
products. What's the percentage of worldwide sales in black
Africa and among blacks in the United States? Aren't they more
scared of losing their markets in the rest of the black world
than they are concerned about the $3 to $4 million in South
Africa.

VERMA: What you're suggesting then is that the decision was more
an economic rather than a moral one.

COMMENT: I think one of the questions there is: Is there tri-
viality when there is a moral issue involved? For example, can
you use the excuse, "Well, if we don't do it, somebody else is
going to do it anyway"? I think that same analogy could be used
for the gas ovens in Germany. So I'm not sure that if you're
talking about a moral issue that the amount of investment is
going to be too relevant.

VERMA: Anybody else?

COMMENT: Just from that Palmer interview, it looked as though
initially they did react in a frightened fashion. They weren't
used to this sort of thing. He said they handled it poorly at
the beginning. But it looks as though they made an honest effort
to abide by the requirements that the South Africans themselves
wanted and that they set up at that time an automatic procedure
for cancelling the distributorship should there be any violation
of the agreement.

VERMA: They did agonize over the decision, and it was not en-

tirely because of economic considerations. But one has to recognize that the company did not have that much to lose. In fact,
the easier decision for them in '71 would have been to just pull
out. So, there is an economic issue only in the sense that if
you have the kind of commitment that a General Motors does, the
decision becomes that much more difficult than if you have a situation where you really don't have that much to lose.

COMMENT: Suppose Idi Amin, who is, I would submit, far worse
that the South African government in the sense of slaughtering
people right and left -- suppose he were using Polaroid film for
security purposes. Where would we be then? This is not white
suppressing black; this is black suppressing white. Did this
ever come up in any of this?

VERMA: No, because I'm not sure that they have any operation in
Uganda, although it would be a legitimate question to raise. The
issue is not white suppression of blacks as much as it is suppression. You have to remember that you're talking about a country (South Africa) which has a total population of about 23
million people. There are approximately 4 million whites and
18 million blacks, and 2½ million coloreds, who are probably
caught in between the two extremes and treated as non-people.

The questions that I asked Mr. Palmer included some of the ones
that you've raised and some others, such as: how thorough were
the annual audits, the timing and the urgency of the decision to
withdraw, the deliberations they went through in making that
decision, the consequences and the impact of their decision.

VIDEOTAPED DISCUSSION

VERMA: If you go back to the initial decision instead of the
one that was just made, Polaroid decided at that time not to
sell to any government agency. My question is: If you know that
the government agencies can buy your products on the open market, aren't you then just denying a direct link between the company and the government?

PALMER: That's correct. There's only one way to stop it completely, and that's for Polaroid to go out of business. Then
you stop it all. There's no way that I know of to control the
indirect or general world market purchase. The problem that we
found with this is the attack that our ID unit was specifically
used for apartheid, the passbook program. The passbook is an
infamous document. It has pages and pages of the person and the
family's history, and inside the front cover is a black and white
print. That was the attack. The Polaroid ID unit, as you know,
does a laminated color card and it wasn't used, can't be used,

for those passbooks. About 10 percent of our film was used in passbooks, where a black would come in to the dealer and say, "I need a picture for my passbook." They could then pick up some other camera company's product and take the picture, or he/she could get a Polaroid for more. (I think it cost a little more right then.) So, about 10 percent of Polaroid black and white film was used that way and that accusation was correct. But the ID system wasn't and the ID unit wasn't.

Now, the second part of the problem is: Did the government get ahold of Polaroid units? They did. They bought some from Frank & Hirsch before this issue broke. They have bought some since and use them for military ID, government agencies, etc. We weren't able to control that and didn't. We did a symbolic thing at the time the issue broke. There were, I think, 62 unsold ID units in South Africa and we took them back, withdrew them, just because we thought the issue was that emotional and that important. What Polaroid did do through this distributor was sell our cameras, film, sunglasses and accessory products. They were then being sold to the dealer and to the public. That was what we did.

VERMA: I'd like to come back to the annual audit which you talked about. My understanding is that once a year somebody from Polaroid went over to South Africa to audit whether the distributorship was meeting the agreement that was set out in 1971. There were some reports that when the Boston Globe interviewed Helmut Hirsch, the distributor, he claimed Polaroid was aware of the sales of products to some government agencies and that there were only a few agencies such as the Bantu (the black enforcement bureau) that were banned by Polaroid's agreement.

PALMER: That's a fair question and one that I have a lot of trouble with. I can only answer in terms of what I went through way back then when we met on it. He is correct in terms of sales that occurred before the issue broke. There was no agreement a-bout them. There was no issue. It's something we should have looked at and did not. We were wrong. We paid very little attention to it and those sales did occur. After we went over and toured and after recommendations were made, that kind of sale still went on for awhile, I think. I don't think there was much but there was some. We then met with Mr. Hirsch in the United States (Cambridge) and said: "No more sales." I was present when the agreement was reached and we just agreed there would be no more sales. There have been since.

Now, in terms of your question about our audits, that's also very fair, because I don't think it really can be called an audit. I think, in retrospect, you'd call it a visit. Our export sales manager would go over, meet with their management and ask questions

like: "Is the agreement going on?" "What efforts have you made
with black employees?" He would meet with the black committee,
white committee, staff, and foundations asking: "Did you get
your grant?" "What is your progress?" etc. But that is not an
audit in that sense of the word. That did not occur until this
evidence was brought to us in November. I might take this opportunity to give Helmut Hirsch public acknowledgement because
he found the evidence. When our export manager was over there,
Hirsch pointed out that he was looking at the wrong books and
brought him the right ones. The guy from Polaroid and the auditor looked in them and attached to some of the orders was evidence of sales to the government that could have easily been
removed. Hirsch was shocked, and I believe that to be true.
But that was the evidence and the decision was made. From my
point of view, that was a real audit.

VERMA: The other question deals with the urgency with which the
decision was made. I believe, if I remember, that the Boston
Globe reporter first approached you on Wednesday, November 16,
and by Monday the decision had been announced that you would
withdraw. And I guess the question comes up: What was the rush?
Given that you had 6 or 7 years of commitment that was being
watched by the world, so to speak, and given that there had been
some discussion about possible sales to the South African government in earlier years, why would the company act so swiftly on
something like this?

PALMER: I think (and I can only speak for myself on this) that
after saying over and over again that there had not been sales
to the government as far as we knew, once the evidence was clear
that there had been, we had no position left. We had no place
to go other than to say in public, "We're wrong," which we
thought would have no credibility. I would have to add that the
decision happening that rapidly, which is remarkable for any
corporation of our size and style, I think showed that there was
a hunger to stop. I think that even though we didn't discuss it,
there was a growing discomfort of selling there, doing business
there, of the problems with the country, its future, and how
hard we felt that we had tried. I think that was part of what
made the decision come more rapidly than it would have otherwise.

VERMA: The reason for the question is that in the November 1977
report that you issued, there was a statement that read something like this: "We believe that constructive engagement is
the responsible course of action for an American company already
there." And you were, in effect, also talking about all the contributions that have been made to black employees, as well as to
educational foundation funds that were made available to blacks
in South Africa. Given all of these commitments and contributions

that Polaroid had made, my question would be: What kinds of factors did management consider in making the decision to withdraw?

PALMER: Well, let's back up to your first part about "constructive engagement." I want to get back to the statement because I made it. I believe we said that the constructive engagement of the investor could still do some good. I think that's maybe true. I don't want to judge it. We were not an investor. We'd been worried about being in what might appear to be a self-righteous position. Back in November of '70, it would have been very tempting to just announce withdrawal because there was nothing to withdraw, and the issue would have been very neatly passed to General Motors or one of the other larger companies. It was very tempting. You couldn't help it. The yelling would stop and we'd go back to work. But we decided to stay in South Africa. I think it was the courageous thing to do. But the danger is that by not being an investor, you do have nothing to lose. So, I worry about that role. I think it might be a different story if we had, in fact, owned our distributorship or bought it and could have controlled it, which we chose not to do. I think that was a major factor. The other factor, which you have to add just for honesty, is that this is a tiny part of Polaroid's sales. You're talking several million dollars out of a billion dollar company. We didn't have the economic problem. We did have the lack of control problem. Those were the two essential factors.

VERMA: Couldn't one make the argument that by withdrawing you're really playing into the hands of the radical element that says that you are to get out, withdraw all investments from South Africa and aren't you, in effect, going against the wishes of the moderate blacks and whites in South Africa?

PALMER: I won't agree with that part. I think 7 years ago the moderate black, the thoughtful white said, "Please try. Here are the things you can do and the government will have to respond to them." Now, I have had a lot of mail in from friends and the company's received mail from people considered to be moderate who are giving up, who are afraid of the future. To me, it's sort of like the proposition that says: Where you have total oppression, really total, and there's no hope for change, there's no problem. Where you create hope and do not produce you get revolution. And where you create hope and produce a little, you get either a very rapid evolution or a revolution. I thought that our very, very tiny effort would have very little effect. But the ripple effect became large, I think. And if you now have a quarter of a million or more blacks with a change in standard of living and major increases in pay and benefits, there are 18 million more that want a piece of that and they aren't going to wait for it. The radical or young are taking over in that sense.

I think that's evidenced in terms of history and I don't see any surprise to it.

VERMA: Except it seems to contradict what some of the large American companies are doing by signing Rev. Sullivan's Statement of Principles saying, "We're going to stay in there and that the only way we'll get change in that society is by staying in there and supporting peaceful equal rights," at least in the South African context.

PALMER: I have a problem with that because the Statement of Principles is, I'm sure, well-intended and well-meaning. I hope it works. It seems to me that it comes six years after a statement of essentially the same goals was made by my company. The other problem is that American investment is not that huge. I think that the question you're raising might be true if, in fact, the American presence was substantial. My own view is that if American investment did leave, and I'm not saying it should, it would be instantly and easily replaceable on the scale that it is now. However, if all South African business, and particularly British and Dutch interests in addition to American, agreed to all of this, then there might be a different future.

VERMA: Okay. Let's get back to your decision to withdraw and look at some of the consequences. It appears that you've made some improvements in the lot of black employees. There are a number of things that I'm interested in getting your reaction to. One is: What happens to your black employees at the distributorship? The other is: What happens to the contributions to scholarships and other black-related funds that were provided? A third is: What happens to the customers that you already had? How do you service them? What happens to the market in South Africa for Polaroid products? And I guess a related question is, if I may ask it now and then let you respond: Does your action set another precedent for other companies?

PALMER: Okay. Let's start with that. I don't think it sets another precedent because we aren't an investor there. I think it would be very different if a large American company with major plants or investments announced withdrawal. But I suspect there are changes coming. I know of companies and banks, as perhaps you do, that are not enlarging their investments. One company has sold out to South African interests, that kind of thing. I doubt that that's Polaroid related at all. I think that's related to the country and the turmoil that it's been in since June of a year ago, the Biko death being just one incident of thousands. I think there's that kind of economic uncertainty and fear.

Now, backing up on the other parts of your question. The employees: Usually when a company is in trouble and they lay off employees, the first to go are the most recently hired or the lower end of the scale. I would assume that black employees will lose jobs. I don't know yet. The sales through Frank & Hirsch, our distributor, were heavily dependent on Polaroid products. It depends on whether he adds or replenishes distribution. He sells lots of products, so he may add others. But it's too early to know that yet. Second, we want to be sure that we can guarantee and repair the products that were sold there. They were bought in good faith. They have a warranty, and they'll be backed up. We are in the process of planning now how that will work. In regard to the question about contributions, they've been made for 1978 and they're continuing at the present time. They are going to be reviewed again in November, as they have been every year. Every fall we review what we've been doing and what the contributions were. So for this year we went ahead with them and they'll be reviewed and audited. I wouldn't be a bit surprised if we stayed involved in that because of some of the efforts we set up.

VERMA: Do you see any circumstances under which Polaroid might be induced to move back into the South African market?

PALMER: No. I don't want to predict the future of the country. I don't see any circumstances now.

VERMA: One other question I'd like you to back up to about the decision. Helmut Hirsch came to Polaroid after you'd made the announcement to withdraw the distributorship and I believe he brought along his attorney. What kind of a case did he make for you to reconsider the decision?

PALMER: He visited shortly afterwards. He asked us to reconsider and review the history, which had been an excellent one, and the relationship, which had been long. I think it was a very difficult discussion for everybody. There had been a long relationship and, for myself, Helmut Hirsch is a good guy and a good person. He has hired political dissidents over there. He's contributed to 'liberal' efforts and where the radicals over here say, "That's the phoney liberal," that's not true over there. It's courageous. I think it was hard on everybody, but we went through the review and stuck with the decision because we felt we could not live with what we had said in public, believing it to be true and finding out that it no longer was. I don't want to discuss it more than that.

VERMA: It's a sensitive issue.

PALMER: Sure. I hope that at some point Polaroid will release

389

a lot of the internal agony in the decision making process. I
think that would be helpful. I think it would contribute. It's
been a very painful process for a company that is respected and
has earned its progressive, if you will, corporate laurels
throughout its history because of a person like Land, the genius
philosopher, and the contributions he's made in American society,
and God knows, within the company.

VERMA: Thank you for coming.

WORKSHOP DISCUSSION

VERMA: An editorial aside just to put this in context. Since
the public statement in November that you see on the first page
of your case, this is the first time that Polaroid has in public
stated its position and some of the thinking that went on behind
it. Would any of you like to react to what you've heard?

COMMENT: A question about Hirsch. There's no information about
how he was shocked that he was dealing with the government. He
didn't know it himself. There's no indication how that sort of
involvement occurs, particularly in a distributorship which is
not that large, without the person who's in charge knowing how
it happened?

VERMA: Well, apparently he was spending a lot of his time
traveling out of the country and his version is that he did not
know what was going on. Some subordinate may have decided to
sell to the government.

COMMENT: I was wondering whether Polaroid can apply the Statement of Principles to other countries, other repressive countries,
because certainly, although South Africa's situation with apartheid separates it from other countries in Africa, the rest of
Africa would certainly benefit from the Statement of Principles.
And it seems that Polaroid made the Statement of Principles during
the six-year period in response to public pressure that was
specifically directed at South Africa.

VERMA: By way of background, I'd like to point out that a lot
of the statements that you see in the Statement of Principles are
very similar to Polaroid's philosophy when they first decided to
stay in South Africa. The impetus for the statement came from
Rev. Sullivan, who happens to be a black minister from Philadelphia and the only black on the Board of Directors of General
Motors. Over the last year he's had 54 companies agree to the
approach suggested by these Principles. This raises another
question: What is the proper role for an American corporation
in South Africa? A number of them have committed themselves to

390

creating change in the context of these principles. Should they be encouraged to stay and continue this work or should they be encouraged to withdraw? A lot of people say Polaroid didn't have that much to lose by pulling out. What does this say for the other companies?

COMMENT: Multinationals should remain in those countries to try, through economic, social and political power, to change the policies of the government.

COMMENT: But you can't overlook the symbolic importance of what they did. The economic impact is miniscule even if all 190 employees, or however many there were, lost their jobs, which is unlikely. Still, in the context of the situation, it was a political act with great significance and I don't think that they would be faulted by the people in South Africa.

VERMA: Let me broaden this a little bit. What do you do in the context of another company that has substantial investments in South Africa? What do you think they should do?

COMMENT: The generalization of this is very surprising because there are a lot of very affluent corporations in the world aside from American corporations, and I think we would really be outraged if they started applying that kind of pressure to our society and making changes in it. As much as I support the efforts Polaroid has made in favor of equality in the treatment of humans, there is something to the principle of interfering in internal affairs. And I think Americans would be especially outraged if a foreign multinational or somebody came here and started contributing money to a very extremist cause, either left or right. And it's hard to straighten out either way, withdrawal or staying there and trying to influence the internal affairs of South Africa, because either principle disturbs me.

VERMA: Well, let me raise another question which is: When do the internal affairs of a sovereign nation stay internal affairs and when does the world community say, "Hey, now wait a minute. That's not appropriate behavior for any country"?

COMMENT: I also thought the objection to IT&T in Chile was outrageous. And yet, isn't this in some important way parallel? I support one and I'm opposed to the other and it's very disturbing to me.

COMMENT: I think we should distinguish between the way in which the multinational corporation practices both the techniques of business that are proper to its own home and also the moral and political standards that are operative there within the employ-

ment of its own people and in the marketing of its products and
its interference in the political processes. I mean, it's not
equivalent to say that just because Polaroid intended to apply
either American or United Nations' standards about human rights
in South Africa that that would be the same as IT&T directly interfering in political elections in Chile. And I think another
thing that is emergent here is that a new set of moral standards
is going to appear as we begin to question the absoluteness of
the sovereignty of the nation state. We're moving into an era
in which there are going to be standards and principles that do
not have their origins in constitutions of various countries but
are going to have to have some kind of basis, either in multinational corporations, in effect, having sovereignty, or else
in a world government.

COMMENT: I think we should bring in some of the theoretical
issues. Let's generalize and say you might conceive morality on
two different models. One would be a universal model. Certain
moral principles apply to everyone regardless of their national
identity and this seems to be the model that, say, Carter is pre-
supposing when he's talking about universal human rights. They'd
be certain basic principles which apply to everyone. If you
accept that sort of model, then it seems to me you have a right,
or perhaps a duty, to interfere in those areas where these basic
first-order principles are not being lived up to, but not to
interfere at a second level. You have a right to interfere in
South Africa if they're not respecting certain basic human rights
but not in Chile where the issue is not covered by these principles. So that would be one model of morality, a model which is
accepted by a lot of people. But on the other side you have a
completely different model which is the model that morality, or
the scope of moral principles, is determined by the sovereignty
of a people or the sovereignty of a nation state. If that is
the model that you're accepting, and I don't think you can mix
the two as some people have been doing, then it's a sovereign
people which are the ultimate determiners of their moral principles and you don't have a right to interfere, regardless of the
abhorrence of what you find.

VERMA: Except you're making an assumption: the sovereignty of
the people.

COMMENT: Okay. If you accept this other model, then there's a
whole bunch of new theoretical questions, namely, what constitutes a sovereignty of the people, and a brand new theoretical
question: Do multinational corporations satisfy a lot of the
conditions for sovereignty? And that's a whole new theoretical
issue which I have no idea how to resolve. But my point is that
it seems to me that you can't mix these two models. You accept

one condition of morality or the other.

VERMA: Let me bring things back. I understand that we're trying to generalize and develop models here, but I'd like to bring your attention back to the issue that I want to resolve if I can, and that is: What does a corporation do in the South African context? A lot of blacks in South Africa think that the time for change has come and that the time for rhetoric is over and that the only way you are going to create change in that society is through revolution. If we accept the premise that the practice of apartheid in South Africa is abhorrent and repressive, then the question is: How do you bring about change?

COMMENT: In this context, those who argue for withdrawal often argue that they are for withdrawal because it will sooner lead to revolution, and an application of the Sullivan principles is a kind of slowing down process and it may prevent or simply postpone the revolution.

COMMENT: But there are also those who support the Sullivan principles and argue that the principles themselves may lead to confrontation. Leon Sullivan would like to see a confrontation without the violence but realizes that they may themselves lead to revolution because they are against South African law, even if an arm of the South African government approved of them. But the point that you were making earlier, I think is very important in this regard too, that a resolution to apply the principles on a worldwide scale, especially by Great Britian, which has the largest investments in South Africa, is needed. If you have increased wages and living conditions for a small part of the black population, you then raise expectations of the rest which may lead to confrontation much sooner.

VERMA: But there is the other question which was raised earlier. If you attempt to change what's going on in any country, this should be through government policy, not corporate policy. Collective action on the part of the British, who have a major stake in the South African economy, and the Dutch and the Americans, should come about as government policy. Apparently this would allow corporations within that framework to say: "The role of the company is not to dictate political philosophy but to operate within the context of government policy, and that the role of the government is to form political philosophy."

COMMENT: I don't think we can say that, on the one hand, companies must resist bribery and, at the same time, they are prohibited from following out their moral principles in dealing with their employees and in marketing their products. Multinational corporations should face the possibility and the neces-

393

sity of their taking a moral position that is, in fact, superior
to the position taken by the nation state. The United States
could be collaborating with South Africa and sustaining that
government because this suits our immediately perceived political
goals. What Polaroid is doing is moving toward an ultimately
more moral position. But there's a second question, and that's
the question that was raised before. Given that it wants to
pursue these moral policies, prudentially, what is the best way
to do that? Should a company like Polaroid have to ask whether
a strategy that it's going to use, either following or not following the Sullivan principles, is going to lead to revolution
or not, and what is its responsibility for precipitating a
political revolution? Does it have a right to do that?

VERMA: In fact, the executives of Polaroid actually wrote to
the government of the United States asking for their opinions as
to what the company should be doing. The fact that you're
talking about a schizophrenic situation that may be created is
the reality. But it is a problem and it's a problem because
you're torn in fifteen different directions. Let me summarize
what we've been talking about here in the South African context.
Let me see if I can focus on some of the issues that, from a
practical standpoint, a company faces today, and especially if
it has investments in South Africa. One problem that is faces
is: Should it leave the country or stay and work for change?
What is the appropriate role of the corporation vis-à-vis the
role of the government? There are also economic issues. What
happens to the investments, to the sales and to the profits that
it is deriving from that type of operation? What happens to
your employees if you desert them and say, "It's a sinking ship,
but that's your problem not ours"? What happens to all the support services -- in South Africa where Polaroid and other countries have made substantial investments in trying to upgrade the
education and the cultural activities of the nonwhites -- what
happens to the contributions that are made by these companies?
In fact, no vacuum may be created -- if you leave, somebody else
from some other country is going to fill that vacuum very easily;
however, you can no longer function as a catalyst for change.
The other side of the coin is what many people in South Africa
are saying, which is: "Hey, if you stay, recognize what you're
doing. You're supporting the apartheid policies by making the
government stronger. You are, in effect, perpetuating the system. You're strengthening the system and you're supporting it."
Now, you may not agree with that, but that's another perspective.
There is the distinct possibility of violence in South Africa
and one has to face that. Then the question arises: What about
the safety and security of your people working there and your
property? And you have another problem, which is that if you

do have upheaval, it depends on the vagaries of the new government that comes in as to what they're going to do with their investment. So you've got some economic problems. You've got
some social problems. You've got some political issues and
you've got some moral issues. What do you do? Obviously, we
don't have the answers, but I think we have raised some of the
issues that need to be resolved. I think we'll all be watching
the situation with a lot of interest.

SESSION XV

"The Corporation and Environmental Regulations:
The Genco, Inc., Case"

Robert Ackerman
Vice President of Finance and Administration
Preco Corporation

ROBERT ACKERMAN

Genco Inc. (A)

The situation that had enveloped the Elkhorn paper mill was
perplexing. John Wilson, a lawyer in the Genco legal department,
circulated a memorandum on September 14, 1972 summarizing his most
recent conversation with a senior official in the regional Environmental Protection Agency (EPA) office. He wrote in part:

1.--If we do not agree by October 4, 1972, to meet the
    criteria in their June 9, 1972 guidelines, suit
    will be filed against us under the 1899 Refuse Act
    seeking to enjoin us from discharging in excess
    of those criteria.

2.--He acknowledged that the EPA cannot give us a permit
    under the Refuse Act under the present status of the
    law.

3.--He acknowledged that their statutory authority-except
    for the Refuse Act-is questionable but the law that
    passes[1] will provide for "best practical control"
    and he believes their guidelines can be shown to be
    the "best practical." If the regulations under the
    law that passes set limits lower than EPA's guide-
    lines, he said that "something" will be worked out.
    Basically, his position is that he is certain their
    guidelines will be the new regulations.

4.--We were the first company he talked to. He has not
    been putting pressure on us and...is aware of the...
    plaudits we received [for the Genco record of achieve-
    ment in pollution control] and recognizes that we
    have been cooperative.

5.--Apparently no one has agreed to their criteria yet
    but he believes they soon will. No suits have been
    filed yet. He is to send me the form of commitment
    letter they want. He said this is a national EPA program.

6.--If we want to negotiate, he suggests the following:

---

[1]The Water Pollution Control Act was then pending in Congress.

399

The average daily production of our mill was used in
their calculations. We can use maximum daily average
production during the highest production week which
will increase our allowable discharges about 20% in his
opinion. No settleable solids will be allowed. Later
on, they will want more reduction.

For over two years, managers in the Paper Products Division
(PPD) of Genco, aided by the corporate Environmental Affairs Department and the legal staff, had been working with the State
Department of Resource Conservation (DRC) to develop a program for
reducing pollution from the Elkhorn mill. Just as that program
was being implemented, EPA issued the guidelines referred to in
the memorandum above and requested the "voluntary" compliance of
firms in the paper industry, supported by a compliance schedule to
be filed within 90 days (e.g., October 4). The EPA standards were
considerably more stringent than the interim emission levels agreed
to earlier with the DRC. The situation was further complicated by
the uncertainties surrounding the Federal Water Pollution Control
Act Amendments then pending before Congress; would the legislation
be enacted and if so, in what form? Moreover, a definition of the
"best practical control" technology and the resultant standards to
be prescribed for the paper industry remained in doubt.

Organizational Factors

PPD was one of six divisions in Genco, a diversified manufacturing company with sales in 1971 of approximately $2.2 billion
and after tax profits of $81 million. PPD had sales of about
$400 million, making it the second largest in the company, and
after tax profits of $11 million. The divisions were managed in-
dependently with little direct involvement from the corporate
offices in operating decisions. Each was held accountable for
the attainment of an annual financial plan agreed to in the fall
in carefully considered negotiations between corporate and division managers. PPD operated six integrated pulp and paper mills,
one of them at Elkhorn, and over 30 box and bag plants, the latter
converting much of the output from the mills. Major products included linerboard, corrugated medium, corrugated shipping containers,
folding boxes, and multi-wall bags.

Wilson's memorandum about the Elkhorn mill was addressed to
Elton Johnson, manufacturing manager of primary operations in PPD,
and an early advocate of environmental protection. Since the late
1950s, first as a mill manager and later in his current position,
Johnson had been actively engaged in proposing and implementing
projects to upgrade the emission profiles of the PPD mills. The
division's record in this regard was generally recognized to be

400

outstanding among paper firms. In 1968 he was given responsibility
for all six paper mills, and the mill managers reported to him.
An organization chart is provided in Exhibit 1.

Johnson's efforts in environmental protection had been partially responsible for the stress given to such matters by Donald
Mason, Chairman of the Board of Genco. During the mid-1960s, Mason
became impressed by the pollution control activities in PPD and
concerned about the ecological impact of Genco operations more
generally. He also foresaw the growing public awareness of environmental issues and the increased governmental involvement
likely to result. His response had been a strongly worded policy
statement in 1966 followed by the creation of the Environmental
Affairs Department, initially that same year as a unit in the corporate engineering organization and in 1970 as an independent department reporting directly to the president.

The other managers receiving copies of Wilson's memorandum
included most of those who had been actively engaged in the Elkhorn deliberations over the preceding two years. First, there was
Peter Kruger, until recently vice president and division manager
of PPD. Although Kruger had been appointed corporate vice president for administration on June 30, 1972, he continued to play an
instrumental role in the management of the division while his
successor, Dan Phillips, wound up his affairs as regional general
manager in another division. (In fact, Phillips had had little to
do with Elkhorn thus far and was not on the distribution list for
the memorandum.) Then there was Fred Skinner, corporate vice
president of environmental affairs, and Jim Peterson, manager of
the seven-person corporate environmental control group. Also receiving copies were Ed Donaldson (vice president of public relations), Bill Comacho (a senior engineer in the PPD engineering
department with special responsibilities in pollution control),
Peter Fitchdorn (Elkhorn mill manager), and Dick French (Elkhorn
technical director).

Early Developments at the Elkhorn Mill

The original Elkhorn mill was constructed in 1888 and through
the years had been expanded and modified on numerous occasions
under a succession of owners. In 1972 it was a large (620 ton/day)
facility utilizing a neutral sulfide semichemical process (NCSS)
for pulp and paper production and employing 350 people. The technology is summarized in Exhibit 3. Shortly after Johnson became
manufacturing manager in 1968, he made a presentation to corporate
and division executives in which he outlined the history of pollution control expenditures for each of the PPD mills and the further
investments that he felt would be necessary to maintain them within
expected regulations. His comments on Elkhorn were in part the

401

following:

> The Elkhorn mill was originally operated as a kraft
> specialty mill. The property was acquired by Western
> Paper Company in 1946[2] and by 1949 the first hardwood
> semichemical pulp for medium was produced. Waste li-
> quor from the process was burned in the kraft recovery
> cycle to avoid discharge to the river. This marked
> the first commercial application for this process.
>
> In 1953 the last kraft operations were discontinued.
> In order to continue recovering the waste liquor, an
> installation of the Institute of Paper Chemistry Direct
> Sulfitation system was made. The use of this unique
> recovery system has allowed the Elkhorn mill to operate
> a semichemical process at a very low level of effluent
> discharge. In 1963, increased discharges of solids
> from the woodyard necessitated the building of 3 ponds
> to treat about 25% of the mill effluent. In 1966, they
> were further enlarged....
>
> In this state, both air and water pollution are under
> the jurisdiction of the Department of Resource Conser-
> vation. The Board is appointed by the Governor. The
> state has submitted criteria and classifications for
> interstate streams to the Federal Government. Hearings
> are being held for the purpose of classifying intra-
> state streams. Although the Elkhorn River is intra-
> state we feel that the interstate criteria will apply.
>
> A general air pollution abatement bill has been passed
> by the state legislature. Standards have not been set
> as yet.
>
> Pollution abatement expenditures to date at Elkhorn,
> based on 1967 replacement costs, have been $2,963,000.
> Anticipated capital expenditures for pollution abate-
> ment equipment for 1968-1972 amount to approximately
> one million dollars.

With the assistance of Bill Comacho, Johnson also constructed
a pollution load chart for each mill which included the impact of
specific abatement projects. The pollution load units were a composite of emissions into both air and water. For the Elkhorn mill,
the most significant proposed expenditures were for enlargements
and improvements in the holding ponds. These projects were to

---

[2]Western Paper Company was acquired by Genco in 1955.

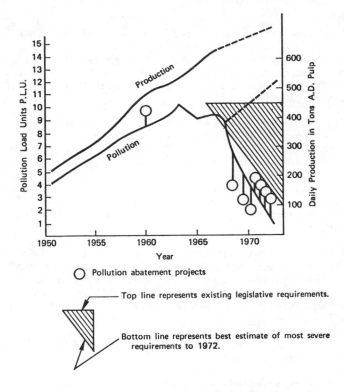

Figure 1   Elkhorn Mill-Load Chart-1968

facilitate the removal of suspended solids and aeration to reduce
the BOD[3] load prior to the release of mill discharge into the river.

Development of an Abatement Program

In August 1970, the DRC conducted public hearings on potential pollution sources on the Elkhorn River. Based on this and
other data, the DRC issued pollution abatement orders on December
1 under state statutes to 64 municipalities and industrial concerns. A DRC official noted that over 90% of the suspended solids

---

[3]Suspended solids are materials floating in the water discharged
from the mill. BOD is a measure of the oxygen needed to break
down dissolved materials in the water.

and BOD load were attributed to pulp and paper mills. He also
said that pulp and paper production in the area had increased
about 80% since 1960, while the BOD discharge remained fairly constant and suspended solids increased roughly 60%. The stated long-
range goal was "to upgrade all waters to a quality suitable for the
propagation of game fish."

Among the items contained in the DRC orders were the following: By Janaury 1, 1971, the recipient was to submit a report of
intention to comply together with a statement of alternatives; by
June 1, 1971, detailed construction plans and specifications were
to be submitted to the DRC; and by December 1, 1971, the facility
was to be operating within the prescribed discharge limits on a
"monthly average" basis. The DRC also indicated that petitions
for review had to be filed within 60 days, to be followed by a
public hearing.

The order sent to Genco was received by Fitchdorn and immediately circulated to other managers in PPD, environmental affairs, and the legal department. The daily limits prescribed for
the mill were 11,160 pounds of suspended solids and 11,600 pounds
of BOD, which compared with actual figures for 1970 of 21,565 and
15,865 pounds respectively.

By December 11, French developed a tentative plan for meeting
the emission limitations encompassing four steps:

1.--Installing aeration in the pond system.
2.--Building a black liquor and evaporator cleanout
    surge pond.
3.--Installing sumps in the paper mill to collect
    press water.
4.--Installing a disc saveall-thickener in the waste
    system.

A plan based on these steps was duly submitted to the DRC. French
also noted that an error had apparently been made by the DRC in
applying the formula for suspended solids and that in fact the
limit should have been 12,444 pounds. However, DRC officials indicated that a petition followed by a hearing would be necessary
to amend the order. It was agreed within Genco that an appeal
should be filed, recognizing that the hearing might result in some
"poor publicity" from the particularly active conservation groups
in the area.

By January 26, the abatement program had been further
specified by French who also summarized for Johnson the assigned
responsibilities for the engineering work. In each case the lead
was to be taken by Elkhorn personnel, assisted in some instances

404

by Comacho. Preparations were also made for the public hearing scheduled for April 1.

Then, on January 28 an environmentalist group petitioned the Attorney General of the United States to bring immediate action against nine industrial firms, among them Genco,, ordering them "to desist from dumping harmful wastes into the Elkhorn River." The environmentalists further charged the DRC with being "permissive with the major pollutors of our [state] waterways." The regional United States Attorney met with the petitioners amid a clamor of newspaper stories on the issue, and subsequently with French and the company's local counsel.

In a later summary of Genco's record at Elkhorn prepared for the United States Attorney, French stressed that during the previous six years production had increased about 10%, while suspended solids had increased 11%, BOD had decreased 47%, and the water usage per ton of output had dropped 25%. He noted that the company had taken steps voluntarily to anticipate negative environmental effects and was actively involved in complying with a state order. The environmentalists remained adamant, however, and the United States Attorney indicated that he intended to follow the company's activities closely.

As French prepared for the April 1 public hearing, he discovered that one of the three paper machines in the mill had been shut down when the DRC tests were taken. As a result, the tests did not reflect the actual discharge from the entire mill. Based on this finding, French argued at the hearings that the allowable discharge should be considerably higher; specifically to 19,000 pounds of suspended solids and 15,000 of BOD per day. The DRC had until June 1 to respond to the Genco petition.

Meanwhile, with the approval of PPD, the Environmental Affairs Department, and counsel, the Elkhorn Engineering Department prepared and filed the detailed specifications for the treatment facilities on May 28. The program itself was not affected by the petition. French was also called upon to submit an air quality control program to the DRC by July 1, as well as file an application for the discharge of wastes into interstate waterways under the Federal 1899 Refuse Act.

The DRC did not act directly on Genco's petition for an increase in discharge limits. Instead, additional engineering data was requested within 90 days on the company's proposed treatment facilities. After conferring with the consulting engineers who had been engaged for the project, PPD officials concluded that this new DRC deadline could not be met. French then asked for and received an extension to February 1, 1972.

As Genco's relationship with the DRC developed over the following months, an understanding evolved on an approach to water pollution abatement at the Elkhorn mill. In essence, the discharge limits in the original order would stand and the company would seek to comply with them. However, because the improvements planned by Genco included some innovative measures, a one-year trial period would be granted from the time the operating permit was approved during which discharges in excess of the limits would not be considered violations unless considered unreasonably disproportionate by the DRC. At the end of that period the limits would be reviewed again.

The expanded water pollution control facilities were initially to be completed by September 1, 1972 at a cost of $750,000; however, because of weather and equipment delivery problems, the date was pushed back to December 1, 1972 with DRC approval. Also scheduled for completion on December 1, 1972 was the first phase of an air pollution control program—a precipitator costing $1.1 million to collect 99.5% of the particulates emitted from the recovery boilers. The second and third phases, each estimated to cost about $1.0 million, were to be undertaken during the succeeding two years.

Enter EPA

On April 14, 1972, two officials from the regional EPA office visited the Elkhorn mill, stating that they wished to see a facility operating a secondary treatment system. They also indicated that the Region had requested approval from EPA in Washington to enter into voluntary agreements with major polluters, which would commit them to the same standards planned in the Water Pollution Control Act legislation then stalled in Congress. On May 22, Kruger received a letter from EPA requesting within three weeks information on the measures being taken to control the discharge of refuse into the Elkhorn River. It stated further that, "Your reply should be as complete as possible, and it is hoped that it will constitute a satisfactory voluntary commitment to an acceptable abatement program. In any event, the need for further action by this Branch will be evaluated in the light of your reply."

The EPA's actions were disturbing to Kruger. It was his understanding that state authorities were to have the responsibility for direct contact and negotiation with those in charge of individual facilities. In view of Genco's established relationship with the DRC, he objected to the need for dealing with a secondary regulatory agency. A second element in his thinking lay in the escalating cost of compliance. At Kruger's request,

406

Comacho estimated that approximately $4.5 million in 1972 dollars would be required to have the "best available" technology for controlling water pollution by 1980, the guideline then being discussed in congressional deliberations. Kruger's reply to EPA on June 9 included the desired information as well as the following suggestion:

> I would respectfully submit that for us to attempt to work with both the state authority and the federal government on the same issues may tend to lead to confusion and all of us tending to work at cross purposes. Accordingly, we hope that your determinations on this matter will be in some manner channeled through the state Department of Resource Conservation.

On June 9, EPA issued voluntary emission level guidelines for water pollution control in the paper industry. French then met with regional EPA officials and was apprised of the specific limitations for the Elkhorn mill. In a letter of confirmation, EPA summarized its position: "We are seeking a firm program by your company to abate its violations of the Refuse Act of 1899 and the resultant pollution of the Elkhorn River. At the meeting, you were advised concerning the effluent limitations which we propose that your plant attain, and the means by which they were determined. We are inviting you to make a voluntary commitment to an undertaking to achieve such limitations." The average daily limits were BOD, 7,500 pounds and suspended solids, 4,600 pounds, both substantially less than called for in the DRC order. In addition, guidelines were proposed for oil and grease, iron and manganese which had not been explicitly covered heretofore.

PPD officials were highly upset by this turn of events. They felt that the demands continued to increase with little evident coordination between federal and state agencies. In addition, the mill had been shut down from time to time due to weakness in the market for corrugated medium, Elkhorn's primary product. By now Kruger was heavily involved in the day-to-day direction of the company's response. However, aside from the environmental affairs group (Skinner and Peterson) and legal counsel (Wilson), the deliberations remained within the division.

EPA had requested an answer to its proposal by July 8. On July 6, a reply was signed by French, containing the following comment written under Kruger's supervision:

> I am thus advising you that in the next 90 days you will receive a definite reply from an authorized officer of our Company on this subject matter. You understand that the economic implication of your

407

Exhibit 1

PARTIAL ORGANIZATION CHART

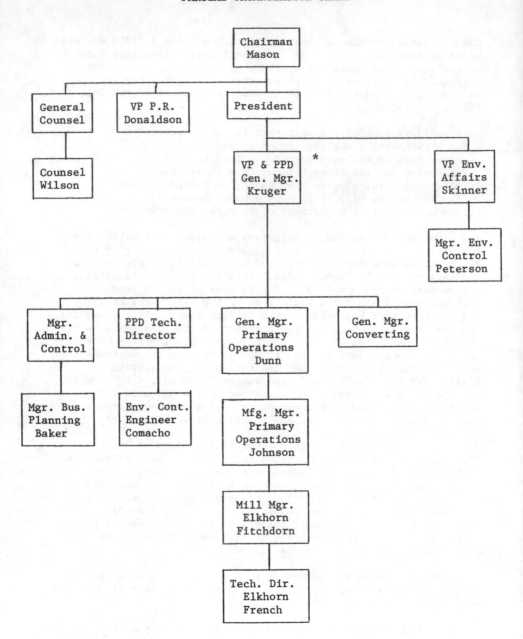

*As of June 30, 1972, Kruger was designated corporate senior vice
president for administration. His place as general manager of PPD
was taken by Phillips.

request makes necessary an in-depth business evaluation of the mill, as well as the environmental considerations.

EPA responded to French's letter by requesting an answer by
the end of August. After a brief review of the situation, the
PPD management group concluded that the 90-day evaluation period
promised originally was already tight enough. French then wrote
to EPA that October 4 continued to be the earliest date that a
reply could be expected. He also prepared the analysis and recommendations shown in Exhibit 2 as a basis for discussion on the
eventual presentation to EPA.

On August 10, Johnson, Wilson, Skinner, Comacho, Peterson,
and Peterson's senior water pollution control engineer met to
establish a position on the Elkhorn mill. It was generally agreed
that Genco should not accept a commitment beyond that made to the
DRC. Moreover, rather than wait the full 90 days to answer EPA
and possibly create the impression that such a commitment would be
forthcoming, the group concluded that Wilson should sign a letter
stating the company's position as soon as possible. Consequently,
with the acquiscence of all concerned, including Kruger, Wilson
wrote in part the following on August 22:

> As I understand the present federal-state water pol-
> lution control effort, the state intrastate water
> quality standards are the only standards applicable
> to our Elkhorn mill and the enforcement of intrastate
> standards is exclusively a state function. The state
> had diligently enforced its stringent intrastate
> standards for the Elkhorn River by a series of orders,
> including the order issued to our Elkhorn mill. Since
> we are in compliance with that order, under my view
> of the law, nothing more is required at this time.
> In addition, if we were to attempt to meet the stan-
> dards you are proposing, revisions to our treatment
> system would be required which might delay our com-
> pliance with the state order.

A Point of Decision

Wilson's discussion with the regional EPA office summarized
in his memorandum of September 14 was far from reassuring. A
degree of urgency appeared to mark EPA's actions. An agreement
had just been reached by the Senate-House conference committee
on the Water Pollution Control Act and passage by Congress seemed

assured.[4] Whether the President would veto the bill or, if he
did, whether sufficient votes would be forthcoming to override
his veto, were considerably less clear. Were the bill to become
law, however, Wilson felt there was a reasonable chance that subsequent suits filed under the 1899 Refuse Act would be prohibited.

Managers at the mill tended to favor exploring the possibility of negotiating a settlement with EPA before the legislative
issues were clarified. In this way, a more acceptable compliance
schedule might result and, were it possible to obtain a five-
year permit, some of the near-term uncertainty would be removed.
On the other hand, Kruger maintained that if the legislation were
enacted, the standards might well be less stringent; by accepting
commitments now when others in the industry did not, the company
might find itself at a competitive disadvantage. For his part,
Wilson was not at all sure that EPA possessed the authority to
negotiate an agreement or issue permits in the first place.
Johnson, manufacturing manager of primary operations, wondered
how his new division manager, Dan Phillips, would approach the
problem.

Exhibit 2

Attention of   Mr.   E.B. Johnson   Intra-Company Correspondence
               cc.   P.K. Kruger   July 23, 1972
                     D.A. Phillips
                     T.A. Dunn
                     J.H. Wilson
                     W.S. Comacho
                     J.M. Peterson
                     P.G. Fitchdorn

---

[4]Under the Water Pollution Control Act, all industries discharging
wastes into the nation's waterways would be required to apply the
"best practical control technology" by July 1, 1977. By July 1,
1983 they would be required to use the "best available technology."
Although no means of enforcement was provided, the Act specified
further that discharge was to be eliminated entirely by July 1,
1985. The standards for particular industries and processes were
to be specified later by EPA.

Response to EPA Requests to Elkhorn

The following are some facts, observations and possible
approaches to be considered when answering the request from the
EPA for a voluntary commitment to a long-term pollution abatement program at the Elkhorn Mill.

BACKGROUND. There are three areas of concern involved in their
request. First, an agreement to follow the state requirements
as given in the DRC order to this mill. Second, an agreement to
immediately lower the iron, manganese and oil content in our discharge. Third, an agreement to reach levels of 7,500 lbs./day
BOD and 4,600 lbs./day of suspended solids by Janaury 1, 1976 and
to include an implementation schedule.

A commitment by this mill to meet the state order would of
course change nothing technically as we are already involved in
doing just that. There are two possible legal problems involved
in adding a voluntary agreement to do the same with the federal
government. First, I can conceive of this concession opening the
door for all others by, in effect, admitting federal jurisdiction.
Second, if we need to apply for an extension of our construction
schedule, as now seems likely, we might have to obtain like permission from the EPA which would be time consuming.

The problem of iron, manganese and oil is potentially much
more serious. Our pond revision is intended to handle surface
oil and should do so. However, our one grab sample analysis made
as part of our 1899 Act license submission showed apparent high
oil contents in our No. 3 pond discharge. This was so in spite
of there being no visible oil sheen on this pond. Further, a
simple material balance of oil use within the mill versus apparent oil discharge indicates about ten times more oil being
discharged than being used. The iron and manganese data also represents only one sample. Further, we have changed our pulping
process which should decrease corrosion. We are now in the process of taking four composite samples of inlet water, No. 3 discharge and main mill discharge over a four-week period for
analysis by the Institute of Paper Chemistry for iron, manganese
and oil. Any further moves regarding these materials should
wait on the results of these analyses.

It should be pointed out, however, that removal of iron
and manganese would require a major investment in flocculation
and settling equipment as there is no simple way to remove these
materials.

The question of reaching the BOD and solids limits is best
handled by a separate analysis. I do not believe that the BOD

411

level specified will be difficult to reach. Our present system varies from 15,000 lbs./day in the winter to under 10,000 lbs./day in the summer. The enlarged system is intended particularly to lower the winter load to be more in line with state requirements.

I believe that it will be possible to meet the 7,500 lbs./day level through a continued program of collecting strong waste streams for complete treatment while at the same time removing all clean water from the strong collection points. In this manner, our Nos. 1, 2 and 3 ponds will operate at higher efficiencies. It may also be necessary to add some additional aeration after we have had time to analyze the operation of the enlarged pond system.

The solids limits of about 4,600 lbs./day may be difficult to reach. Whether it is attainable depends to a large extent upon the efficiency of No. 4 pond as a settling pond. It is difficult to predict as the majority of the material reaching that pond will be of very small size and will not settle rapidly. Recirculation of water within the mill will help as will possible filtration methods. It may well be, however, that in the final analysis some method of clarification will be necessary with recirculation of the solids removed back to No. 1 pond.

CONCLUSIONS. It is not possible at this time to design a least-cost treatment system for Elkhorn. Data is needed on the metals problem and on the operation of the expanded pond system. This information will not be available until late 1973.

If we were to commit the mill today to the 1976 goal and to specify how we would obtain it, I believe we would have to abandon our present approach and use a conventional system of clarifier, standard oxidation basis and secondary clarifier. This immediately implies an additional system for dewatering and burning sludge as we are too land limited to dispose of it by land fill. This additional system could include dewatering filters and presses, a predryer and a new furnace for burning the material.

RECOMMENDATIONS. I recommend that our next response to the EPA should comprise the following points:

1.--That we will continue to comply with the state order as it exists or as it is modified.
2.--That we will commit ourselves to reach the BOD and solids limits specified by January 1, 1976. (I don't believe that we would be conceding anything that won't be federal law long before 1976.)

412

3.—That all other points are to be deferred until we
have had at least one year of operation of our new
and enlarged system.

I do not believe that this type of reply will satisfy the
EPA Region as they are presently operating; however, it is
realistic with regard to our plans and system. It can be defended technically in my opinion. The danger of stronger legal
action by the EPA does exist with this approach but that danger
is present unless we concede to all of their requests.

It also may be that by the time our ninety days have ex-
pired this state and other states will have regained control by
agreements similar to that made by Oregon. I must admit that I
am somewhat pessimistic in this regard as it appears that the
EPA has picked this state and particularly the Elkhorn River to
make their big effort on.

D. L. French

Exhibit 3[1]

TECHNOLOGY, RAW MATERIALS, AND TYPES OF PAPER

PAPER MAKING TECHNOLOGY

The Manufacturing Process

The paper making process has two principal stages; the
first involves converting wood to pulp, and the second is the
conversion of pulp to paper. Ideally, pulp and paper making
facilities should be located together, with pulp in slush form
being pumped with high efficiency through pipes from one operation to the other at very low cost.

There are, however, a relatively large number of paper
mills which do not have adequate pulp-making facilities to match
their paper making requirements. These mills purchase market
pulp to make up their deficiencies. Market pulp is sold in
sheet form, requiring drying, marketing, baling, and handling

---

[1]Adapted with permission from "A Note on the Paper Industry,"
prepared by Richard W. Moxon under the supervision of Associate
Professor Robert B. Stobaugh, Harvard Business School, 1971.

operations which are unnecessary in an integrated operation. Finally, after delivery to the mill, the bales are broken and individual sheets fed into the beaters in order to convert the dry sheets to slushy, free-flowing fibers.

Pulp Manufacture

Pulp is a crude fibrous cellulose raw material which, after suitable treatment can be converted into paper, paperboard, or rayon. Wood pulp is produced by: (1) mechanically grinding up logs (groundwood pulp); (2) chemical fibrization of wood chips (sulfate, sulfite, or soda pulp); or (3) a combination of chemical treatment and mechanical grindings (semichemical pulp).

Sulfate pulp, which accounted for about 67% of 1971 total U.S. pulp production, could be used in making most grades of paper. It is particularly suitable for producing packaging materials-heavy brown wrapping papers and paperboard. Since 1950, virtually all new pulping facilities had been constructed to utilize the sulfate process, both because recovery of chemicals make it a lower-cost process than sulfite, and because technological advances have made it possible to produce a good bleached (white) sulfate product. Sulfite pulp (representing about 8% of total U.S. pulp output) was once the most prevalent process. The pulp is light in color and especially well suited for the higher grades of writing and printing papers. Groundwood pulp (11% of the total) is much cheaper to produce than chemical pulps, since only about 7% of the raw material is lost in processing versus 55% or more in the chemical processes. But its low strength and coarse appearance limits its use to newsprint and low-grade tablet paper. The semichemical process (14% of total) was developed primarily to utilize hardwoods which initally were not well suited to the sulfate or sulfite processes. Semichemical pulp extracted a high yield from the wood input and produced a stiff, resilient paper best suited to corrugated medium, insulating board, egg cartons, and similar formed or molded products.

The cost of entering the pulp making business was high. Estimates in the early 1970s, gathered from various industry sources, placed the initial capital investment for pulp mills at somewhere between $140,000 and $160,000 per ton of daily output, exclusive of supporting forest lands with costs increasing at a rate of 10 to 15% a year. Many persons believed that the smallest economic size for a pulp mill was in the range of 350 to 400 tons a day, making $50 million a minimum capital requirement. Even such a small mill involved upwards of two years to construct and bring on stream.

414

Paper Manufacture

Paper is made by matting together wet cellulose fibers
(the pulp obtained from one of the processes indicated above) to
form a thin sheet of material which, when dried, has the desired
strength, absorption, color, and flexibility specifications. In
the modern day paper mill, the process begins in the beater,
where pulp fibers, suspended in water, are mechanically cut, split,
and crushed. During the beating stage, the fibers develop strong
adhesive properties. When the pulp has been beaten and the necessary dyes, sizing, and resins added, the stock is refined and
then allowed to flow onto the paper-making machine. The most
widely used machine is the Fourdrinier, a machine that mats the
fibers on an endless fine mesh screen, removes most of the excess water, and then dries the newly formed paper by passing it
between a long series of steamheated cylinders.

The required capital investment for even a modest-sized
paper mill was high, but not as great as that required for a
pulp mill. There is a wide range of paper products that a firm
may choose to make, and the choice of product line is the major
determinant of the cost of entry. Paper machines designed to
turn out huge quantities of standardized product, such as newsprint, might cost more than $20 million. On the other hand, a
low-capacity machine, designed to make short runs of a specialty
such as high-grade writing papers, could be built for less than
five million dollars. The greatest restriction on construction
of a paper-making operation of the latter type was the limited
markets available for its output, rather than the magnitude of
the investment.

ROBERT ACKERMAN

Genco Inc. (B)

On October 18, 1972, Congress overrode President Nixon's veto
of the Water Pollution Control Act by a wide margin and it became
law. In the preceding weeks, Genco officials had declined to negotiate a "voluntary" compliance schedule for the Elkhorn pulp and
paper mill with EPA on the basis of guidelines proposed by the
agency in June of that year. Genco's reply to EPA on October 4
was essentially a summary of its efforts to implement a program in
satisfaction of the State Department of Resource Conservation's
orders and an affirmation of the company's intention to maintain
its cooperative posture on environmental matters. Genco was one of
several that had been confronted with a possible suit under the
1899 Refuse Act for the discharge of wastes into navigable waters.[1]

After vacillating for several weeks on whether to initiate
legal action, EPA decided against it. In fact, as soon as the
legislation was passed, the company found the agency reluctant to
discuss the standards to be applied for the "best available technology" required under the Act by July 1, 1977. As a result, the
magnitude of the task ahead remained uncertain.

Toward the end of October, Peter Kruger, then in the process
of disengaging from his job as division manager of the Paper Products Division (PPD) to become corporate senior vice president of
administration, raised a number of fundamental questions. Should
Genco invest upwards of $10 million for pollution control equip-
ment over the next four years in the old Elkhorn mill which at the
time had a book value of only $13 million? If this investment were
made, was the corporation also implicitly committing itself to a
subsequent expansion of the mill at a cost of $25 million? The
division had proposed this expansion on two occasions during the
previous six years and both times the investment had been post-
poned. Was it not better to consider a new mill somewhere else?
Were a new mill to be built, Elkhorn would be phased out and closed
altogether prior to July 1, 1977, the date required for the installation of the "best practical" control technology.

Dan Phillips, the new general manager of PPD, was initially
inclined to agree with the drift of Kruger's thinking. Rather
than take a position on phasing out the mill at the outset, how-

---

[1]See Genco Inc. (A) case for background on these events.

ever, he obtained support for a full review of the Elkhorn mill.
He was aware that managers in Primary Operations were strongly
opposed to phasing out the facility. They maintained that it was
a critical element in PPD's business strategy. Moreover, due in
part to its low investment base, Elkhorn's after tax return on
assets invested of 13.8 per cent was three times the division
average. On the other hand, Phillips knew that the chairman and
president of Genco were both interested in the answers to Kruger's
questions. In late November, responsibility for the study was
assigned to Arthur Baker, manager of business planning in PPD.
(See Exhibit 1 of the (A) case for a partial organizational chart.)

The Elkhorn Mill

PPD had a major market position in corrugated containers as
well as the two products used to make them, linerboard and corrugated medium. The Elkhorn mill produced corrugated medium and
Baker noted that, despite the age of the paper machines, it was
among the largest and lowest cost facilities in this segment of
the industry. He attributed the mill's advantageous position to
a number of factors. First the mill had been managed by highly
capable managers over the previous two decades and consequently
was well-maintained and enjoyed fine labor relations. Second,
company owned woodlands were very convenient to the mill and
capable of supporting half of its needs on a sustained yield basis,
a high proportion for the industry. Third, the woodcutters in
the area were as efficient as any in the country, thus providing
relatively low cost raw material to the pulp mill.

Yet Baker and others in PPD were concerned that Elkhorn's
leadership position in the industry would fade with time. Baker
commented:

There is one problem now that is likely to get worse.
The three paper machines are old and relatively narrow.
They don't trim as well with the newer, wider corrugating machines now being installed to make containers.
A year ago we added some equipment to correct the width
problem, but the process costs money and we sacrifice
some in price. Our costs may have peaked out and at
some point - it may be 2 or 10 or 15 years from now -
they are likely to increase.

To preserve and extend Elkhorn's competitive position, PPD
management had proposed a large paper machine to replace two of
the existing machines and provide a 16 per cent increase in capacity. Elton Johnson, primary operations manufacturing manager,
was among the proponents of this plan. He commented:

417

We applied for a new paper machine in 1969. It would
have cost $13 million then against $25 million now.
But we had just completed an $80 million integrated
mill and the paper business was in the doldrums. The
corporation said we were out of money and the project
was turned down. Elkhorn has always been a low cost
producer and that advantage is being lost. We've let
the old machines go down hill in anticipation of a new
one and our percentage downtime is beginning to show
it. We've been starving the old machines - the mill
manager feels it. . . .

Market Factors: Fall 1972

In the fall of 1972, the paper industry showed signs of re-
covering from the slump that had marred the preceding several
years. Prices appeared to be firming and operating rates and mar-
gins were improving, though in the last instance not to the levels
enjoyed in the 1960's. As reflected in Exhibits 1 and 2, the industry's performance was closely related to the general economic
condition of the country; from 1952 to 1972, tonnage increased at
an annual rate of 4.4%, while real growth in GNP averaged 3.7%.
Profits had been erratic, however, and over-all had not kept pace
with the growth in output. Selected statistics reflecting historical balance sheet and income statement trends for the industry
are summarized in Exhibit 3.

Several explanations for the mediocre profit record among
paper firms were typically offered. Central among them was the
tendency for new mills to come on stream in waves, each wave
creating excess capacity that was only absorbed in time for a new
surge of expansion. Because of the capital intensive nature of
the business and the relatively large number of competitors, producers opted for lower prices under these conditions in an effort
to avoid reduced operating rates. Moreover, to obtain greater
production economies the average size and cost of the new installa-
tions steadily increased thus placing greater competitive pressure
on older mills. Price behavior is shown in Exhibit 4 and an indication of concentration in representative segments of the industry in Exhibit 5. There was also concern in some quarters
about the intrusion of other materials, most notably plastics,
into certain markets traditionally held by paper products, e.g.,
shipping sacks, throwaway cups, etc.

Semichemical paperboard, most of it used in corrugated
medium, accounted for roughly 6.7 per cent of the 55 million tons
of paper and board produced in the U.S. in 1971 as shown in Exhibit 6. The markets for corrugated medium and linerboard were

418

highly competitive and producers had experienced considerable difficulty over the years securing price increases.

In late 1972, Baker described the corrugated market as a
"paradox." An earlier forecast of supply and demand in each of the
industry segments in which PPD competed indicated an expected weakness in operating rates for 1973 for semichemical mills that did
not carry over to either linerboard or corrugated medium as a
whole.

		Operating Rates	
	Linerboard	All Corrugated Medium	Semichemical Mills Only
1966	96%	96%	96%
1968	94	90	92
1970	92	93	93
1971	93	95	95
1972	94 E	94 E	91 E
1973	95 E	93 E	89 E
1974	98 E	96 E	92 E

Although PPD managers expected to outperform the industry, overall operating rates of 90 per cent or less spelled trouble on the
price front. These forecasts had been quite accurate in the past
and were influential in shaping Kruger's thinking on Elkhorn.

On the other hand, by December 1972, Elkhorn production was
edging toward practical capacity. Tom Dunn, manager of primary
operations commented on market conditions:

The market has gotten a lot stronger in the last few
weeks. Right now I'd like to have that new machine
at Elkhorn in operation. I could sell the increased
output this afternoon. We're even in danger of shutting down our own box plants because there isn't
enough corrugated medium to supply them with.

Conclusive explanations for the discrepancy between forecast and
actual conditions were illusive. The economic upturn was obviously
one factor, though Baker was also aware that some mills were shut
down or forced to run at reduced rates because unusual weather
conditions had interrupted wood gathering operations in parts of
the country. He also knew that one large new mill which was supposed to produce corrugated medium had been diverted to other products, at least for the time being, and possibly there were more
in this category. Finally, semi-chemical mills were under pressure from pollution control regulations and Baker suspected that
a certain amount of capacity might have been lost as a result of
mill closings. Prices were firm, but noticeable increases had not

as yet been forthcoming, perhaps as a result of price control limitations.

Pollution control regulations were expected to have a significant impact on capital expenditures in the paper industry during the 1970's. Genco executives had taken special note of a study of the industry prepared by Arthur D. Little for the Council on Environmental Quality and EPA, and published in March 1972. The study indicated that roughly 45% of all U.S. paper mills, accounting for 15% of total capacity were economically marginal and therefore susceptible to closure due to the costs of pollution abatement. Although only a fraction of these facilities were expected to shut down, semichemical mills were among those most likely to be affected. On the other hand, Elkhorn was well above the size considered by ADL to be marginal. Excerpts from this study are contained in Appendix A.

The Elkhorn Study

The evaluation of the Elkhorn mill was completed in early January, 1973. Baker summarized the reasoning behind the study and the methodology employed:

> A number of people at corporate who are concerned about pollution control expenditures are asking in this case if they are not the tail wagging the dog. After we've doubled the book value of the mill, haven't we eliminated any choice on a new paper machine? The feeling that this is bad has been visceral, based on the belief that Elkhorn is an old mill and we might be better off starting all over again somewhere else.
>
> This department [business planning] hasn't been that deeply involved in pollution abatement except in a broad planning sense until this study. It's generally been Comacho[1] and people like that who keep track of budgets and activities. A financial analyst doesn't contribute much to technical decisions; if they say something is needed and Johnson and Dunn[2] agree, we take their word for it. But the Elkhorn question is different.
>
> Our approach has been first to test the accuracy of the statement that after a new machine is installed, we would still have an old mill. We documented all the

---

[1]The chief environmental control engineer in the PPD technical department.
[2]General manager of the Primary Operations Department.

equipment behind the paper machines to determine its age, expected life, capacity and condition. We also evaluated the woodyard and asked how are the costs? Can it handle increased capacity? I believe we established that the mill is in good condition in most areas, though not all.

Then, we compared the capital costs of various alternatives for the period 1973 to 1977. [The alternatives included (a) installing the pollution control equipment and certain maintenance projects without an increase in capacity, (b) making these investments and also eliminating a number of bottlenecks to increase production by 3.3 per cent, (c) installing a new paper machine at Elkhorn, (d) building a new mill in the same area to take advantage of the Genco woodlands and (e) building a new mill in another area.] The last step was to project a P and L for the next 10 years for each of these alternatives and calculate the incremental return on investment.

A summary of the study is contained in Exhibit 7. The results appeared to confirm one point that worried managers in PPD as Baker commented:

Returns on a new integrated pulp and paper mill installation are tough to show at current prices. You just can't get there from here. Numbers I've seen recently in the industry on new mills at today's costs yield a discounted cash flow of maybe 3% - not enough to begin to cover interest.

Johnson reflected on his view of the analysis:

The study has shown that the three old machines are the only bad parts of the mill. The rest is good and the site is ideal. If we put in a new paper machine we'd have a first-rate mill. On the other hand, if we built another mill, we would have to install the "best available" pollution control equipment right away (not the "best practical") which might cost another $4 or $5 million. With an existing facility under the law, the best available isn't necessary until 1977 to 1983.

Additional Considerations

Annual budgets and capital requests for the paper mills were generally initiated by managers in primary operations and reviewed

in detail with the division general manager. They were then submitted to the corporation for comment and approval. By early
January, negotiations had been more or less completed throughout
the company on the 1973 budget. Pending the outcome of the Elkhorn study, the assumption had been made in the PPD budget that
the mill would continue in operation with future investments sufficient to execute the administrative order issued by the state
and to keep up with required maintenance and replacement projects.
Dunn reflected on his dilemma:

> We've been asked by the corporation to live within our
> cash flow as far as capital spending is concerned.
> Yet we're working against time limits on environmental
> control. That means I'm forced to take environmental
> control projects first and let capacity increases and
> cost reductions come later. The fellows at corporate
> won't tell you what to do; you hope like mad you're
> right.

Dunn's thinking on Elkhorn was complicated by the existence of
another older mill in PPD having similar physical characteristics
but a less secure woodlands position and generally lower returns.
In this instance, environmentalist pressure had not been severe
though under the regulations to be promulgated under the Water
Pollution Control Act by the states and approved by EPA, both
mills would presumably have to meet a relatively uniform set of
standards by July 1, 1977.

As the Elkhorn study was being circulated' among PPD managers,
the corporate planning office completed its consolidation and
analysis of the division budgets. The figures revealed that the
aggregate capital spending requests for all divisions for 1973
exceeded the president's guidelines by $18 million, or about 20%.
It was unclear what, if anything, would happen as a result of
this overage.

Negotiations were also proceeding with the State Department
of Resource Conservation on a permit to discharge effluent into
the Elkhorn River. In early January, the DRC drafted a permit for
Genco review which provided for interim emission levels in line
with the original state order, i.e., a monthly average not to ex-
ceed 11,160 pounds of suspended solids and 11,600 pounds of BOD.
It also specified that by July 1, 1976 the company must comply
with the levels suggested the previous June by EPA of 4,600 pounds
of suspended solids and 7,500 pounds of BOD as well as limitations
on iron, manganese and oil and grease. The document stated further that the "permit is issued with the understanding that it does
not stop the state or the U.S. EPA from subsequent establishment
of further requirements for the treatment or control at any

time."[1]

The proposed permit was analyzed in detail by Dick French, Elkhorn technical director. His recommendations to Johnson included the following:

I believe we should attempt to have the permit modified to reflect a July 1, 1977 date for achieving the operational levels and adjust the other compliance dates accordingly. It will be difficult, if not impossible, for us to make a least-cost solution with the schedule in this permit.

We must object to the iron and oil limits as stated. A great deal of our hexane soluble material appears to come from our waste and pressure is on us to increase waste percentage. If we are allowed credit for the river having iron then there would be no problem.

In some fashion we should clarify the question of what protection this permit gives us. It appears to be all one-sided.

A public hearing was scheduled for February during which Genco managers hoped these and other issues might be satisfactorily resolved. In the meanwhile, PPD managers had the task of planning for the over-all future of the Elkhorn mill.

---

[1]EPA had not as yet issued emission level standards for the paper industry under the Water Pollution Control Act.

Exhibit 1

GENCO INC. (B)

SELECTED ECONOMIC AND PAPER INDUSTRY STATISTICS

	Real GNP (billions)	% Change	Paper Industry Demand/ Prod. (1) (000 tons)	% Change	Capacity Additions (1) (000 tons)	% Increase	Paper Industry Operating Rate (2)	Paper Industry Profits (1) (millions)	% Change
1972P	$789.5	+6.4%	59,000	+ 8.9%	1,263	2.1%	96.2%	$883	+72.5%
1971	741.7	+3.0	54,180	+ 1.6	1,750	3.0	90.6	512	−28.8
1970	720.0	−0.6	53,329	− 1.6	580	1.0	90.9	719	−27.2
1969	724.7	+2.6	54,187	+ 5.7	2,131	3.8	94.6	987	+11.0
1968	706.6	+4.7	51,245	+ 9.2	2,262	4.2	93.0	889	+11.7
1967	675.2	+2.6	46,926	− 0.4	2,569	5.0	89.1	796	−12.6
1966	658.1	+6.5	47,113	+ 6.9	3,337	6.9	94.7	911	+ 4.8
1965	617.8	+6.3	44,080	+ 5.7	1,823	3.9	93.5	869	+15.3
1964	581.1	+5.5	41,703	+ 6.3	1,579	3.5	91.7	754	+18.9
1963	551.0	+4.0	38,230	+ 4.5	1,248	2.9	89.1	634	+ 1.0
1962	529.8	+6.6	37,541	+ 5.0	623	1.5	87.1	628	+ 7.7
1961	497.2	+1.9	35,749	+ 3.8	1,466	3.5	85.0	583	− 0.7
1960	487.7	+2.5	34,444	+ 1.3	1,102	2.7	84.5	587	− 5.2
1959	475.9	+6.4	34,015	+10.4	1,591	4.1	86.3	619	+34.6
1958	447.3	−1.1	30,823	+ 0.5	1,290	3.5	81.1	460	−11.7
1957	452.5	+1.4	30,666	− 2.5	2,330	6.7	84.7	521	−20.7
1956	446.1	+1.8	31,441	+ 4.2	1,852	5.6	92.2	657	+ 8.7
1955	438.0	+7.6	30,178	+12.3	996	3.0	92.4	604	+26.1
1954	407.0	−1.4	26,876	+ 1.0	990(3)	3.2	84.8(3)	479	+ 6.4
1953	412.8	+4.5	26,605	+ 9.0	1,324(3)	4.4	87.2(3)	450	+ 3.0
1952	395.1		24,418		1,141(3)	4.0	83.4(3)	437	

20-year Average (4) 3.7%   + 4.4%   + 3.1%

P – Preliminary
(1) American Paper Institute (API) data.
(2) Figured on average capacity that year. Computed from API data.
(3) Smith, Barney estimates based on API data.
(4) Computed by fitting log-liner, least squares trendlines to the figures in this 20-year period.

Source: Smith, Barney, *The Paper Industry—Another Decade of Disappointment?*, New York, 5/18/73.

Exhibit 2

GENCO INC. (B)

APPARENT CONSUMPTION OF ALL GRADES OF
PAPER AND PAPERBOARD

YEAR	LBS./CAPITA	000 TONS PER BILL./ $ REAL GNP.
1899	57.9	
1904	73.7	
1909	90.8	
1914	108.8	N/A
1919	119.6	
1924	162.6	
1929	220.3	
1934	178.6	
1939	243.7	
1944	281.6	
1947	343.4	79.9
1948	355.9	80.6
1949	331.0	76.2
1950	381.1	81.7
1951	394.6	79.7
1952	368.3	73.4
1953	391.6	76.0
1954	385.0	77.1
1955	418.5	79.3
1956	432.2	81.8
1957	410.1	77.9
1958	401.6	78.5
1959	435.5	81.4
1960	433.3	80.3
1961	439.0	81.1
1962	452.7	79.7
1963	462.1	79.3
1964	483.6	79.8
1965	505.6	79.5
1966	536.2	80.0
1967	522.8	76.9
1968	554.7	78.8
1969	581.4	81.3
1970	563.8	80.2
1971P	566.6	79.3

Source: API, "The Statistics of Paper 1972," June 1972, p. 32.

425

Exhibit 3

GENCO INC. (B)

SELECTED FINANCIAL STATISTICS—PAPER AND ALLIED PRODUCTS
1950-1972

Year	Capital Expenditures[1]	Fixed Assets as a % of Total Assets[2]	Debt/Equity Ratios[3]	Return on Sales[4]	Return on New Worth[4]
1950	299	41	13.7	8.8	15.6
1951	389	41	15.8	–	–
1952	371	43	18.2	–	–
1953	397	44	17.6	–	–
1954	533	45	18.2	–	–
1955	556	44	18.6	6.1	11.2
1956	750	46	22.3	6.1	11.4
1957	767	50	22.5	5.0	8.9
1958	618	51	23.7	4.5	7.3
1959	620	61	22.8	5.2	9.3
1960	644	64	23.3	5.0	8.4
1961	685	64	22.6	4.7	7.7
1962	750	64	25.1	4.6	8.1
1963	709	63	24.9	4.5	8.0
1964	901	64	23.7	5.1	9.1
1965	1,185	63	28.1	5.4	10.0
1966	1,422	65	35.6	5.4	10.5
1967	1,585	65	41.5	4.7	8.8
1968	1,238	67	45.1	4.7	9.6
1969	1,420	na	41.9	4.8	9.7
1970	1,397	na	46.8	3.4	7.0
1971	1,197	na	49.7	2.3	4.8
1972	1,421	na	46.8	4.0	8.9

[1] Source: U.S. Bureau of the Census. Annual Survey of Manufacturers, various issues.

[2] Source: Department of the Treasury, Internal Revenue Service, "Statistics of Income, Corporation Income Tax Returns Annual Issues"; From API "A Capital and Income Survey," 1973.

[3] Source: Derived from Federal Trade Commission-Securities and Exchange Commission, Quarterly Financial Report for Manufacturing Corporations, 1950-1973.

[4] Source: FTC percentages calculated from "Quarterly Finanical Report for Manufacturing Corporations," API, "A Capital and Income Survey," 1973.

Exhibit 4

GENCO INC. (B)

Wholesale Price Indexes of Pulp and Paper Products 1961-1971

1957-1959 = 100

	1961	1962	1963	1964	1965	1966	1967	1968	1969	1970	1971
All industrial commodities	100.8	100.8	100.7	101.2	102.5	104.7	106.3	109.0	112.8	116.9	121.2
All pulp and paper	98.8	100.0	99.2	99.0	99.9	102.6	104.0	105.2	108.2	112.5	114.5
Woodpulp	95.0	93.2	91.7	96.1	98.1	98.0	98.0	98.0	98.0	107.4	109.8
Waste paper	80.5	97.5	92.2	92.4	99.4	105.0	78.1	101.5	108.3	97.6	87.4
Paper	102.2	102.6	102.4	103.6	104.1	107.3	110.1	112.7	116.6	122.2	125.6
Paperboard	92.7	93.1	94.7	96.4	96.4	97.1	97.3	92.1	94.4	98.4	99.6
Converted paper and board products	99.5	101.0	99.7	98.3	99.3	102.3	104.8	105.9	108.8	113.1	115.0
Building paper and board	100.8	97.2	96.2	94.0	92.7	92.6	91.9	92.8	97.1	92.8	94.6

Source: Bureau of Labor Statistics

Exhibit 5

GENCO INC. (B)

PERCENT OF VALUE OF SHIPMENTS OF EACH CLASS OF
SELECTED PAPER OR BOARD MILL OUTPUT ACCOUNTED
FOR BY THE LARGEST COMPANIES

	Percent of Value of Shipments			
	4 Largest	8 Largest	20 Largest	50 Largest
Tissue Stock				
1963	56	72	88	99
1958	57	69	83	94
1954	54	64	80	NA
Container Board-Kraft (26311-26312, exc. sp. fd. bd.)				
1963	32	54	82	99+
1958	37	57	84	99
1954	42	59	83	NA
Combination Paperboard: Shipping Containerboard (26314) - old designation as folding boxboard stock				
1963	31	49	75	98
1958	34	50	75	97
Combination Bending and Non-Bending Paperboard (26315, 26316) - once called set-up boxboard				
1963	37	52	79	NA
1958	28	48	78	NA

Source: U.S. Bureau of the Census. Concentration Ratios in
Manufacturing Industry 1963. For Senate Subcommittee
on Antitrust and Monopoly. Vol. I. pp. 168-169. 1966.

Exhibit 6

GENCO INC. (B)

1971 U.S. Production of Paper and Board

	1971		1970	
	(000's tons)		(000's tons)	
All Grades		55,092		53,516
Paper		23,838		23,625
Newsprint, coated, book, and related papers	14,505		14,418	
Packaging & industrial converting papers	5,458		5,439	
Tissue	3,876		3,768	
Paperboard		26,121		25,477
Unbleached linerboard	11,321		10,962	
Bleached packaging	3,501		3,404	
Semi-chemical paperboard (corrugating medium)	3,717		3,414	
Combination shipping containerboard	1,391		1,523	
Combination boxboard	3,635		3,770	
Other paperboard*	2,547		2,404	
Construction paper and board		4,995		4,276
Wet machine board		138		138

*Total corrugated medium was 4,586 and 4,325 thousand tons in 1971 and 1970 respectively. In addition to semi-chemical paperboard produced through a sulfite process, medium was also produced through the sulfate or kraft process. This later production is included in "other."

Source: Adapted from U.S. Department of Commerce, Bureau of the Census, "Current Industrial Reports," 1971

Exhibit 7

GENCO INC. (B)

Elkhorn Mill Study

I. Elkhorn Mill Alternatives - Capital Requirements, 1973-1977 (in thousands)

Mill Production-Tons/Day at 12/31/77#	620 TPD	641 TPD	750 TPD
Pulpmill			
Woodroom	$806	$806	$806
Digester Area	365	365	765
Washer Area	210	210	650
Recovery Area	290	290	290
Miscellaneous Capital (0-25M ea.)	3,250	3,250	3,250
Power Plant	755	755	755
Shipping	15	15	50
Pollution Abatement*			
Air	3,098	3,098	3,098
Water	2,033	2,033	2,033
Solids	825	825	825
Potential Projects	4,000	4,000	4,000
Subtotal Pollution Abatement	9,956	9,956	9,956
Refining and Stock Preparation	325	325	325
Paper Machines-Existing			
Minimum Expenditure	355	355	355
Maintain at 620 TPD	2,124	2,124	
Expand to 641 TPD		2,557	
New Paper Machine & Building			24,400
Total Capital	18,457	21,008	41,602

---

* In addition to identified abatement projects it is possible that up to $750 thousands would be required in 10 years for replacement of existing abatement equipment. Another $1.5 million for pollution abatement might be required depending on the interpretation and implementation of the laws.

Several years are required to add new capacity. A new paper machine would not be in operation until 1977.

Exhibit 7 (continued)

II. Percent After Tax Return on Incremental Investments

	1977	1978	1979	1980	1981	1982
(a) Expansion to 750 TPD vs. no expansion at 620 TPD	6.4	7.6	7.8	8.1	8.3	8.6
(b) Expansion to 641 TPD vs. no expansion at 620 TPD	10.4	8.0	8.0	7.9	7.9	7.9
(c) Expansion to 750 TPD vs. expansion to 641 TPD	5.9	7.6	7.7	8.1	8.4	8.8

III. Differential Profit Requirements – New Mill Versus Elkhorn New Machine (in millions)

	New Mill Same Area	New Mill Another Area
Investment	$67.3	$87.3*
Less: Elkhorn 750 TPD investment	41.6	41.6
Differential investment	$25.7	$45.7
After tax earnings required for 8% return on investment	$ 2.0	$ 3.6
Pre tax earnings required	4.0	7.2
Cost savings required in $ per ton	$15.24	$27.43

* Includes $20 million for the acquisition of timberland.

Exhibit 7 (continued)

IV. Potential Cost Savings per ton Compared with Elkhorn

	New Mill Same Area	New Mill Another Area
Tonnage – all at 750 TPD	–	–
Wood	–	(Higher)
Waste	–	2.00
Chemicals & supplies	(Higher)	(Higher)
Labor	–	1.00
Electric power	(Higher)	1.00
Fuel	–	1.00
Maintenance	2.00	2.00
Depreciation	(4.53)	(4.53)
Freight	–	(Higher)
Taxes	(Higher)	–
Net effect	(2.53)	2.47

APPENDIX A

GENCO INC. (B)

The Economic Impact of Pollution Control
Pulp and Paper Mills[1]

A. Industry Structure

About 45% of all U.S. mills – accounting for some 15% of
total U.S. paper capacity, are economically marginal by current
standards of efficiency.[2] In general, this means that they fall
below the current minimum economic size for mills in their product
sector. These mills will have the greatest difficulty in meeting
the anticipated pollution abatement requirements. Table 1 shows
the distribution of these mills by product sector.

B. Profitability Trend

The paper industry's profitability is at its lowest point
since World War II, with after-tax returns on total assets averaging
about 4% in 1970. Profitability has declined further to about 3%
of total assets in 1971, judging from the financial performance
reported by 39 publicly held companies for the first nine months
of 1971. . . .

Our analysis points to improved operating rates in most
sectors of the industry by 1973, assuming real GNP growth of 5% in
1972 and 1973. Significant overcapacity is expected to continue
through 1973 in three product sectors: insulation board, semi-
chemical corrugated medium, and special industrial paper. Mills
in these sectors will have great difficulty in coping with additional pollution abatement costs because of weak prices and low
profits. For the rest of the industry the market environment will
generally provide increased mill utilization and be conducive to
price increases in the absence of rigid price controls. Between
1974 and 1976 we expect operating rates to decline again judging
from previous cycles in this industry. Industry profitability
will follow the same cyclical trend.

---

[1]Arthur D. Little, Inc., in The Economic Impact of Pollution Control, A Summary of recent studies prepared for the Council on
Environmental Quality, Department of Commerce and Environmental
Protection Agency, March 1972, p 277 ff.
[2]In this report, except as noted, the term "mill" refers to a
single facility that includes both pulp and papermaking facilities;
that is, an integrated facility is considered a single mill.

C. Price Impact

To determine the price increases necessary to absorb the increased pollution abatement costs anticipated by 1976, we compared
the abatement costs for efficient mills with the approximate median
price of each product group. The major price increases relative to
current prices will be in hardboard, newsprint and uncoated groundwood, bleached kraft pulp and unbleached kraft linerboard. Here,
the price increases range from 6.5% to 10% of product value, depending upon the grade. Product sectors that will experience
moderate price increases (3.5% to 6% of current product value) are:
bleached paperboard, semi-chemical corrugating medium, bag and
wrapping paper, combination paperboard, insulation board, printing
papers, and dissolving pulp. The other product sector will require
only modest price increases.

We anticipate that all the above price increases will be obtained (in the absence of price controls) because of the tightening
supply/demand balances projected for most sectors in 1972 and 1973.
Beyond 1974, prices might well decline again should the industry
enter another cycle of overcapacity.

In most cases abatement cost levels for marginal mills will
be appreciably higher than those for larger more efficient mills
since the latter benefit from economies of scale. This factor
adds to the economic difficulties of the marginal mills.

D. Mill Shutdown Probabilities

Table 5 summarizes mill shutdown probabilities between 1972
and 1976 with and without pollution abatement expenditures above
current levels. It indicates that the key impact areas are: sulfite and semi-chemical pulp, tissue paper, printing and writing
paper, special industrial paper, and combination paperboard. In
addition to these we expect less extensive dislocations to occur
in other product groups - mainly newsprint, uncoated groundwood
paper, and packaging paper and board.

Some mills in all of the above sectors will close by 1976
strictly because of economic considerations, but the closure rate
will be increased significantly by the requirement to expend capital to correct a pollution problem. In most cases marginal single-
mill companies in these sectors will be unable to obtain capital
for pollution control equipment because their return on investment
is destined to remain very low. Most such mills are not integrated
to woodpulp and will face a cost/price squeeze since prices for
the market pulp or waste paper upon which they are dependent are
expected to increase at a more rapid rate than the price of the
end products which they produce. The life of many of these mills

434

will be prolonged if they are able to minimize their capital costs
by joining in a municipal water treatment system. For other mills,
particularly tissue paper and special industrial paper companies,
it is still questionable whether they can absorb the increased
operating costs for pollution abatement since these costs are significantly higher for them than for large-scale producers. . . .

Appendix A (continued)

TABLE 1

SUMMARY OF ECONOMICALLY MARGINAL PULP AND PAPER CAPACITY, 1971

Production Sector	Total No. of Mills	Size Criteria (under tons/day)	Economically Marginal Mills		
			No. of Mills	Percent of Total Mills	Percent of Total Capacity
Sulfite Pulp	37*	150**	12	33*	14
Semi-Chemical Pulp	41*	200**	9	22*	6
Tissue	102	50	49	48	18
Printing, Writing and Related	138	200	97	70	48
Special Industrial Paper	38	25	9	25	17
Combination Paperboard	170	100	78	49	27
Other Packaging Paper and Board	97	200-400	17	18	5
Newsprint and Groundwood	32	350	11	29	19
Construction Paper	47	100	31	60	36
Insulation Board	23	100	6	26	9
Hardboard	29	100	10	35	10
Total	752		329	44	15

*Nearly all of these pulp mills are integrated to mills making paper and paperboard.
**Includes some larger mills without chemical recovery systems.

Source: Arthur D. Little, Inc., estimates.

436

Appendix A (continued)

TABLE 5

SUMMARY OF MILL SHUTDOWN PROBABILITIES, 1972-1976

Product Sector	Marginal Capacity (000 tons/yr)	Probability of Closure		Capacity Removal	
		Status Quo* (%)	Additional Abatement (%)	Status Quo* (000 tons)	Additional Abatement (000 tons)
Sulfite and Semi-Chemical Pulp	750	5-10	65	50	485
Tissue	650	15	50	105	345
Printing, Writing and Related	4,730	10	20	490	890
Special Industrial Paper	60	30	85	20	50
Combination Paperboard	2,030	10	25	200	540
Other Products	3,315	5	25	205	775
Total	11,535			1,070	3,085

* Assumes no additional pollution control expenditures above current levels.

Source: Arthur D. Little, Inc., estimates.

437

DISCUSSION

ACKERMAN: We have a situation here that I think managers would recognize as perhaps altogether too common, as they have worked over the last four or five years with EPA and state environmental control agencies. But at this particular point, October of 1972, John Wilson, the lawyer for Genco, has talked with officials at EPA. They've told him what they want, and he has summarized EPA's demands as best he could for the management group in the Paper Products Division. If you were there in that company with this set of issues and the history behind them, what would you do? At this point, what kind of action would you recommend for Genco to take in its response to EPA?

COMMENT: One alternative I'd consider would be to close the plant.

ACKERMAN: Why would you think about doing that?

COMMENT: I think that the investment necessary to build it up isn't worth the effective return the stockholders should expect.

ACKERMAN: So, escalating costs. Why have these costs been escalating?

COMMENT: Because of some of the other work they've had to do.

ACKERMAN: Are these pollution control related things?

COMMENT: Yes, they'd been doing some all along. Still, I'm primarily looking at the type of return they're getting on sales which, corporate-wise, is around 3.6 percent. This represents the second largest division as far as sales are concerned and they're getting something like a 3 percent return and they're facing a big investment, almost $3½ or $4 million. Discount that, depending on what the discount rates are and you could discount that maybe $3, $3½ million. By 1983, I think, they have to put in the best available technology which they estimate would cost another $4 million.

ACKERMAN: Another $4 million by 1985, I guess. It's unclear what the law is going to be at this particular point in time.

COMMENT: That's the other problem, namely, how to react to EPA. They had nothing to react to officially. They are getting caught in the push and pull of state vs. Feds.

438

ACKERMAN: So, "what is the law" is a genuine unknown?

COMMENT: I think one of the other alternatives may be to buy some time. They should try to get the state and the Feds to negotiate to get them off the hook, but that's only going to buy time.

ACKERMAN: You mean you try to get the state and federal people to at least agree with one another?

COMMENT: It seems like right now the state and the federal people are operating on different tracks. They're using different kinds of standards. The state wants about the same levels of BOD and suspended solids, and the EPA wants a much lower level of suspended solids and BOD. It seems like there really isn't any concensus between them about what the standard should be in the future. And it also seems almost like the federal guys are taking a shot in the dark. They say, "Here's a corporate saint that's been trying to do good by the environment all along. Let's take them as our first shot and if we can really get something established with them, then we can use that as leverage with other firms." So it seems like there's room for negotiation or at least that Genco can stall for awhile until those issues get sorted out.

ACKERMAN: Okay. This is where we are at the moment. In terms of pounds per day, there were 15,865 of BOD and 21,585 of suspended solids, and the state has said, "Well, we want you to be 11,600 on BOD and 11,160 on suspended solids." Then EPA has come along and said, "We'd now like you to adopt some voluntary standards which would take you down to 7,850 on BOD and 4,650 on suspended solids." And you're saying that these are pretty steep reductions and it looks like EPA may be asking for something that it really doesn't fully understand.

COMMENT: Yes. They're not only steep, they're out of line with each other. I mean, there's a reduction of one-half on the BOD, but there's a reduction of four times on the suspended solid side.

ACKERMAN: Does the company know how to meet those standards, do you think?

COMMENT: Well, the company's been fiddling with these kinds of things for some time and it's within the company's capacity probably to hold them down there. But the question is whether the cost is going to be too great. It almost looks like they would have to spend close to what their profit from that plant is going to be each year simply to meet the requirements.

ACKERMAN: So, are you then supporting the idea of somehow or another negotiating?

COMMENT: Yeah, I don't like the idea of closing down the plant, because I think that that firm has obligations to more constituencies than the shareholders. There are the employees who have worked for that plant for a long time, and even the woodcutters who are not employees but who sell things to the plant. There's a social system that's built up there, a set of mutual obligations that's built up over time, that I think has to be taken into account. So, I would be against a rash closing of the plant, but I think they are in a situation now where they can buy some time and try to work out a set of arrangements that can allow them to, say, produce a fair return for the stockholders and still play a productive role in that community.

ACKERMAN: Okay, any other views on what the management of this company ought to do?

COMMENT: If the company tries to buy time, the loss would probably, in the end, be fairly stringent. If they decide not to close the plant, and try to buy time, if they're going to have to install the equipment, it's going to be more expensive to install the equipment later than earlier. To get ahead of the game in terms of the capital costs, it may make sense for the company to comply immediately and maybe take a loss for a few years, but ultimately, they will probably be ahead, even ahead of their competitors, because their competitors will have to comply ultimately also.

COMMENT: You have a problem there with the difference between the two kinds of equipment and the two dates that the law prescribes, the most practicable, and the other one, the best available. One consideration might be that if you stall long enough, the equipment you buy later is going to meet the latter part of the law, and if you buy it early, you're going to end up buying another set of equipment later on to meet the last part of the law, not to mention the difficulties of finding the best available and most practicable.

ACKERMAN: And that may change too. Do you suppose that the company has any leverage with either of those agencies?

COMMENT: Probably more with DRC than EPA.

ACKERMAN: More with DRC. You'd like to keep it at the state level, so that people might have a little bit more understanding of some of the immediate employment matters?

440

COMMENT: You'd have more leverage with a state group, but the federal standards are eventually going to be preemptive.

ACKERMAN: They'd have leverage with people who don't have very much power?

COMMENT: Well, part of the answer there might be to get DRC on their side in the fight with the EPA. That's what I was trying to allude to earlier.

COMMENT: In my experience, the EPA officials have nothing but contempt for the state officials, particularly if they view them as being captured by local industry.

ACKERMAN: That business works both ways. So, get DRC' support. And what's DRC's problem? Where do they stand in this little drama that's unfolding? How do you suppose DRC feels about EPA's letter to Genco?

COMMENT: . . .Cutting in on their territory. . .

COMMENT: Well, DRC made early demands and then there were negotiations and Genco worked things out and really developed a working relationship where DRC got a better understanding of what the situation was at that plant. Now EPA has come charging in with a set of what could appear to be arbitrary standards. Not only are they moving in on DRC's territory but they're moving in in a brash uninformed sort of way. DRC would reasonably resent that kind of intrusion.

ACKERMAN: So you could probably get their support, for what it's worth.

COMMENT: But at the same time, as soon as it looks like you two are in harmony, then DRC will lose its credibility. You almost want to maintain a nice adversary relationship with DRC so that they will get credibility in the eyes of the public. You want the tough guy that understands rather than the tough guy that doesn't.

ACKERMAN: So, what's the response to EPA going to be if we conclude that Genco might have some productive discussions with DRC, but the one with the muscle is really the EPA? There's a date here, October 4, and the answer is expected by EPA at that point. EPA has said that they want compliance with a set of voluntary standards. The law sitting before Congress does not actually contain specific standards at all. One of the facts of life in dealing with environmental control regulations, indeed almost all regulations, is that the laws Congress passes are

441

typically very brief. Yet, the Federal Register that finally promulgates what the regulations are may be several inches thick. Actually the law itself has comparatively little to do with the specific standards that companies have to respond to. The law is a kind of broad philosophical statement. What companies really respond to is the interpretation of the law published in the Federal Register which may come out a couple of years later and which finally pins down what EPA's actual demands are going to be. That, unfortunately, is life. But the law is about to be voted on now. What is the response to EPA going to be? How should a company respond to a request of this sort? Does Genco have an obligation to respond?

COMMENT: Is it ethical, maybe you're saying?

ACKERMAN: Is it unethical not to respond to EPA? Unethical to respond to them? Does ethics have anything to do with it? Does Genco have a right not to respond?

COMMENT: Well, I had a case like this in Kentucky, where we just wrote a nice little note that said absolutely nothing. Then we sent someone around to have lunch with the guy to try to find out what it was all about.

ACKERMAN: So, be nice to EPA; buy it lunch, but do nothing - just find out a little more about where they're going at this point?

COMMENT: There's no question that the negotiation approach in a cross-fire of this type is a way to start out. You just don't know what the rules are and you have got to find our where the real demands lie. If they don't do that, how can you really put any numbers together as to what it's going to cost or any long-range returns that project the money you might spend.

ACKERMAN: Are you saying, in a little bit larger vein, that when in doubt, negotiate?

COMMENT: If you don't know what the rules are, you've got to find out the rules. That's No. 1.

COMMENT: I think the first alternative has to be more or less resolved in a very broad, hazy sort of way, because this might be just the excuse you're looking for to get away from some of these other contingencies we've talked about. To get rid of a loser just might be perfect for Genco. It might save Genco from having to go to a consulting firm. Yet somebody else would say that you've got to close the plant down anyway, so let the government take the brunt of it.

COMMENT: And you could make it a good example of what happens whenever EPA comes in with unreasonable demands. The rest of the industry would make you a hero.

COMMENT: So, assuming that you don't want to close the plant, that you do see opportunity for the long-term, then you've got to assume you're going to court and get ready for it.

COMMENT: The second step is to create credibility for the company with the agency; in other words, to try and step out of the adversarial role and move into the kind of role where you're open about your problems in a way in which EPA will believe the facts that you're faced with, the facts that business life is faced with.

COMMENT: Are you suggesting a political approach here?

COMMENT: No. Not at all. I'm saying that in a discussion with the EPA, or any agency for that matter, you may wish to establish the truth of your position by opening your company up, your financial and technological problems up, as far as you possibly can, so that they do not regard your attempt at negotiation as merely an offensive stall.

ACKERMAN: You don't want to create the impression that you're just dragging your feet on this.

COMMENT: Supporting that notion, it seems to me that step one in the negotiation process, which I would opt for, would be a systematic analysis of what the problems are that both sides could agree on. I think the problem solving approach has been best handled by a systematic orderly analysis.

ACKERMAN: What do you suppose EPA and Genco could agree on?

COMMENT: The second memo suggests that it would be pretty easy to meet that BOD limit with very little in the way of additional technology. If you want to create a little credibility with the EPA, a good public relations campaign after meeting the limit might provide you with that opportunity. Take care of one side of this coin first. In effect, you're doing something too because you're reducing pollution. Instead of just talking about doing something, you're doing something. That might create more credibility for you than having lunch or calling up your lawyer.

ACKERMAN: Would you tell EPA that Genco will accept the target for BOD?

COMMENT: Sure, if the plant manager tells you you can. You can

443

also perhaps satisfy an ethical question with the environmental or conservation groups at the same time. In fact, you'd make the Elkhorn River a little better off too, if that counts.

ACKERMAN: In other words, maybe the BOD standard looks okay. And do you think EPA might be willing to say: "Alright, we'll take that as a good faith first step and if you'll do that, we'll raise our limits on suspended solids"?

COMMENT: Well, even if they don't go that far, you might be able to, in effect, negotiate a later compliance date on the suspended solids and wait for better technology.

ACKERMAN: You'd say, in essence, do something. Meet EPA voluntary standards where possible.

COMMENT: Well, isn't this a negotiating, delaying tactic? If you're going to do something that isn't going to cost you too much money to buy time, isn't that, in essence, a continuing negotiation you're committing yourself to, because when time starts to run out, then you have to renegotiate some different numbers and some new dates to meet the standards, and so forth. Is that a long-term solution?

ACKERMAN: Do you think there is a long-term solution?

COMMENT: Well, if you're going to modernize the plant in other ways, you need a long-term solution in order to justify the expenditure. A continuing hassle with these agencies mitigates against any other capital investments here so I think you have to eventually set a date that is going to be the time you're going to quit fiddling and make a long-term deal with EPA.

ACKERMAN: You're saying that the uncertainties here are inhibiting investment?

COMMENT: The whole viability of the operation over the next 10 to 15 years now has a shadow over it as a result of these contingencies on pollution. Therefore, you have to set some date, whether it be one year, two years, three years hence, when this has to be resolved before you can commit yourself to the long-term. But this thing can only be settled over a period of time as I see it. It won't take care of itself in a short period of time.

ACKERMAN: Do you feel that the kind of behavior that's embodied in this line of thought - negotiating, seeking delay, trying to clarify and compromise, perhaps trying to work with some of the standards but push others back, all this sort of thing - is

444

something that critics would use to accuse this corporation of being irresponsible in some way?

COMMENT: It would sure look like that from the outside.

ACKERMAN: Is it "irresponsible" behavior for a corporation to go through the set of activities that we outlined?

COMMENT: Could I go another step? I think from reading this history you've prepared that there are a couple of things missing, such as the problem-solving systematic approach to the problem and the need to communicate with other elements in the environment; for example, the congressional delegation. It seems to me they ought to know what is being done as a matter of information. Perhaps this is a case for the use of some advocacy advertising in the community to explain step by step what Genco is doing as a company; not grinding an axe but just straightforward information, making an acknowledgement that they have goals and that they intend to comply eventually at some point.

ACKERMAN: Well, of course, that's another approach. Instead of buying people lunch, one puts one's position in the newspaper. I suppose that's another way of negotiating.

COMMENT: I don't mean rhetoric now. I mean a straightforward informational account of what they were doing.

ACKERMAN: So, emphasize what they've done. This company has, at least from what they say and from all that one could determine, not been a lagger.

COMMENT: One part is that the company has been a leader in its industry, but the standards of the community have changed. What was once considered very good is now no longer good, even though it's the best of the industry. One of the possibilities is that the insiders have not changed their own attitudes. There are new community standards and further controls are coming. The standards are being raised and much of the problem is not recognizing it. If they want to remain the same sort of company, which is a company that has always felt an obligation to the community, they're going to have to face the fact that costs are going to increase if they want to stay in this industry and that perhaps some long-range planning is necessary.

ACKERMAN: Okay, let's first establish the fact that the regulation is an end point that has its antecedents in public attitudes. Presumably, we live in a political and social context in which attitudes are ultimately reflected in the law. Attitudes and social values have changed. Is this company keeping up to

445

date? That's one question. But you raised something that I
think we ought to get into here, because I think it relates to
the Genco people involved and we really haven't talked about them
much. What if I were to sharpen the question and ask not what
should Genco do, but in particular, what position should Mr.
Phillips take in this affair? Now we must go back to the organization charts, so let me review the situation a little bit.
We have a Chairman, Donald Mason. We have a PPD Division Manager, formerly Peter Kruger and now Dan Phillips. We then have
a fellow by the name of Dunn, who is Manager of Primary Operations, and a man by the name of Johnson, who is in charge of
Manufacturing. Under Johnson, there's a mill manager and finally
we get down to French, who is Technical Director of the Elkhorn
mill. He'd been writing all the memorandums. He's up in Elkhorn, up there in the far regions of the north woods. Mason,
the President, is of course at the corporate office. Kruger, the
former Division Manager, is moving up to a senior corporate staff
job that will put him in the small circle of managers close to
Mason. If you view all this data and the confusion that is present upon Phillips' entry into his new job, what kind of a position does Phillips find himself in? What are the organizational
dimensions of this particular problem? Ultimately, it's going
to be the people involved who are going to make decisions here
about how to respond to this problem, not some abstract corporation. How do you suppose Phillips views what's happening?

COMMENT: He's an outsider who's just come from another division
entirely. He might have different values than those in the Paper
Products Division. He's probably very confused because besides
having all the usual problems of a new manager, he's coming in
at a crisis stage where the plant may be closed. He'd probably
run around for awhile without doing much of anything.

COMMENT: Well, would he have much input into the capital aspect of this, the capital ramifications of either shutting down
or continuing to operate or spending the kind of money that it
might take to meet the new standards?

ACKERMAN: Well, he's running a $400 million business.

COMMENT: It seems to me that he is walking into a major decision
and that he'd have to rely upon Kruger and also the corporate
office regardless.

COMMENT: If I were Phillips, I'd punt.

COMMENT: But the decisions being made here have to do with major
shifts that are taking place in the organization's environment,
and changes which, if they are made, will influence things that

446

are done in other plants and other parts of the organization and probably in other organizations. The EPA is aiming way down at the technical director in one plant, trying to get things sorted out with him, but decisions will be made there that have tremendous impact for the organization as a whole. It would seem to me that Phillips would want the EPA to start dealing with him or with someone on his staff. That's the level in the organization at which these kinds of issues should be sorted out, even if it does breach traditional plant autonomy.

ACKERMAN: So you think then that Phillips really ought to embrace this problem?

COMMENT: Yes, I think he should make it his problem.

COMMENT: I don't think Phillips knows about the problem, because the last memo from Wilson didn't even go to Phillips.

ACKERMAN: He's not even on the distribution list for the memorandum?

COMMENT: Is this Genco's only division that deals with making paper? (Yes) So the rest of the corporation deals with other types of manufacturing? (Yes)

COMMENT: Maybe Phillips ought to take French out to lunch and find out what's going on!

ACKERMAN: We have one alternative for Phillips, "Let Kruger do it" vs. another, "Get involved and make the decisions." Do you suppose Mason wants to get involved in this kind of thing?

COMMENT: He ought to if he wants to keep the plant going.

COMMENT: This is a major crisis. I should think that this ultimately is a corporate, informational if not decisional, type of crisis because if they shut down the plant because of an EPA ruling, the thing can have sky rockets going up all over the place. I just can't help but think this is a major crisis that involves the whole corporation, including the corporate office.

ACKERMAN: We've got six levels of line management here that are involved with this situation plus some corporate lawyers.

COMMENT: Yes, but it has overall corporate significance because these new laws affect all aspects of a corporation. It's not a divisional matter.

COMMENT: Given that too, I'd say this memo was not sent to either

Skinner, who's Vice President of Environmental Affairs, or the PR guy, Anderson.

ACKERMAN: So, the division is trying to handle this thing on its own?

COMMENT: There are two areas that I've always felt are corporate matters in manufacturing operations; one is air and water pollution problems and the other is energy. In other words, these things have effects all across the corporate spectrum and, for all I know, there should be a corporate staff man who would have input on this type of problem, as well as a corporate energy man inside the corporation.

ACKERMAN: Here's a $2 billion corporation coming across a major social issue with lots of apparent ramifications across other divisions, lots of uncertainties, investment decisions that will commit the corporation in the future. Division management, particularly down the line in manufacturing, apparently want to hold that decision to themselves. You can imagine all the reasons why they don't want Mason involved with decisions way down here because there would be absolute chaos if he tried to do it very much. But you can also imagine some of the difficulty in getting a coherent, consistent, rapidly moving corporate response to anything that has as much uncertainty in it as this. Yet, in this case the manufacturing managers tend to harbor the data and the decision points to themselves. So, I guess, as far as Phillips is concerned, he's walking into a difficult organizational situation. There are some views that are pretty well established down in his organization and he's certainly got to contend with them. We don't know a lot about what Mason thinks in detail, but we do know that he has certainly taken a progressive position on environmental matters. One could imagine that he doesn't want the corporation lambasted in the press. That's not his style. He doesn't have that kind of attitude toward the issue. What can Phillips do? Who is he going to lend support to? The managers down the line would like to negotiate. They'd like to somehow or another delay the decision and be able to make the situation something that they can deal with in time.

COMMENT: Isn't Phillips in a position where he can neither win nor lose in one sense. If the forces below him want him to go in one direction, he may have very conservative forces -- let's not rock the boat -- from above, so he steps into a hornet's nest.

ACKERMAN: Do you think he could really duck getting involved?

COMMENT: Not and survive. He's going to get some stings. He

448

can't avoid the inevitable.

COMMENT: I think one thing that may be helpful to him in making the decision would be more information, especially since it's a very technical type of decision based on available technology. It's also going to be based on what the legal situation is going to be and how the law is going to be worked out. It may be helpful if he had some peer or outside consultants look at the technical problem or if he had outside lawyers or company lawyers. I think he needs more independent information, legal information, and technical engineering consultants.

COMMENT: Was Kruger bumped out and Phillips put in to handle this?

ACKERMAN: No, Kruger was, in essence, promoted.

COMMENT: I know. Was he promoted up and out?

ACKERMAN: No, I don't think the implication is that.

COMMENT: It is somewhat unusual in the middle of a controversial matter like this to move the responsible person and then to establish a problem for the corporation by putting in a new manager. Is Phillips a problem-solver type who has been brought in from success in another place? Are we talking about what Phillips might be pushed to do? Does Phillips have a certain style that's going to lead to using consultants, and so forth?

ACKERMAN: Look at the dates involved. It's interesting that the organization change was effective 6/30/72. We're already in October and Phillips is only halfway into his new position at this point. The change must have been announced back about the time that EPA first arrived in April. The company didn't think it had a problem before that. It was working along with DRC, and they seemed to be coming to some kind of an accommodation.

COMMENT: Did they kick Kruger upstairs?

ACKERMAN: If that were the case, then why isn't Phillips in here doing something about it? Or if that wasn't the case, if Kruger was not being kicked upstairs, so to speak, should the reorganization be delayed? At this point in our discussion, let me give you the B Case and you might read just the first page or so of it.

COMMENT: Let me make one quick comment as a total outsider here. I assume that the EPA regulations profess to protect against environmental damage to human beings in the society; but then there

449

is also something bad about people being unemployed which seems to be at odds with the regulations.

COMMENT: The one element that is missing here - it's hard to make a rational decision for the people who are making this decision without considering it - is, how does this society choose among more paper vs. jobs vs. satisfactory environment? All we're dealing with is the cost/profit factor about whether we should keep the plant going. I don't see where or how the other things get factored in.

ACKERMAN: Are you asking, does society need more paper?

COMMENT: Yes. How do you talk about that? It's all missing here. I don't know how to think about it rationally, because I'm missing the elements that I would make a decision on.

ACKERMAN: Do you suppose that the managers involved, as much as they might think about the issues you have raised, have any way of taking action on them?

COMMENT: Not if the lines of authority go up to Mason and then to the stockholders. They don't seem to be interested in that kind of question. I think I'd get fired if I asked that. I don't know. I'm an outsider. But it seems to me that I wouldn't get Phillips' job if I were talking about those questions. And if I had his job and I did that, I would probably get fired.

ACKERMAN: So, these sorts of issues don't really get raised?

COMMENT: It seems to me that these people have been trying to answer these questions for themselves. Earlier on, they voluntarily tried to find ways to reduce the level of pollution that the mill was putting into the environment. They may not have done it as fast as some other people's standards might dictate it should have been done, but they were, in fact, trying to do that. People, at least at the plant level, were very concerned about employees' lives, about maintaining the plant. This may have been one of the many reasons why they didn't want to let the decision be made upstairs. They wanted to deal with the problem at the plant level so that the community could be maintained the way it was. It seems to me that people are making those tradeoffs, but you always come to the point where if the organization cannot survive economically, then you can't make these other decisions and the game is over. And so economic considerations have to have prime consideration, at least to the point of organizational survival.

COMMENT: Let me just ask a general question. I'm a philosopher

450

who doesn't know very much about business, and this would help me understand what we're talking about here. How do environmental regulations hurt a company economically? Presumably, these laws don't put the company at an economic disadvantage because its competitors have to go by the same standards too. So, what is the net effect here? If you have all these environmental controls, people use alternative things besides paper. Is there really anything over and above that?

COMMENT: In this case, everyone doesn't have to meet the same tests. EPA is saying, "You've been a good guy. We want you to go further and we want you to be the example." It's like the paper mill up in New Hampshire which decided to be the example and lost all its business and closed down, but the guy who did it was a real saint.

COMMENT: Well, surely you don't have an obligation to be a martyr. I mean, isn't the thing to do to just steam along and say everybody else should have to do their share?

COMMENT: But they're not saying this. They're saying, "Be the martyr for us and then maybe we can get other people to fall in line voluntarily after you've fallen in line." I mean, that's what's happening in this situation.

COMMENT: How can you apply a model in one company and not in others?

COMMENT: It happens all the time.

COMMENT: This is not a law that's being applied. They're saying, "Come on out and be a saint for us, and then we'll hold you up to the rest of the industry."

ACKERMAN: It's interesting to read what EPA said, or what Wilson said that EPA said. He said the EPA was saying that their pounds per ton figures are really not negotiable. They're standards. And the theory behind them is one that you suggested; namely, if everybody has to meet the same standards, well then presumably the competitive aspect of this will be nullified. Now, what they did say was, "If you want to negotiate with us, we'll negotiate the production rates. We won't negotiate on the standards. We'll take your highest production rate and set the standards around that figure if you play ball with us." So EPA is in some ways being very strict about the way it applies the standards -- so many pounds of BOD per ton of output. But what they are offering to negotiate on is how many tons of product the plant actually made. And that's going to depend on a whole lot of things. So, in essence EPA is offering this company the proposi-

451

tion that, "If you do something with us right now, we'll figure out a way to make things a little better for you, even though our standards are the same." I would doubt very, very much if EPA officials would move off the standards announced for one company and not feel they had to do it for everybody.

COMMENT: Why does a company have a moral obligation to be a martyr?

ACKERMAN: EPA is concerned about equity. They're also concerned about the leverage they have over the people that are willing to move. If they can get somebody to move, they can make others follow. If they can't get anybody to move, well, then they have a problem because they don't know how to run a paper mill. The industry people do. The EPA doesn't and they've got to get at least one credible company to say, "We'll go a little further."

COMMENT: What's wrong with being martyred. I mean, companies try to beat the competition in other things, so why not try to beat the competition in terms of environmental protection. If these standards are going to be applied uniformly and if the best possible control system is to be used to set the standards for the industry, then Genco can also use the willingness to innovate as leverage on other companies. Other companies will be forced to meet the standards as well, but they're going to do it later when the capital costs are higher. Therefore, Genco will have a competitive advantage.

COMMENT: But suppose during that period of martyrdom what happens to martyrs happens to your company. For five years you run at a loss, the plant has to be shut down, and you've just put, let's say, 500 people out of work and maybe destroyed a community. Then the EPA says, "Hey, that's the way it goes, guys."

COMMENT: I'm not advocating shutting down the plant. I'm advocating making technological changes, establishing technological standards for the industry.

COMMENT: Oh, I agree with you. But what happens if part of that involves a couple of communities going broke? It is possible, and it has happened over the past ten years, that companies have shut down and towns have been economically destroyed. The EPA says, "Well, that's the way it goes" and moves on. What happens then? Nobody cited the EPA for being socially irresponsible.

COMMENT: It may involve a temporary, immediate loss.

452

COMMENT: Those words disguise people being out of work. I mean, what temporary economic insufficiency says to some people says starvation to others.

ACKERMAN: I have never heard this argument quite this way. It's an interesting one. If you had the technological capability to go far beyond what your competition could do in pollution control, is it irresponsible to encourage the standards to be set to your specifications, knowing that you are the only one able to meet them and that factories will be shut down as a result?

COMMENT: I think one thing that is very important about this situation is that, before EPA stepped in, there was a voluntary assumption of responsibility on the part of Genco and now it has degenerated into an adversary relationship between Genco and the EPA. Yet both sides are presumably interested in the same ultimate goal, which is solving a problem that's of national, if not international, concern. So why doesn't Genco consult with other companies who are in this industry and say, "Look, here's a common problem that we have," and try to get the industry to adopt a voluntary type of stance.

COMMENT: Someone was saying that that's not legal, that they would be discouraged or maybe even prohibited from consulting with other paper companies along the Elkhorn River who had a similar problem. That is, I guess, somehow collusion in response to EPA.

COMMENT: Well then, I guess the legal structure has effectively prevented adopting what you were referring to before as a rational approach to the problem and that's a very important thing.

ACKERMAN: Could we turn to the B Case for just a minute. I'd like to interject certain elements of it into the discussion because the situation changes pretty dramatically over the next couple of months in terms of the considerations involved. Spend a minute or two, if you haven't already, on the first page and the first paragraph on the next page to get a sense for what's going on.

COMMENT: Before this discussion goes on there's something else that seems to be relevant. Several scholars have suggested that issues of this sort may well be the Achilles heel of the market economy. Short-run profit barriers influence such things as the investment of capital which is obviously necessary to get the best available technology and may make it impossible for a firm to implement that technology because it's not going to be profitable. Yet in the long run -- when you are talking about 10, 20, 30 years -- in an industrial culture, new technology

453

almost surely has to happen.

ACKERMAN: I think that is one of the critical issues of our
time. You're talking about a set of social demands which have
long-term payoffs, but yet are compressed in specific instances
into what happens on the fourth of October given the individual
concerns of the managers involved at that time.

COMMENT: We only compound that problem by having isolated
agencies like EPA. You build an adversary relationship and
that, in effect, undercuts the progress you are trying to make.

ACKERMAN: I don't like to be the one to respond here, but I
will in this particular instance because I do feel strongly about
this point. Very often, if you don't have an adversary process
you end up with bad legislation. We all know that. Is advocacy
basically unhealthy? You know that individual managers, individual companies, attempt to shape the surroundings that are
immediately around them. Are they really in error making their
positions known?

COMMENT: I think the adversary process is necessary. I just
think you don't have a good adversary situation unless it's
broad enough. And pitting EPA against one company isn't useful
when, in fact, at the society level, what you need is an adversary system with a broader sense of issues.

ACKERMAN: My impression is that you would have less advocacy
if you had one super agency, but that's beside the point. What's
happened here in the next couple of months? I'd like to complete the picture and then we can talk about what it all means.
What's happened?

COMMENT: Kruger's helping Phillips step up to his new job.

ACKERMAN: Is he helping him?

COMMENT: Well, he's giving him a set of criteria, some decisions
that have to be made. He hasn't made the decisions, but he's
helping him see the decisions that have to be made when Phillips
takes over.

ACKERMAN: Phillips is now a couple of months further into his
new job. Kruger is getting more and more restless with the people
at the manufacturing level in PPD. And what little parting issue
has Kruger laid in Phillips' lap? He has said, in effect, "Maybe we ought to shut this mill down because once we spend $10 mil-
lion for pollution control equipment, well then I know you are
going to ask for that $25 million paper machine which you have

454

asked for twice before and both times the corporate office has
said no. Have you then got us on the hook? (Us being the people
at Mason's level who ultimately have to allocate the resources.)
Aren't we going to be hoodwinked into the new machine if we put
the pollution control money in that plant? The plant only has
a book value of $13 million; we're going to nearly double it."

COMMENT: I don't see how you can use the term hoodwinked. I
mean after all, if you are going to spend $500 or $5 million or
$10 million, you still have to look at a 10-year span in order
to determine whether it's a good investment. As to the question
of whether or not to phase out Elkhorn, the $10 million for pol-
lution control is just one part of it. I feel it is a tremendous chunk of money for a non-productive investment that doesn't
give any return other than satisfying the law and having some
social use. Doesn't Genco always have that new paper machine
before it in the next expansion and whether or not it is going
to be better off locating in some other spot or market area and
so on. Hoodwinking, I take exception to.

COMMENT: I think there's an assumption made by a number of
people that obeying the law and cutting down pollution somehow
satisfies social needs. I'm not sure that that $10 million,
both in view of the people who run the company and at least one
of the regulatory agencies, wouldn't better be spent in other
ways. I see no reason to think that even regulatory agencies
understand social needs since they disagree with one another
about what they are, at least to some extent. The use of capital, the employment situation, the possible loss of jobs; these
are all social factors which have been assigned no weight either
by the agencies themselves or by anyone in the company. So I
don't see trying to comply with pollution standards as automatically being the right thing to do.

ACKERMAN: What position would you take if you were Phillips
now?

COMMENT: I would suggest that one thing he could do is to question the rationality of putting forward standards of this sort
and what the costs of meeting them are, social and otherwise.
They're ultimately all social costs, but I don't think these
other things are being discussed, and I don't think people have
begun to realize what the social costs are of doing certain
things.

COMMENT: That's not terribly realistic. It's as if you were
making a trip by air from New York to Los Angeles and when you
got over Reno, you started to debate with the crew whether you
should have gone in the first place. The political system has

455

decided that this is a social, economic, and political goal of work.

COMMENT: I don't think that's so.

COMMENT: If it wasn't so, the laws could not have been enacted.

COMMENT: Even the regulatory agencies themselves haven't been able to decide the benefits of the cost.

COMMENT: They are operating under the mandate provided by the water purity law.

COMMENT: Well, I don't know what point in the case you are talking about. When we started out initially there wasn't even a law. There were suggestions about complying with certain standards but those standards were different between the two regulatory agencies.

ACKERMAN: And now we don't know what the standards are because after passage of the law, EPA won't talk to us about what they are going to be.

COMMENT: But I'm saying that all the way through the case, there's some suggestion that it's ethical or socially beneficial to begin to comply or think about complying with those standards and I'm not sure that's fair at all.

COMMENT: There seems to be a mix of technical considerations that come into play here. What is the level of pollution at which people start dying? That's one factor that goes into setting standards. And another factor may well be built in by a kind of a compromise, by saying, "Alright, that's the ideal but if we set it that high now all the plants will have to close down. We can't have that so let's set it at a lower level and rethink that level as new factors come in." What I'm suggesting here is that as these things are rethought in society, you can have the standards being changed as you go along. And that makes it very very difficult to plan 10 years, 15 years, 20 years ahead. I don't know the answer to that because part of it is technical and part of it is social.

ACKERMAN: These are some of the critical factors that are going to determine whether our social, economic system continues to work. We have companies such as Genco making decisions which have long-term ramifications under great uncertainty as to the standards and the available technologies. One additional consideration, which we didn't talk about at all during the A Case but which now becomes extremely relevant, is the market outlook in this case for corrugated medium. All of these factors are changing and interacting with one another. Thus, there's a standard for pollution discharge. The control technology may well demand more costly remedies, which in turn are going to affect prices, which in turn may affect demand and hence the economic fortunes of individual facilities and the outlook for employment. All of those factors have a bearing on where resources are invested. In this instance, we have in the Paper Products Division people who are deathly afraid that this mill might shut down, knowing that they cannot justify a new one. Now I am extending beyond what you read on the first page, but a brand new mill was estimated to yield 3 percent. If division management could never justify a new one and if Kruger calls into question whether they ought to invest further in the old one, they have a real problem. On the other hand, if the mill is modernized and the only parts that are inefficient are the paper machines, then the division managers can argue strongly for a big new one even though the corporation twice before told them they couldn't have it.

Let me extend our discussion just a bit at this point. The issues we have at Genco strike to the core of the problems of managing the large corporation in today's environment. In this case, what Phillips decides to do, what he decides to try to convince other people to let him do, is going to have a major bearing on how Genco responds to pressure from EPA. The manager in this key middle-level general management role has to contend with a lot of environmental uncertainty in forces that are changing around him, and these forces have economic, social, and ethical connotations as well. He's got a series of strategic factors that have to do with where his business is and where it's going and he has a series of organizational factors that have to do with who his superiors, peers and subordinates are, how they feel about matters, and how the administrative systems in the corporation work. All of these are present in this case. We have the combination of these factors and we didn't talk a great deal about how they interact to influence the decision process. We did talk some about the organizational implications of what Phillips has before him. We have a manager with career aspirations and with a set of values unique to him who in some way has got to balance all of these factors. He's not a super government agency; he's a tiny little cog in the great big machine. There are lots of other managers in similar positions all over the country. Every paper company has a series of people who are just like Phillips. They have all kinds of considerations which have an influence on their careers, not the least of which is how much money their divisions make. The situation that we have before us in a broader context begs the question, how can we provide a framework in the

457

large corporation that will permit managers such as Phillips to balance what really has to be balanced here, to come out with decisions that they can accept as being ethical and at the same time not compromise their careers?

COMMENT: There's no conflict between the ethical course of action and the economically prudent course of action in the sense that the manager who acts fiscally irresponsibly is acting morally irresponsibly. So I don't see where the EPA requirements or any other agency requirements are moral requirements, whereas the organizational factors, strategic and so forth, are other than moral.

ACKERMAN: To the extent that the responses to these factors can all be made internally consistent, the manager's problem becomes far simpler. To the extent that Phillips can say that responding to environmental forces from a strategic standpoint is going to produce results which will permit the company to prosper economically and at the same time fit within the organizational context, then the career game that he is playing as he tries to shimmy up the greased pole will be less subject to short-sighted pressures.

COMMENT: What you implied there is an assumption that fiscal irresponsibility is moral irresponsibility, without defining what you mean by fiscal irresponsibility. Is supporting a little league team in Elkhorn fiscal irresponsibility? Well, under the Friedman definition, absolutely; you're disposing of stockholders' money in ways that they may not approve of. They may go for football. Is that, at the same time, immoral? Only if you hold to that a priori assumption, which I certainly don't share. If you mean by fiscal irresponsibility investing in something you know will lose money and provide no good to anyone, okay, but that's unreal.

COMMENT: I have a hypothesis which I argued in the Conference yesterday in terms of my social environment model. When we talk about ethical questions, we usually try and deal with them in anthropomorphic kinds of terms, which I find to be irrelevant from the standpoint of modern psychology and sociology. I like to look at this problem as a cultural system. I have a little proposal here and I would like to hear what some of the businessmen think about it. On the one hand, we have a private enterprise system where short-term kinds of variables govern, say, the relation between environmental regulations, capital, technological changes, and so forth. We have, on the other hand, public concerns. The social good is involved; jobs for people, clean water, long-term sorts of variables. We've got a problem here in the short-term, the private enterprise system. The private enterprise just can't come up with the capital necessary to

458

buy the technological goods. Perhaps what we need are certain
new kinds of institutions, such as one that I have in my mind,
and I don't know how this will go over. It's a federal investment bank that would provide very low interest loans to corporations who are being confronted with this kind of consideration.
It would still preserve some of the virtues of a private enterprise system, namely, even though they're getting low-interest
loans, they're going to have to use that capital efficiently
and productively. And this proposal would serve the public good,
long-term interests.

COMMENT: In some sense, we already have such an institution,
known as tax-loopholes. The investment tax credit is, in a
sense, just what you're suggesting without the setting up of a
formal institution to give the money. And moreover, you don't
have the bureaucracies involved in a bank.

ACKERMAN: So, if we look at all of these long-term programs
requiring investment, and at the forces influencing investment
decisions made in large corporations, how should we try to solve
the problem of justifying distant benefits?

COMMENT: They're going to end up in the price no matter who
pays it, whether it's in taxes or in the price of the product.

COMMENT: But that makes a difference on how it's distributed.
If you do it through taxes, you may distribute it one way. If
you do it through prices, you may through another.

COMMENT: Taxes are more indirect because that ends up in lower
incomes, subtle higher prices and inflation.

COMMENT: You go back to the old proposition that every boat has
to float on its own bottom, and I think you're safer with the
price mechanism than these quick solutions that governments fix.

COMMENT: We already have some institutions like this. First,
there was the consumer bank proposed by President Carter, which
made the federal land bank system for agricultural credit available to cooperatives and production units. And we have some
other mechanisms which do some of these kinds of things in different sectors.

ACKERMAN: I wonder, though, if you don't run into the same
problems in government agencies that exist in corporations, only
more so. Every government agency that I've ever seen has its
own strategic objectives, which have to do with how big it is
and what the size of its budget is. It must relate to a whole
bunch of social forces that are really increasingly similar to

459

those confronted by corporations. And, God knows, government
agencies have their own organizational problems which are far
worse, far more severe than anything known to corporations. Do
you really solve anything by moving this kind of problem into
the public sector? I would suggest that you don't.

COMMENT: You would drop EPA regulations?

ACKERMAN: No. Regulation involves an entirely different set of
mechanisms than direct investment. Regulation influences where
the investment goes, and how and by whom, but indirectly, not
by doing it through government's own direct actions.

COMMENT: But we already have direct action for small companies
through the Small Business Administration. He was talking about
the question of whether you shouldn't have this for executing
other federal goals. He obviously was talking about larger
corporations.

ACKERMAN: I would go a step further. I have a feeling that
what has happened with the SBA is just one example of a general
phenomenon. EPA is another. We have all kinds of subsidies
that are now being talked about in the steel industry; relaxa-
tion of EPA regulations, import support, all kinds of government
assistance. The justification, of course, is the protection of
jobs. In the case of the steel industry in particular, I wonder
if we are really supporting an industry which no longer deserves
to be the same size it used to be, which consumes far too much
in the way of resources, and which is far too expensive in terms
of what the congress has decided for everyone else are reasonable
EPA regulations. Shouldn't we really let the steel industry
shrink, as we've let happen to a lot of our other basic industries? Shouldn't we let that industry contract and provide lots of
money for retraining displaced employees, for in some way encouraging people to move from stagnating industries to growing
industries. Provide economic support in human services, but let
an industry which hogs resources shrink naturally to a size that
we can afford. I submit that probably won't happen, and it's
liable not to happen because we're moving investment decisions
into the public sector where a whole bunch of other environmental
forces will keep it from happening.

COMMENT: Of course, that might be the solution in this case,
but the fact is that all economic activity rests upon a physical
and biological substrata. These problems are simply going to
reappear and reappear ad infinitum, and you can't shut down
everything.

ACKERMAN: That's right. And you have to have a process for re-

allocating resources from places where they're inefficiently
used to places where they're more efficiently used. We've got
some traditional measures by which we determine what efficiency
is, though it's getting to be less and less strictly a matter
of economics. More and more conservation of resources, which
ultimately is reflected in the economic situation of the firm,
is receiving attention. This is nothing really new. We have
permitted industries to atrophy before, but I think we're much
less willing to do it now. If we come across the problem that
you mentioned before, it's in a way because we're not permitting
market forces to determine what we're willing to live with in
terms of quantity, in terms of environment, in terms of safety.
We've set the standards for companies to live by and we should
then let the resources flow to those companies that can best
meet that package of regulations. How the regulation is met
should be sorted out by the supply/demand mechanism of the marketplace. But even in that context, we're going to end up with
the need to create an environment for the manager inside the
organization, whether it is public or private, that is going to
permit that manager to seek out a useful and productive career
while, at the same time, being able to live with himself or herself. Efforts have been made along these lines in a few companies, but the task is not easy. It's time consuming and takes
a lot of direction from the people at the top of the organization
to set the career process and establish ethical standards in the
company that permit managers in middle level positions to wrestle
with the uncertainties all around them in ways that move the
company toward adaptation to social changes.

COMMENT: Just one thing. You discuss environmental uncertainties,
and sometimes I feel there is vagueness in the use of the term.
If you just look at the things we've considered environmental
uncertainties, some of them are less uncertain than others.

ACKERMAN. Yes, that's for sure. That's the analysis that managers have to make.

COMMENT: Social responsibility is vague. We haven't put a number on it and it's going to be very, very tricky to do because
I can see the difficulty in giving a monetary value to asthetic
or environmental types of things. Initially, it would have to
be done very, very crudely. But, in a sense, maybe we're going
to begin to have to do this and realize that the values that
profits measure are not the only values that we're going to have
to use.

ACKERMAN: The person in Phillips' shoes has a budget against
which actual results are reported monthly. The manager may be
in this job for a couple of years, and whether there's a better

job ahead is determined in large part by how well that budget is
met. The forces that drive him can become awfully close and awfully narrow. The financial control systems, if anything, inhibit social responsiveness.

COMMENT: Until we figure out ways to put an end to that budget.

ACKERMAN: Yes. I think a lot has to be done to develop management processes that permit managers to survive and fulfill the
multiple objectives we have discussed this morning in that kind
of a company.

COMMENT: Could you say what some of those things are that organizations have done, or are doing, to change that process?

ACKERMAN: Yes. One, which I think is pretty well established
now, has been the introduction of what I call social issue
specialists, people who try to roll back some of the environmental uncertainties in an attempt to provide substance or clarification to middle managers. They typically exist up in the
stratosphere of the corporate office where they can get the
attention of the chief executive, which, of course, is achieving
an important end in itself. That's one form of adaptation that
both informs the chief executive of social forces affecting the
corporation and sets up an information system and a structure
for gathering data and making judgments about how to respond to
these forces. Most industrial corporations have an office now
for environmental affairs and equal employment. Some also have
one for consumer affairs, depending on the industry. There may
be lots of social issues that are so important that they really
shouldn't be left to a technical director six levels down from
the chief executive who has neither the time nor the experience
to deal with them. A second element is a change in the nature
of the control systems that are applied. When the annual budget
is made up, some companies do not simply focus on the bottom
line with the attitude, "I don't give a damn how you get there,
just deliver it." Instead they attempt to build in a series of
other measures that have to do with the process of adaptation
and what one has to undertake to move along a progressive course.
The objectives are richer than simply earnings per share. A
third element is tougher. It involves rethinking the career
process, so that managers who are promoted are not necessarily
always those that have met the bottom line of the budget. The
rethinking must enrich measures of executive performance so
that they have something to do with the ability to negotiate
responses to social change. In the Genco case, Wilson was instrumental in this company from the legal standpoint in responding to regulation. He subsequently was rewarded for his
skills by being put in charge of another division. Corporate

462

management recognized that here was somebody who was prepared to
manage by a broader set of dimensions than the "blood and guts"
production manager whom he replaced. Once again, the justification for that decision is hard to quantify. It's a more complex
reward system, one that must be intelligently thought about by
the managers in Mason's position. Without these kinds of administrative innovations, I don't think that the corporation is
likely to have a consistently applied, far-reaching approach to
environmental adaptation. I'd say that these elements, or at
least the last two, are far more easily done in the private sector than in a public sector. The leadership of the corporation
still has it in its power, hopefully exercised more responsively
than at times in the past, the authority to set the rules of the
game. It still has the authority to say, "Here are the control
systems we want to have. Here are the performance measurements.
Here is the data we want to collect and here is the problem we
want to solve." That isn't generally true in the public sector.
The corporation has the ability at the moment to align the performance measurement for individual managers with corporate
goals according to criteria which, if established responsibly,
can significantly enhance the corporation's ability to move. In
the pollution-control area, we've seen the results more clearly
than anywhere else. Corporations have been far more responsive
to a changing set of attitudes than governments. I'm not saying
they're perfect, because they certainly haven't been. Nevertheless, the corporation can change the way resources are allocated
through decisions of those on the inside and, further, it has
another capability to reward those managers who are prepared to
act on corporate goals. These are three of the things that a
corporation can do, and I think some of the better ones -- I'd
even say some of the more profitable ones -- are moving in
these directions. Corporate managers are generally not so good
on public display. That's unfortunate in a way. They've never
been rewarded for that, and maybe that ought to be built into
the reward system as well. So, I think there are some things
that can be done. I think that the better corporations are doing
them, and I think in the long run they'll probably come out far
better economically than those that lag behind.

SESSION XVI

"America's Need for an 'Ethical Renaissance'"

Mark O. Hatfield
United States Senate

MARK O. HATFIELD

America's Need for an 'Ethical Renaissance'

I'm still curious as to why a politician was invited to a
conference on ethics. I suppose that we have to have our token
politicians now like other minorities. I'm also, though, very
pleased to get out of Washington for awhile. I think it's good
for us who are in this egocentric profession to step out of that
environment and be accessible to people, not only to hear their
assessments of our work, but also to improve our own.

I was getting ready to make one of many monthly trips back
to Oregon not too long ago and I was in Dulles Airport in Washington.
I needed to wash my hands and went into the facility provided for
that purpose and instead of paper towels, they had one of these
machines that blow dries your hands. And someone had taken a felt
tip pen and printed above this particular one, "Push for a message
from your Congressman." Well, I can assure you I was properly
prepared to meet my constituents. I went to the Kennedy Center
not too long ago to hear a marvelous portrayal of Mark Twain and
I realized that people's attitude toward Washington really has
not changed over the years a great deal. For it was in one of
the readings of 1909 that Mark Twain observed that "Washington
was a stud farm for all the jackasses of the country."

Now that I have properly denigrated and demeaned my profession
I want to assure you that I am certain that many people in public
life and in the business world today are reluctant to talk about
ethics. I think the assumption is that anyone who discusses it
or is used as a resource person in a conference of this kind must
be the epitome of moral virtue. And yet we all realize, as my
wife frequently will remind some enthusiastic supporter when they
will come up to me and say, "Oh, you are Senator Hatfield!" She
will say, "Don't be impressed, I wash his socks!" We are still
mortal and we still have feet of clay.

I know that we have all been turned off many times by the
Elmer Gantrys of the church, by the government and business people
who proclaim a virtuous life and then live by a totally different
standard. And perhaps some of us have also taken out of context
the words of Christ when he said, "Let he who is without sin cast
the first stone." And so we tend to be a little bit sensitive
about setting forth a code or a standard and exhibiting ourselves
as evidence.

I'm not here this morning for any of those purposes. For
I believe that in spite of this reluctance some may have, we still
have a responsibility to define and articulate moral principles and

467

standards toward which we all should be striving. In other words, I'm not sure that any of us have reached perfection and if we think we have, then I'm more concerned than ever. But I do think that we have the right to raise the questions with the understanding that we're all engaged in a mutual journey and struggle.

I think sometimes when we discuss ethical questions in a conference relating to business and politics, there is a tendency to relate it only to the conduct of individuals. We have enacted laws in the Congress placing restrictions on business people in their dealings with government in an effort to assure an ethical relationship, for example, placing limitations on political contributions. Similarly, we have told public officials at every level of government that there are certain dealings with businesses that are forbidden for them. Proposals are being discussed, for example, to tighten the restrictions on the employment possibilities of a former public official within a period of time after leaving office.

But I think sometimes we fail in our ethical task if we confine our discussion and enforcement to individuals. I feel that those of you in business have a responsibility to address the conduct of corporations, not just the actions of executives and employees on the payroll. Similarly, all of us as citizens and those of us who are public officials share an obligation to examine the morality of government. This is not meant as an escape hatch for the crooked official in public office. The task is really both, not either/or; both individual and corporate ethics; individual and corporate accountability.

I would like to discuss with you this morning just a few of the broader ethical principles related to the corporate life of government or of business that I would feel important to consideration. First of all, I want to address the ethic of accountability. Today people are sending thousands of letters and postcards to the Congress expressing their views about the Panama Canal. There is no national constituency in favor of the Panama Canal treaties. But there is a national constituency in opposition to the treaties. So our mail is weighted and out of balance in terms of those who are opposed to the treaties. And the Constitution of the United States becomes a guideline for those of us who hold public office. How do we interpret our accountability to our constituency in this case?

I would suggest that if you look carefully at the founding of our nation, you will find that the drafters of the Constitution did not create the Senate of the United States to parrot what the voters say. The founding fathers knew how difficult it would be to know for sure what the constituents really want, especially

as it relates to a national need or a national concern. They
knew that difficult issues would not lend themselves to shallow
debate or limited samplings of public opinion. They realized
that there were hazards of propaganda, of pressure, of hysteria,
of short-range viewpoints, but they made certain that the
politician, even in the United States Senate, with a six-year
term, indirectly elected initially by the voter, would be protected from those daily pressures in order to maintain the
perspective of distance and time. They retained the ballot box
as a basic tool for accountability.

People may choose to judge candidates and incumbents on
a single issue. I cast over 600 votes in the last Congress of
the United States. And yet there will be those next November,
if I get through the primary, who will say, "I will vote against
him because of his support for the Panama Canal treaties." That
may be true with some of you about other issues. We have labor
reform legislation. We have other very emotional, very controversial issues. But the point is, the public official has an
ethical responsibility to help create public opinion as well as
to reflect public opinion. And again, it's not an either/or.
I am deeply concerned about the mail I receive from my constituents.
I've sent out a team of social science teachers, professors, and
others who have an academic background and knowledge of such controversial issues, to knock on the doors of those who have sent
the most vociferous and perhaps the most vitriolic letters, to
explain the position and to try to understand the position of the
constituents.

I think businesses also have a responsibility and accountability to their partners, to their stockholders, to the customers,
to the clients, and to government. Both business and government
have to live within the tensions of this accountability. Politicians
cannot escape the process by claiming superior wisdom. And business
people cannot cite the doctrines of free enterprise to escape
accountability.

Secondly, I would suggest there is an ethic of sharing. I
believe that this is probably one of the most fundamental of all
of our human impulses. It is not only a very salient part of
the Judeo-Christian ethic but also of the humanistic value systems
and many other religious value systems as well. Our own background in this nation, basically that of the Judeo-Christian ethic,
finds abundant direction in the Scripture toward providing for the
poor and for the widows, for the gleaning after the harvest, for
the year of the jubilee. All of these are examples of the responsibility to share the bounties of life for the necessities of life.

But we should note that there has been a gradual trend towards using public agencies for this sharing responsibility of ethic. This is partly as a result of the great Depression, when those mediating structures of our society collapsed under the pressure of the needs or perhaps the people were at fault because they were not prepared to meet the needs through local community efforts. The trend reached a climax in the United States under the New Deal. Because of the overwhelming economic crisis, the needs of the hungry and the poverty-stricken, the solution was a build-up of federal power and programs.

Thus we had the beginning of modern liberal orthodoxy. That's where it emerged. This liberal orthodoxy, which like any other orthodoxy can be dogmatic, was that anyone with social consciousness was expected to support the new governmental solutions. And any one who raised questions as to the effectiveness of the method was portrayed as callous. This dichotomy was expressed in the election of 1932. For the first time in American history, a president had used the powers of the federal government to interdict an economic cycle. And as our revisionist historians are more accurately portraying today, instead of the Hoover administration being indifferent to the needs of the Depression, it actually laid the foundations for the New Deal.

It was the interjection of that kind of power at the federal level that completely changed the whole relationship of the citizen to his government. The Hoover program was to funnel these federal resources through local governments, rather than bringing the citizen into a dole relationship to the federal government. Hoover warned that a time would come when the federal government will dominate and pervade every aspect of human life.

I once had a visit with my good friend and one of the greatest Senators with whom I have ever served, the late Senator Philip Hart from Michigan. This was a month before he passed away and Senator Hart said, "You know, I have a growing sense of ambivalence. I have been reared and I was party to the philosophy of the New Deal, and I think it was right and I think it was good." But he said, "I have come increasingly to want to participate in the dismantling of the very programs and structures that were created at that time because of my sense of domination, overcentralization of power, that that establishment of the New Deal created and perpetrated." Now this comes from the lips not of a right wing Republican, but an intelligent, highly compassionate, great man of the Senate, a New Deal Democrat.

So it is that we today cannot hang labels upon people as liberal or conservative, New Deal or anti-New Deal. Rather there is a growing concern about our methods of accomplishing the ethic of sharing in our society. How do we share so that the needs of people are met? Again, it's not an either/or proposition. The

470

federal government has a role to play. But have we depended on
federal effort so much that we have undernourished and destroyed
the creativity of the mediating structures that still exist in
our society?

Since the war on poverty was launched by President Johnson
in 1964, we have spent 22 billion dollars of taxpayer's money and
yet there are still 26 million Americans below the poverty level.
Millions have been spent on studies, surveys, consultants, advocacy
groups, but what long term benefits have accrued to the people? If
we are seeking to live and to demonstrate a sound ethical foundation
in our corporate life, should we perhaps look at those we have left
out of the equation; neighborhoods, communities, family, churches,
voluntary associations, and business organizations? I believe that
sometimes we have falsely assumed that government could meet every
need most effectively. The result is a growing sense of powerlessness on the part of the people, a growing sense of the neutralizing
of values, a growing sense of cynicism.

After the Watts riots in Los Angeles, they discovered in
surveys that the second most hated authority figure to the black
person living in the Watts area next to the policeman was the
welfare case worker. Those officials had come to symbolize the
fact that these people had been locked out of the mainstream of
American life and they had been reduced and dehumanized to the
status of wards of the state, even for several generations. The
people in Watts rejected this paternalism of government. They
sensed it had totally taken the dignity out of their life.

At the same time we must realize that our resources are
limited and that we can spend our resources foolishly even with
the highest of motivations. We have to realize that in this fiscal
year, the Administration is asking for 118 billion dollars for
military alone, which is a 3% increase above inflation. They are
asking for 100 million dollars of new money for nuclear weapons
alone. We should remember that when the resources of the federal
government are expended in that way, we receive the least multi-
plier of any federal tax dollar in our whole economy. We should
also realize that there are trade-offs in these expenditures.
For example, $2.8 billion for one Trident submarine and its missiles
is more than we spend on all our child feeding and nutrition
programs. And $1.4 billion for A-15 airplanes is the same as our
'Food for Peace' outlays. So we are motivated by the ethic of
sharing, but not always careful as to how and the methods that we
use to accomplish it.

Still another ethical dimension is the ethic of caring.
Remember the words of Cain, son of Adam, when he asked the classical
question, "Am I my brother's keeper?" God said to him that "his
brother's blood cries out from the ground." To show how very

471

practical the concept of caring is in our government and business, let us use the example of OSHA. When I began to hear of the implementation of OSHA, I had to go back to the voting record to make certain that I had voted for such a monster in the business community. The motivation originally was to protect the health and safety of workers. Many states, unlike my state, had not done well in maintaining reasonable standards in the work place. But in the eight years that I served as governor of Oregon, we had won either first or second place in industrial safety in the nation. Why? Basically not because government had been able to demonstrate a caring concern for the worker, but because the public represented by the government and the employees and the employers had a cooperative responsibility and jointly implemented an ethic of caring. No one questions the need to protect health and safety. But the question is whether the program is reasonable. Is it effective?

What I'm trying to illustrate is that sometimes we can be so ethically oriented that we are totally impractical as far as getting the ethic implemented. It reminds me of those who are so pious on the Sabbath, and so totally indifferent, insensitive to people the other days of the week.

Another illustration is the Affirmative Action program. Very few reasonable people would question the ideal of equal opportunity. Yet we have seen how federal agencies have bogged us down in absurd regulations, quotas and red tape which are as formidable to minorities and women as to employers. Increasingly I find minorities coming to my office saying deliver us from the effort to help us if this is what we have to deal with.

We have all sorts of consumer advocacy groups today and many government agencies have a consumer representative on their agency governing board. But as we think about the ethic of caring for our brother and for our sister, the best consumerism may be voluntary action by producers and processers. Of course they must be accountable to the public and to the law. I believe the government has to do more than flex its muscles and show that it can command the marketplace, that it can regulate the marketplace. I think the goal must be the best available protection possible and this requires us to distinguish the ethic from the methodology.

Lastly, today I would like to mention the ethic of stewardship. I'm not asking your total agreement, perhaps only your understanding. I think we have one of the greatest problems in the nation today in the field of natural resources. Coming from a state that has such abundant natural resources and which we have sought to safeguard from early years, I'm especially sensitive to this. I think one of the real problems we face in the business and political community today is our understanding of ownership. I

472

come out of the Judeo-Christian heritage in which I believe in Creation. And as one who believes in Creation, I do not believe that we can divest the Creator from his Creation and I believe this places a limitation on our ownership.

If you go back to the Scripture again, there is no ownership as we normally think of it, but rather there is stewardship. This is a very sound proposition. We are given the right to manage certain resources within a limited period of time, whatever our life may be. But the ultimate ownership is still vested in the Creator, both before we came into this management/stewardship responsibility as well as when we leave it. We must somehow lift our eyes above the mentality of two children playing in a sandbox, arguing over a toy. It does little good to spend a major part of our life arguing that it's mine or it's not mine, or it's yours or it's not yours, as far as the technical title is concerned.

Let me remind you that there are thirteen basic minerals and raw materials required in our industrial processes. We are increasingly dependent on the rest of the world and other parts of the world to supply us with those resources. We are now having to import over 50% of the supply of at least 4 of those 13. By 1985, it will be over 50% and some as high as 90% of 6 of the 13. By the year 2000, it will have reached 12 of the 13 of the raw materials that we will be importing from the rest of the world. That means that we live on a globe with finite resources and that America can no longer consider that the rest of the world owes us their raw materials to maintain our life style.

This is the relevance of the ethic of stewardship. Creation was not provided just for white anglo-saxon Protestant Americans or any other rational group or category, but for all of humanity. Until we can grasp a global view of stewardship, of resources for which we are ultimately accountable we cannot begin to consider wise utilization. That's the definition of conservation, wise utilization. Of greatest relevance at the moment is our use of energy. We are proceeding as if we had an unlimited supply, which we do not have, of course. I think it's very interesting to note that the largest known reserves at the present time are in Saudi Arabia. And yet they are looking to the day when those reserves will be depleted and they are pursuing many areas of solar research as one alternative.

President Carter has presented us with an energy program which is disastrous in the sense that it is predicated on a continuing dependency on fossil fuels and nuclear fission. That is an illusion we cannot afford to perpetuate. I'm hopeful that by another week the Senate Energy Committee will have a compromise that 3 or 4 of us have been working on for the last month as a transition to a time of full commercialization of renewable

473

sources of energy. Unless we adopt that approach, our nation's future is in jeopardy. We've exceeded 8% over last year's consumption of gasoline even though we've been told that there is a growing shortage.

In a drugstore the other day I noticed a safety razor that you use once and throw away. If you look at the products being marketed today, there is little evidence of a sense of the ethic of stewardship. We have erected false gods in our consumer economy today and, my friends, you in business are party to it. One of your greatest allies is the advertising industry and another ally is government. We're all in it. What we're doing is creating appetites for products that do not exist. We are not concerned about the ethic of stewardship because we are on a wanton rampage of waste. And the two false gods most obvious in our society today are the god of disposability and the god of convenience. We put down our garbage pails and our disposals every year enough waste food to feed the whole country of Canada. We use it and throw it away. It has a built in obsolesence.

I've heard all the arguments. I've heard the arguments about labor costs. I've heard the assertions that you can't repair something because the costs of repair are higher than the costs of replacement. If that is true, where is all the ingenuity of the free enterprise system and all the creativity of people and government working together to correct that? They gave us all those arguments in Oregon when we abolished the throwaway can and the throwaway bottle for beer and soft drinks. We had every executive in the beer and soft drink industries and every labor union leader pounding the table saying, "You're going to destroy jobs in the State of Oregon." We did not destroy jobs. We had an increase in employment and we had a lower cost of highway maintenance. More important than anything, we provided a daily incentive for Oregonians to turn away from the throwaway ethic to a conservative ethic. It's a learning process. It's not the panacea to our energy problems. But we could save enough energy, if we adopted this on a national basis, to provide for the electrical needs of Boston, of New York, and San Francisco.

What I'm saying today is that the ethic of stewardship means that we are given possession for the purpose of management and for the wise utilization of great resources for the benefit of all humanity. We have to start a whole new ethic in this country, an ethic of conservation as it relates to convenience and to our disposability. Of course I like to get off a plane and have a suit that isn't wrinkled, but let me just tell you that the technological choices we have made since World War II have put us on the road toward an energy crisis. We have moved from the use of renewable resources of timber products in the building industry to the greater use of aluminum, plastic, glass, and masonery. We have moved increasingly to dependence upon trucks

474

for moving freight across the country, which consumes 6 times
more energy per mile than by rail. We have allowed our rail
transportation system to fall apart, because of the emphasis
on building highways. These are technological choices, that
have had a heavy impact upon energy and the environment.

These are some of the corporate aspects of ethics that
need to be addressed along with personal ethics. I don't accept
the notion that if you change the individual, you will change
society. I'm afraid that we have some stark examples to refute
that. We have to address both the corporate institutional ethic
as well as the individual ethics. Before the Civil War, the
first institution that broke and divided on the slavery question
between North and South was not the corporation, was not the
business enterprise, was not the political party, was not any
other institution. It was the church that was the first institution that divided because a Southern church was so inculturated
that it could defend from the pulpit the cause of slavery. So
when we talk about an ethic, again we cannot just say, "Make
good spiritual people and good religious people and then they'll
change society automatically." That doesn't work. We have to
address simultaneously the ethics of corporate life, the ethics
of individuals that make up the constituency of that corporate
life.

I'd like to suggest today that we might take note of the
words of Carl Sandburg whenever we grown weary of trying or
the effort that we are making, when we think sometimes we are
making very little progress. This was on the 96th anniversary
of Lincoln's Gettysburg Address, that Carl Sandburg, the Lincoln
Biographer, said: "Always the path of American destiny has been
into the unknown. Always there arose enough reserve of strength,
balance of sanity, portions of wisdom, to carry the nation
through to a fresh start with every renewing vitality."

I have that kind of confidence and trust in the institutions
of this nation, our business institutions, economic institutions,
our political institutions. We have demonstrated many times in
American life the resiliency to come back from wrenching experiences
of civil war, great world wars, depressions, and so forth. I
would only suggest that there may be a slight difference today
from the time Carl Sandburg spoke. That is that time has compressed
us. Geography has compressed us even more. And what we do or
what we fail to do probably has more significant global implications than on the 96th anniversary of Lincoln's Gettysburg Address.

While I feel that a conference of this kind is addressing
one of the fundamental values and problems of this nation, the
solution is not in fiat, or legislation, or law. It must come

from the hearts and minds of the people. John Adams observed about
the American Revolution, "The American Revolution," he said, "was
not the war of 1776. That was but the manifestation of the
revolution that began in the hearts and the minds of the citizens
15 years before a drop of blood was spilled at Lexington." And
so it is that out of this value system, out of the ethic of this
nation, is to be found the real strength, the real sinew of
America.

DISCUSSION

COMMENT: Senator Hatfield, I have two questions, you can choose
one or respond to both. The first question relates to a commonly
heard critique of the ethic of stewardship which is that there
is an historical coupling of gross national product and economic
growth with energy consumption, waste and jobs. If that's the
case historically, and it appears to be, what strategies might
there be for decoupling an attitude of energy consumption from
full employment and growth in the quality of life or standard of
living? The second question is more philosophical. Do you think
that the lack of a fundamental moral consensus of the individuals
in our society, as there appears to be, has reached a point where
the possibility of a coherent and critical ethic for institutions,
like corporations, is practically impossible?

HATFIELD: Let me say that I think the first question carries
with it an assumption that conservation, and this has been perpetrated primarily by conservation-oriented groups, requires a
no-growth philosophy. I reject that. I don't believe that is
a natural coupling, that a conservation ethic must be coupled
with a no-growth policy. And let me indicate to you a little bit
of what I mean by that. I think that many times the politicians
have caught new fads or new catch words, and ecology and environment have been that within the last decade, and they have been
exploited for political purposes. As a consequence, there has
been a polarization, so that if you are for a growth program,
you must be anti-environment, and if you are against a growth program then you must be pro-environment. This is oversimplification, it's superficial, and I think it's unnecessary. What it
does call for, I think, in blending a conservation ethic and a
growth policy, is more careful planning. And when I talk about
planning, don't just think of the stereotype of the community
planner, the professional planner behind some bureau. I'm
talking about planning both in terms of products, and in terms
of the cost factor of energy. I'd like to see a cost/energy
account system established, for instance, in much more of our
marketplace that we have. I think we have to consider raw
materials and the environmental impacts on that. We had in Oregon, if I might be provincial again for a moment, the fastest
rate of new industrial growth because when I became Governor in
1958, we had the lowest employment, we had the highest unemployment. We had a horrible recession in our State in 1958-59. But
in those eight years, we put the thrust on industrial growth and
development. It was deliberate, it was planned. At the same
time we had the fastest expansion of new parks and recreation.

477

We put more teeth in our air/water pollution control, cleaning up the Willamette River, for example. In other words, we paralleled growth and environmentalism because we brought the forces and the people together. Labor unions were not fearful when we talked about this because they knew we had jobs in mind, likewise the environmental groups understood what our objectives were. I think that one of the characteristics of our age is to oversimplify, to get a sort of capsule understanding of something and then we get into these polarized positions. Now, what was the second part of your question?

COMMENT: It was a question about the lack of moral consensus in our society.

HATFIELD: Yes. You were wondering if there was an assumption here again of a lack of a moral base in our society of consciousness.

COMMENT: Well, the call that we're hearing at this Conference and elsewhere, which I take to be an extremely important call, is a call for an institutional ethic, and it's hard for me to understand how that's possible in a circumstance where there is so much individual lack of consensus. How do we fabricate institutional ethics under such circumstances?

HATFIELD: Again, without a vision, the people perish. And if you put that in the context, that homily that you've heard so many times, it means leadership and followership combined. It's not either/or. Let me give you an example. There were a few people, led by Wilburforce many years ago in England, who caught a vision of the evil of slavery. And Wilburforce and this group of people covenanted one with the other that they were going to impact the institutions of government and thereby impact the institution of slavery. And by the kind of commitment that they made and the kind of drive and vision that they had, it led to the abolition of slavery through an orderly process, unlike our own experience here in this country. All I'm saying here is that it's not an either/or. Institutions will reflect the awakening of people. We have had in history the great awakenings, which were spiritual awakenings, which were ethical awakenings, which were moral awakenings. Without exception, those great spiritual awakenings emanated from within the people exercising leadership within the ethical, spiritual community. They had an impact on government. They had an impact on the state. They had an impact on business. They had an impact on education. They had an impact on all the institutions. I think there is a great deal of evidence today of spiritual curiosity in this nation. I don't say spiritual revival but spiritual curiosity. Everything from the Eastern mystical religions, the moonies, and all

478

the other things, the cults, what have you. Let me also say you
can even go into the drug culture and find certain evidences of
spiritual curiosity. They're looking for the real me, the inner
self. Those are spiritual questions. I think it evidences a
reaction against the materialism, the secularism of our culture.
What it provides is an opportunity. How many times in your life
or my life could we think of politicians talking about their personal religious views, from the President of the United States
on down. I think there's a certain fadism in all this, too. I
don't mean to say this is evidence of a great spiritual revival,
but I do think there's enough of this spiritual curiosity that
provides us all with an opportunity to strengthen those moral
and ethical foundations and those moral and ethical principles
within our own relationships, within our own corporate relationships, personal relationships, family relationships. I don't expect it to come from government. Any spiritual, moral, ethical
revival renaissance in this country is going to come from the
mediating structures of our society and from the people.

COMMENT: Senator, I found your last remarks very clarifying because I thought earlier there was something of a contradiction
in what you were saying. You were, on the one hand, advocating
the development of a corporate as opposed to an individual ethic
in addition to, but as really the necessary means for, dealing
with this ethic of conservation as opposed to an ethic of dis-
posal. And, at the same time, you were criticizing the way in
which the government has sought to bring about a corporate ethic
as being ineffectual. And I didn't see how you were going to
put the two together. But in your last remarks, what you seemed
to be saying is that the only thing we can rely upon, the only
institution we can rely upon, is really going to be the church,
that you are really expecting a spiritual reformation rather
than a political reform to be the medium or the institutionalization of this ethic. Now, the comments I would have are: 1)
Your own experience in Oregon would seem to militate against
that, since in the case of the bottles and cans, the government
was able to move in and bring about a significant reform; and
2) while there is evidence of spiritual curiosity, it is certainly the case that our consensus, as an American people, is
not spiritual or religious, but rather political. And it would
seem to me to be illusory to expect the institutionalization of
corporate stewardship to come about through religious reformation,
rather than through political reform.

HATFIELD: Well, I appreciate the opportunity to clarify what I
said. First of all, I would like to say I am not expecting this
to be institutionalized, even in the church. I would want to
clarify that immediately. What I was attempting to do was to
urge us to not restrict our thinking to personal morality and

479

personal piety. We're talking about the need for a renaissance in this country that is fundamental. But we need to broaden that perspective, to look at the ethic of government, or of a corporation, or an institution. Interestingly, throughout church history there were times when the church was very corrupt but its faith, its theology, was still pure. But the people and the institution became corrupt as separate from their ethic. And I think that can happen even in political circumstances. So, all I'm suggesting is that there is a need for the mediating structures, the nonpolitical bodies of our nation, the corporate structures, and the individual to work together toward an integrated concept of relationship. Our ethics are the basis of relationships, whether personal or corporate. That is why we must view government as one institution in terms of its ethics of conservation, stewardship, accountability. And I think, frankly, that government is wasteful. I think it's the leading waster of our money and many other things besides our money. But that usually is the most sensitive of all of our resources that we concern ourselves about.

COMMENT: This is a kind of Conference-related question. I don't know if you're too familiar with advocacy advertising, but I'd like to ask your opinion about this. Could you comment on whether the business community has an undue influence on your colleagues in Congress, perhaps by manipulating public opinion through corporate advocacy advertising, and if you think it does, would you favor some kind of government regulation?

HATFIELD: Well, as our society is pluralistiç, so is the Congress pluralistic, as far as people's reactions and responses are concerned. I would immediately resist the idea of further regulation anywhere. I think this is the time when we have to really try to deregulate rather than to continue regulating. And yet, at the same time, it can't be a categorical judgment. You have to take each case. I much prefer to find that where people are being exposed to advocacy of any kind, that the only thing that we provide there, if government is to play a role, is equal access, or equal opportunity for other viewpoints and other positions. I'd hate to try to regulate to the point where government is almost assuming a dictatorial role in what people will hear or what people will believe. I have to be a civil libertarian in the sense that what I want to see is total access to all information, and I would like to see government remain purely as an umpire if they are to play a role at all. I think that the influence depends a great deal on the location of that industry. You will find that many times those products that are manufactured in a certain constituency will have a great bearing on the reaction of the legislature from that constituency. I have, naturally, a great concern for the forest products industry of

480

this nation. That's the basis of my State's economy. But we have, again, in the pluralism of the Senate, those who are concerned about other values as well, so they have a comingling and a balancing effect.

COMMENT: I just thought you would favor some kind of equal time type guarantee, because of what you said about the returnable bottle debate, and how the bottle industry apparently spent a lot of money opposing returnable bottles.

HATFIELD: Any time that any group is denied access to the same audience, I think there has to be some way to adjudicate that, even though I may resist the role of government.

COMMENT: I'd like to ask you to comment on a case of violation of business ethics, namely, that of J.P. Stevens Corporation which, as you know, has been found guilty 16 times of violations of the National Labor Relations Act. And since this does not seem to stop them from continuing their unfair labor practices, I was wondering whether you could comment on whether you support the Labor Law Reform Bill, which is coming before Congress soon, whether you support the nationwide boycott of J.P. Stevens' products which is now underway, and whether you feel that corporations which are concerned with ethics should also support this nationwide boycott?

HATFIELD: Well, I think that first of all, where there is a violation, a clear violation, there ought to be very diligent enforcement so that it is not repeated. I don't think anyone who believes in a government of law could do other than condemn the whole attitude, the whole lack of ethics within the Stevens Company. I think it has violated not only law, but it has violated the most basic of all ethics, and that is an orderly life under a rule of law. Having said that, I feel it is also well to bear in mind that you don't rush to throw the baby out with the bath water to correct a problem, and I think that is sometimes our tendency to do that. We have seen a violation of this kind, so we rush to correct it, legislatively speaking, or through government, and often times we net up everybody else who has been abiding by the law and who would abide by the law if they were under the same circumstances as Stevens. Now, what is the reasonable approach? What is the proper approach to this? I think this is obviously what gave rise to this present Labor Reform Bill. Let me say to you that there are parts of that bill that I think are extreme and are not in balance, that I think provide a less than proper balance between capital and labor, management and labor. Some of us are attempting to offer amendments to make the bill a better bill. Others want to kill the bill entirely. Therefore, I think that the issue will be de-

481

cided on a procedural vote, a cloture vote, rather than an up or down vote. And it may be doubtful that the bill will even come to the floor. They may not bring it to the calendar, if they don't feel they have the votes for cloture. I shall probably vote for cloture, as I have had an historic pattern of voting for clotures throughout my time in the Senate.

SESSION XVII

"The Corporate Stake in Inner City Survival"

Jay Janis
Undersecretary
U.S. Department of Housing and Urban Development

JAY JANIS

The Corporate State in Inner City Survival

No one would disagree, I suspect, that business ethics, or
at least our view of business ethics, has changed radically over
the past several decades.

The reason for this is simply that corporate attitudes towards the nation and towards the communities in which corporations
are located have changed radically.

I once heard a Southern minister recite the following verse
that might well be applied to modern business enterprises in
America today:

Lord, we ain't what we ought to be.
We ain't what we want to be.
We ain't what we're going to be.
But, thank the Lord, we ain't what we was.

To be specific, look, for instance, at the almost statesman-
like posture of certain trade and professional associations across
the country.

The U. S. Chamber of Commerce issued an interesting booklet
summarizing the consumer affairs activities and programs of many
trade and professional associations. Over ninety associations are
listed as having instituted consumer programs on behalf of their
membership. For instance: programs to evaluate products and services, the sponsorship of consumer advisory panels, testing and
standards programs, consumer education programs involving the
development of educational materials to schools and to the media,
counselling services and complaint handling and resolution programs. This is a far cry from the philosophy that "The business
of America is business."

Business ethics today deals with such topics as the social
performance of corporations. In fact, in many circles, the responsiveness of corporations to social and environmental impact is
perceived to be an important indicia of the quality of management.

Hiring policies, membership on boards, and environmental impact -- all are measures of the social responsiveness of corporate
America.

Many forward looking executives believe that external long

485

range social and economic consequences of management actions must be as carefully and systematically analyzed during the decision making as the more traditional financial and marketing factors which bear on that decision.

And for good reason.

A 1975 Opinion Research Poll indicated the public ranked big business 14th (next to last) in terms of institutions in which they placed their highest trust and confidence. Small business was ranked second; banks were ranked ninth.

So it is entirely appropriate that among the ethical issues which business presently considers are: product design; product performance; sales of products; advertising; consumer affairs; environmental protection; and relationships to employees, to competitors, and to stockholders.

The big question is: Is it enough? Or, is there a further role that business should play in terms of our nation's cities and the problems of urban America?

Here's what CED had to say in 1971 on the subject of corporate responsibility in the arena of social concerns:

"The goals of American society can be realized only through a massive, cooperative effort of government, industry, labor, and education. Increasingly it is felt that the cooperative participation of the private sector is required not only for national defense and space exploration but also for advances in health care, improvement of education, and elimination of poverty.

"Government's basic role through the political process is to determine the nation's goals, set the priorities, develop the strategies, and create the conditions for carrying out the work most effectively to the satisfaction of the public.

"Business, with its profit-and-loss discipline, has an especially significant role in the actual execution of social programs because it is a proven instrument for getting much of society's work done and because its top executives, with their diverse management capabilities and their involvement in community affairs, are normally well fitted to deal with today's socioeconomic problems.

"The incentive for profit is the only practicable way of unleashing the power and dynamism of private enterprise on a scale that will be effective in generating social progress. Social consciousness and good citizenship, while important prerequisites, cannot realistically be expected by themselves to bring business

486

resources to bear on the country's social problems on the massive scale that is needed. To achieve this, government must create the market conditions that will induce business enterprises to apply their operational capabilities to those public tasks they can carry out more efficiently than other institutions."

The CED point of view raises a number of key issues for further consideration. To name just a few: 1/ "What ethical responsibility does business have to upgrade the quality of life in the community in which it operates? How far does ethical responsibility extend in planning, zoning, building regulations, aircraft and construction noise, air and water pollution, other health and safety issues, provision of recreational facilities, promoting civil rights and equal opportunities outside employment areas, promoting civic betterment, helping in areas of transportation, housing, education, cultural opportunities, philanthropy?

"What responsibility does a business have in deciding to locate or relocate plant facilities? What non-economic considerations, if any, should be included in the decision? Should some form of severance payment be offered the community when a plant closes? Should financial aid for added burden on city services be offered to a new community when a plant locates there? Should such decisions consider the "need" of the community or region for employment, taxes, etc.?"

Most of these issues relate to America's urban places.

And well they might. After all, it was the urban riots of the 1960's that galvanized business on many of these subjects. James Roche, then President of General Motors, reports that he stood in his office in 1967 as Detroit went up in flames and thought: "It can't be happening here."

In those years businessmen began to realize that (as Harvey Perloff said): "The ghetto is not just a place with many unemployed and subemployed persons; it is a place that saps motivation, erodes the capacity to learn, pulls young persons out of national mainstream activities by overwhelming them with human temptation and risk. It is also a place where it is difficult, inconvenient, costly, and risky to carry out economic activities (Committee on Science and Astronautics, 1969: 93)."

Let me assure you that our attention at the Federal level, in particular at HUD, is very much focused on the cities. Our recently announced urban policy -- more than anything else --

---

1/ CBBB Ethics Project, December 8, 1976

must be understood as a commitment to the future of the American city.

Surprising new evidence supports the contention that there is a growing nationwide concern about the plight of the cities.

A recent Harris survey reveals that 77 percent agree that "America cannot survive unless the problems of the cities are worked out." These and other comparable statistics are important because they suggest a new attitude toward this Nation's urban ills. Americans are simply not buying the concept of "Natural Selection" when it comes to our urban areas.

Aside from the supporting weight of public opinion, there are other reasons why we should take an objective look at the present condition of our communities, with all of their warts and all of their social problems and decide what must be done to make them more livable.

One reason is that so many Americans live in urban areas, 70 percent, including the poor who need Federal, state and local assistance. Of that 70 percent, 30 percent live in the center city. And these are mainly the unserved or the underserved.

Another reason is the energy crisis. We can substantially reduce the energy drain on our scarce resources by cutting down on the use of automobiles for transportation. Cities can be places where people not only work but enjoy their leisure hours, without wasting time and precious gasoline on travel. More important, cities are vital as places of commerce and industry, and I am convinced that the greatness of America will turn, in years to come, on the greatness of its cities.

Now that I have said all that, let me describe for you where I believe the cities of America generally stand today.

The Harris survey I mentioned earlier paints a clear picture of central city dependence on the suburbs. While people from the suburbs may go to the theater in the city or to a sporting event, they do not pay for the support services which make these attractions possible, the infrastructure, so to speak. They are picking off what they want in terms of services, but not really paying the full cost of those services.

A recent Harris survey reveals the following: "On 9 key activities common to many people, the survey asked people to recount in detail how many of each type of activity they engaged in during the past year and whether they did those activities in the cities or elsewhere. Let me just recount the results for that 40%

488

who live in the suburbs, for it is not news that sizable majorities
of city dwellers do those activities in the cities. Of all the
occasions that suburban residents go to a movie, 53% of the time
they go not to a suburban movie house, but instead to the city.
When suburban residents go to a museum or see a live play or a concert, 53% of those trips are into the city. Of the occasions that
suburbanites buy furniture or a major appliance, 46% of the time
they go to the nearest city. When suburban residents buy new
clothes, 48% of those trips are to the city to buy them. When
those who live in the suburbs want to go out and have a nice dinner,
an even 50% of the time they go to the city to eat. When those in
the suburbs attend a religious service, 44% of the time they do not
go to a place of worship in the suburbs, but instead make the trek
into the city. Of all the occasions when suburban dwellers have
to go to a doctor, a majority of times, 52%, they go not to a doctor in the suburbs, but instead go to a doctor in the city. And
when those who live in the suburbs visit friends, fully 47% of the
time they do not visit friends in the suburbs, but go to cities to
see them. Nationwide, although only 30% of the people live in
cities, as defined in this study, a majority of 53% of all the
visits to friends in the United States are to friends in the city.
This means that the cities in 1978 are the social centers of the
country, as well as the places people feel have superior facilities for most activities. It is not overstating the case to conclude from these results that the much-maligned cities of America
in fact turn out to be not simply indispensable, but are the central pivot for many life activities that people engage in regularly in their lives."

The cities have been put into the position of having to beg
for support from Federal and state governments because of this
very phenomenon, because they provide a set of services to all
people, not just their residents, but which their residents substantially pay for in the long run. That is the central problem
of cities--they are being asked to maintain underlying support
services which a majority of the population uses, but with a
shrinking tax base.

A recent Rand report provides another view of this problem.
That study confirms something that many of us suspected, but which
was contrary to the existing conventional wisdom.

According to the study, jobs follow people and not vice
versa. This means that besides implementing policies which attempt to retain or attract businesses in the city, we must also
institute policies which will provide a move livable environment
for present city residents in order to attract new residents.

Let me quote briefly from the Rand report on that very

significant point.

"The most important single influence on patterns of migration is the prevailing set of conditions in local labor markets. Federal policies that affect local economic growth therefore exert a profound influence on the distribution of population.

"However, households are attracted by cities that also offer a comfortable climate and pleasant physical surroundings, and there is evidence that jobs may follow people to such areas, contrary to an old maxim. . .

"This suggests that Federal policies that lead to the improved environmental quality of older, declining areas may arrest the long-term trends of economic decline more effectively than measures aimed at attracting foot-loose industries. . .

"Thus, from the local perspective, economic development strategies must be related to efforts to improve the quality of life for city residents. From the Federal perspective, urban employment growth will be influenced, not only by direct incentives to business, but also through measures that encourage population growth and improved local services." (Emphasis added.)

The Urban and Regional Policy Group (URPG) report, which was the background document used by the President in determining the National Urban Policy, sheds more light on the conditions of cities today.

For instance, between 1970 and 1975, central cities for the first time lost population. During that time, population losses in central cities totaled 1.2 million people, or 1.9 percent of the population. In contrast, suburban population grew by 8.5 percent or 6.2 million people.

A similar situation exists for the employment picture. While jobs increased in eight major central cities by 335,000 slots between 1962 and 1970--a 17 percent gain--between 1970 and 1974, jobs in those cities declined by 140,000.

As a result of the movement out of the city of its more affluent residents and the general loss of jobs, a striking change has occurred in the income distribution of city residents. During the more prosperous sixties, the number of families in cities who received very low incomes, i.e., incomes under $5,000 in 1973 dollars, declined by about 400,000. This progress was erased during the 1970's. Between 1970 and 1975, the number of city families in this income range grew by 270,000.

490

Those are the hard facts about our cities. Enough good
things are taking place, however--such as some return of middle
income families to the cities and some spatial deconcentration
of minorities to lead me to the conclusion that cities are now
at the crossroads between oblivion or survival. Their future in
large part depends upon how we deal with several basic ethical
issues about fiscal equity, the poor, and urban concerns generally
--issues, I might add, that business must participate in answering:

FIRST, what is the proper role of the suburbs vis à vis the
central city; and what is the role of the state government with
respect to the cities?

As Lou Harris commented recently: "Put bluntly, the cities
have been boxed into the position of being mendicants to beg for
the support from Federal and state governments to save them from
oblivion, largely in order to maintain a system of services that
non-city dwellers join with city dwellers in finding indispensable.
The cities of this country do not need any handouts. The clear
evidence in this study shows that tax bases derived mainly from
where people live is nothing short of a 19th Century anachronism.
Probably the central problem of the cities is that they are being
asked to maintain underlying support services which a majority of
the population in the country uses, but with a tax base that is
shrinking rapidly.

"The only fair and equitable way to balance the scales on
this critical dimension is for the Federal and state governments
to compensate the cities for this service gap. This is not added
monies which the cities have to apologize for one bit. To the
contrary, every piece of evidence in this study indicates that the
cities have earned this kind of added governmental support."

SECOND, can we--as a just and compassionate people--permit
the continuation of a permanent underclass in our society, an
underclass that is located predominately in our cities? The economic and social implications of such a policy surely are devastating. Not only will cities, and their residents, become even more
dependent on the Federal government to keep them alive, the violence and crime and terrorism that so shook the cities of this
country just ten years ago, could once again become an ugly reality.

Can we continue to perpetuate the apartheid society -- one
black, one white, separate but unequal -- which the Kerner Commission saw in the 1960's?

THIRD, can we allow the problems of our cities to go unsolved -- problems of urban crime; urban education; loss of jobs;
fiscal and physical decay; massive unemployment; and human degre-

491

dation?

Or, should business become involved in:

- "downtown" leadership in promoting renewal and re-
  development activities
- locational decisions regarding urban reinvestment
- crime reduction and promoting good government
- tax equalization
- saving urban schools - community relations
                       - discipline
                       - quality of teachers
- fiscal reform at the municipal level
      prudent expenditures
      municipal contracts
      local capacity - accounting, etc.
      hiring practices
- electing responsible officials
- involving neighborhood groups

Obviously, no one institution, no matter how powerful it
might think it is, can solve the problem by itself. As President
Carter said, we must have a new partnership to save our American
cities. We must bring together in a common effort all who have
a stake in the future of our cities, and that is each and every
one of us.

As the President said:

"I call upon all of you, and the institutions and
groups you represent, to join me in building a new
partnership to conserve our communities--a working
alliance of all levels of government with the private sector of our economy and with our citizens
in their communities and neighborhoods."

We can make American cities more attractive places in which
to live and work. We can help the people of urban America lead
happier and more useful lives. But only if we do it together --
and we must do it together.

SESSION XVIII

"Business, Government and Bribery"

George C. S. Benson
Director
The Henry Salvatori Center
Claremont Men's College (California)

Patricia Werhane
Professor of Philosophy
Loyola University of Chicago

John E. Cavanagh
Senior Vice President and General Counsel
Lockheed Aircraft Corporation

Stanley Cleveland
Vice President, International Planning
Bendix Corporation

GEORGE C. S. BENSON

The Role of Business in Political Corruption

Is business to blame for our unduly large amount of political corruption, which probably costs America some scores of billions of dollars? The question is important for at least two
reasons. If it is true that business is the principal corrupter,
then our laws and prosecution practices should be revamped to pro-
secute bribers more than bribees. Business ethics must be radically
changed. Also we should alter our attitude about the political
values of a free enterprise system. If our economic system aids
political corruption there is much less reason to safeguard it in
its present form.

Many writers and groups have assumed that "business" was
the source of the corruption which was so heavy in the 19th century and is still important in American political life. Lincoln
Steffens held this theory in most of his writings in the first
decade of the century. In 1910, Professor Robert Brooks in his
book on corruption argued that business practices and political
corruption were inextricably linked and that competition was the
main reason for most forms of corruption. Brooks, however, failed
to explain why monopolistic industries, such as the railroads and
the public utilities were more anxious than competitive business
to corrupt government. An esteemed political science colleague,
Professor Phillips Bradley, in the 1940s, simply assumed that "a
politician who promotes a private interest in a political 'deal'
is merely following current business practices and ethics." In
1974 the California chapter of Common Cause assumed that limitations on lobbying expenses and business contributions to political
campaigns would end corruption in California. Professor Robert N.
Bellah in The Broken Covenant says that "The present American
economic system, through one of its chief institutions, seems to
be dedicated to the propagation of every one of the classic vices
of mankind."

Are the above mentioned conclusions about business responsibilities for corruption valid?

Business Corruption of Government in Nineteenth Century

With the exception of a few instances, such as Georgia's
Yazoo Land Scandals, there is little evidence of business exten-
sively corrupting government prior to 1860. Indeed, canal and

495

railroad construction, which was financed primarily with government subscriptions, clearly united politics and business in an effort to answer important questions about routes, financing, and use charges, all of which were critical to the economic development of the United States. Most political corruption during the pre-Civil War period related to the sale of public offices, to extortion of funds from businesses shipping goods through custom houses, and to bribes or kickbacks on government contracts.

From 1865 to the early 1900s, however, America experienced one of the most corrupt periods of her history, an era of rapid economic expansion and frontier settlement, in which small and large businessmen were guilty of involvement in corrupt government activities.

A few large businessmen confined their abuses to unethical competitive practices. Standard Oil, for example, was certainly unethical in its treatment of competitors, but most of its practices did not involve political corruption and there is no positive proof that John D. Rockefeller ever agreed to any corrupt transactions. Ida Tarbell does mention Standard Oil's control of the Pennsylvania legislature in 1887, in order to defeat a bill limiting charges for oil, transportation, and storage, but she admits that political corruption was not proven.

Andrew Carnegie was another leading nineteenth century industrialist against whom no charges of political corruption would seem to apply. Carnegie was capable of sharp business practices and was indirectly responsible for the bloody Homestead strike but there is little evidence of his involvement in political corruption.

In sharp contrast to Carnegie and Rockefeller, "Robber barons" such as Jay Gould, Jim Fisk, Daniel Drew, Collis Huntington, David Colton, Thomas Scott and H. O. Havemeyer were actively engaged in many different corrupt activities. Gould, Fisk and Drew bribed legislators, bought judges and cooperated with Tammany Hall in order to further their objectives of plundering the Erie Railroad and of robbing the public. Huntington and Colton of the Central Pacific-Southern Pacific Railroad and Scott of the Pennsylvania and the Texas and Pacific Railroad bribed Congressmen for preferential route legislation. H. O. Havemeyer, founder of the American Sugar Refining Company or the "Sugar Trust," was probably aware of his company's bribing American revenue officers to short-weight raw sugar, thus saving it from paying several million dollars of annual duties.

Quite obviously, the railroads were the major source of political corruption as they expanded across the continent with government aid. The Credit Mobilier construction company of the

496

Union Pacific Railroad distributed shares of stock to prominent Congressmen in such a way that several political careers were abruptly ended when it was discovered. The Central Pacific-Southern Pacific Railroad system bribed or otherwise influenced important political figures in California for over forty years and to a lesser extent influenced legislatures in Arizona and New Mexico. In attempting to secure monopoly control of transportation in California, the Southern Pacific raised and lowered freight rates to obtain exorbitant profits. Much local opposition was aroused by these tactics, but the railroad used its political power freely, securing "the major share of the profit of virtually every business and industry on the coast." The Southern Pacific's domination of California political life ended in 1910 when Progressive Hiram Johnson was elected governor along with a reform legislature.

In an 1884-1885 trial regarding the treatment of a deceased official of the Central Pacific-Southern Pacific system, General David D. Colton, Mrs. Colton (who was the plaintiff) introduced a file of letters to Colton from Collis P. Huntington, one of the Central Pacific's "Big Four" owners, which revealed the railroad's dominance of California politics. In these letters, Huntington named many public officials who were taking instructions from the railroad. Those who voted against the railroad were to be retired to private life at the next election if Huntington had his way. The cost of legislation in Congress or the state legislature was categorized quite frankly as "the price of steel tracks."

A careful study of correspondence of Railroad Leaders, 1845-1890, by Thomas C. Cochran, portrays a point of view somewhat different from that of the Huntington letters. The railroad leaders seemed to recognize that they were in politics and must stay in politics, but several wished that they could get out of the system of distributing free passes to holders of public office. They generally assumed that federal and state legislators lacked understanding of railroad problems. Some of them believed that it was right to bribe a legislator for the sake of better railroad operation, but their remarks about bribery were more guarded than those of Collis Huntington.

Municipal street traction companies also attempted to corrupt municipal and state government in order to secure franchises and to avoid tax payments. Detroit in the 1890s, Chicago in the 1890s and Cleveland in the 1900s are a few examples. In the public sector, the city-owned Philadelphia Gas Trust was a source of major political corruption. Corruption in municipal transportation, however, began to decline sharply after 1917 when automobiles were increasingly being introduced on the road. Street car profits decreased and since then the main difficulty has been to maintain street cars as a means of urban travel.

Despite the railroad experience, most nineteenth century examples indicate a two way movement, in which government was often the first to suggest illegal action. The Tweed Ring, not business, arranged the illegal use of enlarged municipal contracts. Boss Abe Ruef secured his business clients in San Francisco at the suggestion of Mayor Schmitz. Business licenses in San Francisco were granted only after a retainer to Ruef or a bribe to the inspector. The Cox machine in Cincinnati required "donations" from city and county contractors, merchants, and saloonkeepers. In the 1900s, the "Black Horse Cavalry" of the New York legislature demanded $1,000 per vote from Gould and Vanderbilt. The Black Horsemen frequently introduced "strike bills" to force business payments. In Pennsylvania the Quay Machine insisted that banks which had public deposits should contribute the equivalent of the interest to the corrupt machine. A possible exception is that Jay Gould retained Senator Tweed as legal advisor of the Erie Railroad, but it is not sure that Gould initiated this connection.

It has already been mentioned that Lincoln Steffens, in his writings during the early 1900s, was initially inclined to blame most political corruption on business. Before he finished his writing of the muckraking era, however, he was admitting that perhaps management of a railroad requires political corruption. In the same period, he was speculating that business had bosses just as politics did -- a speculation which partly fits with a conclusion of this talk that it is necessary to speak of the standards of all society, not of business alone, or politics by itself.

In his later autobiography, first published in 1931, Steffens became even more tolerant of business. He repeats the thought that railroad management had to run the government. He was interested to learn that the Southern Pacific could not afford to control all California politics.

Business Corruption of Government in the Twentieth Century

American political corruption has declined considerably in the twentieth century, although it is still larger in proportion to population than in other modern democracies, as I demonstrate in a forthcoming book. Business has continued to be a substantial part of it as the following examples show.

The selling of fraudulent securities in "bucket shops," which were named after stores that sold buckets of grain or flour to poorer customers, was a major area of political corruption in the early twentieth century. Arnold Rothstein developed and in-

498

corporated this activity into the network of organized crime which
he established in New York City during the 1910s and 1920s. Bucket
shops obtained protection from police action through bribes, often
distributed through Rothstein to his Tammany Hall friends. Like
the transit companies, bucket shops chiefly corrupted local government. Major business opposed them, and worked to secure laws
against them. Rothstein's rackets could be more appropriately
classified as illicit activities seeking to protect themselves
than as "business" corrupting government.

The Harding Administration provided one of the more blatant
examples of political corruption by a few individual businessmen.
Secretary of the Interior Albert Fall was found to have accepted
thinly-disguised bribes from oil magnates Harry Sinclair and Edward Doheny for oil field leases. Clearly business did the corrupting in this case. However, the larger Truman administration
scandals involved both businessmen and smaller business corporations
in efforts to avoid taxes, to secure Reconstruction Finance Corporation loans, and to secure favors from the Federal Housing Agency;
most of which corruption was at least as much government official
induced as business induced.

More recently, American multinational corporations, such as
International Telephone and Telegraph (ITT), Lockheed Aircraft
Corporation, Gulf Oil Corporation, Exxon and General Motors, were
discovered to have made "illegal" payments to "representatives"
of host governments. While these payments, in the form of bribes,
kickbacks and campaign contributions, were illegal by American
standards, many foreign countries regarded them as ordinary business
transactions. The question arises whether an American company is
acting unethically when, because of corrupt officials or competitive pressures, it pays a foreign government in order to remain in
operation.

Several other examples indicate that political corruption
frequently consists of both political extortion and business bribery with extortion in the lead. The 1972 report of the Knapp
Commission on New York City Police Corruption revealed that police
extortion was a common occurrence. Investigators found that many
bars doing a substantial volume of business made regular biweekly
payments to the police in order to remain in operation. However,
the Commission also found that the Police Department failed to
take adequate measures against construction contractors who offered
bribes to policemen. The most frequent form of misconduct was the
acceptance by police officers of gratuities in the form of free
meals, free goods and cash payments. Officers also sold narcotics,
and extorted bribes from motorists and tow truck drivers. Drugs
were frequently "planted" on suspects.

The Pennsylvania Crime Commission Reports on Philadelphia in the early 1970s indicated that there were more "shakedowns" by police but also recorded "voluntary" contributions. The Commission concluded that systematic corruption resulted from the interaction of many factors, including the Police Department's attitude toward corruption, the vice enforcement policy of the Department, various societal pressures on individual police officers and on other parts of the criminal justice system and the public's tolerant reaction to corruption.

Some elements of the Watergate scandal demonstrated what can result from a mixed business-government relationship. While neither the "third rate burglaries" nor their concealment were directly related to business, Watergate has often been interpreted as a result of excessive business involvement in politics. Common Cause, for example, contends that business contributions to the Committee to Re-elect the President (CREEP) were given so freely that political misdeeds resulted. While it is true that CREEP money was used for the legal defense of several Watergate offenders, it still was hardly the "cause" of Watergate.

The special prosecuting staff working on Watergate investigated many cases of illegal corporate contributions to campaign funds -- to both Republican and Democratic candidates. Although a legal provision against corporate contributions to federal campaigns had been in effect for seventy years, it had not been previously enforced by either party. As a result of this failure, fines and jail sentences for individual defendants were light. In general, both the Republican and Democratic Parties appear to have solicited money from business as much as business had approached them. While business may be rightly criticized for permitting unprincipled politicians to extort money, available evidence supports the view that business cannot be cited as the sole initial corrupter of government. Representatives of CREEP, for example, approached a number of corporations which had problems before federal agencies and asked for substantial contributions.

After reviewing the above evidence, in addition to the mass of evidence elsewhere, one can clearly conclude that there was a two way relationship between government and business corruption. Frequently it becomes a chicken-egg controversy as to whether the official or politician made the demand or a business representative offered the bribe first.

Business Sponsors Government Reform

The fact that many businessmen have actively opposed corruption also argues against the notion that business is solely

500

responsible for corruption. American businessmen firmly supported the establishment of civil service reform organizations in the nineteenth century in order to reduce political corruption. In 1867, the National Manufacturer's Association unanimously supported a Congressional bill for that purpose, primarily to promote tax and revenue reform as well as greater economy in government. Businessmen interested in civil service reform were primarily smaller merchants rather than industrialists, latecomers rather than originators of the reform movement, and followers rather than leaders. They were generally hostile toward "monopolies," some of them arguing that so long as the civil service remained unreformed, legislation to curb the monopolists would be ineffective (since key government positions could be bought with campaign contributions). Business ideals pervaded the thinking of all reformers even those who had little connection with businessmen, and reformers frequently called for "business methods" in government service.

Evidence from abroad also helps negate the view that business is the principal source of political corruption. One of the major books on reform of British politics in the 19th century (Simpkins and Wraith, Corruption in Developing Countries) indicates that some British business led in English political reforms. Switzerland and Sweden have developed highly effective modern business systems with political corruption which is minimal if compared to that of the United States.

Other Ethical Questions About Business and Government

There are many unsolved questions of ethical relationships between business and government. If an aircraft company gives $100,000 to Republican officials just before a decision to buy a new light plane is made by the government, it is clearly a bribe. But is the gift a bribe if it is made by company officials to campaign funds during the campaign? If so, organized labor and farm groups as well as business have been bribing members of Congress and government officials. But is not government supposed to represent the various groups in our society?

The profound effect that government policies can have on the condition of business firms or whole industries often stimulates heavy business involvement in politics. The twenty-seven percent depletion allowance long allowed in certain extractive industries, (such as petroleum) is an excellent example. The oil industry was involved in politics for many years in order to obtain and preserve this and similar tax advantages. As a result of such favors, Wilbur Mills, in 1976 Chairman of the Joint Ways and Means Committee, had little difficulty in securing contri-

butions for his short Presidential campaign from firms which desired favors from his Committee.

A more complex problem is posed by the substantial influence
of organized crime on political life in America through campaign
contributions and other means of political influence. Its methods
and objectives undeniably are shocking and un-American. But what
about a legitimate business which believes it must cooperate with
organized crime to keep its business going? Is it responsible for
the political evil caused by organized crime?

Why did Business and Political Ethics Drop?

It is clear from the above description of the two way relationship in ethics that both American political and business ethics
dropped sharply in the later nineteenth century. It can be added
here, on the basis of other studies, that neither business nor
political ethics rose as sharply as we would desire in the 20th
century.

What is the explanation of this long drop in ethics of both
business and politics in America? We should recall that few people
in business or politics in the nineteenth century had adequate
ethical codes for the problems of a growing industrial America in
the last half of that century. The rapid urbanization and indus-
trialization that the United States underwent from 1865 to 1900 required newer and more comprehensive ethical standards than the
religions and philosophies of early America had developed. Ideas
of "conflict of interest" or careful definitions of "the public
interest" were not known. Unfortunately, the need for these standards was not fully recognized until the beginning of the twentieth
century and even then, no single body was responsible for framing
them. Business, which was ultimately responsible for regulating
its own affairs, possessed few individuals educated to establish
such standards.

The confusion that businessmen and politicians experienced
regarding ethical standards can also be attributed to the emergence of new currents of thought in nineteenth century America.
Darwin's Origin of Species and various trends of "scientism" undoubtedly weakened the influence of religious institutions which,
for many Americans, were essential to the preservation of an
ethical code. The effects of this upheaval were quite visible:
emphasis on individual ethics in school readers declined, business
and political corruption increased, and the climate of ideas was
less friendly for ethical democracy than in 1780. Henry Adams'
writings are adequate proof of the decline.

502

More research needs to be done on America's 19th century drop in political and business ethics. Increasing heterogeneity of the population, the spoils system, political machines, excess of emphasis on profit alone, may all have been contributing causes. But the theory that business was the single cause or a major cause appears to be badly mistaken. Business has basically been a part of American society, shaping the society to some extent but sharing common ideals and common mistakes. The cure to corruption probably lies in education, in better ethical standards for both government and business; not in greater control of business alone.

Answers to the questions posed at the beginning of this article, must reflect our findings that business is only one partner in the process of corruption. I would certainly like to see bribers prosecuted as vigorously as bribees but there are legal difficulties to be faced by prosecuters. I would also like to see business ethical codes changed to forbid any form of bribe of government officials. But I do not believe that the above evidence leads us to assume that political corruption is a necessary concomitant of a relatively free economic system like ours.

PATRICIA H. WERHANE

RELATIVISM AND MULTINATIONAL CORPORATE CONDUCT

The conduct of multinational corporations in foreign countries
has lately been brought under the scrutiny of the SEC, the investigation by the Church Subcommittee on Multinational Corporations
and the criticism of the American public. The subject of controversy
by and large centers around the question of sensitive payments to
political officials, political organizations and private individuals
in foreign countries in order to facilitate business dealings in
that country. Many of these payments are considered illegal and
unethical in this country. But it is often argued that these
payments are consistent with practices of other multinational
corporations, that they are accepted practices in other countries,
and that they are necessary for doing business abroad. The controversy
over sensitive payments raises the following kinds of questions.
What should constitute proper multinational corporate business conduct?
What sorts of transnational activities can be justified? and How
should these activities be evaluated?

Multinational corporations (MNCs) often defend practices such
as sensitive payments in their foreign business operations with
the following kinds of arguments:

(1) When operating in another country, one must adopt the
cultural and ethical mores of that country. One cannot apply one's
own values in another socio-cultural context without morally offending
the host country. One cannot do business profitably in another
country without adjusting to the value scheme and particular business
practices of that country.

(2) American corporations provide technology and economic
services abroad, thus raising the standards of living for citizens
in other countries. These services represent opportunities which
would not be available to these countries otherwise.[1] The means
a MNC may have to employ to make these goods and services available,
e.g., sensitive payments, are thus justified by long-range economic
results.

(3) If American corporations do not provide goods and services
multinationally, other foreign corporations will do so, and they
will do so through the same means, e.g., sensitive payments. The
only business-like way to operate competitively and successfully
abroad is by engaging in transactions which are sometimes labeled
as illegal or immoral by Americans; but these are transactions which

504

are consistent with practices in other countries and "consistent with practices engaged in by numerous other companies abroad."[2]

Let us examine each of these arguments. The first justification of questionable MNC conduct abroad appeals to the principle of cultural relativism. A cultural relativist argues that environmental conditions affect human development in different societies. The resulting socio-cultural disparities between societies are outcomes of different views of human nature. The kinds of social institutions and cultural mores which flow from these differing views of human nature affect the nature of moral reasoning, the substance of moral judgments, and thus the goals and values of a particular society. What counts as right conduct and what one values as good in one society may be considered neither right nor good in another because of differences in personality development, values and styles of moral reasoning. Thus values, value judgements and moral decisions are contextual, relevant to the particular socio-cultural situation in which they arose.[3] Therefore in justifying actions which might be questionable by American value standards the MNC is appealing to the principle that ethical values are culturally relative, and the MNC is arguing that one should respect this principle in judging MNC actions in foreign countries where values and customs are different from our own.

The second justification is based on the principle of ethical absolutism. An ethical absolutist argues that there are at least some moral principles which apply universally and objectively to all people in any situation, regardless of cultural differences existing between human beings. Applying the concept of ethical absolutism to MNCs, when corporations defend their activities abroad by referring to the economic and technological advantages for foreign countries in which they operate, are they not assuming that economic advancement and technological development are in some sense universal values which are held, or should be held by everyone? It might be suggested, then, that MNCs are actually taking an absolutist position by assuming that economic growth and technological advances are values which are, or should be, espoused by all cultures.

Justifications (1) and (2) for MNC conduct are at best inconsistent. For it cannot be argued both that one should operate within cultural and ethical schemes of a particular country and claim at the same time that we should introduce that country to our own economic values because these are "better," more advanced, or because economic development will maximize everybody's happiness. If values are culturally relative we cannot assume that economic advances, universally, will actually enhance all ways of life.

The third justification of questionable MNC conduct abroad argues that actions which are questionable in our value system may be necessary for doing business successfully elsewhere. Pragmatically this argument cannot be supported, since many corporations within and without the United States appear to operate profitably without making sensitive payments of any kind to anyone. More importantly, the third justification erroneously assumes that if some act is an accepted custom in a particular country, that act is also thought to be right or morally acceptable in that country. This assumption misidentifies practice or custom with rightness or principle. It is a confusion one seldom makes in one's own society. For example, pay-offs for building permits are commonly accepted practices in many major American cities. But these pay-offs are both illegal and considered morally unacceptable in this country. In other countries the fact that high governmental officials regularly accept sensitive payments, and that this might be a "commonly accepted practice," does not mean that these practices are considered morally right in these countries. What are commonly accepted customs in many cultures _often_ conflict with moral values of that culture, and both custom and principle need to be taken into account in transnational activities.

In light of this discussion how might one justify MNC conduct abroad, and how might one elicit more ethically appropriate performances by MNCs in alien cultures? If the cultural relativist is correct, then it would be both morally offensive and bad business advice to suggest that MNCs export their ethical mores to foreign, host countries. In the case of sensitive payments I cannot accuse a MNC of bribing an official of a foreign government until (1) I have found out what the payment entailed, (2) I have investigated the cultural situation in which the payment occurred, and (3) I clearly understand what the term "bribe" and other value terms mean in that foreign context.

By the same argument it is also offensive for MNCs to export their own economic and technological values and apply these to another society without first judging the economic and cultural values of that society. Moreover, even if the ethical absolutist is correct that culturally different beliefs, customs and values can be evaluated by some universal standard, for example, "happiness," the ways in which this standard is applied are culturally diverse, because what contributes to happiness in one society might, because of culturally relative differences, produce unhappiness in another society.[4] Thus what might maximize happiness in our culture, e.g., economic advances, might actually create unhappinesses in other societies.

Finally, what is accepted practice in a country is not always what is considered morally right in that country. And sometimes what is morally acceptable or right is a particular society is based on some value or principle which is not identical to the mores of

that society. For example, merely the fact that it is customary for
most people in a society to accept bribes does not imply that this
custom is considered right or good, even within the value structure
of that society. If a MNC is to operate with serious intent in
foreign countries it needs to be informed about the ideals which
people in these countries hold as well as their everyday practices.

What is the role of government in regulating MNC conduct? Any
regulation which requires MNCs to apply American legal and moral
principles without exception to foreign operations commits the same
kinds of cultural errors as the practices the legislation is trying
to reform. Such regulations force MNCs to act illegally in some
foreign contexts. Worse, such regulations assume that American legal
and moral principles are better or more universally applicable
than any others. At most, government can only propose general guidelines for what might constitute improper MNC conduct.

The onus for ethically appropriate international conduct rests
with multinational corporations themselves. To operate trans-
nationally a MNC and its employees need to be aware of the kinds of
values which operate in culturally diverse contexts. And MNCs need
to examine and question the ideal of economic growth as a universal
value before proceeding as if this goal were, or should be held
by everyone. If MNCs were so informed, and if MNCs operated according to this kind of information, I suspect that many issues of
questionable behavior, sensitive payments, and the like would not
arise.[5]

NOTES

1. For example, a vice-president of a large American
multinational bank recently told me that American bankers introduced the concept of household credit to Italy, a concept heretofore unknown in that country. The banker implied that this
kind of credit was good, good for the Italians, and actually enhanced
the Italian way of life.
2. In commenting on Lockheed Aircraft Corporation's recent
payments to high officials in the Japanese government Newsweek
quotes Lockheed management as saying,

The payments..."were made with the knowledge of management
and management believes they were necessary...The company
also believes that such payments are consistent with practices
engaged in by numerous other companies abroad, including
many of its competitors."

Newsweek, August 18, 1975, p. 63
3. See Carl Wellman, "The Ethical Implications of Cultural

507

Relativity," Journal of Philosophy, LX (1963), and Edward Hall, Beyond Culture, New York: Doubleday Anchor Press, 1976.

4. John Hospers, Human Conduct (New York: Harcourt Brace Jovanovich, Inc., 1961, 1972), pp. 36-37.

5. This paper originated as part of the Introduction to Ethical Issues in Business: A Philosophical Approach, an anthology in business ethics I am co-authoring with Thomas Donaldson of Loyola University, forthcoming by Prentice-Hall, Inc. I am deeply indebted to Professor Donaldson's suggestions, revisions and development of many of the ideas.

JOHN E. CAVANAGH

Solutions to today's problems too often have within them
the seeds of tomorrow's problems. When those solutions are in
the form of a new law, the problems which they create result from
the law being complex, sometimes almost unintelligible to anyone
but an expert, and often times unrealistic. The Foreign Corrupt
Practices Act -- which fits rather tidily into our topic of
"Corporations, Government, and Bribery" -- suffers only partially
from these drawbacks. It is not particularly complex, nor unintelligible but it does have some troublesome ambiguities and it
has been sharply criticized as being unrealistic.

The legislation is an aftermath of, a result of, the highly
publicized disclosures of payments in connection with foreign
business which have been variously described as "sensitive,"
"improper," or "questionable" payments. Those descriptive adjectives
are not entirely euphemisms. They reflect the fact that the payments which were disclosed ranged from bribes of officials, to
extortion by officials; from purported political contributions
which may have been thinly disguised bribes or extortion in some
cases to foreign political contributions which were legal in others;
from clear factually supported instances of impropriety in some
cases, to hearsay and unsupported allegations in others.

In any case, the investigations that were conducted by the
Congress, by the SEC, and later by the Department of Justice, over
a period of almost three years and numerous voluntary disclosures
to the SEC revealed hundreds of instances of this kind of conduct.
This finally led to strong pressure for new legislation, a new
law, to restrain U.S. corporations and individuals in their dealings
with foreign officials. There was some considerable debate as to
what form the law ought to take, as to whether requiring disclosure
of any payments to foreign officials would be a sufficient preventative,
or whether bribery of a foreign official should be made a crime
under U.S. law.

The Foreign Corrupt Practices Act, passed in December, 1977,
takes the latter approach. To paraphrase, the law makes it a
criminal offense to corruptly offer or pay money, or offer or give
anything of value to any foreign official, to any foreign political
party or party official or to any candidate for a foreign political
office, for the purpose of influencing his act or decision or
inducing him to use his influence with a foreign government in
order to assist in obtaining or retaining business. The law also
prohibits offers, payments or gifts to any person while "knowing

509

or having reason to know" that all or any portion will be passed on to any such party for such a purpose. You will note, I am sure, the troublesome vagueness of the phrase "having reason to know" and will appreciate the concern a person might have at the prospect of being held criminally liable based on a retrospective judgment as to whether he had reason to know what another person was going to do.

Excluded from the prohibitions of the Act are payments or gifts to officials whose duties are essentially ministerial or clerical. (You would be surprised at how many people think that ministerial refers to ministers; actually it refers to officials whose duties are non-discretionary.) This exclusion is to allow for the so-called facilitating, expediting, or grease payments. There was great concern that the law would place an impossible burden on those who lived and did business in foreign countries if payments to officials necessary to secure routine Government services in foreign countries were made a criminal offense under U.S. law. There seems to be a feeling that bribing officials who do not have any discretionary function to perform is all right -- perhaps a troublesome concept from an ethical and moral standpoint. Interestingly, there's no limitation put on the amount of payments that can be made to officials in that category. Conversely, even a small payment to a foreign official who is not in that category would, under the law, be a violation if made for one of the prohibited purposes even if the service for which the payment was made was routine in nature.

The penalties under the Act are severe, with fines of up to $1 million on a corporation, and up to $10,000 or five years in jail, or both, for individuals. These penalties can be imposed on any officer, director, or employee of the corporation who willfully participates in the violation. The Act is very broad in its prohibition. There is no necessity that a bribe be paid; if it is offered, or authorized corruptly, there is a violation. The Act applies not just to publicly held corporations which the Securities and Exchange Commission has jurisdiction over, but also to any private corporation whose principle place of business is in the United States or that is incorporated within the United States. It applies to any resident, national or citizen, of the United States, even though he might be in a foreign country when the violation occurs.

Does this passage of the law eliminate or supplant the ethical questions that are involved in the practice of bribing foreign officials? Since this is now clearly prohibited as an illegal act, do the ethical questions involved lose their significance? As a minimum we can say that the ethical question is placed in a different context, but ethical questions remain for

the corporation's management to consider. There are problems
of dealing fairly with employees who might be exposed, inadvertently or carelessly, to the impact of this law. And that impact can be severe. The law may be difficult to enforce, but if
it is enforced it can bear harshly on the individuals involved.

Employees of U.S. companies whose employment is in foreign
countries may be in a particularly difficult situation. This
law is addressed after all to operations in foreign countries.
While some of the prohibited activities could take place in this
country, the ultimate objective is to control foreign activities.
Any company that operates in foreign countries may have officers
or employees who are stationed thousands of miles away from
their U.S. headquarters. By definition, they are in a foreign
environment. They may see ample evidence that bribery of government officials is commonplace in that country and may be under
substantial pressure to make such payments. Somehow the corporate management in this country must communicate to those people
and firmly reject any proposal that illegal payments be made.
(Without condoning the practices of the past, there is room for
compassion for some of the practitioners. A man who had been
working for years to consummate a sale, to build a plant or establish a business who was suddenly confronted with an ultimatum
to make a payment or go out of business faced, at best, a painful dilemma.)

Under this law, there is no exclusion for extortion, no
differentiation between bribery and extortion. In the situation,
for example, where a government official threatens to close a
plant unless a bribe is paid, the payment probably would be a
violation of the Act. It is true in the legislative history that
much is made of the concept that the action must be taken "corruptly" and it suggested that to be corrupt, there must be an
intent to have the foreign official misuse his office. But a
person would be ill-advised to make a payment to a foreign
official in response to extortion on the assumption that a pro-
secutor would consider that he had not violated the Act because
his heart was pure.

Here is an example then of an ethical problem company
management must face. If demands for illegal payments are being
made on one of its foreign employees, the management at least
owes him, first, a warning of the dangers of his position and of
the absolute necessity of not making the payment. And, second,
the management must recognize the limitations under which the
employee then operates. If, indeed, in that country extortion
is a way of doing business, then management should and must accept that the foreign business may suffer -- the local manager
cannot make payments in the face of the company policy and of

these criminal limitations and the company may thereby lose business. Another example of a problem under the Act would be presented by an employee attempting to get goods through customs faced with a demand for money from a foreign customs official. The employee must decide then whether he is faced with a ministerial or a clerical official, that is, an official who performs a nondiscretionary function. If he assumes incorrectly that the official is in that category and makes the payment, his company auditor may, months later, pick up the fact of the payment and report to the company that the employee had violated the law. And the management, if it agrees that the payment was a violation, must then decide what action to take. So pity the man who is on the firing line.

The management can address some of these problems. They can and should give explicit instructions to affected employees, even though under this law it is difficult to give guidance. There are no guidelines in the law and apparently none will be furnished by the SEC or the Department of Justice, the responsible Government agencies. There is no minimum amount specified below which there is no violation, no indication that taking an official to dinner, for example, is not a violation. Common sense should be a guide, but it is dangerous in interpreting a criminal statute to apply common sense where the law does not give any guidance. A misjudgment as to what is permitted may lead to prosecution. And even without prosecution there can be investigations and indictment with attendant pain and expense even if there proves to be no criminal violation.

In my company we have faced some of the questions which must be faced under this new law because we have had a policy since 1975 against payments to government officials or use of government officials as sales consultants. Simple though the policy is, its strict enforcement has presented us with an array of questions and problems of interpretation, questions and problems which might seem trivial in the abstract but assuredly will not seem so to a man who is concerned with compliance with a criminal law of the United States.

STANLEY CLEVELAND

We have talked about the philosophical and legal approaches
to our subject. I will be in the middle, and address it from the
viewpoint of a practitioner.

The subject of corporate ethics - particularly bribery -
was until recently exciting, controversial and newsworthy; but
the rejection of bribery as a business practice has now become
generally accepted (at least verbally) by American business. Indeed,
the corporate speeches we hear sometimes remind me of the old
story of the two Yankees discussing the parson's weekly sermon:
Ezra, who sat through it, described it to his friend as long,
involved and complicated. "Well," asked Jed, "what did the
parson talk about?" "Sin." "And what did he have to say?"
"He was agin it."

Perhaps the fact that the subject has reached this level
of platitude is a good sign; perhaps it means that the basic
concept of corporate responsibility and ethics has really been
adopted as being part of the conventional wisdom by corporate
managements in general. But the purpose of this conference, if
I understand it, is to go a little deeper into the problem: to
look at definitions, at some of the dilemmas involved, and the
concrete problems of putting corporate ethics into practice.

Given my own background in government and business, essentially
international and much of it in the field, I would like to address
one particularly difficult question - a philosophical question
which arises out of some very practical problems in the life of
a business and in relations between governments: To what extent is
it proper and indeed possible for U.S.-based corporations, and in
particular for the U.S. government acting through U.S.-based
corporations, to attempt to enforce U.S. conceptions of ethics in
other people's sovereignties?

Before doing so, let me state my credentials - both personal
and corporate. Bendix is well known to have had a long standing
view on the subject of the public responsibility of corporate
management, a view of which Mike Blumenthal as Chairman was an
eloquent exponent. Specifically on the bribery question, well
before the scandals broke we had clear internal directives forbidding not only direct political payments, bribery, etc., but
also indirect activities to the same effect: e.g., excessive
commissions making it possible for others to engage in such
activities without direct involvement of the corporation. In

putting out these directives the management made clear it had considered, faced and accepted that they would mean loss of business, and emphasized that they were to be followed even if that meant loss of business. Sanctions were provided to insure these policies were known, accepted and carried out throughout the various organizations in the company.

Having had for several years the direct line responsibility for some 800 million dollars worth of Bendix business, I've had the experience of trying to carry out these directives in practice in foreign countries. And before that I spent a good many years in the U.S. government with responsibilities in European and South American countries involving the whole range of relationships of U.S. business with local government and local business. It is against this background that I want to make my points.

First, at the risk of admitting to being a "cultural relativist," I would reiterate that government/business relations are different in each country. For example, in the United States we generally consider that there should be an arm's-length relationship between government and business, particularly in the area of government regulation of business, and that it is wrong (even if it often happens) that there should be any serious connection between the regulators and the regulated in an industry. In France, on the other hand, it is considered normal that an industry and the government department concerned with that industry (the so-called "patron" of that industry) should have a close cooperative working relationship, and that the civil servants who have worked in the relevant ministry normally go on to senior positions in one of the companies (nationalized or private) which they have been regulating. This is not only a philosophical but also a practical difference, and occurs in many other areas.

Second, a certain degree of official corruption is tolerated, if not encouraged, in many countries: civil servants are poorly paid and often are more or less expected to supplement their incomes by a certain amount of "bachshish," as long as it is not overdone. In some countries, the receipt of bribes by the second level of the ruling class is considered normal: an inexpensive way of letting them get rich and thus keeping them from making trouble for the people on top. And even where, as in most western European countries, official corruption is not tolerated within the country, the attitude towards this kind of activity outside of the borders, and especially in less developed countries, is very much more tolerant than here.

Third, in many places, and this _does_ include Western Europe, things which are illegal in the United States - for example, corporate contributions to political campaigns - are entirely legal and indeed common in public practice: West Germany is a good example.

514

Now it is a fact of basic importance that most U.S. corporations - those which properly have the name of multinational - work abroad through affiliates, rather than branches (i.e. extensions of the mother company itself). This is particularly true in the manufacturing business. These affiliates are corporate citizens of the country concerned, not of the United States. They are subject to local laws. Their boards are appointed in accordance with local law and practice, and they are expected to conform to local law and in general to local custom. Many have local stockholders; often they have a majority of local stockholders and increasingly they are indeed required by the law or government pressure to have such a local majority.

Where there is local stockholding, even minority, the local company has to take account of the interests of the local stockholders; if it does not, it is subject to stockholder suits or even to criminal prosecution. Even where ownership is 100%, most companies operate with essentially local management, who are usually employees not of the American parent but only of the local company; and usually, if they have any sense, they have a few influential and significant local board members, leading members of the local business community who are accustomed to operating in accordance with the laws and customs of the country.

Moreover, most countries, especially in Europe, take the view that the responsibility of a corporation is not only - sometimes even not primarily - to its stockholders: that the stockholders or their representatives on the board of directors do not in fact have the right to make the major decisions simply in their own interests, but must take account of and be responsive to a number of other constituencies, in particular the labor force. And primarily, that they must be responsive to and carry out national interests and national policy as interpreted by the national government, particularly in the fields of employment and export promotion.

Now all of these factors can create serious problems for an American company if it tries purely and simply to force foreign subsidiaries (even if it controls them) to lose business because they are carrying out the policy of the parent company, whether that policy is on ethical or business grounds. These are real problems; they are not excuses or even necessarily reasons to fail to carry out an ethical policy which most American companies have now accepted and which has now been essentially enshrined in the law. But such policies can only be implemented effectively by a combination of clarity on objectives with a considerable flexibility as to technique and manner. For example, what we have done in Bendix international operations has been to obtain the support of our local boards to adopt policies in each subsidiary against engaging in unusual payments, political contributions, etc., justifying these policies in terms relevant to local requirements and business objectives rather than imposing them as an order from the stockholders.

This kind of an approach, clear in its objectives but flexible in its means, can work. What is difficult and presumptuous, what creates problems, is if these become matters not of local board decision and subsidiary acceptance, but of enforcing U.S. law in a jurisdiction in which U.S. law does not apply. There is now an increasing tendency in the Congress in particular to legislate the conduct of foreign subsidiaries organized under the laws of other people's sovereignties, through control of the multinationals' headquarters. This is not new: the Trading with the Enemy Act dates from the First World War and clearly asserts this same right to extend U.S. law to foreign sovereignties through the U.S. stockholders of foreign subsidiaries. And the Trading with the Enemy Act, as any lawyer can tell you, has created untold problems for us in times of peace in many countries. I know of one case, which I will not go into detail on, (although it is in the public domain) where a subsidiary of an American company with an American majority was told by the U.S. government that it must cancel a contract which its local management had made to sell its only product to its only customer, because the ultimate customer would be Communist China (during the embargo). The French minority stockholders went to court, had the company declared in receivership, took over the company and confirmed the contract, to the loud approval of the local government; it took years for that company to get itself out of trouble, and quite a while for the U.S. government to patch up the intergovernmental relationships which had been broken by this case.

The essential point I want to make is that while company managements can - and in my opinion should - carry out ethical policies abroad, they must do so with due regard for local practice and sensitivities, in a flexible manner that takes account of local law and builds consent among their local partners, boards and employees rather than by the exercise of a corporate sledgehammer. And above all that the U.S. government and Congress should beware of trying to extend U.S. morality, law and sovereignty to other people's countries through the intermediary of U.S.-based multinationals, at the risk of undermining the credibility and authority - and the reputation for good sense not only of U.S. business but of the United States itself.

516

DISCUSSION

COMMENT: I have problems with the continued focus on money –
on bribery. There are other issues.

My question is addressed to Professor Werhane, because she dealt
with the rationale "when in Rome do as the Romans do." I'd like
to recite a case very briefly and invite a comment.

Pharmaceutical companies repeatedly have been found to be selling
drugs abroad with claims of safety and claims of effectiveness
that they're prohibited from making in the United States, because they cannot provide the evidence of safety and effectiveness
specified by law. The most awful example I could think of, off-
hand, involves a combination antibiotic that was produced
starting in 1957 by the Upjohn Company in Kalamazoo.

The antibiotic was called Panalba, the trade name. It combined
tetracycline, which is a very useful broad-spectrum antibiotic
when used correctly, with another antibiotic called novabiacin.

In 1960, Upjohn learned from a study, one that it had sponsored,
and one that was not discovered by the FDA until 1969, that the
useful antibiotic tetracycline was an antagonist of novabiacin,
so that the combination was less useful, less effective, against
an infection than tetracycline alone. In other words, physicians were prescribing Panalba thinking they were helping their
patients with a drug that sometimes was hurting them.

The then commissioner of the FDA, Dr. Herbert Ley, a specialist
in the treatment of infectious diseases, testified before a
Senate subcommittee that the novabiacin component of Panalba
was literally causing, in the United States alone, hundreds of
thousands of needless injuries every year. Most of the injuries
were not serious; you got a rash for a week and wouldn't sleep,
or something like that. Some injuries were very serious, and a
few were fatal.

The FDA finally got the product off the market in 1970. But Upjohn went on selling it abroad under a different name, Albamy-
cin-T.

So much that we've heard concerns useful products that companies
sell abroad. I'm sure that Bendix machinery, Ingersol/Rand
machinery, transport aircraft, are unquestionably useful products. But here we're talking about something that's less than

517

useful, that is, in fact, injurious.

And the defense given by the drug industry generally was, "When
in the United States, we live by the U.S. rules. When we go
abroad, if Zambia or wherever doesn't have rules for safety, we
live by that."

I guess the question is: How does this defense of "when in Rome
do as the Romans do" stand up? How can it help in safety areas,
as illustrated by the Upjohn/Panalba story?

WERHANE: Yes. I think that's a very interesting point. I think
your particular example has brought up two kinds of issues I was
trying to illustrate, or maybe three kinds. First of all, what
do the Romans do, actually -- and, of course, that's always a problem. Also what is prescribed by, say, the Roman legal code? And
I assume that in this case these drugs are not prohibited by the
legal codes where they're sold, obviously. And then, what are
the moral principles in that country and are you respecting them?
It would seem to me that to sell a drug which was harmful to
other individuals is something on almost every moral code that
all people would think was wrong. And I think that Mr. Cavanagh
brought that out, that what is legal is not always what is moral,
or what is immoral. And I think there's a great difference between them, so I can't imagine that the Italians would think it
was right morally to sell a drug which actually harmed their
people, even though it might not be in their legal code.

COMMENT: It seems to me that there you have to invoke an absolutist code, that it is wrong to sell something to people abroad
that you can't sell to people of this country, no matter what
the rules of the other countries are. I guess it really raises
the question: Doesn't there have to be some kind of universal
moral principle?

WERHANE: Well, it also depends on what it is. Because now
you're talking about harming human beings. For example, there are
some food products which are sold in Europe which are not allowed to be sold here because they don't have the preservatives,
which I think is absolutely ridiculous because they really taste
better and they really are better for you without having all those
funny things in them. And yet they're not allowed to be sold in
this country. I don't think that's very much of a moral issue.
It's too bad for the gourmets, but it's not serious. But here
you're talking about harming human beings physically, which seems
to me to be a much different question. It would seem to me that
in almost any human society to harm members of the society is
considered wrong, and that's why I was talking about the difference between "accepted" and "acceptable." So I would think that

518

one was not only not applying American standards universally, but that one was actually conflicting with moral standards of wherever it is you were selling this product.

CAVANAGH: But generally the answers aren't that simple. In your case, it may be. On the other hand, there may be cases where, indeed, a drug would be harmful in 1 out of 1000 cases, but if you denied it in, say, a backward country in Africa where it might help 999, though it might kill the thousandth, then I think you have a different dilemma than you have in this country where there probably are alternative remedies. Or if we say that DDT cannot be exported because it's a health hazard, we may thereby deprive countries that really need DDT to control disease-bearing pests. I do think there's a danger in applying what are proper standards in this country to other countries unquestioningly. I think there have to be different standards. There are different values. There are entirely different problems, and without arguing your point, I do think it would be dangerous and even disastrous to say this whole bureaucracy we have in this country should some-how be transplanted and should have authority over other countries with other needs. So, I think it's a terribly complex question, rather than a simple one, as is true with most problems.

COMMENT: There is one issue, though, that has come up where there is no real difference in the legality of what is done in the United States and what is done in foreign countries, and that's the matter of bribery. Now the difficulties Mr. Cavanagh has raised about the bribery law, as I understand it, are that it is difficult to apply, difficult not for the government to apply it, but difficult for the person in the field to do that. Would he also then eliminate all of the bribery laws in the United States because they were difficult to apply?

CAVANAGH: No, as a matter of fact, the easy part of this law is the fact that you can't make payments to government officials in order to induce them to take official action in your favor. I think that it is a fairly easy thing to state. But when you're in a corporation's office in the U.S. and you're trying to give guidance to a man in a remote foreign country -- to tell him that payments to ministerial or clerical employees are all right, to tell him whether or not it is all right for him to entertain a friend who is in government, trying to give him guidance in specific situations -- it is indeed difficult to be of much help. As I say, there are plenty of problems in the United States. There have been stories of rather interesting regulations in some U.S. agencies on this subject. There was a time, I under-stand, when it was all right to give a 10 pound ham at Christmas to people in one government agency, but not a 12 pound ham. Many of our laws and regulations are crazily complicated because big

519

governments tend to develop complicated rules which seem to defy common sense. Often times they are intended to supplant individual judgment in a whole range of factual situations. And when you take this kind of law and apply it in a foreign setting, again, it can be difficult to give guidance. As I said, I'm not fighting the objective, but I can say that there are problems involved in trying to assure that the application of the law in a foreign country is understood.

COMMENT: Well, there is that problem. And you can see the case being that the problems that we have found with not having a government law forbidding bribery had been so great, and not to point the finger but to point the finger at what occurred with Lockheed in Japan, that it can very well be the sense of the American people that we'd rather have companies deal with that problem of interpreting the law than deal with the enormous repercussions of what has occurred without the law. So that it might very well be that a company would see that the law would be beneficial.

CAVANAGH: I think it would be a lot better if Japan dealt with the problem in Japan than if we tried to deal with it here. It really would be, and as a matter of fact, the steps that the U.S. government did take in trying to cooperate with the Japanese government were right. They had our Department of Justice forward all the material on our case and any other case to Japan for the Japanese to use in deciding what they would do with regard to the Japanese officials allegedly involved. I think that's a right step. As another step, the International Chamber of Commerce and various other groups are trying to stimulate bilateral treaties. Admittedly, the treaty process is slow but, by and large, we're not really going to export our morality unless we persuade people that it's the right thing, the right standard of conduct. This law is all right in its controls on U.S. companies and maybe it will influence other governments, but basically other governments have to do it themselves -- establish their own standards of conduct -- if there is to be a significant change in the conduct of their officials.

COMMENT: But this was a case where the morality and the legality were the same in the United States as Japan, but there was the violation of the law equally in Japan as in the United States.

CAVANAGH: At the top levels of government in Japan, according to what I understand, the alliance between business and politics has always been close and politicians have apparently, over many many years, done precisely this, solicited contributions from companies. The popular morality, indeed, was against it as the public uproar showed, and yet the unofficial under-the-surface

520

morality and practice was apparently quite different. I'm not defending it; I'm just stating what appears to be the case.

COMMENT: I wonder if one of the difficulties is not that there's more absolutism when you're talking about our right to life, and more relativism when you're talking about an exchange of a product for a price. That is, when does the contract of a sale become unjust in a foreign country? If everyone understands that government officials are receiving some type of a stipend so that they can expedite the matter, it almost seems as though you're into an agency contract. Where does the bribe begin in a country in which this agency contract is almost assumed?

CAVANAGH: I never thought of it that way. There are some places where government agencies do indeed represent sellers in selling to the government. I think it's a rarity. I know of two countries that have that arrangement and, apparently, it's legitimate. But I agree with what Professor Benson said, that our Federal Government in this country, with some exceptions, has handled its contracting well from the standpoint of avoiding corruption. We find it out on the fringes but, by and large, the Federal Government has handled it well. There may be other problems but there are relatively few cases of bribery or similar corruption. To my way of thinking, any American business is really going to be more comfortable with that kind of operation. So, if I appear to be arguing against what this law represents, I'm not. I think it's a hell of a way to have to do business, to pay people off or to be subject to extortion. Getting back to your point, I don't know that you could really say there is an agency relationship in most cases, but I know of one country in which a minister in the government was known and recognized and accepted by the other ministers as the man who represented foreign businesses in dealing with the government. He was paid for it and he was responsible for seeing that those companies did, in fact, perform. I don't know what the law provides in that country, but it was plainly the practice and accepted by the government, which is a very stable government.

COMMENT: Something has happened in this country with regard to bribery and society clearly has spoken out: "We don't like what's going on." You have knowledge of what these problems are and how difficult they are to deal with. What is the responsibility of the corporation to cooperate with the government in providing legislation so that, as Senator Hatfield said, we don't lose the objective in the methodology?

CAVANAGH: Well, I don't think we would have been too welcome as spokesmen on this legislation, and we didn't participate in the hearings. We have filed with the Securities and Exchange Commission the policies we now follow to prevent payments to foreign officials. Our policies are carried out. We will have to rewrite policies rather carefully to insure that the mandate of this legislation in all its details is understood by our people. We are in the process of doing that and since we unfortunately have had a little more exposure to the problem, our procedures may serve as a guide to others.

CLEVELAND: At the risk of going against the conventional wisdom, I believe the key is not this kind of prescriptive legislation at all. The thing that broke the back of the problem in the United States was in fact the SEC - the requirements of public disclosure required by the SEC act. Public disclosure is probably the best sanction and the best assurance of ethical corporate conduct. Obviously it is good to have a commitment on the part of corporate leadership generally in the United States to what we consider broadly ethical practices. But the effective sanction is going to be public exposure, the requirement of things being out on the table.

Indeed, when you get into the very tough problem of just what is ethical conduct, it is not a bad definition to say that ethical conduct is what you wouldn't mind seeing on the front page of the newspaper tomorrow. If all corporations were assured that every decision of this sort they take was one that they wouldn't mind seeing published in the newspaper, then you wouldn't need a criminal statute. And the criminal statute - which is perfectly legitimate as far as domestic business is concerned - creates serious problems when you try to take it abroad.

COMMENT: I'd like to address my question to Professor Werhane. I'd like to pursue the very question that Mr. Mintz was also asking earlier concerning the split between so-called absolute values and relative ones. I shy away from the notion of absolutism and would probably prefer to talk about something like the possible existence of universal values. It does strike me that there might be a need to affirm a kind of universal value for certain things; for example, the right to self-determination on the part of the participants in any given country. In other words, that all people in that country have the right to participate in some way in their own government. My question is simply, would you affirm that such a universal value exists, and secondly, is that a kind of value which you believe a corporation should build into its overseas activities?

WERHANE: Yes. I was really shying away myself from talking about absolute values. But I think one could make an argument that indeed there are universal kinds of values. For example, we were talking about the right to human life and I was arguing, at least in a de facto way, that I suspect there aren't any cultures which don't hold that as a value. I suspect that's a universal value. The right to self-determination is more of a

522

political and perhaps universal value, but I'm not sure that corporations have any business in political activities in foreign countries at all. So, I would say that whether or not it is a universal value, I don't think it has much to do with multinational corporations, since I'm not sure they should be in the business of political activities.

COMMENT: The question I have is whether the point about cultural diversity isn't overdrawn and whether it isn't often the case that the practices that are in question are regarded as corrupt on both sides. But there is a temptation on both sides to engage in the practice and we use the issue about cultural diversity as a kind of dodge for going ahead with some recognizably corrupt practice that we're having to engage in. Then the question becomes -- how do you stop it?

BENSON: The Jewish law forbade bribes in the Pentatuch several hundred years before Christ, and I'm sure this is embodied in the Moslem law. I quite agree with you that we ought to be extremely opposed to lowering ethical standards. I thought it was the main point of Professor Werhane's paper, that is, that we should be very careful about taking some position that somebody in some country tells us is the way they act, when really, a great many people in that country will accept a more nearly universal value.

CAVANAGH: I just want to make one final point: It is truly depressing that, as Professor Benson pointed out, in all the years we've had all our enlightened voter power in this country, we haven't been able to stamp out corruption. On the state and local level, it is apparently quite prevalent, particularly in some of the older parts of the country. And since we haven't reformed ourselves, I wonder about the efficacy of our efforts to reform the world. I think we may do some good abroad, but it is humbling to recognize that we haven't been able to correct this problem at home. And that really is pretty bad.

SESSION XIX

"Big Business and the Mass Media"

Chester Burger
President
Chester Burger and Company

Gordon McKibben
Boston Bureau Chief
Business Week

Bernard Rubin
Director
Institute of Democratic Communication
Boston University

Paul J. Wetzel
Regional Manager of Public Relations
General Motors Corporation

CHESTER BURGER

Let's begin with some basic facts first.

Big Business: right there, we have a pejorative term.
People who use the term "Big Business" often don't like the
idea that businesses should be big. To them somehow, the idea
of a mom-and-pop store on the corner seems more in keeping
with the American Way.

But our society can't function with mom-and-pop stores.
People aren't willing to pay the extra costs that a small grocery
store incurs with itty-bitty deliveries every morning. Mom-and-pop
can't affort the modern warehouses, conveyor belts, fleets of
refrigerated trucks, that cut the fat -- or most of it -- out of
the costs of food distribution.

And in other industries, the same is true. Big business
is big because it costs a hundred million dollars to build a paper
mill. Big business is big because it takes almost half a billion
dollars to build a petrochemical plant. Big business is big because
it cost 100 billion dollars to build the nationwide telephone
network -- and it would cost 145 billion to rebuild at today's
inflated prices. That's why business is big.

And what about the media? They aren't as big as the
largest corporation, but they are just as essential to the workings
of our society. Maybe more so. It isn't an accident that the only
industry specifically protected by the Constitution and the Bill
of Rights is not the food industry, not the oil industry, not the
telephone industry, but the press. Thomas Jefferson said,

The basis of our government being the opinion of the people,
the very first object should be to keep that right;
and were it left to me to decide whether we should have
a government without newspapers, or newspapers without
government, I should not hesitate a moment to prefer
the latter.
---Letter to Edward Carrington, 1787---

So here we have two of the great forces in our society.
They are at odds with each other. You can't minimize the profound
distrust which each has for the other. You could almost weigh it
on a scale, it's so -- well, almost tangible.

To hear management people talk, you'd think the media are

527

filled with socialists, or, at least, left-wing reporters out to "get" business, without knowing the consequences, or even worse, without knowing what they are talking about.

And to hear reporters talking, business has been stonewalling it since long before Watergate. Try to get some facts out of a corporation, they say, and you'll get nowhere, if those facts don't make the company look good.

Well, I don't propose to add fuel to the fire of that controversy. It's an easy problem to solve, and I promise you I'll solve it quickly as soon as I solve the problems of the Middle East and the P.L.O., and as soon as I take care of the energy problem and Federal tax reform.

The fact is -- as I see it anyway -- that business can't do much about how the media covers the news. The media has the last word. The media are much better judges of what will interest their readers or viewers than are corporate executives. If you doubt that, look at the research figures. They show much higher ratings for program content (on television) or for editorial matter (in magazines) than for the advertising. In fact, I recently saw one study of readership in a business publication that showed the best-read articles had more than three times the readership of the best-read advertisements in the same issue. That ought to dispose of the myth that editors don't know what their readers are really interested in.

Of course, it's true that many reporters, and many editors, would much rather be covering City Hall than the Boardroom of a corporation. Or be in the streets with a portable TV camera crew, covering a so-called consumer demonstration in front of the super-market against higher meat prices. It's true that most reporters and most editors don't know very much about economics or business. If you think I'm doing them an unkindness, then ask why television news, in particular, covered the United Mine Workers dispute, and the coal strike, without ever explaining what the issue at dispute really was. Since both sides agreed it wasn't about money, then what was the issue? You never found out from television, not because of a conspiracy, but simply because the editors and writers apparently never thought it was important enough for them to find out and report to you.

So clearly, editors and reporters have a job to do, to learn the economic realities of our society. As I said, I'm not the one to teach them that. That's their problem.

But I do want to talk about what the business community can do about biased, unfair, or simply incompetent news coverage. "The fault, dear Brutus, lies not in the stars, but in ourselves." Shakespeare said it. Herb Schmertz of Mobil didn't and probably

528

wouldn't.

It won't be very difficult, in my estimation, anyway, for us
to get our story told more adequately and more fairly. The first
thing we've got to do is to recognize that the press has a right to
know. A right to know, not proprietary information, not confidential
marketing plans, but information about the company's operations
that the public has a legitimate right to know. Take payoffs abroad,
for example. The SEC wants to know. Now, maybe those payoffs are
necessary to make the sale in accordance with the customs of a foreign
country, but they're so unethical by our standards that they shouldn't
be made, even if it means the loss of the sale and the thousands of
jobs for Americans that would result.

I'm not sure I know the answer to that one, although my instincts
are telling me something. But I do think this is a subject that the
public has a legitimate right to know about, especially if the facts
are already on file with the government or regulatory bodies. Thomas
Jefferson wrote,

"The firmness with which the people have withstood the late
abuses of the press, the discernment they have manifested
between truth and falsehood, show that they may safely be
trusted to hear everything true and false, and to form a
correct judgment between them."

--- Letter to Judge Tyler, 1804 ---

Of course, it's unpleasant to talk about. But the answer isn't
to say "no comment" or to evade. The answer for business is, first
of all, to be accessible to the press (by that, I mean, broadcast as
well as print).

The second thing is that corporate executives must play by the
rules of the game -- the media game, that is. If a reporter wants
a 30-second statement on a particular issue, it's up to the executive
to figure out how to tell his story in 30 seconds, not 30 minutes.
Sometimes, the President of the United States doesn't get more than
30 seconds on a network television news program.

The third suggestion is that the executive should understand
that the press doesn't care about his corporate problems. The press
isn't working for his corporation. It's serving the public, its
readers or viewers. So the executive must learn to present things
from the viewpoint of the public, not from the viewpoint of the corporation. He must tell the public how they're affected by an action
or a policy. What's in it for them?

The fourth suggestion is to talk like a human being, not like a corporate bureaucrat. Colloquial, conversational English, "I" or "we," not "The Corporation." "You," not "The Public."

There are other techniques business can use. These are just a few. But the point of them is - before businessmen complain about unfair press coverage, let's make sure we've done everything we can at our end.

GORDON MCKIBBEN

As noted, I'm a reporter, so herewith some reporting based
on about twenty minutes of research on the April 5, 1978 edition
of The Wall Street Journal. I decided to see how many ethics-
related stories the Journal was handling that day. And I must say,
I was surprised. One of the three front page stories involved
IRS efforts to cut down on fraudulent tax shelters and fringes.
A second dealt with "do it yourself" auto shops that are springing
up all over the country because of shoddy work and bogus charges.
On Page 2, two of the four stories dealt with SEC or court
disputes, including Listerine's claim that its mouthwash prevents
colds and another story on an audit of eleven utilities to see if
they cheated consumers by adding on charges related to the coal
strike. On Page 3, one of five stories concerned U.S. Steel agreeing
to roll back prices after being jawboned. On Page 4, there were
six non-ethics stories, and on Page 5, two non-ethics. On Page 6,
one of the two stories involved charges of cheating in a takeover
fight.

Page 7 proved to be a bonanza. Three out of the three stories
involved lawsuits charging, in two instances, improper reporting
during disputed takeovers. A third story was about an FTC inquiry
into alleged illegalities by American Hospitals Supply. Page 8
carried a couple of court fight stories. Page 9 was all ads --
including an advocacy ad. Page 10 carried four non-ethics. On
Page 11, one of the three stories concerned a penalty imposed by the
SEC on a securities firm for what it called 'sham' transactions.
One of three stories on Page 12 involved an auditor who qualified
an annual report because of the company's questionable treatment
of fertilizer assets. One of the six stories on Page 13 was about
Olin Corporation denying it falsified data about dumping mercury
in the Niagara River. One of three stories on Page 14 reported
one corporation charging another with falsifying voting results in
a takeover battle. On Page 15, two of the six stories reported SEC
charges about various rules violations. One of four stories on
Page 16 tells of a stockholder charge of fraud.

None of the stories on Page 17 was really ethics-oriented
unless you noted a one sentence inclusion in a long story on
Goodyear Tire's annual meeting, which reported that less than 5
percent of the shareholders voted in favor of setting up an ethics
committee. One of the two stories on Page 18 reported some fraud
charges still lingering in the long-running financial shennanigans
of Marcel Sindona. There were no ethics-related stories on Page 19,
but on Page 20, two out of the six stories involved ethics. One told
of an out-of-court settlement by Carnation Company with competitors
who claimed marketing antitrust violations. The second story, which

531

shows what you can really get from the business press if you
persevere, reported that a woman employee at Johns-Manville Corporation won a legal battle in which she claimed her boss, who
was a fairly senior executive and who was named, required her to
have sex with him or be fired.

A story about some improper advertising appears on Page 21.
And it could go on and on. I stopped about that point and went
flipping back to Page 46, which is the back page. It had two
stories. One was a lengthy piece about a fraudulent fish farm that
bilked investors out 2½ million dollars. A short piece was head-
lined "Pleasure Trip Deductions Scored by Senator Kennedy." So
that's it. One day chosen at random. I'd estimate that four out
of seven stories in that random Journal sample concerned business
ethics. So what does it prove? Is cheating that fascinating? Is
badness inherent in big business? Is it the tidiness of reporting
the courts which makes it an easy story to report for reporters?
Is it a bias by The Wall Street Journal against business? Is it
the best way to sell ads? If nothing else, it proves that ethical
problems, frequently defined by courts or regulatory agencies, are
the stuff of big business and mass media, which is the subject of
our panel. I should add, I was going to go through this same exercise
with Business Week but I had to get back to work.

I'd like to narrow this down a little bit to a few observations
from my own point of view. And remember, my experiences as a reporter
are with either The Wall Street Journal in Los Angeles or with
Business Week in California, Canada, and Boston -- the elite of the
business press. That bias out of the way, some comments relating
to corporate decision making and the impact of the mass media. I
think observation one might be that the "masser" the media, the
stronger the impact. I'm thinking here of liquified natural gas
and Cabot Corporation, a Boston company which imports liquified
natural gas into this country. I've written several stories about
LNG and Cabot Corp. from one point of view or another, including
some illusions to the safety aspects of it. So has The Wall Street
Journal. So has the Boston Globe. So have a lot of other people.
But along came 60 Minutes the other day, CBS's prime time documentary.
In one 15 minute segment, the TV program stirred up Cabot Corp.
and local, federal, and state regulators. It set in motion all sorts
of problems and road blocks for Cabot Corp. and it's forced Cabot
Corp. to make some decisions. In a public relations sense, their
decision has been to talk openly about LNG safety. From my point
of view, that's excellent, and I think Cabot talks to the press on
the theory that what they perceive as logic is on their side. They've
gone through heaven knows how many regulatory battles and have proved
to the satisfaction of regulators the safety of transport, distribution,
and storage of LNG. But, talking openly about the situation could
be a perilous course for Cabot because who knows, political emotion

532

may override what Cabot perceives as logic. Perhaps they'll have
to take out an advocacy ad or something like that to get their
story across.

A second kind of bombshell story that obviously forces the
corporate decision is the highly specific revelation that forces
a response -- like the United Brands bribery in Central America
which The Wall Street Journal broke, although they were really
just beating the government to the punch by a few days by publishing a lot of SEC leaks. Sometimes the media, certainly The Wall
Street Journal and Business Week, does its own uncovering.
Business Week did a neat job on a charming swindler not long ago,
and more power to us. It forced the swindler's corporation into
bankruptcy, but then he didn't deserve to be in business.

Another ethical consideration that I've run into recently
raises questions for business, media, and government. Should the
media let itself be used by others? I'm thinking in this sense
of the confirmation hearings of G. William Miller, the recently
appointed Federal Reserve Board Chairman. In the process of the
confirmation hearings, you'll recall that Miller, to my mind one
of the most ethical businessmen in the U.S., found his company
charged with various illegal or questionable activities involving
mostly foreign commissions. The point is, he had to read about
it in the New York Times and The Wall Street Journal like all
the rest of us, because the reporters for those papers got leaks
from government officials of supposedly confidential information
that was not available to Textron. Textron didn't have time to
respond and Miller feels that he's been "had" in that sense, that
Textron was damaged to some extent by what he calls "trial by
newspaper." He contends that the same information that was made
available to the reporters should have been made available to
Textron officials so that they could dig into the records and
respond in a meaningful way. Is the media used by people with
an axe to grind? I'm sure it is.

These are examples of the more spectacular types of media/
business confrontations. More important in the long run, I suppose,
is the continuing prod of the press, such as continued writing
about pollution problems until a businessman says, "Okay, enough,
we'll stop dumping poison in the pond." Or, the media as a muck-
raker may force corporations over long periods of time to make
really fundamental changes like improving child labor practices
or forcing governments to pass laws that affect corporate power.
On the other side of the fence, businessmen have a lot of media
allies sharing the business point of view in matters of taxes
or local regulations or special tax breaks -- all sorts of issues
that fall somewhere into the general area of ethics. So, very
frequently, business and media are working the same side of the
street. Business and media are not always adversarial.

Whether big business likes it or not, though, and I don't think it does, most reporters for the mass media consider themselves the conscience of the public, protecting the little man versus big business. Certainly this is a major theme, a long-running drama on the American scene. It's really built into our psychology and I don't think it's going to change and I don't think it really should. I believe business has the resources to survive whatever excesses there are on the part of mass media to overexpose. I believe that the best of the business press, such as _Business Week_ and _The Wall Street Journal_, can be sympathetic to business and the politics that favor business, but at the same time useful and reasonably tough critics of how businessmen conduct their businesses. Think of it this way -- in our day-to-day reporting, we are sort of watch dogs of operational business ethics, and have some impact in the sense of inhibiting unethical behavior through fear of exposure if nothing else.

I am just 40 hours away from my last conference, which is
not as simple a statement as it seems because my last conference
was in Cairo, Egypt. It was a conference on "International News
Media and World Development." I was part of the American delegation to a 30 nation conference backed by such organizations as
The Fletcher School of Law and Diplomacy, Tufts University, the
Middle East News Agency, and The Ford Foundation. The Americans
were among the critics and the criticized at that particular
conference (the head of overseas services of AP, UPI, New York
Times, CBS, NBC were all there). Complaints by developing
world representatives included the high cost of information, and
the high cost of transmission of information. As you may not
know, it costs something like 239 times the price of an American
telephone call to make a telephone call in several of the emerging
nations. Also, the cost of news is set at a very high price, not
as high as it is in the United States, but very high for developing
nations, prone to feel under the dominance of the American news
business at times. The responses were typical and honest American
responses, i.e. that was that we are about to lower the costs
drastically through new technology and so forth. It was suggested
that with modest costs ranging from $250 a month to $4,000, developing states would secure all the wire service information needed.
Forgotten in the rubric was the cold truth that an investment of
millions, indeed billions, in the space satellite paraphernalia
was required in order to get the process going.

At one point the Nigerians, who are going to set up a Nigerian
National News Service called NAN for short, said that they will
probably bar all foreign reporters from Nigeria when NAN is established,
on the grounds that they're extraneous and that the best information
about the developing world should come from within the developing
world. Of course, we had our rejoinders there. For example,
Flora Lewis, the Paris based reporter of the New York Times said
that such an approach was counterproductive. On one hand developing world people say that there is not enough coverage of the
overseas world. On the other hand they say there is the necessity
of keeping out foreign reporters.

The very fact that the conference was held under the auspices
of the Middle East News Agency, with the other sponsors, was very
heartening. Also heartening was the fact that there were 30 countries
represented. Even countries that are well-known in terms of news
reports about squeezes on multinational companies, such as Indonesia,
are quite open to fairly frank conversations on all subjects regard-

ing our country. With that in mind, I would like to now switch
to the more immediate topic of "Big Business and the Mass Media."

Unlike Mr. Burger, I find no rhetoric in that title that
is displeasing. We of the Institute for Democratic Communication
have just published a book called, Big Business and the Mass
Media (D.C. Heath and Company) and all we do is refer to the big
companies. Primarily, they're on the Fortune 500; that is a
pretty good definition, one ball park definition, of big business.
It has nothing to do with any anti-business attitude, but in-
ferences can be drawn at liberty about anti-business attitudes
especially when well-known business consultants are doing the
inference drawing. On the basis of research, I have also
acquired biases. Biases that you may find uncomfortable! First,
we are all going to face enormous changes in the next two or
three decades, and I think that the: recent bribery situations;
the recent creation by Herbert Schmertz of the Mobil Oil Company
of a new kind of advocacy advertising; the recent establishment
of public affairs departments and the taking away of the play
from lobbyists by giant corporations; the desire to deal with
the economy and the ecology at the same time, is reflective of
a basic change in the American economic system. We are going
into something else, and I would say that we are very much akin
to the people in the 1830's and the 1930's. In the 1830's, they
were arguing Henry Clay's American plan, the plan that would tie
the American south to the American west. He didn't understand
at all that the future was to be tied between the American north,
especially the northeast, and the new cities such as Chicago that
were on the railroad lines. He also didn't understand that the
farm community of the new Great Plains was at that time a much
better regional tie than was the American south, which could not
long sustain the slavery system, nor the agricultural system
that was built up in its coastal areas. The American cotton
industry, as he knew it, and the American agricultural scene in
the south, as he knew it, was practically defunct. The costs,
as we know, of that system were prohibitive. Nevertheless, he
argued in terms of an exquisite polemic which did not forecast
the fact that we were on the perilous road to Civil War.

Even as late as the administration of President Lincoln,
I feel that the President did not know that the greatest
industrial revolution that the world has ever seen was well
along. Professor Benson, in the previous panel, referred to
that particular period of history.

I think that in the 1930's, after Wall Street laid its
famous egg, (Do you remember the variety headline, "Wall Street
Laid an Egg?") on October 29, Black Friday, of 1929, we had
no idea that the economic, political and social issues were

536

involved more than getting people back to work. We did not know
that we were about to go into the greatest spurt of industrial
production that the nation had ever seen, that it would all be
based on the pay tomorrow financing system. We did not know
that economic depression would not be stopped by plan but by
preparation for World War II.

We had no idea in the 1930's that microdots, and atomic
energy, and pollution control, and finite natural resources
were all realities for our nearly immediate future.

We have now engaged in, (late 1970's), all sorts of
arguments over the business relationships with the media. This
relationship is going to continue to be difficult. It is going
to be problematical because of two factors: 1) big business
is represented in part by the mass media; and 2) mass media must
criticize all the rest of business because we are now entering
into a new phase of resources, of industrial patterns, of relations,
of relations with the first world, second world, and third world,
of the upcoming uses of industrial production that must be a
tremendous challenge and a burden to all planners and critics.
Secondly we are on the tail end of one complete playing out of
history. There is no going back. We have tried it all. We
began the industrial revolution harvesting machines and machine
guns. We have gone from that combination to mass production of
goods and services and the technology of the H-Bomb. So we are
on the playing out of one fantastic historical era. I think
that if we think of ourselves as uncertain as they were in the
1830's and 1930's, it would be very helpful. There is a new
factor to shape our futures. We do not recognize how totally
bureaucratic our society is and how much more it is likely to
be! The arguments against bureaucracy are nonsense because
bureaucracy is now part of the big business scene. It's part
of the mass media scene and of the government scene. It's part
of everything. It also infers something else in my mind and
that is that a crucial portion of the government of all the
countries of the world, especially the highly technological
countries, consists of big business people. Big business must
now assume its governmental responsibilities both within and
without government. It is no longer possible, as in the 1830's
or 1930's, to assume that some people who are elected to office
or selected for office of a public nature will be able to
handle all of our affairs. Much of the power over what happens
to us is in the hands of big business. This is not an anti-
big business attitude; it is merely a statement of fact. So we
are going to have to look for the political sagacity that we
need from big business as well as from traditional players in
big government. Paul Appleby wrote about it in the early mid
1940's, talking about the expansion of the Department of

Agriculture, little realizing that he might in the 1970's be
talking about enormous expansion of the public affairs departments of some of our giant industries.

The battle for freedom which is an essential media issue
and an essential corporate issue was raised in the last panel.
It is a very practical battle for freedom, not esoteric, not
nebulous, not stratospheric but of daily life. Any one of us,
and there are a number of us in this room who have already reported that they have field experience in a number of countries,
know exactly what you see when people are unable to use the press
to express their opinions. And if any of you want any further
evidence on this, examine congressional committee reports on
civil liberties in the Philippines, civil liberties in Indonesia,
civil liberties in South Korea, civil liberties in countries of
the second world, civil liberties in countries of the developing
world of Africa and so on.

Looking at those situations, we have another problem --
big business does not know how to exercise its social judgment
carefully enough. I have had precious little experience. It is
in its reactive stage. It feels under attack. It feels very
defensive. It knows that it has the power to change things. It
is beginning to feel the responsibility that all political groups
feel when the heat is on them.

In my first chapter of <u>Big Business and the Mass Media</u>, I
wrote in support of the profit motive. I wanted it very clear
in the first sentence that profits is what makes America tick
and if you don't make profits, there's no sense in worrying about
anything else because business would grind to a halt and then
where would we be? But then two paragraphs later I say that
business had no particular credit to assume as a creator of our
Bill of Rights nor enough responsibility for our present condition of freedom. And in my third paragraph I say it's very
necessary for us to understand that business must assume its
responsibilities as a major political factor in protecting the
freedoms that we all cherish.

In looking over the business enterprises, and we polled
most of the Fortune 500, we found some very interesting facts
about the relationship between business and the media. First
there is a great dearth of good business reporting. There is an
amazingly large number of good business magazines and an amazingly
small amount of good business information on the most popular
medium, television. There is very little good reporting considering the breadth and scope of the American newspaper press'
business reporting, including the reporting done in this town
of Boston. If you want to separate good business analysis from

538

the kind of material that comes in over the wires that the editors
just print, there is very little that is originally commissioned
by editors who ask reporters to look into this, that, or the other
thing. There are the stock market reports, the business statements, the statements from this company or that company or the
other company, on whether this new product is promising or not
promising, but no basic business reporting. We also found another
thing. This concentration on Schmertz, (by the way, Professor
Sethi did it in his book, we did it in our book) and Mobil is
overdone. It really is overdone. He is sitting there now presenting a story to a more and more bored audience.

In advocacy advertising, just what rights do people have
who have all the money as against people who have none of the
money? For example, Media Access Project (MAP) as contrasted to
the Chrysler Corporation. Just what rights do corporations have,
outside of the news reports on television, to buy time expressing
company policy? We know full well that if the companies buy all
the time that they want, we will have a new kind of news reporting in this country. They can finance drama. They can
underwrite documentaries. They even can give us news reports
with the best!

Why don't we recognize that the business of America is not
business, but the business of American industry is our civilization, our people, and our hopes. We're dealing with a new economic environment and we don't know exactly where we're going.
We have to do business positively with the third world. We have
to make some adjustments to curtail increasing isolation of the
individuals in our society. If there is a joint role for big
business and for the mass media, it probably has something to do
with government. We are probably beginning to examine a new
phase of the political, social, economic interplay in which all
factors are big business responsibilities.

PAUL J. WETZEL

In his letter inviting me to participate in this panel discussion, Dr. Adamian said we would examine the impact and relationship of the news media on corporate decision making. Recognizing the time constraints placed on us, I was reminded of a Peanuts strip I saw not too long ago. In it, Lucy was taking a history test and the teacher had passed out a sheet of paper with these instructions written across the top -- "Explain World War II. Use both sides of the paper if necessary."

I don't mean to compare General Motors' public relations activities with World War II -- even though we have days when we feel that everybody is shooting at us. But the issue is certainly very broad and general and in discussing anything in general terms we must realize that there are exceptions all along the way. But let me take up the generalities -- as I see them -- and we can get into specifics and exceptions in the discussion period.

In my judgment the question gets to the heart of public relations. We start with the premise that no business in America is born big. We all grew from relatively small beginnings. You don't grow unless you are successful and you won't be successful unless you are satisfying the public. Having arrived at a certain level -- I would also suggest -- that no large company will remain successful without paying careful attention to its many publics.

This of course, is what public relations is all about. Now, General Motors recognized these ideas a long time ago and its efforts at attaining public understanding of its products, policies and actions have grown just as other aspects of our company have grown.

For instance, GM has been a pioneer in many, many areas of public relations. We were the first major firm in America to have a PR professional named vice president. We have introduced many public relations practices now commonly used in corporate public relations. Today we employ more than 100 PR professionals whose responsibility it is to explain our company to our varied publics.

But it doesn't stop there. GM has long held -- as a matter of policy -- that every member of the management group shares in the responsibility for carrying out our various public relations programs. This policy is formally stated in letters from GM chairmen over the past 40 years and continuously reinforced at management conferences and through programs distributed throughout

540

the organization.

Serving a large variety of publics -- stockholders, customers, dealers, employees, governments, suppliers to name some -- means that we have a large communications job to do. And, we employ many communications tools in carrying out that job. The news media ranks as the single most important of those communications tools, in our company and I think in most large companies.

We also use meetings -- large and small -- speeches, booklets, pamphlets and appearances at academic seminars I might add. But our effort to communicate through the news media is by far the biggest effort we make in General Motors to explain ourselves on a daily basis.

I'll take a minute or two to outline some of this effort -- so you can get an idea of our commitment to communicating to the public. We routinely provide more information about ourselves than most people realize. We issue sales reports every ten days, detailed quarterly and annual financial statements and news releases on statements before government agencies, executive speeches, as well as the expected materials in connection with product publicity.

Our top management group -- consisting of eight senior people -- holds five or six major news conferences every year and grants more than 100 other interviews with news people during the course of the year. They make more than 200 public speeches a year at various forums and these are usually open to the news media.

In addition, people such as myself, located in 14 different field offices around the country handle literally hundreds of press queries each year. In all of this press contact, we rarely reply to requests for information by saying "no comment" or refusing to answer in some other manner. Certainly, there are such occasions -- usually forced on us by the legal staff -- and less frequently by a competitive situation -- where we will not or can not reply. But for the most part we welcome and seek out the opportunity to discuss our business and our company with the news media.

I would like to take a minute or two to discuss the results of all this effort and make a few observations on the media side of this question. How do we do with this great publicity effort? As you might expect -- pretty well and not too well.

I think that as an industry -- the automobile industry receives more coverage that anyone else in this country -- although in the past few years the oil people have been running neck and neck. But

when you consider the fact that more than 20 daily newspapers in
the country have auto editors, either full or part-time -- and
virtually every major business publication has a Detroit bureau,
you can see that we are pretty well covered.

Dealing with these specialists during my career with GM
has enabled me to see the obvious advantages of this kind of
media work and to realize also the shortcomings of most other
business news coverage by the press. And let me be specific
about my criticism of business news coverage -- lest I get into
trouble with my many friends in the press.

I would characterize business news coverage today as follows:

With the truly mass media -- television and radio -- it is virtually
non-existent. The nightly network news shows feel business news
consists of the closing Dow Jones averages and once in a while a
recitation of some government statistics on unemployment, cost of
living or inflation. Local radio and television do less than that
unless a local firm is laying people off or going out of business
entirely.

The business press over the past six or eight years, has
grown, prospered and improved. The Wall Street Journal is in a
class by itself. Magazines such as Business Week, Forbes,
Fortune, and the business sections of the general newsweeklies
have prospered and expanded their staffs with better educated,
more experienced reporters who do a better job all the time.

This leaves us with the daily newspapers. With the exception
of a very few such as the NY Times, Washington Post, and the LA
Times, their record runs from unsatisfactory to dismal. I have
discussed this subject with business editors, managing editors,
and publishers in cities such as Chicago, Hartford, Boston,
Milwaukee and smaller places and come to one conclusion. The fault
lies in the lack of a commitment by publishers to spend the money
to cover business news.

Many cite lack of space as the reason for their lack of
coverage but this is a red herring. Newspapers in many of the
cities cited regularly devote four or five pages to business
news. But three or four of them will be filled with the stock
tables, which of course can be transmitted and printed automatically.
If they wished to dispense with the daily tables and hire the
staff to fill that space with stories about business they could
do so. For instance, here in Boston the Herald American runs five
pages of financial news each day. The financial news department
consists of two people -- the editor -- who devotes most of his
time to writing a four times a week column and a reporter who compiles

542

wire copy and compresses it into "roundups." He occasionally covers a local business news conference. This pattern is repeated all too often on papers of this size in cities like Boston throughout the country. When you compare the staff allotment, the budget allotment and the space allotment of business news with the sports news in any major daily newspaper in the U.S. with the exception of those noted earlier -- we can easily see where the priorities lie.

In conclusion then I would say that the press plays an important part in corporate decision making -- a role that grows in importance all the time. The public increasingly wants to know more about why a given company is doing something and most often has a right to that information. The success of the business press reflects that interest.

But the mass media -- major daily newspapers, radio and television -- does not deliver enough of this news. Most major corporations in this country are ready and willing to tell more about ourselves than the media is willing to use.

DISCUSSION

COMMENT: I'd just like to make two very quick comments: First, I think there is a lot of what is being called business news which should not be called that. It should simply be called news. It is a condescending distinction. I think that much of what General Motors Corporation can do is news. The second thing is that if we are to have dialogue about some of these problems we have all been concerned with, there's a certain burden on the columnists and editorial writers in this country. By and large, the major columnists, Reston, Evans, Novak, etc., don't acknowledge the existence of the corporation -- neither negatively nor affirmatively. It just doesn't exist in the mass media. Nobody's dealing with all this and I think it's a shame.

WETZEL: I certainly would agree about the columnists. I think of all the things where there's a gap between the interest to the readers and the disproportion of space -- it is this turning over of virtually 75 percent of the opinions on the opinion page to commentaries on Washington. Our recent studies of the political process indicate the pack journalism aspect of that. First Evans and Novak say it and then Reston says it, and then somebody else says it, and we go on and on, and they're all just talking to themselves. Newsweek has this expression, "the most often quoted," and I wonder when was the last time we ever heard Evans and Novak quoted, or one of these guys quoted outside of Washington. I'd certainly agree with you. When the economy became the major story in the country over the last few years, these people were left with nothing to say, because they didn't know how to cover it.

MCKIBBEN: Actually, Newsweek, as a general magazine, has done a fairly good job of budgeting some space to columnists to comment on business or economics.

COMMENT: I was speaking mainly about daily newspapers.

WETZEL: Yes, the trouble is with daily newspapers. I was thinking, for instance, that in this state, General Electric is either the biggest or the second biggest employer, but where the heck is General Electric. Well, if you want information about General Electric, you're not going to get very much. The local newspaper is going to have a tough time calling Lynn or Pittsfield and getting anything very substantive. By the time he finally finds some spokesman in New York, or wherever, the day is gone. It's almost a structural problem between a local news-

paper's design for a local audience and distribution within a
short distance and big business, pejorative or not, consisting
of very large national companies.

RUBIN: There are two other aspects. The general assignment reporter is not going to give you a good business story. You're
going to have to get people trained in this area. Business is
getting very, very complex, and you have to get your reporters
on special assignment doing nothing but covering business stories.
The average newspaper won't do it. Also, the press has shown
an amazing temerity in regard to business if it's located in its
area, and I'll just give you one example. Sears Roebuck is one
of the largest advertisers in the United States. It was brought
up on charges by the Federal Trade Commission for its "switch
& bait" advertising. Hearings were held in Chicago, its own
headquarters town. It was found guilty. It admitted its guilt.
It was fined and all the rest of it. In Chicago, the major newspapers did not pick up that story until about the fourth day,
and then they picked up the wire service on it -- one or two
paragraphs. The television stations acted as if Sears Roebuck
was somewhere on the moon. That is just one particular story.
The media has to be willing to go after the story, but you have
to know the difference between a stock and a bond to do it.

COMMENT: I wonder how much the papers have been inhibited by the
fact that it's often very difficult to dig out a story from some
of the press releases that come out of many of the big companies.
You pointed this out, Mr. Burger, when you were saying they've
got to talk to us in words we understand. And Mr. Wetzel, as
a reporter going into the PR Department, I've often wondered,
since so many reporters are in PR Departments, why they stop
writing the way they write for newspapers when they become PR
people. They make us have to dig for the angles. Somebody's got
to find them. So why don't you put them on top?

WETZEL: Well, to get to the second part first, the reason you
stop writing that way is you have a different kind of editor than
you do at the newspaper. At the newspaper you've got an ex-
reporter as your editor and at PR you have lawyers and business
executives. But the other point, I just don't buy. That doesn't
stop them when it comes to political corruption. It doesn't stop
them in government stories. It doesn't stop them in any other
kind of story that they feel like going to get. Here in Boston,
you know, the State House hasn't been issuing press releases on
where to go look for all this political corruption that's been
going on. The press goes and finds it. It doesn't happen in
Washington that way. I think that that's a cop-out. By and large,
press releases are their best source. They're a tip that something in this area is going on. These gentlemen alluded to the

SEC. If I was a Washington columnist that hated business, I wouldn't sit in my Bureau, I'd sit at the SEC. You'll find out everything that's going on over there. It's all public. It's written down. That stuff is there if that's what you're looking for. It's all there. The press release is a tip. Call up and start asking the questions. If you can't figure out enough questions from the subject matter of the press release, then I guess you're stuck using our words.

Can I take a minute for an example. This year we brought out new products in our intermediate-size cars. This is an example of what happens and how the way the press discovers a story colors its coverage. On a 4-door, intermediate-size car, the rear windows don't go down -- they're fixed. That comes as news to lots of you. About three weeks ago, I got a call from the local consumer reporter. She claimed that they'd been hearing a lot of complaints from people who bought these cars and then found out that the windows don't go down. She wanted to do a story on it. I said, come on out and we'll talk about it. So she came out and she said to me (and this was while the cameras were rolling), don't you think you have an obligation to tell people this. And I said, we certainly do, and I pulled out of my pocket our press release that we issued, which had been widely ignored. I said, you can have it. It's still an exclusive story. That wasn't quite what she got on the tube that night because she wasn't interested; she was quite upset about my reaction to the story. I said, yes, we do have an obligation and we told it, and nobody wanted to cover it. We didn't bury it. We didn't bury it in a press kit with all the other announcements about new features on our cars. We issued it separately. We gave it a shot all by itself. Then I asked her about these many complaints, and she just stuttered. I asked, can you give me one? Yes, she could give me one. I have my doubts as to whether she had two, three, or four more, but she gave me one. And I said, well, I don't know, we've sold 80,000 of those cars in the Boston area and nobody's called us, and you've got 4 or 5. However, that night the story she ran was her consumer story of a great discovery.

COMMENT: I recently read a book by Silk and Vogel in which they reported that some chief executive officers felt that American business was getting a hard time from the press. But someone else argued that perhaps the press wasn't giving business a hard enough time and that, in fact, the reason was that the American press is itself big business and they don't like to blow the whistle on themselves. I wonder if you'd comment on this.

BURGER: Let me give a specific example. Let me talk about the telephone company. Lots of people hate the telephone company and few people love them. Tell me, how long is it since you last read a story in your newspaper that told the telephone company's side of a controversy affecting them.

Now, the charge that the press is gentle on business because it itself is big business is usually coupled with the charge that the government is pro-business. I think neither statement is true. Consider that two of the corporations that are generally regarded as two of the most honorable, progressive, innovative advanced corporations in America, IBM and the Bell System, are under attack by the government to break them up, on anti-trust grounds.

Now let's go back to the press. Take an example that you're very familiar with: In many states the local Bell Telephone Company has come under attack for proposing to charge you for directory assistance. The so-called consumerists said, "That's a rip-off by the telephone company to take in millions of dollars." The telephone company said, "Most people don't use directory assistance more than two or three times a month." But some people, such as credit bureaus and retail stores, use it heavily. In one case, one particular retail outlet made 2,100 calls for directory assistance within a day or two. Their reason was that if you go in to cash a check, they call directory assistance to make sure you have a telephone number before they'll cash your check. That was the problem.

So the telephone company said, "Why should everybody have to pay for the cost of those who are abusing this service? Suppose we set up a system where everybody gets two or three (or whatever the number is -- it varies around the country) calls free (which is more than enough to cover most users), and if you don't use that quota, we'll give you a refund. But the firm who makes 2,100 calls to directory assistance will have to pay for them." Now, maybe they're right and maybe they're wrong. There are two different perspectives on it. But the point is, where was that story ever told? Did you ever get it in the papers? It wasn't printed. The telephone company told it to everybody who would listen. But the papers didn't print it.

I can give you case after case like that. So to conclude my remarks, I think the press is not biased in favor of business nor, in my opinion, is it biased against business. I think it comes back to what really all the speakers have said: The press doesn't care about business, one way or the other. They are not aware of the fact that what business does affects your income and mine, your standard of living and mine, and they haven't taken the trouble to find out how to explain a complicated issue, like the one I have just mentioned, and treat it as worthy of attention. I think that's the problem -- ignorance and disinterest rather than bias.